145⁰⁰

W9-ARZ-437

# Product Safety
# Evaluation Handbook

# DRUG AND CHEMICAL TOXICOLOGY

### Series Editors

**Frederick J. DiCarlo**
*Senior Science Advisor*
*Environmental Protection Agency*
*Washington, D.C.*

**Frederick W. Oehme**
*Professor of Toxicology, Medicine and Physiology*
*Director, Comparative Toxicology Laboratories*
*Kansas State University*
*Manhattan, Kansas*

*Other Volumes in Preparation*

# Product Safety Evaluation Handbook

*edited by*

## SHAYNE COX GAD

*G. D. Searle and Company*
*Skokie, Illinois*

MARCEL DEKKER, INC.     New York and Basel

ST. PHILIP'S COLLEGE LIBRARY

Library of Congress Cataloging in Publication Data

Product safety evaluation handbook / edited by Shayne Cox Gad.
    p.   cm. -- (Drug and chemical toxicology ; 6)
  Includes bibliographies and index.
  ISBN 0-8247-7829-4
  1. Toxicity testing--Handbooks, manuals, etc. 2. Product safety-
-Handbooks, manuals, etc. I. Gad, Shayne C.
II. Series. Drug and chemical toxicology (New York, N.Y. : 1984) ;
v. 6.
RA1199.P77 1988
615'.19'00289--dc19

Copyright © 1988 by MARCEL DEKKER, INC. All Rights Reserved

Neither this book nor any part may be reproduced or transmitted in
any form or by any means, electronic or mechanical, including photo-
copying, microfilming, and recording, or by any information storage
and retrieval system, without permission in writing from the publisher.

MARCEL DEKKER, INC.
270 Madison Avenue, New York, New York 10016

Current printing (last digit):
10 9 8 7 6 5 4 3 2 1

PRINTED IN THE UNITED STATES OF AMERICA

ST. PHILIP'S COLLEGE LIBRARY

# About the Series

Toxicology has come a long way since the ancient use of botanical
fluids to eliminate personal and political enemies. While such means
are still employed (often with more potent and subtle materials),
toxicology has left the boiling-pots-and-vapors atmosphere of the
"old days" and evolved into a discipline that is at the forefront of
science. In this process, present-day toxicologists adopted a variety
of techniques from other scientific areas and developed new skills
unique to the questions asked and the studies being pursued. More
often than not, the questions asked have never been thought about
before, and only through the advances made in other disciplines (for
example, in analytical chemistry) were the needs for answers raised.
The compounding concerns of society for public safety, the maintenance of environmental health, and the improvement of the welfare
of research animals have expanded the boundaries in which toxicologists work. At the same time, society has spotlighted toxicology as
the science that will offer the hope of safety guarantees, or at least
minimal and acceptable risks, in our everyday chemical encounters.

This *Drug and Chemical Toxicology* series was established to provide a means by which leading scientists may document and communicate important information in the rapidly growing arena of toxicology.
Providing relevant and forward-looking subjects with diverse and
flexible themes in an expedited and prompt publication format will
be our goal. We will strive in this vehicle to provide fellow toxicologists and other knowledgeable and interested parties with appropriate new information that can be promptly applied to help
answer current questions.

Perhaps in no area of toxicology has public concern been so increasingly expressed as in that of consumer product safety. The average shopper has usually expected that any product he/she purchases is
functional and not harmful. Pediatricians, emergency rooms, and
poison control centers now attest to the inaccuracy of this assumption—as will consumers who at one time or another have found that
"it doesn't work like it's supposed to!" Drugs and pharmaceuticals
have been effectively monitored by the Food and Drug Administration,
while the Consumer Product Safety Commission, U.S. Department of

Agriculture, and the Environmental Protection Agency are responsible for the safety, wholesomeness, and appropriate application of the broad field of chemicals, plastics, devices, food, toys, household appliances, and general consumer products. These are not easily tested for safety using $LD_{50}$'s and 90-day feeding trials—and yet what type of tests does one apply to consider the potential problems of allergy from inhaling vapors, hypersensitivity to skin contact, fire hazards, or the potential for birth defects in children born to parents who consumed food stored in newly formulated synthetic freezer bags?

This book explores these areas and more. Although it will not answer all questions and will not have a solution for every future need, the authors provide a good introduction to the safety evaluations available for the wide array of products purchased and used every day by our affluent and demanding consuming society. It also raises the concern for future safety assessment needs in this same society.

*Frederick W. Oehme*
*Frederick J. DiCarlo*

# Foreword

The testing of chemical products and potential new products for safety must be carefully planned, conducted, and analyzed. The disciplines involved in the necessary team effort are many. These include, not necessarily in order of importance, toxicology, pathology, chemistry, statistics, and information science. In each of these, experts must be trained in subspecialties. For example, toxicologists must be knowledgeable in areas such as acute, subchronic, and chronic toxicology; behavioral and neurotoxicity testing; genetic, reproductive, and developmental toxicology; and oral, dermal, and inhalation routes of administration. Pathologists are involved in histo- and clinical pathology.

This handbook, written and edited by authors with many years of experience in their areas of specialty, presents details of the procedures involved in product safety testing. It begins with formulation of the correct questions to be asked. Primary among these is how the product will be used: who might be exposed and by what route(s)? The physical properties of the product must be understood and involved in the design, conduct, and analysis of studies. Will the contact with the product be occasional or often repeated? Will such contact involve only adults, only women? All of these questions and more must be considered in one of the most important phases of this safety evaluation: the design of the experiment.

The next phase, the conduct of the studies, must be exact. Data collected must pass careful tests of quality assurance and must be properly controlled, tabulated, and compared. The resulting reports must accurately present and summarize the information obtained.

The experiments involved are necessarily often conducted using animals such as rats and mice. They must be properly housed and maintained. The purpose of these studies is to predict the degree

of irritation or toxicity for humans.   Therefore, this book concludes
with a chapter on exposure.

   If the information in this handbook is carefully studied, the
degree of safety and/or hazard of products will be properly
delineated.

*Carrol S. Weil*

# Preface

This handbook has been prepared with a single objective—to present a practical guide for those professionals who are (or are planning to be) responsible for ensuring the biological safety of products for consumers and workers in fields where there are no detailed, regulatorily prescribed test methods.

As a practical guide (and not just a workbook), this handbook has been written by professionals who are experienced and currently active in the field. Its chapters clearly set forth the nature of the hazards and the methods for their evaluation. The problems with toxicological methods are clearly delineated, followed by the solutions that have been utilized and a presentation of the scientific and philosophical basis for such guidance. Rigorous development of theoretical concepts or mathematical methods has been avoided. Furthermore, data on specific materials are not presented except to explain or amplify the topic of regulation.

The volume is, by design, aimed at the nonpharmaceutical industries, where there is some regulatory guidance, although it is not of a lockstep nature. It is hoped that the methodologies (though meeting such regulatory requirements as exist in their particular area) provide a flexible and truly scientific approach to evaluation and problem solving.

*Shayne Cox Gad*

# Contents

# Contributors

CAROL S. AULETTA    Bio/dynamics Inc., East Millstone, New Jersey

THOMAS R. BARFKNECHT    Pharmakon Research International, Inc., Waverly, Pennsylvania

BETSY D. CARLTON*    Battelle Columbus Division, Columbus, Ohio

SHAYNE COX GAD    G. D. Searle and Company, Skokie, Illinois

RICHARD A. HILES    Hazleton Laboratories America, Inc., Madison, Wisconsin

MICHAEL A. JAYJOCK    Rohm and Haas Company, Philadelphia, Pennsylvania

HAROLD L. KAPLAN    Southwest Research Institute, San Antonio, Texas

GERALD L. KENNEDY, JR.    E. I. Du Pont de Nemours and Company, Inc., Newark, Delaware

ROBERT W. NAISMITH    Pharmakon Research International, Inc., Waverly, Pennsylvania

CRAIG M. PARKER    Marathon Oil Company, Findlay, Ohio

VINCENT J. PICCIRILLO    NPC, Inc., Sterling, Virginia

JAMES L. SCHARDEIN    International Research and Development Corporation, Mattawan, Michigan

ANN C. SMITH    Allied-Signal Inc., Morristown, New Jersey

---

*Current affiliation: National Sanitation Foundation, Ann Arbor, Michigan.

# 1

# Defining the Objective: Product Safety Assessment Program Design and Scheduling

SHAYNE COX GAD / G. D. Searle and Company, Skokie, Illinois

## I. INTRODUCTION

The most important part of a product safety evaluation program is, in fact, the initial overall process of defining and developing an adequate data package as to the potential hazards associated with the manufacture, sale, and use of a product. This calls for asking a series of questions, and is a very interactive process, with many of the questions designed to identify and/or modify their successors. In fact, this volume should serve as a companion in such a process, and this chapter is a step-by-step guide or map to this question-asking process.

In the product safety evaluation process, we must first determine what information is needed. This calls for an understanding of the way the product is to be made and used, and the potential health and safety risks posed by exposure of humans who will be associated with these processes. This will be covered in this chapter, and is the basis of a hazard and toxicity profile. Once such a profile is established (as illustrated by Fig. 1), a search of the available literature (as presented in the next chapter) is made to determine what is already known. Taking into consideration this literature information and the previously defined exposure potential, a tier approach (Fig. 2) is used to generate a list of tests or studies to be performed. What goes into a tier system is determined by both regulatory requirements imposed by government agencies and the philosophy of the parent organization. How such tests are actually performed is determined on one of two bases. The first (and most common) is the menu approach: selecting a series of standard

| Mixture | Component 1 | Component 2 | Component 3 | Component 4 | Intermediate A | Waste Material B |
|---|---|---|---|---|---|---|
| 1. Literature review | | | | | | |
| 2. Physiochemical properties | | | | | | |
| 3. Use/exposure potential | | | | | | |
| 4. Oral lethality (Rat) (Mouse) | | | | | | |
| 5. Inhalation lethality (Rat) (Mouse) | | | | | | |
| 6. Dermal irritation | | | | | | |
| 7. Ocular irritation | | | | | | |
| 8. Skin sensitization | | | | | | |
| 9. Mutagenesis | | | | | | |
| 10. Teratology | | | | | | |
| 11. Reproduction | | | | | | |
| 12. Repeated exposure studies | | | | | | |
| 13. Carcinogenicity | | | | | | |
| 14. Metabolism | | | | | | |

Figure 1   Mixture toxicity data matrix.

| Tier testing | Mammalian toxicology | Genetic toxicology | Remarks |
|---|---|---|---|
| 0 | Literature review | Literature review | Upon initial identification of a problem data base of existing information and particulars of use of materials are established |
| 1 | Primary dermal irritation<br>Eye irritation<br>Dermal sensitization<br>Acute systemic toxicity<br>Lethality screens | Ames test<br>In vitro SCE<br>In vitro cytogenics<br>Forward mutation/CHO | R&D materials and low volume chemicals with severely limited exposure |
| 2 | Subacute studies<br>Metabolism | In vivo SCE<br>In vivo cytogenetics<br>*Drosophila* | Medium volume materials and/or those with limited exposure |
| 3 | Subchronic studies<br>Reproduction<br>Teratology<br>Chronic studies<br>Specialty studies | — | Any material with a high volume or a potential for widespread human exposure or one which gives indications of specific long-term effects |

**Figure 2** Tier testing.

ST. PHILIP'S COLLEGE LIBRARY

design tests as "modules" of data. The second, which will also be covered in this chapter, is an interactive approach, where studies are designed (or designs are selected) based on both needs and what we have learned about the product. The test designs and approaches presented in the bulk of this text address these identified testing needs.

## II. DEFINING THE OBJECTIVE

The initial and most important aspect of a product safety evaluation program is the series of steps which leads to an actual statement of problems or of the objectives of any testing and research program. This definition of objectives is essential and, as proposed here, consists of five steps: defining product or material use, quantitating or estimating exposure potential, identifying potential hazards, gathering baseline data, and finally, designing and defining the actual research program. Each of these steps is presented and discussed in detail below.

## A. Product/Material Use

Identifying how a material is to be used, what it is to be used for, and how it is to be made are the essential first three questions to be answered before a meaningful assessment program can be performed. These determine, to a large extent, how many people are potentially exposed, to what extent and by what routes they are exposed, and what benefits are perceived or gained from product use. The answers to these questions are generally categorized or qualitative, and become quantitative (as will be reviewed in the next section) at a later step (frequently long after acute data has been generated). Starting with an examination of how a material is to be made (or how it is already being made), it generally occurs that there are several process segments, each representing separate problems. Commonly, much of a manufacturing process is "closed" (that is, occurs in sealed airtight systems) limiting exposures to leaks with (generally) low-level inhalation and dermal exposures to significant portions of a plant work force and to maintenance and repair workers (generally short-term higher level inhalation and dermal exposures to small numbers of personnel). Smaller segments of the process will almost invariably not be closed. These segments are most common either where some form of manual manipulation is required, or where the segment requires a large volume of space (such as when fibers or other objects are spun or formed or individually coated with something) or where the product is packaged (such as powders being put into bags or polymers being removed from molds). The exact manner and quantity of each segment of the manufacturing process, given the development of a categorization of exposures for each of these segments, will then serve to help quantitate the identified categories.

Likewise, consideration of what a product is to be used for and how it is to be used should be of help in identifying who outside of the manufacturing process potentially will be exposed, by what routes, and to what extent.

The answers to these questions, again, will generate a categorized set of answers, but will also serve to identify which particular acts of regular toxicity testing may be operative (such as those for the Department of Transportation or Consumer Product Safety Commission). If a product is to be worn (such as clothing or jewelry) or used on or as an environmental surface (such as household carpeting or wall covering), the potential for the exposure of a large number of people (albeit at low levels in the case of most materials) is very large, while uses such as exterior portions of buildings would have much lower potentials for the number of individuals exposed. Likewise, the nature of the intended use (say, as a true consumer product vs. as an industrial product) determines potential for extent and degree of exposure in overt and subtle manners. For example, a finish for carpets to be used in the home has a much greater potential for dermal and even oral (in the case of infants) exposure than such a product used only for carpeting in offices. Likewise, in general, true consumer products (such as household cleaners) have a greater potential for both accidental exposure and misuse.

## B. Exposure Potential

The next problem (or step) is quantitating the exposure of the human population, both in terms of how many people are exposed by what routes (or means) and what quantities of an agent they are exposed to.

This process of identifying and quantitating exposure groups within the human population is beyond the scope of this chapter, except for some key points. Classification methods are the key tools for identifying and properly delimiting human populations at risk.

Classification is both a basic concept and a collection of techniques which are necessary prerequisites for further analysis of data when the members of a set of data are (or can be) each described by several variables. At least some degree of classification (which is broadly defined as the dividing of the members of a group into smaller groups in accordance with a set of decision rules) is necessary prior to any data collection. Whether formally or informally, an investigator has to decide which things are similar enough to be counted as the same and to develop rules governing collection procedures. Such rules can be as simple as "measure and record exposures only of production workers," or as complex as that demonstrated by the expanded classification presented in Example 1 below. Such a classification also demonstrates that the selection of which variables to measure will determine the final classification of data.

*Example 1*

1. Which groups are potentially exposed?
2. What are segments of groups? Consumers, production workers, etc.
3. What are routes of potential exposure?
4. Which group does each route occur in?
5. Which sex is exposed?
6. Which age groups are potentially exposed?

Data classification serves two purposes: data simplification (also called a descriptive function) and prediction. Simplification is necessary because there is a limit to both the volume and complexity of data that the human mind can comprehend and deal with conceptually. Classification allows us to attach a label (or name) to each group of data, to summarize the data (that is, assign individual elements of data to groups and to characterize the population of the group), and to define the relationships between groups (that is, develop a taxonomy).

Prediction, meanwhile, is the use of summaries of data and knowledge of the relationships between groups to develop hypotheses as to what will happen when further data are collected (as when production or market segments are expanded) and as to the mechanisms which cause such relationships to develop. Indeed, classification is the prime device for the discovery of mechanisms in all of science. A classic example of this was Darwin's realization that there were reasons (the mechanisms of evolution) behind the differences and similarities in species which had caused Linaeus to earlier develop his initial modern classification scheme (or taxonomy) for animals.

To develop a classification, one first sets bounds wide enough to encompass the entire range of data to be considered, but not unnecessarily wide. This is typically done by selecting some global variables (variables all data have in common) and limiting the range of each so that it just encompasses all the cases on hand. One then selects a set of local variables (characteristics which only some of the cases have—say, the occurrence of certain tumor types, enzyme activity levels, or dietary preferences) and which thus serve to differentiate between groups. Data are then collected, and a system for measuring differences and similarities is developed. Such measurements are based on some form of measurement of distance between two cases (x and y) in terms of each single variable scale. If the variable is a continuous one, then the simplest measure of distance between two pieces of data is the Euclidean distance, (d[x,y]) defined as:

$$d(x,y) = (x_i - Y_i)^2$$

For categorical or discontinuous data, the simplest distance measure is the matching distance, defined as:

$$d(x,y) = \text{number of times } x_i \neq y_i$$

After we have developed a table of such distance measurements for each of the local variables, some weighing factor is assigned to each variable. A weighting factor seeks to give greater importance to those variables which are believed to have more relevance or predictive value. The weighted variables are then used to assign each piece of data to a group. The actual act of developing numerically based classifications and assigning data members to them is the realm of cluster analysis. Classification of biological data based on qualitative factors has been well discussed by Glass (3), and Gordon (2) does an excellent job of introducing the entire field and mathematical concepts.

An investigator must first understand the process involved in making, shipping, using, and disposing of a material. EPA recently proposed guidelines for such identification and exposure quantitation (6). The exposure groups can be very large or relatively small populations, each with a markedly different potential for exposure. For di-(2-ethyl-hexyl) phthalate (DEHP), for example, the following at-risk populations have been identified:

IV route: 3,000,000 receiving blood transfusions (50 mg/year)
50,000 dialysis patients (4500 mg/year)
10,000 hemophiliacs (760 mg/year)
Oral route: 10,800,000 children under 3 years of age (434 mg/year)
220,000,000 adults (dietary contamination (1.1 mg/year)

Not quantitated for DEHP were possible inhalation and dermal exposure. The question of routes of potential exposure is a very important one to be resolved, not only because the routes (oral, dermal, and inhalation being the major routes for environmental exposures) each represent different potentials for degree of absorption, but also because the routes dictate potential target organ differences (such as the lung for inhalation exposures) and special toxicity problems (such as delayed contact dermal sensitization). These route-specific concerns are addressed in individual chapters in this book.

All such estimates of exposure in humans (and of the number of humans exposed) are subject to a large degree of uncertainty.

## C. Potential Hazard

Once the types of exposures have been identified and the quantities approximated, one can develop a toxicity matrix by identifying the potential hazards. Such an identification can proceed by one of three major approaches:

1. Analogy from data reported in the literature.
2. Structure–activity relationships.
3. Predictive testing.

Each of these is addressed by one or more chapters elsewhere in this volume. Chapter 2 details how to perform both rapid and detailed literature reviews. Such reviews can be performed either on the actual compounds of interest or on compounds which are similar by structure and/or use. Either way, it is uncommon that the information from a literature review will exactly match our current interests (that is, the same compounds being produced and used the same ways), but an analogous relationship can frequently be developed.

The use of structure-activity relationships (SARs) is addressed in Chapter 13 which covers the current state-of-the-art in mathematical SAR methods and models. There are, however, nonmathematical analogy methods which are still used effectively. These methods are really forms of pattern recognition, starting with a knowledge of the hazards associated with similar or related structures. An example of such a scheme is that of Cramner and Ford (7), where a decision tree based on structural features (or lack of them) is used in a decision tree approach to categorize potential hazards.

The third approach, which is the main focus of this volume, is actual predictive testing. The following section sets forth a philosophy for test and test program design.

It should be noted, however, that each of these approaches has the potential to evaluate hazards in one of two ways: The first is to identify and/or classify existing types of hazards. If the potential for a hazard is unacceptable for the desired use of the material (such as a carcinogen would be for a food additive), then this level of answer is quite sufficient. The second manner in which (or degree to which) a category of potential toxicity may be addressed is quantitatively. In general, quantitative (as opposed to categorical or qualitative) toxicity assessment requires more work and is more expensive. This principle will be stressed in the section on test and program design. In general, it should be recognized that the literature approach can really only categorize potential hazards, and that SAR approaches are most effective as screens to classify potential hazards. Only predictive testing is really effective at quantitative toxicities, and testing may also be designed (either purposely or by oversight) so that it serves to screen or classify toxicities.

It should be noted that there is a major area of weakness in all three approaches. This is the question of mixtures. For neither the literature, nor SAR methods, nor our present testing methods are really effective at evaluating other than pure compounds.

## III. SELECTING AND DESIGNING TESTS AND TESTING PROGRAMS

The majority of the chapters in this book are devoted to the conduct and interpretation of actual tests and studies in toxicology. There are, however, general principles for the design of these tests and before any tests are conducted at all, a program must be designed so that resources are employed in an efficient manner at the same time as all required information is generated.

Finally, there are techniques and guidelines which are necessary to allow scheduling and control of testing programs, whether they be at external contract labs or at an internal facility.

### A. Program Design

As pointed out earlier, there are three approaches to selecting which tests will be included in a safety evaluation: package-battery testing, tier testing, and the special case of SAR approaches to designing programs to test series of compounds. For all three approaches, one must first perform a review of existing data (as outlined in Chapter 2) and then decide whether or not to repeat any of the tests so reported. If the judgment is made that the literature data is too unreliable or incomplete, then a repeat may be in order.

The battery-testing approach, which is not generally recommended or favored by the author, calls for performing all of a set of tests from an existing list. This approach has two advantages: First, it is the most practical and easiest to control for a "factory"-type operation where an overriding concern is completing testing on as many compounds as possible. Second, the results of such test packages are easy to compare to those of other compounds evaluated in identical packages. The main disadvantages are more compelling, however. First, battery programs use up more of every resource (animals, manpower, and test material, for example) except calendar time. Second, the questions asked and answered by the battery approach are not as sharply focused, as the test designs employed cannot be modified in light of data from lower tier tests.

The tier approach, as previously exemplified by the scheme shown in Figure 2, arose in the 1970s when concern about health effects broadened in scope and there were insufficient testing capabilities available to do every test on every material of concern. These schemes are proposed as a means of arriving at and performing an appropriate level and efficient course of testing. The levels of testing, or information generation, are arranged in a hierarchical system. Each tier contains a number of suggested tests which can be chosen as needed to complete information gaps or to establish the appropriate information necessary for safe use or disposal of the material. *It is emphasized that a tier or level of testing does not contain mandatory tests, but that judgment is used, both in moving from one level of testing to another and in selecting the appropriate tests.* Lu (8) has proposed one such scheme. Beck et al. (9) have also developed and published a tier approach type system aimed to include the broader scope questions of environmental effects testing. They provide some valuable points of guidance as to criteria for proceeding to the higher (and more expensive) tier levels.

The last approach is for the special case when one is faced with evaluating a large series of materials which have closely related chemical structures, and desires to be able to rank them as to relative hazard. Frequently, time is a concern in completing such a program for these purposes, and efficiency in use of assets is very much desired. The SAR matrix approach calls for first identifying and classifying the structured features of the compounds. These features frequently vary on a simple basis (for example, length of carbon chain or number of substitutent nitrogens). One can select the compounds at either end of such a linear series (for example, the compounds with 5 and 18 carbon chains) and evaluate them in a tier one (as per Fig. 2) series of tests. From this, one should determine the endpoints (say, sensitization potential and dermal irritation) which are of the greatest concern for the compounds in their intended use. Each compound in the series can then be tested for these endpoints specifically. Those that are then selected for use or further development based on such a methodology should be evaluated fully in a tier approach system.

## B. Study Design

The most important step in designing an actual study is to firmly determine the objective(s) behind it. Based on the broadest

classification of tests, there are generally two major sets of objectives. The first leads to what can be called single endpoint tests.
Single endpoint tests are those for which only one restricted question
is being asked. As will be shown below, such studies are generally
straightforward and generate relatively simple data.

Such tests and their objectives (the questions they ask) are
detailed below.

*Primary dermal irritation (PDI)*: Evaluate potential of a single
dermal exposure to cause skin irritation.
*Primary eye irritation*: Evaluate potential of a single ocular
exposure to cause eye irritation.
*Dermal corrosivity*: Determine if a single 4-hr dermal exposure
will result in skin corrosion.
*Dermal sensitization*: Evaluate the potential of a material to
cause delayed contact hypersensitivity.
*Photosensitization*: Evaluate the potential of a material to cause
a sunlight-activated delayed contact hypersensitivity.
*Lethality screen*: Determine if a single dose of a material, at a
predetermined level, is lethal.
*Mutagenicity*: Determine if the material has the potential to
cause undesirable genetic events.

The second category contains the shotgun tests. The name
"shotgun" suggests itself for these studies because it is not known
in advance what endpoints are being aimed at. Rather, the purpose
of the study is to identify and quantitate all potential systemic effects
resulting from a single exposure to a compound. Once known, specific target organ effects can then be studied in detail if so desired.
Accordingly, the generalized design of these studies is to expose
groups of animals to controlled amounts or concentrations of the
material of interest, then to observe for and measure as many parameters as practical over a period past or during the exposure. Further classification of tests within this category is defined either by
the route by which test animals are exposed/dosed (generally oral,
dermal, or inhalation are the options here) or by the length of dosing. Acutes, for example, imply a single exposure interval (of 24
hours or less) or dosing of test material. Using this second (length
of dosing) scheme, objectives of shotgun studies could be defined
as below.

Philosophy for What We Want Our Studies To Do (Objectives)

Acute
1. Set doses for next studies
2. Identify very or unusually toxic agents
3. Estimate lethality potential
4. Identify organ system affected

Two-week
1. Set doses for next studies
2. Identify organ toxicity
3. Identify very or unusually toxic agents
4. Estimate lethality potential
5. Evaluate potential for accumulation of effects
6. Get estimate of kinetic properties (blood sampling/urine sampling

Four-week
1. Set doses for next studies
2. Identify organ toxicity
3. Identify very or unusually toxic agents
4. Estimate lethality potential
5. Evaluate potential for accumulation of effects
6. Get estimate of kinetic properties (blood sampling/urine sampling)
7. Elucidate nature of specific types of target organ toxicities induced by repeated exposure

Thirteen-week
1. Set doses for next studies
2. Identify organ toxicity
3. Identify very or unusually toxic agents
4. Evaluate potential for accumulation of effects
5. Evaluate pharmacokinetic properties
6. Elucidate nature of specific types of target organ toxicities induced by repeated exposure
7. Evaluate reversibility of toxic effects

"Lifetime studies"
1. Identify potential carcinogens
2. Elucidate nature of specific types of target organ toxicities induced by prolonged repeated exposure

There is also a special group of tests which focus on broad groups of endpoints and which do not fit into either the route or length of exposure categories. These are the reproductive and developmental toxicology studies, each of which is the subject of a separate chapter in this volume.

The other objective in designing studies is to meet various regulatory requirements. A complete review of this objective is beyond the intent of this chapter. As it pertains to various test types, it is addressed in a number of the other chapters, and a short overview of regulatory considerations and their complications was provided earlier.

The approach to the design and conduct of systemic toxicity studies—at least in common practice—has become very rigid and has not been subject to the sort of critical review which is commonly focused on proposed new study designs or test types. The changes made in the last 15 years have been largely restricted to using more animals and rigidly following a standard protocol. The first of these changes, in an attempt to increase the value of the information from such studies by increasing statistical power, is a crude approach to improving study design. The second change is meant to insure the integrity of the data trail and documentation, but by its nature makes sensitive and efficient conduct of investigations more difficult. Clearly, use of some of the approaches described in Gad et al. (11) or Chapter 13 (and more to the point, adoption of the underlying philosophy) would significantly reduce animal usage while increasing both the quantity and quality of information gained.

There is one special case problem that calls for extra thought on the design and conduct of each of the study types discussed. This is the evaluation of the effects of mixtures. As the components of a mixture may have very different physiochemical characteristics (solubility, vapor pressure, density, etc.), great care must be taken in preparing and administering the mixture so that what is actually tested is the mixture of interest. Examples of such procedures are making dilutions (components of the mixture may not be equally soluble or miscible with the vehicle) and generating either vapors or respirable aerosols (components may not have equivalent volatility or surface tension leading to a test atmosphere that contains only a portion of the components of the mixture).

A second problem/concern with evaluating mixtures arises when (as is often the case) one is asked to extrapolate from a set of data on one mixture system (say, one with 79% of A, 8% of B, 7% of C, and 6% of D) to another with the same components in different prevalence (say, 40% of A, 8% of B, 40% of C, and 12% of D). Because of the highly interactive nature of biological systems, without a basis of understanding the actions and interactions of the components in a biological system, one cannot generally make such extrapolations.

The vehicle for translating a study design into the finished product is the protocol. A good protocol details who will do what, when, where, and how. As such, it might well be considered to be like the itinerary for a long and complicated trip. Gralla (12) has provided excellent guidance as to the do's and don'ts of protocol preparation.

## IV. PROGRAM AND STUDY SCHEDULING

The problem of scheduling and sequencing of toxicology studies and of entire testing programs has been minimally addressed in print. Though there are several books and many articles available which address the question of scheduling of multiple tasks in a service

organization (e.g., Ref. 13), and there is an extremely large literature on project management (14–16), no literature specific to a
research testing organization exists. Project management approaches
are a set of principles, methods, and techniques for establishing a
sound basis for scheduling and controlling a multitask project (or,
indeed, a multiproject operation) in the face of complex labor, skill,
and facility requirement, and of modifying such plans and schedules
as esternal requirements change. These techniques also serve to
allow one to reverse the process and give project (study) requirements and time frames and to determine both manpower and facilities
requirements. This is accomplished by identifying and quantifying
networks and the critical paths within them.

For all the literature on project management, a review will quickly
establish that these do not address the rather numerous details that
affect study/program scheduling and management. There is, in fact,
to my knowledge, only a single article (17) in the literature, and it
describes a computerized scheduling system for single studies.

There are available commercial computer packages for handling
the network construction, interactions, and calculations involved in
what, as will be shown below, is a complicated process. These packages are available both on mainframe and microcomputer systems.

The single study case for scheduling is relatively simple. One
begins with the length of the actual study. Then you factor in that
before the study is actually started, several resources must be
ensured.

Animals must be on-hand and properly acclimated (usually for
  at least two weeks prior to the start of the study).
Vivarium space, caging, and animal care support must be
  available.
Technical support for any special measurements such as necropsy,
  hematology, urinalysis, and clinical chemistry must be available on the dates specified in the protocol.
Necessary and sufficient test material must be on hand.
A formal written protocol suitable to fill regulatory requirements
  must be on hand and signed.

The actual study (from first dosing or exposure of animals to
the last observation and termination of the animals) is called the
in-life phase, and many people assume that the length of the in-life
phase defines the time until a study is done. Rather, a study is not
truly completed until any samples (blood, urine, and tissue) are analyzed, slides prepared and microscopically evaluated, data statistically
analyzed, and a report written, proofed, and signed off. Roll all of
this together, and if you are conducting a single study under contract in an outside laboratory, an estimate of the least time involved
in its completion should be

L + 6 weeks + 1/2 L

where L is the length of the study. If the study is a single end-point study and does not involve pathology, then the least time can be shortened to L + 6 weeks.

When one is scheduling out an entire testing program on contract, it should be noted that, if multiple tiers of tests are to be performed (such as an acute, 2-week, 13-week, and lifetime studies), then these must be conducted sequentially, as the answer from each study in the series defines the design and sets the doses for the following study.

If, instead of contracting out, one is concerned with managing a testing laboratory, then the situation is considerably more complex. The factors and activities involved are outlined below. Within these steps are rate-limiting factors which are invariably due to some critical point or pathway. Identification of such critical factors is one of the first steps for a manager to take to establish effective control over either a facility or program.

## A. Prestudy Activities

Before any studies actually start, all the following must occur (and, therefore, these activities are underway currently—to one extent or another—for the studies not yet underway but already authorized or planned this year).

> Sample procurement
> Development of formulation and dosage forms for study
> If inhalation study, development of generation and analysis methodology, chamber trials and verification of proper chamber distribution
> Development and implementation of necessary safety steps to protect involved laboratory personnel
> Arrangement for waste disposal
> Scheduling to assure availability of animal rooms, manpower, equipment, and support services (pathology and clinical)
> Preparation of protocols
> Animal procurement, health surveillance, and quarantine
> Preparation of data forms and books
> Conduct of prestudy measurements on study animals to set baselines as to rates of body weight gain and clinical chemistry values

## B. Designs of Studies Commonly Performed

*90 Day Oral Study.* Groups of animals are given different measured doses of test compound formulation by stomach tube once a day, 5 days a week for 13-14 weeks. Every animal is observed in detail for clinical signs twice a day (7 days a week); weighed at least once a week; has blood and urine collected at least twice during the study (with detailed clinical chemistries and hematology being performed on each sample); has a detailed necropsy performed on it (10 to 12 organs are weighed; 40+ tissues are collected, slides prepared, and a detailed microscopic examination is performed); detailed special measures (renal function, neurologic function, etc.) may also be performed. A minimum of 220,000 pieces of data are collected on a minimum of 240 animals.

*90-Day Inhalation Study.* As above, however, instead of oral dosing, the animal groups are exposed in chambers to gases, vapors, or aerosols of very tightly controlled concentration and nature for six hours a day. Performing a 90-day study by this route adds no animals but does add at least 1200 additional pieces of information.

*Reproduction Study.* Groups of animals are dosed with, fed with, or exposed to (by inhalation) several levels of a test compound and to a positive control material. Pairs of animals are mated and the resulting pregnant females are allowed to go to term. The resulting offspring are assessed as to their development. All aspects of reproductive performance and of viability of the offspring are assessed in detail. Selected members of the offspring generation continue to be dosed and are also mated. The reproductive performance of this generation of animals and the viability of the resulting offspring are assessed. Histopathology is performed on reproductive organs and tissues. At least 320 animals are involved in breedings and at least 185,000 pieces of data are generated.

*Special Target Organ Studies* (e.g., a renal toxicity study). Route and length of dosing/exposure of animals is variable, dependent on the particular problem being evaluated. Renal function is assessed by histopathology, clinical chemistry, specialized biochemical studies, and by a series of studies requiring microsurgical manipulations. These studies can involve some 700 animals and can produce some 210,000 pieces of data.

*Two-Week Oral.* The design is the same as that for the 90-day oral study, however, animal group sizes are smaller and dosing is once a day, 5 days a week for 2 weeks. This study will involve at least 80 animals and 70,000 pieces of data.

*Two-Week Inhalation.* This, too, is the same as the 90-day inhalation study, however, animal group sizes are smaller and exposure is 6 hr a day, 5 days a week, for 2 weeks. This study will involve at least 80 animals and 70,300 pieces of data.

*Acute Inhalation.* Separate groups of animals are exposed for (depending on the design) 2, 4, or 6 hours (four is most common) to different concentrations of a test gas, vapor, or aerosol; the animals are then observed over 2 weeks for effects before being

terminated and necropsied. Detailed clinical observations are performed twice daily on every animal. Each animal is weighed at least
seven times during the study. A detailed necropsy and microscopic
examination of tissues is performed, organ weights are determined,
and special observations or tests may also be performed. If at all
possible, an $LC_{50}$ is determined. Between 20 and 70 animals are
utilized, generating on the average 13,000 pieces of data.

*Acute Oral Study.* This procedure is the same as that for the
acute inhalation study, however, instead of exposure to an atmosphere containing the test compound, the animals are given a single
dose of the formulation by stomach tube.

*Acute Dermal Study.* This follows the same procedure as the
acute inhalation study, however, instead of exposure to an atmosphere containing the test compound, the animals have a portion of
their back shaved. Measured amounts of the test material are applied to these shaved areas and covered with an occlusive patch for
24 hours, after which time the patches are removed and any remaining test material is washed off.

*Primary Dermal Irritation Study.* A group of six animals each
have separate large areas of their backs shaved, onto which a 0.5 g
or 0.5 ml portion of test material is placed. The test substance is
then covered by an occlusive patch and removed 4 hours later, at
which time excess test material is washed off. Separate regions of
the back are also used for positive and vehicle control sites. The
different skin regions which had been exposed are then evaluated
for irritation (erythema and edema) at 24, 48, and 72 hr after the
patch is removed. If significant irritation is observed, additional
observations are made up to one week after the removal of the patch.
Six animals are utilized to generate from 108 to 252 pieces of data.

*Primary Eye Irritation Study.* This test is only performed if a
material has a pH of 3.1–10.9 and has proven not to be a severe
skin irritant. The primary dermal irritation study for a particular
compound is therefore always conducted first. Nine rabbits are used
to evaluate the potential of test substance to irritate or damage the
eye and to determine what value water may have in reducing damage.
For 6 of the rabbits, the material is instilled into the eye and left
for a period before being washed out. For thr other 3 rabbits,
20 sec after the material is instilled into the eye, the eye is vigorously rinsed with a stream of water. The eyes are then examined
at every other day with an ophthalmoscope, with all observations
being scored on the Draize system. Nine rabbits generate some 126
pieces of data.

*Guinea Pig Sensitization Study.* A group of guinea pigs have
patches of their skin shaved regularly, patched with test and control materials, and read for edema and erythema over a period of
6–7 weeks (a negative test result requires an additional week of

testing). A separate group of animals is always concurrently exposed to a similar positive control substance.

The laboratory should always run batteries of these tests together to achieve an economy of mass by sharing one control group of animals for all of the studies. A group of 13–21 animals are used to generate 648 pieces of data.

*Guinea Pig Maximization Study.* A group of guinea pigs (larger than the number used in the preceding study) have test substance and immunological adjutant solution subcutaneously injected repeatedly during the induction phase. They are then exposed via patching to the above test substance during the challenge phase. Skin regions are evaluated for edema and erythema as above over a period of 6–7 weeks. A separate concurrent positive control group is also always used here. As many as 20–40 animals are used to generate 1200+ pieces of data.

### 1. Poststudy Activities

After completion of the in-life phase (that is, the period during which live animals are used) of any study, significant additional effort is still required to complete the research. This effort includes the following:

Preparation of tissue slides and microscopic evaluation of these slides
Preparation of data tables
Statistical analysis of data
Preparation of reports

There are a number of devices available to a manager to help improve/optimize the performance of a laboratory involved in these activities. Four such devices (or principles) are general enough to be particularly attractive.

*Cross Training.* Identification of rate-limiting steps in a toxicology laboratory over a period of time usually reveals that at least some of these are variable (almost with the season). At times, there is too much work of one kind (say, inhalation studies) and too little of another (say, dietary studies). The available staff for inhalation studies cannot handle this peak load and as the skills between these two groups are somewhat different, the dietary staff (which is now not fully occupied) cannot simply relocate down the hall and help out. However, if early on one identifies low and medium skill aspects of the work involved in inhalation studies, one could cross-train the dietary staff at a convenient time so that staff could be redeployed to meet peak loads.

*Economy of Mass.* Especially for acute studies, much of the effort involved in study preparation, conduct and completion is baseline. That is, whereas it takes hours to set up for a single irritation study, it takes only 7 to set up for two, 8 for three, and so on. Such studies are most efficiently performed in groups or batteries.

*Flexibility and Prioritization.* All too many laboratories let themselves be caught up in bulky systems for study start-up, such that any change in schedule means going back to the beginning and losing substantial effort along the way. Systems for study preparation should be studied to insure that they are flexible enough to allow for changes in priority that frequently occur. Likewise, prioritization of studies should be performed so that the results of planning efforts are as stable as possible.

*Shared Controls.* Acute studies frequently include a control group receiving either vehicle (to guard against "background noise") or a positive control (to ensure system sensitivity). If such studies are performed in battery (that is, two or three) guinea pig sensitization studies at a time, one can legitimately use one common ("shared") control group of animals for the entire battery of studies. This will both save labor and reduce the number of animals employed.

Chapter 14 should be consulted for detailed guidance as to contracting out studies. When doing so, it should be kept in mind that comparative shopping for toxicology studies is very tricky. A detailed examination of protocols is essential to ensure that the different prices are for two different things (apples and oranges) that are called the same thing. Small variations in such factors as numbers of animals used and length of postdosing observational period can make large differences in both the cost and information value of a study.

## V. RISK AND HAZARD ASSESSMENT

Once one has the complete package of information resulting from a testing program, and must determine what it means in terms of the potential sales packaging and use of the project, a risk or hazard assessment is called for. Chapter 15 has addressed the nonmathematical aspects of such efforts. For guidance on the special case of mathematical risk assessment, one should refer to Gad and Weil (18). Beginning a meaningful risk or hazard assessment, however, must start with an understanding of what is acceptable in the case of the use for which a product is intended.

## VI. GREAT DISASTERS IN PRODUCT SAFETY ASSESSMENT

No attempt to address the topic this chapter (or, indeed, this entire volume) is aimed at would be complete without providing the reader with some guidance as to common pitfalls to avoid.

Indeed, there are a number of common mistakes (in both the design and conduct of studies and in how such information is used) that have led to unfortunate results, ranging from losses in time and money and the discarding of perfectly good potential products to serious threats to people's health. Such outcomes are indeed the great disasters in product safety assessment—especially since many of them are avoidable if attention is paid a few basic principles.

## VII. FALLACIES AND FAILURES

### A. Program Design

1. All too many people believe that if a material is polymer based, that no toxicities can be associated with it. Based on this assumption, polymers then may not be evaluated at all for safety. The basis for this assumption is the premise that molecules of greater than approximately 10,000 MW cannot gain entry to the body by traditional routes of exposure.

   The errors in this assumption are that very few polymers are the products of reactions that have gone to completion (and therefore contain contaminants of lower molecular weight which may gain entry to the body) and that polymers may burn (therefore decomposing into smaller and more reactive molecules).

2. A generalization of the above "molecular weight rule" holds that monomers are more toxic than dimers, which in turn, are more toxic than the trimers, and so on. This is not true; dicyclopentadiene, for example, is much more toxic than cyclopentadiene. Another way of saying this is that SAR models provide guidance as to trends in effects within structural series, but not hard and fast rules.

3. It has also been assumed by a number of people that if a material is handled only within a closed system, there is no product safety concern because there is no exposure potential. This assumption has always been fallacious; dosed systems must be opened up to be cleaned and maintained. And they leak—sometimes disasterously, as at Bophal.

4. The best model for studying effects of materials in humans is the human itself. What is seen in animal models should never be expected to be exactly the same in humans, and seeing nothing adverse in tightly controlled animal studies does not guarantee that the same material will be "safe" in the hands of humans.

### B. Study Design

It is quite possible to design a study for failure. Common shortfalls include:

1. Wrong animal model.
2. Wrong route.
3. Wrong vehicle or form of test material.
4. In studies where several dose levels are studied, the worst thing that can happen is to have an effect at the lowest level tested (not telling you what dosage is safe in animals, much less in humans). The next worst thing is to not have an effect at the highest dose tested (generally meaning, you won't know what the signs of toxicity are and invalidating the study in the eyes of many regulatory agencies).
5. Making leaps of faith. An example is to set dosage levels based on others' data and to then dose all your test animals. At the end of the day, all animals in all dose levels are dead. The study is over, the problem remains.
6. Using the wrong concentration of test material in a study. Many effects (including both dermal and gastrointestinal irritation, for example) are very concentration dependent.
7. Failure to include a recovery group. If you find an effect in a 90-day study (say, gastric hyperplasia), how do you interpret it? How does one respond to the regulatory question, "Will it progress to cancer?"? If an additional group of animals were included in dosing, then were maintained for a month after dosing had been completed, recovery (reversibility) of such observations could be both evaluated and (if present) demonstrated.

## REFERENCES

1. Hartigan, J. A. (1983). Classification. In *Encyclopedia of Statistical Sciences*, Vol. 2. Edited by S. Katz and N. L. Johnson. New York, John Wiley.
2. Gordon, A. D. (1981). *Classification*. New York, Chapman and Hall.
3. Glass, L. (1975). Classification of biological networks by their qualitative dynamics. *J. Theor. Biol.* 85-107.
4. Schaper, M., Thompson, R. D., and Alarie, Y. (1985). A method to classify airborne chemicals which alter the normal ventilatory response induced by $CO_2$. *Toxicol. Appl. Pharmacol.* 79: 332-341.
5. Kowalski, B. R. and Bender, C. F. (1972). Pattern recognition. A powerful approach to interpreting chemical data. *J. Am. Chem. Soc.* 94: 5632-5639.
6. EPA (1984). *Proposed Guidelines for Exposure Assessment*, F R 49 No. 227, November 23, 46304-46312.
7. Cramner, C. M., Ford, R. A., and Hall, R. L. (1978). Estimation of toxic hazard—a decision tree approach. *Fed. Cosmet. Toxicol. 16*: 255-276.

8. Lu, Frank C. (1985). *Basic Toxicology*. New York, Hemisphere Publishing Corp., pp. 68–95.
9. Beck, L. W., Maki, A. W., Artman, N. R., and Wilson, E. R. (1981). Outline and criteria for evaluating the safety of new chemicals. *Reg. Toxicol. Pharmacol. 1*: 19–58.
10. Page, N. P. (1986). International harmonization of toxicity testing. In *Safety Evaluation of Drugs and Chemicals*. Edited by W. E. Lloyd. New York, Hemisphere Publishing, Inc., pp. 455–467.
11. Gad, S. C., Smith, A. C., Cramp, A. L., Gavigan, F. A., and Derelanko, M. J. (1984). Innovative designs and practices for acute systemic toxicity studies. *Drug Chem. Tox.* (5): 423–434.
12. Gralla, E. J. (1981). Protocol preparation design and objectives. In *Scientific Considerations in Monitoring and Evaluating Toxicological Research*. (Edited by E. J. Gralla.) New York, Hemisphere Publishing Corporation, pp. 1–26.
13. French, S. (1982). *Sequencing and Scheduling*. New York, Halsted Press.
14. Kaufman, A. and Desbazeille, G. (1969). *The Critical Path Method*. Gordon and Breach Science Publishers.
15. Martin, C. C. (1976). *Project Management: How to Make It Work*. New York, Animal Management Association.
16. Kerzner, H. (1979). *Project Management: A Systems Approach to Planning, Scheduling and Controlling*. New York, Van Nostrand Reinhold Company.
17. Levy, A. E., Simon, R. C., Beerman, T. H., and Fold, R. M. (1977). Scheduling of toxicology protocol studies. *Comput. Biomed. Res. 10*: 139–151.
18. Gad, S. C. and Weil, C. S. (1986). *Statistics and Experimental Design for Toxicologists*. Caldwell, NJ, Telford Press, pp. 176–243.

# 2

# Available Toxicology Information Sources and Their Use

CRAIG M. PARKER / *Marathon Oil Company, Findlay, Ohio*

## I. INTRODUCTION

Even before enactment of the Occupational Safety and Health Administration (OSHA) Federal Hazard Communication Standard on November 25, 1985, the industrial toxicologist was frequently called upon by his employer to quickly review his collection of published reference sources and make a "quick and dirty" hazard assessment of the toxicologic potential of a specific chemical substance and/or mixture. Frequently in these "quick and dirty" hazard assessments, important pieces of toxicology information were omitted because the toxicologist was not given the proper information about the compound to be evaluated or he/she was not familiar with the published information sources that were available either by hand search or on-line computer.

The purpose of this chapter is threefold:

Section II contains an overview of the older and more commonly used published information sources on general toxicology, industrial hygiene, and first aid/medical treatment information that are available. Each text will be briefly summarized with respect to its scope, usefulness/applicability, and the variety and number of chemical substances covered. This chapter is written for the new professional in industrial toxicology; especially if he or she is in a situation that limits access to an adequate toxicology library.

Section III addresses those criteria helpful in conducting a meaningful literature search. It outlines the types of on-line data bases that are available and helps identify some of the questions that need to be considered prior to initiating the search. This will not only improve the quality of the search, but reduce the number of incomplete or inadequate searches.

Section IV discusses an approach one can use to monitor the published literature and identify research in progress.

However, before any review of the literature (hand search or on-line computer) is initiated, it is important to obtain as much of the following product composition and exposure information as practical:

1. Chemical composition and major impurities.
2. Chemical production and use information (i.e., manufacturing process, exposure patterns, and other commercial uses).
3. Correct chemical identity including formula, Chemical Abstract Service Number, common synonyms, and trade names.
4. Selected physical properties (i.e., physical state, vapor pressure, chemical reactivity, and pH).
5. Other chemical substances exhibiting similar toxicity and/or structure/activity relationships.

Collection of the aforementioned information is not only important for hazard assessment (high vapor pressure would indicate high inhalation potential just as high and low pH would indicate high irritation potential), but the prior identification of all product uses and exposure patterns can identify other alternative information sources, for example, chemicals formerly used as anesthetics, food additives, or pesticides may have extensive toxicology data obtainable from government or private sources.

## II. PUBLISHED INFORMATION SOURCES

There are numerous published texts that should be considered for use in literature-reviewing activities. An alphabetic listing of 17 of the more commonly used texts is provided in Table 1. Obviously, this is not a complete listing and consists of only the general multi-purpose texts that have a wider range of applicability for industrial toxicology. Texts dealing with specialized classes of chemicals, namely petroleum hydrocarbons, plastics, or specific target organ toxicity (neurotoxins and teratogens), although not considered to be within the scope of this chapter are briefly discussed under Miscellaneous Reference Sources (Sect. II.R).

### A. Annual Report on Carcinogens (1)

The 1985 *Fourth Annual Report on Carcinogens* prepared by the National Toxicology Program (NTP) contains "a list of all substances (1) which are known to be carcinogens or which may reasonably be anticipated to be carcinogens and (2) to which a significant number of persons residing in the United States are exposed." The report

Table 1  Published Information Sources

| Reference | Title |
|-----------|-------|
| (1) | *Annual Report on Carcinogens* (NTP) |
| (2) | *Chemical Hazards of the Workplace* |
| (3) | *Clinical Toxicology of Commercial Products* |
| (4) | Criteria Documents (NIOSH) |
| (5) | Current Intelligence Bulletins (NIOSH) |
| (6) | *Dangerous Properties of Industrial Materials* |
| (7) | *Documentation of the Threshold Limit Values* (ACGIH) |
| (8) | *Handbook of Toxic and Hazardous Chemicals* |
| (9) | *Hygienic Guide Series* (AIHA) |
| (10) | *Industrial Toxicology* |
| (11) | International Agency for Research on Cancer (IARC) |
| (12) | *Merck Index* |
| (13) | *Occupational Health Guidelines for Chemical Hazards* (NIOSH/OSHA) |
| (14) | *Patty's Industrial Hygiene and Toxicology* |
| (15) | *Registry of Toxic Effects of Chemical Substances* (RETECS) |
| (16) | *Toxicology: The Basic Science of Poisons* |
| (17) | *Toxicology of the Eye* |

lists 150 individual substances, mixtures of chemicals, or exposures associated with technological processes which fall into one of the two categories mentioned above. Scientists from the National Institute for Occupational Safety and Health, Consumer Product Safety Commission, Environmental Protection Agency, Food and Drug Administration, National Library of Medicine, Occupational Safety and Health Administration, and National Toxicology Program are represented on the review panel. Although the NTP *Annual Report on Carcinogens* does not contain a review of the carcinogenicity of the substance in question, it does cite the primary literature upon which the scientific panel made its determination. Compounds listed by the panel are considered to be carcinogens under the OSHA Hazard Communication Standard.

## B. Chemical Hazards of the Workplace (2)

This 500-plus page text contains information on over 400 industrial chemicals including solvents, metals, pesticides, and organic chemicals. Written in 1978, this text was intended primarily for physicians and other health professionals treating individuals in industrial work settings. Data for these chemicals were obtained from the Joint National Institute for Occupational Safety and Health (NIOSH)/ Occupational Safety and Health Administration (OSHA) Standards Completion Project. The emphasis of the text is directed toward effects reported in humans. Data from animal tests have been included when appropriate to point out potential target organs or in some cases as supplemental information in the absence of human data. Chapter 4 contains a chemical classification according to principal target organ or systemic effect. The First Aid and Medical Treatment information on individual chemicals is comprehensive and sufficiently detailed for use in counseling in medical emergencies.

## C. Clinical Toxicology of Commercial Products (3)

This 2000-plus page text is one of the best reference books on commercial products presently available. The fifth edition contains toxicity data on over 1642 substances. Manufacturer-verified composition information covers over 16,000 consumer products such as drugs, chemicals, solvents, and household products. The book is divided into seven sections as follows: First Aid and General Emergency, Ingredients Index, Therapeutics Index, Supportive Treatment, Trade Name Index, General Formulations, and Manufacturers' Names and Addresses.

The Ingredients Index provides an alphabetical listing of over 1642 substances including CAS Registry Numbers. The Therapeutic Index provides a more detailed review of human poisoning information on 85 compounds, including pharmaceuticals. The Trade Name Index contains specific composition information on over 15,000 nonfood products; it is one of the best compendiums of trade names available. The General Formulations section provides several hundred formulas for products and preparations commonly found in households and on farms. The last section of the text provides names, addresses, and telephone numbers of the manufacturers of these products, from whom additional available toxicology information may be obtained.

## D. Criteria Documents (NIOSH) (4)

The National Institute for Occupational Safety and Health (NIOSH) had a program to develop Criteria Documents for the purpose of establishing standards for the occupational exposure to various chemical and physical hazards in the workplace. The "Criteria For a Recommended Standard for Occupational Exposure to . . . (a hazardous substance)" are prepared from all known, relevant published or otherwise publicly available occupational health information, including but not limited to, the concentration of the substance in the environment found to not cause an adverse effect in people exposed for a normal working lifetime. Over 100 Criteria Documents have been prepared by contract assistance or by NIOSH staff and are reviewed by professional occupational health personnel from selected backgrounds of industry, government, organized labor, and universities. The resulting documents serve to provide the detailed support for the standards recommended by NIOSH for the Department of Health, Education and Welfare to be used by the Department of Labor as a basis for its promulgation of a standard. NIOSH Criteria Documents are usually available from the Government Printing Office or the National Technical Information Service or both. The NIOSH Publications Catalog (18) provides a comprehensive index, ordering forms, and helpful instructions for obtaining these documents.

## E. Current Intelligence Bulletins (NIOSH) (5)

Current Intelligence Bulletins are reports issued by the National Institute for Occupational Safety and Health (NIOSH) for the purpose of disseminating new scientific information about occupational hazards. The bulletin may either: (a) draw attention to a hazard previously unrecognized, or (b) report new data suggesting that a known hazard is either more or less dangerous than previously reported, or (c) update information from a NIOSH Criteria Document (4). Although relatively few in number (less than 50) and relatively short in length (5-10 pages), these bulletins contain useful toxicology and human exposure sections that document the most current information available. NIOSH Current Intelligence Bulletins are usually available from the Government Printing Office or the National Technical Information Service or both. The NIOSH Publications Catalog (18) provides a comprehensive index, ordering forms, and helpful instructions for obtaining these documents.

## F. Dangerous Properties of Industrial Materials (6)

This 3000-plus page text contains over 18,000 industrial and laboratory materials. It also contains over 40,000 synonyms for aid to referencing. It contains both CAS Registry and NIOSH identification numbers. The major difference between Sax's previous editions and the newer fifth and sixth editions is that the newer editions include acute toxicity information from the NIOSH Registry (14). Since many of the toxicity hazard ratings were derived from unrefereed journal citations in the NIOSH RTECS, the use of these data without first securing the original published material is cautioned.

## G. Documentation of the Threshold Limit Values [ACGIH) (7)

This text contains published literature references used to support the over 600 chemicals that currently have established 8-hr threshold limit values (TLV) and/or 15 minute short-term exposure limits (STEL) by the American Conference of Governmental Industrial Hygienists (ACGIH). These 1-2 page literature summaries provide the pertinent inhalation toxicity, respiratory irritation, and skin absorption data used to set the current TLVs. It is important that supplements to this document containing the latest revisions and updates also be obtained. The *TLV Threshold Limit Values and Biological Exposure Indices for 1985-86* (19) contains the latest revisions and intended changes proposed by ACGIH.

## H. Handbook of Toxic and Hazardous Chemicals (8)

This 700-plus page text covers over 600 chemicals commonly encountered in the industrial workplace. Included are those chemicals assigned allowable air concentrations as set by the American Conference of Governmental Industrial Hygienists (ACGIH) and National Institute for Occupational Safety & Health (NIOSH). It also (as of 1981) includes all the EPA priority toxic water pollutants and most of the EPA "Hazardous Wastes" and "Hazardous Substances" as contained in the EPA Chemical Hazard Information Profiles (CHIPS) and NIOSH information documents. In addition to CAS and NIOSH number identification, Department of Transportation labeling information, exposure and use information, and established EPA water concentration can also be obtained from this source.

## I. Hygienic Guide Series (AIHA) (9)

The two-volume publication published in 1978 by the American Industrial Hygiene Association (AIHA) contains human exposure and toxicity information of approximately 184 industrial chemicals commonly found in the workplace. Although many of the hygienic guides were actually published much earlier, these literature summaries contain much of the early information that had been developed that would not normally be discovered via an on-line published literature search.

Published references have been evaluated by each review committee and the extent of their review was adequate for that time period. Two shortcomings of the series are the limited number of chemicals reviewed and the fact that many of the guides need updating.

## J. Industrial Toxicology (10)

Originally published in 1929 and now in its fourth edition, this 400-plus page text was written for physicians and nurses working in occupational medicine. This text contains useful animal toxicity information for a variety of metals, industrial chemicals, and plastics, but its main empahsis is more toward reporting occupational exposure, epidemiology, and human poisoning incidents.

## K. International Agency for Research on Cancer (11)

Since 1971, the International Agency for Research on Cancer (IARC) has had a continuing program of critically evaluating groups of chemicals for carcinogenicity. Through international working groups of scientific experts in chemical carcinogenesis and related fields, the review of the published literature is summarized in the form of monographs. These monographs are probably the largest collection of critical reviews of toxicology with voluminous lists of literature citations. Classes of chemicals covered in these 35 volumes are provided in Table 2. Supplement 4 is a summary document which contains short descriptive summaries of all the chemicals, industrial processes, and industries that were evaluated for carcinogenicity in the first 29 volumes (1). Appendix 2 of Supplement 4 contains a listing of those chemicals for which there is considered to be sufficient evidence of carcinogenicity in experimental animals. Currently, a supplement and appendix (carcinogen list) for Volumes 30 to 35 has not been developed. Compounds listed by IARC are determined to be carcinogenic under the OSHA Hazard Communication Standard.

## L. Merck Index (12)

The *Merck Index* is probably the most widely recognized biochemical encyclopedia, containing over 10,000 chemicals, drugs, and biological substances of current interest and importance. More than 55,000 synonyms, including titles, CAS names, alternate names, trade names, and derivatives are contained in the Cross Index and over 10,000 entries appear in the Formula Index. Its original purpose was to provide basic chemical information and use data to the chemist and biochemist. In the tenth edition, the scope of the *Index* has been broadened to incorporate more information relating to the pharmacology, toxicology, and metabolism of the compound. Although toxicity

**Table 2** IARC Monographs: Classes of Chemicals Evaluated

| Volume | |
| --- | --- |
| 1 | Inorganics, chlorinated hydrocarbons, aromatic amines, N-nitroso compounds, and natural products |
| 2 | Inorganic and organometallic compounds |
| 3 | Polycyclic aromatic hydrocarbons and heterocyclic compounds |
| 4 | Aromatic amines, related hydrazines, N-nitroso compounds, and alkylating agents |
| 5 | Organochlorine pesticides |
| 6 | Sex hormones |
| 7 | Antithyroid substances, nitrofurans, and industrial chemicals |
| 8 | Aromatic azo compounds |
| 9 | Aziridines, N-, S-, and O-mustards and selenium |
| 10 | Naturally occurring substances |
| 11 | Cadmium, nickel, epoxides, miscellaneous industrial chemicals, and volatile anesthetics |
| 12 | Carbamates, thiocarbamates, and carbazides |
| 13 | Miscellaneous pharmaceuticals |
| 14 | Asbestos |
| 15 | Fumigants, 2,4-D and 2,4,5-T herbicides chlorinated dibenzodioxins, and miscellaneous industrial chemicals |
| 16 | Aromatic amines, hair dyes, coloring agents, and miscellaneous industrial chemicals |
| 17 | N-nitroso compounds |
| 18 | Polychlorinated biphenyls and polybrominated biphenyls |
| 19 | Monomers, plastics, and synthetic elastomers and acrolein |
| 20 | Halogenated hydrocarbons |
| 21 | Sex hormones (II) |

Table 2 (Continued)

| Volume | |
|---|---|
| 22 | Nonnutritive sweetening agents |
| 23 | Metals and metallic compounds |
| 24 | Pharmaceutical drugs |
| 25 | Wood, leather, and associated industries |
| 26 | Anticancer and immunosuppressive drugs |
| 27 | Aromatic amines, anthraquinones, nitroso compounds and inorganic fluorides |
| 28 | Rubber industry |
| 29 | Industrial chemicals and dyestuffs |
| 30 | Miscellaneous pesticides |
| 31 | Feed additives, food additives, and naturally occurring substances |
| 32 | Polynuclear aromatic compounds (PNAs), Part 1 |
| 33 | PNAs Part 2, carbon blacks, mineral oils, and nitroarenes |
| 34 | PNAs Part 3, aluminum, coal gasification, and coke production, iron and steel founding |
| 35 | PNAs Part 4, bitumens, coal-tars, shale-oils, and soots |

data are sparse for most compounds, references to literature reviews and original literature are often present to complement other information sources. As mentioned in the Introduction, it is extremely important to obtain basic chemical and use information prior to initiating any search and the *Merck Index* is unsurpassed as the first information source for obtaining these basic data.

## M. Occupational Health Guidelines (NIOSH/OSHA) (13)

The National Institute for Occupational Safety and Health and the Occupational Safety and Health Administration under the Standards Completion Project summarized and reviewed data for approximately 333 chemicals that had existing permissible exposure limits. *Occupational Health Guidelines for Chemical Hazards* was intended primarily

for the industrial hygiene and medical surveillance personnel responsible for initiating and maintaining occupational health programs, but
does contain published information on the chemical and physical
properties, toxicology, signs and symptoms of overexposure, and
emergency first aid treatment. Most of the information contained
therein would not be picked up through an on-line literature search.
The major limitation of this source is that updates are not provided.

### N.  Patty's Industrial Hygiene and Toxicology (14)

This three volume, 5000-plus page text is probably the premier published reference source for industrial chemicals. Volumes 2A, 2B,
and 2C collectively consist of 59 chapters of referenced literature
reviews on specific classes of industrial chemicals written by noted
toxicologists in their field of expertise. Classes of chemicals covered
are listed in Table 3. The interpretive evaluation that it contains
on many of these chemicals is extremely useful. The numerous reference citations contain many older citations not normally available
through on-line computerized literature searching sources. Since
the third edition was published in 1981, it should be understood
that data published within the last five years would need to be
sought out from more recent literature reviews and/or on-line reference sources.

### O.  Registry of Toxic Effects of Chemical Substances (15)

The eleventh edition of the National Institute for Occupational Safety and Health's Registry of Toxic Effects of Chemical Substances
(RTECS) is a three-volume 2500-plus page document containing toxicology information on 59,224 substances with their 159,522 associated
synonyms. The RTECS is updated continually and supplements to
it are published between editions. The *Registry* not only contains
basic toxicity information (i.e., $LC_{50}$ and Draize irritation indexes),
but serves as an introductory review of the toxicological literature.
The document is also quite helpful in identifying other available published toxicology reviews. However, since many of the citations
give only lowest reported doses or originate from foreign literature
or from unreferenced citations, caution should be exercised in using
these data without first reviewing the primary reference sources.

### P.  Toxicology: The Basic Science of Poisons (16)

This 700-plus page text is the most widely used text in toxicology
courses. Although it contains much information, its original primary objective was to teach the general principles of toxicity. The
specific chapters on toxic agents (e.g., metals, solvents, and

**Table 3**  Patty's Industrial Hygiene and Toxicology:
Classes of Chemicals Evaluated

---

Metals

Organic sulfur compounds

Phosphorus, selenium, and tellurium

Epoxy compounds

Ethers, esters

Aromatic nitro and amino compounds

Alcohols, ketones

Phenols and phenolic compounds

Aldehydes and acetals

Heterocyclic and miscellaneous nitrogen compounds

Occupational carcinogens

Halogens (including baron and silicon)

Alkaline materials

Organic fluorine compounds

N-nitrosamines

Aliphatic and alicyclic amines

Aliphatic and alicyclic hydrocarbons

Aromatic hydrocarbons

Halogenated aliphatic and cyclic hydrocarbons

Glycols and glycol derivatives

Inorganic oxygen, nitrogen, and carbon compounds

Aliphatic nitro compounds (nitrates, nitrites)

Polymers

Organic phosphates

Cyanides and nitriles

Aliphatic carboxylic acids

---

plastics) are extremely useful in characterizing the toxicity of these classes of chemicals. If the particular chemical you are searching has specific systemic or target organ effects, the systemic effects section may contain useful mechanistic information (if known) on mode of action. The literature citations at the end of each chapter usually provide excellent review articles and other primary literature sources that should be consulted for further information.

## Q.  Toxicology of the Eye (17)

Even though this two-volume 1200-plus page text has not been updated since 1974, it remains the most comprehensive text available describing, on an individual chemical basis, the toxicologic effects of a wide variety of drugs, chemicals, plant venoms, and other substances on the eye. The author has included an excellent cross referencing and index section which includes (when available) both a Draize Irritation Index Score and a published literature citation for each substance given.

## R.  Miscellaneous Reference Sources

There are some excellent published information sources covering some specific classes of chemicals, for example, heavy metals, plastics, resins, or petroleum hydrocarbons. The National Academy of Science publishes the "Medical and Biologic Effects of Environment Pollutants" series (20) covering 10–15 substances considered to be environmental pollutants (Table 4). *CRC Critical Reviews in Toxicology* is a well known scientific journal, that over the years has compiled over 16 volumes of extensive literature reviews of a wide variety of chemical substances. A photocopy of this journal's topical index will prevent overlooking information that may be contained in this important source. Trade organizations such as the American Petroleum Institute and the Chemical Manufacturers Association have extensive toxicology data bases from their research programs that are readily available to toxicologists of member companies. Texts that deal with specific target organ toxicity—neurotoxicity, hepatotoxicity, or hematotoxicity—often contain detailed information on a wide range of industrial chemicals. Published information sources like the "Target Organ Toxicity" series (Raven Press) or *Neurotoxicity of Industrial and Commercial Chemicals* (CRC Press) are just a few examples of the types of publications that often contain important information on many industrial chemicals that may be useful. Upon discovery that the chemical you are evaluating may possess target organ toxicity, a cursory review of these types of texts is warranted.

Table 4 Chemicals Evaluated in the National
Academy of Sciences Environmental Pollutant
Program

---

Asbestos

Chlorine and hydrogen chloride

Chromium

Copper

Fluorides

Hydrogen sulfide

Lead

Manganese

Nickel

Ozone and other photochemical oxidants

Particulate polycyclic organic matter

Selenium

Vanadum

Vapor-phase organic pollutants

---

Lastly, since new texts are continuously being prepared and printed, it is important to be on the mailing lists of all the major publishing companies to be aware of the new toxicology information as it comes into circulation.


## III.  ON-LINE LITERATURE SEARCHES

In the last decade, the use of on-line literature searches for many toxicologists has changed from an occasional, sporadic request to the semicontinuous need for computerized search capabilities.  Usually nontoxicology-related search capabilities are already in place in many companies.  Therefore, all that is needed is to expand the information source to include some of the data bases that cover the types of toxicology information you desire.  However, if no capabilities exist within your company, you can approach a university or a private contract laboratory and utilize their on-line system at a rate reasonable to your level of use.

## A. National Library of Medicine

The National Library of Medicine (NLM) information retrieval service (21) contains the well-known and frequently used Medline, Toxline, and Cancerline data bases. Data bases commonly used by industrial toxicologists in the NLM service are identified in Table 5 and explained below.

1. Toxline (Toxicology Information Online) is a bibliographic data base covering the pharmacological, biochemical, physiological, environmental, and toxicological effects of drugs and other chemicals. It contains approximately 1.7 million citations; most of which are complete with abstract, index terms, and Chemical Abstracts Service (CAS) Registry Numbers. Toxline citations have publication dates of 1981 to present. Older information is on Toxback 76 (1976–1980) and Toxback 65 (pre-1965 through 1975). Information on Toxline comes from 13 secondary subfiles listed in Table 6.

2. Medline (Medical Information Online) is a data base containing approximately 800,000 references to biomedical journal articles published since 1980. These articles, usually with an English abstract, are from over 3000 journals. Coverage of previous years (back to 1966) is provided by back files searchable online that total some 3.5 million references.

3. Toxnet (Toxicology Data Network) is a computerized network of toxicologically oriented data banks. Toxnet offers a sophisticated search and retrieval package which accesses the following three subfiles:

Table 5 Some of the Databases Utilized Through the National Library of Medicine (NLM) Information Retrieval System

| Acronym | Information and/or citation source |
| --- | --- |
| Cancerlit | Cancer literature citations |
| Cancer Proj | Ongoing cancer research projects |
| CHEMLINE | Chemical dictionary file |
| HSDB | Hazard substances data base on Toxnet |
| MEDLINE | *Index Medicus* abstracts |
| RTECS | Registry of toxic effects of chemical substances |
| TDB | Toxicology data bank |
| TOXLINE | Toxicology literature references |

Table 6  Secondary Subfiles Utilized on the Toxline Data Base

| Acronym | Information and/or citation source |
| --- | --- |
| TOXBIB | Toxicity bibliography |
| CBAC | Chemical-biological activities |
| BIOSIS | Toxicological aspects of environmental health |
| IPA | International pharmaceutical abstracts |
| ILO | International labour office |
| HMTC | Hazardous materials technical center |
| EMIC | Environmental mutagen information |
| ETIC | Environmental teratology information center file |
| TD3 | Toxicology document and data depository |
| RPROJ | Toxicology research projects |
| PESTAB | Pesticides abstracts |
| HAYES | Hayes file on pesticides |
| TMIC | Toxic materials information center file |

a. HSDB (Hazardous Substances Data Bank) is a scientific-ally reviewed and edited data bank containing toxicological information strengthened with additional data related to the environment, emergency situations, and regulatory issues. Data is derived from a variety of sources including government documents and special reports. This data base contains records for over 4100 chemical substances.

b. TDB (Toxicology Data Bank) is a peer-reviewed data bank focusing upon toxicological and pharmacological data, environmental and occupational information, manufacturing and use data, and chemical and physical properties. References have been extracted from a selective list of standard source documents.

c. CCRIS (Chemical Carcinogenesis Research Information System) is a National Cancer Institute-sponsored data base derived from both short- and long-term bioassays on 1200 chemical substances. Studies cover carcinogenicity, mutagenicity, promotion, and cocarcinogenicity.

4. RTECS (Registry of Toxic Effects of Chemical Substances) is the NLM online version of NIOSH's annual compilation of substances with toxic activity. The original collection of data was derived from the 1971 Toxic Substances Lists. RTECS data contain threshold limit values, aquatic toxicity ratings, air standards, NTP carcinogenesis bioassay information, and toxicological/carcinogenic review information. NIOSH is responsible for the file content in RTECS, and for providing quarterly updates to NLM. RTECS currently covers toxicity data on more than 61,000 substances.

5. Cancerlit (Cancer Literature) is a data base containing more than 300,000 National Cancer Institute references dealing with cancer. All references have English abstracts. This data base covers over 3000 U.S. and foreign journals as well as cancer-related articles from various scientific books, reports, and meeting abstracts.

6. Cancerproj (Cancer Research Projects) is a data base also sponsored by NCI covering a large collection of summaries on on-going cancer research projects.

## B. Material Safety Data Sheet Information Systems

With the new federal and state requirements for Material Safety Data Sheets (MSDSs) on all hazardous chemicals in the workplace, a number of data bases containing toxicology, material safety data sheet (MSDS), and hazard communication information have been developed. Most of this information is derived from secondary sources, that is, not primary literature citations; therefore, these databases may or may not be sufficient for the needs of the toxicologist in making "health hazard" determinations. Some of these MSDS collections contain substantial information on lesser known chemicals. Occupational Health Services (22), Information Handling Services (23), Genium Publishing Corporation (24), VCH Publishers (25), and Hazardous Material Information Services (26) are some of the better known systems that contain information for approximately 1000–9000 chemicals.

## C. Search Procedure

As mentioned in the Introduction, chemical composition and identification information should already have been obtained before the chemical is to be searched. With most information retrieval systems this is a relatively straightforward procedure. Citations on a given subject may be retrieved by entering the desired free text terms as they appear in titles, key words, and abstracts of articles. The search is then initiated by entering the chemical CAS number and/or synonyms. If you are only interested in a specific target organ effect, for instance, carcinogenicity, or specific publication years, searches can be limited to a finite number of abstracts before requesting the printout.

Often it is not necessary to request a full printout (author, title, abstract). You may choose to review just the author and title listing before selecting out the abstracts of interest. In the long run, this approach may save you computer time, especially if the number of citations being searched is large.

Once you have reviewed the abstracts, the last step is to request photocopies of the articles of interest. Extreme caution should be used in making any final health hazard determination based solely upon an abstract or nonprimary literature source.

## IV. MONITORING PUBLISHED LITERATURE AND OTHER RESEARCH IN PROGRESS

Although there are a few other publications offering similar services, the *Life Sciences* edition of *Current Contents* (27) is the publication most widely used by toxicologists for monitoring the published literature. *Current Contents* monitors over 1160 major journals and provides a weekly listing by title and author. Selecting out those journals you wish to monitor is one means of selectively monitoring the major toxicology journals.

Aids available to the toxicologist for monitoring research in progress are quite variable. The National Toxicology Program Annual Plan for Fiscal Year 1985 (28) highlights all the accomplishments of the previous year and outlines the research plans for the coming year. The Annual Plan contains all projects in the president's proposed fiscal year budget that occur within the National Cancer Institute/National Institutes of Health, National Institute of Environmental Health Sciences/National Institutes of Health, National Cancer for Toxicological Research/Food and Drug Administration, and National Institute for Occupational Safety and Health/Centers for Disease Control. This report includes a list of all the chemicals selected for testing which includes but are not limited to research areas of mutagenicity, immunotoxicity, teratology/reproduction, neurotoxicity, pharmacokinetics, subchronic toxicity, and chronic toxicity/carcinogenicity.

The Annual Plan also contains a bibliography of NTP publications from the previous year. A companion publication is the 1985 NTP *Review of Current DHHS, DOE and EPA Research Activities* (29). Similar to the Annual Plan, this document provides detailed summaries of both proposed and ongoing research.

Another mechanism for monitoring research in progress is by reviewing abstracts presented at the annual meetings of the professional societies such as the Society of Toxicology, Teratology

Society, Environmental Mutagen Society, and American College of Toxicology. These societies usually have their abstracts prepared in printed form, for example, the 1986 *Toxicologist* (30), contained over 1300 abstracts presented at the annual meeting. Copies of the titles and authors of these abstracts are usually listed in the societies' respective journals, which in many cases, would be reproduced and could be reviewed through *Current Contents* (27).

## REFERENCES

1. National Toxicology Program, (1985), *Fourth Annual Report on Carcinogens.* Washington, D.C., Department of Health and Human Services, PB 85-134633.
2. Proctor, N. H. and Hughes, J. P. (1978), *Chemical Hazards of the Workplace*, Philadelphia, J. B. Lippincott.
3. Gosselin, R. E., Smith, R. P., and Hodge, H. C. (1984). *Clinical Toxicology of Commercial Products*, Fifth Edition. Baltimore, Williams and Wilkens.
4. National Institute for Occupational Safety and Health, *NIOSH Criteria for a Recommended Standard for Occupational Exposure to . . .* Cincinnati, OH, Department of Health, Education and Welfare.
5. National Institute for Occupational Safety and Health. *NIOSH Current Intelligence Bulletins.* Cincinnati, OH, Department of Health, Education and Welfare.
6. Sax, N. I. (1985). *Dangerous Properties of Industrial Materials*, Sixth Edition. New York, Van Nostrand Reinhold.
7. American Conference of Governmental Industrial Hygienists. (1986). *Documentation of the Threshold Limit Values*, Fifth Edition. Cincinnati, OH, ACGIH.
8. Sittig, M. (1981). *Handbook of Toxic and Hazardous Chemicals.* Park Ridge, NJ. Noyes Publications.
9. American Industrial Hygiene Association. (1980). *Hygienic Guide Series*, Volumes I and II. Akron, AIHA.
10. Finkel, A. J. (1983). *Hamilton and Hardy's Industrial Toxicology*, Fourth Ed. Boston, John Wright PSG Inc.
11. International Agency for Research on Cancer (1982). *Evaluation of the Carcinogenic Risk of Chemicals to Humans*, monograph supplement 4, Volumes 1-29. Lyon, France.
12. Windholz, M. (1983). *The Merck Index*, Tenth Ed. Rahway, NJ, Merck and Company, Inc.
13. Mackinson, F. National Institute for Occupational Health and Safety/Occupational Safety and Health Administration. (1981). *Occupational Health Guidelines for Chemical Hazards.* Department of Health and Human Services (NIOSH)/Department of

Labor (OSHA) DHHS No. 81-123, Washington, D.C., Government Printing Office.

14. Clayton, D. G. and Clayton, F. E. (1981). *Patty's Industrial Hygiene and Toxicology*, Third Revised Ed., Volumes 2A, 2B, and 2C. New York, John Wiley & Sons.
15. National Institute of Occupational Safety and Health. (1984). *Registry of Toxic Effects of Chemical Substances*, Eleventh Ed. Volumes 1–3. Washington, D.C., Department of Health and Human Services DHHS No. 83–107, 1983 and RTECS Supplement DHHS 84–101.
16. Doull, J., Klaassen, C. D., and Amdur, M. O. (1980). *Casarett and Doull's Toxicology; The Basic Science of Poisons*, Second Ed. New York, Macmillan Publishing Company.
17. Grant, W. M. (1974). *Toxicology of the Eye*, Second Ed., Volumes I and II. Springfield, IL., Charles C. Thomas.
18. National Institute for Occupational Safety and Health (1984). *Publications Catalog*, Sixth Ed. Cincinnati, OH, Department of Health and Human Services, DHHS No. 84–118.
19. American Conference of Governmental Industrial Hygienists. *TLVs® Threshold Limit Values and Biological Exposure Indices for 1985-86.* Cincinnati, OH, ACGIH.
20. National Academy of Sciences, National Research Council, Committee of Medical and Biologic Effects of Environmental Pollutants. Washington, D.C., NAS Printing and Publishing Office.
21. National Library of Medicine, Office of Inquiries and Publications Management, 8600 Rockville Pike, Bethesda, MD, 20209.
22. Occupational Health Services, Inc., 400 Plaza Drive, Secaucus, NJ, 07094.
23. Information Handling Services, 15 Inverness Way East, P.O. Box 1154, Englewood, CO, 80150.
24. Genium Publishing Corporation, 1145 Catalyn Street, Schenectady, NY, 12303.
25. VCH Publishers, 303 N.W. 12th Avenue, Deerfield Beach, FL, 33442.
26. Hazardous Materials Information Service. Department of Defense, 605.5L, Washington, D.C., Government Printing Office.
27. Institute for Scientific Information. (1986). *Current Contents- Life Sciences*. Philadelphia, ISI, Inc.
28. National Toxicology Program. (1985). *Annual Plan for Fiscal Year 1985*. Department of Health and Human Services, NTP-85-055. Washington, D.C. Government Printing Office.
29. National Toxicology Program. (1985). *Review of Current DHHS, DOE, and EPA Research Related to Toxicology*. Department of Health and Human Services, NTP-85-056. Washington, D.C. Government Printing Office.
30. Abstracts of the 25th Anniversary Meeting, Society of Toxicology (1986). *Toxicologist 6*(1), 1986.

# 3

# Acute Systemic Toxicity Testing

CAROL S. AULETTA / *Bio/dynamics Inc., East Millstone,
New Jersey*

## I. INTRODUCTION

Acute systemic toxicity studies evaluate the biological effects of a
single exposure to a material, generally in a large amount, and most
frequently as a result of an accident. Exposure can occur as a result of an industrial accident, a shipping mishap (train derailment,
tank car leak, etc.), a chemical spill, misuse of a household product,
a faulty container, a curious child left unsupervised for a moment,
a wide variety of other accidents, or, occasionally, as a result of
intentional ingestion (suicide attempt). It is the responsibility of
the manufacturer and supplier of a material to adequately characterize the nature of the hazards likely to result from such exposures
and to use this information to (1) assure that appropriate precau-
tions are taken to prevent accidental exposures and (2) make available all appropriate information for use in providing first aid and
treatment for persons exposed to the material. Likewise, if a material is essentially nonhazardous, it is important that this information be available to prevent needless concern.

Acute systemic toxicity studies are designed to provide this
information. Acute (accidental) exposures are generally oral (by
mouth), dermal (through the skin), or by inhalation. This chapter
discusses methods for the evaluation of acute oral and dermal toxicity; inhalation toxicity testing is discussed in a separate chapter.

## II. REGULATIONS, GUIDELINES, AND REGULATORY AGENCIES

Manufacture, distribution, packaging, labeling, and use of chemicals and other materials are regulated or monitored on the basis of acute toxicity data by a diverse and frequently confusing number of agencies, guidelines, and regulations. Several of these are discussed below.

### A. United States

#### 1. Consumer Product Safety Commission (CPSC)

This group is responsible for assuring that the consumer is not exposed to any unduly hazardous products and that any potentially hazardous products are labeled appropriately.

The CPSC administers the Federal Hazardous Substances Act (FHSA), passed in 1967, which replaced the earlier Federal Hazardous Substances Labeling Act (FHSLA). The current law, found in the Code of Federal Regulations as 16 CFR 1500, defines "hazardous substances" based on several characteristics, including toxicity, and applies to a wide range of consumer products. Some exemptions are made for substances regulated by other laws: economic poisons subject to the Federal Insecticide, Fungicide and Rodenticide Act; food, drugs, and cosmetics subject to the Federal Food, Drug and Cosmetic Act; substances intended for use as fuels when stored in containers and used in the heating, cooking, or refrigeration system of a house; and radioactive materials, which are regulated under the Atomic Energy Act.

A substance is considered "toxic" under the FHSA if it "has the capacity to produce personal injury or illness to man through ingestion, inhalation, or absorption through any body surface." A material is defined as "highly toxic" by ingestion or dermal absorption, on the basis of acute toxicity tests, if it: "produces death within 14 days in half or more than half of a group of 10 or more laboratory white rats each weighing between 200 and 300 grams, at a single dose of 50 milligrams or less per kilogram of body weight [mg/kg] when orally administered" or "produces death within 14 days in half or more than half of a group of 10 or more rabbits tested in a dosage of 200 milligrams or less per kilogram of body weight, when administered by continuous contact with the bare skin for 24 hours or less."

"Toxic" substances are defined similarly except that death must be produced in half or more than half of animals receiving oral doses between 50 and 5000 mg/kg or dermal doses between 200 and 2000 mg/kg. A further provision "to provide flexibility in the

number of animals tested" deletes the specific number of animals per
dose (10), but states that the number "should be sufficient to give
a statistically significant result and shall be in conformity with good
pharmacological practices."

Substances defined as highly toxic must be labelled as poison
and carry a "DANGER" label. Other hazardous substances must
carry "WARNING" or "CAUTION" labels and comply with additional
labeling requirements as defined in the FHSA regulations. Exemptions to labeling requirements for orally toxic substances may be
made if it can be demonstrated that such labeling is not necessary
because of "the physical form of the substance (solid, thick plastic,
emulsion, etc.), the size or closure of the container, human experience with the article or any other relevant factors."

It should be noted that this is a labeling act only. The CPSC
does not register materials, and there is no requirement for submission of toxicity data to the commission. The manufacturer or
distributer's sole obligation is to comply with the labeling regulations.

### 2. *Department of Transportation (DOT)*

Materials transported on U.S. roadways, railways, or airways
must be shipped in appropriately labeled vessels. Regulations for
labeling, packaging, transporting, and storing materials are presented
in 49 CFR 173 and are based on the hazard classification of a material,
also defined in this regulation. Class A poisons, "extremely dangerous poisons," represent inhalation hazards and are defined (in 49
CFR 173, Section 173.326) as "poisonous gases or liquids of such
nature that a very small amount of the gas, or vapor of the liquid,
mixed with air is dangerous to life." They include such materials
as phosgenes and cyanogenic materials. Class B poisons are classified based on hazards resulting from ingestion or dermal absorption
as well as by inhalation. Based on acute oral and dermal toxicity,
a material is considered by the DOT to be a Class "B" poison (and
thus subject to specific shipping and packaging regulations) if it
"produces death within 48 hours in half or more than half of a group
of 10 or more white laboratory rats weighing 200 to 300 grams at a
single dose of 50 milligrams or less per kilogram of body weight when
administered orally" or "produces death within 48 hours in half or
more than half of a group of 10 or more rabbits tested at a dosage
of 200 milligrams or less per kilogram body weight, when administered
by continuous contact with the bare skin for 24 hours or less" (49
CFR 173.343).

Exemptions to this classification can be made "if the physical
characteristics or the probable hazards to humans as shown by experience indicate that the substances will not cause serious sick-
ness or death."

### 3. Environmental Protection Agency (EPA)

The Environmental Protection Agency has responsibility for registration and labeling of pesticides under the Federal Insecticide, Fungicide and Rodenticide Act (FIFRA) and for regulation of chemicals and other potentially hazardous materials under the Toxic Substances Control Act (TSCA).

*Labeling.* Labeling and packaging standards for pesticides are established on the basis of toxicity categories and are detailed in 40 CFR 162.10. Categories range from IV (no significant toxicity) to I (very toxic) and are defined on thr basis of results of acute toxicity and irritation testing. Proposed changes in the regulations, redefining the hazard categories based on dermal toxicity, were published in the *Federal Register* (Vol. 49(188), September 26, 1984) but, as of this writing, have not been formally adopted. Current and proposed toxicity category criteria for acute oral and dermal toxicity are presented in Table 1.

*Testing Guidelines.*

1. *FIFRA and TSCA.* Some of the most recent and most comprehensive testing guidelines have been published by the EPA under FIFRA (*Pesticide Assessment Guidelines*, Subdivision F; Hazard Evaluation: Human and Domestic Animals; Office of Pesticide Programs, United States Environmental Protection Agency, Office of Pesticide and Toxic Substances, October 1982) and TSCA (*Health Effects Test Guidelines*; Office of Toxic Substances; Office of Pesticides and Toxic Substances, United States Environmental Protection Agency, August 1982). Guidelines are updated as needed, and guidelines for acute oral and dermal toxicity were updated in October 1984 to address public concern about the LD50 test and to clarify the agency's policy in this area. These guidelines also have become part of the Code of Federal Regulations (40 CFR Part 798) and were published in final form in the *Federal Register* (September 27, 1985).

In contrast to previously-cited regulations which provide minimal specifications (generally species, weight, dose, and duration of exposure and observation periods), the FIFRA and TSCA guidelines provide several pages of detailed information and testing procedures. The advantage of this approach is the increased consistency of studies performed in a variety of laboratories. However, because materials and circumstances differ, it is important to keep in mind that these are guidelines only (not rules), and regulators should be careful not to assume that studies which do not adhere to every detail of the guidelines are flawed.

Major provisions of these testing guidelines are summarized in Tables 2 and 3 and discussed in more detail below.

A number of specialized regulations and guidelines are also administered by the EPA.

**Table 1** Toxicity Category Criteria for Pesticide Labeling—EPA (FIFRA)[a]

| Hazard indicator | Category I | Category II | Category III | Category IV |
|---|---|---|---|---|
| Oral $LD_{50}$ | Up to and including 50 mg/kg | 50–500 mg/kg | 500–5000 mg/kg | >5000 mg/kg |
| Dermal $LD_{50}$ current: | Up to and including 200 mg/kg | 200–2000 mg/kg | 2000–20,000 mg/kg | >20,000 mg/kg |
| Dermal $LD_{50}$ proposed:[b] | Up to and including 200 mg/kg | >200–2000 mg/kg | 2000–5000 mg/kg | >5000 mg/kg |
| Human hazard signal word(s) | Danger, poison | Warning | Caution | Caution |

[a]U.S. Environmental Protection Agency: Federal Insecticide, Fungicide and Rodenticide Act; Subpart A: Registration, Re-registration and Classification Procedures (40 CFR 162.10).
[b]*Federal Register*, 49(188): September 28, 1984: Proposed Rules.

Table 2  Summary of Testing Guidelines/Regulations—Acute Oral Toxicity Tests

| | FHSA | DOT | TSCA | FIFRA | OECD | J MAFF |
|---|---|---|---|---|---|---|
| *Test animals* | | | | | | |
| Species | Rat | Rat | Rat[a] | Rat | Rat[a] | Rat plus one other |
| Age | NS | NS | Young adult | Young adult | Young adult | Young adult |
| Weight(g) | 200–300 | 200–300 | NS[b] | NS[b] | NS[b] | NS |
| *Limit test* | | | | | | |
| Amount (mg/kg) | 5000[c] | 50[d] | 5000 | 5000 | 5000 | 5000 |
| Acceptable mortality | Less than half | Less than half | None | None | None | None |
| *LD50 determination* | | | | | | |
| Minimum no. animals per group | 10 | 10 | 10[e] | 10[e] | 10[e] | 10[e] |
| No. of groups | NA | NA | 3 | At least 3 | At least 3 | 5 |
| Vehicle control | NR | NR | Yes[f] | No[g] | No[g] | NS[g] |
| *Dosing solution* | | | | | | |
| Volume | NS | NS | Constant | Constant | Constant | NS |
| Concentration | NS | NS | Variable | Variable | Variable | NS |

*Observations*

| | | | | | | |
|---|---|---|---|---|---|---|
| Observation period | 14 Days | 48 hr | 14 Days[h] | 14 Days[h] | 14 Days[h] | 14 Days[h] |
| Body weights | NS | NS | Weekly[i] | Weekly[i] | Weekly[i] | Weekly[i] |
| Necropsy | NR | NR | Yes | Optional[j] | Optional[j] | Optional[j] |
| Histopathology | NR | NR | Optional[k,l] | NS | Optional[k] | Optional[k] |

[a]Preferred species (several mammalian species acceptable).

[b]Weight not specified, but weight variation not to exceed ± 20% of the mean weight for each sex.

[c]To be considered not "toxic."

[d]To define Class B poison.

[e]5 Males and 5 females.

[f]Required unless historical data are available to determine acute toxicity of vehicle.

[g]The toxic characteristics of the vehicle should be known.

[h]14 Days is minimum duration; study may be extended if delayed mortality is seen.

[i]Body weights pretest, weekly and at death.

[j]Should be considered where indicated.

[k]Should be considered for animals surviving more than 24 hours.

[l]Clinical chemistry studies should also be considered.

Abbreviations: FHSA = Federal Hazardous Substances Act; DOT = Department of Transportation Regulations; TSCA = Toxic Substances Control Act (EPA); FIFRA = Federal Insecticide, Fungicide and Rodenticide Act (EPA); OECD = Organization for Economic Cooperation and Development—Toxicity Testing Guidelines; J MAFF = Japanese Ministry of Agriculture, Forestry and Fisheries—Requirements for Safety Evaluation of Agricultural Chemicals; NS = not specified; NR = not required; NA = not applicable.

Table 3  Summary of Testing Guidelines/Regulations—Acute Dermal Toxicity Tests

|  | FHSA | DOT | TSCA | FIFRA | OECD | J MAFF |
|---|---|---|---|---|---|---|
| *Test animals* | | | | | | |
| Species | Rabbit | Rabbit | Rat, rabbit, or guinea pig[a] | Rat, rabbit, or guinea pig[a] | Rat, rabbit, or guinea pig | One mammalian species, (rat, rabbit, guinea pig, etc.) |
| Age | NS | NS | Young adult | Adult | Adult | Adult |
| *Weight* | | | | | | |
| Rat (g) | NA | NA | 200–300 | 200–300 | 200–300 | 200–300 |
| Rabbit (kg) | 2.3–3 | NS | 2–3 | 2–3 | 2–3 | 2–3 |
| Guinea pig (g) | NA | NA | 350–450 | 350–450 | 350–450 | 350–450 |
| *Limit test* | | | | | | |
| Amount (mg/kg) | 2000[b] | 200[c] | 2000 | At least 2000 | 2000 | 2000 |
| Acceptable mortality | Less than half | Less than half | None | None | None | None |
| *LD50 determination* | | | | | | |
| Minimum no. animals per group | 10 | 10 | 10[d] | 10[d] | 10[d,e] | 10[d] |

| | | | | | |
|---|---|---|---|---|---|
| No. of groups | NA | NA | 3 | At least 3 | At least 3 | At least 3 |
| Vehicle control | NR | NR | Yes[f] | No[g] | No[g] | No[g] |
| *Observations* | | | | | | |
| Observation period | 14 Days | 48 hr | 14 Days[h] | 14 Days[h] | 14 Days[h] | 14 Days[h] |
| Body weights | NS | NS | Weekly[i] | Weekly[i] | Weekly[i] | Weekly[i] |
| Necropsy | NR | NR | Yes | Optional[j] | Optional[j] | Optional[j] |
| Histopathology | NR | NR | Optional[k,l] | NS | Optional[k] | Optional[k] |

[a]Rabbit is preferred.
[b]To be considered not "toxic."
[c]To define Class B poison.
[d]5 Males and 5 females.
[e]Smaller numbers may be used, especially in the case of the rabbit.
[f]Required unless historical data are available to determine acute toxicity of vehicle.
[g]The toxic characteristics of the vehicle should be known.
[h]14 Days is minimum duration; study may be extended if delayed mortality is seen.
[i]Body weights pretest, weekly and at death.
[j]Should be considered where indicated.
[k]Should be considered for animals surviving more than 24 hours.
[l]Clinical chemistry studies should also be considered.
Abbreviations: See Table 2.

2. Biorational Pesticides. The new generation of "biological" pesticides which rely on specific pathogens, presumably hazardous only to the target species, are regulated under Subpart M of the FIFRA regulations. Separate sets of tests are proposed for biochemical and microbiological materials. However, the acute oral and dermal toxicity/infectivity studies are similar for all categories and essentially duplicate the Subdivision F guidelines, with the addition of an "infectivity" analysis of fluids and tissues and the specification of the rat as the species of choice for acute dermal toxicity testing. Additional acute infectivity studies are required in mice and hamsters with administration by injection (intravenous or intraperitoneal) and observations for up to 4 weeks after dosing.

3. Hazardous Waste. CFR 40 (Protection of Environment, Environmental Protection Agency), Subpart B, 261.11: Criteria for Listing Hazardous Waste, presents criteria for listing hazardous waste, based in part on acute toxicity data. Section (a) (2) of this paragraph states that:

The Administrator shall list a solid waste as a hazardous waste only if it has been found to be fatal to humans in low doses or, in the absence of data on human toxicity, it has been shown in studies to have an oral $LD_{50}$ toxicity (rat) of less than 50 milligrams per kilogram . . . or a dermal $LD_{50}$ (rabbit) of less than 200 milligrams per kilogram or is otherwise capable of causing or significantly contributing to an increase in serious irreversible, or incapacitating reversible, illness. (Waste listed in accordance with these criteria will be designated Acute Hazardous Waste.)

4. United States Forest Service (USFS). This group has established its own set of testing protocols for flame retardants used in combatting forest fires. These protocols generally follow FIFRA guidelines, but the Forest Service requires a more direct involvement in testing than other agencies, by actually providing materials directly to the testing laboratory for evaluation and requesting that reports be submitted directly to the agency by the testing laboratory.

*4. Department of Health, Education and Welfare (HEW)*
*Food and Drug Administration (FDA)*

In addition to regulating pharmaceuticals, which are not within the scope of this book, the FDA is responsible, through its Bureau of Foods, for the safety of direct food additives and color additives used in food. Materials which are to be directly added to foods and which are not considered to meet GRAS criteria (generally recognized as safe) must be approved by the FDA. Under the Food, Drug and

Cosmetic Act, the safety of a food or color additive must be established prior to marketing. (Natural foods are not regulated.) Indirect food additives (materials which leach through packaging, pesticide residues, residues of animal feed additives) are regulated separately, by the FDA (packaging components), the EPA (pesticide residues), the U.S. Department of Agriculture (animal feed additives), and other agencies. The safety of food and color additives is defined in the Code of Federal Regulations (21 CFR 170.3) as a reasonable certainty that a substance is not harmful under the intended conditions of use. Safety evaluation by the FDA includes estimates of probable consumer exposure and evaluation of appropriate toxicological information. In 1982 the FDA Bureau of Foods published "Toxicological Principles for the Safety Assessment of Direct Food Additives and Color Additives used in Foods." This document, which has a red cover and has come to be known as "The Redbook," was developed to provide guidelines for use by FDA personnel in evaluating food additive petitions submitted for review.

One of the premises of this document is that, because additives are substances that people ingest intentionally, the agency should possess at least some toxicological or other biological safety information for each additive intended for addition to the food supply. Although an acute oral toxicity study is not required for safety evaluation of direct food additives, guidelines for this study are presented in the "Redbook" for use when the acute toxicity of an additive is of concern or when acute toxicity data are required for the design of longer-term studies.

### 5. United States Pharmacopeia (USP)

The USP XX specifies certain biological tests "designed to test the suitability of plastic materials intended for use in fabricating containers or accessories thereto, for parenteral preparations, and to test the suitability of polymers for medical use in implants, devices and other systems." One of the required tests is a "systemic injection test," which is performed by intravenously injecting extracts of the test plastic in various vehicles into mice (ten per group) and comparing response over 72 hours with that of mice injected with vehicle alone.

## B. International

### 1. Organization for Economic Cooperation and Development (OECD)

Member nations include the United States and much of the European Economic Community. OECD has formed expert groups on

short-term and long-term toxicology to review toxicity testing requirements of the member nations and formulate testing guidelines
which would be acceptable to all members. "Test Guidelines for
Toxicity Testing" were issued in draft form in December 1979 by
prominent member countries (United States and the United Kingdom).
Most acute toxicity testing for products to be registered, sold, or
distributed in Europe is performed according to these guidelines,
whose aim was stated as follows:

> The aim of the present work has been to produce a framework
> for each toxicity test which is sufficiently well-defined to en-
> able it to be carried out in a similar manner in different
> countries and to produce results that will be fully acceptable
> to various regulatory bodies. The growing demands for
> testing and evaluating the toxicity of chemical substances
> will place increasing pressure on personnel and laboratory
> resources. A harmonized approach, promoting the scientific
> aspects of toxicity testing and ensuring a wide acceptability
> of test data for regulatory purposes, will avoid wasteful
> duplication or repetition and contribute to the efficient use of
> laboratory facilities and skilled personnel.

On April 11, 1986, the OECD published draft updates of its
guidelines for acute oral and dermal toxicity testing. These updates, discussed in more detail in the section on alternatives (Sect.
II.B.3), propose several procedures which are intended to reduce
numbers of animals used in experiments and limit the amount of pain
to which they are subjected.

### 2. Japan

In Japan, regulations exist for toxicity testing of medicinal
products and for agricultural chemicals. Agricultural chemicals are
regulated by the Japanese Ministry of Agriculture, Forestry and
Fisheries (MAFF), which updated its requirements and testing guidelines, effective April 1, 1985. "Requirements for Safety Evaluation
of Agricultural Chemicals" states that acute oral toxicity testing in
at least two species and acute dermal toxicity testing in at least one
species, using both the end-use product and the technical grade of
the active ingredient are required for registration of agricultural
chemicals used on either food or nonfood crops. "Testing Guidelines for Toxicology Studies" state that if limit tests (10 animals)
demonstrate no compound-related mortality at an oral dose of 5000
mg/kg or a dermal dose of 2000 mg/kg, "no further testing might
be necessary."

## III.  CONDUCT OF ACUTE TOXICITY TESTS

After the applicable regulations and/or guidelines have been established, one must then design and conduct appropriate studies and, finally, interpret the results.

### A.  Study Protocols

Study protocols, specifying materials and methods to be used in performing toxicity evaluations, can be obtained from testing laboratories or may be designed by the manufacturer of the material to be tested.  Fortunately, it is not necessary to perform separate tests for each regulatory agency, since requirements are essentially similar, and one test can be designed which satisfies all of the requirements. If cost is critical and only one of the less comprehensive regulations is applicable, a smaller, less expensive study design will frequently suffice.  However, one cannot later attempt to apply the limited information obtained for purposes other than those for which it was originally intended.  Thus, some forethought may result in a slightly higher initial expenditure but can ultimately save time, money, and animals.

Major provisions of several of the testing guidelines presented above are summarized in Tables 2 and 3 and discussed below, along with other factors to be considered in establishing protocols for acute toxicity studies.

### B.  Study Design/Number of Animals

#### 1.  Limit Test

Virtually all regulatory and labeling guidelines accept the concept of the limit test, a study in which a large amount of the test product is administered to several laboratory animals, generally 5 males and 5 females.  If no mortality is seen at this "limit" dose, then no further testing is required.  Some confusion exists, however, about interpretation of the limit test when some mortality is seen, but less than half of the animals die, in other words, the apparent median lethal dose ($LD_{50}$) is greater than the amount administered.

#### 2.  $LD_{50}$ Determination

If a material produces mortality in the limit test, additional doses are usually administered to determine the approximate median lethal dose ($LD_{50}$), or the dose which will kill approximately half of the animals.  If only one or two animals die after receiving the amount specified for the limit test, our laboratory does not generally recommend additional doses. However, persons submitting materials for EPA registration or review may feel obligated to proceed to a full $LD_{50}$ study because of the wording of the regulations, which indicate that a full $LD_{50}$ test should be performed if any mortality is seen during the limit test and because of the general inflexibility of EPA reviewers in interpreting these guidelines.

For materials of unknown toxicity or for those with an anticipated $LD_{50}$ value below the limit test, it is often useful to perform a preliminary range-finding test to provide guidance in selecting dose levels. Four or more different dosage levels are generally administered to two animals (one male and one female) per level. If no information is available, a wide range of doses, for example, from 50 to 5000 mg/kg should be selected. It is usually possible to select doses for $LD_{50}$ determination based on one range-finding study, although, occasionally, additional studies are necessary. Animals used for range-finding studies are generally observed for mortality only and are held for 7 days after dosing. Clinical observations may provide useful information about anticipated effects in the definitive study.

Based on results of range-finding, doses are selected for the $LD_{50}$ study. An attempt should be made to select one dose which will produce little or no mortality, one dose which will produce mortality of approximately 50%, and one dose which will be lethal to most of the animals. Traditionally, five or more dosage levels have been used for $LD_{50}$ studies; however, current regulations accept as few as three dosage levels, and attempts are usually made to use as small a number of animals as possible. However, dose selection based on a small group size (2 animals) is not always accurate. The 2 animals in the range-finding study may represent either end of the spectrum of effects. Therefore, mortality of 50% (1 of 2) in the range-finding study may represent mortality of 10% (1/10) or 90% (9/10) in a study with a larger group size. It is sometimes necessary to add additional groups if an appropriate mortality range is not achieved initially. Care should be taken to maintain conditions of the additional doses as close as possible to those of the initial doses. Variables in body weights, age, environmental conditions, test material conditions/preparation, etc. may produce confusing results and present difficulties in data interpretation. Thus, while this step-wise approach decreases the total number of animals used in $LD_{50}$ studies, it can sometimes lead to variable results and must be administered carefully. The judgement and experience of the laboratory are important factors in determining the initial and total numbers of dosage levels to be used for $LD_{50}$ determination. For rabbits, a step-wise approach, giving one dose at a time to 10 animals, will usually produce a reasonable $LD_{50}$ estimate with three doses.

A variety of methods can be used to calculate the actual $LD_{50}$ value (the dose which is lethal to half of the animals) with 95%

confidence limits, that is, the range of doses which would be expected to include the $LD_{50}$ value 95% of the time (1–6). The precision of the $LD_{50}$ value and the extent of the 95% confidence limits vary with the method used and the number of animals tested. In general, precision increases with increasing numbers of animals. However, the $LD_{50}$ study has been criticized by several responsible toxicologists who question the validity and usefulness of a precise number ($LD_{50}$ value) generated by using a biological system and a test design with so many variables that may affect the actual numerical value (7,8). The consensus among toxicologists is that a precise (but frequently nonreproducible) $LD_{50}$ value is of limited usefulness and that significant information can be obtained by using fewer animals treated at doses producing little or no lethality (7–10). This approach has been encouraged and supported by various animal rights groups dedicated to "abolishing the $LD_{50}$" or, at least, decreasing animal use in experiments and unnecessary pain and suffering.

## 3. Alternatives

Several innovative alternative approaches have been suggested to reduce animal use or to replace animals entirely and still provide useful information.

*Alternative Studies Using Animals.* Some procedures which use fewer animals than the so-called "classical $LD_{50}$" study are currently performed routinely. These are the limit test and the $LD_{50}$ study using as few as three dose groups (30 animals), discussed above. Other study designs have been proposed but are not currently in common use.

In an acknowledgment that much acute toxicity testing is performed in order to classify materials and place them in hazard categories, some authors (10) suggest a "classification scheme" in which groups of animals are dosed in a step-wise manner at various regulatory-designated dosage levels until the appropriate classification is obtained. This is a variation of the limit test and, if a material is of low toxicity, may require only 10 animals if most or all survive an initial upper dose in the classification scheme. Our laboratory performs MSDS studies, which are abbreviated designs using 4 to 6 animals per dose, designed to place materials in hazard categories for Material Safety Data Sheets. The disadvantage of such studies is that, although they achieve the desired purpose of classifying the materials, they do not provide much, if any, detailed information about toxicity of the material.

Most proposed alterations in study design emphasize evaluation of toxicity, rather than lethality, while obtaining this information with fewer animals. As early as 1943 (11,12), procedures for determining an approximate lethal dose (ALD) using as few as 6 animals were suggested. The "up-and-down" study, designed by R. Bruce

(13), is a more current published version (1985), incorporating similar principles. The concept of staggering doses, or observing for effects in animals dosed initially, prior to administering further doses, is also an integral part of several approaches designed to reduce laboratory animal use (9,14). Based on studies demonstrating that sex-related differences are relatively rare in acute toxicity studies (15-17), some authors suggest that acute studies be performed using animals of one sex only (5 animals per dose), preferably the more sensitive sex. Administration of one dose to the opposite sex, to confirm absence of sex-related differences, is usually recommended. This approach essentially halves the number of animals required and is one of the suggestions incorporated in the revised OECD draft (April 1986).

Although most government agencies still require numerical values for lethal and nonlethal doses, most of the alternative methods emphasize that a determination of an approximate lethal dose, or even a range of toxic but nonlethal doses, provides adequate or superior information for characterization of potential hazards. Some regulatory acceptance of this concept is apparent. The revised OECD draft (April 1986) suggests that animals "showing severe and enduring pain may be humanely killed" and that doses "known to cause marked pain and distress . . . need not be administered, even when no mortality has been observed at tolerated doses." Many alternative methods incorporate "multiple end-point testing" for evaluation of acute toxic effects. Thus, while fewer animals may be tested, it is hoped that more meaningful information will be obtained from each animal.

Many of these alternative approaches have been developed and/or adopted in various industrial laboratories, and their use is increasing. The problem faced by the manufacturer or supplier of a product, however, is the general inflexibility of rules and regulators which perpetuate studies using more animals and higher doses than appear warranted by good science.

*Nonanimal Tests.* The search for "alternatives" includes, in addition to the alternative approaches to classical study designs discussed above, investigations of nonanimal systems which might replace animal testing or reduce the number of animals used. A wide and fascinating variety of approaches have been suggested.

In vitro methods using various types of cells and organs in culture and evaluating a variety of effects on growth, viability, and metabolism abound. Studies using lower organisms (bacteria, algae, fungi, plants, insects, lower vertebrates) have also been developed. Mathematical models, based on structure-activity relationships and computer modeling are available as well. The major difficulty with these alternatives is the problem of validation, a term on which there is still much disagreement among toxicologists. Validation of a procedure should include some comparison to currently accepted in vivo methods and some agreement that results generated by the new procedure can provide information which is reasonably equivalent to that provided by current methods. Most methods currently under development have not reached this stage of validation.

Thus, while much research continues into alternative methods, the consensus among toxicologists and regulatory agencies is that currently no acceptable methods exist which will eliminate entirely the need for animal testing.

## C. Test Animals

### 1. Species/Strain

*Acute Oral Toxicity.* The rat is the animal used most commonly for acute oral toxicity testing. If a second species is required, the mouse is generally selected. Rabbits and hamsters are used occasionally, but such studies are relatively rare. If data on a large animal species are required, generally by special request of certain agencies and usually to provide preliminary information for longer-term studies, dogs and (rarely) nonhuman primates may be tested. Such studies would almost always be done using the up-and-down method (13), which requires only a small number of animals, usually 6–10.

The three commonly used strains of albino rat are the Sprague-Dawley-derived, the Fisher 344, and the Wistar. The hooded (Long-Evans) rat is also used occasionally, but one of the three albino strains is more likely to be selected. Most laboratories have a strain and animal supplier(s) which they use routinely and, thus, have historical experience with a specific strain. Because strain-related differences in response to various materials have been demonstrated, it is generally best to test the strain with which the laboratory has had experience.

*Acute Dermal Toxicity.* The New Zealand White (albino) rabbit has historically been the species of choice for acute dermal toxicity testing, although use of albino rats or guinea pigs has become increasingly accepted. Because of their size, rats and guinea pigs are easier (and less expensive) to test. However, they are also generally less sensitive to topically administered materials than are rabbits, and there is no significant historical data base available for comparison with other materials. Thus, based on the extensive data base available and its superior skin permeability, the rabbit continues to be the species of choice for acute dermal toxicity evaluations.

### 2. Husbandry/Housing

Guidelines exist which define facilities and environmental conditions appropriate for standard laboratory species (18). Laboratories which are accredited by the American Association for Laboratory

Animal Care (AALAC) are inspected periodically and must adhere to appropriate standards to maintain accreditation. Facilities housing rabbits, guinea pigs, and hamsters must adhere to specifications of the Animal Welfare Act and are subject to periodic inspection by the U.S. Department of Agriculture (USDA). (Rats and mice are not regulated.) Cage sizes are specified based on the size and activity patterns of each species. Temperature ranges of 18–26°C (64–79°F) for rats and 16–21°C (61–70°F) for rabbits are specified; desired relative humidity values are usually in the range of 40–70%.

The intent of husbandry guidelines is to assure that standard conditions are maintained and to minimize environmental stress which might complicate interpretation of study results. Newer facilities are designed to adhere to these standards. However, one must keep in mind that acute toxicity studies have been performed for several decades and that many older facilities cannot always maintain the exact environmental conditions specified in some of the guidelines. Temperature and humidity variations are only two of the multiple variables which may influence results of acute toxicity studies (7,8). Thus, while reasonable care should be exercised, deviations from desired environmental conditions are likely to occur and, unless they are severe and sustained over a long period, they will generally not compromise an acute toxicity study or preclude meaningful interpretation of results. Rodents and guinea pigs may be housed as a group or individually. Individual caging provides easier identification and observation of animals and prevents loss by cannibalism of animals which die. Rabbits are generally housed individually.

### 3. Age, Sex, and Weight

Most current guidelines specify the use of adult or young adult animals; some also suggest weight ranges (200–300 g for rats, 2–3 kg for rabbits).

Because there is a sex-related size difference in rats, males and females of the same weight will be of different ages. Thus, one or the other will be variable. In our laboratory, we have defined "young adult" as approximately 9–12 weeks old and specify weight ranges based on these ages (approximately 250–360 g for males, 200–270 g for females) (19) for the Sprague-Dawley-derived albino rat. Young adult male and female rabbits are generally comparable in size; a weight range of approximately 2–3 or 3.5 kg is appropriate.

Equal numbers of animals of each sex are usually tested. Most current guidelines specify that females should be nulliparous and nonpregnant. Although males and females will give equivalent responses to most materials tested, sex-related differences are sometimes seen. Many materials are more toxic to females than to males. In cases where a sex-related difference is apparent, it is necessary to adjust the doses given to the different sexes and to report the

$LD_{50}$ separately, by sex. Although a total $LD_{50}$ can generally be calculated if data are combined, this will usually represent a dose which will kill most or all animals of one sex and few or none of the opposite sex.

### 4. Animal Health

Healthy laboratory rats are generally readily available, and maintaining healthy rats for acute oral toxicity studies is usually not a problem. However, rats are particularly susceptible to sialodacryo-adenitis virus (SDAV), a disease characterized by enlargement of the salivary glands with resultant cervical swelling and often accompanied by ocular abnormalities (drying of the cornea) (20). This disease is acute, self-limiting, and seldom fatal. However, it frequently appears just as animals are completing quarantine and are ready to be tested and may create delays in initiating studies. Serological surveillance and strict quarantine procedures will help to reduce the incidence of SDAV infections.

Identifying and maintaining a source of consistently healthy rabbits is a major difficulty in assuring that suitable animals are available for acute dermal toxicity studies. Rabbit breeding facilities are generally not as large or sophisticated as those maintained by rodent suppliers, and large rabbit suppliers often supplement their stock by purchasing locally raised animals from small farms or family enterprises. Thus, the purchaser, attempting to adhere to accepted standards of husbandry and environmental conditions, has little or no control over the conditions to which the animals were exposed prior to receipt at the laboratory. An additional problem is the practice of many rabbit suppliers of medicating feed and/or water with antibiotics (generally tetracycline) to control outbreaks of disease. Rabbits removed from this prophylaxis upon receipt at the laboratory frequently exhibit signs of illness within several days. Diseases commonly found in laboratory rabbits include respiratory problems (snuffles) or intestinal disease generally associated with pasteurellosis or coccidiosis (21). It is important to monitor carefully for such diseases and assure that animals placed on acute toxicity studies are free of any abnormal clinical signs. It is not uncommon, however, for animals harboring diseases subclinically to exhibit signs of illness after the stress of test material administration. Experience in observing clinical and morphological manifestations of common rabbit diseases is useful in deciding whether or not death of an animal is a toxic response to the test material.

### D. Administration of Materials

#### 1. Oral Administration

Oral administration of materials is generally performed by using a syringe fitted with a ball-tipped intubation needle or a flexible rubber or tygon tube. This delivery technique, known as oral intubation or gavage, requires practice and skill; it is important to use well-trained, experienced technicians. However, even experienced technicians sometimes have "dosing accidents" (intratracheal delivery of material or perforation of the esophagus), especially when administering viscous materials. It is standard procedure in our laboratory to prepare one additional rat per sex per dose level to be used as a replacement in case of dosing accidents. Such accidents are usually apparent immediately by the animal's response, but may take several hours (or, occasionally, a few days) to produce death. It is important, therefore, to carefully examine animals which die for evidence of injuries sustained during dosing. Animals in which the cause of death is determined to be accidental should be replaced, if possible, and excluded from mortality estimates and calculations. If death is delayed, it is frequently not possible or practical to dose a replacement animal because the dosing solution and suitable animals are no longer available and the replacement animal(s) would be on a different time schedule than those dosed originally.

The physical form of a material designated for oral administration often presents unique challenges. Liquids can be administered as supplied or diluted with an appropriate vehicle, and powders or particulates can often be dissolved or suspended in an appropriate vehicle. However, selection of an appropriate vehicle is often difficult. Water and oil (usually a vegetable oil, such as corn or peanut oil) are used most commonly. Materials which are not readily soluble in water or oil can frequently be suspended in a 1% aqueous mixture of methylcellulose, which is essentially nontoxic. Occasionally a more concentrated methylcellulose suspension (up to 5%) may be necessary. Materials for which appropriate solutions/suspensions cannot be prepared using one of these three vehicles often present major difficulties.

Limited solubility/suspendability of materials often dictates preparation of dilute mixtures, which require large volumes to be administered. The total volume of liquid dosing solution or suspension which can be administered to a rat is limited to the size of its stomach. However, because a rodent lacks a gagging reflex and has no emetic mechanism, any material administered will be retained. Current guidelines state that the maximum volume which can be administered to a rodent is 20 ml/kg of body weight for aqueous solutions and 10 ml/kg for other vehicles (oils), although some references have indicated that volumes of aqueous solutions as high as 64 ml/kg can be given (22). We have administered volumes of up to 30–35 ml/kg of aqueous suspensions of methylcellulose to control rats in our laboratory with no adverse effects and feel this is a reasonable maximum volume for aqueous mixtures. Although similar volumes of oil mixtures can be physically administered, a maximum volume of 10 ml/kg appears reasonable because of the cathartic effect of oils. Dose volumes of 10 and 30 ml/kg are equivalent to total volumes of 2-3.5 ml and 6-10.5 ml for rats in the 200-350 g weight range.

Limitations on total volume, therefore, present difficulties for materials which cannot easily be dissolved or suspended. The most dilute solutions which can be administered for a limit test (5000 mg/kg), using the maximum volume discussed above, are 17% for aqueous mixtures and 50% for other vehicles. In cases where it is necessary to administer larger volumes, two or more smaller doses can be given over a period of several hours.

Although vehicle control animals are not required for commonly used vehicles (water, oil, methylcellulose), most regulations require that the toxic characteristics should be known and/or that historical data be available. Our laboratory periodically generates control data by selecting 10 animals (5 of each sex) from shipments of rats used for acute oral toxicity studies. These animals are dosed with 1.0% methylcellulose (the vehicle most commonly used in acute oral studies) at a volume of 30 ml/kg (the maximum volume administered in any study) and observed following a standard protocol. Data are used for reference in preparing the final report and are appended to the report if applicable. Unfortunately, the best solvents are generally toxic and, thus, cannot be used as vehicles. Ethanol and acetone can be tolerated in relatively high doses but produce effects which may complicate interpretation of toxicity associated with the test material alone. It is sometimes possible to dissolve a material in a small amount of one of these vehicles and then dilute the solution in oil.

Gels and resins often present problems because of their viscosity at room temperature. Warming these materials in a water bath to a temperature of up to 50°C will frequently facilitate mixing and dosing. However, it is important to ascertain that no thermal degradation occurs.

Another possibility for insoluble materials is to mix the desired amount of material with a small amount of the animal's diet. The difficulty with this approach is the likelihood that the animal will not consume all of the treated diet or that it may selectively not consume chunks of test material. In some cases, if all of these approaches fail, it may not be possible to test a material by oral administration.

Rats are usually fasted overnight prior to oral dosing in order to assure an empty stomach. Mice, because of a more rapid metabolic rate, may be fasted for a shorter interval. Some toxicologists feel that fasting is undesirable because absorption of the material is altered from that which would most likely occur during accidental exposure. However, this has been the traditional procedure and represents the most conservative approach. Doses can be calculated using weights obtained prior to or after fasting. Because a rat can exhibit a large decrease in weight (up to 20%) after an overnight fast, the dose received can vary significantly depending on which weight is used. The fasted weight represents the truest weight, while dosing based on the unfasted weight represents the more conservative approach, in other words, it errs on the side of safety.

Most current guidelines suggest that concentrations of dosing mixtures be varied so that animals at different dose levels are given the same volume of dosing solution. This presents some practical problems in the laboratory and raises some scientific questions; arguments can be made both for and against this approach. Administering a different concentration of solutions or suspensions to each dose level requires preparation of several different mixtures, and is thus more time consuming and labor intensive. Preparing multiple mixtures also requires more test material and increases the possibility of error. Primarily for practical reasons, our laboratory prefers to prepare one mixture for all groups of animals and vary the dose volume as necessary. It is also not clear whether liquid materials should be diluted. However, testing liquids in the form to which the consumer or worker would be exposed seems to be the most reasonable approach (23) and, unless necessary to achieve a reasonable dose volume, our laboratory does not dilute liquid materials.

### 2. Dermal Administration

Materials administered dermally are applied to the skin of the back, sides, and/or entire trunk. Fur is usually removed using a veterinary clipper on the day prior to dosing. Care should be taken to avoid nicks, cuts, or "clipper burns" which would disrupt the integrity of the skin and could alter permeability or enhance irritation. Clipping rats and guinea pigs is relatively easy, but rabbits require additional care because of their larger size, long fine hair, and delicate skin. A band extending from the shoulders to the pelvic girdle and exposing the back and sides comprises approximately 600 cm$^2$ in an average-sized (3 kg) rabbit and represents approximately 10–20% of the body surface.

An area of this size is generally adequate to accommodate most test materials. However, it is sometimes necessary to remove the fur on the abdomen as well so that the band of exposed skin encircles the animal. Special care must be taken to avoid the nipples and to avoid damaging the delicate abdominal skin. Although administering materials to intact skin is the most common procedure, some study designs specify that the skin of some or all of the animals should be abraded prior to test material administration. This is accomplished in our laboratory by using a hypodermic needle with a blunted point. The skin is lightly scored longitudinally every few centimeters over the exposure area. Abrasions are made deep enough to penetrate the outer layer of skin (the stratum corneum) but not deep enough to penetrate the dermis or to produce bleeding. Administration of materials to abraded skin simulates exposure to damaged skin and is probably a realistic assumption in the case of factory workers who may have cuts or scratches on the skin.

Dermal administration presents fewer logistic difficulties than oral administration. Liquids can be administered as supplied and powders or solids can be moistened with saline to form a thick paste or slurry or applied dry and moistened with saline. Solid materials (sheets of plastic, fabric, etc.) can also be administered dermally. Liquid materials or slurries are applied directly to the skin, taking care to spread the material evenly over the entire area or as much of the area as can reasonably be covered, and then covered with a strip of 8-ply gauze. If a large amount of material is being administered and the abdominal skin will be exposed, it is sometimes necessary to apply material to the gauze as well as to the skin. Dry materials are weighed out, then placed on the gauze strip, and moistened with physiological saline (generally 15 ml) so that they will adhere to the gauze. The gauze is then wrapped around the animal. This porous gauze dressing is then held in place by an additional wrapping, generally of an impervious material, to create an "occlusive" covering. This occlusion enhances penetration and prevents ingestion or evaporation of the test material.

In our laboratory, a plastic sleeve, consisting of a rectangle cut from a plastic garbage bag, folded, and reinforced with masking tape on both ends, is used. This rectangular band is wrapped (overlapped) over the gauze band and secured in place by masking tape. Application is performed by two technicians. One applies the material and secures the gauze and plastic covering; the second grasps the rabbit by the shoulders and pelvis and lifts it to allow the wrapping procedure. Other types of covering used are Saran Wrap, athletic bandages, or other surgical wrapping materials.

Most guidelines specify a 24-hr exposure period. Although animals may be immobilized (restrained in stocks) during this exposure period to prevent ingestion of test material or disturbance of the wrapping, it is preferable not to inhibit mobility. This can be accomplished by using Elizabethan-type collars. These can be purchased commercially from veterinary suppliers. We use collars fabricated from plastic (approximately 1/4 inch thick) and consisting of two semicircular pieces drilled with several holes in each end. The two pieces are secured with wing nuts; the holes allow the collars to be adjusted to fit each individual rabbit. These lightweight collars are tolerated well and serve their purpose by preventing the rabbits from disturbing the test site. They are generally worn throughout the exposure period and for the entire postdose period.

Although excess test material is wiped or washed after termination of the exposure, it is not uncommon for residual material to remain. The collars remove the possibility of ingestion. Occasionally an animal will catch a collar in its lower jaw and cut its mouth. Animals are checked frequently and any instances of injury from the collar are noted in the data so observations related to such injuries can be distinguished from test material-related effects. Materials administered dermally to rats and guinea pigs are generally secured by a flexible overlapping adhesive bandage (Elastoplast).

Doses are administered on the basis of animal body weight, although some toxicologists feel that dosing based on amount of skin surface covered is a more scientifically sound procedure. Although literature references exist indicating $LD_{50}$ values of 20 g/kg or higher and some toxicity classifications refer to values in this range, it is difficult to imagine how such a large amount of material could be applied and kept in contact with the skin. (The revision in the FIFRA pesticide labeling standards (24) attempts to address this issue.) Experiments in our laboratory indicate that approximately 8 g (or ml) of material is the maximum amount which can reasonably be administered and absorbed, depending on the nature of the material. This represents a total volume of 16–32 ml for animals in the 2–4 kg body weight range and is still too high for many materials.

## E.  Experimental Evaluation

Acute toxicity testing is generally the first, and frequently the only, evaluation of mammalian systemic toxicity performed on a product. Therefore, studies should be designed to obtain the maximum amount of information possible. Although a few studies of the "kill 'em and count 'em" variety are still performed, most acute toxicity studies attempt to provide some characterization of the nature and extent of the hazard of accidental exposure in addition to estimates of lethality.

### 1.  Clinical Signs

Animals should be observed for mortality and unusual signs several times on the day of dosing and at least once daily thereafter (twice daily for mortality). Animals which appear to be moribund (close to death) should be checked frequently to preclude postmortem autolytic changes which occur if an animal dies unobserved and mortality is not discovered for several hours. Contrary to common practice in other types of toxicity studies, moribund animals are generally not killed in acute toxicity studies. Because mortality is one of the major endpoints and because some animals which appear to be moribund do recover, animals are generally held until death or recovery is seen. Animals should be observed for effects on behavior (increased or decreased activity, etc.), neurologic function (tremors, convulsions, ataxia), respiratory parameters (alteration in rate or character, secretions), secretory and excretory functions (salivation, lacrimation, diarrhea, urination, fecal, or urinary staining of the fur), physiologic state (hypothermia, etc.), and any other unusual signs. Although food consumption is generally not measured in acute toxicity tests, animals which are not eating or which are eating poorly can be identified and these observations noted. "Cageside" observations will detect mortality and extreme abnormalities. However, detailed observations generally require that the animal be handled, observed closely for behavioral/locomotor changes, and evaluated for such abnormalities as unusual respiratory sounds (rales). Recording forms or systems which provide the previous observations for each animal are preferable; this allows the technician to ascertain if unusual signs seen previously are still present and helps prevent oversights and data inconsistencies. Each laboratory develops a set of terminology and definitions which are used to describe unusual signs. Some observations are fairly unambiguous (convulsions), while others are more likely to vary from laboratory to laboratory. Such terms as lethargy, hypoactivity, depression and (possibly) sedation, and prostration are probably describing the same essential observation. It is important, therefore, to obtain a general sense of the types of abnormalities seen and not to attempt to make too fine a distinction between individual terminologies.

Neurologic effects may be seen for some materials. Specific regulatory guidelines (Neurotoxicology Functional Observational Battery Guidelines, TSCA Health Effects Test Guidelines, October 1983), exist for evaluation of neurotoxic effects, generally for repeated-dose studies. However, for materials which may only be subjected to acute testing some toxicologists (9) suggest the inclusion of a neurologic screen (25). One must be careful, however, to distinguish true neurotoxic effects from manifestations of the overwhelming general toxic effects of a lethal or near-lethal dose of a material.

Some indication of severe dermal effects (necrosis, eschar formation) is warranted for dermal studies, although the systemic, rather than the local, effects are of primary importance in this type of study. Assignment of dermal scores (26) can be done, but this may be misleading because of the large surface area covered and the possible variability from area to area. Materials which are severely irritating and/or corrosive may produce such severe skin damage that alterations in activity, locomotion, and food consumption are seen. In extremely severe cases, secondary septicemia of damaged skin may intervene. If such severe local tissue damage is seen, it is generally advisable to sacrifice the animals, not only for humane reasons, but also because any systemic toxic manifestations would be secondary to the skin destruction and evaluation of the hazard should be made based on the irritant, rather than the toxic potential of this type of material.

## 2. Body Weights

Most guidelines recommend that body weights be obtained at least weekly as well as at the time of death. More frequent weighing may help to distinguish between levels of toxicity and speed of recovery for different materials or for different doses of the same material. Animals which die generally exhibit antemortem weight losses. Weight changes are generally calculated from the pretest weight obtained prior to fasting. Changes are usually not calculated for animals which die during the first 24 hours, since these animals were fasted prior to dosing and probably did not consume any food after dosing. Recovery of weight to pretest values or higher is usually apparent after the first week or, occasionally after two weeks in survivor rats. Failure to recover weight, especially when accompanied by continuing signs of toxicity, may indicate a delayed effect. In such cases, the postdose observation period should be extended for one or more weeks to characterize the nature and time course of toxic effects and recovery.

Weight changes in rabbits are not as marked as those in rats, and it is not unusual to see little or no weight change ($\pm$ 0.2 kg) in untreated rabbits over a 1- or 2-week interval. However, some materials do produce marked weight decreases indicative of systemic toxicity.

## 3. Clinical Laboratory Studies

The EPA guidelines suggest that clinical laboratory studies should be considered. Although such studies increase the cost of acute toxicity evaluations, they may provide important information about possible target organs and the nature of the hazards. Certain classes of materials with known effects would be likely candidates for such studies, for example, cholinesterase evaluations for pesticides; methemoglobin determinations for anilines; hematology studies for benzenes; liver and kidney function studies for some solvents. Correlation of blood effects with lethal and nonlethal dosage levels can provide useful information for personnel monitoring and other industrial hygiene considerations.

## 4. Postmortem Examinations

Most guidelines suggest that gross postmortem examinations be considered, and these are generally performed, although the usefulness of information obtained is sometimes questionable. It is seldom possible to determine a specific cause of death (except in the case of intubation accidents). Examination of animals which are found dead is usually complicated by postmortem autolytic changes (discoloration of several organs). Severe gastrointestinal damage may be indicated by red or black discoloration of the stomach and intestinal walls and the presence of red or black material in the gastrointestinal tract. However, similar changes can be seen with advanced autolysis. A common finding in male rats which are found dead in our laboratory is the presence of one or both testes in the body cavity. No relationship to specific types of materials has been evident, and we have concluded that this represents a nonspecific response to antemortem stress rather than an effect on the reproductive system.

Animals which survive to study termination (usually 14 days) have generally recovered from any acute toxic effects and seldom exhibit any remarkable postmortem findings. Adhesion of abdominal viscera sometimes provides evidence of severe gastrointestinal irritation. The presence of historical control data is useful in interpreting postmortem observations. It is important to distinguish changes resulting from the method of killing the animals (i.e., red foci in the lungs as a result of carbon dioxide asphyxiation) from true toxic effects. Necropsy observations seen in control animals in our laboratory consist primarily of uterine alterations (swelling, redness) and ovarian cysts which appear to represent normal physiological variations. A finding which we see occasionally in rabbits, with no apparent relationship to test material administration, is the presence of necrotic adipose tissue in the abdominal viscera or wall.

In some cases, obtaining organ weights may provide useful information on target organ toxicity. However, unless concurrent control values are available, it may be difficult to interpret these data. Obtaining weights of spleen and thymus as a measure of immunotoxic effect has been suggested, and accumulation of such data would probably provide useful information in this relatively new area of toxicology.

Microscopic pathology is seldom performed for acute toxicity studies and tissues are rarely saved. In some cases, histopathological examination of target organs may provide useful information, however, and this option should be considered. Treated skin from animals used for acute dermal toxicity tests is sometimes preserved for possible microscopic examination; however, such examinations are not likely to provide information on the acute systemic toxicity of a material.

## ACKNOWLEDGMENT

Grateful acknowledgment is given to Ms. Kathryn H. Kolupanowich for typing this manuscript.

REFERENCES

1. Bliss, C. I. (1938). *Quart. J. Pharm. Pharmacol.* 11: 192–216.
2. Finney, D. G. (1971). *Probit Analysis*, 3rd ed. London, Cambridge University Press.
3. Litchfield, J. T. and Wilcoxon, F. (1949). *J. Pharmacol. Exp. Ther.* 96: 99–113.
4. Miller, L. C. and Tainter, M. L. (1944). *Proc. Soc. Exp. Biol. Med. NY* 57: 261–264.
5. Thompson, W. (1947). *Bact. Rev.* 11: 115–141.
6. Weil, C. S. (1952). *Biometrics* 8: 249–263.
7. *Acute Toxicity Tests, LD$_{50}$ (LC$_{50}$) Determinations and Alternatives.* European Chemical Industry Ecology and Toxicology Centre (ECETOC) Monograph No. 6, May 1985.
8. Steelman, R. L. (1965). *Factors Influencing Acute Toxicity Values.* Presented at the East$_2$ Subcommittee Meeting, Pharmaceutical Manufacturers Association Drug Safety Evaluation Committee, New York City, February 11, 1965.
9. Gad, S. C., Smith, A. C., Cramp, A. L., Gavigan, F. A., and Derelanko, M. J. (1984). Innovative designs and practices for acute systemic toxicity studies. *Drug Chem. Toxicol.* 7(5): 423–434.
10. A New Approach to the Classification of Substances and Preparations on the Basis of their Acute Toxicity. A Report by the British Toxicology Society Working Party on Toxicity. *Human Toxicol.* 3: 85–92, 1984.
11. Deichmann, W. B. and Leblane, T. J. (1943). Determination of the approximate lethal dose with about six animals. *J. Indust. Hyg. Toxicol.* 25: 415–417.
12. Smyth, Jr., H. F. and Carpenter, C. P. (1944). The place of the range finding test in the industrial laboratory. *J. Ind. Hyg. Toxicol.* 26: 269.
13. Bruce, R. D. (1985). An up-and-down procedure for acute toxicity testing. *Fund. Appl. Toxicol.* 5: 151–157.
14. LeBeau, J. E. (1983). The role of the LD$_{50}$ determination in drug safety evaluation. *Reg. Toxicol. Pharmacol.* 3: 71–74.
15. Depass, L. R., Myers, R. C., Weaver, E. V., and Weil, C. S. (1984). *Alternative Methods in Toxicology*, Vol. 2. *Acute Toxicity Testing: Alternative Approaches.* New York, Mary Ann Liebert Inc., publishers.
16. Schultz, F. and Fuchs, H. (1982). A new approach to minimising the number of animals used in acute toxicity testing and optimising the information of test results. *Arch. Toxical.* 51: 197.
17. Tattersall, M. C. (1982). Statistics and the LD$_{50}$ study. *Arch. Toxicol. (Suppl.)* 5: 267.

18. *Guide for the Care and Use of Laboratory Aniamls.* U.S. Department of Health and Human Services, Public Health Service, National Institutes of Health, NIH Publication No. 85-23, Revised 1985.
19. Growth Charts. Charles River Breeding Laboratories, Inc. Publication 6/80/3500.
20. Baker, H. J., Lindsey, J. R., and Weisbroth, S. H. (eds.). (1979). *The Laboratory Rat.* New York, Academic Press.
21. Weisbroth, S. H., Flatt, R. E., and Kraus, A. L. (Eds.). (1974). *The Biology of the Laboratory Rabbit.* New York, Academic Press.
22. Appraisal of the Safety of Chemicals in Foods, Drugs and Cosmetics. (1959). Association of Food and Drug Officials of the United States.
23. Principles and Procedures for Evaluating the Toxicity of Household Substances. (1977). Washington, D.C. National Academy of Science.
24. Proposed Rules—Toxicity Category for Criteria for Pesticide Labeling—EPA (FIFRA). (1984). *Fed. Reg. 49*(188):
25. Gad, S. C. (1982). A neuromuscular screen for use in industrial toxicology. *J. Toxicol. Env. Health 9:* 691–704.
26. Draize, J. H. (1959). The Appraisal of Chemical in Foods, Drugs, and Cosmetics. Austin, TX, Association of Food and Drug Officials of the United States.

# 4

# Evaluating Products for Their Potential to Cause Dermal and Ocular Irritation and Corrosion

SHAYNE COX GAD / *G. D. Searle and Company, Skokie, Illinois*

## I. INTRODUCTION

Among the most fundamental assessments of the safety of a product or, indeed, of any material that has the potential to be in contact with a significant number of people in our society, are tests in animals which seek to predict potential eye and skin irritation or corrosion. Like all the other tests in what is called a range-finding, tier I, or acute battery studies, the tests used here are both among the oldest designs and are currently undergoing the greatest degree of scrutiny and change. All currently established test methods for these endpoints use the same model—the rabbit (almost exclusively the New Zealand White). These tests have become the first focus point of concern and protest by those concerned with the humane treatment and rights of animals. Because of this, the design of and technique used in these tests are being modified. Also, alternatives are being developed that use models other than the rabbit or other mammals.

## II. DERMAL TESTING

Virtually all man-made chemicals have the potential to come into contact with human skin. In fact, many (cosmetics and shampoos, for example) are intended for skin contact. The greatest number of industry-related medical problems are skin conditions, indicating the large extent of dermal exposure where none is intended. The testing procedures that are currently used are basically those proposed by Draize et al. (1), and have changed little since their initial use in 1944.

Testing is performed to evaluate the potential occurrence of two different, yet related endpoints. The broadest application of these is an evaluation of the potential to cause skin irritation, characterized by erythema (redness) and edema (swelling). Severity of irritation is measured in terms of both the degree and duration of these two parameters. There are three types of irritation tests, each designed to address a different concern.

1. Primary (or acute) irritation, a localized reversible dermal response resulting from a single application of or exposure to a chemical without the involvement of the immune system.
2. Cumulative irritation, a reversible dermal response which results from repeated exposure to a substance (each individual exposure not being capable of causing acute primary irritation).
3. Photochemically induced irritation, which is a primary irritation resulting from light-induced molecular changes in the chemical to which the skin has been exposed.

Though most regulations and common practice characterize an irritation that persists 14 days past the end of exposure as other than reversible, the second endpoint of concern with dermal exposure, corrosion, is assessed in separate test designs. These tests start with a shorter exposure period (4 hours or less) to the material of concern, and then evaluates simply whether tissue has been killed or not (or, in other words, if necrosis is present or not).

It should be clear that, if a material is found to have less than severe dermal irritation potential, it will not be corrosive and therefore need not be tested separately for the corrosion endpoint.

## A. Objectives

The first step in undertaking a dermal testing program is developing a clear statement of objective, that is, understanding exactly what question is being asked for what purpose. The three major objectives for such testing are presented below.

1. Providing Regulator Required Baseline Data. Any product now in commerce must both be labeled appropriately for shipping (2) and accompanied by a material safety data sheet (MSDS) which clearly states potential hazards associated with handling it. Department of Transportation (DOT) regulations also prescribe different levels of packaging on materials found to constitute hazards as specified in the regulations. These requirements demand absolute identification of severe irritants or corrosives and adherence to the

basics of test methods promulgated by the regulations. False positives (type I errors) are to be avoided in these usages.

2. Hazard Assessment for Accidents. For most materials, dermal exposure is not intended to occur, yet will in cases of accidental spillage or mishandling. Here we need to correctly identify the hazard associated with such exposures, being equally concerned with false positives or false negatives.

3. Assessment of Safety for Use. The materials at issue here are the full range of products for which dermal exposure will occur in the normal course of use. These range from cosmetics and hand soaps to bleaches, laundry detergents, and paint removers. No manufacturer desires to market a product which cannot be used safely and will lead to extensive liability if entered in the market place. Accordingly, the desire here is to accurately predict the potential hazards in humans, that is, to have neither false positives nor false negatives.

Table 1 sets forth the regulatory mandated test designs, which form the basis of all currently employed test procedures.

All of these methods use the same scoring scale: the Draize scale (1,3), which is presented in Table 2. However, although the regulations prescribe these different test methods, most laboratories actually perform some modified methods. Below are two recommended modifications (one for irritation, the other for corrosion) which reflect laboratory experience by the author.

## B. Primary Dermal Irritation Test

*Rabbit Screening Procedure*

1. A group of at least 8–12 New Zealand White rabbits are screened for the study.
2. All rabbits selected for the study must be in good health; any rabbit exhibiting snuffles, hair loss, loose stools, or apparent weight loss is rejected and replaced.
3. One day (at least 18 hr) prior to application of the test substance, each rabbit is prepared by clipping the hair from the back and sides using a small animal clipper. A size No. 10 blade is used to remove the long hair and then a size No. 40 blade is used to remove the remaining hair.
4. Six animals with skin sites that are free of hypermia or abrasion (due to shaving) are selected. Skin sites that are in the telogen phase (resting stage of hair growth) are used; those skin sites that are in the anagen phase (stage of active growth) are not used.

Table 1  Regulatory-Mandated Test Designs

| Agency | Test material | | Exposure time (H) | Number of rabbits | Sites per animal (intact/ abraded) |
|---|---|---|---|---|---|
| | Solid | Liquid | | | |
| Department of Transportation (DOT) | Not specified | Not specified | 4 | 6 | 1/0 |
| Environmental Protection Agency (EPA)[a] | Moisten | Undiluted | 24 | 6 | 2/2 |
| Consumer Product Safety Commission (CPSC) | Dissolve in appropriate vehicle | Neat | 24 | 6 | 1/1 |
| OECD | Moisten | Undiluted | 4 | 3[b] | 1/0 |

[a]Most recent EPA guidelines are the same as OECD.
[b]But additional animals may be required to clarify equivocal results.

*Study Procedure*

1. As many as four areas of skin, two on each side of the rabbit's back, can be utilized for sites o/ administration.
2. Separate animals are not required for an untreated control group. Each animal serves as its own control.
3. Besides the test substance, a positive control substance (a known skin irritant, 1% sodium lauryl sulfate)* and a negative control (untreated patch) are applied to the skin. When a vehicle is used for diluting, suspending, or moistening the

*Distilled water is used as the vehicle for sodium lauryl sulfate.

| At end of exposure | Scoring intervals postexposure | Note | References |
|---|---|---|---|
| Skin washed with appropriate vehicle | 4 and 48 hr | Endpoint is corrosion in 2 of 6 animals | (3) |
| Skin wiped, but not washed | 24 and 72 hr; May continue until irritation fades or is judged irreversible | Toxic Substance Act test | (4) |
| Not specified | 24 and 72 hr | Federal Hazardous Substances Act (FHSA) | (5) |
| Wash with water or solvent | 30–60 min, 24, 48, 72 hr or until judged irreversible | European Common Market | (6) |

test substance, a vehicle control patch is required, especially if the vehicle is known to cause any toxic dermal reactions or if there is insufficient information about the dermal effects of the vehicle.

4. The four intact (free of abrasion) sites of administration are assigned a code number:

   #1  Test Substance
   #2  Negative Control
   #3  Positive Control
   #4  Vehicle Control (if required)

5. The following diagram illustrates the pattern of administration used in each study. This pattern of administration makes certain that the test substance and controls are applied to each position at least once.

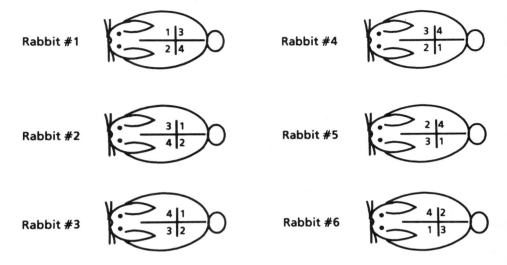

Rabbit #1

Rabbit #2

Rabbit #3

Rabbit #4

Rabbit #5

Rabbit #6

6. Each test or control substance is held in place with a 1 × 1 inch square 12-ply surgical gauze patch. The gauze patch is applied to the appropriate skin site and secured with 1 inch wide strips of surgical tape at the four edges, leaving the center of the gauze patch nonoccluded.

7. If the test substance is a solid or semisolid, a 0.5 g portion is weighed and placed on the gauze patch. The test substance patch is placed on the appropriate skin site and secured. The patch is subsequently moistened with 0.5 ml of physiological saline.

8. When the test substance is in flake, granule, powder, or other particulate form, the weight of the test substance that has a volume of 0.5 ml (after compacting as much as possible without crushing or altering the individual particles, such as by tapping the measuring container) is used whenever this volume weighs less than 0.5 g.

   When applying powders, granules, and so on, the gauze patch designated for the test sample is secured to the appropriate skin site with one of the four strips of tape at the most ventral position of the animal. With one hand, the appropriate amount of sample measuring 0.5 ml is carefully poured from a glycine weighing paper onto the gauze patch which is held in a horizontal (level) position with the other hand. The patch containing the test sample is then placed carefully in position on the skin by raising the remaining three edges with tape dorsally until they are completely secured. The patch is subsequently moistened with 0.5 ml of physiological saline.

**Table 2** Evaluation of Skin Reactions

| Skin Reaction | Value |
|---|---|
| Erythema and eschar formation: | |
|   No erythema | 0 |
|   Very slight erythema (barely perceptible) | 1 |
|   Well-defined erythema | 2 |
|   Moderate to severe erythema | 3 |
|   Severe erythema (beet redness) to slight eschar formation (injuries in depth) | 4 |
|   Necrosis (death of tissue) | +N |
|   Eschar (sloughing) | +E |
| Edema formation: | |
|   No edema | 0 |
|   Very slight edema (barely perceptible) | 1 |
|   Slight edema (edges of area well defined by definite raising) | 2 |
|   Moderate edema (raised approximately one millimeter) | 3 |
|   Severe edema (raised more than one millimeter and extending beyond the area of exposure) | 4 |
| Total possible score for primary irritation | 8 |

9. If the test substance is a liquid, a patch is applied and secured to the appropriate skin site. A 1 ml tuberculin syringe is used to measure and apply 0.5 ml of test substance to the patch.
10. If the test substance is a fabric, a 1 × 1 inch square sample is cut and placed on a patch. The test substance patch is placed on the appropriate skin site and secured. The patch is subsequently moistened with 0.5 ml of physiological saline.
11. The negative control site is covered with an untreated 12 ply surgical gauze patch (1 × 1 inch).

12. The positive control substance and vehicle control substance are applied to a gauze patch in the same manner as a liquid test substance.

13. The entire trunk of the animal is covered with an impervious material (such as Saran wrap) for a 24-hr period of exposure. The Saran wrap is secured by wrapping several long strips of athletic adhesive tape around the trunk of the animal. The impervious material aids in maintaining the position of the patches and retards evaporation of volatile test substances.

14. An Elizabethan collar is fitted and fastened around the neck of each test animal. The collar remains in place for the 24-hr exposure period. The collars are utilized to prevent removal of wrappings and patches by the animals, while allowing the animals food and water ad libitum.

15. The wrapping is removed at the end of the 24-hr exposure period. The test substance skin site is wiped to remove any test substance still remaining. When colored test substances (such as dyes) are used, it may be necessary to wash the test substance from the test site with an appropriate solvent or vehicle (one that is suitable for the substance being tested). This is done to clean the test site to facilitate accurate evaluation for skin irritation.

16. Immediately after removal of the patches, each 1 × 1 inch square test or control site is outlined with an indelible marker by dotting each of the four corners. This procedure delineates the site for identification.

*Observations*

1. Observations are made of the test and control skin sites 1 hr after removal of the patches (25 hr postinitiation of application). Erythema and edema are evaluated and scored on the basis of the designated values presented earlier in Table 2.

2. Observations again are performed 48 and 72 hr after application and scores are recorded.

3. If necrosis is present or the dermal reaction needs description, this should be done. Necrosis should receive the maximum score for erythema and eschar formation (4) and a (+N) to designate necrosis.

4. When a test substance produces dermal irritation that persists 72 hr postapplication, daily observations of test and control sites are continued on all animals until all irritation caused by the test substance resolves or until day 14 postapplication.

*Evaluation of Results*

1. A subtotal irritation value for erythema or eschar formation is determined for each rabbit by adding the values observed at 25, 48, and 72 hr postapplication.
2. A subtotal irritation value for edema formation is determined for each rabbit by adding the values observed at 25, 48, and 72 hr postapplication.
3. A total irritation score is calculated for each rabbit by adding the subtotal irritation value for erythema or eschar formation to the subtotal irritation value for edema formation.
4. The primary dermal irritation index is calculated for the test substance or control substance by dividing the sum of total irritation scores by the number of observations, 18 (3 days × 6 animals = 18 observations).
5. A test/control substance producing a primary dermal irritation index (PDII) of 0.0 is a nonirritant: >0.0 to 0.5 is a negligible irritant; > 0.5 to 2.0 is a mild irritant; > 2.0 to 5.0 is a moderate irritant; and > 5.0 to 8.0 is a severe irritant. This categorization of dermal irritation is a modification of the original classification described by Draize.

| PDII = | 0.0 | Nonirritant |
|---|---|---|
| | > 0.0 − 0.5 | Negligible irritant |
| | > 0.5 − 2.0 | Mild irritant |
| | > 2.0 − 5.0 | Moderate irritant |
| | > 5.0 − 8.0 | Severe irritant |

*Limitation of the Test*

The results of this test are subject to considerable variability due to relatively small differences in technique, such as how snugly the occlusive wrap is applied. Weil and Scala (7) arranged and reported on an intralaboratory study (by 25 laboratories) which clearly established this fact. However, the method outlined above has proven to give reproducible results in the hands of the same technicians over a period of years (8) and contains some internal controls (the positive and vehicle controls) against large variabilities in results or the occurrence of false negatives or false positives. However, it should be recognized that the test is designed with a bias to preclude false negatives, and therefore tends to exaggerate results in relation to what would happen in humans. Findings of ngeligible (or even very low range mild) irritancy should therefore not be of concern unless the product under test is to have large-scale and prolonged dermal contact.

## C. Dermal Corrosivity Test

This procedure is based on the Department of Transportation "Method of Testing Corrosion to Skin" (9).

*Rabbit Screening Procedure*

1. A group of at least 8–12 New Zealand White rabbits are screened for the study.
2. All rabbits selected for the study must be in good health; any rabbit exhibiting snuffles, hair loss, loose stools, or apparent weight loss is rejected and replaced.
3. One day (at least 18 hr) prior to application of the test substance, each rabbit is prepared by clipping the hair from the back and sides using a small animal clipper. A No. 10 blade is used to remove the long hair and then a No. 40 blade is used to remove the remaining hair.
4. Six animals with skin sites that are free of hyperemia or abrasion (due to shaving) are selected. Skin sites that are in the telogen phase (resting stage of hair growth) are used; those skin sites that are in the anagen phase (active stage of hair growth) are not used.

*Study Procedure*

1. Separate animals are not required for an untreated control group. Each animal serves as its own control.
2. In addition to the test substance, a negative control (un-treated patch) is applied to the skin.
   a. If the test substance is a liquid, it is applied undiluted.
   b. If the test substance is a solid or a semisolid, it is applied as such.
   c. If information about the effects of moistening a solid or semisolid test substance is required, a third optional site can be added to the test.
3. The intact (free of abrasion) sites of administration are assigned a code number:

   #1 Test substance
   #2 Negative control
   #3 (Optional) test substance moistened with 0.5 ml of physiological saline
4. The following diagram illustrates the pattern of administration used in each study.

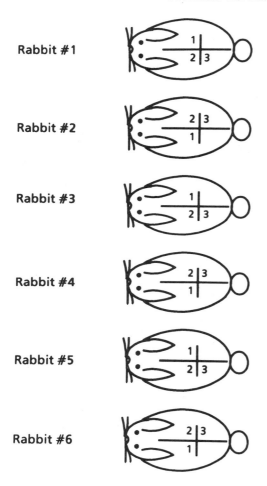

Rabbit #1

Rabbit #2

Rabbit #3

Rabbit #4

Rabbit #5

Rabbit #6

5.  The test substance is held in place with a 1 × 1 inch square
    12 ply surgical gauze patch. The gauze patch is applied to
    the appropriate skin site and secured with 1 inch wide strips
    of surgical tape at the four edges, leaving the center of
    the gauze patch nonoccluded.
6.  If the test substance is a solid or semisolid, a 0.5 g portion
    is weighed and placed on the gauze patch. The test sub-
    stance patch is placed on skin site 1 and secured.
    a.  When the test substance is in flake, granule, powder,
        or other particulate form, the weight of the test sub-
        stance that has a volume of 0.5 ml (after compacting as
        much as possible without crushing or altering the

        individual particles, such as by tapping the measuring container) is used whenever this volume weighs less than 0.5 g.

    b. When applying powders, granules, and so on, the gauze patch designated for the test sample is secured to the appropriate skin site with one of four strips of tape at the most central position of the animal. With one hand, the appropriate amount of sample measuring 0.5 ml is carefully poured from a glycine weighing paper onto the gauze patch which is held in a horizontal (level) position with the other hand. The patch containing the test sample is then carefully positioned, on the skin by raising the remaining three edges dorsally until they are completely secured with tape.

7. As an option, the effects of moistening a solid or semisolid can be investigated. If this is done the test substance is applied to site 3 (as described above) and the patch holding the test substance is subsequently moistened with 0.5 ml of physiological saline.

8. If the test substance is a liquid, a patch is applied and secured to skin site 1. A 1 ml tuberculin syringe is used to measure and apply 0.5 ml of test substance to the patch.

9. The negative control site 2 is covered with an untreated 12 ply surgical gauze patch.

10. The entire trunk of the animal is covered with an impervious material (such as Saran Wrap) for a 4-hr period of exposure. The Saran Wrap is secured by wrapping several long strips of athletic adhesive tape around the trunk of the animal. The impervious material helps to keep the patches in position and retards evaporation of volatile test substances.

11. An Elizabethan collar is fitted and fastened around the neck of each test animal. The collar remains in place for the 4-hr exposure period. The collars are utilized to prevent removal of wrappings and patches by the animals, while allowing the animals food and water ad libitum.

12. The wrapping and patches are removed at the end of the 4-hr exposure period. When colored test substances (such as dyes) are used, it may be necessary to wash the test substance from the test site with an appropriate solvent or vehicle (one that is suitable for the test substance being tested). This is done to clean the test site to facilitate accurate evaluation.

13. Immediately after removal of the patches, each 1 × 1 inch square test or control site is outlined with an indelible marker by dotting each of the four corners. This procedure delineates the site for identification purposes.

## Observations

1. After 4 hours of exposure, observations of the test and control sites are described. Observations are made again at the end of a total of 48 hr (44 hr after the first reading).
2. In addition, the Draize grading system (3) for evaluation of skin reactions was used to score the skin sites and 4 and 48 hr after dosing (Table 2).

## Evaluation of Results

1. Corrosion would be considered to have resulted if the test substance caused destruction or irreversible alteration of the tissue on at least 2 of the 6 rabbits tested. Ulceration or necrosis of the tissue at either 4 or 48 hr postexposure would be considered permanent tissue damage (i.e., tissue destruction does not include merely sloughing of the superficial epidermis, or erythema, edema, or fissuring) (9).
2. If a conclusive assessment of the extent of damage to the skin can not be made after 48 hr (it is difficult to determine whether or not permanent, irreversible damage is present), daily observations of the skin sites will be made and recorded, either until a determination can be made about the extent of skin damage or until day 14 after exposure. Photographs will be taken at those time intervals after exposure that are most meaningful for documentation purposes.
3. If the test continues to day 14 after exposure, a final evaluation of the skin is made, resulting in a conclusive assessment of the test substance's potential to cause corrosion to skin. Scar tissue formation at this time is indicative of permanent tissue damage.

## Limitations of the Test

Unlike the primary dermal irritancy test, the results from the corrosivity test should be taken at face value. There is some lab-to-lab variability and the test does produce some false positives (though these are almost always at least severely irritating compounds), but does not produce false negatives.

## D. Alternatives

The state of development for any alternative models for dermal irritation or corrosion is very minimal. Although there have been attempts to utilize other animal models, these have not led to better or more economical results.

The major attempts to modify the actual test designs themselves centered on the use of abrasion as a means of increasing sensitivity and therefore further precluding false negatives. However, the results of comparative studies of materials on both abraded and unabraded skin have not established that abrasion consistently increase sensitivity (8).

Finally, there are no real in vitro models under development for dermal irritation or corrosion tests.

## III. OCULAR TESTING

Evaluating chemicals for their potential to cause eye irritation in animals and extrapolating to potential results in humans did not start with, as is popularly believed, Draize et al. (1). Animal models had been utilized and the results reported prior to this 1944 publication.

In 1942, Mann and Pullinger (10) reported on the use of a rabbit model to predict eye irritation in humans. No specific scoring system was presented to grade the results, and the use of animals with pigmented eyes (as opposed to albinos) was advocated. Early in 1944, Friedenwald et al. (11) published a method using albino rabbits in a manner very similar to that of the original Draize publication, but still prescribing description of the individual animal response as the means of evaluating and reporting the results, though a scoring method was provided.

What the method developed and published in 1944 by Draize, Woodward, and Calvery did was to provide a new numerical scoring system for the observations resulting from the test. This scoring system provided a basis for classification of agents as to their potential to cause ocular irritation and it became widely accepted. This scoring system, shown in Table 3, gives the greatest weight to corneal changes (80 out of 110 points), and is based on observations at 24, 48, and 72 hr. Both of these points are weaknesses of the original test method, as will be discussed later.

Since the introduction of the Draize test, ocular irritation testing in rabbits has both developed and diverged. Indeed, clearly there is no longer a single test design that is used and there are different objectives that are pursued by different groups using the same test. This lack of standardization has been recognized for some time and attempts have been made to address standardization of at least the methodological, if not the design aspects of the test.

The common core design of the test calls for instilling either 0.1 ml of a liquid or 0.1 g of a powder (or other solid) into one eye of each of 6 rabbits. The material is not washed out, and both eyes of each animal (the nontreated eye acting as a control) are graded

**Table 3** Scale of Weighted Scores for Grading the Severity of Ocular Lesions

I. Cornea

   A. Opacity: Degree of density (area which is most
      dense is taken for reading)

      Scattered or diffuse area-details of iris clearly
        visible    1

      Easily discernible translucent areas, details of iris
        slightly obscured    2

      Opalescent areas, no details of iris visible, size of
        pupil barely discernible    3

      Opaque, iris visible    4

   B. Area of cornea involved

      One quarter (or less), but not zero    1
      Greater than one quarter—less than one-half    2
      Greater than one half less than three quarters    3
      Greater than three quarters, up to whole area    4

      Scoring equals $A \times B \times 5$   Total maximum = 80

II. Iris

   A. Values

      Folds above normal, congestion, swelling, circumcor-
      neal injection (any one or all of these or combina-
      tion of any thereof), iris still reacting to light
      (sluggish reaction is positive)    1

      No reaction to light, hemorrhage; gross destruction
      (any one or all of these)    2

      Scoring equals $A \times B$   Total maximum = 10

III. Conjunctivae

   A. Redness (refers to palpabral conjunctivae only)

      Vessels definitely injected above normal    1
      More diffuse, deeper crimson red, individual vessels
        not easily discernible    2
      Diffuse beefy red    3

   B. Chemosis

      Any swelling above normal (includes nictitating
        membrane)    1
      Obvious swelling with partial eversion of the lids    2
      Swelling with lids about half closed    3
      Swelling with lids about half closed to completely
        closed    4

Table 3 (Continued)

---

C. Discharge

Any amount different from normal (does not include small amount observed in inner canthus of normal animals)     1

Discharge with moistening of the lids and hair just adjacent to the lids     2

Discharge with moistening of the lids and considerable area around the eye     3

Scoring (A + B + C) × 2   Total maximum = 20

---

The maximum total score is the sum of all scores obtained for the cornea, iris, and conjunctivae.

according to the Draize scale at 24, 48, and 72 hr. The resulting scores are summed for each animal.

Although the major objective of the Draize scale was to standardize scoring, it was recognized early on that this was not happening and that different people were reading the same response differently. To address this, two sets of standards using the modified Draize scale (to provide guidance by comparison) have been published. In 1965 the Food and Drug Administration (FDA) published a guide featuring color illustrations as standards (12). The quality of the color in their prints was fair to begin with, and the prints have since faded with age. In 1974 the Consumer Product Safety Commission (CPSC) published a second illustrated guide (13) which provided 20 color photographic slides as standards. The color quality on these is better and the slides have retained their original color quality well through time.

A second course of methodological variability has been in the procedure utilized to instill test materials into the eyes. There is now consensus that the substance should be dropped into the cul de sac formed by pulling the lower eye lid gently away from the eye, then allowing the animal to blink and spread the material across the entire corneal surface.

There are also variations in the design of the "standard" test. Most laboratories observe animals until at least 7 days after instillation any may extend the test to 21 days after instillation if any irritation persists. These prolonged postexposure observation periods are designed to allow for evaluation of the true severity of damage and for assessing the ability of the ocular damage to be repaired. The results of these tests are evaluated by a descriptive classification scale (Table 4) such as that described in NAS publication 1138 (14) which was derived from that reported by Green et al. (15).

This classification is based on the most severe response observed in a group of 6 nonirrigated eyes and data from all observation periods are used for this evaluation.

## A. Objectives

Any discussion of current test protocols must begin with a review of why the tests are done. What are the objectives of those causing eye irritation testing to occur and how are these different objectives reflected not only in test design and interpretation, but also in the regulations prescribing testing and in the ways that test results are utilized?

Table 4  Severity and Persistence (14)

---

Inconsequential or complete lack of irritation. Exposure of the eyes to a material under the specified conditions caused no significant ocular changes. No staining with fluorescein can be observed. Any changes that did occur clear within 24 hr and are no greater than those caused by normal saline under the same conditions.

Moderate irritation. Exposure of the eye to the material under the specified conditions causes minor, superficial, and transient changes of the cornea, iris, or conjunctivae as determined by external or slit-lamp or subsequent grading of any of the following changes is sufficient to characterize a response as moderate irritation: opacity of the cornea (other than a slight dulling of the normal luster), hypermia of the iris, or swelling of the conjunctivae. Any changes that are seen to clear within 7 days.

Substantial irritation. Exposure of the eye to the material under the specified conditions causes significant injury to the eye, such as loss of the corneal epithelium, corneal opacity, iritis (other than a slight injection) conjunctivitis, pannus, or bullae. The effects clear within 21 days.

Severe irritation or corrosion. Exposure of the eye to the material under the specified conditions results in the same types of injury as in the previous category and in significant necrosis or other injuries that adversely affect the visual process. Injuries persist for 21 days or more.

Different regulatory agencies within the United States have prescribed slightly different procedures for different perceived regulatory needs (37). These are looked at in more depth in the text.

---

There are four major groups of organizations (in terms of their products) which require eye irritation studies to be performed. These can be generally (though not absolutely, as for all such classifications) classified as the pharmaceutical, cosmetic, consumer product, and industrial chemical groups.

For the pharmaceutical industry, eye irritation testing is performed when the test material is intended for use in the eye, as a matter of course. There are a number of special tests applicable to pharmaceutical or medical device applications. In general, however, it is desired that an eye irritation test that is utilized by this group be both sensitive and accurate in predicting the potential to cause irritation in humans. Failure to identify irritants (lack of sensitivity) is to be avoided, but of equal concern is the occurrence of false positives. The products here have a real value and benefit to the user in terms of better health and alleviation of discomfort, and prohibiting their use based on a faulty identification as significant irritants, would be an error with unacceptably high costs to society. Rather, a cost/benefit analysis based on an accurate prediction of human hazard is desired.

Similarly, in the cosmetics industry, products of interest are frequently intended for direct contact with the eye or at least to be used in a manner that such contact is unavoidable. At the same time, the benefit to the user is not as clear. In this case the objective is a test that is as sensitive as possible, even if this results in a low incidence of false positives. Even a moderate irritant would not be desirable.

Consumer products (such as soaps, detergents, and shampoos) have a different perspective. These products are not intended to be used in a manner that causes them to get into eyes, but because they are used by a large population and since their modes of use do not include active measures to prevent eye contact (such as the use of goggles and face shields), and the benefit derived from using the products is relatively moderate, accurate identification of severe eye irritants is desirable. A mild or moderate eye irritant would still be a viable product—a severe irritant would not. Only in the case of children's shampoos would there be major interest in identifying mild irritants to preclude their use.

Finally, there are industrial chemicals. These are handled by (relative to consumer products) a smaller population. Eye contact is never intended, and in fact, active measures are taken to prevent it. The use of eye irritation data in these cases is to fulfill labeling requirements for shipping and to provide hazard assessment information for accidental exposures and their treatment. The results of such tests do not directly effect the economic future of a material or product. It is desirable to identify accurately moderate and severe irritants (particularly those with irreversible effects) and to determine if rinsing of the eyes after exposure will improve or aggravate the consequences of exposure. False negatives for mild reversible irritation are acceptable.

To fullfil these objectives, a number of basic test protocols have been developed and mandated by different regulatory groups. Table 5 gives an overview of these as previously presented in part by Falahee et al. (16).

The philosophy underlying these test designs almost universally, equates maximization of the biological response with production of the most sensitive test. As our review of objectives has shown, the greatest sensitivity (especially at the expense of false positive findings which is an unavoidable consequence) is not what is universally desired, and, as we shall see later, maximizing the response in rabbits does not *guarantee* sensitive prediction of the results in humans.

## B. Ocular Irritation Test

*Test Article Screening Procedure*

1.  Each test substance will be screened in order to eliminate potentially corrosive or severely irritating materials from being studied for eye irritation in the rabbit.
2.  If possible, the pH of the test substance will be measured.
3.  A primary dermal irritation study will be performed prior to the study.
4.  The test substance will not be studied for eye irritation, if it is a strong acid (pH is 2.0 or less) or strong alkali (pH 11.0 or greater), and/or if the test substance is a severe dermal irritant (with a primary dermal irritation index of 5 to 8) or causes corrosion of the skin.
5.  If it is predicted that the test substance does not have the potential to be severely irritating or corrosive to the eye, continue to Rabbit Screening Procedure.

*Rabbit Screening Procedure*

1.  A group of at least 12 New Zealand White rabbits of either sex are screened for the study. The animals are removed from their cages and placed in rabbit restraints. Care should be taken not to accidentally cause mechanical damage to the eye during this procedure.
2.  All rabbits selected for the study must be in good healty; any rabbit exhibiting snuffles, hair loss, loose stools, or apparent weight loss is rejected and replaced.
3.  One hour prior to instillation of the test substance, both eyes of each rabbit are examined for signs of irritation and

Table 5  Regulatory Ocular Irritation Test Methods

| Reference: | Draize et al., 1944 (1) | FHSA, 1964 (36) | NAS, 1977 (14) |
|---|---|---|---|
| Test species | Albino rabbit | Same | Same[a] |
| Age/weight | NS[b] | NS | Sexually mature/ less than 2 yr old |
| Sex | NS | NS | Either |
| Number animals/group | 9 | 6-18 | 4 (minimum) |
| Test agent; volume and method of instillation liquids | 0.1 ml; direct instillation into lower conjunctival sac | Same as Draize (1) | Liquids and solid; two or more different doses within the probable range of human exposure[d] |
| Solids | NS | 100 mg or 0.1 ml equivalent when this volume weighs less than 100 mg; direct instillation into lower conjunctival sac | Manner of application should reflect probable route of accidental exposure |
| Aerosols[e] | NS | NS | Short burst at distance approximating self-induced eye exposure |
| Irrigation schedule | At 2 sec (3 animals) and at 4 sec (3 animals) following instillation of test agent | Eyes may be washed after 24 hr reading | May be conducted with separate experimental groups |

| OECO, 1981 (6) | IRLG, 1981 (17) | EPA, 1981 (18) |
|---|---|---|
| Same | Same | Same |
| NS | Young adult/2.0 3.0 kg | NS |
| NS | Either | NS |
| 3 (minimum) | 3 (preliminary test);[c] (6) | 6−18 |
| Same as Draize (1) | Same as Draize (1) | Same as Draize (1) |
| Same as FHSA (36) | Same as FHSA (36) | Same as FHSA (36) |
| 1 sec burst sprayed at 10 cm | 1 sec burst sprayed at approx. 4 inches | NS |
| Same as FHSA (36); in addition, for substances found to be irritating: wash at 4 sec (3 animals) and at 30 sec (3 animals) | Same as FHSA (36) | Same as FHSA (36) |

Table 5 (Continued)

| Reference: | Draize et al., 1944 (1) | FHSA, 1964 (36) | NAS, 1977 (14) |
|---|---|---|---|
| Irrigation treatment | 20 ml tap water (body temp.) | Sodium chloride solution (U.S.P. or equivalent) | NS |
| Examination times (post-instillation) | 24 hr<br>48 hr<br>72 hr<br>4 days<br>7 days | 24 hr<br>48 hr<br>72 hr | 1 day<br>3 days<br>7 days<br>14 days<br>21 days |
| Use of fluorescein | NS | May be applied after the 24 hr reading (optional) | May be used |
| Use of anesthetics | NS | NS | NS |
| Scoring and evaluation | Draize et al., 1944 (1) | Draize et al., 1944 (1), or a slit lamp scoring system | CPSC, 1976 (5) |

[a]Tests should be conducted in monkeys when confirmatory data are required.
[b]Not specified.
[c]If the substance produces corrosion, severe irritation or no irritation in a preliminary test with 3 animals, no further testing is necessary. If equivocal responses occur, testing in at least an additional 3 animals should be performed.
[d]Suggested doses are 0.1 and 0.05 ml for liquids.
[e]Currently no testing guidelines exist for gases or vapors.
[f]Eyes may also be examined at 1 hr, 7, 14, and 21 days (at the option of the investigator).

| OECD, 1981 (6) | IRLG, 1981 (17) | EPA, 1981 (18) |
|---|---|---|
| Wash with water for 5 min using volume and velocity of flow which will not cause injury | Tap water or sodium chloride solution (U.S.P. or equivalent) | Same as FHSA (36) |
| 1 hr<br>24 hr<br>48 hr<br>72 hr | 24 hr[f]<br>48 hr<br>72 hr | 24 hr<br>48 hr<br>72 hr |
| Same as FHSA (36) | Same as FHSA (36) | Same as FHSA (36) |
| May be used | May be used | NS |
| CPSC, 1976 (5) | CPSC, 1976 (5) | CPSC, 1976 (5) |

corneal defects with a hand-held slit lamp. All eyes are stained with 2.0% sodium fluorescein and examined to confirm the absence of corneal lesions.

*Fluorescein Staining.* Cup the lower lid of the eye to be tested and instill one drop of a 2% sodium fluorescein solution onto the surface of the cornea. After 15 seconds, the eye is thoroughly rinsed with physiological saline. The eye is examined employing a hand-held long wave ultraviolet illuminator in a darkened room. Corneal lesions, if present, appear as bright yellowish-green fluorescent areas.

4. Only 9 of the 12 animals are selected for the study. These 9 rabbits must not show any signs of eye irritation and must show either a negative or minimum fluorescein reaction (due to normal epithelial desquamation).

*Study Procedure*

1. At least 1 hour after fluorescein staining, the test substance is placed on one eye of each animal by gently pulling the lower lid away from the eyeball to form a cup (conjunctival cul de sac) into which the test material is dropped. The upper and lower lids are then gently held together for 1 sec to prevent immediate loss of material.
2. The other eye remains untreated and serves as a control.
3. For testing liquids, 0.1 ml of the test substance is used.
4. For solids or pastes, 100 mg of the test substance is used.
5. When the test substance is in flake, granular, powder, or other particulate form, the amount that has a volume of 0.1 ml (after gently compacting the particles by tapping the measuring container in a way that will not alter their individual form) is used whenever this volume weighs less than 100 mg.
6. For aerosol products, the eye should be held open and the substance administered in a single, short burst for about one second at a distance of about 4 inches directly in front of the eye. The velocity of the ejected material should not traumatize the eye. The dose should be approximated by weighing the aerosol can before and after each treatment. For other liquids propelled under pressure, such as substances delivered by pump sprays, an aliquot of 0.1 ml should be collected and instilled in the eye as for liquids.
7. The treated eyes of 6 rabbits are not washed following instillation of the test substance.
8. The treated eyes of the remaining 3 rabbits are irrigated for 1 min with room temperature tap water, starting 20 sec after instillation.

9. In order to prevent self-inflicted trauma by the animals immediately after instillation of the test substance the animals
   are not immediately returned to their cages. After the tests
   and control eyes are examined and graded at 1 hr postexposure, the animals are returned carefully to their respective cages.

*Observations*

1. The eyes are observed for any immediate signs of discomfort
   after instilling the test substance. Blepharospasm and/or
   excessive tearing are indicative of irritating sensations
   caused by the test substance and the duration should be
   noted. Blepharospasm does not necessarily indicate that the
   eye will show signs of ocular irritation.
2. Grading and scoring of ocular irritation are performed in
   accordance with modified Draize's scale (1) (Table 3). The
   eyes are examined and grades of ocular reactions are
   recorded.
3. If signs of irritation persist at 7 days, readings are continued on day 10; and if the toxic effects are not resolved
   after 10 days, readings are made on day 14.
4. In addition to the required observations of the cornea, iris,
   and conjunctiva, serious effects (such as pannus, rupture
   of the globe, or blistering of the conjunctivae) indicative of
   a corrosive action are reported.
5. Whether or not toxic effects are reversible depends on the
   nature, extent, and intensity of damage. Most lesions, if
   reversible, will heal or clear within 21 days. Therefore, if
   ocular irritation is present at the 14-day reading, a 21-day
   reading is required to determine whether the ocular damage
   is reversible or nonreversible.

*Evaluation of Results*

The results are evaluated by the following two methods:

1. Federal Hazardous Substances Act (FHSA) Regulations (12):
   Interpretation of data is made from the 6 test eyes which
   are not irrigated with water. Only data from days 1, 2,
   and 3 are used for this evaluation; data from the 1 hr observation and days 4, 7, 10, 14, and 21 are not used. An
   animal shall be considered as exhibiting a positive reaction
   if the test substance produces at any of the readings ulceration of the cornea (other than a fine stippling) (grade 1),
   or opacity of the cornea (other than a slight dulling of the

normal luster) (grade 1), or inflammation of the iris (other than a slight deepening of the rugae or a slight circumcorneal injection of the blood vessels) (grade 1), or if such substance produces in the conjunctivae (excluding the cornea and iris) an obvious swelling with partial eversion of the lids (grade 2) or a diffuse crimson red color with individual vessels not easily discernible (grade 2).

The test shall be considered positive if four or more of the animals in the test group exhibit a positive reaction.

If only one animal exhibits a positive reaction, the test shall be regarded as negative.

If two or three animals exhibit a positive reaction, the test is repeated using a different group of 6 animals. The second test shall be considered positive if 3 or more of the animals exhibit a positive reaction.

If only 1 or 2 animals in the second test exhibit a positive reaction, the test shall be repeated with a different group of 6 animals. Shoul w a third test be needed, the substance will be regarded as an irritant if any animal exhibits a positive response.

2. A modified Classification Scale of Ocular Responses is based on severity and persistence [derived from NAS, 1977 (4) and Green (15)]. The most severe response seen in a group of 6 test animals is used for the classification.

*Inconsequential or nonirritation.* Exposure of the eye to the material under the specified conditions caused no significant ocular changes. No tissue staining with fluorescein was observed. Any changes that did occur cleared within 24 hr.*

*Moderate Irritation.* Exposure of the eye to material under the specified conditions caused minor, superficial, and transient changes of the cornea, iris, or conjunctivae as determined by external or slit-lamp examination with fluorescein staining. The appearance at any grading interval of any of the following changes was sufficient to characterize a response as irritation: opacity of thee cornea (other than a slight dulling of the normal luster), hyperemia of the iris, or swelling of the conjunctivae. Any changes that were seen cleared within 7 days.

---

*Slight conjunctival injection (grade 1, some vessels definitely injected) that does not clear within 24 hr is not considered a significant change. This level of change is inconsequential as far as representing physical damage to the eye and can be seen to occur naturally for unexplained reasons in otherwise normal rabbits.

    *Substantial Irritation.* Exposure of the eye to the material under the specified conditions caused significant injury to the eye, such as loss of the corneal epithelium, corneal opacity, iritis (other than a slight injection), conjunctivitis, pannus, or bullae. The effects healed or cleared within 21 days.

    *Severe Irritation or Corrosion.* Exposure of the eye to the material under the specified conditions resulted in the types of injury described in the former category and resulted in significant tissue destruction (necrosis) or injuries that probably adversely affected the visual process. The effects of the injuries persisted for 21 days or more.

Figure 1 gives a diagramatic presentation of the prescreening step incorporated into this test to preclude undue discomfort on the part of the test animals.

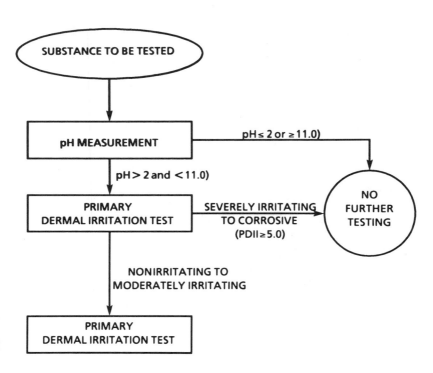

Figure 1   Tier approach for eye irritation testing.

*Limitations*

Commonly used methodological variations to improve the sensitivity and accuracy of describing damage in these tests are inspection of the eyes with a slit lamp and instillation of the eyes with a vital dye (very commonly, fluorescein) as an indicator of increases in permeability of the corneal barrier. These techniques and an alternative scoring system which is more comprehensive than the Draize scale are reviewed well by Ballantyne and Swanston (19) and Chan and Hayes (20).

To assess the adequacy of the currently employed eye irritation tests to fulfill the objectives behind their use, we must evaluate them in terms of (a) their accuracy (how well do they predict the hazard to humans) and (b) can comparable results be obtained by different technicians and laboratories, and finally (c) what methods and designs have been developed and are being employed as alternatives to rabbit eye irritation tests.

Assessing the accuracy of rabbit eye irritation tests—or indeed, of any predictive test of eye irritation—requires that the results of such tests be compared to what happens in humans. Unfortunately, the human data base for making comparisons is not large. The concerns, however, have been present almost as long as the tests have been performed (21).

There are substantial differences between the eye of humans and rabbits, and indeed, other species that have also been considered as test models. Beckley (22) presented the following comparison of corneal thickness and area (as a percentage of the total area of the globe) of four species, as shown in Table 6.

The aqueous humor of the rabbit also has a different pH (7.6 vs. 7.1–7.3 for humans), a less effective tearing mechanism, and a nicitating membrane. Calabrese (23) presents a comprehensive review of the anatomical and biochemical differences between the ocular systems of humans and rabbits.

Some have claimed that the rabbit, as the test is currently performed, is more sensitive than man. Anionic formulations, for ex-

**Table 6** Corneal Thickness and Area

| Species | Thickness | Area (%) |
|---------|-----------|----------|
| Humans | 0.53–0.54 | 7 |
| Rabbit | 0.4 | 25 |
| Mouse | 0.1 | 50 |
| Rat | ? | 50 |

**Table 7** Summary of Rabbit Eye Studies

| Study | Results | Reference |
|---|---|---|
| 1. Three materials by 3 readers under two separate conditions | 90% Reproducibility of irritant/nonirritant classification | (27) |
| 2. 7 Materials evaluated in duplicate | Tests results reproducible | (28) |
| 3. 56 Materials evaluated in three separate protocols | Each protocol reproducible—variations between tests by different protocols | (29,30) |
| 4. 29 Materials (detergents) evaluated in 2 rabbit, 2 monkey and 1 human test | Results for all tests more severe than human but low volume rabbit test data were rank comparable to human data | (31) |

ample, are severe irritants to rabbit eyes, but are nonirritants in humans. However, generally the rabbit is no more sensitive than man. Rather, the relative sensitivities vary from class to class of chemical. Alexander (1965) and Calabrese (23) have provided reviews of materials for which rabbits are more sensitive than humans. MacDonald et al. (24) published a review of materials that were either more or less irritant in rabbits than in humans. Swanston (25) has also published a comparative review of seven different species, including humans.

It should be noted, however, that rabbit eye tests do not detect ocular toxicities associated with some ocular anesthetics and eye drops (26).

A second long-standing concern regarding the adequacy of the rabbit tests is its reproducibility. Weil and Scala (7) published the most frequently cited study, in which 25 labs evaluated a common battery of 12 materials. The results did show variability between laboratories, with a number of labs reporting consistently either more or less severe results than the other labs. The causes and cures for such variability are multiple, but we have already mentioned differences in protocols and methodologies (to name just two major sources).

Since the Weil and Scala study (7) a number of authors have published comparative studies which have shown a greater degree of reproducibility. Some of these are summarized in Table 7.

Several authors have made the point that reproducible predictability of nonirritants and strong irritants is easier to achieve. For other materials, several authors have made the point thattthe use of concurrent reference materials (32) or semiannual refresher training of readers versus a set of standards (24) improves reproducibility of results and gives a set of standard results against which we can evaluate a drift in test or reading practices.

## C. Alternatives

The alternatives which have been proposed and adapted for the performance of rabbit eye irritation tests themselves should be reviewed. These alternatives have been directed at the twin objectives of making the tests more accurate in predicting human responses and at reducing both the use of animals and the degree of discomfort or suffering experienced by those that are used. Some of these alternatives have already been touched on in our review of how much testing is performed (Table 5 and its footnotes).

  1. Alternative Species. Dogs, monkeys, and mice (25) have all been suggested as alternatives to rabbits that would be more representative of humans. Each of these, however, also has shown differences in responses compared to those seen in humans, and pose additional problems in terms of cost, handling, lack of database, etc.

  2. Use of Anesthetics. Over the years, a number of authors have proposed that topical anesthetics be administered to the eyes of rabbits prior to their use in the test. Both OECD and IRLG regulations provide for such usage. However, numerous published [such as Falahee et al. (16)] and unpublished studies have shown that such use of anesthetics interfere with test results usually by increasing the severity of eye irritation findings.

  3. Decrease Volume of Test Material. An alternative proposal (one which a survey showed has been adopted by a number of labs) is to use a reduced volume/weight of test material.

  In 1982, Williams et al. (28) reported a study in which they evaluated 21 different chemicals at volumes of 0.1, 0.03, 0.01, and 0.003 ml. These are materials on which there human data was already available. It was found that the volume reduction did not change the rank order of responses, and that 0.01 ml (10 μl) gave results which best mirrored those seen in humans.

  In 1984, Freeberg et al. (31) published a study of 29 detergents (for which human data was available), each evaluated at both 0.1 and 0.01 ml test volumes in rabbits. The results of the 0.01 ml tests were reported to be more reflective of results in humans.

  In 1985 Walker (33) reported an evaluation of the low volume (0.01 ml) test which assessed its results for correlation with those in humans based on the number of days until clearing of injury, and reported that 0.01 ml gave a better correlation than did 0.1 ml.

While it must be pointed out that there may be some classes of chemicals for which low volume tests may give results less representative of those seen in humans, it seems clear that this approach should be seriously considered by those performing such testing.

4. Use of Prescreens. This alternative may also be considered a tier approach. Its objective is to avoid testing severely irritating or corrosive materials in many (or, in some cases, any) rabbits. This approach entails a number of steps which should be considered independently.

First is a screen based on physicochemical properties. This usually means pH, but also should be extended to materials with high oxidation or reduction potentials (hexavalent chromium salts, for example).

Though the correlation between low pHs (acids) and eye damage in the rabbit has not been found to be excellent, all alkalis (pH 11.5 or above) tested have been reported to produce opacities and ocular damage (34). Many laboratories now use pH cutoffs for testing of 2.0 or lower and 11.5 or 12.0 and higher. If a material falls outside of these cutoffs (or is so identified due to other physicochemical parameters), then it is either (a) not tested in the rabbit eye and assumed to be corrosive, or (b) evaluated in a secondary screen such as an in vitro cytotoxicity test or primary dermal irritation test (35), or (c) evaluated in a single rabbit before a full-scale eye irritation test is performed. It should be kept in mind that the correlation of all the physicochemical screen parameters with acute eye test results is very concentration dependent, being good at high concentrations and marginal at lower concentrations (where various buffering systems present in the eye are meaningful).

The second commonly used type of level of prescreen is the use of primary dermal irritation (PDI) test results. In this approach the PDI study is performed before the eye irritation study, and if the score from that study (called the primary dermal irritation index (PDII) and ranging from 0 to 8) is above a certain level (usually 5.0 or greater), the same options already outlined for physicochemical parameters can be exercised. There is no universal agreement on the value of this prescreen. Gilman et al. (37) did not find the PDII a good predictor, but made this judgment based on a relatively small data set and a cutoff PDII of 3.0 or above. In 1984 and 1985, Williams (38,39) reported that severe PDII scores (5.0 or greater) predicted severe eye irritation responses in 39 of 60 cases. He attributed the false positives to possible overprediction by current PDI test procedures. On the other hand, Guillot et al. (29,30) reported good prediction of eye irritation based on skin irritation in 56 materials and Gad et al. (8) reported good prediction of severe eye irritation results based on PDIIs of 72 test materials.

5. Staggered Study Starts. Another approach, which is a form of screen, calls for starting the eye test in 1 or 2 animals, then offsetting the dosing of the additional animals in the test group for 4 hr a day. During this offset period, if a severe result is seen in the first 1 or 2 animals, the remainder of the test may be cancelled. This staggered start allows one to both limit testing severe eye irritants to a few animals and yet have confidence that a moderate irritant would be detected.

6. Alternative Models. There is intensive work underway to develop models which are either in vitro or use lower order living organisms. This has recently been reviewed in detail by Frazier et al. (40).

## REFERENCES

1. Draize, J. H., Woodard, G., and Calvery, H. O. (1944). Methods for the study of irritation and toxicity of substances applied topically to the skin and mucous membranes. *J. Pharmacol. Exp. Ther.* *82*:377–390.

2. Department of Transportation Code of Federal Regulations (1980). Title 49, 173.240.

3. Draize, J. H. (1959). Dermal toxicity. In *Appraisal of the Safety of Chemicals in Foods, Drugs and Cosmetics*. Austin, TX, Association of Food and Drug Officials of the U.S.

4. Environmental Protection Agency. (1979). *Acute Toxicity Testing Criteria for New Chemical Substances*. Washington, D.C., Office of Toxic Substances, EPA 560/13-79-009.

5. Consumer Product Safety Commission. (1980). Federal Hazardous Substances Act Regulations. CFR 1500. 41.

6. Organization for Economic Cooperation and Development. (1981). *OECD Guidelines for Testing of Chemicals*, Sect. 404, Acute Dermal Irritation/Corrosion, Paris.

7. Weil, C. S., and Scala, R. A. (1971). Study of intra- and interlaboratory variability in the results of rabbit eye and skin irritation tests. *Toxicol. Appl. Pharmacol.* *19*:276–360.

8. Gad, S. C., Walsh, R. D., and Dunn, B. J. (1986). Correlation of ocular and dermal irritancy of industrial chemicals. *Ocular Dermal Toxicol.* *5*(3):195–213.

9. Code of Federal Regulations, Transportation, Title 49: Part 173, Appendix A—Method of Testing Corrosion to Skin, Revised; November 1, 1984.

10. Mann, I., and Pullinger, B. D. (1942). A study of mustard gas lesions of the eye of rabbits and men. *Proc. R. Soc. Med.* *35*:229–244.

11. Friedenwald, J. S., Huges, W. F., and Hermann, H. (1944). *Arch. Ophthalmol.* *31*:279.

12. *Illustrated Guide for Grading Eye Irritation by Hazardous Substance.* (1965). Washington, D.C., Food and Drug Administration.

13. CPCS. (1976). *Illustrated Guide for Grading Eye Irritation Caused by Hazardous Substances.* 16 CFR 1500.

14. National Academy of Sciences. (1977). *Principles and Procedures for Evaluating the Toxicity of Household Substances.* NAS Publication 1138. Washington, D.C., National Academy of Sciences.

15. Green, W. R., Sullivan, J. B., Hehir, R. M. Scharpf, L. F., and Dickinson, A. W. (1978). *A Systematic Comparison of Chemically Induced Eye Injury in the Albino Rabbit and the Rhesus Monkey.* New York, The Soap and Detergent Association.

16. Falahee, K. J., Rose, C. S., Siefried, H. F., and Sawhney, D. (1982). Alternatives in toxicity testing. *Product Safety Evaluation.* Edited by A. M. Goldberg. New York, Mary Ann Lieber, pp. 137–162.

17. Interagency Regulatory Liaison Group. (Jan. 1981). Testing Standards and Guidelines Work Group. Recommended Guideline for Acute Eye Irritation Testing.

18. Environmental Protection Agency. (1981). *Eye Irritation Testing.* EPA-560/11-82-001.

19. Ballantyne, B., and Wanston, D. W. (1977). The scope and limitations of acute eye irritation tests. *Current Approaches in Toxicology.* Edited by B. Ballantyne. Bristol, John Wright & Sons, pp. 139–157.

20. Chan, P. K., and Hayes, A. W. (1985). Assessment of chemically induced ocular toxicity; a survey of methods. *Toxicology of the Eye, Ear, and Other Special Senses.* Edited by A. W. Hayes. New York, Raven Press, pp. 103–143.

21. McLaughlin, R. S. (1946). Chemical burns of the human cornea. *Am. J. Ophthalmol.* 29:1355–1362.

22. Beckley, J. H. (1965). Comparative eye testing: Man vs. animal. *Toxicol. Appl. Pharmacol.* 7:93–101.

23. Calabrese, E. J. (1984). *Principles of Animal Extrapolation.* New York, John Wiley & Sons, pp. 391–402.

24. McDonald, T. O., Seabaugh, V., Shadduck, J. A., and Edelhauser, H. F. (1983). Eye irritation. *Dermatotoxicology.* Edited by F. N. Marzulli and H. I. Maibach. New York, Hemisphere Publishing, pp. 555–610.

25. Swanston, D. W. (1985). Assessment of the validity of animal techniques in eye irritation testing. *Food Chem. Toxicol.* 23:169–173.

26. Andermann, G., and Erhart, M. (1983). *Meth. Find. Exptl. Clin. Pharmacol.* 321–333.

27. Bayard, S., and Hehir, R. M. (1976). Evaluation of proposed changes in the modified Draize rabbit irritation test. *Toxicol. Appl. Pharmacol.* 37(1):186.

28. Williams, S. J., Graepel, G. J., and Kennedy, G. L. (1982). Evaluation of ocular irritancy potential: Intralaboratory variability and effect of dosage volume. *Toxicol. Letters 12*:235–241.

29. Guillot, J. P., Gonnet, J. F., Clement, C., Caillard, L., and Trahaut, R. (1982). Evaluation of the cutaneous-irritation potential of 56 compounds. *Food Chem. Toxicol. 201*:563–572.

30. Guillot, J. P., Gonnet, J. F., Clement, C., Caillard, L., and Truhaut, R. (1982). Evaluation of the ocular-irritation potential of 56 compounds. *Food Chem. Toxicol. 20*:573–582.

31. Freeberg, F. E., Griffith, J. F., Bruce, R. D., and Bay, P. H. S. (1984). Correlation of animal test methods with human experience for household products. *J. Toxicol. Cut. Ocular Toxicol. 1*:53.64.

32. Gloxhuber, C. H. (1985). Modification of the Draize eye test for the safety testing of cosmetics. *Food Chem. Toxicol. 23*:187–188.

33. Walker, A. P. (1985). A more realistic animal technique for predicting human eye responses. *Food Chem. Toxicol. 23*:175–178.

34. Murphy, J. C., Osterberg, R. E., Seabaugh, V. M., and Bierbower (1982). Ocular irritancy response to various pHs of acids and bases with and without irrigation. *Toxicology 23*:281–291.

35. Jackson, J., and Rutty, D. A. (1985). Ocular tolerance assessment-integrated tier policy. *Food Chem. Toxicol. 23*:309–310.

36. *Federal Register.* (1973). *Federal Hazardous Substances Act.* 38 No. 187, Section 1500, September 27.

37. Gilman, M. R., Jackson, E. M., Cerven, D. B., and Moreno, M. T. (1985). Relationship between the primary dermal irritation index and ocular irritation. *J. Toxicol. Cut Ocular Toxicol. 2*:107–117.

38. Williams, S. J. (1984). Prediction of ocular irritancy potential from dermal irritation test results. *Food Chem. Toxicol. 2*:157–161.

39. Williams, S. J. (1985). Changing concepts of ocular irritation evaluation: Pitfalls and progress. *Food Chem. Toxicol. 23*:189–193.

40. Frazier, J., Gad, S. C., Goldberg, A. M., and McCaulley, J. (1987). *A Critical Appraisal of Alternatives to the Rabbit Eye Irritation Test.* New York, Mary Ann Liebert.

# 5

# Predicting Hypersensitivity Responses

RICHARD A. HILES / *Hazleton Laboratories America, Inc.*, *Madison, Wisconsin*

## I. INTRODUCTION

Delayed contact hypersensitivity is the expression of the ability of a chemical to cause a greater dermal response than would have been anticipated based on simple irritancy. Unlike the inflammatory response in irritation, the responsiveness to an allergen is highly variable within a population. As Jackson (1) stated, irritation tells us about how we are similar while sensitivity tells us about how we are different. That is, everyone is irritated by strong acids, alkalis, and solvents, but only a select number of people respond to 3-pentadecylcatechol in poison ivy. Sensitization responses can be very undesirable in humans, the allergens difficult to avoid, and in the case of persistent sunlight-activated reactions, can be totally disabling.

The outward expression of irritation and sensitization are often similar (erythema, edema, heat, etc.) but the mechanisms leading to these two inflammatory responses are very different (2). Skin sensitization and dermal photosensitization are delayed humoral immune responses mediated by T cells. A chemical hapten or incomplete allergen passes into the dermis and complexes with dermis protein to form a hapten—protein complex. The Langerhans' cells in the area interact with this allergen as if it were completely foreign protein. The Langerhans' cells migrate to the thymus gland to "educate" the naive T cells about the allergen. The now educated T cells proliferate and leave the thymus as sensitized cells. With the proper stimulus they can initiate the inflammatory process through the release of lymphokines.

All assays for delayed contact hypersensitivity have common elements: induction phase, primary challenge phase, rechallenge phase, and irritation/toxicity screens. The *induction phase* involves exposing the test animals to the test material several times over a period of days or weeks. A number of events must be accomplished during this phase if a sensitization response is to be elicited. The test material must penetrate through the epidermis and into the dermis. There it must interact with dermis protein. The protein test material complex must be perceived by the immune system as an allergen. Finally, the production of sensitized T cells must be accomplished. Some assays enhance the sensitivity of the induction phase by compromising the natural ability of the epidermis to act as a barrier. These enhancement techniques include irritation of the induction site, intradermal injection, skin stripping, and occlusive dressings. In contrast, events such as the development of a scab over the induction site can reduce penetration. Light is used in the photosensitization assays to produce a chemically active species for interaction with the dermis protein. The attention of the immune system can be drawn to the induction site by the intradermal injection of oil-coated bacteria (Freund's complete adjuvant).

The *primary challenge phase* consists of exposing laboratory animals to a concentration of the test material which would normally not be expected to cause a response (usually an irritation-type response). The responses in the test animals and of the control animals are then measured.

A *rechallenge phase* is a repeat of the challenge phase and can be a very valuable tool if used properly. Sensitized animals can be rechallenged with the same test material at the same concentration used in the challenge in order to assist in confirming sensitization. Sensitized animals can be rechallenged with different concentrations of the allergen to evaluate dose versus response relationships. Animals sensitized to an ingredient can be challenged to a formulation containing the ingredient to evaluate the potential of the formulated product to elicit a sensitization response under adverse conditions. Conversely, animals which responded (sometimes unexpectedly) to a final formulation can be challenged with formulation without the suspected sensitizer or to the ingredient which is suspected to be the allergen. Cross reactivity can be evaluated. That is, the ability of one test material to elicit a sensitization response following exposure in the induction phase to a different test material. A well-designed rechallenge is important and should be considered at the same time that the sensitization evaluation is being designed, since the rechallenge must be run within 1 to 2 weeks after the primary challenge. Unless plans have been made for a possible rechallenge, one may have to reformulate a test material or obtain

additional pure ingredient and perhaps run additional irritation/
toxicity screens before the rechallenge can be run. The ability of
the sensitized animals to respond at a rechallenge can fade with
time, thus the necessity that the rechallenge be run shortly after
the challenge. In addition, some assays use sham-treated controls,
and these must be procured while the induction phase is in progress.
One additional piece of information must be kept in mind when evaluating a rechallenge. The animal does not differentiate between an
induction exposure and a challenge exposure. If one is using an
assay which involves three induction exposures and one challenge
exposure, then at the rechallenge, the animal has received four
induction exposures. This "extra" induction may serve to strengthen
a sensitization response.

All assays require knowledge of the dermal irritancy and systemic toxicity of the test material(s) to be used in the induction,
challenge, and rechallenge. These properties are defined in the
*irritation/toxicity screen*. Most assays will allow mild irritation in
the induction phase, but no systemic toxicity. Generally, a nonirritating concentration is required for the challenge and the rechallenge. As will be discussed in the sections on the individual
assays, even a carefully designed screen does not always provide
the desired guidance in selecting workable concentrations.

And what does one do with the results of the assay for delayed
contact hypersensitivity? The plan of action depends on the nature
of the material, how it will be used, and how conservative a risk
factor the investigator is using. The author has seen responses
ranging from refusal to use any ingredient which gave any positive
results, to one which does not worry unless all test animals exhibit
strong (+2) reactions. One can use the percentage of the animals
responding as a guide:

| % Responding | Classification |
| --- | --- |
| 0–10 | Nonsensitizer |
| 11–30 | Weak to mild |
| 31–60 | Moderate |
| 61–90 | Strong |
| 91–100 | Extreme |

A "responding animal" is one that exhibits a response at the challenge which is definitely greater than that observed in the controls.
The system denotes the ease with which the test material can elicit
a sensitization response in a population, not the strength of the

response. As previously discussed, the responsiveness of the animals can be a function of the particular assay used, solvents, vehicles, and concentration. In cases where human exposure is not intended or expected, then a warning to avoid dermal contact may be sufficient. (It is interesting that the EPA labeling guidelines (3) do not address sensitizers.) In situations where human contact is probable or desirable, then even weak sensitizers require careful consideration; human patch testing may be in order, but this subject is beyond the scope of this discussion. If one does not obtain a sufficient number of positive responders to classify a material as a sensitizer, it does not always mean that one does not have to be concerned about the potential of a test material being a sensitizer. Especially with final formulations, one should consider additional evaluations if, for example, all of the control animals have skin grades of "0" and all of the test animals exhibit grades of "±."

Positive controls are available for each assay for delayed contact hypersensitivity. A good positive control is one which gives predictable positive results only when the assay is run properly. A control that yields 100% responders is not impressive, as the assay may be run in a flawed manner and still yield 100% responders. Each laboratory should consider running control assays every 6 months. If a company places a significant amount of work at outside contract testing laboratories, then the sponsoring company would be wise to send "blind" positive controls on a regular basis. Some sponsors believe that a positive control should be run with every assay. If the testing laboratory has a collection of historical data generated with a consistant source of animals as well as data generated within the last 6 months, then the running of a positive control with each assay is not necessary. Experience would indicate that regulatory agencies do not require that a positive control be run with each evaluation and will accept historical data.

Over the past 50 years, a number of investigators have evaluated the usefulness of different animal models and assays for predicting dermal hypersensitivity responses in humans. To the credit of each investigator, and almost without exception, the method devised by each investigator worked better for the investigator's purpose than did the method devised by someone else. Since the author has not invented any new assays for this biological response, but has had experience in running several of the assays, it is the purpose of this chapter to inform rather than to contribute to the debate. Specifically, this presentation will provide insight into the Buehler assay (4) and the maximization assay (5) for detecting dermal sensitizers in the guinea pig, the Armstrong assay (6) for detecting photosensitizers in guines pigs, and the mouse ear swelling test assay (7) for detecting dermal allergens in the mouse. These four assays use almost all of the techniques which would be involved in the numerous other assays for delayed contact hypersensitivity.

## II. BUEHLER ASSAY FOR DETECTING DERMAL ALLERGENS

### A. Background

Buehler originally published his method for evaluating potential sensitizers in 1965 (4). He noted that his goal was to devise an assay method which would provide good prediction of human responses with a low number of false negatives. There have been many modifications of the original "Buehler assay" and almost any closed-patch exposure of guinea pigs not using adjuvant is referred to as the "Buehler assay." There are, however, several key elements which must be used to properly evaluate a material with this method. These elements along with various modifications of the original method as described by Ritz and Buehler (8) and some more recent changes not yet published are described here.

### B. Patching

The single most important technique in this assay is patching. Unlike some dermal sensitization assays, the Buehler assay does not potentiate the penetration of material into the dermis by damaging the skin through the application of irritants or by stripping away the epidermis, nor is the response potentiated through the injection of adjuvant or test material. The Buehler assay relies on holding the test material tightly against the skin with very good occlusion. A special restrainer which is still the key to obtaining good and consistent occlusion was described in the original paper. Stated very simply, one cannot execute the Buehler assay properly without the use of the restrainer. One cannot obtain the same degree of occlusion and thus penetration by simply wrapping the animal with an elastic bandage. Figure 1 shows an animal properly situated in a restrainer with an induction patch in place. Restrainers can be custom fabricated or can be purchased (Suburban Equipment, Chicago, IL). The material to be tested is applied to a patch before being applied to the skin of the animal. Two commercial patches are commonly used: Professional Medical Products, Inc. (PMP) patches which are a 20×20 mm Webril pad on adhesive tape and the 25 mm Hill Top chamber (both types of patches are available through Hill Top Research, Miamiville, OH). (The original PMP patch was a 20×20 mm Webril pad on adhesive tape and was available from Professional Medical Products, Inc., Greenwood, SC.) However, their standard production patch now uses a nonstick pad which will not work for the assay. Hill Top Research orders sufficient quantity of the old style PMP patch for a custom run and has them available for resale. The PMP patch has a capacity of 0.4 ml and the Hill Top chamber 0.3 ml. Data have been presented demonstrating that the PMP patch provides better sensitization than the Hill Top

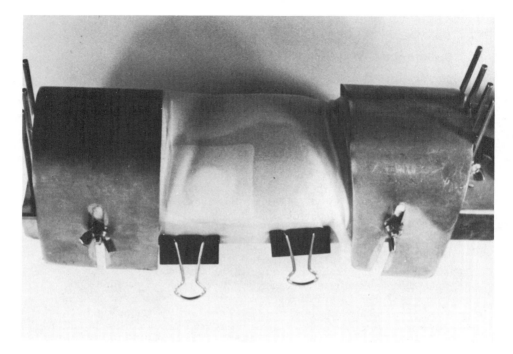

**Figure 1**  A guinea pig properly situated, occluded, and patched for induction in a restrainer for the Buehler assay.

chamber and visa versa.  The Hill Top chamber probably provides better occlusion while the PMP patch provides more material to react with the dermis protein.  Figure 2 compares the results of patching guinea pigs with water using the guinea pig restrainer and either the PMP patch or the Hill Top chamber.  The evaluation was run at three different laboratories.  The water (0.4 or 0.3 ml) was applied to the patch, the patch weighed, and quickly applied to the skin. The patch was occluded, removed after 6 hours, and reweighed. The percentage of weight loss during the exposure period was calculated.  The data demonstrate that good occlusion can be obtained with both patches, and of equal importance, the inter- and intralaboratory variations in technique can be a significant factor in reproducibility.

The occlusive material is a medium-weight rubber dental dam. The 6-inch wide roll cut into pieces of approximately 6 inches in length works well.  It is convenient to clip one side of the dental

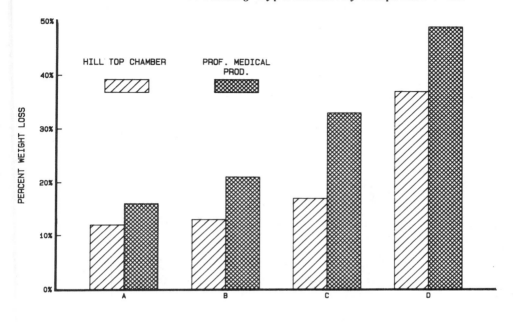

**Figure 2**  Comparison of water loss during 6 hr of occlusion using PMP patches and Hill Top chambers.  The study was run at three different laboratories (A, B, and C+D).  Laboratory C+D represents two separate attempts by the same laboratory to perform the Buehler assay.  (Courtesy of the Proctor & Gamble Co., Cincinnati, OH.)

dam to the bottom of the restrainer before placing the animal in it. The patch (freshly prepared with test material) is applied to the prepared test site, the dam pulled over the upper part of the animal and then clipped to the restrainer on the opposite side.  Adjustments are then made to give a firm restraint by the rubber without over-stressing the animal.  One should be able to just pinch a bit of the rubber on the back.  If the dental dam squeezes the test material out from under the pad or if the animal begins to lachrimate during the exposure, the dental dam is too tight.  The final adjustment is to snug the animal down with the steel restrainer straps.  The dental dam must be secured under the restrainer straps to assure good occlusion.  Animals should be checked frequently, especially the first time they are placed in the restrainer, to assure that they have not twisted into a position where the patch is no longer occluded. Repositioning of the animal may be required.

## C. Site Preparation

The test site must be prepared before each induction exposure, prior to the challenge or rechallenge, the irritation screens, and before grading. The hair is removed from the area to be patched the day before in order to provide time for any small surface injuries to the skin to close. Care should be taken to avoid injury to the skin. A #80 clipper blade provides for close removal of the hair. Complete removal of hair is required only before grading the test sites. This is accomplished using a depilatory such as Neet (Whitehall Laboratories, New York, NY). Since depilatories are themselves irritants, they should not be left in contact with the skin for more than 15 minutes and must be completely rinsed away with warm running water. The animals are dried with a towel, the sides of the cage wiped clean of any depilatory and the animals held in the cage at least 2 hours before grading.

## D. Grading

Grading is based on the visual perception of redness. Thus, it can be extremely subjective. Careful training of persons involved in the grading must be done in order to assure intralaboratory consistency. Written descriptions of the grades used are as follows:

    0 = No reaction
    ± = Slight, patchy erythema (barely perceptible or questionable)
    1 = Slight, but confluent or moderate but patchy erythema
    2 = Moderate erythema
    3 = Severe erythema with or without edema

A better alternative is a set of color plates to use as a guide (these may be obtained from the author). Lighting is a critical part of color perception. It is advisable to have a grading cart equipped with an overhead set of four 40-W fluorescent-type lights (GE Watt-Miser 11, F40LW P>S> WM11 Lite White or equivalent) suspended 3 feet above a flat black background. Grading should be done by two investigators, and the control animals should be graded before the test animals. The importance of good consistent grading cannot be overemphasized. The critical grade is often the decision between a ± and a 1 score, as a ± is not considered a "positive responder" while a grade of 1 is often considered a positive response. Scores of 0 or 2 or 3 are easily discerned. Since a material is considered to have elicited a sensitization response if 3 of 20 animals have a positive score, the decision between a ± and a 1 is critical. Sometimes dermal responses which are not erythema are observed (pinpoint red spots, brown crusty surface, etc.). These should be described but not used in determining the score.

## E. Vehicles

Often it is desirable or necessary to use a diluted form of the test material. Whenever possible, water is the most desirable solvent since there is no concern of the solvent causing a sensitization reaction. Other solvents which have been used are acetone, 95% ethanol, ethanol/water(80/20 v/v), petrolatum, and propylene glycol. With the exception of water, it is undesirable to use the same vehicle for the induction as is being used for the challenge, since it is possible to elicit a sensitization response to the vehicle or to impurities in the vehicle during the induction phase and obtain a false positive at the challenge. When deciding on the vehicle, one should keep in mind the effect the vehicle can have on the penetration of material through the epidermis and how the results of the sensitization assay with a particular vehicle will relate to the intended final use.

## F. Irritation Screens

A preliminary evaluation to determine the irritancy of the test material is often done prior to the actual evaluation of the sensitization potential. The Buehler assay requires a concentration of test material for the induction that will not cause a level of irritation which will result in eschar formation and that will not cause systemic toxicity. The concentration used at the challenge should not produce more than the slightest irritation (i.e., not more than 50%± in the control animals). The typical irritation screen uses 4 animals with 4 patches and thus 4 concentrations on each animal. The locations of the various concentrations on each animal are varied to correct for any site-to-site variations. Based on the results, a none-to-slightly irritating concentration of test material can be selected for the induction. If all of the concentrations are too irritating, the screen is repeated. In the past, this screen was often used to select the concentration of test material to be used in the challenge. However, it was found that the "nonirritating" level selected was sometimes irritating at the challenge in the control animals. Thus, a second irritation screen is now suggested. This second screen uses 8 animals and only 2 patches or concentrations per animal. This second screen has been found to be an excellent predictor of the results that will be observed in the control animals at the challenge and reduces the number of times that a rechallenge has to be run because of high background levels of irritation in the controls. It is obvious that if a solvent is being used in the induction which is different from the solvent which is being used in the challenge, then a second irritation screen must be run.

## G. Animals

The Hartley outbred guinea pig is the animal of choice. No differences between the responsiveness of sex to known sensitizers has been documented, but as a matter of principle, groups containing approximately equal numbers of males and females are used. All test and control animals should be weighed at the start of the induction and should be between 300 and 400 g. This weight range allows a workable size at the start of the study (i.e., large enough to obtain a good occlusive patching) and one that will still fit into the restrainer at the challenge (7 weeks later if a rechallenge is run). Animals are reweighed at the time of the challenge. Test and untreated control animals should gain about the same amount of weight if they are healthy and if there is no systemic toxicity to the test material. Guinea pigs used for the screens can weigh between 300 and 500 g. Animals are never identified by ear punch, toe clip, ear tag, or tattoo, as all of these have the potential of compromising the assay. Animals are identified by cage cards only. When they are placed in the restrainers, the restrainers are identified with the animal number using a marking pen. A useful aide is to use colored stickers on the cage card when more than one test is being done in the same room and to use a matching colored marking pen to mark the hair on the nose of the test animals and the rump of the control animals when they are in the restrainers.

## H. Conducting the Buehler Assay

The foregoing discussion has provided insight into the reasons for and the details of many of the steps in the Buehler assay. The following scheme combines these into an evaluation.

1. *Preinduction Irritation/Toxicity Screen*
   *(4 Animals)*

Day −1. Remove the hair from entire back with clippers.
Day 0. Prepare 4 different concentrations of test material. Patch each animal with 4 patches for 6 hours (±15 min).
Day 1. Depilate the patched area 18–22 hr after removal of the patches. Grade a minimum of 2 hr after depilation (24-hr grade).
Day 2. Repeat the grading 24 hr (±2 hr) later (48-hr grade).

2. *Induction (20 Test + 10 Control Animals +*
   *Any Rechallenge Controls)*

Day −1. Weigh the test and control animals and remove hair from the left shoulder with clippers of only the test animals.

Day 0.  Patch 20 test animals only for 6 hr (±15 min).

Weeks 2 and 3.  Repeat the clipping and patching twice more on the test animals only with a 5- to 9-day interval between patchings.  Check the induction site during clipping for eschar damage; move patches to a new site if escher is present.

## 3.  *Prechallenge Irritation Screen*
   *(8 Animals)*

Run this screen during the induction phase.  Run using the same procedure as the prestudy screen except use two patches per animal.  The lowest concentration which caused slight irritation in the prestudy screen is used as the highest concentration in the prechallenge screen.

## 4.  *Challenge (20 Test + 10 Control Animals*
   *12 to 16 Days After the Last Induction)*

Day −1.  Remove the hair from the area to be patched on the test and the naive control animals (never the area used for the induction) using the animal clippers.

Day 0.  Challenge the test and control animals with a non-irritating concentration of the test material using an occluded patch and an exposure time of 6 hr (±15 min).

Day 1.  Depilate and grade as in the irritation screens.  Grade control animals first (24-hr grade).

Day 2.  Grade a second time (48-hr grade).

## 5.  *Rechallenge (6–10 Days After the*
   *Primary Challenge)*

All or selected animals may be rechallenged with the same material used in the challenge at the same or a different concentration or a new test material may be used.  Use 10 new control animals, naive test sites on all animals, and the same procedures used in the challenge phase.

## 6.  *Report*

Determine the number of positive responders (number of animals with a score ⩾1 at either the 24- or 48-hr grading or with a score one unit higher than the highest score in the control group).  Determine the average score (scores at face value and ± = 0.5) at 24 hr and at 48 hr for the test and the control group (4 values).

## I. Advantages, Disadvantages, and Problems

The Buehler assay has been in use for 20 years. In this time, a large quantity of data have accumulated which indicate that the assay provides good predictability of what can be expected in humans. Some confusion exists because the original paper by Buehler used 10 induction patchings and 10 animals and not the 3 inductions on 20 animals as presented here. Some regulatory agencies give the impression that they require the 10 patching/10 animal procedure. However, work referenced in the Introduction (Section I) demonstrates that the 3 patch/20 animal method provides equal sensitivity at less cost. Another advantage of the latter method relates to the decision which must be made from the results. The normal criterion for a positive sensitizer is 3 or more of 20 animals with positive scores. This would mean that only 1 animal of 10 in a 10 animal assay would need to exhibit a positive score for the judgement to be made that the material elicits a sensitization response. The major problem with the assay is that it is very technique dependent; false negatives can be obtained if the technique is flawed. The use of a subjective grading system for erythema is an obvious source of potential problems.

## J. Positive Control

A positive control should yield responses *only* if the assay has been run correctly. The positive control for the Buehler assay is a solution of 3-chloro-2,4-dinitrobenzene (DNCB). A 0.3% w/v solution in ethanol:water 80:20 v:v on a PMP patch (0.4 ml) is used for the induction. Test and control animals are challenged with a 0.2% and a 0.02% w:v solution in acetone. Typical results are as follows:

| Group | Challenge level | Incidence[a] | Severity 24 hr | Severity 48 hr | Maximum score 24 hr | Maximum score 48 hr |
|---|---|---|---|---|---|---|
| Test | 0.2% | 20 of 20 | 2.7 | 2.3 | 3 | 3 |
| | 0.02% | 6 of 20 | 0.6 | 0.5 | 1 | 1 |
| Control | 0.2% | 0 of 10 | 0.1 | 0.1 | ± | ± |
| | 0.02% | 0 of 10 | 0.0 | 0.0 | 0 | 0 |

[a] Animals with score ⩾1 at 24 or 48 hours.

## III. MAXIMIZATION ASSAY FOR DETECTING DERMAL ALLERGENS

### A. Background

Magnusson and Kligman published a procedure for evaluating the potential for chemicals to elicit a delayed contact hypersensitivity response (5). This procedure attempted to "maximize" the potential for a response through the use of Freund's complete adjuvant, intradermal injection of the test material, and the use of a pretreatment to produce irritation at the induction site. The epidermis was initially bypassed by intradermally injecting adjuvant, adjuvant mixed with test material, and test material in vehicle. The second phase consisted of irritating the skin over the injection sites with a surfactant and then applying the test material to the skin under an occlusive patch. The stated purpose of the assay was to determine if a chemical has *any* potential as a dermal allergen. It was recommended for testing individual chemicals and not complex mixtures, finished products, or formulations. Except in cases where the maximization assay gives negative results, the results cannot be directly applied to the potential for human risk as the assay tends to overestimate the risk. A positive result merely warns the toxicologist of the possibility of harmful effects.

### B. Induction Site

#### 1. Injections

Each test animal receives three pairs of injections of 0.1 ml each, high on the back just behind the shoulders, with the paired injections separated by the backbone (Fig. 3). The position of the 6 injections must be limited to an area which can be covered by a 20 × 40 mm patch. The hair is removed on the day of the injections using small animal clippers with a #80 blade. One pair of injections is a 1:1 v:v dilution of Freund's complete adjuvant (Calbiochem-Behring, San Diego, CA or Difco, Detroit, MI) and water. The second pair is the test article in vehicle and the third pair is test article mixed with adjuvant and brought to a final dilution of 1:1. The injections *must* be intradermal. A 1 cc syringe with a 1/4 inch 25 or 28 gauge needle works well. However, some test material preparations (especially suspensions) may require a larger needle; leakage from the needle hole may occur. The sham-treated controls receive adjuvant, vehicle, and adjuvant with vehicle but no test material.

#### 2. Booster Patch

The original published paper used a piece of filter paper for the booster patch, but PMP patches are easier and provide more

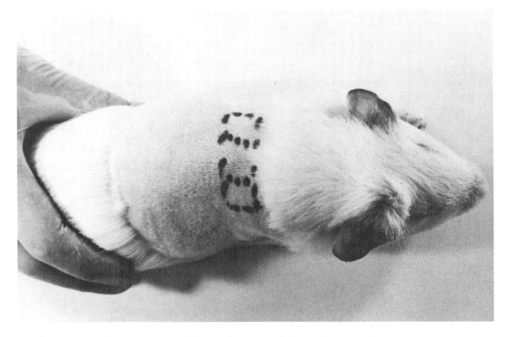

**Figure 3**  Placement of the intradermal injections and booster patch in the maximization assay.  Black ink was used to denote the 6 sites for the injections within an area (dashed lines) which will be covered by the 20 × 20 mm booster patch.  (Courtesy of Hazleton Laboratory, Inc., Madison, WI.)

consistency (see Sect. II.A).  The 20 × 40 mm patch is obtained by cutting the tape away from one edge of a 20 × 20 mm PMP patch and sticking this patch adjacent to a second uncut patch.  Test material in petrolatum can be smeared onto the pad, or in the case of a test article in a liquid form, the pad readily accommodates 0.8 ml of substance.  The assay requires the use of an irritating concentration of test material, or if the test material is not irritating, that the skin irritation be induced by a surfactant prior to the application of the booster patch.  The surfactant irritation step uses a 10% w/w preparation of sodium lauryl sulfate in petrolatum.  Both the test and the control animals are exposed when sodium lauryl sulfate is used.  The 20 × 40 mm patch is coated with the surfactant preparation and applied over the injection sites.  The patch is then occluded with a piece of dental dam which is held in place with a piece of hypoallergenic tape.  The trunk of the animal is wrapped with elastic tape for a period of 24 hours. Just prior to initiating the booster patching, the surfactant patch is removed. The booster patch (containing test material or vehicle for the controls) is placed over the injection sites and occluded as described for the surfactant patch. This booster patch remains in place for 48 hours.

## C. Patching

The PMP patch and the Hill Top chamber as discussed in the Buehler assay can be used in the irritation screens and the challenge phase. The use of the modified PMP patch in the induction phase was discussed in the previous section. Unlike the Buehler assay, no restrainers are used in the maximization assay as the length of the restraint period (up to 72 hr) would far exceed the stress limits of the animals. Occlusion is accomplished by covering the patch with a piece of medium-weight rubber dental dam which is secured with a piece of hypoallergenic adhesive tape and then wrapping the trunk of the animal with elastic adhesive tape. The elastic tape prevents the animal from bending in a normal manner and can present problems with certain types of feeders. That is, they can climb part of the way into the feeder but cannot get out because they cannot bend enough for their feet to reach the bottom of the cage.

## D. Site Preparation

The procedures for clipping the hair and for depilation are the same as described for the Buehler assay.

## E. Grading

The grading system for dermal irritation and sensitization responses is the same as described in the Buehler assay.

## F. Preliminary Screens

The maximization assay involves two types of screens: one for the intradermal injections and one for dermal irritation. A concentration for the intradermal injections which does not cause systemic toxicity or necrosis within 48 hours is required. Eight male or female guinea pigs are used in this screen. Each of 4 different concentrations of test material is tested in a pair of animals. The four concentrations must be prepared both in vehicle and in Freund's complete adjuvant. A pair of animals is then given two 0.1 ml injections of the test material in vehicle and two 0.1 ml injections of test material in adjuvant (4 injections per animal). The injections must be intradermal and are given in the back over the shoulder region after the hair

has been clipped away. The injection sites are evaluated for irritation and necrosis and the animals for systemic toxicity 24 and 48
hours after the injections. A descriptive evaluation, rather than a
formal grading, is made, as one is only interested in a dose concentration which can be tolerated.

A dermal irritation screen must be run in order to select, if possible, a slightly irritating level for the booster patch phase of the
induction and a nonirritating concentration for the challenge. The
hair is removed from the backs of 4 male or female guinea pigs the
day before the test material is to be applied. Four concentrations
are tested on each animal (4 patches per animal) with the location
of the different concentrations varied to correct for any site-to-site
variations. PMP patches (0.4 ml) or Hill Top chambers (0.3 ml) can
be used. The patches are placed on the back, covered with a piece
of dental dam which is secured with a piece of hypoallergenic tape,
and then the trunks of the animals wrapped with a piece of elastic
adhesive tape. The patches are removed 24 hr (±30 min) later.
Approximately 21 hr after the patches are removed, the remaining
hair is removed with depilatory. The sites are graded 24 hr (±1 hr)
and 48 hr (±2 hr) after removal of the patches. As discussed more
fully in the Buehler assay, a more accurate prediction of the background irritation which will be observed at the challenge can often
be obtained if a second irritation screen is run using only two patches
per animal.

## G. Vehicles

The vehicles to be used in preparing the various concentrations of
the test material must be given careful consideration. As many as
three different vehicles may be required: One for the injection of
test material in vehicle, one for the preparation of test material in
adjuvant, and one for the dermal application. Water-soluble test
materials present the least problem as this single vehicle can be used
in all phases. When a water-soluble material is to be mixed with
adjuvant, it is first dissolved in water and this solution is then
mixed with an equal volume of adjuvant. Complete dispersion is accomplished by rapid stirring. One must observe that the mixing of
the test material preparation with adjuvant has not disrupted the
emulsion of the adjuvant. Oil-soluble or insoluble test materials can
often be dissolved or suspended directly in the adjuvant and then
the mixture diluted with water to a final 1:1 dilution. In some cases,
it has been found advantageous to first dissolve a test material in
acetone or ethylacetate and then add up to 0.1 ml of the solution to
the adjuvant. Under these conditions, the adjuvant should be stirred
rapidly and the organic solution added in very small drops.

The injection of the test material in vehicle without adjuvant may use water, mineral oil, vegetable oil, or propylene glycol as the vehicle. The use of many organic solvents such as acetone or alcohol generally cause an excess of tissue damage.

Test material is prepared for dermal application (booster patch, irritation screen, and challenge) by dissolving it in an appropriate solvent such as water, ethanol:water (80:20 v:v), or acetone or by dispersing it in petrolatum. If one must work with a suspended solid, the solid should be micronized before use.

## H. Animals

The animals are the same as discussed in the Buehler assay.

## I. Running the Maximization Assay

The foregoing discussion has provided insight into the reasons for and the details of many of the steps in the assay. The following scheme combines these into an evaluation:

### 1. *Irritation/Toxicity Screen (12 Animals)*

Intradermal injections (8 animals)

Day 0. Prepare 4 concentrations of test material in adjuvant and 4 concentrations in vehicle. Clip the hair from the back over the shoulders. Inject a pair of animals with each of the concentrations—2 injections of one of the adjuvant concentrations and 2 injections of the corresponding concentration of test material in vehicle.

Days 1 and 2. Evaluate the injection sites grossly for irritation and necrosis and the animals for systemic toxicity.

Dermal Irritation (4 animals)

Day −1. Remove the hair from the back using a clippers.

Day 0. Patch each animal with 4 different concentrations of test material. Occlude the patches and wrap the animals with elastic tape. Use either PMP patches or Hill Top chambers depending on which one will be used at the challenge.

Day 1. Remove the patches 24 hr (±30 min) after the start.

Day 2. Remove the hair with depilatory approximately 21 hr after removing the patches. Grade the test sites for irritation 24 hr (±1 hr) after removing the patches.

Day 3. Grade the test sites 48 hr (±2 hr) after removing the patches.

2. *Induction (20 Test, 10 Sham Controls +*
   *Rechallenge Controls)*

Day 0. Weigh the test and control animals. Remove the hair
from the shoulder region with clippers, inject each test
animal with 2 intradermal 0.1 ml shots each of diluted
adjuvant, adjuvant containing test material, and test material in vehicle (6 injections per animal). Inject each control animal in a similar manner except do not use test
material.

Day 6. If the test article concentration to be used for the
booster patch was not irritating in the screen, treat the
injection sites with 10% sodium lauryl sulfate in petrolatum
under occluded dressing for 24 hr. Remove the hair with
clippers prior to the treatment. If the test article was
irritating, omit this step.

Day 7. Remove the hair from the injection sites with clippers
if this was not done on day 6. Place 0.8 ml of liquid test
material preparation on a 20 × 40 mm PMP patch or coat the
patch with test material in petrolatum if it is a solid. Place
the patch over the injection sites of the test animals, cover
with dental dam and wrap the animal with elastic tape.
Treat the controls with vehicle only.

Day 9. Remove the booster patches 48 hr (±2 hr) after initiating the patching.

3. *Prechallenge Irritation*

Repeat the dermal irritation screen during the induction phase,
if desired. Use only two patches per animal.

4. *Challenge*

Day 19. Weigh the test and control animals. Remove the hair
from the entire back of each test and control animal using
a clipper.

Day 20. Patch each test and control animal with test material
on a PMP patch or with a Hill Top chamber on a naive test
site with a concentration of test material as determined in
the irritation screen. Use a vehicle control patch if appropriate. Occlude the patches with dental dam and wrap the
animals with elastic tape.

Day 21. Remove the patches and any excess test material 24 hr
(±30 min) after application.

Day 22. Remove any remaining hair with depilatory starting
approximately 21 hr after the patches were removed. Grade
the test sites 24 hr (±1 hr) after patches were removed
(24-hr grade).

Day 23. Grade the sites again 48 hr (±2 hr) after the patches were removed (48-hr grade).

## 5. Rechallenge

All or selected animals may be rechallenged with the same test material at the same or a different concentration or with a different test material within 7–14 days after the primary challenge. Use new control animals and naive test sites on all animals.

## 6. Report

Determine the number of positive responders (animals with a score ≥1 at either the 24- or the 48-hr grading or with a score one unit higher than the highest score in the control group). Determine the average score (with ± = 0.5) at 24 and 48 hr for the test and control groups (4 scores).

## J. Advantages, Disadvantages, and Problems

Maximization assay provides a very sensitive determination if a test material has any potential to be a dermal sensitizer. Because of the use of adjuvant, intradermal injections, and skin irritants, all of which compromise the epidermal barrier, it is difficult to relate the results to potential danger in "normal" human exposure. On the other hand, a negative result tends to be very reassuring that there is little concern for sensitization in humans. If the investigator is interested in determining if a single component in a complex mixture which is a recognized sensitizer might elicit a sensitization response when in the mixture, then a group of animals can be sensitized to the pure component and challenged with the final formulation. As with any assay which involves the injection of adjuvant, there is often a problem with using the results of the irritation screen in naive animals to accurately predict the results that will be seen in the sham controls at the challenge. If the material being tested is a nonirritant or if one selects a concentration of an irritant which is far below the irritating concentration, then the screen does an adequate job of predicting the background irritation level in the challenge controls. However, if a slightly nonirritating concentration of an irritant is used, the screen often underpredicts the response and a high background level of irritation is observed at the challenge in the sham-treated controls. The interpretation of the challenge results become difficult. Thus, it is often necessary to rechallenge the test animals at a lower concentration and therefore additional sham-treated controls must be available. The possible need for rechallenge control animals adds additional cost to the assay. The use of adjuvant injections causes a significant increase in the stress to the animals.

## K. Positive Control

The positive control for the assay uses 1-chloro-2,4-dinitrobenzene. The intradermal injections are made with a final concentration of 0.1% using propylene glycol as the vehicle. The booster patch (20 × 40 mm PMP patch) and the challenge patch (Hill Top chamber) use a 0.1% (w:v) solution of test material in 80:20 ethanol:water (v:v). Typical results are as follows:

| Group | Incidence[a] | Severity 24 hr | Severity 48 hr | Maximum score 24 hr | Maximum score 48 hr |
|---|---|---|---|---|---|
| Test | 20 of 20 | 2.5 | 2.3 | 3 | 3 |
| Sham control | 0 of 10 | 0.0 | 0.0 | 0 | 0 |
| Naive control | 0 of 10 | 0.0 | 0.0 | 0 | 0 |

[a]Animals with score ⩾1 at 24 or 48 hr.

## IV. ARMSTRONG ASSAY FOR DETECTING PHOTOALLERGENS

### A. Background

The interaction of light [generally ultraviolet (UV)] with certain chemicals can lead to a reactive species. Under the proper circumstances, some of these reactive chemicals can result in a sensitization response. Ichikawi and colleagues (6) published a testing method for evaluating the potential of a chemical to be a photosensitizer. Evaluating the potential for photosensitization has become of significant interest to the cosmetic industry since two widely used fragrance materials, musk ambrette and 6-methyl coumarin, have become recognized as photoallergens in humans. The Armstrong assay has been recommended by the Cosmetic, Toiletries and Fragrances Association. It is interesting that the EPA has not made public a concern about photoallergens since several pesticides have similar structures to the aforementioned fragrances and numerous pesticides are known to form reactive species in the presence of UV light.

### B. Lights

The Armstrong assay uses UVA light (320–400 nm) in the induction and challenge phase. UVA lights are commonly known as "black lights" and can be purchased as "BLB" fluorescence-type bulbs from major light manufacturers. However, the selection of the light

source is critical since the range of wave lengths emitted by the
bulb is controlled by the phosphor coating and different manufacturers use different phosphors to produce BLB lights. Sometimes
different phosphors are used by the same manufacturer and there
is no code on the bulbs to indicate which phosphor is being used.
Cole et al. (9) reported an excellent study of this problem. Figure
4 shows the photoemission spectrum of General Electric and Sylvania
BLB lights. General Electric bulbs emit effective energy only at
wave lengths longer than 350 nm while the entire spectrum between
315 and 400 nm is covered by the Sylvania bulb. Less than 2% of
the total energy emitted by the General Electric light is between 250
and 350 nm while 42% of the energy from the Sylvania light falls in
this range. There are known photoallergens which require the energy
contained in the spectrum below 345 nm for activation and thus give
a false negative if the incorrect light source is used. The best pre-
caution is to determine the emission spectrum of the lights which are

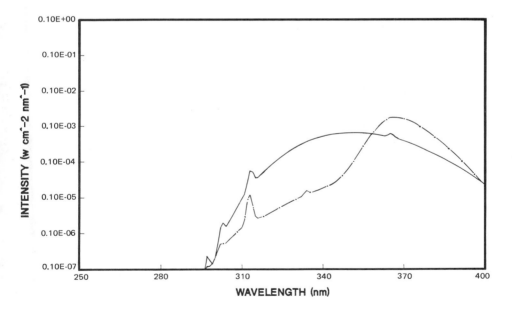

**Figure 4** Energy spectra of GE F40 BLB lights (solid line) and Sylvania F40 BLB lights (dashed line). Spectra were measured with an
Optronics Model 742, dual holographic grating, spectral radiometer
fitted with a teflon diffuser. (Courtesy of Schering-Plough, Inc.,
Memphis, TN.)

to be used in the assay. However, at a cost of $15,000, a photo-radiometer may be a bit over budget for many laboratories. When pressed, the manufacturer will provide emission spectrum data.

It is necessary to determine the total energy being emitted by the lights in order to calculate the proper $J/cm^2$ exposure. An international Light Model 700 provides a relatively inexpensive means of measuring the light energy when fitted with a cosine-corrected UVA detector (W150s quartz diffuser, UVA-pass filter SEE015 detector). The device has a peak sensitivity of 360 nm with a band width of 50 nm. A bank of 8 bulbs is readily prepared by bolting together two industrial 4-bulb (48 inch long) reflectors. Two sets of these will allow 40 animals to be treated at one time. The lights are allowed to warm 30 minutes before use. They are turned off just before the animals are placed under them and then turned back on. The light intensity is measured at several locations at the level of the top of the backs of the animals and the correct exposure time then calculated. The lights are adjusted to be between 4 and 6 inches above the back and 10 $J/cm^2$ is the proper exposure.

## C. Patching

The Hill Top chamber (see Buehler assay) provides a good patching system in this assay. A volume of 0.3 ml is used. The animal restrainers described in the Buehler assay work well for holding the animals during the patching and the exposure to the light as well as assist in providing excellent occlusion.

## D. Induction Site Preparation

The majority of hair is removed from the intended patching site with a small animal clippers fitted with a #80 blade. The assay has a frequent requirement for the complete removal of hair using a depilatory. Neet (Whitehall Laboratories, New York, NY) cream or lotion is applied and left in contact with the skin for no more than 15 minutes. It must be washed away completely with a stream of warm running water. The animals are dried with a towel and the inside of the cages wiped clean of any depilatory before returning the guinea pigs to the cages.

When required, the epidermis is partially removed with transparent adhesive tape [3M brand (3M Company, St. Paul, MN) or similar]. The skin must be completely dry or the stripping will be ineffective. A length of tape approximately 8 inches long is used. Starting at one end, the tape is placed against the skin and rubbed with the finger a few times to cause good adhesion. It is then peeled away, taking with it some dry epidermis cells. A new section of the tape is then applied to the skin and the procedure is repeated 4 or 5 times. The skin will have a shiny appearance due to the leakage of moisture from the dermis. The tape should not be jerked away from the skin as this can cause rupture to dermal capillaries.

The potential of the animal to respond to a sensitizer is enhanced by the injection of Freund's complete adjuvant (Calbiochem-Behring, San Diego, CA or Difco, Detroit, MI). The adjuvant is diluted 1:1 with sterile water before using. The injections *must* be intradermal. In the Armstrong assay a pattern of four 0.1 ml injections are given just prior to the first induction patching in the nuchal area. All 4 injections should fit under the edge of the area to be covered by the Hill Top chamber. It is advisable to perform the skin-stripping operation before the injections, since adjuvant can leak onto the skin and prevent good stripping.

The occlusion of the patches is done in the same manner as described in the Buehler assay. The test site(s) is exposed to the UVA light after 2 hours of occlusion. The animal is left in the restrainer and the dental dam above the test site to be exposed is cut and the patch removed. Sites not to be exposed are left patched. Excess material is wiped from the site of exposure and the remaining parts of the animal are covered with aluminum foil. All patches are removed after the light exposure step, the patched areas wiped free of excess material, and the animal returned to the cage.

## E. Grading

Grading is the same as in the Buehler assay.

## F. Vehicles

With the exception of water, it is desirable to use a vehicle for the inductions which is different from the one used at the challenge (see Buehler assay). Since the control animals in the Armstrong assay are sham treated (including any vehicle), one can patch the test and control animals with vehicle at the challenge if the same vehicle must be used for both the induction and the challenge. It is advantageous to use a vehicle which dissolves the test material, though suspensions may not be avoided in all cases.

## G. Irritation Screens

The irritation screen is used to determine acceptable concentrations for the induction phase (i.e., should not produce eschar with repeated exposures or systemic toxicity) and the challenge phase (no more than slightly irritating). Each concentration must be tested with and without exposure to UVA light, as both conditions are used in the challenge. Thus, to evaluate 4 concentrations requires that 8 animals be used. Each animal receives a pair of patches with each pair being a different concentration (i.e., each concentration is patched on 4 animals). One of each pair of patches is placed on the left side and the corresponding concentration on the remaining patch is placed on the right side. The hair is removed by depilation on the day of patching. The patches on the right side are removed after 2 hours of occlusion, the remaining parts of the animal covered with foil, and the right side exposed to 10 J/cm$^2$ of UVA light. Animals are returned to their cages after the exposure. If different solvents are being used in the induction and challenge phase, then two separate screens need to be run.

## H. Animals

The animals are the same as described in the Buehler assay.

## I. Running the Armstrong Assay

Combining the discussed techniques in a specific regimen yields the assay as follows:

### 1. Irritation/Toxicity Screen (8 Animals)

Day 0. Remove the hair from the lumbar region by clipping and depilation. Apply 2 concentrations on each animal on adjacent left-side/right-side locations for a total of 4 dose concentrations. Occlude the patches for 2 hours (±15 min). Expose the right side to 10 J/cm$^2$ of UVA light after removing the patches on the right side. Remove the remaining patches and excess material after the exposure.

Day 1. Grade all test sites 24 hr (±1 hr) after removal of all patches (24-hr grade).

Day 2. Repeat the grading 48 hr (±2 hr) after removing the patches (48-hr grade).

### 2. Induction (20 Test + 10 Sham Controls + Any Rechallenge Controls)

Day 0. Weigh all test and control animals. Remove the hair from the nuchal area with clippers and depilatory. Remove the epidermis by stripping 4 to 5 times with tape. Make four 0.01 ml injections of a 1:1 dilution of Freund's complete adjuvant in an area to be covered by the patch. Cover this area on the test animals with a Hill Top chamber which has 0.3 ml of test material preparation. Patch the sham controls with water or solvent on the patch. Occlude with dental dam

and restrain the animal in a holder for 2 hr (+15 min).
Remove the patches, cover the nonpatched areas with foil,
and expose to 10 J/cm$^2$ of UVA light.

Days 2, 4, 7, 9, 11. Repeat the activities of day 0 with the
following exceptions: Do not weigh animals and do not inject
adjuvant. Move the patch back when the original induction
site becomes too damaged but remain in the nuchal area.
Dipilation may not be needed at each induction.

3. *Challenge (20 Test + 10 Sham Control Animals*
*9–13 Days After Last Induction Exposure)*

Day 0. Weigh all animals, clip the lumbar region free of hair,
and dipilate. Do not strip the skin. Patch each animal with a
with a pair of adjacent patches (one on the left side and one
on the right side) containing 0.3 ml of a nonirritating concentration of test material on a Hill Top chamber. Occlude
the patches and restrain the animal for 2 hr (±15 min).
Remove the patches from the right side and cover the rest
of the animal with foil. Expose the right side to 10 J/cm$^2$
of UVA light. Remove the remaining patch and any excess
material.

Day 1. Grade all challenge sites keeping separate the grades
of the sites exposed to light and those not exposed to light
24 hr (±1 hr) after removal of the patches (24-hr grade).

Day 2. Repeat the grading 48 hr (±2 hr) after removal of the
patches (48-hr grade).

4. *Rechallenge*

All or selected animals may be rechallenged with the same or a
different test material 7–12 days after the challenge. Use 10 new
sham-treated controls and naive test sites on all animals following the
same procedure as used in the challenge.

5. *Report*

Determine the number of positive responders (number of animals
with a score ≥1 at either the 24- or 48-hr grading or with a score
one unit higher than the highest score in the control). Determine
the average score at 24 and at 48 hr for the test and control groups
using face values and ± = 0.5. Keep the data for the sites exposed
to light separate from the data for sites not exposed to light.

## J. Advantages, Disadvantages, and Problems

The Armstrong assay was found to give responses in the guinea pig
which were consistent with what has been observed in humans:

positive responses for 6-methyl coumerin and musk ambrett. One major disadvantage is that the procedure is time consuming with six induction exposures; additional work might demonstrate that fewer exposures will yield the same results. The procedure is very stressful on the animals because of the injection of adjuvant and the multiple skin strippings and depilations. As with any assay involving the intradermal injection of adjuvant, there is often a problem with using the results of the irritation screen in naive animals to accurately predict the results that will be seen in the sham controls at the challenge. If the material being tested is a nonirritant or if one selects a concentration of an irritant which is far below the irritating concentration, then the screen does an adequate job of predicting the background irritation level in the challenge controls. However, if a slightly nonirritating concentration of an irritant is used, then the screen often underpredicts the irritation response and a high background level of irritation is observed at the challenge in the sham controls. The interpretation of the results of the challenge becomes difficult. The use of animals in the irritation screen which have had a prior injection of adjuvant might provide a viable alternative and reduce the number of times that rechallenges must be run because of high background levels of irritation. The Armstrong assay was designed to evaluate materials for their photoactivated sensitization potential and not their potential to be nonphotoactivated dermal sensitizers. At this time there is no background data which will allow for properly positioning results of the Armstrong assay with regard to human risk if the assay indicates that a test material is a sensitizer or that a material is both a sensitizer and a photoallergen. Thus, it is highly recommended that a "standard" sensitization assay which can be related to humans be run before or in conjunction with the photosensitization assay. The use of a subjective grading system can be a source of significant variation.

## K. Positive Control

The recommended positive control is musk ambrett. TCSA (3,3,4,5-tetrachlorosalicylanilide) will also give positive results, but this material has been reported to be an allergen without UV light activation. Animals are induced with a 10% w/v solution of musk ambrett in acetone and sham controls are patched with acetone alone. The Hill Top chamber is used for all patchings. The challenge is also done in acetone. A note of warning. Both types of UVA lights yield the same results. Typical results are as follows:

| Group | Challenge level | Incidence[a] | Severity | | Maximum score | |
|---|---|---|---|---|---|---|
| | | | 24 hr | 48 hr | 24 hr | 48 hr |
| Test | | | | | | |
| no UV light | 0.1% | 0 of 20 | 0.0 | 0.0 | 0 | 0 |
| UV light | | 17 of 20 | 2.0 | 1.8 | 3 | 3 |
| no UV light | 0.01% | 0 of 20 | 0.0 | 0.0 | 0 | 0 |
| UV light | | 17 of 20 | 0.6 | 0.4 | 2 | 1 |
| Control | | | | | | |
| no UV light | 0.1% | 0 of 10 | 0.0 | 0.0 | 0 | 0 |
| UV light | | 0 of 10 | 0.0 | 0.0 | 0 | 0 |
| no UV light | 0.01% | 0 of 10 | 0.1 | 0.0 | ± | 0 |
| UV light | | 0 of 10 | 0.1 | 0.0 | ± | 0 |

[a]Animals with a score ≥1 at 24 or 48 hr.

## V. MOUSE EAR SWELLING TEST (MEST) ASSAY FOR DETECTING DERMAL ALLERGENS

### A. Background

The guinea pig has historically been the animal of choice, and methods such as the Buehler and maximization assays have traditionally been used to evaluate the potential of a chemical or mixtures to elicit a sensitization response. Since guinea pigs are relatively expensive to purchase ($12 to $28) and maintain and the assays require weeks to complete, investigators have sought an alternative assay. Gad has presented an assay called the mouse ear swelling test (MEST) (7,10). The mouse was shown to exhibit the capability for delayed-type contact hypersensitivity in 1959 (11). Asherson and Ptak (12) developed the technique of quantitatively assessing contact delayed hypersensitivity by measuring the swelling of the mouse ear with a micrometer. Chapman et al. (13) demonstrated that an excellent correlation exists between ear swelling and histological changes. Gad's group performed an extensive evaluation using a variety of exposure conditions, animal strains, and test materials in order to elucidate the conditions for optimum response. The MEST results compared favorably with the results of maximization assay when 72 test materials were identified as sensitizers or nonsensitizers. Several laboratories have participated in a validation of the procedure (14).

### B. Animals

Female CF-1 mice are used in the assay. They should be 6–8 weeks of age when the study is initiated. The sex of the animal is not critical from a sensitization criterion. However, there is a cost advantage to group housing (5 per cage) and the use of females avoids the fighting problems often found with male mice. Both CF-1 and BALB/C mice respond well to known sensitizers while several other strains of mice are not sensitive responders; the CF-1 mice are much less expensive than the BALB/C strain. Animals less than 4 weeks old and greater than 13 weeks old are not as responsive as the 6–8-week-old animals. Animals are not given an ear tag or notch for identification as this would compromise the assay. Extra care must be taken not to confuse the test and control animals.

### C. Induction Site Preparation

The abdominal region is used for the induction applications as it was found that very poor or no induction could be achieved when the back was used. An enhancement of responsiveness is obtained by the use of both Freund's complete adjuvant (Calbiochem-Behring, San Diego, CA or Difco, Detroit, MI) and skin stripping. On the day of the first induction exposure (day 0), the hair is removed from the abdominal region using a clipper fitted with a No. 40 or 80 blade. An evaluation of the use of a depilatory to remove the last traces of hair has not been reported. Two intradermal injections of 20 μl each of undiluted Freund's complete adjuvant are made in the belly region using a 30 gauge needle. It is important that these injections be intradermal. The epidermis is then compromised by tape stripping 10 times or until the skin is shiny using Dermiclear transparent tape (1 inch wide) (Johnson and Johnson Products, Inc., New Brunswick, NJ). The stripping is best accomplished with one person holding and supporting the mouse and a second person firmly pressing the tape to the belly region and quickly removing it. Both the test and control animals are stripped and injected.

## D. Induction

Four exposures to the test material on four consecutive days consti- tute the induction. The concentration of the test material is one which, if possible, causes slight irritation but no systemic toxicity. The belly skin is tape stripped 5 times or until shiny on days 1, 2, and 3 (10 times on day 0 as discussed) but no adjuvant is given. Test animals receive 100 μl of test material preparation and control animals are dosed with 100 μl of vehicle on each day of the induction. The dosed volume is spread over the stripped area with the side of the dosing needle. It is recommended that a blunt needle be used to assure avoidance of unscheduled skin damage. It is necessary to rapidly dry the induction site before returning the animal to the cage. This is readily accomplished using a hair dryer for vehicles of low volatility though care must be taken not to use heat, just air flow.

## E. Challenge

The challenge is done on the seventh day after the last induction. Shorter or longer waiting periods do not provide as much sensitivity as the 7-day period. The challenge consists of applying 20 μl of vehicle to the right ear and 20 μl of test material to the left ear. The 20 μl dose is divided such that 10 μl is applied on the dorsal side of the ear and 10 μl is applied to the ventral side. The sub- stances are carefully applied evenly over the ear from a microliter pipetter and dried in a stream of warm air. Both the test and con- trol animals are dosed with test substance in vehicle and vehicle only.

## F. Evaluation of Response

Unique to the MEST assay is the use of a thickness gauge rather than a subjective irritation response used in other dermal allergen assays to measure the elicited sensitization response (Fig. 5). The gage is an Oditest D-1000 Thickness Gage (Dyer Company, Lancaster, PA) equipped at the factory with a fixed 5-mm diameter contact surface. The thickness of both the left and right ears is determined 24 hr (±1 hr) and 48 hr (±2 hr) after the application of the challenge dose. It is important to measure the thickness of the ear toward the outer edge and not in the cartilage area. The spring load of the gage can cause a redistribution of edemic fluid in the ear. Thus, the animal is anesthetized lightly with ether or other volatile anesthetic, which easily facilitates a rapid and consistent measurement of the ear thickness. The measurement at 48 hr is important, as some test materials exhibit a response at this time which is not fully developed at 24 hr. A responder is considered an animal which has a thickness of the test ear which is 20% greater than the thickness of the control ear at either 24 or 48 hr after the challenge. Gad et al. (7) determined that the variation between ear thickness of any one animal was always 4% or less and that low levels of simple irritation rarely caused a 10% increase in thickness (responses of >10% occurred at a frequency of approximately 0.5%). Thus, the 20% criteria is a strong indication of a sensitization response in that particular animal (i.e., a positive responder):

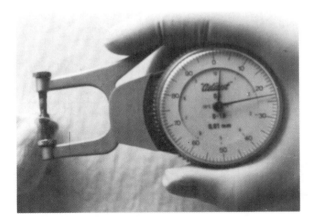

Figure 5    Measurement of ear thickness in the MEST Assay. (Courtesy of Allied Corporation, Morristown, NJ.)

$$\% \text{ Ear change} = \frac{(\text{test ear} - \text{control ear})}{\text{control ear thickness}} \times 100$$

The measurement of the ears of the control animals is used as an indicator of background response of a nonallergic nature. The swelling of the test ears of the animals compared to the control ears is also calculated as follows:

$$\% \text{ Ear swelling} = \frac{\text{sum of test (left) ear thickness}}{\text{sum of control (right) ear thickness}} \times 100$$

## G. Rechallenge

The mice can be rechallenged to the same concentration of test material to confirm sensitization, to weaker concentrations to evaluate dose versus response relationships, to a finished product containing the allergen, or to a different material to evaluate cross reactivity. The mouse assay must rechallenge on a previously exposed skin site (the left ear) which could cause problems if previous exposures have compromised this site. One must plan for any rechallenges by providing 5 additional sham-treated control animals for each rechallenge. Rechallenges should be done approximately 7 days after the previous challenge. Since the induction of sensitization is relatively short for the MEST assay, it may be advisable to induce additional animals if one has absolute plans for rechallenges.

## H. Prestudy Screens

Preliminary data must be obtained before starting the induction and challenge portion of the study. A screen must be run to determine a slightly irritating but nontoxic concentration for the induction and to determine a nonirritating level for application to the ear at the challenge. Two mice are used to test each concentration of test material; both the belly region and the ears of each animal are used. The hair is clipped from the belly region and tape-stripped 10 times on day 0. A volume of 100 µl is applied to the belly and 20 µl of the same concentration is applied to the left ear. The right ear is dosed with 20 µl of vehicle. The thicknesses of the test ear and the control (right) ear are measured 24 hr (±1 hr) and 48 hr (±2 hr) after the application. The belly region skin is stripped 5 times on days 1, 2, and 3 and an additional 100 µl of test material applied after each stripping. At 24 hours after the last dose, the belly skin is observed for irritation. Animals are observed daily for signs of systemic toxicity. An acceptable level for the induction should cause no more than slight irritation while the challenge dose should cause less than a 10% increase in the test ear thickness when compared to the control ear.

## I. Vehicles

Water is the ideal vehicle since it is neither irritating nor an allergen. Other acceptable vehicles which have been used successfully include acetone, ethanol:water (70:30, 80:20 or 95:5 v:v), methyl ethyl ketone, propylene glycol, petrolatum, and vegetable oils. It is best, with the exception of water, to use different vehicles for the induction and the challenge in order to avoid any possible allergic responses due to impurities in the vehicle. It is also desirable to have the test material dissolved in the vehicle rather than suspended. One must keep in mind that some vehicles can have a dramatic effect on the penetration of an allergen and thus on the results of the assay.

## J. Running the MEST Assay

Combining the discussed techniques in a specific regimen yields the assay:

1. *Irritation/Toxicity Screen (8 Animals for 4 Concentrations)*

Day 0. Prepare 4 concentrations of test material in the vehicle(s) to be used in the induction and challenge phases. Remove the hair from the belly region of a pair of animals for each of the concentrations. Tape strip the belly region until shiny and apply 100 µl of one of the concentrations to a pair of the animals. Apply 20 µl of the same concentration (in the same or a different vehicle) to the left ear of the same pair of animals and vehicle to the right ear.

Day 1. Measure the thickness of the left and right ears of each animal 24 hr (±1 hr) after the application. Tape strip the belly skin 5 times and apply 100 µl of test material in vehicle.

Day 2. Measure the thickness of the left and right ear 48 hr (±2 hr) after application of the challenge dose. Tape strip the belly region 5 times and apply 100 µl of test material.

Day 3. Tape strip the belly region 5 times and apply 100 µl of test material.

Day 4. Evaluate the belly for irritation and necrosis and the animals for systemic toxicity.

2. *Induction (15 Test + 5 Control + Rechallenge Control Animals)*

Day 0. Remove the hair from the belly of all animals with a clipper. Give each animal two 20 µl intradermal injections in the belly region of Freund's complete adjuvant. Tape strip the region until shiny. Apply 100 µl of test material

in vehicle to the test animals and 100 µl of vehicle to the
sham-control animals.

Days 1, 2, 3. Tape strip the animals until shiny and dose with
test material or vehicle as on day 0.

3. *Challenge (15 Test + 5 Sham-Control Animals)*

Day 10. Apply 20 µl of test material in vehicle to the left ear
and 20 µl of vehicle to the right ear of both the test and
control animals.

Day 11. Determine the thickness of the left and right ears of
each animal 24 hr (±1 hr) after the challenge application.

Day 12. Repeat the ear measurements 48 hr (±2 hr) after
application of the challenge dose.

4. *Rechallenge*

All or selected test animals and new sham-control animals may be
rechallenged 7 days after the first challenge.

5. *Report*

Report the number of positive responders (test animals with left
ear thickness ≥20% of the right ear provided the left ear of the control animals is <10% thicker than the right ear of the control) and the
% swelling for the test group.

## K. Advantages/Disadvantages and Problems

The MEST assay offers a very economical means of rapidly screening
materials for their potential to elicit a delayed contact-type hypersensitivity response. The assay requires relatively inexpensive
animals, economy of vivarium space, a small amount of test material,
and less time than any of the more commonly used guinea pig assays.
The assay results have been shown to correlate well with known human
sensitizers. The major problem with the assay is its lack of history.
The procedure is new and has not been accepted by all of the regulatory agencies (the FDA is now accepting the assay) and has not
been tested in court. It should provide an efficient screening tool
until such time as it has appropriate patina to be acceptable to the
toxicology community at large. The use of adjuvant often causes a
hypersensitivity of the skin to irritation in the guinea pig assays and
the effects of adjuvant on the responsiveness of the ear to swelling
are unknown. Another possible problem in the assay is the need to
reuse the test-skin site (left ear) in rechallenges that was used in
the challenge; some test materials may compromise the ear and lead
to confusing results. An alternative for one rechallenge is to switch

and use the ear which was used for the vehicle in the primary challenge.

## L. Positive Control

Typical results using a 0.5% solution of 1-chloro-2,4-dinitrobenzene in 70% ethanol/water (v/v) for induction and a 1% preparation for the challenge are shown as follows:

| Left (test) ear thickness | Right (control) ear thickness |
|---|---|
| Test group | |
| 30[a] | 21 |
| 26 | 23 |
| 26[a] | 21 |
| 24 | 22 |
| 29[a] | 24 |
| 26[a] | 20 |
| 30[a] | 21 |
| 29[a] | 23 |
| 29[a] | 22 |
| 32[a] | 21 |
| 38[a] | 23 |
| 31[a] | 22 |
| 31[a] | 23 |
| 26 | 24 |
| 34[a] | 24 |

Sum: 441                334

Responders: 80%

% Swelling: 132%

| Control group | |
|---|---|
| 22 | 21 |
| 23 | 23 |

| Left (test) ear thickness | Right (control) ear thickness |
|---|---|
| Control group (continued) | |
| 25 | 24 |
| 24 | 24 |
| 25 | 24 |

[a]Responder = test ear ⩾20% thicker than control ear.

# REFERENCES

1. Jackson, E. M. (1985). Difference between irritation and sensitization. *J. Toxicol. Cut. Ocular Toxicol.* 4:1.
2. Jackson, E. M. (1984). Cellular and molecular events of inflammation. *J. Toxicol. Cut. Ocular Toxicol.* 3:347.
3. Labeling Requirements for Pesticides and Devices. *Fed. Reg.* (40 CFR Parts 156 and 167) September 26, 1984.
4. Buehler, E. V. (1965). Delayed contact hypersensitivity in the guinea pig. *Arch. Dermatol.* 91:171.
5. Magnusson, B. and Kligman, A. M. (1964). The identification of contact allergens by animal assay. The maximization test. *J. Invest. Dermatol.* 52:268.
6. Ichikawa, H., Armstrong, R. B., and Harber, L. C. (1981). Photoallergic contact dermatitis in guinea pigs: Improved induction technique using Freund's complete adjuvant. *J. Invest. Dermatol.* 76: 498.
7. Gad, S. C., Dunn, B. J., and Dobbs, D. W. (1985). Development of an alternative dermal sensitization test: mouse ear swelling test (MEST). In *Alternative Methods in Toxicology*, vol. 3. New York, Mary Ann Liebert, Inc., p. 539.
8. Ritz, H. L. and Buehler, E. V. (1980). Planning, conduct and interpretation of guinea pig sensitization patch test. In *Current Concepts in Cutaneous Toxicology*. New York, Academic Press, p. 25.
9. Cole, C. A., Forbes, P. D., and Davies, R. E. (1984). Different biological effectiveness of blacklight fluorescent lamps available for therapy with psoralens plus ultraviolet A. *J. Am. Acad. Dermatol.* 11:599.
10. Gad, S. C., Dunn, B. J., Dobbs, D. W., Reilly, C., and Walsh, R. D. (1986). Development and validation of an alternative sensitization test: the mouse ear swelling test (MEST). *Toxicol. Appl. Pharmacol.* 84:93.

11. Crowle, A. J. (1959). Delayed hypersensitivity in mice: Its detection by skin test and its passive transfer. *Science 130*: 159.
12. Asherson, G. L. and Ptak, W. (1968). Contact and delayed hypersensitivity in the mouse 1. Active sensitization and passive transfer. *Immunology 15*:405.
13. Chapman, J. R., Ruben, Z., and Butchko, G. M. (1986). Histology of and quantitative assays for oxazolone-induced allergic contact dermatitis in mice. *Am. J. Dermatopathol. 8*: 130.
14. Gad, S. C., Auletta, C. S., Dunn, B. J., Hiles, R. A., Reilly, C., Reagan, E., and Yenser, B. (1986). A double blind intralaboratory validation of the mouse ear swelling test (MEST). *Toxicologist 6*:242.

# 6

# Practical Mutagenicity Testing

THOMAS R. BARFKNECHT and ROBERT W. NAISMITH / *Pharmakon Research International, Inc., Waverly, Pennsylvania*

## I. JUSTIFICATION FOR MUTAGENICITY TESTING

There are approximately 70,000 synthetic chemicals in commerce in the United States at this time and of these, 25,000 are produced in large quantities (1,2). In addition, 1000-2000 new chemicals are introduced into the environment each year (3). A recent review of the results of several studies has suggested that 80-90% of all human cancers are induced by environmental agents (4). Since synthetic chemicals contribute to this cancer burden it is necessary to screen these chemicals for their potential to induce mutagenic and/or carcinogenic events.

### A. Risk Prevention for Humans

Exposure of human populations to mutagenic chemicals may result in the induction of a variety of disease states. Human afflictions that appear to be affected directly or indirectly by mutagenic agents are cancer, teratogenesis, impaired reproductive capacity, heart disease, and aging (4-9). Major areas of concern are the effects of mutagenic chemicals upon human germ cells and the induction of cancer in humans.

#### 1. Genetic Risk to Humans

A multitude of heritable human genetic diseases are known (10). These diseases are caused by two major classes of genetic events; gene point mutations and chromosomal aberrations (11). Gene point mutations occur at the molecular level and involve base-pair changes, while chromosome aberration events can be observed using traditional cytological procedures. Most chromosome mutational events that occur in either the sperm or ova produce dominant lethal effects which are not transmitted to the next generation (12). However, point mutational events can result in recessive mutations that pose a more serious threat to the human gene pool since they may accumulate in the undetected heterozygous carrier state (11).

### 2. Carcinogenic Risk to Humans

Evidence from a variety of studies establishes a correlation between chemical mutagens and their ability to induce cancer (5,13–15). Because of this relationship, a research effort has been undertaken resulting in the development of approximately 100 short-term tests for detecting genotoxic events (2). Some of the assay systems developed are presented in Table 1. These genotoxicity assay systems utilize bacterial cells, eukaryotic cells such as yeast and fungi, the common fruit fly, *Drosophila melanogaster*, mammalian cells in culture and whole mammals. The genetic endpoints that these various assay systems detect include not only gene point mutations, but chromosomal events and DNA damage. These genetic endpoints comprise the array of genotoxic events. In addition to those genotoxicity assay systems presented in Table 1 which can be employed to predict both somatic cell and germ cell mutational events, several mammalian cell assays have been developed which can detect the ability of a test chemical to induce oncogenic events in vitro. These are the in vitro cellular transformation assays. Currently, four such assay systems have received the most attention. They are the baby hamster kidney (BHK 21/Cl 13) soft agar clonal assay, the Syrian hamster embryo fibroblast clonal assay, the Balb c/3T3 mouse embryo fibroblast focus assay and the C3H 10T$_{1/2}$ mouse embryo fibroblast focus assay (16–18). In theory these in vitro cellular transformation assays would be most suitable for predicting in vivo tumorigenesis. However, these systems are fraught with reproducibility problems and inadequate metabolic capabilities (16–18).

### B. Financial Considerations

The definitive means of predicting the carcinogenic potential of a chemical is the rodent cancer bioassay. This bioassay system employs both sexes of rats and mice and is currtently estimated to cost between $400,000 and $600,000 (11,15) and require up to 36 months to complete (5). Not only is the rodent cancer bioassay costly in the amount of dollars and time expended, it may not be an accurate predictor of human carcinogenic potential (15,19). Due to the cost and time restrictions of the rodent cancer bioassay, a

**Table 1** Common Genetic Toxicology Assays [a]

| Assay type | Organism and/or cell type | Endpoints measured |
| --- | --- | --- |
| Bacterial mutation | *Salmonella typhimurium* | Reverse mutation (Ames assay) |
| | *Salmonella typhimurium* | Forward mutation |
| | *Escherichia coli* | Forward and reverse mutations (WP2) |
| Bacterial DNA Repair | *Escherichia coli polA$^+$/polA$^-$* | Differential toxicity due to DNA damage not repaired |
| | *Bacillus subtile Rec$^+$/Rec$^-$* | Differential toxicity due to DNA damage not repaired |
| Fungal/yeast mutation | *Saccharomyces cerevisiae* | Reverse mutation |
| | *Schizosaccharomyces pombe* | Forward mutation |
| | *Neurospora crasse* | Forward and reverse mutations |
| Yeast chromosome effects | *Saccharomyces cerevisiae* | Mitotic recombination |
| | *Saccharomyces cerevisiae* | Mitotic aneuploidy and meiotic nondisjunction |
| Mammalian cell point mutation | L5178Y Mouse lymphoma cells | Forward mutation |
| | Chinese hamster cells (CHO/V79) | Forward mutation |

Table 1 (Continued)

| Assay type | Organism and/or cell type | Endpoints measured |
|---|---|---|
| Mammalian cell point mutation (continued) | Human fibroblasts | Forward mutation |
| Mammalian cell cytogenetic damage | CHO/V79 and human lymphocytes | Chromosomal aberrations |
| | CHO/V79 and human lymphocytes | Sister chromatid exchange |
| Mammalian cell DNA repair | Human fibroblasts, rat hepatocytes, and continuous cell lines | Unscheduled DNA synthesis (UDS) |
| Insect mutation | Drosophila melanogaster | Sex-linked recessive lethal mutations |
| Insect chromosomal effects | Drosophila melanogaster | Translocations and sex chromosome loss |
| Whole animal mutation | Mouse/specific locus | Forward mutation and deletions |
| | Mouse/spot test | Forward mutation and deletions |
| Whole animal cytogenetic damage | Mouse or rat | Bone marrow chromosomal aberrations |
| | Mouse or rat | Lymphocyte chromosomal aberrations |

| | Mouse or rat | Bone marrow or lymphocyte sister chromatid exchange |
|---|---|---|
| | Mouse | Micronucleus test |
| Whole animal DNA repair | Rat | Unscheduled DNA synthesis in hepatocytes |
| Whole animal germ cell cytogenetic damage | Mouse | Spermatocyte chromosomal rearrangements |
| | Mouse/heritable-translocation | Sterility and detection of translocations |
| | Mouse/dominant lethal | Chromosomal damage |
| Whole animal germ cell DNA damage | Mouse or rat | Spermatocyte unscheduled DNA synthesis |
| Host-mediated | Mouse or rat | Gene mutation in bacterial test system |
| Body fluids analysis | Urine samples from mouse, rat or man most common | Various genetic endpoints in bacterial and/or cell culture |

[a] Adapted from Ref. 44.

multitude of short-term genotoxicity assays have been developed
to screen chemicals for their mutagenic/carcinogenic potential.
Initially, mutagenesis testing was intended to serve as a cost-effective
means for screening the carcinogenic potential of compounds in development. However, as Clive (20) has so eloquently pointed out,
a promising chemical should not be "killed" based solely on the result from a single short-term genotoxicity assay. A single positive
result could represent a false positive (able to induce genotoxicity
but negative in a cancer bioassay) finding. In addition, other factors should be considered, such as risk-benefit analysis and in vivo
toxicological/pharmacological parameters.

In screening a chemical for its ability to induce heritable mutation damage, the mouse specific locus test (for gene mutation events)
and the mouse heritable translocation test (for chromosomal damage)
are considered standard (21). However, little data currently exists
for these two mammalian mutation assays (21) and it is generally
agreed that the cost of performing these two tests will prevent them
from becoming routinely employed as mutation screening assays (22).
Therefore, the genotoxicity assays presented in Table 1 may also be
employed to screen test chemicals for their ability to induce germ
cell mutational damage.

## C. Regulatory Requirements

The original objective of short-term genotoxicity assays was as a
cost-effective means for screening chemicals under development for
their mutagenic/cercinogenic potential. However, regulatory agencies
on a national and international basis have seen fit to include mutagenesis testing as part of the overall toxicological assessment of
chemicals intended for a variety of uses.

It is a legal requirement that many chemicals be evaluated for
their ability to induce mutagenic/carcinogenic events with established
short-term genotoxicity testing systems. Additional discussion of
the legal requirements for the genotoxic assessment of chemicals will
be presented in the following section.

## II. NATIONAL AND INTERNATIONAL REGULATIONS REQUIRING GENOTOXICITY TESTING

### A. Federal Regulations in the United States

Most countries, including the United States, have separate legislation
at various levels of government to regulate the manufacture and release of, and exposure to environmental contaminants, including
chemicals in the occupational environment, drugs, food and feed
additives, cosmetics, household chemicals, pesticides, and newly

synthesized chemicals (3). In the United States there are over a dozen federal statutes concerned with protecting the human population from unnecessary exposure to chemicals and industrial processes that may represent a carcinogenic and/or mutagenic risk (23). The major federal government regulatory agencies involved with mutagenesis/carcinogenesis evaluation and hazard assessment are the Environmental Protection Agency (EPA), the Food and Drug Administration (FDA), and the Occupational Safety and Health Administration (OSHA). Each of these agencies have issued proposed and/or required mutagenicity/genotoxicity testing guidelines. However, due to the rapid development and validation of short-term genotoxicity assays, the requirement for specific tests and the complexity of testing schemes and batteries is constantly in a state of flux. The significant federal legislation or regulatory orders and administering agencies involved with mutagen/carcinogen assessment and regulation are presented in Table 2.

**Table 2** U.S. Federal Laws and Regulations Requiring Mutagenicity Testing

| Act or regulation | Administering body |
| --- | --- |
| Federal Insecticide, Fungicide Rodenticide Act (FIFRA) | Environmental Protection Agency |
| Toxic Substances Control Act (TOSCA) | Environmental Protection Agency |
| Resources Conservation Recovery Act (RCRA) | Environmental Protection Agency |
| Animal Drugs: Sensitivity of the Method | Food and Drug Administration |
| Medical Devices | Food and Drug Administration |
| Identification, classification and Regulation of Toxic Substances Posing a Potential Occupational Carcinogen Risk | Occupational Safety and Health Administration |
| Principles and Procedures for Evaluating the Toxicity of Household Substances | Consumer Products Safety Commission |

### 1. EPA-Administered Program

Under the Toxic Substances Control Act (TOSCA), a manufacturer must submit to the EPA all information necessary for the agency to define any foreseeable risk for a new chemical intended for release into the environment (26). After the premanufacturing notice (PMN) is submitted, the EPA may request additional information. Under the auspices of TOSCA and the Federal Insecticide, Fungicide, Rodenticide Act (FIFRA), the EPA has proposed a guideline for genotoxic evaluation of chemicals which fall under the regulation of these two federal statutes. The initial proposed testing scheme is shown in Table 3. The assay systems included in the proposed

**Table 3** Genotoxicity Testing Requirements Proposed by the U.S. Environmental Protection Agency for FIFRA and TOSCA[a]

---

Gene mutation assays, three tests must be selected

1. Bacteria with and without metabolic activation

2. Eukaryotic micro-organisms (yeast, fungi) with and without metabolic activation

3. *Drosophila* sex-linked recessive lethal assay

4. Mammalian cells in culture with and without metabolic activation

5. Mouse Specific locus test

Chromosomal aberrations in vivo, each test is required

1. Chromosomal aberration assays in rats or mice

2. *Drosophilia* translocation assay

3. Dominant lethal and heritable translocation assay in rodents

DNA damage, two tests must be selected

1. DNA repair in bacteria with and without metabolic activation

2. Unschedule DNA synthesis in mammalian cells with and without metabolic activation if not performed with primary hepatocytes

3. Mitotic recombination and gene conversation in yeast with and without metabolic activation

4. Sister cromatid exchange in mammalian cells in culture with and without metabolic activation

---

[a]Adapted from Ref. 11.

Table 4  Environmental Protection Agency Proposed Genotoxicity
Assays for the Evaluation of Hazardous RCRA Samples[a]

| Protocol | Assay system |
|----------|--------------|
| Preliminary screen | Bacterial mutation assay |
| Confirmatory screen in vitro assays | DNA damage in hepatocytes, gene mutation, and sister chromatid exchange in mammalian cells |
| In vivo/in vitro assays | Bioassay of body fluids and tissues from treated animals, sister chromatid exchange in bone marrow, lymphocytes, and embryo liver |

[a]From Ref. 25.


EPA genotoxicity battery were selected to detect three basic genetic
endpoints, namely, gene point mutation, chromosomal damage, and
DNA damage (11).  However, following review by the scientific and
industrial communities it was generally agreed that this testing scheme
was too costly.  In addition, it was felt that some of the in vivo assays should be used for risk estimation and not at the screening
level (11).  Therefore, a core battery approach has been taken in
which all chemicals are evaluated in a stepwise manner.  If the chemical of interest is negative, it may proceed through a series of the
Ames/*Salmonella* mutation assay, mammalian cell in culture point mutation assay, and a DNA damage test, unscheduled DNA synthesis
(UDS) or the chemical may first be evaluated in an in vitro cytogenetic assay followed by an in vivo cytogenetic test (11).  If a positive
result is encountered along the way, a cell transformation test or
various in vivo genotoxicity assays are required depending upon
which core assay gave the positive results (11).

The Resource Conservation and Recovery Act (RCRA Section 3001)
directs the federal government to "develop and promulgate criteria
for identifying the characteristics of hazardous waste, and for listing hazardous waste . . . taking into account toxicity."  The EPA
has issued proposed guidelines for evaluating the genotoxicity of
hazardous waste samples (25).  These proposed guidelines are shown
in Table 4.  The evaluation scheme consists of a preliminary screen,
the Ames/*Salmonella* mutation assay and a confirmatory screen.  The
confirmatory screen is composed of in vitro and in vivo/in vitro
genotoxicity tests.  The in vitro assays included in the confirmatory
screen are detection of DNA damage expressed as UDS in rat primary
hepatocytes, gene mutation in mammalian cells in culture, and

assessment of sister chromatid exchange (SCE) in mammalian cells. The in vivo/in vitro assays consist of the analysis of body fluids and tissues from treated animals employing a detecting test such as the Ames/Salmonella mutation assay. Other recommended in vivo tests include the assessment of SCE in the bone marrow and lymphocytes of the treated dams and in the hepatocytes of the embryos. The information gathered from the genotoxicity screen and other toxicological assessments will be used to classify RCRA samples as to whether they pose a hazard sufficient to require regulation and listing as hazardous wastes.

### 2. FDA-Administered Programs

The FDA has proposed two sets of genotoxicity testing programs. One is for the evaluation of tissue residues from domesticated animals given various veterinary drugs. The genotoxicity requirements for this program consists of a simple battery comprised of the Ames/ Salmonella mutation assay and either the L5178Y mouse lymphoma cell mutation assay or the Drosophila melanogaster sex-linked recessive lethal test. In addition, an in vitro UDS assay is also required (11).

The second FDA-proposed genotoxicity evaluation scheme is somewhat more complex and is presented in Table 5. This mutagenesis testing battery was intended for the evaluation of medical devices and is divided into three different levels depending upon the use of the medical device (11). As one proceeds through the screening levels the genotoxicity tests required increase in number and complexity. Once level three has been reached, the sophistication and cost required for mutagenesis screening appear unreasonable for medical devices. Since the actual materials to be evaluated in the proposed testing scheme are extracts of inert medical devices, there is little possibility that these extracts will be mutagenically active (11). In addition, large volumes of extracted material would be required for level three screening.

In its administration of other federal statutes such as the Food, Drug and Cosmetic Act and the Saccharin Study and Labeling Act (3) that are under its jurisdiction, the FDA has established an unofficial policy to request, recommend, or require mutagenicity testing (20). Therefore, the decision is based on individual cases.

### 3. Other Federal Government-Administered Programs

OSHA has issued policy statements establishing means, including mutagenesis testing for the identification and regulation of chemical substances that may pose a potential carcinogenic risk in the workplace environment (27,28). The Consumer Product Safety Commission (CPSC) has issued a report entitled Principles and Procedures for Evaluating the Toxicity of Household Substances in which it is

**Table 5** FDA Proposed Genotoxicity Assays for the Evaluation of Medical Devices[a]

| Type of device | Genotoxicity assay |
|---|---|
| External devices external exposure only | Level I<br>Gene mutation<br>  bacterial or fungal<br><br>DNA damage<br>  SCE analysis in vitro or UDS or<br>  in vitro cellular transformation |
| Internal devices limited short-term exposure | Level II<br>Level I assays plus:<br>In vivo mutation assays<br>  dominant lethal test in mice or<br>  *Drosophila* sex-linked recessive<br>  lethal<br><br>Chromosome damage<br>  In vivo rat bone marrow cytogene-<br>  tics or in vitro human lymphocytes |
| Internal devices long-term exposure | Level III<br>Level I and Level II assays plus:<br>in vivo mouse genotoxicity assays<br>  heritable translocation or specific<br>  locus assay or two-generation<br>  reproductive study |

[a]Adapted from Ref. 11.

proposed that a genotoxicity testing battery composed of a gene mutation assay, a chromosome aberration test, and a test for DNA damage be performed on new products (29).

## 4. Updated EPA Testing Requirements

Recently, the Environmental Protection Agency issued a revised set of proposed guidelines for mutagenicity risk assessment (22). It is the agency's intention that the currently proposed genotoxicity testing guidelines can be employed to assess risks associated with exposure of the human population to potentially mutagenic chemicals (30). The proposed guidelines define the terms of sufficient, suggestive, and limited evidence for potential human germ cell mutagenicity and the terms sufficient and suggestive for relative indication of the interaction of the test chemical with the gonads (30). For sufficient evidence to exist that a test chemical is a potential human germ cell mutagen, positive results must be observed in either two gene point mutation assays (one of which should be performed in mammalian cells) or in two cytogenetic studies (one of which should be performed in mammalian cells) (30). In addition, sufficient evidence of germ cell interaction is required in both cases. An alternative approach which may be taken is evaluation of the test chemical in a mammalian cell gene mutation assay and a mammalian cell cytogenetics test. Again, a positive result in each study is required and sufficient evidence of germ cell interaction is also required. Sufficient evidence of germ cell mutation also exists when a positive response occurs in a single mammalian germ cell in vivo genotoxicity assay (30). Suggestive evidence exists for germ cell mutation when a positive response is observed in a gene point mutation assay or a cytogenetics test coupled with evidence for chemical interaction in the gonads (30). If the chemical of interest induces a mutagenic event or interacts with the gonads this constitutes limited evidence for human germ cell mutational risk (30). Although no specific battery of genotoxicity tests is now proposed by the EPA, the assay systems presented in Table 6 could be employed to meet the testing requirements.

It is worth noting that the newly proposed genotoxicity testing guidelines place a significant amount of emphasis on the possibility that some chemicals may induce changes in chromosome number. These aneuploidy events would not be detectable by the traditional genotoxicity assays. Therefore, it is considered important to include tests which would detect chromosome nondisjunction events in the overall evaluation scheme. Standard cytogenetic tests are available for such determinations. However, in a report of a recent workshop sponsored by the EPA to assess the role of aneuploidy in human health risk, it was concluded that many short-term tests for aneuploidy are not yet well enough developed to serve as screening assays (31).

In order for sufficient evidence to exist for the interaction of the test chemical with mammalian gonads the EPA-proposed guidelines state that direct interaction of the test material with germ cell DNA must be demonstrated or that positive responses in tests for UDS, SCE, or chromosome aberrations in germ cells must be observed (30). In a review of the EPA document, Ashby (32) has pointed out that UDS measurement in sperm is most closely correlated with the heritable germ cell mutagenicity data compiled by Russell et al., (21). However, UDS in sperm is not considered a substitute for germ cell mutation tests by the EPA (32).

While the issuance of these newly proposed guidelines the EPA has established a ranking system for assay systems of varying

**Table 6** Current Proposed Guidelines of the Environmental Protection Agency for Assessment of Genotoxicity Risk to Germ Cells

| Gene mutation | Chromosome damage | Chromosome number (aneuploidy) |
|---|---|---|
| Bacterial assays *Salmonella* or *E. coli* | Mammalian cells in culture rodent cells (CHO,V79) | Fungal assays *Saccharomyces* and *Neurospora* |
| Fungal assays *Saccharomyces* or *Neurospora* | Human lumphocytes | Mammalian cells in cultures |
| Mammalian cells in culture CHO/V79 mouse lymphoma and human fibroblasts | Insects *Drosophila* heritable trans- location | CHO/V79 or human lymphoctes karyotype analysis |
| Insects *Drosophila* sex- linked recessive lethal | Mammals in vivo mouse micronucleus test mouse hertiable translocation | Insects *Drosophila* sex-chromosome loss |
| Mammals in vivo mouse specific locus test | Mouse or rat bone marrow cytogenetics mouse spermatocyte cytogenetics | Mammals in vivo mouse or rat bone marrow or lymphocyte karyotype analysis |

complexity. This hierarchical approach taken by the agency places greater weight on studies performed with germ cells rather than somatic cells, on assays performed in vivo versus in vitro, on tests with eukaryotic cells as apposed to prokaryotic cells, and in mammalian species rather than submammalian species (22,30). However, since the two well established mammalian in vivo assays for heritable genetic damage, the mouse specific locus test and the mouse heritable translocation test (21), are complex and costly, it is not likely that they will become routine screening assays (22,30). Other tests, such as in vivo sperm UDS may be developed further to meet the new-EPA proposed genotoxicity testing requirements (32).

## B. Foreign and International Regulations

Several international organizations and/or conventions have issued recommended guidelines or required mutagenicity screening programs for chemical materials intended for a variety of uses (Table 7).

### 1. ECC Requirements

The European Economic Community (EEC) has established mutagenicity testing requirements under the sixth amendment of the Directive on Dangerous Chemical Substances (3,11,26). This directive requires that chemicals intended for use in the member states (Belgium, Denmark, France, Federal Republic of Germany, Greece, Ireland, Italy, Luxembourg, The Netherlands, and the United Kingdom) must have mutagenicity testing data submitted as part of the technical dossier for the premarketing notification. The EEC has issued proposed genotoxicity evaluation guidelines for chemicals that will be used as food additives, pharmaceuticals, pesticides, and new chemicals not falling into the other three categories (3). For new

Table 7 International Groups/Conventions with Proposed or Established Mutagenicity Testing Requirements

| | |
|---|---|
| International Agency for Research on Cancer | (IARC) |
| International Program on Chemical Safety | (IPCS) |
| United Nations Environment Program | (UNEP) |
| Organization for Economic Co-operation and Development | (OECD) |
| European Economic Community | (EEC) |
| Council for Mutual Economic Assistance | (CMEA) |

chemicals, the technical dossier must be submitted with results from
a bacterial mutation assay, either the Ames/*Salmonella* mutation assay
or an *Escherichia coli* mutation assay. In addition, results from one
of the three following tests are required; (1) in vitro mammalian cell
cytogenetics, (2) in vivo bone marrow cytogenetics, or (3) the mouse
micronucleus assay (26). For the other classified chemical substances,
a somewhat more detailed mutagenicity testing scheme is required.
The EEC recommends that the results from one test in each of the
categories listed in Table 8 be submitted as part of the notification
dossier. The final decision as to which tests are to be performed
is left to the applicant. However, the applicant must supply complete justification for the individual genotoxicity tests selected and
include an explanation of the overall testing strategy.

### 2. OECD Proposed Guidelines

The Organization for Economic Cooperation and Development
(OECD) has prepared mutagenicity testing guidelines to be employed
in the evaluation of toxic chemicals in general (3,11). The OECD
recommended genotoxicity testing battery is shown in Table 9. To
meet the minimal testing requirements an assay representing each
genetic endpoint of the initial screen must be performed. Additional
test results may be submitted along with the minimal test data if accompanied by scientific justification. These additional genotoxicity
tests can be chosen from those listed as confirmatory or supplemental
assays in Table 9. Following review of the genotoxicity data and
other toxicological data, additional tests may be required. Manufacturing methods, proposed use, disposal methods, and the potential of exposure of the human population will be taken into consideration in determining if additional genotoxicity testing is required.
Selection of the appropriate confirmatory test and/or the supplemental genotoxicity assays listed in Table 9 can then be employed to extend and/or confirm the results observed in the minimal series of
tests. Mammalian genotoxicity tests such as the mouse specific locus
test or the mouse heritable translocation test may be necessary (11).

### 3. Requirements for Evaluation of New Chemicals

In addition, to the requirements for genotoxicity screening of
new chemicals established by the EEC in Europe and TOSCA in the
United States, other individual countries have promulgated regulations calling for the genetic evaluations of new chemicals. Countries
requiring the submission of results from genotoxicity tests in order
to register the new chemical substance are listed in Table 10. In a
manner similar to the sixth amendment of the EEC Directive on Dangerous Substances and TOSCA (26), the manufacturer is required
to submit a detailed technical dossier containing information on the

Table 8 European Economic Community Genotoxicity Testing Requirements

| Bacterial gene mutation | In vitro mammalian cell chromosome aberrations | In vitro mammalian cell gene mutation | In vivo genotoxicity |
|---|---|---|---|
| Ames/Salmonella reverse mutation | Chinese hamsters ovary or V79 cell | Chinese hamster ovary or V79 cell HGPRT | Mouse micronucleus |
| Escherichia coli reverse mutation | Human lymphocytes | Mouse lymphoma cell TK locus | Drosophila sex-linked recessive lethal |
| | | Human fibroblast HGPRT | Rat bone marrow cytogenetics |
| | | | Mouse heritable-translocation or dominant-lethal |

Table 9 OECD[a] Guidelines for the Genotoxic Evaluation of Chemicals[b]

| Testing sequence | Gene mutation | Chromosome damage | DNA damage |
|---|---|---|---|
| Initial screening | Bacterial assays Ames/Salmonella or E. coli reverse mutation | Mammalian cells in culture or in vivo assays mouse micronucleus or bone marrow cytogenetics | |
| Confirmatory assays | Yeast or fungal mammalian cells in culture CHO/V79, mouse lymphoma Mammalian in vivo mouse specific locus test | In vivo cytogenetics mouse micronucleus bone marrow cytogenetics mouse spermatocyte cytogenetics mouse heritable translocation test | |
| Supplement assays | | | E. coli polA$^+$/polA, B. subtilis RecA/RecA$^-$, UDS in mammalian cells, sister chromatid exchange in vitro or in vivo |

[a]Organization for Economic Cooperation and Development.
[b]Derived from Ref. 11.

**Table 10** International Regulations for Mutagenicity/Carcinogenicity Evaluation[a]

| Country or group | Product or class |
| --- | --- |
| EEC member states and United States | Food additives |
| 18 countries including United States | Pesticides |
| Italy, Venezuela, Federal Republic of Germany | Cosmetics and/or additives |
| Over 50 countries as compiled by International Federation of Pharmaceutical Manufacturers Association | Pharmaceuticals/medicants |
| Britain, Canada, The Netherlands, United States | Household chemicals |
| Japan, Federal Republic of Germany United States, Denmark, Britain, France, and The Netherlands | New chemicals |

[a]Derived from Ref. 3.

new chemical material including toxicological data (33,34). The notification registration process, in most cases, allows the administrating agency to request additional information if deemed necessary (33,34).

In the United Kingdom, guidelines for the mutagenicity testing of new chemical substances have been published (35,36). Screening of chemicals for genotoxicity has been established by the United Kingdom Health and Safety Commission in its Draft Approved Code of Practice on the Classification and Labeling of Dangerous Substances (37). Both The Netherlands and France have formal regulations requiring mutagenicity screening of new chemicals in respect to notification procedures (3).

4. *Requirements for Food Additives, Pharmaceuticals, and Pesticides*

Table 10 lists the countries that recommend or require mutagenicity testing of chemical substances that are intended to be used as food additives, pharmaceuticals, pesticides, household chemicals, and cosmetics. The EEC member states and the United States recommend and/or require genotoxicity screening of chemical materials intended for use as food additives (38,39).

Pesticides are one of the most well regulated groups of chemical substances in regards to requirements for genotoxicity screening. Eighteen countries including the United States require studies to be conducted on the mutagenicity and/or carcinogenicity of pesticides in support of applications for registration (3).

Pharmaceuticals have received the most attention from authorities concerning evaluation for genotoxic effects. More than 50 countries require mutagenicity and/or carcinogenicity data in support of applications for new drugs to be manufactured (40). The World Health Organization (WHO) has issued a report dealing with the testing of pharmaceuticals for mutagenicity (41), which has had substantial influence upon national legislation and guidelines for mutagenicity screening of drugs.

In the United Kingdom, only the Ames/*Salmonella* mutation assay is specifically required for the evaluation of medicinal products. However, the Department of Health and Social Security has provided guidelines for other genotoxicity testing. An in vitro mammalian cell point mutation assay or a *Drosophila* sex-linked recessive lethal mutation assay is recommended. In addition, an in vivo cytogenetics study such as a bone marrow metaphase analysis or a micronucleus test is recommended. Alternatively, the mouse dominant lethal mutation assay can be substituted for the in vivo cytogenetics tests.

The Committee on Proprietary Products of Belgium recommends the following minimal testing requirements for evaluating the genotoxicity of pharmaceutical products, a bacterial mutation assay, an in vitro chromosome aberration test in mammalian cells, an in vitro gene mutation assay in mammalian cells, or the *Drosophila* sex-linked recessive lethal mutation test, and in vivo bone marrow cytogenetic analysis (42).

Sweden has also established requirements for the submission of mutagenicity testing data as part of the supporting materials for registration of new medical products. The required genotoxicity tests are the Ames/*Salmonella* mutation assay, a mammalian cell gene mutation assay, and an in vivo cytogenetics test.

The Health Protection Branch of the Department of National Health and Welfare of Canada has issued Final Pre-clinical Toxicologic Guidelines requiring mutagenicity testing of new pharmaceutical products (43).

Other countries that have established legislation requiring or recommending the genotoxic evaluation of new chemicals intended for use as pharmaceuticals as part of the licensing/registration process are Japan, Hungary, Poland, and the German Democratic Republic (3).

This section has presented a review of the national and international recommendations and requirements for the mutagenicity screening of new chemicals before their manufacture or release into the environment. However these genotoxicity evaluation schemes do not conform to one overall testing pattern, although progress is being made toward this goal by the OECD in cooperation with the EPA. In Section V, strategies for the development and evaluation of genotoxicity screening programs will be presented.

## III.  ROLE OF METABOLISM

### A.  General Considerations

Initially it was believed that xenobiotic chemicals underwent only detoxification in whole animal systems.  However, now it is well documented that chemicals can undergo metabolic conversion to toxic species as well (44).  The liver is the most active organ in mammals for the metabolic conversion of xenobiotics.  Some of the metabolic steps performed in the liver are listed in Table 11.  Oxidative metabolism is principally carried out by the cytochrome/mono-oxygenase enzyme system, various reductive metabolic steps may also be catalyzed by the cytochrome mono-oxygenases (44).  It is the metabolic conversion of chemicals to highly reactive electrophilic species which can bind with DNA that appears to be responsible for mutation and/or cancer induction (45–47).

In the early development of bacterial mutation assay systems for the screening of chemical mutagens/carcinogens, many well known chemical carcinogens did not induce bacterial mutation.  It soon became apparent that bacterial cells did not possess the metabolic capabilities of mammalian cells for the conversion of chemicals to genotoxic species.  It was Ames et al. (48) who first incorporated a simple mammalian cell-derived liver homogenate into a bacterial mutation assay system.  The use of the liver homogenate greatly enhanced the ability of the *Salmonella* mutation test to detect carcinogens that have mutation-inducing activity (49).

### B.  Mono-oxygenase/Cytochrome System

Most of the oxidative metabolic reactions presented in Table 11 are carried out by the cytochrome P-450 family of mono-oxygenase (44). The cytochrome P-450 mono-oxygenase system is comprised of a group of hemoproteins.  The mono-oxygenases catalyze the insertion of one atom of oxygen into the substrate (44).  The mono-oxygenase/cytochrome enzyme system is composed of an NADPH-cytochrome P-450 reductase, phosphatidyl choline, and cytochrome P-450 which functions as the terminal oxygenase (47).  This enzyme system is inducible by a variety of agents and this inducibility to enhance the mutagen-activating capacity of liver and other organ homogenates has been used to advantage (50,51).

Table 11  Metabolic Events Involved in the
Conversion of Chemicals to Genotoxic
Agents[a]

---

Oxidative metabolism:

    Aromatic or aliphatic C oxygenation
        (epoxidation or hydroxylation)

    N-, O-, or S- dealkylation

    N-oxidation or N-hydroxylation

    S-oxidation

    Deamination

    Dehalogenation

    Desulfuration

Reductive metabolism:

    Azo reduction

    Nitro reduction

    Arene oxide reduction

    N-hydroxyl reduction

    Quinone reduction

Metabolic conjugation:

    Glucuronidation

    Sulfate conjugation

    Glutathione conjugation

    Acetylation

    Glycoside conjugation

---

[a]Adapted from Ref. 44.

The mono-oxygenase/cytochrome enzyme system is found within the mammalian cell endoplasmic reticulum. Upon removal of the organ (usually the liver) from the animal, homogenation and centrifugation at 100,000 × g for one hour are performed, the resulting pellet containing the enzyme activity is referred to as the microsomal pellet (44). In the preparation of the microsome-containing liver homogenate utilized by Ames et al. (48), the liver is homogenized and centrifuged at 9000 × g. The resultant postmitochondrial microsome-containing supernatant is commonly referred to as the S-9 fraction (48,52). The S-9 fraction with appropriate cofactors is routinely employed as the source of mammalian cell-derived metabolizing enzymes for a variety of in vitro genotoxicity assay systems.

The liver has the highest levels of mono-oxygenase and other enzyme systems (44) and, therefore, has been the organ of choice in the preparation of microsome-containing subcellular fractions for the metabolic activation of xenobiotic chemicals. Rat liver is generally employed for the preparation of the S-9 fraction. However, species differences do exist for levels of enzyme activity, with hamster liver yielding the highest values (53). Although rodent livers are generally used as the source of the S-9 fraction for in vitro genotoxicity assays, preparations of human liver microsomes on the average possess lower levels of metabolic activity relative to rodent liver preparations (47). Difference in metabolic activation capacity also occur for sex, age, and means of pretreatment enzyme induction of the animal (44,47,51).

## C. Detoxification

Xenobiotic mutagens can also be detoxified by metabolic systems. The principal means for inactivating the reactive electrophilic agents are conjugation with glutathione or sulfate via reaction with glutathione transferases or sulfotransferases (44,47). In addition, epoxide hydratases are the major enzymes involved in the detoxification of arene oxides and epoxides including polycyclic aromatic hydrocarbons via addition of water to form nonreactive dihydrodiols (44, 47). The epoxide hydratases are primarily found associated with microsomes, while the glutathione and sulfotransferases exists as cytosolic enzymes (44,47). These enzymes increase the water solubility of potentially genotoxic metabolites via the conjugation reactions which then allows them to be excreted (44,47).

## D. Metabolizing Systems for Genotoxicity Assays

Many tests for genotoxicity lack the necessary enzymatic capabilities to convert xenobiotic chemicals to genotoxic species. Therefore, several means of providing the proper source of metabolizing enzymes for genotoxicity assays have been developed.

### 1. Subcellular Fractions

The microsome-containing S-9 liver homogenate originally incorporated by Ames et al. (48,52) into the *Salmonella typhimurium* histidine reversion mutation assay has also been employed for the conversion of xenobiotic chemicals to genotoxic metabolites in a variety of other in vitro genotoxicity assays. However, it is generally agreed that S-9 fractions yield an overbalance of genotoxic metabolites (44, 47). This is in part due to the loss or inactivation of the necessary cofactors required for detoxification, such as conjugation with glutathione (47). In addition, the use of S-9 fractions results in the generation of metabolite profiles and DNA adducts that are different from those observed in intact cells following treatment with the promutagens/procarcinogens aflatoxin $B_1$, benzo(a)pyrene and 7,12-dimethylbenz(a)anthracene (54–59). These data suggest that the use of S-9 fractions may result in the production of mutagenic metabolites that do not reflect the in vivo situation. Another problem is that normally, microsome-containing S-9 fractions are prepared from the livers of rats pretreated with enzyme inducers such as Aroclor 1254, phenobarbital, and 3-methylcholanthrene which results in enhanced levels of certain enzymes, particularly the mono-oxygenases which can lead to overproduction of genotoxic metabolites (44,47). Therefore, the interpretation of a positive result obtained with an in vitro genotoxicity assay employing an S-9 fraction for xenobiotic metabolism should be made with caution.

### 2. Whole Cells in Culture

Isolated hepatocytes maintain most of their xenobiotic chemical-metabolizing capabilities for up to 24 hr in culture (44). This fact has been used advantageously in the development and validation of the primary hepatocyte DNA repair assay (60–64). This genotoxicity assay system employs primary hepatocyte cultures as both the drug-metabolizing cells and the target cells for DNA damage. Primary hepatocytes have also been utilized as a source of whole cell metabolic capabilities in association with other genotoxicity indicator assays such as mammalian cell point mutation and the Ames/*Salmonella* mutation assays (65–69).

Primary hamster embryo fibroblasts have also been utilized as the metabolically competent cells for the activation of xenobiotic chemicals in association with in vitro genotoxicity tests (70,71). In addition, a variety of other cell types including primary lung, bronchus, bladder, kidney, rat liver cell lines, and human hepatoma cell lines have also been employed as the metabolically competent cells or metabolizing and target cells for in vitro genotoxicity tests (72–76). Currently, however, primary rodent hepatocytes are the cells of choice for providing intact cell-metabolizing capabilities for in vitro genotoxicity studies.

### 3. In Vivo Animal Bioassays

It has been established for some time that xenobiotic metabolism in primary hepatocytes and continuous hepatoma cell lines differs from that of the intact liver (77,78). The use of whole animals for treatment and evaluation brings into play a spectrum of physiological events such as chemical half-life, distribution, metabolism, and organ specificity that can have a profound effect upon the genotoxicity of the test chemical. Since the entire metabolic capabilities of the test organism are involved in the activation/detoxification of the test chemical, in vivo genotoxicity assays have recently been highly touted as being more relevant for safety evaluation (22,30,79,80). In vivo genotoxicity assays that are routinely employed in the safety assessment of chemicals and drugs are the mouse micronucleus tests, cytogenetic analysis of rat bone marrow, Drosphila melanogaster sexlinked recessive lethal assay, and the dominant lethal assay in rats (11,79–81). A further discussion of routinely employed genotoxicity tests and their metabolic capabilities is presented in the next section.

## IV. ROUTINELY EMPLOYED GENOTOXICITY ASSAYS

In this section a brief description of the genotoxicity assays routinely employed for product safety evaluation is given. The assay systems chosen were based on the list compiled by the Environmental Protection Agency Gene-Tox Program (91), a survey by the Genetic Toxicology Association, and a review of genotoxicity evaluation programs established by 6 major U.S. pharmaceutical firms. The genotoxicity testing systems to be discussed are presented in Tables 12 and 13. The assay systems are classified as bacterial mutation assays, mammalian cell gene point mutation assays, DNA damage/DNA repair assays, in vitro cytogenetic screens, and in vivo assays.

## A. Bacterial Mutation Assays

### 1. Ames/Salmonella Mutation Assay

The Salmonella typhimurium histidine-independence reversion assay developed by Ames and co-workers (48,52,82) is the most widely employed genotoxicity testing screen. This assay system routinely uses five histidine auxotrophs of S. typhimurium, TA1535, TA1537, TA1538, TA98, and TA100. Strains TA1535 and TA100 respond to mutagens that induce base-pair mutational events while strains TA1537, TA1538, and TA98 are mutated by mutagens which induced frameshift-type events. All strains lack the normal DNA excision repair system due to a deletion of the uvrB gene. Therefore, they are extremely sensitive to DNA-damaging agents. Tester strains TA98

**Table 12** In Vitro and In Vivo Genotoxicity Assays Routinely Employed for Product Evaluation[a]

| Genetic endpoint | Gene mutation | Chromosome damage | DNA repair |
|---|---|---|---|
| | Ames/*Salmonella* reverse mutation | Cytogenetic analysis in mammalian cells; CHO/or human lymphocytes primarily | *E. coli* $polA^+/polA^-$ |
| | *E. coli* reverse mutation | Micronucleus test | Sister chromatid exchange in CHO cells or human lymphocytes |
| | L5178Y Mouse lymphoma $TK^-$, Chinese hamster ovary $HGPRT^-$ | Bone marrow cytogenetic analysis | UDS in mammalian cells in culture |
| | Chinese hamster V79 $HGPRT^-$ | Rodent dominant lethal test | Sister chromatid exchange in rats or mice |
| | *Drosophila* sex-linked recessive lethal | | |

[a] As compiled by the U.S. Environmental Protection Agency Gene-Tox Program (1985) and the Genetic Toxicology Association Survey (1983).

**Table 13** Genotoxicity Tests Routinely Employed by U.S. Pharmaceutical Firms[a]

| Bacterial gene mutation | No.[b] | Mammalian cell gene mutation | No. | Cytogenetics | No. | DNA damage | No. |
|---|---|---|---|---|---|---|---|
| Ames/*Salmonella* mutation assay | 6 | Chinese hamster ovary HGPRT | 3 | In vitro chromosome abberations | 1 | In vitro hepatocyte UDS | 4 |
| | | Chinese hamster V79 HGPRT | 1 | In vivo chromosome aberrations | 5 | | |
| | | Mouse lymphoma TK | 2 | Micronucleus test | 2 | | |
| | | | | In vivo sister chromatid exchange | 1 | | |

[a]Based on a survey of 6 major pharmaceutical manufacturing firms in the United States.
[b]Number of companies employing the test.

and TA100 also contain the pKM 101 plasmid which further increases the sensitivity of these two strains to many mutagens. Recently, two new tester strains, TA97 and TA102, have been designed for addition to the standard set of five tester strains. Strain TA97 which contains the pKM 101 plasmid may replace strain TA1537 (83). Strain TA102 contains the pKM 101 plasmid, the multicopy plasmid pAQ1 and is excision repair proficient (84). Strain TA102 detects mutagenic damaged induced by such agents as formaldehyde, glyoxal, various hydroperoxides, bleomycin, x-rays, ultraviolet-light, and DNA cross-linking agents which are not readily detected by the other tester strains (84,85). As discussed earlier, the Ames/*Salmonella* mutation assay routinely utilizes a rodent liver S-9 fraction with appropriate cofactors as a source of mammalian cell activating enzymes. Detailed methods and recommendations for the performance of the Ames assay have been published (52,85). Essentially, each bacterial culture is treated with a range of concentrations of the test article in the presence and absence of the S-9 metabolic activation preparation. Appropriate dilutions of the test chemical are added to test tubes containing 0.1 ml aliquots of the tester strain culture and approximately 2 ml of molten top agar. The contents of the tubes are mixed and poured over minimal glucose agar plate. Normally, 2–3 plates are poured per treatment point. Solvent and standard positive controls are also employed. The plates are incubated for 48–72 hr at 37°C before being scored. Spontaneous and induced histidine-independent revertant mutants are now routinely scored with the aid of an automatic colony counter. The colony counter output can be directly interfaced with a computer for data acquisition and analysis.

The OECD, EPA, and the United Kingdom Environmental Mutagen Society (UKEMS) have established guidelines for performing the Ames/ *Salmonella* mutation assay (87–90). In addition, the American Society of Testing and Materials (ASTM) committee on genetic toxicology is currently in the process of preparing guidelines for the performance and evaluation of this assay. The advantage of this short-term bacterial mutation assay is its ability to screen a large number of test chemicals over a relatively short period of time in an economical manner. However, extrapolation of the results from the Ames mutation assay for human risk assessment is difficult due to the bacterial nature of the test system.

### 2. *Escherichia coli* WP2 *trp* Mutation Assay

*Escherichia coli* WP2 and derivatives thereof have been utilized to study the molecular events of mutagenesis and DNA repair for over 20 years. In terms of screening test chemicals for their mutagenic potential the strains of *Escherichia coli* employed are WP2 (wild type), WP2 *uvrA*, and WP2 *uvrA* pKM 101. All three tester strains require tryptophan due to an *ochre* nonsense mutation in a gene coding for an enzyme necessary for tryptophan biosynthesis (91). The three tester strains can be reverted to tryptophan independence by treatment with chemicals that induce primarily base-pair substitution mutational events (91,92). The mutation can occur at the original mutant site or in external suppressor loci that code for transfer RNA molecules (92).

The wild-type strain WP2 is excision repair proficient while strains WP2 *uvrA* and WP2 *uvrA* pKM 101 are mutants in the *uvrA* gene which codes for an excision repair enzyme. Therefore, tester strains WP2 *uvrA* and WP2 *uvrA* pKM 101 are extremely sensitive to most DNA-damaging chemicals. In addition, strain WP2 *uvrA* pKM 101 carries the pKM 101 plasmid which confers additional mutagen sensitivity to this tester strain. Methods for performing the *E. coli* WP2 *trp* mutation assay for the screening of mutagenic potential have been presented and reviewed (91–93). Aliquots of 0.1 ml bacterial broth culture are treated in duplicate or triplicate in test tubes containing approximately 2.0 ml of molten agar with a dose range of the test chemical. Solvent and appropriate positive controls are also evaluated. After addition of the test chemical dilution, the test tubes are mixed and the contents of the tubes poured over minimal glucose agar plates. The three tester strains are plated in the presence and absence of the standard Aroclor 1254-induced rat liver S-9 metabolic activation preparation, 0.5 ml/test tube. The plates are allowed to incubate at 37°C for 48–72 hr. We recommend incubation for 72 hr to assure that may of the slow growing trp[+] suppressor revertants are of sufficient size to be scorable by automatic colony counters. Guidelines for performing the *E. coli* WP2 *trp* mutation assay have been issued by the OECD and the EPA (87–89). A review of the *E. coli* WP2 *trp* mutation assay has suggested that it is of limited use for the genotoxicity screening of chemicals due to the mutational specificity and engineering of the tester strains (92). However, data from the *E. coli* mutation assay are still required by the regulatory bodies of various countries when test chemical information is submitted for safety evaluation.

## 3. Escherichia coli PolA[+]/PolA[−] Differential Toxicity

Genotoxic chemicals are known to interact with DNA which may ultimately result in the production of DNA strand breaks. DNA polymerase is involved in the repair of DNA strand breaks, and bacterial mutants lacking DNA polymerase I are more sensitive to DNA damaging agents (94–97). This fact is used to advantage in the *E. coli* PolA[+]/PolA[−] DNA damage test. A wild-type (PolA[+]) and a DNA polymerase I-deficient mutant (PolA[−]) strain of *E. coli* are treated with the test chemical. If the PolA[−] mutant of *E. coli* is more sensitive to treatment with the chemical of interest than is the wild-type (PolA+) tester strain, the test chemical is presumed to be a DNA-damaging agent with mutagenic potential. The *E. coli* PolA+/ PolA- DNA damage assay does not screen for the mutagenicity of the test chemical directly, but suggests that the chemical under study has DNA damaging activity which may result in various mutational events.

Procedures have been established for carrying out the *E. coli* PolA+/PolA- DNA damage test (98,99): 0.1-ml aliquots of an exponential culture of the *E. coli* PolA+ or PolA- strain are added to 2-3 ml of molten top agar, which is then poured over a nutrient medium agar plate. After the top agar has been allowed to harden, a sterile filter paper disc carrying a dilution of the test chemical is placed on the center of the plate. After incubation at 37°C for approximately 16 hr the zone of growth inhibition is measured. In order to perform the assay in the presence of a metabolic activation system, 0.1 ml aliquots of the *E. coli* tester strains are spread over the surface of the nutrient agar plates. Once the plates have been allowed to dry, a well, approximately 0.8 cm in diameter is cut into the center of the plates. To the well is added 50 µl of the rat liver-derived metabolic activation preparation. For those test chemicals that induce a large zone of growth inhibition for the *E. coli* PolA- tester strain relative to the wild-type strain, the results are considered to indicate that the test chemical is capable of producing DNA damage.

EPA has published guidelines for performing and evaluating the data from the *E. coli* PolA+/PolA- DNA damage test (88,89).

## B. Mammalian Cell Gene Point Mutation Assays

### 1. Chinese Hamster Cell HGPRT Mutation Assays

Two lines of Chinese hamster cells are routinely employed to evaluate the ability of a test chemical to induce gene point mutations. These lines are the Chinese hamster ovary (CHO) $K_1$ line which has 20 chromosomes and the V79 cell line which has a modal chromosome number of 22± 1 (100,101). Both cell lines have near diploid, relatively stable chromosome numbers, doubling times of 12-16 hr, cloning efficiencies of 75-95% and low spontaneous background mutant frequencies (100,101). Procedures for maintaining the cell lines, performing the HGPRT mutation assay, and evaluating the results have been published and reviewed for each cell line (100-102).

The basis of the HGPRT mammalian cell mutation assays is the inactivation of the hypoxanthine-guanine phosphoribosyl transferase (HGPT) enzyme coded for by the HGPT gene. The HGPT enzyme catalyzes the conversion of hypoxanthine and guanine to the corresponding nucleoside-5-monophosphate. The HGPT enzyme also catalyzes the conversion of the purine analogs 6-thioguanine (6TG) and

8-azaguanine (8AG) into their cytotoxic nucleoside-5-monophosphates (100,101). Therefore, mutant cells which lack HGPT enzyme activity will survive in the presence of these toxic purine analogs and form clones in media supplemented with either 6TG or 8AG.

Normally, in a genotoxicity screening program, the chemical of interest is evaluated for its cytotoxic nature in a preliminary toxicity screen with the cell line of choice. Most protocols for either the CHO or V79 HGPRT mutation assay suggest performing the study with a dose range of the test chemical which would yield % survival values of between 100 and 10% (100,101).

Exponential phase cells are seeded the day before use at a density such that on the day of treatment $1.0-1.5 \times 10^6$ cells are treated per culture. Treatment is normally for 4–5 hr in the presence and absence of a rodent liver-derived metabolic activation preparation. However, both the CHO and V79 hamster cell lines have been seeded in the presence of metabolic competent cells such as hamster embryo fibroblasts or rodent primary hepatocytes which serve to metabolize the test chemical. When the CHO or V79 hamster cells are seeded with feeder layer metabolizing cells, treatment times can be extended up to 24 to 48 hr (100,101).

Following treatment the CHO or V79 hamster cells are allowed to grow for 6–8 days in order to express the induced 6TG- or 8AG-resistant mutants. Normally, the treated cultures are subcultured 2–3 times during the expression period. Approximately $10^6$ cells are passaged at each subculture. However, the number of cells subcultured is dependent on the toxicity of the treatment. If too few viable cells are subcultured an insufficient number of induced mutant cells may be transferred and subsequently not recovered (100,101).

Following the expression period the cells are seeded in culture medium in the presence of 6TG or 8AG. For the CHO/HGPT mutation assay normally $10^6$ cells are seeded per culture for selection (101). With the Chinese hamster V79 cell mutation assay, up to $3 \times 10^6$ cells are normally seeded for selection per culture (100). For both hamster cell mutation assays a suspension of diluted cells from each culture is seeded in nonselective medium to determine the cloning efficiency at the time of selection. Mutant selection and cloning efficiency culture dishes are incubated for 6–8 days under specified conditions (100,101) before being stained.

Mutant clones and cloning efficiency dishes can be scored with the aid of automatic colony counters. The colony counter output may be interfaced to a computer for data calculation and evaluation. Criteria for the evaluation of the data generated by the CHO/HGPRT and V79/HGPRT mutation assays have been reported (100–102). In terms of product safety evaluation, these two in vitro gene point mutation assays offer the advantage of being mammalian in nature.

However, each still relies on the exogenous rodent liver S-9 metabolic activation preparation for the metabolism of the test chemical.

OECD, UKEMS, and EPA have established general guidelines for performing and evaluating the data from mammalian cell mutation assays (87–90). In addition, the ASTM Genetic Toxicology Committee has prepared draft guidelines for the CHO/HGPRT mutation assay.

### 2. *L5178Y Mouse Lymphoma Cell Mutation Assay*

A third mammalian cell gene point mutation assay that is used routinely for the evaluation of the mutagenic potential of test chemicals is the L5178Y mouse lymphoma cell mutation test developed by Clive and co-workers (103–105).

The L5178Y mouse lymphoma cell line was originally isolated from a murine ascitic tumor and adapted to growth in culture by G. Fischer (106). These cells exhibit rapid growth in culture (generation time of 10–12 hr) high cloning efficiency (80–100%) and a stable near-diploid chromosome number of 40±1 (106). The thymidine kinase (Tk) heterozygote subclone, −3.7.2C, is utilized for mutation assay screening (103–105).

The mouse lymphoma cell mutation assay is based on the loss of the thymidine kinase enzyme. $Tk^{-/-}$ mutants are selected for in the presence of the toxic thymidine analog, trifluorothymidine (TFT) which is phosphorylated by the Tk enzyme (104–106). Many mutagens induce two sizes of TFT-resistant clones in the mouse lymphoma cell mutation assay, small colony mutants, and large colony mutants as determined by incremental colony size determinations (107–109). Data suggest that many of these small colony mutants carry a chromosome aberration in chromosome 11 which codes for the Tk enzyme (107,108,110).

Detailed protocols for performing the mouse lymphoma cell mutation assay have been published (104–106,111). Approximately 6 × $10^6$ mouse lymphoma cells are treated in suspension culture with the test article in the presence and absence of a rodent liver-derived S-9 fraction and cofactors preparation. Rodent primary hepatocytes have also been employed as a source of xenobiotic metabolizing enzymes for the mouse lymphoma cell mutation assay (112,113). Normally, duplicate or triplicate cultures are treated per dose point including appropriate solvent and positive controls. The treatment period is usually 4 hr at 37°C when an S-9 metabolic activation preparation is employed for metabolic activation. However, this treatment period can be extended when rodent primary hepatocytes are utilized for metabolic activation of the test chemical. Following the treatment period, the suspension cultures are washed free of the test chemical by repeated centrifugation and resuspension. Finally the treated cell cultures are resuspended in a volume of 20 ml of medium to a cell density of approximately 3 × $10^5$ cells/ml. The cell cultures are incubated with shaking at 37°C for approximately 24 hr. At this time the cell density of each culture is enumerated by counting a diluted aliquot of the culture with an electronic particle counter or a hemocytometer. If necessary, the cultures are diluted back to a cell density of $3 \times 10^5$ cell/ml. All cultures are reincubated with shaking for an additional 24 hr to allow for the expression of the induced TFT-resistant mutants. Following the second 24 hr period of incubation, the cultures are again counted. A total of $3 \times 10^6$ cells must be present for the culture to be clonable. If insufficient cells are present, an additional day of recovery/expression growth may be employed. In order to select TFT-resistant clones the mouse lymphoma cells are cloned in soft agar. Approximately $3 \times 10^6$ cell from each clonable culture are centrifuged and resuspended in 100 ml of soft agar medium. An aliquot of this cell suspension is further diluted and suspended in soft agar medium at a cell density of approximately 3 cells/ml to determine the cloning efficiency of the culture. The cells at high density ($3 \times 10^4$ cells/ml) are treated with TFT to select the TFT-resistant mutant clones. Three soft agar plates are poured per culture to determine the cloning efficiency and three are poured to select the TFT-resistant clones. Soft agar plates are incubated at 37°C for 10–12 days to allow the colonies to develop. The scoring of clones is normally performed by an automatic colony counter. The TFT-resistant mutant clones may be sized with an automatic colony counter following established procedures (107,109, 111). Methods for data calculation, statistical analysis, and interpretation have been presented (104,106,111).

Although the L5178Y mouse lymphoma cell mutation assay has technical manipulations that differ somewhat from those of the hamster cell HGPRT mutation assays discussed above, the amount of time required to perform these mammalian cell gene point mutation tests is similar. The use of the mouse lymphoma cell mutation assay may give an indication of the ability of the test chemical to induce chromosomal damage as well as point mutation DNA damage if colony sizing is performed.

General guidelines for the performance of mammalian cell gene point mutation assays have been established by the OECD, UKEMS, and EPA (87–90). Recently, the ASTM Genetic Toxicology Committee has prepared draft guidelines specifically for the L5178Y mouse lymphoma cell mutation assay.

## C. DNA Repair Assays

### 1. Primary Hepatocyte DNA Repair Assay

The rodent primary hepatocyte DNA repair assay developed by Williams (61–63) employs nondividing, rodent, primary hepatocytes to detect unscheduled DNA synthesis (UDS) induced by chemical mutagens. As discussed in Section III, primary hepatocytes retain their full metabolic capabilities for a period of time in culture which results in the production of a more realistic profile of xenobiotic metabolites relative to that generated in vivo.

The primary hepatocyte DNA/repair assay (PH DNA/repair) has been well validated as to its predictive value for discriminating non-carcinogens from genotoxic carcinogens (60,63,64). Methods for the PH DNA/repair assay including a recent review of the literature have been published (114–117).

Isolation of hepatocytes is accomplished by perfusion of the liver in situ with an EGTA solution followed by a buffered collagenase solution which results in the dissociation of the hepatocytes from the liver connective tissues. Following perfusion, the liver is removed. Young adult male Fischer 344 rats are the animals of choice for hepatocyte culture preparation. However, other species have been employed (114).

Once the liver is removed from the animal, the hepatocytes are gently brushed or combed from the liver connective tissue into cell culture medium. Viability of the dissociated hepatocyte suspension is normally determined by trypan blue dye exclusion. Preparations with viabilities of 80% or greater are normally considered acceptable for the evaluation of test chemicals. Hepatocyte suspensions are seeded onto coverslips, normally in multiwell dishes containing culture medium with serum. The hepatocytes are allowed to attach to the coverslips for $1\frac{1}{2}$–$2\frac{1}{2}$ hr at 37°C. Following attachment, unattached hepatocytes are rinsed from the wells and the medium is replaced with serum-free medium containing [3H]thymidine and the test article, solvent control, or positive control. Normally, three cultures are treated per dose point and treatment is normally for 18–24 hr at 37°C. Following treatment, the test chemical is removed by successive rinsing and the cells are then fixed to the coverslips. The coverslips are allowed to dry and then mounted to microscope slides. The following steps for autoradiography to determine if DNA repair has been induced by the test chemical should be performed in a well equipped photographic dark room. The slides are dipped into NTB photographic emulsion and allowed to dry. After drying the slides are allowed to develop the [3H]thymidine grains for 7–10 days at 0–4°C. Following this, the slides are developed and stained.

In order to establish if the test chemical has induced DNA repair as evidenced by a net increase in nuclear photographic grains caused by an incorporation of the [3H]thymidine into the DNA excision repair gaps in the nuclear DNA, the slides are scored with the use of a microscope and an automatic colony counter. The nuclear area of hepatocytes are scored as well as the adjacent nuclear size cytoplasmic areas. Cytoplasmic grain counts are subtracted from nuclear grain counts to determine if there has been a net increase of [3H]thymidine grains in the nucleus. Depending upon the protocol, 20–50 cells are scored per coverslip.

Methods for data calculation and evaluation have been published (60,64,115,116). In addition, variations to the standard rat hepatocyte DNA/repair assay have recently been presented (117). Guidelines for general UDS assays have been published by the EPA and the UKEMS (88,89,118). Specific draft guidelines for the performance and evaluation of the primary hepatocyte DNA/repair assay have been prepared by the ASTM Committee on Genetic Toxicology.

The major advantage of including the PH DNA/repair assay in a genotoxicity screening program is that currently it is the only in vitro assay system routinely employing whole cells for the metabolic conversion of test chemicals. Therefore, the primary hepatocyte system may avoid positive results that are obtained in other genotoxicity tests from metabolites that are detoxified by whole cell enzyme systems.

### D. Mammalian Cell Cytogenetic Analysis

The genotoxicity assay systems to be discussed in this section rely on the evaluation of cytogenetic damage in mammalian cells in vitro. Test systems for the quantitation of sister-chromatid exchange (SCE) and chromosome aberrations generally use Chinese hamster cells or human lymphocytes. Both cell types can be employed to evaluate the ability of test chemicals to induce chromosome aberrations and/or SCE. Normally, a study is carried out in the presence of a metabolic activation system.

#### 1. Chromosome Aberrations

Chromosome aberrations are structural alterations of normal chromosomes that can be detected by light microscope techniques. Formation of structural chromosome aberrations requires production of DNA strand breaks which may be followed by DNA repair (119). Many of these chromosome aberration events are believed to be lethal to the cells carrying them (120). However, it is assumed that test chemicals capable of inducing visible aberrations also induce nonlethal chromosomal structure changes such as translocations, inversions, and small deletions that could represent a genetic hazard. In addition, visible chromosomal aberrations have been implicated in the neoplastic process (121,122). Therefore, evaluation of a test chemical's ability to induce chromosomal aberrations is one of the major endpoints in genotoxicity screening programs.

Basic procedures for carrying out chromosome aberration analysis in vitro have been published (123–126). A variable that can play a major role in determining the outcome of an in vitro cytogenetic analysis is the time of sampling the cell population after treatment with the test chemical. If too many cell cycles are allowed to occur between treatment of the cells with the test chemical and evaluation for chromosome aberrations, most visible aberrations will be lost due to their lethal nature. However, if the time of sampling the treated cell population for chromosome aberrations is shortly after chemical treatment, false negative results may occur. This situation results because many chemical clastogens (agents which induce chromosome aberrations) are not active in the latter stages of the cell cycle and clastogens can also delay the cell cycle. Therefore, a sampling interval which is $1\frac{1}{2}$ times the normal cell cycle period is recommended for routine genotoxicity screening. Multiple sampling times may also be employed if no preliminary measure of cell cycle kinetics is made to assure that sufficient metaphase cells are recovered for chromosome analysis.

Currently, the Chinese hamster ovary (CHO) cell line or human peripheral blood lymphocytes are routinely employed for the evaluation of the induction of chromosomal aberrations by test chemicals (90,126). CHO cells are normally treated with the chemical of interest in the exponential phase of growth to assure that there are cells in all stages of the cell cycle and that there is a sufficient number of metaphase cells for analysis. Since the normal untreated cell cycle time for CHO cells is 12–14 hr (126), a sampling time of 18–21 hr is considered appropriate. When employing human peripheral blood lymphocytes it is necessary to establish short-term in vitro cultures with blood samples obtained from healthy donor individuals. In culture, the normally nondividing lymphocytes are stimulated to divide by the addition of a mitogen, usually phytohemagglutinin to the culture medium (124). Mitotic activity normally begins approximately 40 hr after stimulation and reaches a maximum at about 3 days. For routine genotoxicity screening, stimulated human lymphocytes are treated with the test chemical approximately 48 hr after cultures have been established. Cells are then harvested for chromosome analysis after 24 hr of treatment.

The standard rodent liver-derived S-9 metabolic activation preparation is routinely utilized for the metabolism of test chemicals in both the CHO and human lymphocyte assay systems (90,127,128). However, due to problems with toxicity of the S-9 cofactor preparations to the cell cultures, the exposure time of the test chemical in the presence of exogenous metabolic activation must be limited to a maximum of 3–4 hr. In addition, the same problems arise with the use of liver homogenates for the metabolism of xenobiotics in cytogenetic assays as discussed in Section III. Therefore, the use of metabolically competent "feeder layer" cells for metabolism of test chemicals in in vitro chromosome aberration test systems has been explored (129,130).

Since there is a close relationship between chromosome aberration induction and cytotoxicity, it is necessary to demonstrate cytotoxicity in the chromosome aberration assay in order to establish that the test chemical is negative in this assay. Many clastogens (chromosome breaking agents) may damage the cells at any stage of the cell cycle. Some of these damaged cells may be incapable of repairing the lesions and die, while others may repair the damage enough to traverse the cell cycle and reach mitosis. These lesions seem to require DNA misrepair to be expressed as chromosome aberrations at mitosis.

Cytotoxicity of a test substance is determined by cell proliferation kinetics which is a measure of mitotic delay. The average proliferation time is determined by a shift in the ratios of first, second, and third division metaphase ($M_1$, $M_2$, $M_3$) as characterized by the staining patterns of the chromosomes when stained for sister chromatid differentiation. If the chemical induces mitotic delay, there will be an increase in $M_1$ and $M_1^+$ metaphases as compared to the solvent control resulting in an increase in the average proliferation time. The harvest time may be adjusted based on mitotic delay so that most of the cells of the high dose will be in first mitotic division after treatment and adequate time will have lapsed for transgression of the damaged cells through the cell cycle phases. The highest dose chosen should be one which shows a cytotoxic effect, but which allows sufficient metaphases for a reliable analysis. Generally, this dose will be one which gives approximately 80% or greater increase in average proliferation time as compared to the solvent control.

Once dosage levels have been selected for study, cell cultures are treated with the appropriate concentrations of the test chemical; cultures are also treated with the solvent and positive control. Cultures are then harvested at one or more intervals after treatment. To harvest the treated cultures, they are exposed to a metaphase-arresting agent such as colcemid and treated with a hypotonic solution to enlarge the cells. The cells are fixed, cell suspensions dropped onto microscope slides, and stained for observation. Scoring of the various chromosome aberrations is a critical step of the study and must be performed by a well trained, experienced individual. Methods of nomenclature and classification of chromosome aberrations have been recommended (90,131).

The OECD, EPA, and the UKEMS have developed guidelines for the performance and evaluation of in vitro chromosome aberration tests (87–90).

## 2. Sister-Chromatid Exchanges (SCE)

An SCE event is believed to represent a symmetrical exchange of chromosomal material at one locus between sister chromatids. This exchange, which is presumed to involve the breakage and reunion of DNA strands does not alter overall chromosome morphology as does induction of chromosome aberrations. Many chemical agents that induce chromosome aberrations and/or gene-point mutations also induce SCEs (118,132–137). Studies have shown that many DNA-damaging agents induce SCEs at concentrations that are orders of magnitude lower than those dosage levels required to induce visible chromosome aberrations. In addition, less technical training is required to evaluate the slides for SCE induction. Therefore, the evaluation of the ability of a test chemical to induce SCEs has been employed as a screen for genotoxicity. However, caution must be used in the evaluation of SCE test results since a clear relationship between SCE formation and the induction of mutational damage has not yet been established (118,132,136,137).

The mechanism of the formation of SCEs is not clear at this time. However, it is believed that DNA repair is involved in the process which results in the exchange of chromatid material (136,138,139). In order to visualize these symmetrical exchanges, it was necessary to develop staining methods that could differentiate the two sister chromatids. The procedure that is now employed routinely to visualize SCEs utilizes the ability of DNA-incorporated BrdUrd to quench the fluorescence of DNA binding dyes such as Hoechst 33258. Cells in culture are exposed to BrdUrd during the last two rounds of DNA replication. Following incorporation of BrdUrd into the DNA, the cells are stained with Hoechst dye and exposed to an exciting light source. Following light exposure, the cell preparations are stained with Giemsa stain. The differential staining mechanism for SCE detection and general staining procedures have been reviewed (118,135, 136,138,139).

General methods for performing and evaluating the data generated by in vitro SCE assays have been reviewed in the literature (118, 135,140). In addition, detailed protocols for carrying out SCE studies have recently been published (141,142). CHO cells and human peripheral blood lymphocytes are routinely employed in the evaluation of the ability of test chemicals to induce SCEs (118,135,136,137–142). However, diploid human fibroblasts and Chinese hamster V79 fibroblasts have also been utilized to study SCE induction (118,135,136, 140).

When CHO cells are to be used for the evaluation of SCE induction, they are subcultured the day before use to assure that the cells are in the exponential phase of growth for chemical treatment and incorporation of the BrdUrd photosensitizer. Normally, cultures are treated for intervals of 2–4 hr in the presence and absence of the standard rat liver S-9 metabolic activation preparation before addition of the BrdUrd. Cultures are incubated for an additional 24–30 hr in the dark to allow the necessary two rounds of DNA replication to occur. If the test chemical induces significant mitotic delay, additional incubation time is required to assure that two rounds of DNA replication have occurred. A metaphase-arresting agent such as colcemid should be added to the cultures 2–3 hr before harvest.

CHO cells in metaphase are harvested by the mitotic shakeoff technique. The cells are swollen with hypotonic KCl followed by washing with fixative. Cell suspensions are dropped onto microscope slides and stained for SCE differentiation by the fluorescence plus Giemsa technique.

When human lymphocytes are used in the analysis of SCE formation, short-term cultures are initiated from freshly drawn blood samples. Since human lymphocytes are normally in an arrested phase of growth ($G_0$) while in circulation, a mitogen such as phytohemagglutinin (PHA) must be added to the cultures. Treatment with the test chemical is normally initiated at 24 or 48 hr following the mitogenic stimulation. The treatment interval is 1-4 hr, and harvest time is between 60 and 72 hr post-PHA stimulation. Lymphocytes are fixed and stained in a manner similar to that employed for CHO cells.

Results of SCE analysis are normally reported as the mean number of SCEs per cell. The statistical test most routinely employed in the evaluation of SCE data is the two tailed $t$-test (118,135). However, the use of other statistical methodologies for the analysis of SCE data has recently been reviewed (144).

The EPA and the UKEMS have published guidelines to establish proper procedures for conducting and evaluating data from in vitro SCE studies (88,89,118). Since the molecular mechanism for the formation of SCEs is unknown, the significance of SCE induction to a test chemical's genotoxicity is not well established. Therefore, the results of an in vitro SCE study for a test chemical must be considered in light of results from other genotoxicity assays.

## E. Cellular Transformation Assays

Although they are not considered routine genotoxicity screening tests, in vitro cellular transformation assays have been employed in the evaluation of test chemicals for their potential oncogenicity. The use of several cell transformation assay systems for predicting the carcinogenicity of test chemicals has recently been reviewed (16–18, 145,146). The endpoint that is most widely applied in evaluation of in vitro transformation is loss of density-dependent growth. Transformed cells grow in piled up, disorganized, criss-cross colonies or foci. Cells at the periphery of transformed foci often appear to be invading the surrounding normal cells as occurs in invasive tumors in vivo (18). There are four in vitro transformation assays that have been utilized to screen the oncogenic potential of test chemicals. They are, the Syrian hamster embryo fibroblast clonal morphology assay system, the BHK 21 clonal growth in soft agar system, and two transformation systems that rely on the development of morphologically altered transformed foci. The transformed foci tests use either the Balb c/3T3 mouse embryo fibroblast cell line or the C3H/10T1/2 clone 8 mouse embryo fibroblast cell line.

The Syrian hamster embryo fibroblast clonal morphology assay relys on the ability of chemical carcinogens to induce a transformed morphology of individual colonies. The scoring of such colonies is subjective. This transformation assay system has been developed and validated in the laboratory of Pienta (147–149). The hamster embryo fibroblasts apparently retain their ability to metabolize many carcinogens and this transformation assay system has been demonstrated to have a 92% concurrence with animal cancer bioassay data. However, the reproducibility of the Syrian hamster embryo fibroblast transformation test system has not been well documented outside of Pienta's laboratory (16,17).

The BHK 21 clonal growth in soft agar transformation assay employs as an endpoint of in vitro transformation the ability of cells to form clones in soft agar. This ability is considered indicative of oncogenic potential (18). The standard rodent liver S-9 metabolic activation system is employed to metabolize the test chemicals. The BHK 21 clonal assay system has been demonstrated (primarily in one laboratory) to have an accuracy of 94% in discriminating between 120 carcinogens and noncarcinogens (150,151). However, if not properly maintained in culture, the BHK 21 cell line can have an unacceptably high spontaneous transformation frequency (16,17). In addition, the BHK 21/clone 13 cell line will induce tumors following the injection of $10^3$ cells into newborn Syrian hamsters (16). This invitro transformation assay system has not yielded reproducible results in independent laboratories (16–18) and is, therefore, not a reliable screen for determining the oncogenic potential of candidate chemicals at this time.

The Balb c/3T3 mouse embryo fibroblast transformation assay relies on the development of morphologically transformed foci atop a confluent monolayer of normal cells to serve as an indicator of in vitro malignancy. Only a few clones of Balb c/3T3 cells are suitable for transformation studies and these clones have unstable karyotypes and cellular morphologies (17,152). In addition, Balb c/3T3 cells lines are deficient in metabolic capabilities and a reliable means of incorporating an exogenous source of metabolism into the Balb c/3T3 transformation assay has not yet been developed (17,146).

A second transformation assay system that relies on the development of transformed foci as the indicator of oncogenic potential is the mouse embryo fibroblast C3H/10T½ clone 8 cell line originally developed by Reznikoff and co-workers (153,154). Methods of employing the C3H/10T½ transformation assay have recently been reviewed (18,145).

The C3H/10T½ mouse embryo fibroblast cell line is highly sensitive to postconfluent inhibition of growth and has an essentially nondetectable level of spontaneous transformation in relatively low passage cultures (up to passage numbers 13–15). Many of the induced transformed foci of $C3H/10T_{\frac{1}{2}}$ cells develop the invasiveness observed for malignant tumors in vivo (155).

Normally, a preliminary cytotoxicity study is performed to establish a dosage range with significant toxicity at the higher dose levels. For the transformation assay, low passage (p. 8–p. 15), cells are seeded at predetermined cell densities, usually 10–20 cell culture dishes per point. At approximately 24 hr following seeding, the cell cultures are treated with the test chemical for 24 hr. The test chemical is removed by washing the culture dishes. The culture dishes are incubated at 37°C for 6–7 weeks posttreatment. The culture medium is changed weekly until the culture dishes are fixed and stained. Specific criteria have been established for scoring the transformed foci (18,145,154).

The $C3H/10T_{\frac{1}{2}}$ cell line is only partially competent for the metabolism of xenobiotic chemicals. Therefore, the use of rodent liver S-9 fractions and rat hepatocytes for metabolic activation has been explored (18). Currently, no validated metabolic activation system has been developed for the $C3H/10T_{\frac{1}{2}}$ transformation assay (18). However, it is recommended that if exogenous metabolic activation is incorporated into the test protocol, that rodent liver S-9 with appropriate cofactors be employed (18). Due to the problems associated with the development of a suitable metabolic activation system for the mouse $C3H/10T_{\frac{1}{2}}$ cell transformation assay, this system has not yet been well validated as to its carcinogen predictive potential.

When evaluating the data from an in vitro cellular transformation assay, one must be aware that the events resulting in morphologic transformation may not be relevant to the oncogenic process in vivo. In theory, cellular transformation assay systems are highly relevant for determining the oncogenic potential of test chemicals. However, in terms of establishing a chemical's potential genetic risk, other genotoxicity tests with more well defined genetic endpoints could be more appropriate.

## F. In Vivo Assay Systems

In vivo genotoxicity assays utilize whole animals with the test chemical being administered via a variety of routes. Genetic endpoints similar to those described in the section on in vitro assays can be examined. The in vivo genotoxicity assays that are routinely employed in the evaluation of candidate chemicals are the *Drosophila melanegaster* Sex-linked recessive lethal assay, mouse micronucleus assay, rat bone marrow cytogenetic analysis, rat bone marrow SCE test, and the rodent dominant lethal assay.

*1. Drosophila Melanogaster Sex-linked Recessive Lethal Assay*

This genotoxicity test employing *Drosophila melanogaster* as the test organism includes a variety of genetic endpoints: intragenic changes, small deletions, and chromosomal aberrations that result in in lethality. It has been estimated that 500–800 genes on the *Drosophila* X chromosome are subject to lethal mutational events (156,157). Both direct-acting and mutagens requiring metabolic conversion can be detected in this *Drosophila* mutation assay.

The test chemical may be administered by a variety of routes that include, in the feed, by injection, or via inhalation. Administration of the test chemical in the food is the most routine method followed by body injection (157–159), although larval feeding has been employed. Procedures for carrying out the *Drosophila* sex-linked recessive lethal mutation assay have been published and reviewed (157–159).

The assay is initiated following a preliminary toxicity screen by treating a laboratory stock of male flies with the test chemical of interest. The treated males are mated to Muller-5 (base) virgin females. The $F_1$ females from the initial cross are individually mated with several sibling males. The $F_1$ females carry both a treated X chromosome derived from the treated males and the tester X chromosome with recognizable genetic markers. Two classes of $F_2$ males are expected, wild-type and mutant tester males. If wild-type males are observed, the treatment was nonmutagenic for that particular X chromosome. If no wild-type males were observed, but at least 8 mutant males are seen, a recessive lethal mutation has occurred in the treated X chromosome. Approximately 7000 $F_2$ cultures are required to determine if a treatment has induced a doubling of the spontaneous recessive lethal mutation frequency (44).

Advantages of the *Drosophila* sex-linked recessive lethal mutation assay are; intact cell metabolism of the test chemical, stable spontaneous mutant background, and a wholly objective means of scoring; the absence of a specific phenotype of male represents a mutagenic response. In addition, this assay is designed to detect germ cell mutational events giving it higher weight in light of the Environmental Protection Agency's recently issued updated *Mutagenicity Testing Guidelines* (22,30). Some of the disadvantages associated with this genotoxicity assay system are that many test chemicals that are routinely evaluated for mutagenic potential such as insecticides, are too toxic for this system. Also, although it appears that *Drosophila* performs many metabolic functions similar to mammals, it has been reported that the metabolism of several drugs and chemican carcinogens in *Drosophila* is different from that in rat liver (44). Finally, only a relatively few laboratories are proficient in the performance of this assay. Since the *Drosophila* sex-linked recessive lethal mutation assay is an in vivo germinal cell mutation test, guide-lines for performing it have been published by the OECD, EPA, and UKEMS (87–89,157).

### 2. *Mouse Micronucleus Test*

The micronucleus assay is an in vivo genotoxicity test that is routinely performed in the mouse for product safety evaluation. Al-though other systems are available (160), the mouse micronucleus test is the only well-validated micronucleus assay system. The mi-cronucleus test is an indirect determination of a test chemical's ability to induce chromosomal damage. Micronuclei are formed when chromosomal fragments or entire chromosomes do not migrate to the poles of daughter nuclei during anaphase of cell division (160,161). The chromosome fragment or whole chromosome will appear in bone marrow polychromatic erythrocytes (PCEs) as a micronucleus, that is, a small, round chromatin-containing body which stains like a normal cell nucleus (161, 162).

Schmid (163,164) initially developed the micronucleus protocol employing PCEs. However, continued evaluation of this protocol sug-gested that it was not optimal for the detection of micronuclei. Therefore, the revised protocol developed by Heddle and co-workers is currently employed for routine genotoxicity screening (165–167).

For normal genotoxicity evaluation, a minimum of two dosage levels should be employed with multiple sampling times for the bone marrow PCEs (166,168). Multiple sampling times are necessary to assure that the maximum number of induced micronuclei are detected. This is particularly important for test chemicals that are absorbed slowly and/or not metabolized rapidly (166,168,169). Salamone et al. (169) have demonstrated that sampling times of 24, 48, and 72 hr are necessary to cover the interval when recovery of micronuclei are at the maximum. For a minimum acceptable protocol, sample times of 24 and 48 hr are necessary after treatment with a single dosage level (166). Generally, 4–5 animals per sex are put on study per each experimental point and 1000–2000 PCEs are scored per animal (161,166,167).

Micronucleus studies can be scored by technical staff having less formal training then that required to evaluate the traditional bone marrow cytogenetic metaphase analysis, although considerable expertise is necessary to differentiate artifacts based upon shape, size, refractability, and color from micronuclei. Because the micro-nucleus assay is an in vivo mammalian study, it has considerable weight in the EPA's rank-ordering of genotoxicity assays (22,30).

The OECD, UKEMS, and the EPA have established guidelines for performing and evaluating the data from the mouse micronucleus test (87–89,161). In addition, the ASTM Committee on Genetic Toxicology has prepared draft guidelines for the mouse micronucleus assay.

## 3. Rat Bone Marrow Cytogenetic Analysis

The rodent bone marrow metaphase analysis is the one most routinely employed in vivo assay for assessing a test chemical's ability to induce chromosomal damage in the whole animal. The rat, mouse, and Chinese hamster have all been widely utilized for such studies (170,171). However, the rat has become the animal of choice due to its use in many other toxicological studies. The bone marrow is the most widely utilized tissue due to the well-established procedures that exist for studying the induction of chromosomal aberration in this tissue, its high mitotic index, and the fact that test articles that enter the peripheral circulation are readily available to the bone marrow (123,126,161,172). However, a negative response with a particular test chemical in a bone marrow metaphase analysis does not preclude the possibility that the test chemical could induce a positive effect in another tissue of the animal.

Normally, a bone marrow metaphase analysis study is initiated with three dose levels over a one log interval (11,89,161). Dose levels should be selected based upon the ability of the chemical to influence cell proliferation kinetics as a measure of mitotic delay. A pilot study using subcutaneously incorporated paraffin-coated BrdUrd pellets which allows for scoring of sister chromatids can be utilized to gain an indication of cell proliferation kinetics in the bone marrow. Average proliferation time (APT) is calculated from the shift in metaphase ratios. The high dose used in the metaphase analysis study should give approximately 80% or greater increase in APT with sufficient scorable metaphases. The preferred routes of administration of the test chemical are by intraperitoneal injection or orally. Normally, the test chemical is administered as a single dose at each level to be evaluated. However, subchronic or chronic dosing regimens can also be established (11,89,161). When single dose studies are performed, multiple sample times are required to assure that genotoxic effects on different stages of the cell cycle are detected and to avoid missing chromosome aberrations due to mitotic inhibition (126,161,172). Recommended sampling times are 6–12 hr, and 48 hr posttreatment. Methods for the harvesting of bone marrow cells, staining, and the evaluation of the preparation for chromosome aberrations have been described (11,170,173,174).

Results of the rat bone marrow cytogenetic study can be expressed as frequency of aberrations per cell and/or percent aberrant cells. An appropriate statistical analysis such as the two-tailed t-test (11) should be applied to the data.

Guidelines have been published by OECD, UKEMS, and the EPA establishing criteria for carrying out and evaluating data generated by the rat bone marrow cytogenetic assay (87–89,161). Currently ASTM is preparing a guide for minimal acceptable criteria.

### 4. In Vivo Sister Chromatid Exchange Analysis

As for other in vivo genotoxicity assays, the major advantage of the in vivo sister chromatid exchange test is that it brings into play the entire metabolic capabilities of the whole animal in the activation and detoxification of the test chemical. Though a variety of common laboratory rodents such as mice, hamsters, and rats have been employed for in vivo SCE studies; the mouse is the most widely used species (135,142). Several tissues including bone marrow, spermatogonia, spleen, thymus, and regenerating liver have served as the source of cells for SCE analysis following in vivo administration of the test chemical (135,142). The bone marrow is the tissue of choice for performing routine SCE analysis due to its high mitotic index, the large data base that exists for this tissue, and the well-established methods that are available for preparation of bone marrow cells for staining (135,142,173). However, the regenerating liver may prove to be a more sensitive indicator of SCE-inducing ability relative to the bone marrow, presumably due to the liver's enhanced metabolic capabilities (175,178).

Several routes of administration of the test chemical, including inhalation, oral gavage, and intravenous or intraperitoneal (i.p.), injection have been utilized for in vivo SCE assays (136,142). For routine genotoxicity screening purposes, oral gavage or intraperitoneal injection are the recommended routes of administration. However, the decision on which route of administration is most appropriate can be based upon the projected means of human exposure. Normally, a minimum of three dosage levels of the test chemical over a 100-fold concentration range are required for a study (135,142). The highest dosage level should induce significant signs of animal morbidity and/or target cell toxicity (135,142). Dosage selection follows similar methodology employed in the metaphase analysis; however, the high dose should give 50% or greater increase in APT with sufficient $M_2$ metaphases for analysis. It is recommended that at least five (5) animals of each sex constitute a treatment group (89).

In order to achieve incorporation of BrdUrd into the sister chromatids in vivo, several methods have been developed to overcome the rapid debromination that occurs in vivo (136,138). Continuous intravenous infusion of BrdUrd or implantation of BrdUrd in tablet form during the treatment period have overcome this problem (135,136, 138,142). For the last 2 hr of treatment, colchicine (colcemid) must be administered either by intravenous infusion or i.p. injection to arrest cells in metaphase. Bone marrow cells are harvested and processed for staining following established procedures (142,173). Chromosomes are routinely stained and differentiated for sister chromatid exchanges by the fluorescent plus Giemsa method developed by Perry and Thomson (142) and described in Section IV.D.2. A minimum of 25 cells should be scored per animal (135,142).

In evaluating the results of an in vivo SCE study, the 2-tailed t-test is recommended for establishing significance (135). Particular attention should also be paid to the occurrence of a dose-related increase in the frequency of SCEs/cell.

The EPA has established test guidelines for performing and evaluating the data from in vivo SCE assays (88,89).

### 5. The Rodent Dominant Lethal Assay

The advantage of the rodent dominant lethal assay over other genotoxicity assays that are routinely employed to assess a test chemical's potential genetic effect to humans is that it is an in vivo mammalian screen for genetic damage induced in the germ cells. A dominant lethal mutation occurs in the germ cells and does not inhibit the function of the gamete, but results in the death of the fertilized egg or developing embryo. It is believed that dominant lethal mutations occur due to chromosome damage (179). Although, strictly speaking the rodent dominant lethal test is not a measurement of heritable genetic damage, the relevance of making extrapolations concerning transmissible mutations is enhanced by the finding that dominant lethal mutations and heritable translocations occur in parallel (180,181).

Rats and mice are the species of choice for performing dominant lethal studies (89,182). Rats offer the advantage of allowing reliable scoring of corpora leutea as a measure of preimplantation loss. For routine screening purposes, the male animal is selected for treatment in order to reduce the number of animals that must be dosed and to reduce nongenetic effects upon ovulation, fertilization, implantation, and embryonic development in the female (182,183). Normally, the test chemical is administered as a single dose or by a subacute dosing scheme over a 5–7 day period (182,183). To achieve maximum absorption of the test chemical, intraperitoneal injection is recommended as the route of administration. However, if the data from the study is to be utilized in risk assessment for determining a potential human hazard, the route of human exposure may be employed for treatment (182,183).

For an initial dominant lethal study, a minimum of three dosage levels is customary with the top level being the maximum tolerated dose which can be half the $LD_{50}$ or a dosage level that has a small effect upon fertility (182,183). The doses should range over at least a single log interval.

Following treatment, the males are mated to untreated virgin females. Normally, if mice are employed in the dominant lethal study, the males are mated at 7-day intervals for 8 weeks, while a period of 10 weeks is required if rats are utilized for the study (182,183). This prolonged mating schedule is required to assure that all stages of sperm maturation are sampled (182,183). An alternative treatment is to continually treat the male animals over an 8–10 week period followed by two weeks of mating (184). This method offers significant cost advantages over the 8–10 week mating scheme and, therefore, is often used for the dominant lethal study (182).

To accumulate a sufficient amount of data for statistical evaluation, 30–50 pregnant females are required (89). Generally, if CD-1 mice are used for the study, approximately 50 pregnant females per treatment group per week will allow the detection of a doubling over the spontaneous dominant lethal mutant frequency (5%) at the 95% confidence limit (182). Protocols are designed in which 25 or fewer males per experimental group are mated to 2–3 females per male animal (182,183).

At 15–16 days following introduction of the males to the females, the females should be sacrificed and the uterus evaluated for live fetuses, early and late deaths. Preimplantation losses evaluated only be if corpora lutea determinations were made. Postimplantation loss which is an expression of the dominant lethal effect is calculated by determining the ratio of dead to total implants from the various treatment groups compared to the ratio of dead to total implants from the vehicle control group. A variety of statistical methods have been presented for the evaluation of dominant lethal data (182,183).

A positive result in the rodent dominant lethal assay will have a high level of significance in terms of risk assessment in the United States since it is an in vivo mammal germ cell mutation test and is, therefore, given a high ranking in the recent genotoxicity evaluation scheme proposed by the EPA (22,30).

Guidelines for the rodent dominant lethal assay have been prepared by the EPA, the OECD, and the UKEMS (87–89,182). ASTM is currently also preparing guidelines.

## G. Summary

The genotoxicity assays presented in this section represent those assay systems that were at one time, or are now, routinely employed by government and industry in product safety evaluation. As test systems are validated and product safety regulations are established, particular genotoxicity tests may fall in and out of favor. In the final section (Sect. V), we will discuss testing strategies and the role that the computer can play in genotoxicity test selection and data evaluation.

## V. MUTAGEN TESTING STRATEGIES

### A. Development of a Practical Approach to Mutagen Screening

A variety of schemes for evaluating the genotoxic/carcinogenic potential of a test chemical have been proposed/promoted. Most have incorporated short-term tests representing the three major endpoints of genotoxic damage, namely, gene point mutations, chromosomal aberrations, and DNA damage/DNA repair. Different genotoxicity evaluation strategies have normally been composed of a battery of assays, a tiered testing structure, and/or a decision point scheme. The development of these various genotoxicity testing strategies has been reviewed (11,185).

One approach taken in the evaluation of the genotoxicity of a test chemical is to employ a battery of short-term assays. Usually, a battery consists of test systems representing the major endpoints of genotoxicity and utilizes both in vitro and in vivo models. A representative genotoxicity testing battery is presented in Table 14. Results are normally evaluated by the "weight of evidence" approach with all tests having the same weight. However, no guidelines specify how many positive responses from the battery of tests constitute a positive result for the test chemical. Evaluation of data from such a battery of short-term genotoxicity tests as those listed in Table 14 could result in confusion, making it more difficult to perform risk assessment on the chemical of interest.

Another, somewhat more structured means for evaluating the genotoxic potential of test chemicals is the application of a tiered/ decision point approach. This means of evaluating the genotoxic potential of a test chemical has been taken by Weisburger and Williams (15,185). In their scheme, the structure of the test compound is first considered to determine if it is similar in structure to known mutagens and/or carcinogens. Once this analysis has been applied, the test chemical is moved into an in vitro genotoxicity testing program. The in vitro genotoxicity tests recommended by Weisburger and Williams (15,185) are shown in Table 15. Their in vitro, short-term testing battery consists of the Ames/*Salmonella* mutation assay, a mammalian cell gene point mutation assay, the primary hepatocyte DNA/repair test, an evaluation of SCE-inducing ability and an in vitro cellular transformation assay. In terms of establishing strict genetic risk potential, the in vitro transformation assay would not be necessary. If all in vitro tests yielded negative results, it is likely that the test chemical represents little or no health risk. If this is the case, priority for further testing depends upon the test chemical's structure and potential human exposure (15,185). If the results from one or more of the in vitro genotoxicity assays is positive, the test chemical is moved to the next testing tier. In the Weisburger and Williams scheme, tier two consists of four in vivo bioassays for tumorigenesis (15,185). If one is strictly interested in the ability of the test chemical to induce heritable genetic changes, the tier two tests of Weisburger and Williams would require substitution with one or more of the in vivo assays designed to detect heritable mutagenic events. Assays that could be employed for this purpose are the *Drosophila* sex-linked

Table 14 Proposed Weight of Evidence Genotoxicity Evaluation Battery

| Gene mutation | Chromosome damage | DNA damage | In vitro transformation |
|---|---|---|---|
| Ames/*Salmonella* mutation assay | In vitro cytogenetic analysis CHO cells Human lymphocytes | UDS in vitro human fibroblasts Primary hepatocytes | Primary cells in culture Syrian hamster Embryo cells |
| Mammalian cell mutation assay CHO HGPRT, V79 HGPRT Mouse lymphoma cell TK | In vivo cytogenetic analysis Rat bone marrow | SCE induction in vitro CHO cells or human lymphocytes | Established cell lines mouse embryo fibroblast 10T$\frac{1}{2}$ Balb/c 3T3 |
| In vivo mutation *Drosophila* sex-linked recessive lethal | | | |

Table 15  Decision Point/Tier In Vitro Genotoxicity Testing Battery[a]

| Bacterial mutation | Mammalian cell mutation | DNA repair in vitro | Chromosome evaluation | In vitro transformation |
|---|---|---|---|---|
| Ames/*Salmonella* Histidine Reversion Mutation Assay | Chinese hamster ovary HGPRT | Unscheduled DNA synthesis in primary hepatocytes | Detection of SCEs in vitro CHO cells or human lymphocytes | Primary cells Syrian hamster embryo fibroblasts |
| | Chinese hamster V79 HGPRT | | | Established cell lines |
| | Mouse lymphoma cell TK | | | Mouse embryo Fibroblast 10T$\frac{1}{2}$ BHK fibroblasts |

[a] Adapted from Ref. 15.

recessive lethal test, rodent dominant lethal assay, mouse specific locus test, or the mouse heritable translocation test (21,44). If the oncogenic potential of the test chemical is to be assessed, one or more of the "limited" in vivo bioassays proposed by Weisburger and Williams in their testing scheme could be employed. The limited in vivo bioassays are; pulmonary tumor induction in mice, skin tumor induction in mice, breast cancer in female rats and altered foci induction in rodent liver (15,185). Bull and Pereira have also recommended that these limited in vivo bioassays be included in the second tier of a carcinogen evaluation program (196). A detailed description of these four limited in vivo tumorigenesis bioassays can be found in the *Handbook of Carcinogen Testing* edited by Milman and Weisburger (187).

For application of the tiered/decision point approach to test chemical evaluation, Weisburger and Williams consider that any chemical giving a positive result in one of the in vitro genotoxicity assays and a positive result in one of the limited in vivo bioassays has carcinogenic potential. Two positive results in limited bioassay tests is unequivocal evidence of carcinogenic activity (15,185). However, the limited in vivo bioassays for tumorigenicity are not highly validated. In addition, very few laboratories are capable of performing such assays. Therefore, in practical terms, these assays would not be suitable for routine mutagen screening programs.

The U.S. National Research Council (NRC) has published recommendations for assessing the heritable mutagenic potential of test chemicals (44). The NCR-proposed genotoxicity screening scheme is a two tiered system and is shown in Table 16. The first tier is composed of the Ames/*Salmonella* mutation assay, a mammalian cell gene point mutation assay and a mammalian cell chromosome aberration test (44,188). If the test chemical is negative in all three tier I level genotoxicity assays, it is presumed a nonmutagen. If two of the in vitro tests yield positive results, the test chemical is considered to be a mammalian mutagen. A single positive result in tier I testing results in the chemical being advanced to the tier II level which is a *Drosophila* sex-linked recessive lethal assay (44, 188). A problem with the NCR mutagen assessment program is a lack of an assay for DNA damage/DNA repair at the tier I level. In addition, the NCR tier I genotoxicity assays all rely on exogenous S-9 metabolic activation preparations for the metabolism of the test chemical. As pointed out in Section III, conversion of the test chemical to active metabolites by subcellular liver S-9 preparations can result in artifactual positive results. If a positive result occurs in the tier I level testing scheme only in the presence of exogenous metabolic activation preparation, we recommend that a rodent primary hepatocyte DNA/repair study be included in the initial evaluation of mutagenic potential. Also, the NCR genotoxicity screening program

**Table 16** National Research Council Recommended Genotoxicity Testing Scheme[a]

| | Bacterial mutation | Mammalian cell gene mutation | Mammalian cell cytogenetics |
|---|---|---|---|
| Tier I | Ames/*Salmonella* Histidine independence | Chinese hamster ovary or V79 cell HGPRT or mouse lymphoma cell TK | In vitro Chinese hamster ovary or V79 cell or human lymphocytes |
| Tier II | *Drosophila* sex-linked recessive lethal assay for gene mutations | | |

[a]Adapted from Ref. 44.

offers no alternative to the *Drosophila* sex-linked recessive lethal assay in tier II. For practical mutagen testing programs, more flexibility is required at the tier II level in order to select the proper genotoxicity assays which will yield the necessary information to make risk estimation and production decisions.

The recent EPA-proposed guidelines for heritable mutation risk assessment give a high weighting to in vivo mammalian assays (21, 22,30) and therefore such studies should be included in the tier II level. Recently, Ashby (79) has proposed a two-tiered mutagen screening scheme which is presented in Table 17. The first tier is composed of the Ames/*Salmonella* mutation assay, a mammalian cell chromosome aberration test and a test for DNA damage, either an in vitro SCE assay or a primary hepatocyte DNA/repair study. An in vitro chromosome aberration test is included in tier one as a complementary study to the Ames assay based on the recommendation of the International Program for Chemical Safety (79,189). An in vitro SCE study or a primary hepatocyte DNA/repair test may be employed to reduce the false positive rate (79). Whole cell metabolic activation performed by primary hepatocytes will reduce false positive responses due to S-9 fraction activation artifacts while in vitro SCE study results may be used to screen out false positive results obtained with the Ames/*Salmonella* mutation assay since SCE studies are performed in mammalian cells in culture. In an SCE study, the test article must interact with the complex mammalian cell genome to induce a positive result. A test compound yielding negative results in the three assays of the in vitro tier is considered to be nonmutagenic and testing is terminated (79).

Table 17  In Vitro and In Vivo Short-Term Genotoxicity Battery[a]

|  | Gene mutation | Chromosome aberration | DNA damage |
|---|---|---|---|
| In vitro tier | Ames/*Salmonella* mutation assay | Chinese hamster ovary or V79 cells | Sister chromatid exchange or UDS in primary hepatocytes |
| In vivo tier |  | Mouse micronucleus assay | In vivo/in vitro hepatocyte UDS assay |

[a]Adapted from Ref. 79.

**Table 18** Recommended Genotoxicity Screening Program

|  | Gene point mutation | Chromosome aberration | DNA damage |
|---|---|---|---|
| Tier I | Ames/*Salmonella* mutation assay or mammalian cells in culture, i.e., CHO/ HGPRT or mouse lymphoma TK⁻ | Chinese hamster ovary cells, V79 cells or human lymphocytes, or mouse micronucleus test | Primary hepato- cyte DNA/ repair |
| Tier II | *Drosophila* sex- linked recessive lethal assay | Mouse micronu- cleus test, bone marrow meta- phase analysis or rodent dominated lethal | In vivo/in vitro hepatocyte DNA/repair or sperm DNA/ repair |

A confirmed positive response in any of the three in vitro genotoxicity tests results in the test chemical being evaluated in the two
in vivo tier assays, the mouse micronucleus test and the in vivo/
in vitro hepatocyte DNA/repair assay (79,116). These two organo-
tropically independent in vivo genotoxicity assays are considered to
be complementary by Ashby (79). A positive result in either of the
two in vivo assays suggests that the test chemical is a potential
mammalian mutagen and/or a carcinogen. At this point, financial
considerations, potential use, and risk assessment come into play in
determining if additional mutation screening is necessary. To determine if there is a definite risk of heritable mutation associated with
the chemical of interest, the mammalian germ cell mutation assays
recommended by Ashby and the EPA's proposed mutation testing
guidelines must be considered (21,22,30,32,79). Results from one
or more of the following assays; sperm DNA/repair, germ cell cytogenetics, *Drosophila* sex-linked recessive lethal, and/or a rodent
dominant lethal study (21,22,32,44,79) would provide information for
making a final decision.

For routine mutagen assessment, we recommend a genotoxicity
screening program similar to that of Ashby. Our testing screen is
composed of a two-tiered structure and is shown in Table 18. Tier
one is composed of three in vitro mutation tests representing the
three major endpoints of genotoxicity. Three genotoxicity assays

were selected to make up tier one based on the recommendations made by Heinze and Poulsen and Rosenkranz and co-workers (190, 201,203) in their studies on the optimal design of mutation screening batteries and by Ashby (79).

Our tier I level recommends performing one of two gene point mutation assays, the Ames/*Salmonella* mutation assay or a mammalian cell mutation test. For routine, rapid, economical screening of many test chemicals the Ames mutation assay is still the genotoxicity test of choice. In addition, depending upon where the test chemical will be manufactured, sold, and its usage, many countries require that the Ames mutation assay data be submitted for regulatory purposes (3,20,26). However, a positive result in the Ames/*Salmonella* mutation test should not be sufficient to "kill" a promising chemical with much potential benefit (20,80). A positive Ames test should trigger an in vitro mammalian point mutation assay for a "weight of evidence" approach to potential genotoxicity or carcinogenicity determination.

If the Ames/*Salmonella* mutation assay is to be used for screening in the research and development phase of chemical evaluation, we recommend that the protocol developed by the National Toxicology Program (NTP) be utilized. The NTP screening program utilizes the preincubation modification of the standard Ames/*Salmonella* mutation assay and both Aroclor 1254-induced hamster and rat liver S-9 metabolic activation preparations (191,192). These modifications increase the sensitivity of the Ames mutation assay, thereby reducing the number of false negative results that can occur. Elimination of false negative results should be a primary objective of an initial genotoxicity screening program.

When genotoxicity data is to be used to make risk assessments for potential heritable mutagenic damage in accordance with the EPA's proposed guidelines (22,30) we recommend that an in vitro mammalian cell mutation assay support the Ames/*Salmonella* mutation test. Results from a mammalian cell mutation test is given considerably more weight in terms of risk assessment than results from the Ames/*Salmonella* mutation assay (21). In addition, if false positive results are generated by the Ames mutation assay, a mammalian cell mutation test plus one or more of the more costly and time-consuming tier II in vivo genotoxicity screening assays would be required to "refute" the false positive results of the Ames assay.

An in vitro chromosome aberration assay is included in our tier I level screen since it is considered to be complementary to the gene point mutation study (79,189). However, we can equally support the inclusion of the micronucleus test in tier I because of our experience with "false" positives with the in vitro chromosome aberration assay. Finally, we recommend that a rodent primary hepatocyte DNA/repair test be performed at the tier I level. This genotoxicity assay system has a well defined endpoint closely related to genetic damage and utilizes whole cells for metabolism of the test chemical. Therefore, as pointed out in Section III, the primary hepatocyte DNA/repair assay is less prone to false positive results induced by artifactual enhancement of activation pathways encountered when induced, subcellular liver S-9 preparations are employed for the metabolism of test chemicals.

Our tier II level in vivo mutation screening scheme is somewhat more flexible than the one proposed by Ashby (79). However, it is still primarily, based on routine assays. The genotoxicity tests listed in our tier II level would only be employed if a reproducible positive response is observed in one or more of the tier I level screening assays. The test or tests chosen from the tier II level will be dependent upon which assay(s) at the tier I level gave positive results. If the test chemical induced an increase in gene mutations, the *Drosophila* sex-linked recessive lethal assay is recommended. However, another in vivo test that should be considered in all cases is the mouse micronucleus test due to the well documented concurrance of rodent bone marrow cytogenetic studies with the results of mammalian germ cell mutation assays (21,79,193).

A positive result in the in vitro chromosome aberration test requires confirmation in one of the in vivo cytogenetic studies of tier II. If one is concerned with making risk estimations for heritable genetic damage, either the *Drosophila* sex-linked recessive lethal or a rodent dominant lethal study should also be considered.

The in vivo/in vitro hepatocyte DNA/repair assay should be used to confirm a positive finding in the tier I in vitro, primary hepatocyte DNA/repair study. A positive result in both of these assays is highly suggestive of the test chemical's ability to act as a hepatocarcinogen. In order to make risk assessments for the test chemical's ability to induce germ cell mutational damage after a positive DNA/repair result is observed, an additional test from tier II is recommended. The specific test to be performed could be selected by risk vs. benefit analysis for the chemical of interest.

For data interpretation, a positive result in one or more of the tier I level in vitro assays that is confirmed by one of the tier II level in vivo tests suggest that the test chemical may be a mammalian germ cell mutagen and is highly likely to be a carcinogen as well (79,194). Confirmation of a positive result in vitro by two of the in vivo genotoxicity assays is almost certain evidence that the test chemical is a mammalian carcinogen. Two positive in vivo results also provide sufficient evidence that the test chemical is a mammalian germ cell mutagen. However, for risk-benefit analysis, an additional in vivo study may be necessary, such as a rodent dominant lethal test or a sperm DNA/repair assay.

Our recommended genotoxicity screening program will allow a rapid, economical evaluation of a test chemical's ability to induce genetic damage. It also provides a means for meeting regulatory requirements at the national and international level. When our screening program is used in consultation with a well trained genetic toxicologist, the proper assays can be selected which will allow the resulting data to be utilized in risk-assessment analysis.

## B. Computer–Assisted Genotoxicity Analysis

The performance of individual genotoxicity tests to predict the carcinogenicity of test chemicals can be expressed by the test's sensitivity (ability to detect carcinogens as positive responses), specificity (ability to yield negative results with noncarcinogens), and accuracy or selectivity (number of correct results observed/number of chemicals tested) (195). Data bases of the National Cancer Institute, National Toxicology Program, Environment Protection Agency, International Agency for Research on Cancer, and the International Program for the Evaluation of Short-Term Tests for Carcinogenicity have been utilized in the evaluation of the accuracy of genotoxicity assays (196–199). However, a major problem that currently exists with the evaluation of the performance of genotoxicity assays in this manner is that the preponderance of the data is only for documented animal carcinogens (196,197,199). Of the approximately 550 chemicals that have been adequately tested in rodent carcinogen bioassays, 465 or 85% are carcinogens (196,199). Therefore, the overall predictive accuracy of a given short-term genotoxicity assay is primarily based upon its sensitivity. Although a list of 70 chemicals that have proven to be animal noncarcinogens based upon the results of rodent carcinogenicity bioassays has been published (197), much additional testing would be necessary to complete validation studies on selected genotoxicity tests. A means of overcoming this problem in the evaluation of the accuracy of genotoxicity tests is the application of cluster analysis. Several investigators have utilized cluster analysis to estimate the predictive accuracy of short-term genotoxicity tests and establish optimal screening batteries (198,200–203). Essentially, cluster analysis classifies or groups initially unclassified data. The object or individual (genotoxicity test) to be classified is described by a set of variables. Cluster analysis groups the objects (tests) into classes such that the tests within a given class are similar in respect to the majority of variables. In terms of short-term genotoxicity assays, cluster analysis provides a means for estimating the accuracy of an individual test when there is little or no information available for direct calculation. Cluster analysis also provides for determining the dependence or independence of a pair or groups of assays. The selection of independent tests is essential in the construction of a genotoxicity screening battery (190,201,202).

Benigni and Giuliani have applied the technique of cluster analysis to the data generated by the International Program for the Evaluation of Short-Term Tests for Carcinogenicity on the 42 test chemicals in the study (198). The results from 20 individual genotoxicity assay systems were initially evaluated. Benigni and Giuliani found that the assays fell into three clusters with the genotoxicity tests being grouped together irrespective of their phylogenetic origin or mutational endpoint detected. Cluster three consisted of the in vivo tests: *Drosophila melanogaster* sex-linked recessive lethal assay, mouse micronucleus test, SCE induction in mouse bone marrow, and the mouse sperm morphology assay. As might be expected, the in vivo test cluster was the least sensitive in terms of correctly identifying carcinogens. However, it had the highest degree of specificity or lowest false positive rate.

Applying cluster analysis to establish an assay's accuracy along with the a priori probability that a test chemical is a carcinogen, the predictive indices of genotoxicity assays can be computed using Bayes' formula (201,203). That a priori probability that the test chemical is a carcinogen may be arrived at based upon an expert genetic toxicologist's estimation or with the aid of information provided by a structure to activity analysis such as that of the computer-automated structure-evaluation (CASE) program developed by Klopman and co-workers (196,204,205). The CASE system is self-learning and can be used to evaluate the activities of untested chemicals. The system has the ability to determine if chemical fragments responsible for activity or inactivity in one chemical system are identical or not with the fragments determining activity in another system. In terms of genotoxicity data and estimating potential carcinogenicity risk, the CASE system will allow one to determine if genotoxicity and induction of cancer in animals is due to similar chemical structures (196). Also, the CASE program can aid in the construction of genotoxicity testing batteries by including assays that respond to different structural moieties or by utilizing only those genotoxicity tests that respond to structural determinants that are also responsible for the induction of cancer in rodent bioassays (196).

In constructing a genotoxicity screening program based on information provided by computer analysis such as the CASE program, in combination with Bayes' formula it is essential that the assays be statistically independent (190,201,203). In addition, the initial genotoxicity screening battery should be composed of an odd number of assays in order to establish a "weight of evidence" criteria for evaluating the data. After applying Bayes' formula to data generated by the Environmental Protection Agency's Gene-Tox data base, Rosenkranz and co-workers (201,203) have recommended that initial screening be conducted with three genotoxicity assays from different cluster groups. The carcinogenicity predictive potential of a screening battery composed of three independent genotoxicity tests was determined to be approximately 88% following evaluation with Bayes' formula (201).

The carcinogenicity prediction and battery selection (CPBS) program developed by Rosenkranz and co-workers (201,203,206) may not only be used to construct specific genotoxicity screening batteries, but may also be employed to evaluate data from a variety of short-term tests. Application of the CPBS program to conflicting data generated from a number of genotoxicity tests performed due to regulatory requirements will prove to be useful in making risk assessments. As an example, the pesticide Kathon was recently evaluated in 6 genotoxicity studies; Ames/*Salmonella* mutation assay, L5178Y mouse lymphoma cell mutation assay, primary hepatocyte DNA/repair test, C3H mouse fibroblast morphologic transformation assay, *Drosophila melangaster* sex-linked recessive lethal assay, and a bone marrow cytogenetics test. Positive results were obtained with the Ames/*Salmonella* mutation assay and mouse lymphoma cell mutation assay, the other tests yielded negative results (196). Applying the CPBS program, the probability that Kathon is a noncarcinogen was 96% (196). Another example of the application of the CPBS program is evaluation of the genotoxicity data for dopamine. Dopamine was evaluated in the following 6 short-term studies; Ames/*Salmonella* mutation assay, L5178Y mouse lymphoma cell mutation assay, DNA strand breakage in human fibroblast, SCE in human lymphocytes, *Drosophila melanogaster* sex-linked recessive lethal test, and a mouse micronucleus test (207). Results were positive for the in vitro, DNA strand breakage test and the mouse lymphoma cell mutation assay. The results for the other 4 studies were negative. Based on CPBS analysis the probability that dopamine is a noncarcinogen was 98.5% (203).

The CASE/CPBS program may provide methodology for developing efficient and accurate genotoxicity screening batteries and evaluating the data generated from mutagen screening programs. When data from the National Toxicology Program's rodent cancer bioassay and genetic toxicology validation studies are available for study, the validation of the CASE/CPBS program can be continued. In addition, independent evaluation of the CASE/CPBS program for assessment of genotoxicity data and risk estimation can be implemented. There are several caveats that must be considered when employing the CASE/CPBS system, especially when the data is to be used for risk assessment. Due to the lack of genotoxicity data for many well documented noncarcinogens, the specificity of many short-term genotoxicity tests must be estimated by cluster analysis. Also, the use of Bayes' formula requires that an a priori probability of the test chemical's carcinogenicity be established by either expert judgment or computer estimation techniques. If one wishes to use the worst case possibility, the a priori probability can be set to 0.50 (191, 193). However, the use of computer-assisted techniques, such as the CASE/CPBS program in the development of genotoxicity testing screens and evaluation of the data appears to have the potential to offer much benefit in chemical safety evaluation.

## ACKNOWLEDGMENT

The authors wish to express their appreciation to Mrs. Betty Good, Miss Mary Alice Naughton, and Mrs. Ann Swartwood for the preparation of the manuscript.

## REFERENCES

1. Fishbein, L. (1980). Potential industrial carcinogenic and mutagenic alkylating agents. In *Safe Handling of Chemical Carcinogens, Mutagens, Teratogens and Highly Toxic Substances*. Edited by D. B. Walters. Ann Arbor, Ann Arbor Science, p. 329.

2. Hollstein, M., McCann, J., Angelosanto, F. A., and Nichols, W. W. (1979). Short-term tests for carcinogens and mutagens, *Mutat. Res. 65*:133.

3. International Commission for Protection Against Environmental Mutagens and Carcinogens. (1983). Regulatory approaches to the control of environmental mutagens and carcinogens, *Mutat. Res. 114*:179.

4. Barfknecht, T. R., and Naismith, R. W. (1984). Methodology for evaluating the genotoxicity of hazardous environmental samples. *Haz. Waste 1*:93.

5. Ames, B. N. (1979). Identifying environmental chemicals causing mutations and cancer. *Science 204*:587.

6. Benditt, E. P. (1977). The orgins of otherosclerosis. *Sci. Am. 235*:74.

7. Burnet, F. M. (1974). *Intrinsic Mutagenesis: A Genetic Approach to Aging*. Lancaster, England, Medical and Technical Publishing.

8. Brash, D. E., and Hart, R. W. (1978). DNA damage and repair in vivo. *J. Environ. Path. Tox. 2*:79.

9. Manson, J. M. (1981). Developmental toxicity of alkylating agents: mechanism of action. *The Biomedical Basis of Chemical Teratogenesis*. Edited by M. R. Juchau. New York, Elsevier/North Holland Press, p. 95.

10. McKusick, V. A. (1978). *Mendelian Inheritance in Man: Catalogs of Autosomal Dominant, Autosomal Recessive and X-linked*

*Phenotypes*, 5th ed. Baltimore, The John Hopkins University Press.

11. Brusick, D. (1982). Genetic toxicology. *Principles and Methods of Toxicology.* Edited by A. W. Hayes. New York, Raven Press, p. 223.

12. Brusick, D. J. (1979). Alterations of germ cells leading to mutagenesis and their detection. *Environ. Health Perspect.* *24*:105.

13. Miller, E. C., and Miller, J. A. (1971). The mutagenicity of chemicals. In *Chemical Mutagens: Prinicples and Methods for their Detection.* Edited by A. Hollaender. New York, Plenum Press, p. 83.

14. Brusick, D. J. (1978). The role of short-term testing in carcinogen detection. *Chemosphere 5*:403.

15. Weisburger, J. H., and Williams, G. M. (1981). Carcinogen testing: Current problems and new approaches. *Science* *214*:401.

16. Brookes, P. (1981). Cricital assessment of the value of in vitro cell transformation for predicting in vivo carcinogenicity of chemicals. *Mutat. Res. 86*:233.

17. Meyer, A. L. (1983). In vitro transformation assays for chemical carcinogens, *Mutat. Res. 115*:323.

18. Meyer, A. McGregor, D., and Styles, J. (1984). In vitro cell transformation assays. *Report of the UKEMS Sub-Committee on Guidelines for Mutagenicity Testing,* Part II. Edited by B. J. Dean. Swansea, United Kingdom Environmental Mutagen Society, p. 123.

19. Salsburg, D. (1983). The lifetime feeding study in mice and rats—an examination of its validity as a bioassay for human carcinogens. *Fund. Appl. Toxicol. 3*:63.

20. Clive, D. (1985). Mutagenicity in drug development: interpretation and significance of test results. *Reg. Toxicol. Pharmacol. 5*:79.

21. Russell, L. B., Aaron, C. S., de Serres, F., Generoso, W. M., Kannan, K. L., Shelby, M., Springer, J., and Voytek, P. (1984). Evaluation of mutagenicity assays for purpose of genetic risk assessment. *Mutat. Res. 134*:143.

22. Anon, A. (1984). Proposed guidelines for mutagenicity risk assessment. *Fed. Reg. 49*:46314.

23. Council on Environmental Quality (1980). Environmental quality. *The Eleventh Annual Report of the Council on Environmental Quality.* Washington, D. C., p. 192.

24. OSHA (1980). Identification, classification and regulation of potential occupational carcinogens. *Fed. Reg. 45*:5001.

25. Health Effects Research Laboratory (1983). *Hazardous Waste Health Effects Resarch Program.* Research Triangle Park, U.S. Environmental Protection Agency.

26. Loprieno, N. (1983). Control of commercial chemicals: The sixth amendment to the directive on dangerous chemical substances (79/831/EEC) adopted by the council of the European communities. *Chemical Mutagens: Principles and Methods for their Detection*, Vol. 8. Edited by F. J. de Serres. New York, Plenum Press, p. 343.

27. *Federal Register* (1980) 45:5001.

28. *Federal Register* (1981) 46:7402.

29. National Academy of Sciences (1977). Principles and Procedures for Evaluating the Toxicity of Household Substances, *Prepared for the Consumer Product Safety Commission by the Committee for the Review of NAS, Publication 1138*. Washington, D.C., National Academy of Sciences, p. 86.

30. Sobels, F. H. (1985). Personal comments on "Environmental Protection Agency" proposed guidelines for mutagenicity risk assessment. *Mutat. Res. 147*:211.

31. Dellarco, V. L., Mavournin, K. H., and Tice, R. R. (1985). Aneuploidy and health risk assessment: current status and future directions. *Environ. Mutagen. 7*:263.

32. Ashby, J. (1985). Gonadal genotoxicity assays as practical surrogates for germ-cell mutagenicity assays. *Environ. Mutagen. 7*:263.

33. Mattes, M. A. (1977). *Permarket Testing of Industrial Products: A Means of Controlling Unrecognized Environmental Hazards*. Morges, Switzerland, International Union for Conservation of Nature and Natural Resources.

34. Wilson, E. R. (1981). Outline and criteria for evaluating the safety of new chemicals. *Reg. Toxicol. Pharmacol. 1*:19.

35. Culbert, M. F. (1981). Guidelines for testing of chemicals for mutagenicity. *Health Trends 13*:76.

36. Committee on Mutagenicity of Chemicals in Food Consumer Products and the Environment (1981). *Guidelines for the testing of chemicals for Mutagenicity*. London, Department of Health and Social Security, HMSO.

37. *Intern. Environ. Reporter*. (1982). 5:21.

38. Vettorazzi, G. (ed.). (1980). *Handbook of International Food Regulatory Toxicology*, Vol. I Evaluations. New York, Spectrum Publications.

39. Vettorazzi, G. (ed.). (1981). *Handbook of International Food Regulatory Toxicology*, Vol. II *Profiles*. New York, Spectrum Publications.

40. *Legal and Practical Requirements for the Registration of Drugs (Medicinal Products) for Human Use*. (1980). International Federation of Pharmaceutical Manufacturers Associations, Zurich.

41. *Evaluation and Testing of Drugs for Mutagenicity: Principles and Problems*. (1971). WHO Technical Report Series, No. 482.

42. Draper, M. H. and Griffins, J. P. (1980). Draft guidelines on mutagenicity testing of new drugs issued by the CPMP. A four test screen. *Archs Toxicol. 46*:9.

43. *International Drug Regulatory Monitor.* (1981). *100*:1.

44. National Research Council. (1983). *Identifying and Estimating the Genetic Impact of Chemical Mutagens.* Washington, D.C., National Academy Press.

45. Miller, E. C., and Miller, J. A. (1976). The metabolism of chemical carcinogens to reactive eletrophiles and their possible mechanisms of action in carcinogenesis. In *Chemical Carcinogens.* Edited by C. S. Searle. Washington, D.C., American Chemical Society, p. 737.

46. Miller, E. C. (1978). Some current perspectives on chemical carcinogenesis in humans and experimental animals: Presidential address. *Cancer Res. 38*:1479.

47. Wright, A. S. (1980). The role of metabolism in chemical mutagenesis and chemical carcinogenesis. *Mutat. Res. 75*:215.

48. Ames, B. N., Durston, W. E., Yamasaki, E., and Lee, F. D. (1973). Carcinogens are mutagens: A simple test system combining liver homogenates for activation and bacteria for detection. *Proc. Natl. Acad. Sci. (U.S.A.) 70*:2281.

49. McCann, J., and Ames, B. N. (1977). The *Salmonella*/microsome mutagenicity test: predictive value for animal carcinogens. In *Origins of Human Cancer.* Edited by H. H. Hiatt, J. D. Watson, and J. A. Winsten. Cold Spring Harbor, N.Y., Cold Spring Harbor Laboratory, p. 1431.

50. Conney, A. H. (1967). Pharmacological implications of microsomal enzyme induction. *Pharmacol. Rev. 19*:317.

51. Ullrich, V., and Kremers, P. (1977). Multiple forms of cytochrome P-450 in the microsomal mono-oxygenase system. *Arch. Toxicol. 39*:41.

52. Ames, B. N., McCann, J., and Yamasaki, E. (1975). Methods for detecting carcinogens and mutagens with the *Salmonella*/mammalian-microsome mutagenicity test. *Mutat. Res. 31*:347.

53. Litterst, C. L., Mimnaugh, E. G., Reagan, R. L., and Gram, T. E. (1975). Comparison of in vitro drug metabolism by lung, liver and kidney of several common laboratory species. *Drug Metab. Disposition 3*:259.

54. Bigger, C. A., Tomaszewski, J. E., and Dipple, A. (1978). Differences between products of binding of 7,12-dimethylbenz-[a]anthracene to DNA in mouse skin and in a rat liver microsomal system. *Biochem. Biophys. Res. Commun. 80*:229.

55. Bigger, C. A., Tomaszewski, J. E., and Dipple, A. (1980). Limitations of metabolic activation systems used with in vitro tests for carcinogens. *Science 209*:503.

56. Decad, G. M., Hsieh, D. P., and Byard, J. L. (1977). Maintenance of cytochrome P-450 and metabolism of aflatoxin $B_1$ in primary hepatocyte cultures. *Biochem. Biophys. Res. Commun.* *78*:279.
57. Newbold, R. F., Wigley, C. B., Thompson, M. H., and Brookes, P. (1977). Cell-mediated mutagenesis in cultured Chinese hamster cells by carcinogenic polycyclic hydrocarbons: Nature and extent of the associated hydrocarbon-DNA reaction. *Mutat. Res. 43*:101.
58. Schmeltz, I., Tosk, J., and Williams, G. M. (1978). Comparison of the metabolic profiles of benzo[a]pyrene obtained from primary cell cultures and subcellular fractions derived from normal and methylcholanthrene induced rat liver. *Cancer Lett.,* *5*:81.
59. Selkirk, J. (1977). Divergence of metabolic activation systems for short-term mutagenesis assays. *Nature 270*:604.
60. Probat, G. S., McManhont, R. E., Hill, L. E., Thompson, C. Z., Epp, J. K., and Neal, S. B. (1981). Chemically-induced unscheduled DNA synthesis in primary rat hepatocyte cultures: A comparison with bacterial mutagenicity using 218 compounds. *Environ. Mutagen. 3*:11.
61. Williams, G. M. (1976). Carcinogen-induced DNA repair in primary rat liver cultures: A possible screen for chemical carcinogens. *Cancer Lett. 1*:231.
62. Williams, G. M. (1977). Detection of chemical carcinogens by unscheduled DNA synthesis in rat liver primary cell cultures. *Cancer Res. 37*:1845.
63. Williams, G. M. (1980). The detection of chemical mutagens/carcinogens by DNA repair and mutagenesis in liver cultures. In *Chemical Mutagens, Principles and Methods for Their Detection*, Vol. 6. Edited by F. J. de Serres and A. Hollander. New York, Plenum Press, p. 61.
64. Williams, G. M., Laspia, M. F., and Dunkel, V. C. (1982). Reliability of the hepatocyte primary culture/DNA repair test in testing of coded carcinogens and noncarcinogens. *Mutat. Res. 97*:359.
65. Langenbach, R., Freed, H. J., and Huberman, E. (1978). Liver cell-mediated mutagenesis of mammalian cells by liver carcinogens. *Proc. Natl. Acad. Sci. (U.S.A.) 75*:2864.
66. Glatt, H. R., Billings, R. Platt, K. L., and Oesch, F. (1981). Improvement of the correlation of bacterial mutagenicity with carcinogenicity of benzo(a)pyrene and four of its major metabolites by activation with intact liver cells instead of cell homogenate. *Cancer Res. 41*:270.

67. Michalopoulos, G., Strom, S. C., Kligerman, A. D., Irons, G. P., and Novicki, D. L. (1981). Mutagenesis induced by procarcinogens at the hypoxanthine-guanine phosphorlbosyl transferase locus of human fibroblasts cocultured with rat hepatocytes. *Cancer Res. 41*:1873.

68. Poiley, J. A., Raineri, R., and Pienta, R. J. (1979). Use of hamster hepatocytes to metabolize carcinogens in an in vitro bioassay. *J. Natl. Cancer Inst. 63*:519.

69. Raineri, R., Poiley, J. A., Andrews, A. W., Pienta, R. J., and Lijinsky, W. (1981). Greater effectiveness of hepatocyte and liver S9 preparations from hamster than rat preparations in activating N-nitroso compounds to metabolites mutagenic to *Salmonella. J. Natl. Cancer Inst. 67*:1117.

70. Huberman, E., and Sachs, L. (1974). Cell-mediated mutagenesis of mammalian cells with chemical carcinogens. *Int. J. Cancer 13*:326.

71. Huberman, E., and Sachs, L. (1976). Mutability of different genetic loci in mammalian cells by metabolically activated carcinogenic polycyclic hydroacrbons. *Proc. Natl. Acad. Sci. (U.S.A.) 73*:188.

72. Langenbach, R., Nesnow, S., Malick, L., Gingell, R., Tompa, A., Kuszynski, C., Leavitt, S., Sasseville, K., Hyatt, B., Cudak, C., and Montgomery, L. (1981). Organ specific activation of carcinogenic polynuclear aromatic hydrocarbons in cell culture. In *Polynuclear Aromatic Hydrocarbons*. Edited by M. Cooke and A. J. Dennis. Columbus, Ohio, Battele Press, p. 75.

73. Huh, N., Nemoto, N., and Utakoji, T. (1982). Metabolic activation of benzo(a)pyrene, aflatoxin $B_1$, and dimethylnitrosamine by a human hepatoma cell line. *Mutat. Res. 94*:339.

74. Hsu, I. C., Stoner, G. D., Autrup, H., Trump, B. F., Selkirk, J. K., and Harris, C. C. (1978). Human bronchus mediated mutagenesis of mammalian cells by carcinogenic polynuclear aromatic hydrocarbons. *Proc. Natl. Acad. Sci. (U.S.A.) 75*:2003.

75. Tong, C., and Williams, G. M. (1978). Induction of purine analog-resistant mutants in adult rat liver epithelial lines by metabolic activation-dependent and independent carcinogens. *Mutat. Res. 58*:339.

76. Tong, C., Brat, S. V., and Williams G. M. (1981). Sister-chromatid exchange induction by polycyclic aromatic hydrocarbons in an intact cell system of adult rat-liver epithelial cells. *Mutat. Res. 91*:467.

77. Owens, I. S., and Nebert, D. W. (1975). Aryl hydrocarbon hydroxylase induction in mammalian liver-derived cell cultures.

Stimulation of cytochrome $P_1$ 450-associated "enzyme activity" by many inducing compounds. *Mol. Pharmacol.* *11*:94.

78. Owens, I. S. and Nebert, D. W. (1976). Aryl hydrocarbon hydroxylase induction in mammalian liver-derived cell cultures. Effects of various metabolic inhibitors on the enzyme activity in hepatoma cells. *Biochem. Pharmacol.* *25*:805.

79. Ashby, J. (1986). The prospects for a simplified and internationally harmonized approach to the detection of possible human carcinogens and mutagens. *Mutagenesis* *1*:3.

80. Vanparys, Ph., and Marsboom, R. (1985). Genetic toxicology in the pharmaceutical industry. *Food Chem. Toxic.* *23*:19.

81. Brusick, D., and Auletta, A. (1985). Developmental status of bioassays in genetic toxicology: A report of phase II of the U.S. Environmental Protection Agency gene-tox program. *Mutat. Res.* *153*:1.

82. Ames, B. N., Lee, F. D. and Durston, W. E. (1973). An improved bacterial test system for the detection and classification of mutagens and carcinogens. *Proc. Natl. Acad. Sci. (U.S.A.)* *70*:782.

83. Levin, D. E., Yamasaki, E., and Ames, B. N. (1982). A new *Salmonella* tester strain for the detection of frameshift mutagens: A run of cytosines as a mutational hot-spot. *Mutat. Res.* *94*:315.

84. Levin, D. E., Hollstein, M. C., Christman, M. F., Schwiers, E. A., and Ames. B. N. (1982). A new *Salmonella* tester strain (TA102) with A:T base pairs at the site of mutation detects oxidative mutagens. *Proc. Natl. Acad. Sci. (U.S.A.)* *79*:7445.

85. Maron, D. M., and Ames, B. N. (1983). Revised methods for the *Salmonella* mutagenicity test. *Mutat. Res.* *113*:173.

86. de Serres, F. J., and Shelby, M. D. (1979). The *Salmonella* mutagenicity assay: Recommendations. *Science* *203*:563.

87. Organization for Economic Co-Operation and Development. (1981). *OECD Guidelines for Testing of Chemicals*. O.E.C.D., Paris, France.

88. Office of Pesticides and Toxic Substances. (1984). *Health Effects Test Guidelines*. EPA 560/6-82-001, U.S. Environmental Protection Agency, Washington, D.C.

89. U.S. Environmental Protection Agency. (1985). Toxic substances control act test guidelines: Subpart F - genetic toxicity. *Fed. Reg.* *50*:39435.

90. Dean, B. J. (ed.) (1983). *Report of the UKEMS Sub-Committee on Guidelines for Mutagenicity Testing*. Swansea, Wales, United Kingdom Environmental Mutagen Society.

91. Green, M. H. L., and Muriel, W. J. (1976). Mutagen Testing using trp[+] reversion in *Escherichia coli*. *Mutat. Res.* *38*:3.

92. Brusick, D. J., Simmon, V. F., Rosenkranz, H. S., Ray, V. A., and Stafford, R. S. (1980). An evaluation of the *Escherichia coli* WP2 and WP2 *uvrA* reverse mutation assay. *Mutat. Res. 76*:169.

93. Matsushima, T., Sugimura, T., Magao, M., Yahag, T., Shirai, A., and Sawamura, M. (1980). *Short-Term Tests for Detecting Carcinogens*. Edited by K. H. Norlooch and R. C. Garner. Berlin-Heidelberg, New York, Springer, p. 273.

94. D'Alisa, R. M. Carden III, G. A., Carr, H. S., and Rosenkranz, H. S. (1971). "Reversion" of DNA polymerase-deficient *Escherichia coli*. *Mol. Gen. Genet. 110*:23.

95. DeLucia, P., and Cairns, J. (1969). Isolation of an *E. coli* strain with a mutation affecting DNA polymerase. *Nature, 224*:1164.

96. Gross, J., and Gross, M. (1969). Genetic analysis of an *E. coli* strain with a mutation affecting DNA polymerase. *Nature 224*:1166.

97. Kelly, R. B., Atkinson, M. R., Huberman, J. A., and Kornberg, A. (1969). Excision of thymine dimers and other mismatched sequences by DNA polymerase of *Escherichia coli*. *Nature 224*:495.

98. Rosenkranz, H. S., Gutter, B., and Speck, W. T. (1976). Mutagenicity and DNA-modifying activity: A comparison of two microbial assays. *Mutat. Res. 41*:61.

99. Slater, E. E., Anderson, M. D., and Rosenkranz, H. S. (1971). Rapid detection of mutagens and carcinogens. *Cancer Res. 31*:970.

100. Bradley, M. O., Bhuyan, B., Francis, M. C., Langenbach, R., Peterson, A., and Huberman, E. (1981). Mutagenesis by chemical agents in V79 Chinese hamster cells: A review and analysis of the literature. *Mutat. Res. 87*:82.

101. Hsie, A. W., Casciano, D. A., Couch, D. B., Krahn, D. F., O'Neill, J. P., and Whitefield, B. L. (1981). The use of Chinese hamster ovary cells to quantify specific locus mutation and to determine mutagenicity of chemicals. *Mutat. Res. 89*:193.

102. Bartsch, H., Malaveille, C., Camus, A. M., Martel-Planche, G., Brun, G., Hautefeuille, A., Sabadie, N., Barbin, A., Kuroki, T., Drevon, C., Piceoli, C., and Montesano, R. (1980). Validation and Comparative studies on 180 chemicals with *S. typhimurium* strains and V79 Chinese hamster cells in the presence of various metabolizing system. *Mutat. Res. 76*:1.

103. Clive, D., and Spector, J. F. S. (1975). Laboratory procedures for assessing specific locus mutations at the TK locus in cultured L5178Y mouse lymphoma cells. *Mutat. Res. 31*:17.

104. Clive, D., Johson, K. O., Spector, J. F. S., Baston, A. G., and Brown, M. M. M. (1979). Validation and characterization of the L5178Y /TK /+/- mouse lymphoma mutagen assay system. *Mutat. Res. 59*:61.

105. Moore-Brown, M. M., Clive, D., Howard, B. E., Batson, A. G., and Johnson, K. O. (1981). The utilization of trifluorothymidine (TFT) to select for thymidine kinase-deficient (TK$^{-/-}$) mutants from L5178Y /TK$^{+/-}$ mouse lymphoma cells. *Mutat. Res. 85*:363.

106. Clive, D., McCuen, R., Spector, J. F. S., Piper, C., and Mavournin, K. H. (1983). Specific gene mutations in L5178Y cells in culture. *Mutat. Res. 115*:225.

107. Clive, D., Batson, A. G., and Turner, N. T. (1980). The ability of L5178Y /TK$^{+/-}$ mouse lymphoma cells to detect single gene and viable chromosome mutations: Evaluation and relevance to mutagen and carcinogen screening. In *The Predictive Value of Short-Term Screening Tests in Carcinogenicity Evaluation.* Edited by G. W. Williams, et al. Amsterdam, Elsevier /North-Holland, p. 103.

108. Hozier, J., Sawyer, J., Moore, M., Howard, B., and Clive, D. (1981). Cytogenetic analysis of the L5178Y /TK$^{+/-}$ --- TK$^{-/-}$ mouse lymphoma mutagenesis assay system. *Mutat. Res. 84*:169.

109. Moore, M. M., and Howard, B. E. (1982). Quantitiation of small colony trifluorothymidine resistant mutants of L5178Y / TK$^{+/-}$ mouse lymphoma cells in RPMI-1640 medium. *Mutat. Res. 104*:287.

110. Hozier, J., Sawyer, J., Clive, D., and Moore, M. (1982). Cytogenetic distinction between the TK$^{+}$ and TK$^{-}$ chromosome in the L5178Y TK$^{+/-}$ mouse lymphoma mutagen assay system. *Mutat. Res. 105*:451.

111. Turner, N. T., Batson, A. G., and Clive, D. (1984). Procedures for the L5178Y /TK$^{+/-}$ TK$^{-/-}$ mouse lymphoma cell mutagenesis assay. In *Handbook of Mutagenicity Test Procedures.* Edited by B. J. Kilbey et al. New York, Elsevier Science Publishers, p. 239.

112. Amacher, D. E., and Paillet, S. C. (1982). Hamster hepatocyte-medicated activation of procarcinogens in the L5178Y /TK mutation assay. *Mutat. Res. 106*:305.

113. Amachar, D. E., and Paillet, S. C. (1983). The activation of procarcinogens to mutagens by cultured rat hepatocytes in the L5178Y /TK mutation assay. *Mutat. Res. 113*:77.

114. Maslansky, C. J., and Williams, G. M. (1982). Primary cultures and the levels of cytochrome P450 in hepatocytes from mouse, rat, hamster and rabbit liver. *In Vitro 18*:683.

115. Mitchell, A. D., Casciano, D. A., Meltz, M. L., Robinson, D. E., San, R. H. C., Williams, G. M. and Von Halle, E. S. (1983). Unscheduled DNA synthesis test. *Mutat. Res. 123*:363.

116. Mirsalis, J. C., and Butterworth, B. E. (1980). Detection of un-scheduled DNA synthesis in hepatocytes isolated from rats treated with genotoxin agents: An *in vivo-in vitro* assay for potential carcinogens and mutagens. *Carcinogenesis 1*:621.

117. Barfknecht, T. R., Naismith, R. W., and Kornbrust, D. J. (1987). Variations on the standard protocol design of the hepatocyte DNA repair assay. *Cell Biol. Toxicol. 3*:193.

118. Dean, B. J. (ed.). (1984). *Report of the UKEMS Sub-Committee on Guidelines For Mutagenicity Testing.* Swansea, Wales, United Kingdom Environmental Mutagen Society.

119. Bender, M. A. (1980). Relationship of DNA lesions and their repair to chromosomal aberration production. In *DNA Repair and Mutagenesis in Eukaryotes.* Edited by W. M. Generoso et al. New York, Plenum Press, p. 245.

120. Joshi, G. P., Nelson, W. J., Revell, S. H., and Shaw, C. A. (1982). X-ray-induced chromosome damage in live mammalian cells and improved measurements of its effects on their colony-forming ability. *Int. J. Radiat. Biol. 41*:161.

121. Cairns, J. (1981). The origin of human cancers. *Nature 289*:353.

122. Radman, M., Jeggo, P., and Wagner, R. (1982). Chromosomal rearrangement and carcinogenesis. *Mutat. Res. 98*:249.

123. Evans, H. J. (1976). Cytological methods of detecting chemi-cal mutagens. In *Chemical Mutagens, Principles and Methods for Their Detection,* Vol. 4. Edited by A. Hollander. New York, Plenum Press, p. 1.

124. Evans, H. J., and O'Riordan, M. L. (1975). Human perpheral blood lymphocytes for the analysis of chromosome aberrations in mutagen tests. *Mutat. Res. 31*:135.

125. Nichols, W. W., Miller, R. C., and Bradt, C. (1977). *In Vitro* anaphase and metaphase preparations in mutation testing. In *Handbook of Mutagenicity Test Procedures.* Edited by B. J. Kilbey et al. Amsterdam, Elsevier Science Publishers, p. 225.

126. Preston, R. J., Au, W., Bender, M. A., Brewen, J. G., Carrano, A. C., Heddle, J. A., McFee, A. F., Wolff, S., and Wassom, J. S. (1981). Mammalian in vivo and in vitro cytogenetic assays. *Mutat. Res. 87*:143.

127. Madle, S., and Obe, G. (1980). Methods for analysis of the mutagenicity of indirect mutagens/carcinogens in eukaryotic cells. *Human Genet. 56*:7.

128. Natarajan, A. T., Tates, A. W., VanBuul, P. P. W., Meijers, M. and De Vogel, N. (1976). Cytogenetic effects of mutagens/carcinogens after activation in a microsomal system *in vitro* I. Induction of chromosome aberrations and sister chromatid ex-changes by diethylnitrosamine (DEN) and dimethylnitrosamine (DMN) in CHO cells in the presence of rat-liver microsomes. *Mutat. Res. 37*:83.

129. Ray-Choudhuri, R. S., Kelley, S. and Iype, P. T. (1980). Induction of sister-chromatid exchanges by carcinogens mediated through culture rat liver epithelial cells. *Carcinogenesis* 1:779.

130. Wojciechowski, J. P., Kaur, P., and Sabharwal, P. S. (1981). Comparison of metabolic systems required to activate promutagens/carcinogens *in vitro* for sister-chromatid exchange studies. *Mutat. Res. 88*:89.

131. Savage, J. R. K. (1979). Annotation: Classification and relationships of induced chromosomal structural changes. *J. Med. Genet. 13*:103.

132. Bradley, M. O., Hsu, I. C. and Harris, C. C. (1979). Relationship between sister chromatid exchange and mutagenicity, toxicity and DNA damage. *Nature 232*:318.

133. Carrano, A. V., Thompson, L. H., Lindl, P. A., and Minkler, J. L. (1978). Sister chromatid exchange as in indicator of mutagenesis. *Nature 271*:551.

134. Galloway, S. A., and Wolff, S. (1979). The relation between chemically induced sister-chromatid exchanges and chromatid breakage. *Mutat. Res. 61*:297.

135. Latt, S. A., Allen, J., Bloom, S. E., Carrano, A., Falke, E., Kram, D., Schneider, E., Schneider, R., Tice, R., Whitfield, B., and Wolff, S. (1981). Sister-chromatid exchange: A report of the gene-tox program. *Mutat. Res. 87*:17.

136. Perry, P. E. (1980). Chemical mutagens and sister-chromatid exchange. In *Chemical Mutagens: Principles and Methods for Their Detection*, Vol. 6. Edited by F. J. de Serres and A. Hollaender. New York, Plenum Publishing, p. 1.

137. Perry, P., and Evans, H. J. (1975). Cytological detection of mutagen-carcinogen exposure by sister chromatid exchange. *Nature 258*:121.

138. Latt, S. A., Schreck, R. R., Loveday, K. S., Dougherty, C. P., and Shuler, C. F. (1980). Sister chromatid exchanges. *Adv. Human Genet. 10*:267.

139. Wolff, S. (1977). Sister chromatid exchange. *Ann. Rev. Genet. 11*:183.

140. Takehisa, S. (1982). Induction of sister chromatid exchanges by chemical agents. In *Sister Chromatid Exchange*. Edited by S. Wolff. New York, John Wiley and Sons, p. 87.

141. Galloway, S. M., Bloom, A. D., Resnick, M., Margolin, B. H., Nakamura, F., Archer, P., and Zeiger, E. (1985). Development of a standard protocol for in vitro cytogenetic tests with Chinese hamster ovary cells: Comparisons of results for 22 compounds in two laboratories. *Environ. Mutagen. 7*:1.

142. Perry, P. E., and Thomson, E. J. (1984). Sister chromatid exchange methodology. In *Handbook of Mutagenicity Test Procedures*, 2nd Ed. Edited by B. J. Kilby et al. New York, Elsevier Science Publishers, p. 495.

143. Langenbach, R., and Oglesby, L. (1983). The use of intact cellular activation systems in genetic toxicology assays. In *Chemical Mutagens: Principles and Methods for their Detection,* Vol. 8. Edited by F. J. de Serres. New York, Plenum Press, p. 55.

144. Tice, R. R., and Hollaender, A. (eds.) (1984). *Sister Chromatid Exchanges: 25 Years of Experimental Research,* Part B, New York, Plenum Press.

145. Heidelberger, C., Freeman, A. E., Pienta, R. J., Sivak, A., Bertram, J. S., Casto, B. C., Dunkel, V. C., Francis, M. W., Kakuhaga, T., Little, J. B., and Schectman, L. M. (1983). Cell transformation by chemical agents. A review and analysis of the literature. *Mutat. Res. 114:*283.

146. Sivak, A., Charest, M. C., Rudenko, L., Silveira, D. M., Simons, I., and Wood, A. M., (1981). Mammalian cell transformation by chemical carcinogens. In *Advances in Modern Environmental Toxicology,* Vol. I. Edited by N. Mishra, V. Dunkel, and M. Hehlman, Princeton Junction, Senate Press, p. 133.

147. Pienta, R. J. (1979). A hamster embryo cell model system for identifying carcinogens. In *Carcinogens: Identification and Mechanisms of Action.* Edited by A. C. Griffin and C. R. Shaw. New York, Raven Press, p. 121.

148. Peinta, R. J. (1980). A transformation bioassay employing cryopreserved hamster embryo cells. In *Advances in Modern Environmental Toxicology,* Vol. I. Edited by N. Mishra, V. Dunkel, and M. Mehlman. Princeton Junction, N.J., Senate Press, p. 47.

149. Pienta, R. J., Poiley, J. A., and Lebherz III, W. B. (1977). Morphological transformation of early passage golden Syrian hamster embryo cells derived from cryopreserved primary cultures as a reliable in vitro bioassay for identifying diverse carcinogens. *Int. J. Cancer 19:*642.

150. Purchae, I. F. H., Longstaff, E., Ashby, J., Styles, J. A., Anderson, D., Lefevre, P. A., and Westwood, F. R. (1976). Evaluation of six short-term tests for detecting chemical carcinogens and recommendations for their use. *Nature 264:*624.

151. Purchase, I. F. H., Longstaff, E., Ashby, J., Styles, J. A., Anderson, D., Lefevre, P. A., and Westwood, F. R. (1978). An evaluation of six short-term tests for detecting organic chemical carcinogens. *Br. J. Cancer 37:*873.

152. Sivak, A., Rudenko, L., and Simons, I. (1977). Variability of physiological and karyotypic characteristics of Balbc/3T3 cell populations. *In Vitro 13:*198.

153. Reznikoff, C. A., Brankow, D. W., and Heidelberger, C. (1973). Establishment and characterization of a cloned line of C3H mouse embryo cells sensitive to post confluence inhibition of division. *Cancer Res. 33:*3231.

154. Reznikoff, C. A., Bertram, J. A., Brankow, D. W., and Heidelberger, C. (1973). Quantitative and qualitative studies of chemical transformation of cloned C3H mouse embryo cells. *Cancer Res. 33*:3239.

155. Heidelberger, C. (1980). Mammalian cell transformation and mammalian cell mutagenesis in vitro. *J. Environ. Pathol. Toxicol. 3*:69.

156. Abrahomson, S., Wurgler, F. E., DeJongh, C., and Meyer, H. V. (1980). How many loci on the x-chromosome of *Drosophila melanogaster* can mutate to recessive lethals. *Environ. Mutagen. 2*:447.

157. Bootman, J., and Kilbey, B. (1983). Recessive lethal mutations in Drosphilia. In *Report of the UKEMS Sub-Committee on Guidelines for Mutagenicity Testing*, Part I. Edited by B. J. Dean. Swansea, Wales, United Kingdom Environmental Mutagen Society, p. 103.

158. Kilbey, B., MacDonald, D. J., Auerbach, C., Sobels, F. H., and Vogel, E. W. (1981). The use of *Drosophilia melanogaster* in tests for environmental mutagens. *Mutation Res. 85*:141.

159. Wurgler, F. E., Sobels, F. H., and Vogel, E. (1977). *Drosophila* as an assay system for detecting genetic changes. In *Handbook of Mutagenicity Test Procedures*. Edited by B. Kilbey et al. Amsterdam, Elsevier Science Publishers, p. 335.

160. Salamone, M. F., and Heddle, J. H. (1983). The bone marrow micronucleus assay: Rational for a revised protocol. In *Chemicals Mutagens: Principles and Methods for their Detection*, Vol. 8. Edited by F. J. de Serres. New York, Plenum Press, p. 111.

161. Topham, J., Bootman, J., Scott, D., and Tweats, D. (1983). *In Vivo* cytogenetic assays. In *Report of the UKEMS Sub-Committee on Guidelines for Mutagenicity Testing*. Edited by B. J. Dean. Swansea, Wales, United Kingdom Environmental Mutagen Society, p. 119.

162. Heddle, J. A., and Salamone, M. F. (1981). Chromosomal aberration and bone marrow toxicity. *Environ. Health Perspect 39*:23.

163. Schmid, W. (1975). The micronucleus test. *Mutat. Res. 31*:9.

164. Schmid, W. (1976). The micronucleus test for cytogenetic analysis. In *Chemical Mutagens: Principles and Methods for their Detection*. Edited by A. Hollaender. New York, Plenum Press, p. 31.

165. Heddle, J. A., Benz, R. D., and Countryman, P. J. (1978). Measurement of chromosomal breakage in culture cells by the micronucleus technique. In *Mutagen-Induced Chromosome Damage in Man*. Edited by H. J. Evans and D. C. Lloyd. New Haven, Yale University Press, p. 191.

166. Heddle, J. A., and Salamone, M. F. (1981). The micronucleus assay: *In Vivo*. In *Short-Term Tests for Chemical Carcinogens*. Edited by H. Stich and R. H. C. Sans. New York, Springer-Verlag, p. 243.

167. Heddle, J. A., Stuart, E., and Salamone, M. F. (1984). The bone marrow micronucleus assay. In *Handbook of Mutagenicity Testing Procedures*. Edited by B. Kilbey. New York, Elsevier Science Publishers.

168. Salamone, M., Heddle, J., Stuart, E., and Katz, M. (1980). Towards an improved micronucleus test—Studies on 3 model agents, mitomycin C, cyclophosphamide and dimethylbenzanthracene. *Mutat. Res. 74*:347.

169. Salamone, M., Heddle, J., and Katz, M. (1981). Mutagenic activity of 41 compounds in the *in vivo* micronucleus assay. In *Evaluation of Short-Term Tests for Carcinogens*. Edited by F. J. de Serres and J. Ashby. New York, Elsevier Science Publishers, p. 686.

170. Dean, B. J. (1969). Chemical-induced chromosome damage. *Lab. Anim. 3*:157.

171. Goetz, P., Sram, R. J., and Dohnalova, J. (1973). Relationship between experimental results in mammals and man. I Cytogenetic analysis of bone marrow injury induced by a single dose of cyclophosphamide. *Mutat. Res. 31*:247.

172. Kilian, J. D., Moreland, F. E., Benge, M. C., Legator, M. S., and Whorton, E. B., Jr. (1977). A collaborative study to measure intralaboratory variation with the *in vivo* bone marrow metaphase procedure. In *Handbook of Mutagenicity Test Procedures*. Edited by B. J. Kilbey et al. Amsterdam, Elsevier Science Publishers, p. 243.

173. Legator, M. S., Palmer, K. A., Green, S. and Peterson, K. W. (1969). Cytogenetic studies in rats of cyclohexalamine, a metabolite of cyclamate. *Science 165*:1139.

174. Schmid, W., Arakaki, D. T., Breslau, N. A., and Culbertson, J. C. (1971). Chemical mutagenesis. The Chinese hamster bone marrow as an *in vivo* test system, I Cytogenetic results on basic aspects of the methodology obtained with alkylating agents. *Humangentik 11*:103.

175. Conner, M. K., Alarie, Y., and Dombroske, R. L. (1979). Sister chromatid exchange in murine alveolar macrophages, regenerating liver and bone marrow cells a simultaneous multicellular *in vivo* assay. *Chromosoma 74*:51.

176. Schreck, R. R., Paika, I. J., and Latt, S. A. (1979). *In Vivo* induction of sister chromatid exchanges in liver and marrow cells by drugs requiring metabolic activation. *Mutat. Res. 64*:315.

177. Roberts, G. T., and Alken, J. W. (1980). Tissue specific induction of SCEs by ethyl carbamate in mice. *Environ. Mutagen. 2*:17.

178. Cheng, M., Conner, M. K., and Alarie, Y. (1981). Potency of some carbamates as multiple tissue sister chromatid exchange inducers and comparison with known carcinogenic activities. *Cancer Res. 41*:4489.

179. Brewen, J. G., Payne, H. S., Jones, K. P., and Preston, R. J. (1975). Studies on chemically induced dominant lethality. I. The cytogenetic basis of MMS-induced dominant lethality in post meiotic germ cells. *Mutat. Res. 33*:239.

180. Generoso. W. M., Cain. K. T., Huff, S. W., and Gosslee, D. G. (1977). Heritable translocation test in mice. In *Chemical Mutagens, Principles and Methods for their Detection.* Edited by A. Hollaender. New York, Plenum Press, p. 55.

181. Anderson, D., Hodge, M. C. E., Palmer, S., and Purchase, I. F. H. (1981). Comparison of dominant lethal and heritable translocation methodologies. *Mutat. Res. 85*:417.

182. Anderson, D., Bateman, A., and McGregor, D. (1983). Dominant lethal mutation assays. In *Report of UKEMS Sub-Committee on Guidelines for Mutagenicity Testing.* Edited by B. J. Dean. Swansea, Wales, United Kingdom Environmental Mutagenicity Society, p. 143.

183. Bateman, A. J. (1984). The dominant lethal assay in the male mouse. In *Handbook of Mutagenicity Test Procedures.* Edited by B. J. Kilbey et al., New York, Elsevier Science Publishers, p. 471,

184. Green, S., Moreland, F. M., and Flamm, G. W. (1977). A more refined approach to dominant lethal testing. *Toxicol. Appl. Pharmacol. 39*:549.

185. Williams, G. M., and Weisburger, J. H. (1981). Systematic carcinogen testing through the decision point approach. *Ann. Rev. Pharmacol. Toxicol. 21*:393.

186. Bull, R. J., and Pereira, M. A. (1982). Development of a Short-term testing matrix for estimating relative carcinogenic risk. *J. Am. Coll. Toxicol. 1*:1.

187. Milman, H. A., and Weisburger, E. K. (1985). *Handbook of Carcinogen Testing.* Park Ridge, N.J., Noyes Publications.

188. Crow, J. F. (1983). Chemical mutagen testing: A committee report. *Environ. Mutagen. 5*:255.

189. de Serres, F. J., and Matsushima, T. (1984). Environmental mutagenesis and carcinogenesis: Test method development, validation and utilization. *Mutat. Res. 130*:353.

190. Heinze, J. E., and Poulsen, N. K. (1983). The optimal design of batteries of short-term tests for detecting carcinogens. *Mutat. Res. 117*:259.

191. Haworth, S., Lawlor, T., Mortelmans, K., Speck, W., and Zeiger, E. (1983). *Salmonella* mutagenicity test results for 250 chemicals. *Environ. Mutagen. 5*(Suppl. I):3.

192. Mortelmans, K., Haworth, S., Lawlor, T., Speck, W., Tainer, B., and Zeiger, E. (1986). *Salmonella* mutagenicity tests: II. Results from the testing of 270 chemicals. *Environ. Mutagen. 8*(Suppl. 7):1.

193. Holden, H. E. (1982). Comparison of somatic and germ cell models for cytogenetic screening. *J. Appl. Toxicol. 2*:196.

194. Tennant, R. W., Stasiewicz, and Spalding, J. W. (1986). Comparison of multiple parameters of rodent carcinogenicity and in vitro genetic toxicity. *Environ. Mutagen. 8*:205.

195. Purchase, I. F. (1982). An appraisal of predictive tests for carcinogenicity. *Mutat. Res. 99*:53.

196. Rosenkranz, H. S., Klopman, G., Chankong, V., Pet-Edwards, J., and Haimes, Y. Y. (1984). Prediction of environmental carcinogens: A strategy for the mid-1980s. *Environ. Mutagen. 6*:231.

197. Shelby, M. D., and Stasiewicz, S. (1984). Chemicals showing no evidence of carcinogenicity in long-term, two-species rodent studies: The need for short-term data. *Environ. Mutagen. 6*:871.

198. Benigni, R., and Giuliani, A. (1985). Rational approach to the evaluation of short-term tests: Analysis of a homogeneous data base. *J. Toxicol. Environ. Health 16*:333.

199. Palajda, M. and Rosenkranz, H. S. (1985). Assembly and preliminary analysis of a genotoxicity data based for predicting carcinogens. *Mutat. Res. 153*:79.

200. Benigni, R., and Giuliani, A. (1985). Cluster analysis of short-term tests: A new methodological approach. *Mutat. Res. 147*:133.

201. Chankong, V., Haimes, Y. Y., Rosenkranz, H. S., and Pet-Edwards, J. (1985). The carcinogenicity prediction and battery selection (CPBS) method: a Bayesian approach. *Mutat. Res. 153*:135.

202. Pet-Edwards, J., Rosenkranz, H. S., Chankong, V., and Haimes, Y. Y. (1985). Cluster analysis in predicting the carcinogenicity of chemicals using short-term assays. *Mutat. Res. 153*:167.

203. Pet-Edwards, J., Chankong, V., Rosenkranz, H. S., and Haimes, Y. Y. (1985). Application of the carcinogenicity prediction and battery selection (CPBS) method to the Gene-Tox data base. *Mutat. Res. 153*:187.

204. Klopman, G. (1984). Artificial intelligence approach to structure-activity studies, Computer automated structure evaluation of biological activity of organic molecules. *J. Am. Chem. Soc. 106*:7315.

205. Klopman, G., and Rosenkranz, H. S. (1984). Structural requirements for the mutagenicity of environmental nitroarenes.
*Mutat. Res. 126*:227.
206. Rosenkranz, H. S., Pet-Edwards, J., Chankong, V., and
Haimes, Y. Y. (1984). Assembling a battery of assays to
predict carcinogenicity: A case study. *Mutat. Res. 141*:65.
207. Moldeus, P., Nordenskjold, M., Bolesfoldi, G., Eiche, A.,
Haglund, U., and Lambert, B. (1983). Genetic Toxicology of
dopamine. *Mutat. Res. 124*:337.

# 7

# Repeated-Dose Toxicity Studies

VINCENT J. PICCIRILLO / *NPC, Inc., Sterling, Virginia*

## I. INTRODUCTION

Repeated-dose toxicity studies are designed to characterize the effects of a test chemical following multidose exposures to the experimental model over a specified duration. The test animals are observed regularly for mortality, signs of clinical toxicity, and changes in body weight and food consumption. The design of the study may include assessment of hematological, biochemical, physiological, neurological, and ophthalmological parameters. Morphological evaluation is generally conducted on organs and tissues collected at necropsy to ascertain any exposure-related alterations.

These exposure studies may range from a few days duration and up to the lifetime of the study animal. For both historical and regulatory reasons, studies other than pilot range-finding tests are generally conducted with at least three dosage levels. The highest dosage level is selected so that toxicity or alterations in one or more measured parameters are observed. No evidence of toxicity should be seen at the lowest dose.

Under the Toxic Substances Control Act (1), the choice of route of administration for a test chemical in repeated-dose studies depends on the physical and chemical properties of the test article as well as the route that most typifies human exposure. The principal routes of exposure are oral, dermal, and inhalation. This chapter will discuss the methodologies involved in repeated-dose toxicity studies by the oral and dermal routes of exposure. The following discussion is intended as a guide to, hopefully, avoid some of the pitfalls in the various testing regimes.

## II. ORAL TOXICITY

The standard dosing regimens via the oral route are test chemical/diet admixture, test chemical/drinking water admixture, and oral gavage.

### A. Dietary Exposure

Because of concerns regarding both the intentional and nonintentional addition of chemicals to foodstuffs as well as biological accumulation via the food chain, the dietary route has served as the standard bearer for oral exposure. Its simplicity of presentation to the animals has also enhanced its preferred status.

The most critical factor to dietary studies is the proper preparation of the test chemical/diet admixtures. The range of physical and chemical characteristics of test materials requires that considerations regarding appropriate mixing techniques should be determined on an individual basis. Standard practices generally dictate the preparation of a premix, to which is added appropriate amounts of feed to achieve the proper concentrations. However, direct addition of the test chemical to the untreated feed is often the exception rather than the rule.

Dietary preparation involving liquid materials frequently results in either wet feed in which the test article does not disperse or formation of "gumballs," feed and test material that form discernible lumps and chemical "hotspots." Drying and grinding of the premix to a free-flowing form prior to mixing the final diets may be required, however, these actions could affect the chemical nature of the test article.

Solid materials require special techniques prior to or during addition to the diets. Materials that are soluble in water may be dissolved and added as described above for liquids. Nonwater-soluble materials may require several preparatory steps. The test chemical may be dissolved in corn oil, acetone, or other appropriate vehicles prior to addition to the weighed diet. When an organic solvent such as acetone is used, the mixing time for the premix should be sufficient for the solvent to evaporate. Some solids may require grinding in a mortar and pestle with feed added during the grinding process.

Prior to study initiation, test chemical stability in the diet should be determined over a test period at least equivalent to the time which animals are exposed to a specific diet mix. Stability of test samples under the conditions of the proposed study is preferable. Labor and expense can be saved when long-term stability data permit mixing of several weeks of test diet in a single mixing interval.

Homogeneity and concentration analysis of the test article/diet admixture are performed by sampling at 3 or 4 regions within the freshly mixed diet (e.g., samples from the top, middle, and bottom of the mixing bowl or blender).

A variety of feeders are commercially available for rats and mice. These include various-sized glass jars, and stainless steel or galvanized feed cups, which can be equipped with restraining lids and food followers to preclude significant losses of feed due to the animals digging in the feeders. Slotted metal feeders are designed so that animals cannot climb into the feed and also contain mesh food followers to prevent digging.

## B. Oral Intubation in Rats and Mice

Oral gavage dosing is an effective alternative to dietary presentation especially in cases where the test material may be unstable in a dietary admixture or when the dietary admixture is unpalatable or unacceptable to the test animal. The accuracy of dosage level is more precise than that of the dietary regimen, however, the toxicological responses of the animal to a single bolus may differ from that seen with ad libitum feeding.

The presence or absence of food in the stomach may influence the response of the animal to the test chemical as well as the acceptability of the gavage technique. Stomach components may interact with the test article, potentially altering both the absorption and toxicological response of the test chemical. Food content in the stomach also limits the volume of dosing solution that can be given to the animal, thereby influencing the maximum achievable dose level that can be presented to the animal. This is an important consideration for materials with low vehicle solubility or those that must be prepared in dilute form for animal acceptability. Test chemicals that cause significant gastrointestinal irritation must be prepared in dilute form or dosed to nonfasted animals to lessen this effect.

Oral intubation in rats and mice is commonly used in acute oral toxicity studies and has been used more frequently in subchronic and chronic toxicity studies over the last several years. Standard dosing needles depend on the size of the animal. A 20-gauge oral dosing needle approximately 1.5 inches (3.8 cm) long with a blunt tip of 1.25 mm diameter is generally used for mice.

Successful gavage dosing requires immobilization of the animal's head such that the esophagus forms a straight line from the mouth to the stomach. The mouse is grasped by the skin behind the neck using the thumb and forefingers. The back of the animal is held against the palm of the hand by the remaining fingers.

Recommended dosing needles for rats are the 16 gauge, 3 inch (7.6 cm) long needle with a blunt tip of 3 mm diameter or a 14 gauge, 3 inch (7.6 cm) long needle with a blunt tip of 4 mm diameter. The rat is held in one hand with the thumb placed under the animal's foreleg pushing the leg upward toward the head. The forefingers hold the animal's body against the palm of the hand.

The tip of the needle is placed in the animal's mouth on either side of the incisors and guided toward the esophagus. With slight pressure and gentle rotation of the needle from side to side, the needle should slide into the esophagus and down toward the stomach. The material is injected into the stomach and the needle is retracted. Forcing the needle may cause esophageal rupture or entry into the trachea and lungs. These trauma injuries may result in infection, clinical symptomatology, and even death of the animal.

## C. Exposure to Drinking Water

Industrial, agricultural, and domestic chemical uses are the primary sources of water contamination. Under the auspices of TSCA, the potential effects and associated risks of this contamination on human health and the environment are evaluated.

Physicochemical properties of the test material should be a major consideration in selection of drinking water as a dosing matrix. Unlike diet preparation or preparation of gavage dose solutions and suspensions where a variety of solvents and physical processes can be utilized to prepare a dosable form, preparation of drinking water solutions are less flexible. Water solubility of the test chemical is the major governing factor and is dependent on factors such as pH, dissolved salts, and temperature. The animal model itself sets limitations for these factors (acceptability and suitability of pH and salt-adjusted water by the animals as well as environmental specifications such as animal room temperature).

Stability of the test chemical in drinking water under study conditions should be determined prior to study initiation. Consideration should be given to conducting stability tests on test chemical/drinking water admixtures presented to some test animals. Besides difficulties of inherent stability, changes in chemical concentrations may result from other influences. Chemicals with low vapor pressure can volatilize from the water into the air space located above the water of an inverted water bottle, thus, a majority of the chemical may be found in the "dead space" not in the water.

Certain test chemicals may be degraded by contamination by microorganisms. A primary source of these microorganisms is the oral cavity of the rodents. Anyone who has worked with guinea pigs realizes that bacterial contamination can be significant. Although rats and mice are not as notorious as the guinea pig in spitting back into water bottles, significant bacteria can pass via the sipper tubes and water flow restraints into the water bottles. Sanitation and sterilization procedures for water bottles and sipper tubes must be

rigorously maintained to prevent further bacterial growth. A sub-
standard water bottle washer may in fact supply temperature and
humidity conditions that may facilitate bacterial growth.

Water bottles should be considered as the least important equipment needed in a drinking water study. Properly fitting rubber
stoppers, properly shaped sipper tubes, water restraints, and suitable bottle holders working in conjunction should be considered more
important. Worn, poorly fitting, hardened rubber stoppers are the
main reason for water spillage. Slight movement of the animal cage
racks or activity such as the animal drinking, provide sufficient
force to pop these stoppers from the bottle and spill its contents.

Water bottle holders should permit easy accessibility to the animal
room staff in changing and replacing the bottles, yet be secure
enough to keep the water bottle in place when a rack is moved.

Sipper tubes should be shaped so that access to water is not impaired when the sipper tube is used in conjunction with the bottle,
stopper, and holder. Water restrainers are stainless steel ball bear-
ings of sufficient size to preclude water flow and dripping from the
bottle and readily moveable by the animal to permit it to drink. Water
restraints should be checked frequently to assure that water is accessible and that no dripping occurs. Animal saliva and food particles may cause the water restraints to become inoperable so that
either water is not accessible to the animal or the water drips continuously from the bottle.

Accurate water consumption data is necessary to calculate meaningful compound intake data. The technical staff involved in the
study should be aware of the need for properly fitting equipment and
the necessity to prevent water spillage. Whether preparing a few or
several hundred bottles, a lack of consistency in the amount of water
is generally apparent. The tendency in water bottle filling is to
overfill the bottles to assure sufficient water for a specified duration.
Technical staff should be aware that an air space above the water in
an inverted bottle is essential for the free flow of water. It is
frustrating to an investigator to lose study animals to dehydration
when an excess of water was available.

## III. MOUSE SKIN PAINTING BIOASSAYS

Although skin painting bioassays have been conducted on a multitude
of various chemical types for many years, no specific testing guidelines have been proposed by any regulatory body. Under the Toxic
Substance Control Act, standard testing guidelines for dermal oncogenicity studies are those utilized for any other route of administration. No distinction is made in the study design for feeding, dermal,

or intubation studies except for the route of administration. Details of dermal tumor appearance are not considered in this design.

The usefulness of the mouse skin painting bioassay has been evaluated extensively. The dermal carcinogenicity of many types of products such as tobacco smoke condensates and oil-related products have demonstrated that continuous application of these classes of materials to the skin of mice produces skin tumors ranging from papillomas to carcinomas. The ability of test chemicals to act as initiators or promoters of dermal tumors can also be demonstrated by proper design of the test protocol. The ability of the mouse skin to respond positively to various test chemicals is thought to be related to the presence of dermal enzymes necessary for producing those intermediates capable of acting as initiators or promoters.

The key point in the design of any skin painting bioassay is to determine the purpose of the study. As discussed above, these studies can be designed to determine the dermal oncogenic potential of the test material itself, as well as the potential of test chemicals to act as initiators and/or promoters. After the purpose of the study has been established, the frequency of test material application must be evaluated. Dosing in skin painting studies can range from daily to weekly applications for study durations ranging from several weeks up to the lifetime of the animal. Unlike standard mouse oncogenicity studies, a single dose level of the test material is generally used rather than multiple dose levels. Each test material should be independently evaluated when determining the dose level and treatment frequency. Criteria for treatment selection should include potential human exposure patterns, dermal toxicity, dermal irritation potential, and historical data from test materials within a similar class. The methods described in this chapter are for the generic procedures in the conduct of skin painting bioassays and are not intended as guidelines for determining the purpose or the dose regimens to be followed.

## A. Animal Preparation and Test Material Administration

Since these studies are via the dermal route, the hair must be removed from the intended site of application. The test material is generally dosed to the intrascapular area of the mouse in order to prevent potential oral ingestion and to provide a distinct area for observation for the appearance of dermal tumors. Approximately a 1 in.$^2$ area is shaved free of hair using an electric clipper equipped with a size 40 clipper blade. The predose shaving should be completed a few days prior to the initiation of treatment so that any minor nicks or abrasions have sufficient time for healing. Follow-up shaving should be as needed and once per week is generally sufficient.

Care must be taken in the reshaving process so that neither the skin nor any dermal masses are disrupted by the shaving process.

Dosing volumes typically used in the skin painting bioassay are in the microliter range (50–100 μl doses are standard). These small dose volumes can be achieved by using either plastic-tipped calibrated micropipettes or automatic dosing syringe dispensers. Both types of dispensers are commercially available. However, for efficiency in the dosing procedure, the syringe dispenser is preferable. Standard syringe dispensers contain 2500 μl of a test article and precise 50 μl doses can be applied. In this manner a full syringe permits dosing of a group of 50 animals with each receiving a 50 μl dose. These syringes can be cleaned easily, however, it is recommended that one syringe be used for each test article during the course of the study. For both the shaving and dosing procedures, the animal is removed from the cage and allowed to firmly grip the bottom of the wire-mesh cage with its front legs. Gentle pressure is applied to the tail of the animal stretching the animal to a semi-immobile position. In this position, the back can be shaved or the test material can be applied. During the dosing procedure, the tip of the syringe is used to spread the test material evenly in the dosing region.

## B. Tissue Mass Observations

The frequency of observation of the animal for the appearance for dermal tumors depends on the needs of the investigator. Observation of the animal for dermal tumors on at least a weekly basis is necessary for determination of the latency period. Any skin irregularities that are less than 1 mm and larger masses that do not protrude above the skin surface are generally disregarded. Lesions that measure at least 1 mm but less than 2 mm in diameter are defined as such and are carefully observed since masses of this type have a relatively high incidence of spontaneous regression. A dermal skin lesion is considered to be significant if it reaches or exceeds 2 mm in diameter and protrudes above the surrounding skin. The time previously recorded for a lesion reaching 1 mm in diameter is assumed to be the time of first appearance. Once a lesion has grown to 2 mm the animal is considered to be a lesion bearer even if that lesion regresses or subsequently disappears.

Accurate records of the disposition of each mass are essential. Figure 1 demonstrates a system for maintaining tissue mass data. At the time of appearance, the position and size of the mass is drawn onto the diagram. The first mass is numbered 1, and the measurements and location of the mass are recorded on the data record. As additional masses appear, they are numbered sequentially and the locations and measurements recorded. In most cases, this procedure is very simple, however, certain procedures must be followed to

Figure 1    Tumor observation sheet.

prevent loss of mass identification under certain circumstances. It is not uncommon for a single animal to bear as many as 6–20 tissue masses in initiation/promotion studies or with positive control substances. Small masses may increase in size to the point where two or more masses may merge. In order that the identity of individual masses be maintained, the merged mass should carry the numbers of the individual masses. For example, if masses 1 and 2 merge, the data for the merged mass is recorded as mass 1, 2. If a mass regresses or disappears, these data are also recorded. It is not uncommon for the wartlike lesions noted from benzo-(a)-pyrene treatment to disappear. Histological evaluation of the underlying skin shows evidence of a squamous cell carcinoma. The careful maintenance of the tissue mass data through the time of necropsy permits complete accountability so that gross to microscopic determination can be made. In the histopathological evaluation of these tumors, the pathologist should be consulted regarding the necessity of evaluation of all observed masses.

## IV.  REPEATED PERCUTANEOUS TOXICITY STUDIES

Guidelines for repeated percutaneous toxicity studies have been designed by the Environmental Protection Agency (EPA) under both the Federal Insecticide, Fungicide and Rodenticide Act (FIFRA, 1982) and TSCA as well as the Organization for Economic Cooperation and Development (OECD, 1981). These studies are commonly conducted in the rat and rabbit and occasionally in the guinea pig. Although the design for these studies is the same, the techniques for shaving and dosing are species specific.

### A.  Shaving

Approximately 24 hr prior to the first application of the test material, the backs of the test animals are clipped closely of hair using standard small animal clippers. The clipping should be completed so that no abrasions or other disruption of the dermis occurs. It is essential that the clippers be in good condition (not dull) to prevent these types of dermal damage.

The small motor of the clippers tends to overheat and lose efficiency, therefore several sets of clippers should be available so that they can be alternated, avoiding overheating and eventual breaking of the clippers. Dull blades also contribute to shaving difficulty. Additional sets of sharpened blades should be available. A stiff brush should be used to remove excess hair and avoid clogging the blades. A clipper lubricant spray used between each animal

also assists in the easy removal of hair. Hair should always be
clipped in the direction opposite to the hair growth pattern.

For rabbits, clipping is facilitated by using two technicians. One
technician removes the rabbit from its cage and places it on a hard
flat surface. The rabbit is grasped firmly by the skin at the nape
of the neck and at the lower back just above the hind legs. The
second person can then clip the hair from the animal. Because of
seasonal variations in hair growth for rabbits, a two-step clipping
procedure may be necessary. In the first step, an Angra blade is
used to shorten the length of the hair. The remaining hair is removed using a size 40 animal clipper blade. The clipped area should
approximate 10 to 15% of the body surface area.

Rats can be held and clipped in the same manner as rabbits.
This is particularly required for large rats which have not been
placed on study. Clipping of young rats can be completed by one
person. Either of two procedures can be utilized. In one procedure,
the rat is held by the nape of the neck with the legs hanging. The
technician can then remove the hair from the back. In the second
procedure, the animal is gently cradled in the palm of the technician's
hand. The animal is then clipped. Guinea pigs can be clipped in
the same manner as rats.

## B. Test Article Application

Liquid test articles are applied directly to the skin and spread evenly
over the body surface. If a large volume of liquid is required, the
test material can be applied under gauze patches to prevent the test
material from flowing to the flanks and abdominal regions of the
animal. For test articles in the form of flakes, powders, granules,
or other particulates, the appropriate amount of test material can be
placed on a gauze pad which has been moistened with a vehicle such
as physiological saline and applied to the animal. The design of the
study will dictate whether the test sites are occluded or nonoccluded.
When occlusion is not required the animal may be fitted with an Elizabethan collar to prevent ingestion of the test chemical. The collars
should be used only during the exposure period if possible. Collars
should be firm fitting but not so tight that breathing or the animal's
ability to eat or drink is impaired. A properly fitting collar for
a rat will slide over the animal's head with gentle pressure but be
tight enough so that it cannot be easily removed by simple forelimb
pressure by the animal. Attachment of the collar is completed by
placing it in front of the rat so that the animal explores it with his
nose. As the nose pokes through the central hole, the collar is
gently pushed over the head and neck with a twisting motion. The
collar should be checked for proper fit once it is in place.

In cases where collars are not used, oral ingestion can be pre-
cluded by either occlusive or nonocclusive dressings. Nonocclusive

dressings include cotton flannel, additional gauze, and elastic bandages. Occlusive dressings include rubber dental dam and impervious plastic sheeting. The entire trunk of the animal is covered with
the wrapping material which is secured in place with several long
strips of adhesive tape at the anterior and posterior ends. The area
of taping should be as distant from the dosing area as possible since
tape burns may preclude the appropriate evaluation of the skin for
irritation reactions. The tape should not be applied in such a manner to affect the animal's ability to move in its cage or to breathe
properly. It is a common mistake for animal technicians to apply
the tape so tightly that animals succumb to the dosing and wrapping
techniques. At the end of the exposure period the wrappings are
cut with scissors and removed. Any test material remaining on the
skin may be wiped or washed if required by the study protocol.

## C. Dermal Observations

Exposure sites may be graded for appearance of dermal irritation by
several different systems. The most frequently used system is that
of Draize (2). The design for the study should give consideration
as to the frequency of these observations. It is also important to
include a provision in the protocol for the early sacrifice of the
animals for humane reasons. If excessive irritation, fissuring, or
necrosis are observed and these findings are deemed to have an
adverse effect on the animal, sacrifice should be considered.

## V.  OBSERVATIONS

During the course of repeated-dose toxicity studies, the animals are
observed on a regular basis for mortality, moribundity, signs of
generalized toxicity, and changes in body weight and food consumption. Additional tests may be included in the experimental design to assess potential effects on hematological, biochemical, physiological, neurological, and ophthalmological parameters. The selection
of the appropriate tests depends on the use of the chemical, the
regulatory body for which the test is conducted, and suspected
organ systems that may be affected by ingestion of the chemical.

## A.  Generalized Toxicity

Every animal is observed at regular intervals for differences in the
physical condition and behavior of the animal and for the location
and character of specific abnormal findings. Commonly, all animals
are observed at least twice daily, once in the morning and once in
the late afternoon, for mortality and general physical appearance.
These observations should be made on a frequent enough basis to

limit the numbers of unobserved animal deaths in which tissues are lost to autolysis.

The frequency of complete physical and clinical examinations for all animals should be defined by the study design. The OECD test guidelines require a careful clinical examination of all animals daily. TSCA guidelines require daily handling and physical evaluation of all animals.

Physical examinations include observations for pharmacological and toxicological effects, behavioral abnormalities, and digital palpation for tissue masses. Most laboratories have, as standard operating procedure, defined those clinical findings considered appropriate for each animal specie. Terminology for clinical findings should be standardized by the laboratory. These observations are generally comprised of those obvious signs that can be readily identified by a skilled technician rather than diagnostic evaluations reserved for the study director or other specialists.

Digital palpation of the test animals for suspected tumors is completed on a regular basis and records regarding the time to appearance and disposition of the lesions can be maintained. These records should include the location, size, and any changes that may have occurred since the previous interval. A system for tracking tissue masses has been previously described in the dermal toxicity section. Some laboratories measure tissue masses to include length, width, and height while other laboratories use descriptive terms to serve this purpose (e.g., peasized).

## B. Clinical Pathology

Changes in hematology, clinical biochemistry, and urinalysis parameters are assessed on a regular basis in repeated-dose toxicity studies. The frequency of clinical intervals and the parameters evaluated depends on the purpose of the study and the regulatory body for which the study is required. The minimum requirements are specified by the TSCA, FIFRA, and OECD guidelines.

## C. Ophthalmology

Ophthalmological evaluations are performed to determine changes in the ocular tissues of the animals. The pupils are dilated and evaluations are made by an observer skilled in the use of a slit-lamp biomicroscope, funduscope, or other appropriate equipment.

## D. Neurological Assessments

Evaluation of potential neurotoxic effects of test chemicals involves four specific areas: functional deficits, motor activity, behavioral responses, and neuropathology. Screening procedures such as those discussed by Irwin (3) detect changes in sight, sound, and other sensory functions. Techniques for evaluation of motor activity have been described by Finger (4) and by Reiter and MacPhail (5). Techniques for schedule-controlled operant behavioral assessment are described by Laties (6) and by the National Academy of Science (7).

## VI. DATA INTERPRETATION

The primary step in the evaluation of data from repeated dose toxicity studies should include a review of the purpose for which the study was conducted. Since these studies provide the basis upon which regulatory bodies assess the potential risks to humans associated with chemical exposure the most current reporting requirements of that agency should be reviewed. Specific reporting and evaluation requirements can be found in the FIFRA or TSCA test guidelines or in test rules for the specific chemical. The EPA has also prepared data evaluation guidelines for several types of studies.

Data evaluation requires appropriate statistical comparisons of the data from the treated groups to the collateral control groups. Statistically significant differences between the control and treated groups are considered as an indication of chemical-related effect but not as definitive proof.

Because of the limited numbers of animals used in toxicity studies, statistical comparisons of study data to both published and in-house historical control data permits a more valid assessment of potential treatment effects. An organization can provide no better service to their professionals for data evaluation than a properly controlled, statistically compared base of historical laboratory data.

Upon completion of the statistical evaluation of the data, the toxicologist can make an interpretation and evaluation of the study data. This evaluation involves the professional opinion of the study director and other scientists. Therefore, no simple rules or procedures exist or can be provided. Knowledge of dose-response criteria and of "normal" values coupled with the statistical evaluations are most frequently the basis for decision making. In the final analysis, however, it is the experience and intuition of the scientists that arrive at the final conclusions.

## VII. COMMON MISTAKES

Some common mistakes and problems associated with the various test procedures have been included in the sections above.

The most basic premise in the conduct of any toxicity study is that the correct animal must receive the correct dose for the duration

specified in the protocol.  The most serious mistake that can occur
in the conduct of a study is the misdosing of the test animals.  Errors in observations or procedural errors in dosing (with the exception of animal death or irreversible damage) can generally be corrected without the loss of the entire study.  Misdosing of the animals
cannot be corrected.

Procedures for the correct identification of the animal and for the
test chemical are essential.  A simple procedure entails color coding
of dosing solution containers and animal cage cards.  The labels on
the dosing solution containers should include, as a minimum, the
study number, the concentration of the test chemical in the solution
(diet), the treatment group number, and the mixing date.  Animal
cage cards should include the permanent animal number, study number, group number, sex, dose level, and study initiation date.

Proper calculations of compound and matrix needs are necessary
for proper preparation.  These calculations can be made and verified
in one step.  Two technical personnel (e.g., the study director and
the lab supervisor) independently perform the calculations by whatever method each is most familiar with, the results are compared and
any discrepancies resolved.  Final calculations should be reverified
by each person.

The procedures for the preparation of the dosing solution should
be written in recipe form so that anyone could, if the need occurred,
be able to properly mix the dosing vehicle.  This procedure should
be readily accessible also.  It serves no purpose to have a detailed
procedure that cannot be found when needed.  Analytical verification of the dose media should be done prior to initiation of the study
to assure the acceptability of the mixing procedures.

An embarrassing situation that occurs more frequently than one
would admit is discovering that an insufficient quantity of test chemical is available.  This finding usually occurs when the most current
dosing matrix is being prepared for use the following day.  This
problem can be avoided by determining the quantity of test material
required for the study prior to study initiation and making the necessary arrangements to assure test compound is available before running
out.  This is particularly important for chronic studies where a
single lot of the material should be used, if possible, for the entire
test or battery of tests.  The required amount should be set aside
for delivery to the testing lab on an established scheduled basis.

## VIII.  SUMMARY

The purpose of this chapter was to discuss some of the methods involved in the conduct of repeated-dose toxicity studies by the oral
and dermal routes.  The information was not intended to serve as a
"how to" for these types of studies but rather to supply helpful

suggestions for conducting these tests and avoiding some of the common problems associated with repeated-dose tests.

## REFERENCES

1. EPA (1985). Toxic Substances Control Act Test Guidelines: Final Rules. 40 CFR Part 798, *Fed. Reg.* *50*(188):39397–39471.
2. Draize, J. H. (1959). Dermal toxicity. In *Appraisal of the Safety of Chemicals in Foods, Drugs and Cosmetics.* Association of Food and Drug Officials of the United States (3rd printing 1975) pp. 46–59.
3. Irwin, S. (1968). Comprehensive observational assessment: Ia. A systematic quantitative procedure for assessing the behavioral and physiological state of the mouse. *Psychopharmacologia 13*: 222–257.
4. Finger, F. W. (1972). Measuring Behavioral Activity. In *Methods in Psychobiology*, Vol. 2. Edited by R. D. Myers. New York, Academic, pp. 1–19.
5. Reiter, L. W. and MacPhail, R. C. (1979). Motor activity: A survey of methods with potential use in toxicity testing. *Neurobehav. Toxicol.* (suppl.) 1:53–66.
6. Laties, V. G. (1978). How operant conditioning can contribute to behavioral toxicology. *Environ. Health Perspect. 28*:29–35.
7. National Academy of Science. (1982). Strategies to determine needs and priorities for toxicity testing. Appendix 3B. *Reference Protocol Guidelines for Neurobehavioral Toxicity Tests. 2*:123–129.
8. Organization for Economic Co-operation and Development. (1981). *OECD Guidelines for Testing of Chemicals.*

# 8

# Neurological and Behavioral Toxicology Testing

SHAYNE COX GAD / *G. D. Searle and Company, Skokie, Illinois*

## I. INTRODUCTION

Though nervous system toxicity has been with us since antiquity
(in such forms as mercury and lead poisoning), and there were significant incidents associated with specific synthetic chemicals earlier
in this century ("ginger jake" paralysis due to cresyl phosphates in
1930 and polyneuritis associated with exposure to carbon disulfide
in the 1940s, for example), it is only in the last 20 years that
awareness of the scope and importance of the problem has become
generally acknowledged.  In the last 15 years this domain, originally restricted to a few researchers, has broadened to a vast field
for scientists from such diverse disciplines as biochemistry, physiology, pharmacology, neurology, psychiatry, psychology, occupational health, epidemiology, and internal medicine.  The increased
interest stems mainly from advances in the field of neuroscience and
from enhanced public awareness of the major problems arising from
deliberate or unintentional exposure to potentially neurotoxic chemicals.  Such exposure might involve substance abuse, neurological
and psychiatric disorders caused by drugs, and poorly controlled
or unavoidable levels of chemicals present in the work place or in
the environment.

Research and test evaluations developed and approaches applied over the last 10 years (neurophysiology, morphological techniques, neurochemistry, and behavioral measures) have both greatly
increased our ability to detect abnormalities and led to confusion
over their interpretation.

Our limited understanding of both the mechanisms underlying
neurotoxic-induced diseases and of the structure–activity relationships involved with neurotoxicity at least complicates (and perhaps

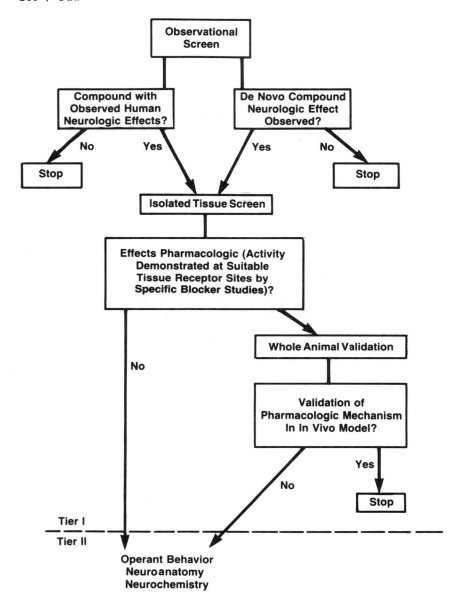

Figure 1    Tiered-decision-tree approach to neurotoxicity screening.

**Table 1** Known Neurotoxic Agents

| Agents | Effects |
| --- | --- |
| Methylmercury | Purkinje cell loss<br>Sensory deficits |
| Lead | Parietal pyramidal cell loss<br>Learning deficits<br>Motor deficits |
| X-irradiation | Cortical pyramidal cell loss<br>Hyperactivity |
| Arsenic | Sensory and motor deficits |
| Organic phosphates | Peripheral neuropathy<br>(sensory and motor deficits) |
| DDT | Hyperexcitability |
| Carbon disulfide | Polyneuropathy; central nervous<br>system effects (acute psychosis<br>and motor and sensory effects) |
| Acrylamide | Sensory and motor deficits |
| Hexachoraphene | Convulsions; central nervous sys-<br>tem effects |
| Methyl n-butyl ketone<br>(and n-hexane) | Peripheral neuropathy<br>(sensory and motor) |
| Thallium | Peripheral neuropathy |
| Triethyltin<br>(Organotins) | Hyperexcitability; motor deficit |
| Kepone (Chlorodecone) | Tremors; central nervous system<br>effects |
| Styrene | Central nervous system, sensory,<br>and motor effects |
| Dimethylaminoproprionitrile | Sensory and motor deficits |
| 5, 7, 11-Dodecatriyn-1-01 | Sensory and motor deficits; cen-<br>tral nervous system effects |
| Cadmium | Central and peripheral nervous<br>system effects |
| Carbon monoxide | Sensory and central nervous sys-<br>tem effects |
| Clioquinol | Optic nerve; central nervous sys-<br>tem effects; sensory deficits |

precludes) any firm classification of neurotoxicants based on either changes they produce (in structure or function) or on structural similarities between neurotoxic compounds on their active components. Indeed, in most cases, the actions of neurotoxic compounds are arrays of damage or dysfunction in various portions of the nervous system, and not single discrete target actions.

One can, however, consider a working classification of neurotoxicants based on their primary or first seen target site. One such classification is:

Sensory
Motor
Peripheral (both sensory and motor)
Central (integrative or behavioral)

The approach to identifying and evaluating potential neurotoxicants that will be presented in this chapter is a tier-type approach. This approach is presented in diagramatic form in Figure 1. This particular approach is from Gad (1), but others (2,3) have made similar recommendations.

The front end of this tier approach is a neurobehavioral observational screen, the tool of choice for initial (and for most of the compounds covered by this volume, the only screening test for) identification of potentially neurotoxic chemicals. The use of such screens, other behavioral test methods, or what are generally called clinical observations does, however, warrant one major caution or consideration. That is that short-term (within 24 hours of dosing or exposure) observations are insufficient on their own to differentiate between pharmacologic (reversible in the short term) and toxicological (irreversible) effects. To so differentiate, it is necessary to either use additional means of evaluation (such as inciated in Fig. 1, and including morphological evaluations) or to have the period during which observations are made extended through at least 3–4 days.

Table 1 presents a summary of neurotoxic agents identified to date.

## II. GENERAL TEST DESIGNS

The most generally useful test or detector for a neurotoxicant is enhanced careful observation of animals during such traditional toxicology studies as acute and subchronic oral and reproductive and teratology studies. A formal means of ensuring such a set of observations is to use an observational screen as proposed by several researchers (4–6,45). Such a screen, integrated into the normal course of other systemic toxicity studies, is the initial step in evaluating the potential for neurotoxicity of a compound and the one step

I believe is essential for all new materials in terms of protecting against possible neurotoxicity.

There are many variations on the design and conduct of such a screen. All have their origin in the work of neurologic and behavioral pharmacologists such as Smith (7), Irwin (8, 9), and Campbell and Richter (10). The approach presented here is based on the author's own proposed methodology (6) which has been cited as a starting point for such a screen by the Environmental Protection Agency (EPA) and Food and Drug Administration (FDA).

The following set of observations/measures are performed on animals (rats and/or mice) that constitute the experimental and control groups in standard acute, subacute, subchronic, reproductive, developmental, and chronic toxicity studies. Technicians can be trained to screen animals after approximately 6 hr with reinforcement conducted over one week. The screen replaces clinical observations performed prior to dosing, and, in the case of an acute study at 1 hr, 24 hr, 4, 7, and 14 days after dosing/exposure (unless a vehicle such as propylene glycol, which masks neurological effects by its transitory character is used, in which case the 1 hr measurement is replaced by a 6 hr measurement). For a repeated dosage study, as appropriate, the screen can be performed at 1 hr, 1, 7, 14, 30 days, and once a month thereafter. A trained technician takes from 3 to 5 min to screen a single animal. Table 2 gives a listing of all the procedures utilized, along with their probable neural correlates and the nature of the data generated by the observation. Each specific test procedure is then briefly described.

In preparation for the screen, a sufficient number of scoring sheets are filled in with the appropriate information. Then the cart employed as a mobile testing station is checked to ensure that all the necessary equipment (empty wire-bottom cage, blunt probe, penlight, 1/2 in. diameter steel rod, force transducer, ink pad, pad of blotting paper, ruler, and electronic probe thermometer) are on the cart and in working order. Each animal is then evaluated by the following procedures.

*Locomotor Activity.* The animal's movements (walking, jumping) while on the flat surface of the cart are evaluated quantitatively on a scale of 1 (hypoactive) to 5 (hyperactive), with 3 being the normal state. The data can be upgraded to interval data if one has and utilizes one of the electromagnetic activity-monitoring instruments.

*Righting Reflex.* For rats and mice, the animal is grasped by its tail and flipped in the air ($\sim$2 ft) above the cart surface so that it turns head over heels. The normal animal should land squarely on its feet. If it lands on its side, score 1 point; if on its back; score 2 points. Repeat 5 times and record its total score. For a rabbit, when placed on its side on the cart, does the animal regain its feet without noticeable difficulty?

Table 2 Observational Screen Components

| Observation | Nature of data generated[a] | Correlates to which neutral component |
| --- | --- | --- |
| Locomoter activity | S/N | M/C |
| Righting reflex | S | C/M |
| Grip strength (fore limb) | N | M |
| Body temperature | N | C |
| Salivation | Q | P |
| Startle response | Q | S/C |
| Respiration | S | M/P/C |
| Urination | S | P/M |
| Mouth breathing | Q | S |
| Convulsions | S | C |
| Pineal response | Q | Reflex |
| Piloerection | Q | P/C |
| Diarrhea | S | G.I. tract/P/M |
| Pupil size | S | P/C |
| Pupil response | Q | P/C |
| Lacrimation | Q | S/P |
| Impaired gait | S | M/C |
| Stereotypy | Q | C |
| Toe pinch | S | S (surface pain; spinal reflex) |
| Tail pinch | S | S (deep pain) |
| Wire maneuver | S | C/M |
| Hind-leg splay | N | P/M |
| Positional passivity | S | S/C |
| Tremors | S | M/C |
| Extensor thrust | S | C/M |

**Table 2** (Continued)

| Observation | Nature of date generated[a] | Correlates to which neutral component |
|---|---|---|
| Positive geotropism | Q | C |
| Limb rotation | S | M/C |

[a]Data quantal (Q), scalar (S), or interval (N). Quantal data· is characterized by being of either/or variety, such as dead/alive or present/absent. Scalar data is such that one can rank something as less than, equal to, or greater than over values, but cannot exactly quantitate the difference between such rankings. Interval data is continuous data where one can assign (theoretically) an extremely accurate value to a characteristic that can be precisely related to other values in a quantitative fashion.
Abbreviations: P, peripheral; S, sensory; M, muscular; C, central.

*Grip Strength.* For rats and mice, the animal is placed on top of the overturned wire-bottomed cage. The tail is grasped at the base and the animal is pulled along the surface to determine its ability to hold on to the wire surface. If a number of animals are observed to have markedly reduced strength, grip strength is measured by the method of Meyer (51).

*Body Temperature.* The electronic probe thermometer (with a blunt probe) is used to take a rectal temperature, allowing equilibration for 30 sec before the reading is recorded.

*Salivation.* Discharge of clear fluid from mouth, most frequently seen as beads of moisture on lips in mice and rats or as a fluid flow from the mouth in rabbits. Normal state is to see none, in which case the score sheet space should be left blank. If present, a plus sign should be recorded in the blank.

*Startle Response.* With the animal on the cart, the metal cage is struck with the blunt probe. The normal animal should exhibit a marked but short-duration response, in which case the space on the scoring sheet should be left blank. If present, a plus sign should be entered.

*Respiration.* While at rest on the cart, the animal's respiration cycle is observed and evaluated on a scale from 1 (reduced) to 5 (increased), with 3 being normal.

*Urination.* When returning the animal to its case, examine the pan beneath the cage for signs of urination and evaluate on a scale of 1 (lacking) to 5 (polyurea).

*Mouth Breathing.* Rats and mice are normally obligatory nose breathers. Note whether each animal is breathing through its mouth (if it is, place a check in the appropriate box).

*Convulsions.* If clonic or tonic convulsions are observed, they should be graded for intensity (1, minor, 5, marked) and the type and intensity recorded.

*Pineal Response (Rabbits Only).* When a blunt probe is lightly touched to the inside of the ear, the normal animal should react by moving its ear and head reflexively. If this response is present (normal case), the space should be left blank. If absent, a minus sign should be entered in the blank.

*Piloerection.* Determine whether the fur on the animal's back is raised or elevated. In the normal case (no piloerection), leave the space blank. If piloerection is present, a plus sign should be entered in the blank.

*Diarrhea.* In examining the pan beneath an animal's cage, note if there are any signs of loose or liquid stools. Normal state is for there to be none, in which case a 1 should be recorded on a scale of 1 (none) to 5 (greatly increased).

*Pupil Size.* Determine if pupils are constricted or dilated and grade them on a scale of 1–5, respectively.

*Pupil Response.* The beam of light from the pen light is played across the eyes of the animal, and changes in pupil size are noted. In the normal animal, the pupil should constrict when the beam is on it and then dilate back to normal when the light is removed. Note only if there is no response (in which case a minus sign is recorded in the blank space).

*Lacrimation.* The animal is observed for the secretion and discharge of tears. In rats and mice the tears contain a reddish pigment. No discharge is normal, and in this case the box should be left blank. If discharge is present, a plus sign should be entered.

*Impaired Gait.* The occurrence of abnormal gait is evaluated. The most frequent impairments are waddling (W), hunched gait (H), or ataxia (A, the inability of all the muscles to act in unison). Record the extent of any impairment on a scale of 1 (slight) to 5 (marked).

*Stereotypy.* Each animal is evaluated for stereotypic behavior (isolated motor acts or partial sequences of more complex behavioral patterns from the repertoire of a species, occurring out of context and with an abnormally high frequency). These are graded on a scale of 0–5 (as per Sturgeon et al. (11) if such signs are present.

*Toe Pinch (Rats and Mice Only).* The blunt probe is used to bring pressure to bear on one of the digits of the hind limb. This

should evoke a response from the normal animal, graded on a scale
from 1 (absent) to 5 (exaggerated).

*Tail Pinch.* The procedure detailed above is utilized with the
animal's tail instead of its hind limb, and is graded on the same scale.

*Wire Maneuver (Rats and Mice).* The animal is placed on the
metal or wooden rod suspended parallel to the cart 2 feet above it.
It ability to move along the rod is evaluated. If impaired, a score
of from 1 (slightly impaired) to 5 (unable to stay on the rod) is
recorded. The diameter of the rod relative to the animal is critical.
Larger animals need thicker rods.

*Hind Leg Splay.* After the method of Edwards and Parker (52),
the hind paws are pressed on a stamp pad and marked with ink.
The rat or mouse is then held 30 cm above a sheet of blotting paper
placed on the cart, and dropped, and the distance between the
prints of the two hind paws is measured.

*Positional Passivity.* When placed in an awkward position (such
as on the edge of the top of the wir-bottom cage) on the cart surface, does the animal immediately move into a more normal position?
If not, a score should be recorded on a scale of 1 (slightly impaired)
to 5 (cataleptic).

*Tremors.* These are periods of continued fine movements, usually starting in the limbs (and perhaps limited to them). Absence
of tremors is normal, in which case no score is recorded. If present,
they are graded on a scale of 1 (slight and infrequent) to 5 (continuous and marked).

*Extensor Thrust.* The sole of either hind foot is pressed with
a blunt object. A normal animal will push back against the blunt
object. If reduced or absent, this response should be graded on a
scale of 1 (reduced) to 5 (absent).

*Positive Geotropism.* The animal is placed on the inclined (at an
angle of -30°) top surface of the wire cage with its head facing
downward. It should turn 180° and face "uphill," in which case
the space on the form should be left blank. If this occurs, a negative sign should be recorded in the blank.

*Limb Rotation.* Take hold of the animal's hind limbs and move
them through their normal plane of rotation. In the normal state,
they should rotate readily but there should be some resistance. The
variations from normal are no resistance (1) to markedly increased
resistance or rigidity (5), with 3 being normal.

There are a number of other tests which may be added to a behavioral screen to enhance its sensitivity. These methods tend to
require more equipment and effort, so if several compounds are to
be screened, their inclusion in a screen must be carefully considered.
An example of such methods is the "narrowing bridge" technique,
all these methods require some degree of training of animals prior
to their actual use in test system. This approach has served the

author well in the case of a number of varied industrial chemicals (48-50).

The narrowing bridge test measures the ability of a rat to perform a task requiring neuromuscular control and coordination. Any factor which renders the neuromuscular system of the rat less effective will be expected to result in the rat obtaining a higher score in this test. Therefore, the test cannot by itself discriminate between injuries to the brain (e.g., degenerative changes or tumors), spinal cord, muscle, or peripheral nerve. In addition, compounds which exert a pharmacological action on the central or peripheral nervous systems will be expected to alter the performance of rats on this test. However, a study of the manner in which the performance of the rat alters with time plus clinical examination will enable, in many cases, a distinction to be made between these different possibilities.

The main use of the test is in the study of peripheral neuropathy. It has been demonstrated that this test will detect acrylamide neuropathy 1 week before any clinical signs of neuropathy are apparent. It also claimed that this test is the most sensitive method for detecting hexane neuropathy.

The narrowing bridge consists of three 1.5 m wooden bridges, 23 cm above the ground arranged at right angles. The widths of the three bridges are 2.5, 2.0, and 1.8 cm, respectively. The rat is placed at the end of the 2.5 cm wide bridge and must traverse the three bridges to get to the home cage. The number of times the rat slips is counted. The score on each section of the bridge is calculated as follows:

Score on 2.5 cm wide bridge = number of slips × 3
Score on 2.0 cm wide bridge = number of slips × 2
Score on 1.8 cm wide bridge = number of slips × 1

The total is calculated by adding the scores from the three sections of the bridge. The test is repeated 3 times and the measure of the performance of the rat in the test is the mean of the three total scores. Animals are trained to navigate the bridge system for 5 consecutive days prior to receiving any test compound.

## A. Isolated Tissue Assays

The second phase in the tier I screen is a series of isolated tissue preparation bioassays, conducted with appropriate standards, to determine if the material acts pharmacologically directly on neural receptor sites or transmission properties. Though these bioassays are normally performed by a classical pharmacologist, a good technician can be trained to conduct them. The required equipment consists of a Magnus (or similar style) tissue bath (12,13,46), a physiograph or kymograph, force transducer, glassware, a stimulator, and bench spectrophotometer. The assays utilized in the screening battery are listed in Table 3, along with the original reference describing each preparation and assay. The assays are performed as per the original author's descriptions with only minor modifications, except that control standards (as listed in Table 3) are always used. Only those assays that are appropriate for the neurological/muscular alterations observed in the screen are utilized. Note that all these are intact organ preparations, not minced tissue preparations as others (14) have recommended for biochemical assays.

The first modification in each assay is that, where available, both positive and negative standard controls (pharmacological agonists and antagonists, respectively) are employed. Before the preparation is utilized to assay the test material, the issue preparation is exposed to the agonist to ensure that the preparation is functional and to provide a baseline dose-response curve against which the activity of the test material can be quantitatively compared. After the test material has been assayed (if a dose-response curve has been generated), one can determine whether the antagonist will selectively block the activity of the test material. If so, specific activity at that receptor can be considered as established. In this assay sequence, it must be kept in mind that a test material may act to either stimulate or depress activity, and therefore the roles of the standard agonists and antagonists may be reversed.

Commonly overlooked when performing these assays is the possibility of metabolism to an active form that can be assessed in this in vitro model. The test material should be tested in both original and "metabolized" forms. The metabolized form is prepared by incubating a 5% solution (in aerated Tyrodes) or other appropriate physiological salt solution with strips of suitably prepared test species liver for 30 min. A filtered supernatant is then collected from this incubation and tested for activity. Suitable metabolic blanks should also be tested.

## B.  Electrophysiology Methods

There are a number of electrophysiological techniques available which can be used to detect and/or assess neurotoxicity. These techniques can be divided into two broad general categories; those focused on central nervous system (CNS) function and those focused on peripheral nervous system function (47).

First, however, the function of the individual components of the nervous system, how they are connected together, and how they operate as a complete system should be very briefly overviewed.

Data collection and communication in the nervous system occurs by means of graded potentials, action potentials, and synaptic coupling

Table 3 Isolated Tissue Pharmacologic Assays

| Assay system | Endpoint | Standards (agonist/antagonist) | References |
|---|---|---|---|
| Rat ileum | General activity | None (side-spectrum assay for intrinsic activity) | 15 |
| Guinea pig vas deferens | Muscarinic<br>nicotinic | Methacholine/atropine<br>Methacholine/hexamethonium | 16 |
| | or Muscarinic | Methacholine/atropine | |
| Rat serosal strip | Nicotinic | Methacholine/hexamethonium | 17 |
| Rat vas deferens | Alpha adrenergic | Norepinephrine/phenoxybenza-mine | 18 |
| Rat uterus | Beta adrenergic | Epinephrine/propranol | 19 |
| Rat uterus | Kinin receptors | Bradykinin/none | 20 |

| | | | |
|---|---|---|---|
| Guinea pig tracheal chain | Dopaminergic | Dopamine/none | 15 |
| Rat serosal strips | Tryptaminergic | 5-Hydroxytryptamine (serotonin)/dibenzyline or lysergic acid dibromide | 21 |
| Guinea pig tracheal chain | Histaminergic | Histamine/benadryl | 22,23 |
| Guinea pig ileum (electrically stimulated) | Endorphan receptors | Methenkephaline/none | 24 |
| Red blood cell hemolysis | Membrane stabilization | Chlorpromazine (not a receptor-mediated activity) | 25 |
| Frog rectus abdominis | Membrane depolarization | Decamethonium iodide (not a receptor-mediated activity) | 26 |

of neurons. These electrical potentials may be recorded and analyzed at two different levels depending on the electrical coupling
arrangements: individual cell (that is, intracellular and extracellu-
lar) or multiple cell (e.g., EEG, evoked potentials (EPs), slow
potentials). These potentials may be recorded in specific central
or peripheral nervous system areas (e.g., visual cortex, hippocampus, sensory and motor nerves, muscle spindles) during various behavioral states or in in vitro preparations (e.g., nerve-muscel,
retinal photoreceptor, brain slice).

## C.  CNS Function:  Electroencephalography

The electroencephalogram (EEG) is a dynamic measure reflecting the
instantaneous integrated synaptic activity of the CNS, which most
probably represents, in coded form, all ongoing processes under
higher nervous control. Changes in frequency, amplitude, variability, and pattern of the EEG are thought to be directly related to
underlying biochemical changes, which are believed to be directly
related to defined aspects of behavior. Therefore, changes in the
EEG should be reflected by alterations in behavior and vice versa.
    The human EEG is easily recorded and readily quantified, is
obtained noninvasively (scalp recording), samples several regions
of the brain simultaneously, requires minimal cooperation from the
subject, and is minimally influenced by prior testing. Therefore,
it is a very useful and recommended clinical test in cases in which
accidental exposure to chemicals produces symptoms of CNS involvement and in which long-term exposures to high concentrations are
suspected of causing CNS toxicity.
    Since the EEG recorded using scalp electrodes is an average of
the multiple activity of many small areas of cortical surface beneath
the electrodes, it is possible that in situations involving noncortical
lesions, the EEG may not accurately reflect the organic brain damage
present. Noncortical lesions following acute or long-term low-level
exposures to toxicants are well documented in neurotoxicology (27).
The drawback mentioned earlier can be partially overcome by utilizing activation or evocative techniques, such as hyperventilation,
photic stimulation, or sleep, which can increase the amount of information gleaned from a standard EEG.
    As a research tool, the utility of the EEG lies in the fact that
it reflects instantaneous changes in the state of the CNS. The pattern can thus be used to monitor the sleep-wakefulness cycle activation or deactivation of the brainstem, and the state of anesthesia
during an actue electrophysiological procedure. Another advantage
of the EEG, which is shared by all CNS electrophysiological techniques, is that it can assess the differential effects of toxicants (or
drugs) on various brain areas or structures. Finally, specific CNS

regions (e.g., the hippocampus) have particular patterns of after-discharge following chemical or electrical stimulation which can be quantitatively examined and utilized as a tool in neurotoxicology.

The EEG does have some disadvantages, or, more correctly, some limitations. It cannot provide information about the effects of toxicants on the integrity of sensory receptors or of sensory or motor pathways. As a corollary, it cannot provide an assessment of the effects of toxicants on sensory system capacities. Finally, the EEG does not provide specific information at the cellular level and therefore lacks the rigor to provide detailed mechanisms of action.

Rats represent an excellent model for this as they are cheap, resist infection during chronic electrode and cannulae implantation, and are relatively easy to train so that behavioral assessments can be made concurrently.

Depending on the time of toxicant exposure, the type of scientific information desired, and the necessity of behavioral correlations, a researcher can perform acute and/or chronic EEG experiments. Limitations of the former are that most drugs that produce general anesthesia modify the pattern of EEG activity and thus can complicate subtle effects of toxicants. However, this limitation can be partially avoided if the effect is robust enough. For sleep-wakefulness studies, it is also essential to monitor and record the electromyogram (EMG).

Excellent reviews of these electrophysiology approachs can be found in Fox et al. (28) and Takeuchi and Koike (29).

## D. Neurochemical and Biochemical Assays

Though some very elegant methods are now available to study the biochemistry of the brains and nervous system, none has yet discovered any generalized marker chemicals which will serve as reliable indicators or early warnings of neurotoxic actions or potential actions. There are, however, some useful methods. Before looking at these, however, one should understand the basic problems involved.

Normal biochemical events surrounding the maintenance and functions of the nervous system centers around energy metabolism, biosynthesis of macromolecules, and neurotransmitter synthesis, storage, release, uptake, and degradation. Measurement of these events is complicated by the sequestered nature of the components of the nervous system and the transient and liabile nature of the moieties involved. Use of measurements of alterations in these functions as indicators of neurotoxicity is further complicated by our lack of a complete understanding of the normal operation of these systems and by the multitude of day to day occurrences (such as diurnal cycle, diet, temperature, age, sex, and endocrine status) which are constantly modulating the baseline system. For detailed discussions of these difficulties, the reader is advised to see Damstra and Bond (30,31).

There are two specific markers which may be measured to evaluate the occurrence of specific neurotoxic events. These are neurotoxic esterase (NTE; the inhibition of which is a marker for organophosphate-induced delayed neuropathy) (44) and β-galactosidase (which is a marker for Wallerian degeneration of nerves). Johnson and Lotti (32-34) have established that inhibition of 70-90% of normal levels of NTE in hens 36 hours after being dosed with a test compound is correlated with the development some 15 days later of ataxia and the other classic physiologic signs of delayed neuropathy. Johnson's 1977 (33) article clearly describes the actual assay procedure.

β-galactosidase is associated not with a single class of compounds but rather with a particular expression of neurotoxicity—Wallerian degeneration. In nerves undergoing Wallerian degeneration following nerve section, the activity of β-galactosidase increases by over a thousand percent. There is also evidence that this enzyme is elevated in the peripheral nerves and ganglia of rats suffering from certain toxic neuropathies. This assay, therefore, can be used as a biochemical method for detecting neurotoxic effects of compounds (35).

β-galactosidase is a constituent of lysosomes whose function is to split β-galactosides, for example, it will convert lactose into galactose and glucose. The assay method below utilizes an artificial substrate, 4-methylumbelliferyl β-D-galactopyranoside (MUG). At an acid pH, β-galactosidase will split galactose from this compound to leave a product which fluoresces in alkaline solution.

In summary, animals exposed to or dosed with the chemical are necropsied and peripheral nervous tissue is collected. The β-galactosidse activity of peripheral nervous tissue homogenates is determined by incubating 0.2 ml of 1% w/v homogenates with $1 \times 10^{-3}$ M methylumbelliferyl β-galactoside in 0.1M glycine buffer, pH 3.0 for 1 hr at 37°C. The enzyme releases methylumbelliferone which can be measured fluorimetrically in alkaline solution (excitation wavelength 325-380 nm, emission wavelength 450 nm) (36).

Progress in the more generalized methodologies of evaluating alterations in neurotransmitter levels has not been as conclusive and is reviewed by Bondy (37,38) and specific methodologies are presented by Ho and Hoskins (39). That such methodologies can be useful is demonstrated by the compendium of results presented by Damstra and Bondy (31) that many neurotoxicants have been shown to be associated with alterations in nervous tissue metabolism or in vivo levels of neurotransmitters or neurotransmitter binding.

## E. Pathology

Just as there are special biochemical measurements associated with the study of neurotoxicity, the methodology used in evaluating morphological alterations is also specific. The newly introduced techniques of tissue preparation and examination have been adopted slowly by neuropathologists and, to this day, conventional histological methods are overwhelmingly utilized for the routine examination of human nervous tissue. Toxicologists have been slow to exploit the potential of these new techniques to detail pathological changes and to illuminate the mechanisms by which toxic damage is effected. Modern techniques of tissue preparation and examination will be more heavily utilized for experimental neurotoxicology, and many even become accepted as the method of choice for routine pathological examination of all organs.

Many of these new techniques are presented or reviewed in detail by Spencer et al. (40) and Spencer and Bischoff (41). Three additional generalized methodologies for collection and staining of nervous tissue will be presented in brief below.

### Sciatic Nerve Dissection

1. Terminate animal by appropriate rapid and humane means.
2. Remove fur from the hind limb and lower dorsal surface.
3. Make incisions at perpendicular angles in the region of the new joint to expose the sciatic nerve from the spinal cord to the foot.
4. Raise the limb away from the abdomen to reveal a small white section of sciatic nerve.
5. Make two cuts to either side of the nerve mare to produce a plug for well of tissue.
6. Carefully remove the resulting circular area of nerve and muscle and fix in appropriate preservative or process for biochemical analysis.

### Rat Trigeminal Ganglion Dissection

1. Terminate animal by appropriate rapid and humane means.
2. Remove the scalp from the top of the skull.
3. Using bone scissors, puncture the skull along the edges of the region from which the scalp has been removed, and carefully and remove the top of the skull, exposing the brain.
4. Using a blunt probe, carefully tease the brain from the skull.
5. Identify the trigeminal nerves on either side of the bottom of the brain. These are two cream-colored triangles of tissue.

6. Hold each ganglion with forceps and detach any connective tissue.
7. Remove the ganglia and preserve the process them as appropriate.

Rat Dorsal Root Ganglion Dissection

1. Terminate animal by appropriate rapid and humane means.
2. Remove the fur and skin from the dorsal surface.
3. Remove the muscle layers from the above the spinal cord to reveal the terminal vertebra.
4. Remove all connective tissue so that the bone is exposed.
5. Remove the upper section of the neural arch by cutting through the bone on either side of the neural spine. Then cut through the vertebrae so that the bone can be lifted away.
6. Remove the sympathetic nerve processes and clear all connective tissue from the central canal. Separate the connective tissue to expose each dorsal root ganglion.
7. Remove as many ganglia as needed to cold (below 10°C) saline, then process further as needed.

## F. Nerve Cell Culture

Over the last 10 years numerous cultured cell models have been developed for screening for study of specific target organ toxicities. Nervous system toxicity has been no exception: there are a number of very active groups in this area. Some of these studies focus on single forms of neurotoxicity (such as that of Fedalei and Nardone (44) on cultured cells to screen for organophosphate neuropathy via NTE inhibition), while most are designed or intended as generalized screens for particular mechanistic forms of neurotoxicity.

Culture of nervous system components was pioneered in the early 1960s. Various methodologies, each with specific advantages and drawbacks, were developed by different laboratories. The major difficulty has been that neurons, as soon as they are sufficiently differentiated to be recognizable as such, probably are not capable of significant additional multiplication in the culture milieu. This purification and cloning of neurons is difficult and very tedious at best. The more complex the culture system, and thus the closer to normality the surrounding nervous system cells, the less likely are the neurons to be capable of multiplication. Although the use of several nervous system tumors in culture and the appearance of cultures of purified cell types have reduced dependence on primary cultures, the disadvantages of isolating any nervous system cell type out of an organ in which the intercellular interdependencies of function are so great are frightening. The mystique of the culture of nervous system components has been reduced to the degree that, although all of the details have not been explained, any well-equipped laboratory should be able to reproduce most of the culture systems that have been reported.

The original promise projected for the culture techniques, that of rapid and complete dissection of complex nervous system functions within a few years, has not yet been realized. In fact, it seems as if the capacity to produce useful experimental systems has outstripped the capacity of the investigators to ask meaningful questions with those systems. The brain and its functions may be so complex that our minds cannot be stretched sufficiently to make meaningful or reasonable hypotheses and test them out? One hopes that these culture systems are simply poised for the time, when they will be employed to raise and answer fundamental questions about the nervous system, its functions, and its development. Such breakthroughs will only come after more investigation to find the weakest point.

Neurotoxicology has provided this effort with some essential tools in developing this model, as agents with known neurotoxic effect on the intact organism can be used as probes in cultured cell systems to correlate organism level effects with cellular mechanisms.

Cultured screening systems used in neurotoxicology include whole embryos, intact organs, explants (i.e., portions of organs, primary cells, and cell lines, that is, tumor cells). Each of these in turn has strengths and weaknesses. Interested readers should see Schrier (42) or Vernadakis et al. (43) for indepth presentations in this area.

### G. Old Hen Test for Organophosphate-Induced Delayed Neuropathy

The most established (and until recently, the only regulatorly recognized) test method in neurotoxicology is the "old hen test," or delayed neurotoxicity test in hens following acute (single) exposure to a test compound.

A basic design for this test may be summarized as:

Three groups of adult hens are selected and treated as follows:
Experimental group: dosed orally with the test compound.
Positive control group: dosed orally with tri-o-tolyl phosphate.
Negative control group: not dosed.

If the hens are to be dosed with a compound possessing a pronounced cholinergic effect, they are given an intramuscular injection of atropine sulfate and pralidoxime chloride prior to dosing, these helps ensure sufficient survivors.

The birds are observed daily for signs of locomotor ataxia, and birds showing persistent signs of ataxia are sent for pathology. If no persistent ataxia is observed in the experimental group after 21 days, the dosing regime is repeated and the hens observed for a further 21 days after which they are sent for pathological investigation.

## REFERENCES

1. Gad, S. C. (1981). A sensory/neuro screen for use in industrial toxicology. *Toxicologist* 1:150.
2. Weiss, B. (1975). Behavioral methods for investigating environmental health effects. In *Proc. Intl. Symp. Recent Adv. Assessment Health Effects*. Environ. Pollution, Paris, 1974, Luxembourg; Community of European Committees, pp. 2415–33.
3. Evans, H. L. and Weiss, B. (1978). Behaviroal toxicology. In *Contemporary Research in Behavioral Pharmacology*. Edited by D. E. Blackman and D. J. Sanger. New York; Plenum, pp. 449–87.
4. Zbinden, G. (1981). Experimental methods in behavioral teratology. *Arch, Toxicol.* 48:69–88.
5. Mitchell, C. L., and Tilson, H. A. (1982). Behavioral toxicology in risk assessment: Problems and research needs. *Crit. Rev. Toxicol.* 10:265–274.
6. Gad, S. C. (1982). A neuromuscular screen for use in industrial toxicology. *J. Toxicol. Environ. Hlth.* 9:691–704.
7. Smith, W. G. (1961). Pharmacological screening tests. In *Progress in Medicinal Chemistry*, vol. 1. Edited by G. Ellis and G. West, Washington, D. C.; Butterworth, pp. 1–33.
8. Irwin, S. (1962). Drug screening and evaluation procedures. *Science* 136:123–128.
9. Irwin, S. (1964). Drug screening and evaluation of new compounds in animals. Animal and clinical pharmacologic techniques. In *Drug Evaluation*. Edited by J. Nodine and P. Siegler. Chicago, Year Book Medical Publishers, Inc., pp. 36–54.
10. Campbell, D., and Richter, W. (1967). Whole animal screening studies. *Acta Pharmacol.* 25:345–363.
11. Sturgeon, R. D., Fessler, R. G., and Meltzer, H. Y. (1979). Behavioral rating scales for assessing phencyclidine induced locomotor activity, stereotyped behavior and ataxia in rats. *Eur. J. Pharmacol.* 59:169–179.
12. Turner, R. A. (1965). *Screening Methods in Pharmacology*, vols. I and II. New York, Academic, pp. 42–47, 60–68, 27–128.
13. Offermeier, J., and Ariens, E. J. (1966). Serotonin I. Receptors involved in its action. *Arch. Int. Pharmacodyn. Ther.* 164:92–215.

14. Bondy, S. C. (1979). Rapid screening of neurotoxic agents by in vivo means. In *Effects of Food and Drugs on the Development and Function of the Nervous System: Methods for Predicting Toxicity.* Edited by R. M. Gryder and V. H. Frankos. Washington, D.C., Office of Health Affairs, FDA, pp. 133–143.

15. Domer, F. R. (1971). *Animal Experiments in Pharmacological Analysis.* Springfield, IL; Charles C. Thomas, pp. 98, 115, 155, 164, 220.

16. Leach, G. D. H. (1956). Estimation of drug antagonisms in the isolated gui pig was deferens. *J. Pharm. Pharmacol.* 8:501.

17. Khayyal, M. T., Tolba, N. M., El-Hawary, M. B., and El-Wahed, S. A. (1974). A Sensitive Method for the Bioassay of acetylcholine. *Eur. J. Pharmacol.* 25:287–290.

18. Rossum, J. M. van (1965). Different types of sympathomimetic β-receptors. *J. Pharm. Pharmacol.* 17:202.

19. Levy, B., and Tozzi, S. (1963). The adrenergic receptive mechanism of the rat uterus. *J. Pharmacol. Exp. Ther.* 142:178.

20. Gecse, A., Zsilinsky, E., and Szekeres, L. (1976). Bradykinin antagonism. In *Kinins; Pharmacodynamics and Biological Roles.* Edited by F. Sicuteri, N. Back, and G. Haberland. New York, Plenum Press, pp. 5–13.

21. Lin, R. C. Y., and Yeoh, T. S. (1965). An improvement of Vane's stomach strip preparation for the assay of 5-hydroxytryptamine. *J. Pharm. Pharmacol.* 17:524–525.

22. Castillo, J. C., and De Beer, E. J. (1947). The guinea pig tracheal chain as an assay for histamine agonists. *Fed. Proc.* 6:315.

23. Castillo, J. C., and De Beer, E. J. (1947b). The tracheal chain. *J. Pharmacol. Exp. Ther.* 90:104.

24. Cox, B. M., Opheim, K. E., Teschemach, H., and Goldstein, A. (1975). A peptide-like substance from pituitary that acts like morphine 2. Purification and properties. *Life Sci.* 16: 1777–1782.

25. Seeman, P., and Weinstein, J. (1966). Erythrocyte membrane stabilization by tranquilizers and anithistamines. *Biochem. Pharmacol.* 15:1737–1752.

26. Burns, B. D., and Paton, W. D. M. (1951). Depolarization of the motor end-plate by decamethonium and acetylcholine. *J. Physiol.* (London) 115:41–73.

27. Norton, S. (1980). Toxic responses of the central nervous system. In *Toxicology: The Basic Science of Poisions*, 2nd edition. Edited by J. Doull, C. D. Klaassen, and M. O. Amdur. New York, Macmillan, Inc.

28. Fox, D. A., Lowndes, H. E., and Bierkamper, G. G. (1982). Electrophysiological techniques in neurotoxicology. In *Nervous System Toxicology*. Edited by C. L. Mitchell. New York, Raven Press, pp. 299–336.

29. Takeuchi, Y., and Koike, Y. (1985). Electrophysiological methods for the in vivo assessment of neurotoxicology. In *Neurotoxicology*. Edited by K. Blum and L. Manzo. New York, Marcel Dekker, Inc., pp. 613–629.

30. Damstra, T., and Bondy, S. C. (1980). The current status and future of biochemical assays for neurotoxicity. In *Experimental and Clinical Neurotoxicology*. Edited by P. S. Spencer and H. H. Schaumburg. Baltimore, Williams and Wilkins, pp. 820–833.

31. Damstra, T., and Bondy, S. C. (1982). Neurochemical approaches to the deletion of neurotoxicity. In *Nervous System Toxicology*. Edited by C. L. Mitchell. New York, Raven Press, pp. 349–373.

32. Johnson, M. K. (1975). The delayed neuropathy caused by some organophosphorus esters: Mechanism & challenge. *Crit. Rev. Toxicol.* 3L289–316.

33. Johnson, M. K. (1977). Improved assay of neurotoxic esterase for screening. Organophosphates for delayed neurotoxicity potential. *Arch. Toxic.* 37:113–115.

34. Johnson, M. K., and Lotti, M. (1980). Delayed neurotoxicity caused by chronic feeding of organophosphates requires a high-point of inhibition of neurotoxic esterase. *Toxicol. Letts.* 5: 99–102.

35. Dewar, A. J., and Moffett, B. J. (1979). Biochemical methods for detecting neurotoxicity—a short review. *Pharmacol. Ther.* 5:545–562.

36. Dewar, A. J. (1981). Neurotoxicity testing with particular references to biochemical methods. In *Testing for Toxicity*. Edited by .. W. Gorrod. London, Taylor & Francis, Ltd., pp. 199–217.

37. Bondy, S. C. (1982). Neurotransmitter binding interactions as a screen for neurotoxicity. In *Mechanisms of Actions of Neurotoxic Substances*. Edited by K. N. Prasad and A. Vernadakis. New York, Raven Press, pp. 25–50.

38. Bondy, S. C. (1984). Especial consideration for neurotoxicological research. *Crit. Rev. Toxicol.* 14(4):381–402.

39. Ho, I. K., and Hoskins, B. (1982). Biochemical methods for neurotoxicological analyses of neuroregulators and cyclic nucleotides. In *Principles and Methods of Toxicology*. Edited by A. W. Hayes. New York, Raven Press, pp. 375–406.

40. Spencer, P. S., Bischoff, M. C., and Schaumburg, H. H. (1980). Neuropathological methods for the detection of neurotoxic disease. In *Experimental and Clinical Neurotoxicology*.

Edited by P. S. Spencer and H. H. Schaumburg. Baltimore, Williams and Wilkins, pp. 743–757.

41. Spencer, P. S., and Bischoff, M. C. (1982). Contemporary neuropathological methods in toxicology. In *Nervous System Toxicology*. Edited by C. L. Mitchell. New York Raven Press, pp. 259–276.

42. Schrier, B. K. (1982). Nervous system cultures as toxicological test systems. In *Nervous System Toxicology*. Edited by C. L. Mitchell. New York, Raven Press, pp. 337–349.

43. Vernadakis, A., Davies, D. L., and Gremo, F. (1985). Neural culture: A tool to study cellular neurotoxicity. In *Neurotoxicity*. Edited by K. Blum and L. Manzo. New York, Marcel Dekker, Inc., pp. 559–583.

44. Fedalei, A. and Nardone, R. M. (1983). An in vitro alternative for testing the effect of organo-phosphates on neurotoxic esterase activity. In *Product Safety Evaluation*. Edited by A. M. Goldberg. New York, Mary Ann Liebert, Inc., pp. 253–269.

45. Mitchell, C. L., Tilson, H. A., and Cabe, P. A. Screening for neurobehavioral toxicity: Factors to consider. In *Nervous System Toxicology*. Edited by C. L. Mitchell. New York, Raven Press, pp. 237–245.

46. Nodine, J. H., and Siegler, P. E. (eds.) (1964). *Animal and Clinical Techniques in Drug Evaluation*. Chicago, Year Book Medical Publishers, Inc.

47. Seppalainen, A. M. (1975). Applications of neurophysiological methods in occupational medicine: A review. *Scand. J. Work Environ. Health 1*:1–14.

48. Gad. S. C. McKelvey, J. A., and Turney, R. A. (1979). NIAX catalyst ESN- subchronic neuropharmacology and neurotoxicology. *Drug and Chem. Toxicol. 3*(3):223–236.

49. Gad, S. C., Conroy, W. J., McKelvey, J. A., and Turney, R. A. (1978). Behavioral and neuropharmacological toxicology of the macrocyclic ether 18-Crown 6. *Drug Chem. Toxicol. 1*:339–354.

50. Gad, S. C., Dunn, B. J., Gavigan, F. A., Reilly, C., and Peckham, J. C. (1987). Acute and Neurotoxicity of 5, 7, 11-dodecatriyn-1-ol and 4, 7, 11, 13-octadecatetrayne-1, 18-Diol. *J. Appl. Toxicol.* (in press).

51. Meyer, O. A., Tilson, H. A., Byrd, W. C., and Riley, M. T. (1979). A method for the routine assessment of fore- and hind-limb grip strength of rats and mice. *Neurobehav. Toxicol. 1*:233–236.

52. Edwards, P. M., and Parker, V. H. (1977). A simple, sensitive and objective method for early assessment of acrylamide neuropathy in rats. *Toxicol. Appl. Pharmacol. 40*:589–591.

# 9

# Techniques for Evaluating Hazards of Inhaled Products

GERALD L. KENNEDY, JR. / *E. I. Du Pont de Nemours and Company, Inc., Newark, Delaware*

## I. INTRODUCTION

Starting any presentation with a definition or two is like turning the light out in a late afternoon seminar–part of the audience misses the message entirely due to a lack of consciousness. To avoid this problem, I'll begin by stating the obvious and will spend the rest of this chapter developing the theme, and then I'll sneak a few definitions into the next paragraph. For a chemical to present a hazard, it must be capable of entering and interacting with the biological system. For agents that are very toxic but not present in the breathing atmosphere, the inhalation hazard approaches zero. Conversely, relatively inert materials present in the atmosphere either in high concentrations or for long periods of time might present a significant inhalation hazard. The evaluation of the safety of an agent then depends on the relative toxicity of the material as well as the possibilities for exposure. Materials then can be placed into proper perspective based on their intended usage patterns. Please note here that safety (freedom from hazard) is a continuum and that there are no examples which absolutely define the outer bounds.

## II. TOXICITY AND HAZARD

Our goal as toxicologists working in the area of safety evaluation is twofold. First, we need to define the toxicity of the chemical (or physical agent) and second, we must define the conditions under which humans (and other biological species) might come in contact with the agent. Toxicology is the science dealing with the adverse effects of chemical and physical agents on living systems. This includes identification of the target organ or organ system which is affected by contact with the agent and what amounts of agent are needed to produce the change. By amounts we refer to both daily (or weekly or any usual time frame) amounts and the length of exposure or treatment. It is important to note that there are interactions between chemicals and biological systems that are not necessarily adverse (macrophage infiltration, for example) but in the general setting of toxicologic hazard evaluation, it is appropriate to consider that the interactions likely to occur are those which should be prevented.

Agents come into contact with humans via three major routes, oral, dermal, or by inhalation. I will focus on inhalation but a brief discussion on the relationships between these other routes of exposure will be included. Regardless of physical form, chemicals can become airborne and thus present a potential hazard to humans. Hazard is defined as the probability that a substance will produce injury when used in a particular quantity and manner. Materials which are easily transferred to the atmosphere (such as gases and low boiling liquids) have a greater potential to present a hazard than do either solids or high boiling liquids but, very importantly, the inherent toxicity of the agent has a great impact on that determination. The purpose of this chapter will be specifically to discuss considerations necessary to be taken into account when establishing the procedure to follow to determine the inhalation hazard associated with chemicals. Since most of my experience is in asking this question as it applies to industrial chemicals, the emphasis will reside in this area, but the principles and methods of testing should have enough similarities to be broadly applicable.

## III. ROUTES OF EXPOSURE

We need to remember that situations rarely exist where the exposure to a chemical is solely by inhalation. Chemicals in the air can enter the body by all three major routes of exposure. Traditionally animals have been exposed in an acute (usually single dose or exposure) manner to the chemical and values such as the effective or lethal concentrations have been determined. All three routes are tested and one can get a general idea of how toxic (1), on an acute basis, the chemical is following each route of administration. Where similar quantities of a given chemical produce the same response, it may be inferred that the agent has entered the system in similar amounts (at the target site). In this manner, a rough comparison of the potency of the chemical as a function of exposure route can be obtained.

The response of animals exposed whole-body to agents in the air reflects not only the amount of chemical absorbed through the lungs but that amount absorbed through the skin and the gastrointestinal tract as a result of oral ingestion (rodents preening for example). We tend to lose sight of noninhalation routes as factors in the measurement of responses produced during inhalation experiments, but must keep these in mind. For example, in our laboratory, we found the lethal concentration 50% ($LC_{50}$) to rats following a 4-hr inhalation exposure to aniline to be 478 ppm when the animals were exposed whole-body (Table 1). When only the head of the rat was allowed into the exposure chamber, the resulting $LC_{50}$ was considerably greater, 839 ppm. This was also the case for two other substituted anilines, N-ethyl and N,N-diethyl (2,3). The amount of chemical absorbed through the skin or ingested during the former inhalation tests apparently contributed to the observed responses.

The contribution of dermal contact during inhalation exposures has been measured in humans. Krivanek et al. (4) exposed human volunteers to 10 ppm dimethylformamide for 6 hr. They then measured the amount of the major urinary metabolite, monomethylformamide (MMF), appearing in the urine both during and following exposure. One group wore short-sleeved shirts and no respirators; the second group wore short-sleeved shirts but also wore fitted respirators to prevent inhalation exposure. The amount of urinary MMF measured in the subjects exposed only by the dermal route to the vapors was low but measurable (0.8 mg MMF per 24-hr urine sample). Those exposed both by inhalation and by dermal contact excreted approximately 4.2 mg MMF, a fivefold increase. This experiment gives some idea of relative contribution of the absorbed dose from these two contact routes and points out that dermal contact with small amounts of this chemical, which penetrates the skin relatively easily, did contribute measurably to the overall absorbed dose (5).

**Table 1**  Effect of Inhalation Exposure Route on Toxicity of Anilines

| Compound | LC50 in ppm | | Ratio whole/body head-only |
|---|---|---|---|
| | Whole-body | Head-only | |
| Aniline | 478 | 839 | 0.57 |
| N-ethylaniline | 263 | 424 | 0.62 |
| N,N-diethylaniline | 315 | 679 | 0.46 |

## IV. RESPIRATORY TRACT AND DEPOSITION

Any discussion on inhalation hazard must consider the various compartments of the respiratory tract since the ultimate biological response will, to a great extent, reflect the degree of penetration and sensitivity of the different cell types making up the system. The most useful compartmentalization of the respiratory tract considers it as three regions based upon anatomy and upon particle deposition and clearance features that occur within each compartment (6). These regions, shown in Figure 1, are the nasopharyngeal (NP), the tracheobronchial (TB), and the pulmonary (P).

The NP region begins at the anterior nares and extends to the larynx. Deposition here is usually restricted to larger particles which impact and are entrapped in the nasal hairs. Relatively soluble particles transfer into the circulation and insoluble particles transfer to the stomach via the mucociliary transport mechanism. Both clearance rates are relatively short, estimated to be approximately 4 minutes. The anterior portion of the nose collects most of the larger particles and clears them essentially by physical removal to the outside (7). The posterior portion clears particulate via the mucociliary escalator with clearance times of 6–8 hr (8).

The TB region begins in the larynx and includes the trachea and ciliated bronchial airways and extends to the terminal bronchioles. Particles deposit here from inertial impaction at bifurcations, by

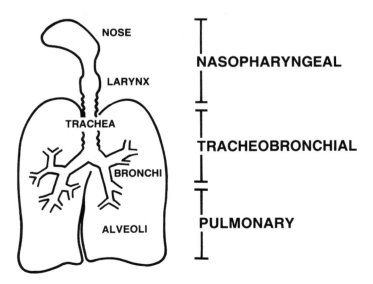

Figure 1    Compartmental model of the respiratory tract.

sedimentation, and by Brownian movement (small particles only).
Interception is an important deposition mechanism for fibrous dusts.
Particles in this region distribute according to size with smaller particles tending to go deeper into the lung. Clearance rates have been
described for the airways in terms of their relative size with half-
times of 0.5, 2.5, and 5 hr for the large, intermediate, and fine airways, respectively (9).

The pulmonary region (P) contains the functional gas exchange
units of the lung (respiratory bronchioles, alveolar ducts, alveolar
sacs, and alveoli). Particles passing the upper regions deposit here
following either settling, diffusion, or interception. Small particles
are trapped in this region with clearance mechanisms thought to
involve one or more of the following: dissolution of insolubles, direct transfer to blood, phagocytosis, or transfer to lymphatics.

Deposition patterns are quite complex but measurement of the
concentration of particles deposited (difference between the distribution of particles inhaled and exhaled) and particle size yields the
curve shown in Figure 2. The minimum total deposition occurs with
a particle size of approximately 0.5 μm with pulmonary and tracheobronchial deposition falling sharply when particles are 10 μm or more.

The preceding characteristics of the respiratory system have
been worked out both in humans and in experimental animals. De novo
determinations of inhalation toxicity must involve the experimental
animal, usually the rat, whose respiratory tract is quite similar to

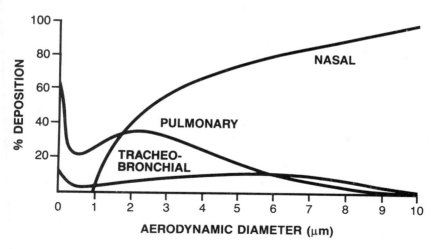

Figure 2   Particle size deposition probabilities for particles of varying sizes.

Table 2   Morphometrics of Human and Rat Lung

|  | Human | Rat |
|---|---|---|
| Age (yr) | 60 | 1 |
| Weight (kg) | 80 | 0.33 |
| Tracheal diameter (cm) | 2.0 | 0.3 |
| Tracheal flow velocity (cm/sec) | 372 | 231 |
| Terminal bronchioles: |  |  |
| Number | 32,800 | 2,500 |
| Diameter (mm) | 0.6 | 0.2 |
| Flow velocity (cm/sec) | 13 | 27 |
| Alveoli: |  |  |
| Number | $3 \times 10^8$ | $3 \times 10^9$ |
| Diameter (mm) | 0.3 | 0.09 |
| Surface area ($m^2$) | 70 | 0.7 |

humans in many ways.  Morphometric determinations of the respiratory tract of humans and rat are compared in Table 2 (10).

## V.  ANIMAL MODELS

The choice of an animal species selected for an inhalation study is important.  It is apparent that there is not one ideal human surrogate but that each species presents its own advantages and disadvantages.  The most commonly used species are rodents and include the rat, mouse, guinea pig, and hamster (probably in that order). The extensive use of these species in inhalation toxicology has provided a large body of background information available to the investigator as well as, on a practical note, a wide variety of apparatus needed to physically conduct such studies.  Rodents have been used in toxicologic tests, as models for particle deposition and clearance, and as models for infectivity and immunologic function.  The relatively short lifespan of rodents can be both an advantage and a disadvantage for various biologic monitoring but certainly allows a reasonable approach to chronic toxicity evaluations and carcinogenesis bioassays.  An important and sometimes overlooked fact is that rodents frequently show greater sensitivity to toxic gases than do larger animals including humans (11,12).

The guinea pig model has been used in studies of the immune function and respiratory sensitization. This model has been particularly useful in determination of the relative potencies of inhaled isocyanates (13–15). This species also has unusually abundant bronchial smooth muscle which makes it a useful model to study bronchoconstriction.

The hamster has also been used for studies involving respiratory tract cancer. This rodent has a very low spontaneous rate of lung tumors and is highly resistant to pulmonary infection. Some investigators feel that the hamster is the best animal model for the study of experimental lung cancer (16). This may be true for comparative studies in which materials are directly administered into the trachea but actual inhalation experiments have not yielded data to allow such conclusions.

There are a number of major disadvantages in using the rodent as an inhalation model for humans. The nasal/pharyngeal anatomy with the tortuous anterior chambers of the rodent is not similar to humans and particle deposition here may be quite different. In addition, these species are obligate nose breathers, hence, their filtering efficiency at the nasal level is superior. Evaluation of pulmonary function in nonanesthetized animals is difficult although recent miniaturization of probes and detectors has allowed some success here (although the work is still tedious and labor intensive) (17–19). The most serious problems with rodents are those involving spontaneous respiratory infections and the sequelae. This is especially true with the rat.

The dog presents a number of advantages including the presence of a large amount of background data (especially for the beagle). The animal is a convenient size for a number of laboratory measurements including evaluation of pulmonary function. A great diversity of natural disease states exist in the dog making it a good model for evaluation of impact of the agent against such conditions as asthma. An obvious disadvantage is cost and the facilities needed to properly care for the dog. Technically the nasal anatomy of the dog is unlike that of humans and the subgross lung type is different. Furthermore, the dog may be relatively insensitive to certain inhaled gases such as ozone (11).

Monkeys have a nasal anatomy similar to humans, are commonly used in inhalation experiments, and hence there is extensive background literature available. Invasive and noninvasive methods to determine lung function can easily be conducted. The long lifespan can be both an advantage and a disadvantage depending on the endpoints measured and the need for timely information. There is considerable cost involved in obtaining and maintaining monkey colonies and lack of general availability is a problem. The subgross pulmonary anatomy does differ from that of humans (20). A further and potentially more serious limitation to the use of monkeys is the extreme care that must be taken to prevent the transmission of serious disease from monkey to the human species.

Other species such as the ferret, horse, donkey, sheep, cat, rabbit, and pig have been suggested for use in inhalation studies. However, these models are generally used for special applications which take advantage of a particular anatomical feature, chemical sensitivity, or research curiosity (for a more complete discussion see Refs. 21, 22).

## VI. TYPES OF EXPOSURE

Three general types of inhalation exposure chambers have been used: nose-only, head-only, and whole-body (Fig. 3). The nose-only and head-only exposure systems avoid contamination of the animal's body. This is important in evaluating the effects of particulate since the actual inhalation dose received through respiration could be augmented by additional exposure through ingestion (preening) and absorption. Each exposure type has its advantages and disadvantages and the one selected should reflect the questions being asked.

The whole body chamber can be as simple as an appropriately sized bell jar or as complex as desired. It really serves only as an enclosure to which a material can be introduced and in which a controlled uniform atmosphere can be maintained. The advantage of this type exposure system is that large numbers of animals can be exposed simultaneously under conditions which involve no confinement stress. This design is most practical for prolonged, repeated-dose studies. A few observations that relate to design are appropriate here. The chambers themselves must be constructed of materials which do not react with the chemical(s) being tested and should contain as much translucent area as possible to allow observation of the animals during exposure. Stainless steel and glass are commonly used. Glass surfaces present a dust or aerosol build-up problem due to static charge accumulation. Plexiglas or other plastic materials have been used with some success but the possibility of organic vapor and static electricity build-up exists and the material might not stand up well to repeated use.

The distribution of chemical within the chamber is of particular importance and whole-body exposure units, because of their large size, require that great attention be paid to interchamber chemical concentration differences. This problem is greater with dusts (particularly fibers) and aerosols. MacFarland (23), however, notes that the variations encountered with these physical forms are similar and stresses the importance of knowing the chamber distribution characteristics. The concentrations should be measured at various points within the chamber before animals have been introduced,

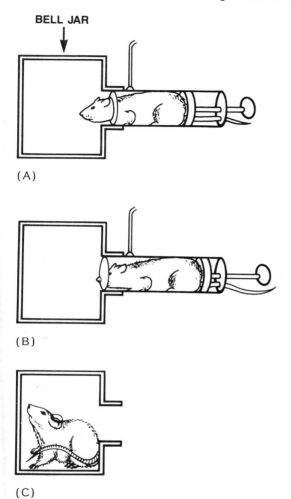

**BELL JAR**

(A)

(B)

(C)

**Figure 3** Exposure types. (A) head-only; (B) nose-only; (C) whole body.

using a sampling strategy which best analyzes the distribution. It is not usually practical to use the same strategy once animals are in place in the chamber but the concentrations needed to be determined frequently (at least once each half-hour for a 6-hr exposure) at locations indicated as representative in the preliminary survey. These samples need to be taken near the breathing zone of the animals.

The ventilation rate in the chamber should be comparable to that of the animal rooms and a rate that introduces 8–12 chamber volumes of air per hour is usually sufficient. To prevent the build-up of heat and humidity within the chamber, the total animal body volume should not exceed 5% of the chamber volume (24).

The advantages of the whole body system include equipment that is easy to fabricate, can house a large number of animals and simultaneously expose multiple species (if desired), requires limited handling of the animals, maintains adequately constant and uniform concentrations of the test agent, and is relatively easy to clean and maintain. The disadvantages include the high cost of materials such as stainless steel used for the larger chambers, the large amount of test agent which must be obtained, analyzed, generated, reanalyzed, collected, and disposed of, and the contributions of skin (and oral) contact to the total absorbed dose of the chemical.

The head-only design usually involves smaller chambers and, as such, uses considerably less test agent. The movement of air and chemical into and out of this system is relatively easy. The uniformity of exposure doses animal to animal requires a large airflow to prevent downstream animals being exposed to chemically depleted atmospheres. These systems can involve helmut-type exposures although more typical designs include tubes with cutouts to allow insertion of the head. Rats, mice, guinea pigs, and hamsters can be exposed easily in this system but dogs, monkeys, and larger mammals cannot be accommodated so easily. The typical exposure unit consists of a cylinder, generally constructed from rigid plastic, placed inside a protective casing. Animals are then placed in restrainers which are either plastic or stainless steel and designed to allow the escape of body heat. Conical head pieces are then placed into the cylinder and are sealed loosely with rubber port inserts or the equivalent. We have used this system to evaluate the toxicity of a number of aerosols (25–27) and to measure the respiratory rate change associated with exposure to known nasal tumorigens (28).

Nose-only systems are similar but only the anterior tip of the nares is inserted into a similarly designed exposure cylinder (or chamber). These exposures limit the entry of the agent to the respiratory tract, require very little test chemical, allow easy containment of the test agent, and allow concentrations to be altered easily and quickly. We have used this system to determine acute lethal doses over time periods as short as 15 sec (29). For larger species such as the dog or the monkey, specially fitted masks can be used to accomplish the same type of exposures.

## VII. GENERATION OF AGENT

Generation of test atmospheres needs to be carefully considered to obtain the most consistent uniform distribution of the test agent in the exposure system over the duration of the experiment. The physical form of the material (gases, liquids, and solids) determines the degree of difficulty the experimenter will have in attaining that goal.

A gas is a state of matter in which the molecules are practically unrestricted by cohesive forces and have neither shape or volume. It is a substance which has a critical temperature below 20°C and thus cannot be condensed at any pressure equal to this temperature. A vapor is a substance dispersed in air as individual molecules which could be condensed to a liquid at 20°C by increasing the pressure. Vapor pressure is the pressure exerted by the gaseous state over its normal liquid or solid state. It should be noted that the term vapor is most correctly applied to describe a substance which exists normally as a liquid or solid at room temperature and at normal atmospheric pressure. Liquids with lower boiling points then either exist normally in two physical forms with both a liquid and a gaseous component. Adding heat (or lowering pressure) to the system creates a greater gaseous fraction.

An aerosol is a relatively stable two-phase system consisting of finely divided condensed particulate matter in a gaseous medium. The condensed phase can be either liquid or solid (or a combination of the two). Thus, generation of either solids or higher boiling liquids in the air can be accomplished rather easily or sometimes only with great difficulty.

Generation of gaseous atmospheres is usually quite simple. If it is contained in a pressurized cylinder, it is metered through a calibrated flowmeter into the airstream entering the chamber. The entry should involve a thorough mixing of the test gas with air by means of baffles, duct configurations, or pre-entry mixing reservoirs. When it is necessary to generate low concentrations, it may not be possible to add the gas directly to the chamber. For these situations a reservoir of test gas in nitrogen can be established, which can be metered into the testing chamber using an appropriate precision pumping system. Syringe-driven entry allows accurate introduction of very small amounts of the test gas into air streams which can then be metered into the chamber.

Vapors are generated in a similar manner except that the liquid (only rarely does a solid fit into this category) needs an energy source to attain the heat of vaporization. For very volatile liquids this may only involve passing the liquid into a preheated reservoir where the heat of the surrounding air is enough to volatilize the liquid. In other cases it may be necessary to preheat the reservoir. Care must be taken to use as little heat as possible in the generation of vapors. This is best accomplished by providing a large heated surface to get efficient transfer of heat to the liquid. In addition to thermal decomposition, unnecessarily high temperatures at this stage can produce supersaturated vapor streams which then condense in the cooler downstream air, particularly in the animal exposure chamber.

When a liquid sample is completely vaporized, the proportion of volatile components in the resulting vapor is similar to that in the liquid sample. This then reflects the conditions which exist where the liquid is being used. This is especially important when evaluating the inhalation hazard of liquids for which there is no (or relatively little) possibility for aerosol formation.

Vapors can be generated directly from a liquid reservoir, a convenient and frequently used method. The purity of the test agent must be ascertained, since this method often results in fractional distillation with the lower boiling materials coming off and entering the inhalation chamber first. This may not accurately reflect the type of exposures experienced by humans. The entire sample may be heated to generate sufficient vapor. A schematic showing the sample being a syringe driven into a heated flask allowing flash evaporation of the test sample directly into the exposure chamber is shown in Figure 4. This method can lead to thermal decomposition. Samples with more than one component again will distribute such that the component with highest volatility will come off first, thus leading to vapor atmospheres whose character changes during the course of the exposure. A volatilization system described by Potts and Steiner (30) allows the production of almost completely saturated atmosphere without creating heated surfaces on which decomposition could occur. This system passes the liquid down through a distillation column (jacketed to prevent cooling) and is an excellent method for generation of high boiling liquids.

Aerosol generators have been designed to deliver either solids or liquids (wet or dry). Wet-dispersion generators break up bulk liquid into droplets. If the droplets are nonvolatile, the resulting aerosol consists solely of liquid droplets. If the liquid is volatile, the resulting droplet will be considerably smaller than the originally generated droplets. Dry generators will disperse previously ground materials by mechanical means, usually with the aid of an air jet. The rate of generation depends on a number of factors including the hardness of compound, the packing density, the uniformity of the feeding mechanism, and the air jet pressure.

Compressed air nebulizers find great use in generating test aerosols. A nebulizer is a type of atomizer that produces an aerosol

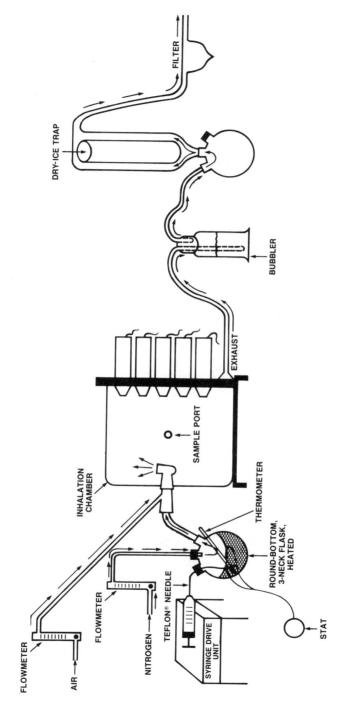

**Figure 4** Liquid being driven at constant rate into heated flask to flash evaporate material directly into an inhalation chamber.

of small particle size by removing larger spray droplets by impaction within the device. As a class, nebulizers produce aerosols at concentrations of 5–50 g/m$^3$ and with mass median diameters of 1–10 μm and geometric standard deviations of 1.5–2.2. Ultrasonic nebulizers are also available but their use in inhalation studies has been limited.

Numerous dry-dispersion devices have been used in inhalation studies. The Wright dust feed, popular in the past, is capable of delivering a constant amount of dry solid particulate for entry into the chamber. However, a limited number of test agents have the physical characteristics necessary for optimal use of this apparatus (low packing density, need for very dry, almost anhydrous dispersion air). Many other mechanical devices, consisting of equipment to carry solid materials to a point where they can be suspended in an air jet, are also available (31,32). A fluidizing bed, created by the use of a high-speed four-blade fan, which then aspirates a preground dust from the bed through a baffling chamber into an inhalation chamber, was described by Drew and Laskin (33). Air-activated fluidized beds are commercially available and have been used to generate aerosols of both particulates and fibers (34) to overcome mechanical entanglement and electrostatic charge properties. We used a high-pressure air-impingement device to separate aramid fiber fibrils from the matrix then deliver the fibrils to a prechamber separating cyclone to conduct long-term inhalation studies (Fig. 5, Ref. 35).

Most particulate-generating devices produce a range of particle sizes, only some of which are small enough to penetrate to the alveoli.

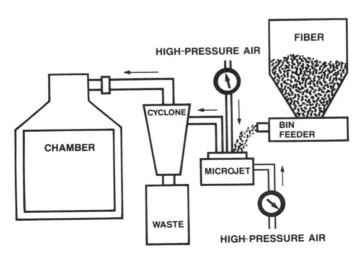

**Figure 5**    Generation system used to produce airborne Kevlar fibrils.

Because this distribution may change with time, careful analysis of both particle concentration and size distribution is critical to adequately characterize the exposure conditions.

The physics of these generating systems often precludes the testing of particulates at very high concentrations. Furthermore, the respiratory tract does have a limited capacity to handle particulates, especially insoluble dusts, so that the use of very high levels may lead to excessive accumulation in the respiratory system in a manner which is not reflective of the situation occurring under real-world exposure conditions for human beings.

## VIII. CHAMBER ANALYSIS

All analytical monitoring systems must accomplish two basic tasks, collection of a representative sample and accurate analysis. Samples may be collected directly from the chamber, a technique which is efficient, rapid, easily automated, and less prone to error. Extractive techniques may need to be used which, although more time-consuming and hence less efficient, are able to concentrate low level atmospheric samples in order to increase analytical sensitivity (Table 3).

The most commonly used analytical techniques for analyzing gases and vapors are gas chromatography and infrared spectroscopy. Aside from the need to accurately measure the test atmosphere, these readings are needed to control the intended concentrations during the test.

Direct samples may be collected in evacuated glass or metal containers, inflatable bags of polymeric (nonreactive) material, or most commonly by gas-tight syringe. These may also be taken remotely by the use of transfer lines fed directly into the analytical instrument. Extractive sampling involves passing the test atmosphere through a solvent, adsorption onto a collecting surface, or condensation onto a cold surface.

Gas chromatography (GC) is the most versatile and frequently used analytical technique for monitoring gases and vapors. GC offers chemical separation of components for specific analysis, low detection limits, and rapid turnover of data for feedback control. Infrared spectroscopy works well since most gases and vapors give reasonably intense and unique spectra. The Miran portable gas analyzer is particularly useful for continuous monitoring. Other techniques shown to be useful include the use of ion-specific electrodes, UV-visible spectrophotometers, and scrubbing colorimeters. As is always the case, frequent calibration of analytical instruments is essential (36).

Aerosols present a special case in that the investigator needs to measure the mass concentration of the chemical, the chemical

**Table 3** Analysis of Inhalation Chamber Concentrations

---

Vapors

1.  Gas chromatography
    a.  Direct sampling
    b.  Extracted samples

2.  Infrared spectroscopy

3.  Ion-selective electrodes

4.  UV-visible spectrophotometers

Aerosols

1.  Concentration
    a.  Gravimetric
    b.  Forward-scatter detectors
    c.  Back-scatter detectors
    d.  $\beta$-attenuation detector
    e.  Quartz crystal microbalance detector

2.  Particle size
    a.  Cascade impactors
    b.  Microscopy (fiber morphology)
    c.  Laser/Doppler type

---

composition as a function of particle size, and the particle size distribution of the aerosol. No continuously sampling instruments are available to measure both particle size and chemical concentration. Particle detection can be accomplished using both forward and back-scatter detectors. Moss and Decker (37) describe their experience with the forward-scatter detectors to be of limited use for the usual purposes of toxicity testing. The back-scatter described allows for noninvasive determinations over a range from 6 to 10,000 mg/m$^3$. An infrared light beam is projected through a 1.5-mm lucite window into the chamber. The light back-scattered from a sensing volume of about 12 cm$^2$ is detected, in the same unit, containing the light beam by the outer edges of the light focusing optics. The unit is capable of monitoring without invading the chamber to remove an aliquot of the test atmosphere.

The quartz crystal mass monitor reflects the mass change on the face of the crystal when particles are drawn through an orifice and are deposited on the face by electrostatic precipitation (38). Mass concentration instruments can detect the collected mass by the attenuation of β radiations. The aerosol is drawn through an orifice and particles impact on a surface positioned between a source and a counter (39).

For particle sizing, many varieties of cascade impactors perform well, although care must be taken to avoid errors introduced by sampling (such as collection in sampling lines). The laser/Doppler-type particle size device can be used to measure aerodynamic size at low concentrations with a rapid readout. In a system described by Cook (40), a powerful pulsed laser using temporal analysis of back-scattered light indicates the spatial distribution of particles.

## IX. STUDY TYPES

The type of inhalation test conducted will depend on the question being addressed, but generally we look to determine what happens when biological systems are exposed infrequently or frequently and are the exposures to high or low concentrations. Studies can be described as either acute, chronic, or subchronic depending on number of test exposures. Acute effects usually occur rapidly as a result of short-term exposures (most often single) and are of short duration. Chronic studies involve repeated exposures which may need to be continued for the duration of an animal's lifetime. These studies are generally conducted at relatively low concentrations.

Acute studies are generally conducted at a relatively high concentration and are useful in determining the approximate range of toxicity of a chemical. Acute studies can be used as a starting point in the determination of dose levels for longer term tests. The clinical signs evoked at these high exposures often allow determination of the nature of the toxic effect induced. The two most common numerical values that come from an acute study are the ALC (approximately lethal concentration) and the $LC_{50}$. The ALC is defined as the lowest concentration that produces death in at least 1 of a group of exposed animals, while the $LC_{50}$ is the calculated concentration at which 1/2 of the exposed population would be expected to die. Generally the exposures are conducted for a single 4- or 6-hr period and the animals are observed for 14 days after treatment.

Subchronic studies generally precede lifetime studies and are conducted to determine what the target organ or organ system might be and what exposure regimen (concentration × time) is required to produce this change. For this purpose, our practice is to expose groups (n = 10) of male rats to three test concentrations (Table 4). The highest concentration tested is set at 1/5 the ALC (or the $LC_{50}$ depending on the steepness of the mortality dose-response curve) and the lower 2 would be 1/15 and 1/50. Rats are exposed 6 hr a day for 5 days, given a 2-day rest period, and are again exposed

Table 4    Design of Subchronic Inhalation Study

---

Test species:  Rat

Sex:  Male

Number of test groups:  3 (1/5, 1/15, 1/50 ALC)

Number per group:  10

Exposures:  6 hr/day, 5 days/wk, 2 wks

Animal sacrifice:  5/group after 10th exposure
                   5/group after 14 day recovery period

Parameters measured:  Growth and in vivo responses
                      Clinical pathology
                      Urine analyses
                      Gross pathology with organ weights
                      Microscopic pathology
                      Chemical index of exposure (where possible)

---

for 5 days.  In vivo observations, including body weight measurements are made daily.  Following the 10th exposure, all rats are subjected to hematological, clinical blood chemistry, and urine analysis evaluations.  Half of the rats are sacrificed at that time and a complete pathological examination including histological evaluation is conducted.  The remaining rats are held without additional exposures for 2 weeks and the parameters altered in rats sacrificed immediately following the 10th exposure are evaluated to determine the reversibility of the change(s).

A variation of this design uses an increasing exposure regimen which continues until severe biologic effects are observed.  This provides target organ toxicity data using fewer animals (only 1 group is treated), but the quantitative aspects can be masked in cases where chemical build-up in the body occurs or change occurs only after some protective function in the body has been depleted (41). In both of the subchronic studies, the importance of adequate concurrent control animals needs to be underscored.

Chronic studies are conducted to determine effects of long-term exposures at levels where acute toxicity is not obvious.  Chronic exposure patterns generally follow those encountered in the workplace, animals exposed 6 hr/day, 5 days/week for their lifetime.  For environmental contaminants, continuous exposures of 23 hr/day (allowing 1 hr/day to feed the animals and clean the exposure chambers) for 7 days/week might be considered more appropriate.

In both chronic study types, exposures are designed to be as constant as possible with minimal deviation from the target or design concentrations. Investigators go to great lengths to be able to report test concentrations of × ppm with ×/100 standard deviations. This needs to be contrasted with the work or living environment where chemical pollutant levels fluctuate greatly depending on released amounts, ventilation, meteorological conditions, and many other important factors. Investigators measuring effects of airborne chemicals in confined spaces such as a submarine would more likely choose continuous exposures (12), while evaluation of materials in industrial atmospheres would likely involve intermittent exposures similar to those described previously (42–44).

Chemicals irritating to the sensory apparatus of the upper respiratory tract can be identified by measuring the reflex-induced decrease in respiratory rate (45). The basic design uses an apparatus which translates changes on thoracic body cavity volume into tracings that can determine the depth and rate of respiration. The animal, usually a rat or mouse, is placed into a whole-body tube connected to an inhalation chamber such that only the nose protrudes into the exposure area (Fig. 3). Animals are then exposed to various concentrations of the agent and a plot of respiration rate against concentration is made. Dose-response curves and minimum effect levels can be determined, the data usually being expressed in terms of the $RD_{50}$ (concentration required to lower the respiration rate by 50%). The method is quite simple and detects the effects of irritation at concentrations where no associated pathological modifications occur.

Intratracheal instillation of materials is a popular alternative to inhalation exposure of animals. The advantages of this type of exposure include the need for very small amounts of test agent (hence safety feature in terms of handling and containment of the chemical), extensive chambers are not required, and the complex technical support needed to generate and maintain experimental exposure conditions is avoided. These factors make this type of study very inexpensive to conduct. Furthermore, the dose can be delivered very precisely to the respiratory tract tissues. However, dose distribution to the respiratory tract tissues does not accurately simulate an inhaled dose and hence, does not reflect the real-life response very clearly. Inhalation of airborne toxins generally results in a relatively well-distributed dose throughout the respiratory system. Intratracheal instillation tends to lead to a less uniform deposition and to favor the lower portions of the lung due to gravimetric settling of material. Brain et al. (46) exposed rats and hamsters to radioactive particles and examined the distribution following both inhalation and instillation. The resulting distributions were strikingly different with instillation producing heavy deposits in the medium-sized bronchi. Instilled materials seldom reached the alveoli whereas inhalation led to considerable deposition in the small airways. High local concentrations following instillation can lead to localized tissue damage which would not be seen following more uniform deposition. The use of this technique then is basically limited to situations where tissue reactions, both of an acute (inflammation) and chronic (neoplasia, fibrosis) nature, to a variety of materials are to be compared side-by-side.

## X. LOCAL VS. SYSTEMIC RESPONSES

The type of damage produced by materials as they enter the body via the respiratory tract needs to be considered briefly. Materials, particularly gases and vapors, can produce irritation at the point of contact. In the lung, these irritants can interact with pulmonary membranes to produce edema, pleural effusion, and a hyperemic reaction. With the loss of the pulmonary barrier, the passage of fluid and protein becomes altered, leading ultimately to the loss of the ability to appropriately oxygenate blood. The inflammatory process is essentially the same within the lung but different sites may be affected, due to differences in the solubility, boiling point, and volatility of the irritant chemical. The solubility of a compound is probably the most important factor in determining the site of action. Highly soluble materials such as ammonia and hydrogen chloride affect primarily the upper respiratory tract producing rhinitis and related inflammatory changes. Compounds of intermediate solubility such as ozone affect both the upper respiratory tract and the pulmonary tissue, while less soluble materials such as nitrogen dioxide and phosgene affect primarily the deep lung.

Irritants can produce changes both at the site of contact and systemically. Those which act only locally at the point of contact are considered primary irritants. These exert little systemic toxicity since they are either metabolized to products which are nontoxic, or the local effects far exceed any systemic reaction. Examples of primary irritants are hydrogen chloride and sulfuric acid. Another type of primary irritant is characterized by reactive materials such as mustard gas. These compounds are extremely toxic if absorbed but produce such a severe degree of irritation that death occurs before systemic poisoning can be produced. Secondary irritants are agents which have a significant irritating effect on mucous membranes, but following absorption have a more profound systemic effect. Hydrogen sulfide and many organic compounds fall into this category. There are materials which are irritants but also produce systemic injury—hydrogen fluoride, for example, produces severe injury at the point of contact but also produces kidney damage.

Inhalation of a wide variety of particulates produces pulmonary disease. Pneumoconiosis is a term used to designate a fibrotic condition of the lung caused by inhaled dust. The character of the fibrosis depends on the type of dust inhaled, with the more important

**Table 5** Silicosis and Related Pneumoconiosis

| Dust | Chemical | Reaction site | Response | Designation |
|------|----------|---------------|----------|-------------|
| Asbestos | Fibrous silicates | Lung parenchyma | Diffuse fibrosis | Asbestosis |
| Coal | Coal | Lung parenchyma<br>Lymph nodes | Collagen nodules | Anthracosis |
| Diatomaceous earth | Amorphous $SiO_2$ | Lung parenchyma | Diffuse fibrosis | Kieselguhr lung |
| Graphite | Coal particles | Lung parenchyma<br>Lymph nodes | Collagen nodules | Graphite lung |
| Kaolin | $Al_2(SiO_2O_5)OH_4$ | Lung parenchyma<br>Lymph nodes | Collagen nodules | Kaolinosis |
| Quartz | Silica, $SiO_2$ | Lung parenchyma<br>Lymph nodes | Collagen | Silicosis |
| Talc | $Mg_6(SiO_2)OH_4$ | Lung parenchyma<br>Lymph nodes | Collagen nodes | Pleural sclerosis |

agents being crystalline silica (silicosis), asbestos (asbestosis), talc, and coal that contains silica (Table 5). Deposition of metals and their compounds in the lung leads to a variety of disease states. The pulmonary response to particulates is determined by factors such as : (1) the nature of the dust particles, (2) the site of dust deposition in the respiratory tract, (3) the amount of dust deposited in the lung, (4) the exposure period, and (5) individual variation and immunologic status. Lee (47) describes five categories based on the lung tissue reaction to inorganic (mineral) dusts. These include the macrophage reaction produced by so called nuisance dusts such as soot, iron, and titanium dioxide, foreign body granuloma produced by beryllium and talc, sarcoid-type granuloma produced by beryllium, collagenized fibrosis both diffuse (from hard metals, asbestos) and nodular (from quartz and silica), and neoplasia produced by nickel and asbestos.

The systemic changes produced by inhalation reflect the wide variety of biologic targets within any living system and need to be detected using the usual tools of the toxicologist. In this case, the dose-response characteristics of the lesion following systemic absorption via the respiratory tract should be measured against the target organ or target organ system.

## XI. AIR MEASUREMENTS: INDUSTRIAL HYGIENE

Since the extent of an inhalation hazard is both a function of the inherent toxicity and the amount of human contact, accurate determination of the latter is essential. In the occupational setting, the respiratory tract is the most common route of entry for chemicals. Most of the health standards such as the ACGIH TLV are based primarily on this route of entry.

Methods for collection of environmental data on airborne contaminants are based primarily on their physical characteristics and methods of analysis are based primarily on their chemical characteristics. Gases and vapors can be collected by physical entrapment usually by collecting the air to be analyzed in an evacuated container such as a bottle or plastic bag. Chemical collection reacts the contaminated air with an absorbing or adsorbing medium by passing the contaminated air over or through the medium which may be a solvent or a sorbent such as activated carbon or silica gel.

Particulates have been more difficult to assess. The amount present in the contaminated air needs to be characterized on both a mass basis (mg/m$^3$ as determined by the amount trapped by a filter of a given pore size) and on a physical basis relating to the respiratory tract (what amount of the total is respirable). The usual lung retention models used for aerodynamic spherical-like particulates have to be modified when other physical forms, for example fibers, are being evaluated. Chemical analysis of the material following removal from the filter media is needed to identify specifically the contaminant being measured.

Under certain conditions, gases or vapors are adsorbed onto particulates while they are airborne and may be inhaled in conjunction with those particulates. For such situations (aluminum reduction and coke oven operations are examples), consideration must be given to the collection and analysis of both the particulate and the gases and vapors. The biological response produced from such exposures also needs to be considered, since, in this fashion, gases and vapors, which might be readily soluble and subsequently removed by the upper respiratory tract, can now penetrate into the lung. An example of this is seen in sulfuric acid mist (48).

## XII.  SAFETY

The safety of persons working in an experimental area dealing with generation and maintenance of airborne chemicals needs to be carefully protected. Standard measures to prevent contact or spread of chemicals within the laboratory need to be enforced. Specifically, to prevent inhalation of test agents by those working on the experiment, a number of additional considerations are needed. Dust masks provide only minimal protection to larger dust particles such as animal dander and hair. For chemical protection, half-face cartridge respirators can be used against certain organic vapors and dusts during times for potential exposure (transfer of agents, removing animals from exposure chambers, observing animals following whole-body inhalation exposures). Air-supplied respirators should be used when handling open containers of highly toxic materials and these transfers should be made within a laboratory hood. The respirators should be fit tested and personnel should be trained in their proper use.

Provisions for isolation of animals following exposure to test agents should be made (walk-in storage areas for animal racks, portable hoods). The type of monitoring necessary in any experimental situation needs to be geared to that particular chemical. Area monitoring before, during, and after daily exposures should be conducted at reasonable intervals to establish the appropriate conditions for avoiding exposure and to ensure that the worker is protected.

The best practice in conducting experimental inhalation tests is to remember that the subjects of the test need to be isolated. The working area itself should be isolated so that only those directly involved with the experiment have access to the facility. Potential for human contact should be appropriately controlled prior to initiation of the experiment. This often is best accomplished by enclosing the entire generation and exposure system (including the exhaust) within a laboratory hood. The specific measures taken will follow from the type of test, the amount of chemical being handled during the test, and the toxicity of the chemical.

## XIII. COMMON PROBLEMS AND POSSIBLE SOLUTIONS

The inhalation toxicity test is a complex endeavor involving chemical, engineering, and biological skills. As such, there are many points in the experiment which need constant attention or the results will be of little or no use to those needing the information for safety evaluation purposes. I will discuss a few of the problems we have encountered and will suggest either generic answers or questions that need to be asked and answered before and during the conduct of such studies. This section is, of necessity, not all-encompassing as the next unknown problem probably awaits in the laboratory today. Those problems discussed here are frequently encountered and do need appropriate attention at all phases of the inhalation experiment.

The reactivity of the test chemical itself needs to be considered. Interaction with containment vessels, transfer lines, exposure chambers, humidity, and air can result in achieved concentrations much lower than desired or exposures to reaction products rather than the intended test chemical. Awareness of potential reactivity and use of equipment that will not favor reaction, as well as restricting the contact points for the chemical prior to introduction into the breathing zone of the animal, will minimize this potential problem. Hydrolysis of chemicals in both the test atmosphere and in the aqueous environment of the respiratory tract can occur and the extent and rate of the reaction should be known to fully appreciate the hazard involved in breathing the material.

Good chemical analysis is mandatory for relating quantity of chemical inhaled with effects produced. Inhalation exposures generally involve the introduction of a single agent into the atmosphere which then needs to be measured. Although interfering substances are less likely to exist here than in real-world situations (where chemicals exist potentially among concentrations of other agents), the need to use a specific analytical method is important. Methods that are relatively quick are most useful so that deviations from desired concentrations can be readily corrected. However, situations arise in which more lengthy analytical procedures are necessary for accuracy. In some cases, the use of more than one method, that is, one as a rough screen to monitor the chamber to prevent excursions and a second to quantitate exactly for actual concentrations, may be used. An example of this practice may be seen in studies involving solid particulates where the total airborne particulate concentration may be measured gravimetrically every half hour and particle sizing and analytical determination of the particulate trapped on the filter may be done at selected time intervals (often at the beginning, in the middle, and at the end of the exposure period).

When working with mixtures of materials with different boiling points, care needs to be taken not to generate atmospheres which are initially enriched in the more volatile components. Continuing exposures of this type follow the laws of fractional distillation and may produce atmospheres which are both much different from that of the starting mixture and which change considerably as the exposure continues (and depletion of the more volatile material(s) occurs). This can be prevented by either testing the material as an aerosol and directing the total fluid into the chamber or by flash evaporating the liquid on a heated surface, for example, prior to entry to the chamber.

The problem of actual versus nominal concentration should be a thing of the past but, occasionally, experiments continue to report concentrations in terms of material used as a function of air flow to the chamber (nominal concentration). This practice in itself is a problem since the values arrived at by that calculation represent maximum concentrations possible rather than that concentration actually presented to the animal. For certain materials such as gases, the difference between actual and nominal may not be great. However, for particulates, the difference may be several orders of magnitude. Specifically, the concentration in the breathing zone of the animal needs to be determined analytically.

With both liquid and solid aerosols, the amount of material in the breathing zone needs to be present in respirable sizes to produce a response. Hence, with such materials, it is important to accurately define the test atmosphere both in terms of chemical concentration and particle size. Experiments using particulates with mass median diameters much in excess of 10 µm really are not measuring the toxicity of the material. Unless the material produces local irritation of the mucous membranes of the respiratory tract, there is little possibility of the material entering the system (the lower respiratory tract) and doing damage. With materials whose physical form is such that the dusts exist mainly in the form of large non-respirable particles, the method for testing should involve either concentrating those particles at the respirable end of the size distribution or using physical means to reduce them to that size. This allows the determination of toxicity, what the chemical can do when it enters the lungs. The hazard determination then will involve knowing what portion of the material normally exists in respirable sizes and relating that concentration to the effects seen. For example, you find little toxicity in a test after, with heroic effort, you are able to generate and maintain a respirable test atmosphere of 50 mg/m$^3$.

Only a very small fraction of the naturally occurring particles of this material are of respirable size and you find much less than 1 mg/m$^3$ in the workplace. In this situation, the inhalation hazard of this material would be considered quite low.

The type of exposure system chosen can also present problems when one is trying to measure only the effects of materials entering via the lung. Whole-body exposures can also involve absorption through the skin and through the gastrointestinal tract (following preening). The contribution of other routes to that amount absorbed via inhalation can be minimized by exposing only the nose of the animal to the test atmosphere. As discussed earlier, this type of exposure is not difficult but does have some limitations that need to be kept in mind—for one, it is difficult to observe the response of an animal while it is restrained in the equipment necessary to accomplish nose-only exposures.

This section has highlighted only some of the problem areas which are frequently encountered in inhalation hazard determinations. The procedures which can be applied to generate and analyze test atmospheres in the wide variety of experimental set-ups which are used in the field makes the application of common sense and sound scientific principles a necessity in producing information which is genuinely useful for hazard determination purposes.

## XIV. SUMMARY

This chapter has considered the techniques used in the testing of materials for their inhalation toxicity. As is true in most areas of endeavor, there are many appropriate procedures for gathering the information necessary for making scientific judgements. The experimental details, although widely divergent, need to be carefully evaluated before, during, and especially after conduct of each particular experiment or series of experiments. We need to be critical of our experimental design and results to be sure that further use of the information developed is not being undertaken against an inappropriate background.

Note that the preceding paragraph referred to the techniques covered as those which are used in toxicity testing, not directly in the evaluation of product hazard which is the topic of the chapter. I come again to the point of separating toxicity from hazard. Once we know what potential a chemical (or physical agent or chemical process) has for producing toxicity following inhalation exposure, we may proceed to the evaluation of hazard. This encompasses the inherent toxicity of the material against the background of exposure potential. Of two materials with equal toxicity (considering both acute and chronic response), the one which is more easily airborne will most likely present a greater hazard.

Gases can readily become airborne and when not contained will result in inhalation exposures. The need to know the toxicity of such materials following inhalation is obvious. Liquids with low boiling points (high vapor pressures) present a similar situation where relatively high concentrations of chemical can be inhaled easily under normal (standard temperature and pressure) conditions.

High boiling liquids and solids, both dusts and fibers, can become airborne and present inhalation hazards as well. As with all inhaled materials, the response obtained is proportionate to the dose. However, with aerosols the deposition of a few particles with a large mass may have a greater impact than the deposition of numerous smaller particles. For example, the deposition of a single 1 μm diameter particle (assume a sphere) is equal in mass burden to 1000 particles of 0.1 μm diameter. Furthermore, a given amount of mass deposited in the respiratory tract may be distributed among many small or among few large particles and the resultant toxicity may be quite different.

For these reasons, knowledge of the particle size of aerosols generated in inhalation experiments is essential. First, the toxicity profile should be developed using aerosols which are respirable. Inhalation tests conducted by temporary suspension of large (greater than 10 μm diameter aerodynamically) particles will always understate the toxicity (perhaps not the hazard) of the agent. Carbon fibers with diameters of 7 μm and aerodynamic properties that make them nonrespirable lead, as expected, to little in the way of biologic response (49). Certain situations may exist where particles of respirable size cannot be generated but this situation is unusual. More commonly, a distribution of particles including those in both the respirable and nonrespirable range can be generated. Taking the response obtained from this test, with full characterization of the particle size distribution, and referencing it against both the concentration and the particle size distribution seen under actual use conditions, an estimate of the hazard the material poses can be obtained. In our laboratory we needed to refine and concentrate the small fibrils which make up only a very small portion of a fibrous product under study as is normally produced and encountered in use situations. This allowed us to attain exposure concentrations of airborne fibrils which were respirable. This, in turn, enabled us to estimate the degree of hazard under actual use conditions where the concentration of respirable fibers is exceedingly low (35).

The final assessment of risk posed by inhaled materials then becomes a function of the inherent toxicity of the material (tested in such a way as to determine target organs, systemic and local respiratory tract involvement) and the extent to which the material will be inhaled by humans under use conditions (concentration, time, particle size). These factors evaluated by the appropriate professional should result in establishment of exposure conditions which allow, as best as possible, safe use of the product.

## REFERENCES

1. Gosselin, R. E., Hodge, H. C., Smith, R. P., and Gleason, M. N. (1984). *Clinical Toxicology of Commercial Products,* 4th Ed. Baltimore, Williams and Wilkins Co.
2. Kennedy, Jr., G. L. (1982). Problems facing the petrochemical industry in regard to dermal and inhalation exposures. Presentation at the Toxicology Forum, Aspen, CO, July 1982.
3. O'Neal, F. O. (1982). Cited in "Problems facing the petrochemicals industry in regard to dermal and inhalation exposure." Presented by G. L. Kennedy, Jr., at the Toxicology Forum, Aspen, CO, July 1982.
4. Krivanek, N. D., McLaughlin, M., and Fayerweather, W. E. (1978). Monomethylformamide levels in human urine after repetitive exposure to dimethylformamide vapor. *J. Occup. Med.* 20:179.
5. Maxfield, M. E., Barnes, J. R., Azar, A., and Trochimowicz, H. J. (1975). Urinary excretion of metabolite following experimental human exposures to DMF or to DMAC. *J. Occup. Med.* 17:506.
6. Task Group on Lung Dynamics. (1966). Deposition and retention models for internal dosimetry of the human respiratory tract. *Health Phys.* 12:173.
7. Walsh, P. J. (1970). Radiation dose to the respiratory tract of uranium miners-and review of the literature. *Environ. Res.* 3:14.
8. Morrow, P. E. (1972). "Theoretical and experimental models for dust deposition and retention in man." *UR-3490-169,* University of Rochester, Rochester, NY.
9. Morrow, P. E., Gibb, F. R., and Gazioglu, K. M. (1967). A study of particulate clearance from the human lungs. *Am. Rev. Respir. Dis.* 96:1209.
10. Mauderly, J. L. (1985). "Relationship of structure and function of the respiratory tract to responses to inhaled toxicants." Refresher Course, 24th Meeting Society of Toxicology, San Diego, CA.
11. Stokinger, H. E., Wagner, W. D., and Dobrogorski, O. J. (1959). Ozone toxicity studies. III. Chronic injury to lungs of animals following exposure to a low level. *Arch. Ind. Health* 16:514.
12. Jones, R. A., Jenkins, Jr., L. J., Coon, R. A., and Siegel, J. (1970). Effects of long-term continuous inhalation

of ozone on experimental animals. *Toxicol. Appl. Pharmacol.* 17:189.

13. Weyel, D. A. and Schaeffer, R. B. (1985). Pulmonary and sensory irritation of diphenylmethane-4,4'- and dicyclohexyl-methane-4,4'-diisocyanate. *Toxicol. Appl. Pharmacol.* 77:427.
14. Karol, M. H. and Magreni, C. M. (1982). Extensive skin sensitization with minimal antibody production in guinea pigs as a result of exposure to cyclohexylmethane-4,4'-diisocyanate. *Toxicol. Appl. Pharmacol.* 65:291.
15. Wong, K. L. and Alarie, Y. (1982). A method for repeated evaluation of pulmonary performance in unanesthetized, unrestrained guinea pigs and its application to detect affects of sulfuric acid mist inhalation. *Toxicol. Appl. Pharmacol.* 63:72.
16. Saffiotti, U. (1970). *Morphology of Experimental Respiratory Carcinogenesis, A.E.C. Symposium Series 21*, U.S.A.E.C. Division of Technical Information, p. 245.
17. Ellakkan, M. A., Alarie, Y. C., Weyel, D. A., and Karol, M. H. (1985). Concentration-dependent respiratory response of guinea pigs to a single exposure of cotton dust. *Toxicol. Appl. Pharmacol.* 80:357.
18. Costa, D. L., Schafrank, S. N., Wehner, R. W., and Jellett, E. (1985). Alveolar permeability to protein in rats differentially susceptible to ozone. *J. Appl. Toxicol.* 5:182.
19. Drew, R. T., Kutzman, R. S., Costa, D. L., and Iwai, J. (1983). Effects of sulfur dioxide and ozone on hypertension-sensitive and resistant rats. *Fundam. Appl. Toxicol.* 3:298.
20. McLaughlin, R. F., Tyler, W. S., and Canada, R. O. (1961). A study of the subgross pulmonary anatomy in various mammals. *Am. J. Anat.* 108:149.
21. Phalen, R. F. (1984). *Inhalation Studies: Foundations and Techniques.* CRC Press, Boca Raton, FL, p. 228.
22. Stuart, B. O. Selection of animal models for evaluation of inhalation hazards in man. *Air Pollution and the Lung.* Edited by E. F. Aharonson, A. Ben-Davis, and M. A. Klingberg. J. Wiley and Sons, New York, p. 268.
23. MacFarland, H. N. (1983). Designs and operational characteristics of inhalation exposure equipment—a review. *Fund. Appl. Toxicol.* 3:603.
24. Rampy, L. W. (1981). Generating and controlling atmospheres in inhalation chambers. In *Scientific Considerations in Monitoring and Evaluating Toxicological Research.* Edited by E. J. Gralla. Washington, D.C., Hemisphere Pub. Co., p. 57.
25. Kennedy, Jr., G. L. and Chen, H. C. (1984). Inhalation toxicity of dibutylhexamethylenediamine in rats. *Food Chem. Toxicol.* 22:425.

26. Kinney, L. A., Burgess, B. A., Stula, E. F., and Kennedy, Jr., G. L. (1985). Acute and subchronic inhalation toxicity of 1,4-butanediol in rats. *Toxicologist* 5:130.

27. Burgess, B. A., Ashley, P. A., and Kennedy, Jr., G. L. (1983). Acute toxicity and upper respiratory tract irritation of carbonyl sulfide and carbon disulfide in rats. *Toxicologist* 3:63.

28. Gardner, R. J., Burgess, B. A., and Kennedy, Jr., G. L. (1985). Sensory irritation potential of selected nasal tumorigens in the rat. *Food Chem. Toxicol.* 23:87.

29. Smith, L. W., Gardner, R. J., and Kennedy, Jr., G. L. (1982). Short-term inhalation toxicity of perfluoroisobutylene. *Drug Chem. Toxicol.* 5:295.

30. Potts, W. J. and Steiner, E. C. (1980). An apparatus for generation of vapors from liquids of low volatility for use in inhalation toxicity studies. *Am. Ind. Hyg. Assoc. J.* 41:141.

31. Dimmick, R. L. (1959). Jet dispenser for compacted powders in the one-to-ten micron range. *Arch. Ind. Health* 20:8.

32. Laskin, S., Drew, R. T., Cappiello, V. P., and Kuschner, M. (1972). Inhalation studies with freshly generated polyurethane from dust. In *Assessment of Airborne Particles*. Edited by T. T. Mercer, P. E. Morrow, and W. Stober. Springfield, IL, Charles C. Thomas Publisher, p. 382.

33. Drew, R. T. and Laskin, S. (1971). A new dust generating system for inhalation studies. *Am. Ind. Hyg. Assoc. J.* 32:327.

34. Carpenter, R. L., Pickrell, J. A., Mokler, B. V., Yeh, H. S., and DeNee, P. B. (1981). Generation of respirable glass fiber aerosol using a fluidized bed aerosol generator. *Am. Ind. Hyg. Assoc. J.* 42:777.

35. Lee, K. P., Kelly, D. P., and Kennedy, Jr., G. L. (1983). Pulmonary response to inhaled Kevlar® aramid synthetic fibers in rats. *Toxicol. Appl. Pharmacol.* 71:242.

36. Burgess, B. A. and Kelly, D. P. (1984). Monitoring vapor concentrations in test atmospheres. In *Chemistry for Toxicity Testing*. Edited by C. W. Jameson and D. B. Walters. Stoneham, MA, Butterworth Publishers, p. 139.

37. Moss, D. R. and Decker, J. R. (1984). Chemical monitoring of aerosols in inhalation chambers. In *Chemistry for Toxicity Testing*. Edited by C. W. Jameson and D. B. Walters. Stoneham, MA, Butterworth Publishers, p. 149.

38. Lundgren, D. (1976). Aerosol mass measurement using piazoelectric crystal sensors. In *Fine Particles*. Edited by B. Y. N. Liu. New York, Academic Press.

39. Macias, E. S. and Husar, R. B. (1976). A review of atmospheric particulate mass measurement via the beta attenuation technique. In *Fine Particles*. Edited by B. Y. N. Liu. New York, Academic Press.

40. Cook, C. S. (1976). Remote measurement of smoke plume transmittance using Lidar. *Appl. Optics 11*:127.

41. Calandra, J. C. and Fancher, D. E. (1979). Target organ studies. In *New Concepts in Safety Evaluation*, Part 2. Edited by M. A. Mehlman, R. E. Shapiro, and H. Blumenthal. New York, John Wiley & Sons, p. 179.

42. Rowe, V. K., McCollister, D. D., Spencer, H. C., Adams, E. M., and Irish, D. D. (1952). Vapor toxicity of tetrachloroethylene for laboratory animals and human subjects. *Arch. Ind. Hyg. Occup. Med. 5*:566.

43. Lee, K. P., Trochimowicz, H. J., and Sarver, J. W. (1977). Inhalation of nasal tumors in rats exposed to hexamethylphosphoramide (HMPA). *Lab. Invest. 36*:344.

44. Lee, K. P., Trochimowicz, H. J., Reinhardt, C. F. (1985). Pulmonary response of rats exposed to titanium dioxide ($TiO_2$) by inhalation for two years. *Toxicol. Appl. Pharmacol. 79*:179.

45. Alarie, Y., Lin, C. K., and Geary, D. L. (1974). Sensory irritation evoked by plastic decomposition products. *Am. Ind. Hyg. Assoc. J. 35*:654.

46. Brain, J. D., Knudson, D. E., Sorokin, S. P., and Davis, M. A. (1976). Pulmonary distribution of particles given by intratracheal instillation or by aerosol inhalation. *Environ. Res. 11*:13.

47. Lee, K. P. (1985). Lung response to particulates with emphasis on asbestos and other fibrous dust. *CRC Crit. Rev. Toxicol. 14*:33.

48. Amdur, M. O. (1957). The influence of aerosols on the respiratory response of guinea pigs to sulfur dioxide. *Am. Ind. Hyg. Assoc. Q. 18*:149.

49. Ballantyne, B., Clary, J. J., Owen, P. E., and Glaister, J. R. (1985). Carbon fibers—a subchronic inhalation toxicology study. *J. Occup. Med. 27*:676.

# 10

# Reproductive Hazards

JAMES L. SCHARDEIN / *International Research and Development Corporation, Mattawan, Michigan*

## I. INTRODUCTION

The toxic effects of chemicals and drugs on the human reproductive system have become a major health concern to scientists and the populace alike, due to several factors. First, the number of reproductive hazards to which we are being exposed in the environment is increasing. Best estimates indicate over 58,000 chemicals in common use at present with 650 added each year. The near global use of pesticides and accounts of incidents such as Love Canal, Three Mile Island, Minamata Bay, Times Beach, Seveso, Hopewell, Bhobal, and countless other industrial chemical spills, leaks, and other accidents, both real and exaggerated, fortify the perception of potential hazards in the environment. Unfortunately, only scant data exist on the reproductive effects of the large array of existing chemicals. The information that is available usually relates to accidental overexposures, whereas most real-life exposures are low level (which may impart greater significance as hazards to reproductive health).

Second, a relatively large number of individuals are exposed more directly because of occupational exposure in the workplace, through manufacture, packaging, or handling of manmade chemicals than through the environment. In this regard, 50% of pregnant American women are employed during at least part of their gestation (1), thus, while emphasis has been directed toward protection of the *pregnant woman and conceptus* when potential industrial risks have been suspected, exposure of either males or nonpregnant females may cause abnormalities which result in reproductive failure. Disorders of reproduction, infertility, abortion, and teratogenesis are in fact, the sixth leading cause of work-related disease according to OSHA (1982).

Finally, it is generally perceived that sensitive biological indicators of such toxic exposures (i.e., impotency, infertility, stillbirths, abortions, malformations and cancers) are on the increase. In addition, it is generally recognized that human reproductive processes may be reactive to a wide variety of other conditions, including climate, altitude, social class, parity, age, diet, infections, stress, and social habits. Thus, there is heightened concern over environmental hazards being added to an already overburdened number of potentially detrimental factors.

It is very likely that environmental toxins have taken their toll on reproductive capacity in the human species. For instance, approximately 10–12% of couples who desire children fail to achieve pregnancy (2); this number rises to 20–25% if those who conceive but who do not have live offspring and those that fail to conceive a second time are included (3). Then, only 1/4 to 1/3 of all embryos conceived develop to become liveborn infants (4). From a different clinical perspective, it has been speculated that "normal" sperm counts in American men may have been decreasing in the recent past: In 1950, 44% of men sampled had sperm counts in excess of 100 million, while in 1977, only 22% of men assayed had sperm counts of this magnitude (5). To the extent that reduction in sperm counts affect reproduction, these data may reflect a serious decline in reproductive potential. An associated problem here is that basic physiologic parameters of normalcy have not yet been established with respect to human male reproduction (3).

Consider for a moment the critical prerequisites for successful reproduction: It requires the completion, in both sexes, of a series of complex interdependent cellular, molecular, and physiological events, involving the capacity of a male to produce and release viable sperm in adequate numbers, a female to produce and release viable ova, and the union to produce a conceptus, through gametic interaction, which will flourish and develop (6). Is it any wonder that every sexual union does not result in a perfect outcome?

## II.  TARGET ORGANS AND SPECTRUM OF REPRODUCTIVE OUTCOMES

For our purposes, reproductive toxicity shall be defined simply as adverse effects of chemicals that interfere with the ability of males or females to reproduce. It is important in this context to realize that effects to either sex may result in the same endpoint of reproductive failure. Because miscarriage/abortion, stillbirth, intrauterine growth retardation (IUGR)/low body weights at birth and congenital malformations are important reproductive outcomes and at the same time represent developmental toxicity, there can be no clearcut separation of these events from strictly reproductive toxicity. However, this presentation shall be directed toward reproductive hazards as defined above, rather than developmental ones. The discussion thus will be largely confined to preconception and pregnancy reproductive outcomes (Table 1).

## A. Characteristics of Gonadotoxins and Their Outcomes

The range of reproductive outcomes possible is depicted in Table 1. The background frequencies for these events in the human are given in Table 2.

In general, damage to gonads and their function by chemicals can result from any of several mechanisms including direct actions on germ cells, actions affecting the accessory sex organs, or inhibition of

**Table 1**  Range of Reproductive Outcomes

| Prior to conception | During pregnancy | After delivery |
|---|---|---|
| Altered libido | Maternal toxicity | Low birth weight (IUGR) |
| Abnormal sperm production/transport | Miscarriage | Congenital malformation |
| Impotence (males) | Spontaneous abortion | |
| Ejaculatory disorders (males) | Premature labor | |
| Ovulatory disorders (females) | Altered/prolonged gestation | Developmental disability |
| Abnormal menses (females) (dys-, oligo-, amenorrhea, dysfunct. uterine bleeding) | Dystocia | Death (late fetal, neonatal, childhood) |
| | | Behavioral disorders |
| Effect on fertility (reduced, infertility/ sterility) | | Altered reproductive capacity |

hormonal-controlling mechanisms at either the gonadal or the hypo-
thalamic-pituitary level. It should be kept in mind that a reproductive toxin in one species may not be toxic in another, because of
differences in reproductive or toxicological mechanisms. In this
respect, gender differences in toxicity are crucial: As a result of
the accessibility of gametes and gonads, more compounds have been
demonstrated to be toxic in males than in females (15).

Evidence to date indicates that the most likely outcome of exposure to environmental toxicants is *infertility* in the male and
*spontaneous abortion* in the female (16). In laboratory animals as
well as in humans, fertility rates are commonly used as reproductive
endpoints, but these are hampered by a large number of variables
influencing reproductive potential, especially in the human. This
is because of psychological and physiological factors in the latter,
and in addition, personal habits (i.e., smoking, alcohol, and caffeine

**Table 2**   Background Frequency of Reproductive Outcomes (Human)

| Parameter | Reported normal (approximate) rate (U.S.) | Reference |
|---|---|---|
| Maternal mortality | 0.7/10,000 | 7 |
| Infertility[a] | 15% | 8 |
| Spontaneous abortion[b] | 15% | 8 |
|   karyotypical abnormal | 60% | 9,10 |
| Livebirths[k] | 86.7% | 11 |
| Prematurity | 6.4–9.2% | 7 |
| Prolonged labor | 2.4% | 7 |
| Low birthweight[d] | 7% | 8 |
| Birth defects | | |
|   minor[e] | 140/1000 | 12 |
|   major[e] | 4% | 8 |
|   minor mental retardation[e] | 3–4/1000 | 12 |
|   severe mental retardation[e,j] | 0.4% | 8 |
|   among deaths after | | |
|     gestation of:   2–8 wks | 3.4% | 12 |
|               9–15 wks | 8% | 12 |
|              14–18 wks | 5.7% | 12 |
|   at birth[e] | 20–30/1000 | 12 |
|   at 1 year | 60–70/1000 | 12 |

**Table 2**   (continued)

| Parameter | Reported normal (approximate) rate (U.S.) | Reference |
|---|---|---|
| Death | | |
| early embryonic/fetal[h] | 11–25% | 12 |
| late fetal[c] | 9.8/1000 | 12 |
| stillbirth[c] | 2% | 8 |
| neonatal[g] | 9.9/1000 | 12 |
| infant[e,f] | 14.1/1000 | 12 |
| childhood, 1–4 years | 0.95/1000 | 13 |
| Chromosomal abnormalities[e] | 5–6/1000 | 12 |
| among early fetal deaths[i] | 50% | 12 |
| among stillbirths | 6% | 9,12 |
| among nonmalformed | 1.7% | 14 |
| among lethally malformed | 13–33% | 9 |
| Physically handicapped, age 2 | 16.7% | 13 |

[a]Impaired fecundity.   Defined as failure to achieve pregnancy after 1 year without contraceptive use.
[b]<20 Weeks gestation.
[c]21+ Weeks gestation.
[d]<2500 g.
[e]Of livebirths.
[f]<1 year old.
[g]28 Days.
[h]End of 4th week on.
[i]8–20 Weeks.
[j]IQ < 50.
[k]As % of total pregnancies.

use) may affect reproductive outcome (17).   Additionally, infertility appears not to be gender specific:   Male factors have been identified in approximately 40% of the cases, and female dysfunction in 35–50%; unknown causes account for 10–20% of the cases of infertility in human populations (18).

Abortion has been suggested as one of the most useful outcomes for the evaluation of occupational reproductive hazards (19).   Because of the frequency of their occurrence, the power of studies to detect an effect of an exposure is much greater than for other adverse pregnancy outcomes (20).

Reproductive failure in the form of abortion, stillbirth, or birth defects alone is not an adequate measure of the extent of reproductive hazards from toxic agents among humans (16). Reproductive toxins can manifest themselves in a variety of ways, including adversely affecting the male or female reproductive cycle, possibly leading to infertility; causing the production of insufficient or defective sperm; preventing the successful implantation of fertilized ova; or inducing functional defects not readily observed at birth and hence, not associated with reproductive failure. Thus, reproductive toxins may have subtle as well as overt effects on reproduction.

### 1. Male

Specifically in the male, dysfunction can be reflected in altered hypothalamo-pituitary-gonadal interactions, spermatogenesis, Sertoli cell function, hormone synthesis and action, accessory sex organ function, gene integrity, libido, potency, and ejaculation (21,22).

It is vital to know the mechanism by which chemicals interfere with gonadal function, because the severity of, and in some cases the reversibility of, the toxicity depends on the process being disrupted. Some of these have been reviewed specifically in the male (23,24). For instance, a number of toxicants, in particular hormones, inhibit gonadal function through negative feedback, based on the androgen dependency of the testis. A number of others, including antihypertensive drugs, tranquilizers, and neuroleptics, may interfere with gonadotropin secretion. Some, like spironolactone and aminoglutethimide, inhibit enzymes involved in androgen biosynthesis. Still others, like the heavy metals, destroy the blood–testis barrier. Antimetabolites cause irreversible nutritional disturbances that affect testicular function. The antimitotic and anticancer drugs act directly on the germ cells, especially those cells most active in nucleic acid synthesis (i.e., the spermatocytes).

A large number of chemicals have been reported to affect male reproduction. More than 100 chemicals have shown this potential in male laboratory animals, while fewer than 15 of this number have been shown conclusively to have this effect in the human (25). A list of steroids, therapeutic agents, metals and trace elements, pesticides, food additives and contaminants, industrial chemicals, investigational antispermatogenic drugs, and miscellaneous chemicals have been tabulated as inferred reproductive toxicants in males in several recent publications (4,23–31).

Physicochemical characteristics of reproductive toxins in the male have been reviewed elsewhere (32). In general, the stereotypic gonadotoxin is usually lipophilic, of diverse chemical structure, and has avidity for androgen receptors and a propensity for rapidly dividing cells. Its molecular weight is frequently less than 400, thus it can permeate the testes-blood barrier.

## 2. *Female*

In the female as well as in the male, the ways in which reproductive dysfunction can be expressed are multitudinous. Female reproductive dysfunction can appear as altered hypothalamo-pituitary-gonadal interactions; oogenesis, steroidogenesis, and ovulation; and accessory sex organ function (21). Some 30 potential reproductive processes have been identified as potentially susceptible to toxicants in nonpregnant subjects and at least half that number in pregnant women (33).

In the larger dimension, the reproductive hazards to which the female is exposed may precede fertilization, occur between fertilization and implantation, or placentation and parturition, at parturition, postnatally, or through accelerated reproductive senescence. Each of these events are vulnerable to the adverse effects of toxins.

Damage to primary oocytes usually occurs through cell death, but sublethal injury may result in oocytes capable of fertilization but culminate in early abortion (34). Some gonadotoxins, polycyclic aromatic hydrocarbons for instance, may not be so directly, but become metabolized by the ovary to reactive intermediates that are cytotoxic (35). Exposure of ova to chemicals near meiosis may result in death of the ova or affect fertilizability. However, ovarian toxicity which produces periods of infertility or subfertility may be difficult to identify (36). Tabulations of chemicals affecting reproductive function in the female have been summarized elsewhere (4,15,21, 27,28,36-39).

## B. Origin and Differentiation of Gonads and Gametes

It is important that fundamentals of germ cell development in both males and females be well understood if we are to devise methods and evaluate meaningfully reproductive events and gonadal toxicity in laboratory animals in order to extrapolate these into realistic assessments of human hazard. The development of reproductive capacity occurs during a critical period in time, and while undergoing development, the reproductive system is a highly vulnerable target for toxic injury (40).

### 1. *Male*

In mammals, gonadal origins occur early in embryonic development, prior to sexual differentiation (41). Thus the initial stages described here are equally pertinent to male and female alike. Descriptions of development and differentiation of the duct system and external genitalia in either gender will not be discussed in this presentation, since an understanding of their embryology is not critical to considerations of gonadal toxicity.

*Derivation*. The gonads appear initially as a pair of longitudinal genital ridges formed by proliferation of the coelomic epithelium and a condensation of the underlying mesenchyme of the mesonephros renal system. The *primordial germ cells* appear at an early stage of development among the endoderm cells in the wall of the yolk sac close to the allantois, migrate along the dorsal mesentery of the hindgut, and invade the genital ridges. This occurs in the sixth week of development in the human or days 10 1/2-12 in the rat.

Shortly before and during the arrival of the primordial germ cells, the coelomic epithelium of the genital ridge proliferates and epithelial cells penetrate the underlying mesenchyme, forming a number of irregularly shaped elements, the primitive sex cords. At this time, it is impossible to differentiate between the male and female gonad: It is thus known (at about 8 weeks in the human or day 12.5 in the rat) as the *indifferent gonad*. It should be emphasized that it is the Y chromosome in the male and the XX chromosome configuration in the female that cause the development of the respective gonadal structures.

In genetically male embryos (carrying an XY sex chromosome complex), the primitive sex cords of the indifferent gonad continue to proliferate and penetrate deep into the medulla to form the medullary cords or *testis*. The secondary cortical cords typical of the female constitution regress at this time. Toward the hilus of the gland, the testis cords break up into a network of strands which later give rise to the tubules of the rete testis; during further development, the testis cords become separated from the surface epithelium by the tunica albuginea.

Later on, the extremities of the testis cords are continuous with those of the rete testis. They are now composed of primitive germ cells (spermatogonia) and Sertoli cells, derived from the surface of the gland. The interstitial cells (Leydig cells) develop from the mesenchyme located between the testis cords: They are particularly abundant in months 4-6 of development in man (day 15 in the rat). The male gonad is now able to influence the sexual differentiation of the genital ducts and external genitalia. The cords remain solid until puberty, when they acquire lumens, thus forming the seminiferous tubules.

*Spermatogenesis*. Spermatogenesis is a two-phase process comprised of spermatocytogenesis and spermiogenesis (42). The spermatogenesis process is the sum of transformations that result in formation of spermatozoa from spermatogonia while maintaining spermatogonial numbers. The process begins at puberty and continues almost throughout life. Spermatogonia are dormant following birth until puberty when proliferative activity begins again. In simplistic terms, the process evolves as follows: The *spermatocytogenesis* phase is the spermatogenic tissue growth phase of the testis; in it, proliferation occurs through mitotic division of germ cells to form spermatids.

In the testis there exist a number of germ cells recognized as cellular associations: Depending on the species and the observer, 6–14 different cellular associations have been discerned. Each contains 4 or 5 types of germ cells organized in a specific layered pattern within the seminiferous tubules of the testis, with each layer representing one cell generation. The entire series of cellular associations is termed the cycle of the seminiferous epithelium. Progression through the series of cellular associations occurs in a predictable, sequential fashion and continues repeatedly over and over. The interval required for one complete series of cellular associations to appear at a fixed point within a tubule is termed the duration of the cycle of the seminiferous epithelium. This duration is uniform for each species and ranges from 8.6 days in the mouse to 16 days in man (see Table 8).

The process of spermatogenesis is initiated when type A stem spermatogonia become committed to produce a cohort of spermatids. The onset accompanies functional maturation of the testes; the germ cells proliferate in a protected environment created in part by the blood-testis barrier (43). Type A spermatogonia germ cells periodically differentiate at a given point within a seminiferous tubule and divide to give rise to more differentiated spermatogonia and ultimately, primary spermatocytes. The spermatogonial stem cell population in its development stages is far more vulnerable to chemical injury than differentiated spermatogonia (44). The duration of spermatogenesis is the interval from this point until release of the resulting spermatozoa at spermiation. The interval between commitment of a stem A spermatogonium to differentiation and formation of the resulting primary spermatocytes is not known with certainty, but probably requires between 1.3 and 1.7 cycles of seminiferous epithelium, and the interval between formation of primary spermatocytes and spermiation is close to 3.0 cycles in the common mammalian species. Thus, the duration of spermatogenesis is 4.3–4.7 cycles of the seminiferous epithelium, or about 35–70 days in the common species (see Table 8).

As this transformation is in progress, reduction occurs through meiotic division, to ensure that the haploid number of chromosomes in each gamete is maintained (Fig. 1a). Because of the complexity of the process, meiosis is one of the most susceptible stages of the entire process for chemical toxicity to occur.

In the *spermiogenesis* phase, the spermatids complete their development into spermatozoa by undergoing reorganization: The nucleus condenses and becomes the sperm head; the two centrioles form the axial filament (flagellum); the Golgi in part becomes the acrosome; and the mitochondria concentrate into the sheath. It is not until the sperm reach the lower corpus or cauda epididymis, a process lasting 10–15 days in most species, that they finally achieve the potential to fertilize the mature oocyte. The immature, immotile spermatozoa transformed by this process depend on follicle-stimulating

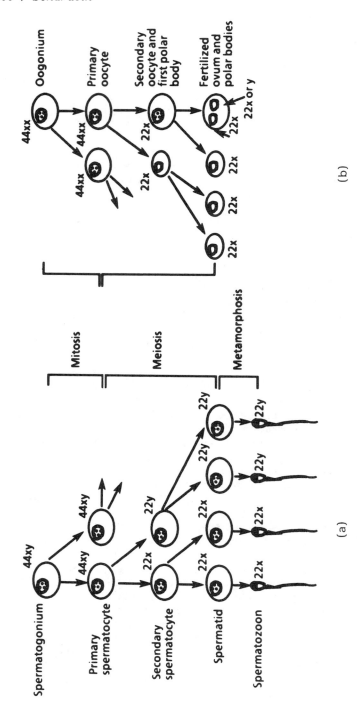

Figure 1  The processes of spermatogenesis (a) and oogenesis (b) (from Ref. 26).

hormone (FSH) secreted by the pituitary and subtle biochemical and morphological changes acquired during epididymal transit for final maturation into fertile spermatozoa. In the case of the human male's reproductive lifespan of more than 60 years, approximately one quadrillion spermatozoa are produced in this manner (26). This is a superlatively efficient process, even in biologic terms, to say the least!

Sperm storage is within the caudal segment of the epididymis, and upon ejaculation, only sperm present in this region of the duct are discharged (43). Surplus unejaculated sperm are discharged during spontaneous emissions, voided in the urine, and in rodents, emerge in the form of seminal plugs in the urethra; others may also disintegrate in the cauda and vas deferens.

### 2. Female

*Derivation.* In embryos predetermined to be female (XX sex chromosome complement), the primitive sex cords comprising the indifferent gonad described above, break up into irregular cell clusters. These contain groups of primitive germ cells, and are located primarily in the medullary part of the designated ovary. Later they disappear and are replaced by a vascular stroma which forms the ovarian medulla.

Unlike that of the male, the surface epithelium of the female gonad continues to proliferate, giving rise to a second generation, the cortical cords. These penetrate the underlying mesenchyme and in the 4th month in the human (day 13.5 in the rat), these cords are also split into isolated cell clusters, each surrounding one or more primitive germ cells. The germ cells subsequently develop into the oogonia, while the surrounding epithelial cells, descendents of the surface epithelium, form the follicular cells.

*Oogenesis/Folliculogenesis.* In contrast to the process of spermatogenesis in the male, oogenesis in the female is a discontinuous process. The process is outlined below (26,39).

As previously mentioned, the oogonia proliferate during the fetal period within the cortex of the ovary and become surrounded by epithelial cells to form the primary follicle. Shortly after birth, oogonia cease to proliferate and become oocytes, folliculogenesis begins, with formation of the follicle complex.

The follicle complex is the smallest functional unit of the ovary, and consists of oocyte, granulosa cells, basement membrane, and thecal cells. Oocytes require the follicular complex for support. Those oocytes which are not a part of a follicular complex following completion of folliculogenesis are lost through extrusion from the surface of the ovary or by cell death within the ovary. After sexual maturation, three types of follicular complexes are found in the ovary: Resting or primordial follicles, growing follicles, and preovulatory follicles, and are distinguished on the basis of size of oocyte and zona pellucida, and number of granulosa cells. This classification is important because follicle complexes of different size have varying susceptibility to reproductive toxins.

In mammals, germ cells in the ovary are arrested at the primary oocyte stage (diplotene), where they remain until just before they are ovulated. During the 30 years or more that constitute the human reproductive period (or in the 1-year breeding interval in the rat), follicles in various stages of growth can always be found. Following this (menopause in the human), follicles are no longer present in the ovary.

Follicular growth requires recruitment of follicles from a resting pool into a growing pool, the mechanisms of which are poorly understood at this time. Further growth and ultimate ovulation of the oocyte from the follicle complex requires the presence of gonadotropins and steroid hormones produced by dynamic interactions between the ovary, hypothalamus, and pituitary. Ovulation occurs predictably in the various species (see Table 10); in the human it is 28-32 hours after the onset of the luteinizing hormone (LH) surge (45). The final event of this process, follicle rupture, is probably the result of the action of prostaglandins. Following ovulation, the follicle complex differentiates into the corpus luteum, and those follicle complexes recruited into the growing pool which do not ovulate undergo atresia.

While in the ovary, the primary oocyte undergoes two specialized meiotic divisions: In the first stage, the primary oocyte is in preparation for entering prophase. Each prophase chromosome doubles and each doubled chromosome is attracted to its homologous mate to form tetrads; chromosomes of the same parental origin are connected to one another by their centromeres. The members of the tetrads synapse, but before separation, the chromosomes exchange genetic material by a "crossing-over" process, which accounts for most of the qualitative differences between the resulting gametes. The subsequent meiotic stages distribute the members of the tetrads to the daughter cells so that each cell receives haploid chromosomes. At telophase, one secondary oocyte and polar body have been formed which are no longer genetically identical, and the mature ovum is released from the ovary at this stage.

The second meiotic division in the oocyte is triggered in the oviduct by the entry of the sperm. The stimulus of sperm penetration into the mature ovum and decondensation of the sperm chromatin initates the resumption of meiosis and extrusion of the second polar body. Meanwhile, the first poalr body attempts division shortly before degenerating. The early product of ovulation and fertilization is thus one large ovum with maternal and fraternal haploid chromosome complements and three rudimentary ova known as polar bodies each with haploid chromosomes (Fig. 1b).

In humans, between 300,000 and 400,000 follicles are present at birth in each ovary. Under normal conditions, there is a continual reduction in the number of viable ovarian follicles: About half the number of oocytes present at birth remain at puberty; the number is reduced to about 25,000 by 30 years of age, and further loss occurs to menopause. Thus, on an average during the reproductive life of a woman, only about 400 primary follicles will yield mature ova, and only a very few of these are likely to be fertilized. This disparity in female and male gametogenesis is depicted in Figure 2.

With respect to ovarian toxicity induced by various chemicals, it is clear from the description of the oogenesis and folliculogenesis processes, that several stages in the process are particularly vulnerable to toxins. Obviously any chemical agent that blocks the process in toto will decrease the number of oocytes and thus may affect fertility. Likewise, any agent that damages the follicles or oocytes proper will accelerate the depletion of the follicle pool and lead to

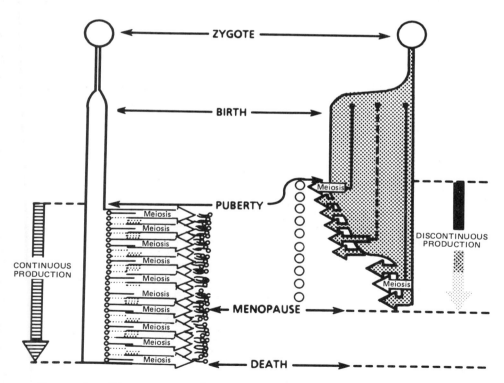

Figure 2   The contrast of the gametogenesis process between males (left) and females (right) (from Ref. 411).

reduced fertility. Further, in both experimental animals and humans, follicle complexes have differing sensitivity to ovarian toxins, depending on the strain, species, agent, and dosage used. Effects on dominant follicles are immediate, while resumption in fertility occurs following repopulation of the preovulatory pool and selection of another dominant follicle (36). Toxicity to growing gonadotropin-independent follicles will cause a delay in onset of infertility proportionate to the time necessary for follicles to progress through the gonadotropin-dependent pool. Finally, toxicity to resting follicle complexes is most delayed with respect to effects on reproductive function. Hypothetical effects on fertility based on the type of oocyte destruction in the female are shown in Figure 3.

## C. The Processes of Fertilization and Implantation

The formation, maturation, and intersection of gametes produced by the male and female are all preliminary to their actual union into a zygote by the process of fertilization. Fertilization can be arbitrarily divided into three phases: Penetration of the egg by the sperm; activation of the egg; and union of egg and sperm nuclei (26). The process is short-lived, ranging from about 0.25–12 hours in duration, depending on the species (46).

A proper state of maturity of both male and female germ cells must exist for union of sperm and egg. In almost all mammals, the first polar body must be extruded and the second polar body must be in a state of arrest before penetration of the sperm can take place. As mentioned above, the second meiotic division is completed only during the preliminary events of fertilization. The sperm, to be successful, must possess high motility and also must be in a functionally potent phase. The actual site of fertilization is in the ampulla of the oviduct within one day of ovulation.

Preparation of the sperm for fertilization requires the initiation of complex events termed capacitation and involves labilization of the sperm plasma membrane, requiring about 5 hours. Subsequent to this, sperm membrane changes allow breakdown of the acrosome and release of enzymes instrumental in passage of sperm through the follicular cells prior to penetration of the sperm cell through the zona pellucida into the egg cytoplasm. This process, the acrosomal reaction, is thought to be prerequisite for fertilization in mammals (45). The sperm pass through the cumulus, then the zona pellucida, and enter the eperivitelline space. In the great majority of animals, only one sperm finds its way into the egg. Upon attachment of the fertilizing spermatozoan to the egg, rapid changes take place in the membrane composition of the egg which reduce the possibility of penetration by a second sperm. Finally, the sperm penetrates the plasma membrane of the oocyte, and intense nuclear activity ensues,

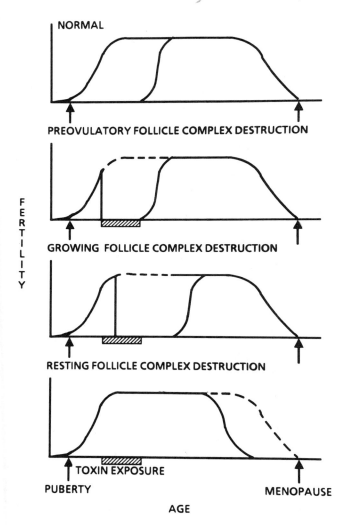

**Figure 3** Effect of ovarian toxins on fertility. The cross hatched area represents the period of ovotoxin exposure: (−) the expected fertility; (− −) the normal fertility in absence of toxin exposure (from Ref. 39).

with eventual formation of a male pronucleus. At the same time, a female pronucleus forms and the two join (syngamy), restoring the diploid state and establishing the sex of the individual. This is followed almost immediately by the first cleavage division, signaling the end of fertilization. As with a number of reproductive processes already described, any of the sequences of steps in the process of fertilization may be a target for insult by chemically hazardous agents (47).

In the mammal following fertilization, the cleaving ova pass through the oviducts into the uterus, and after a variable period in its lumen, adhere to the endometrium. Tubal passage is relatively constant, generally lasting about 3-4 days. Adherence is followed by firm attachment, or implantation, and formation of a placental connection from the fusion of maternal and fetal tissues. During this phase the developing conceptus is nourished, first by its own yolk substance and the tubal fluids, then by the secretions of the uterine glands. Once formed, the placenta becomes chiefly responsible for maintenance and growth of the embryo.

On arriving in the uterus, in polytocous species, the eggs distribute through the two horns: Attachment of the blastocyst is a relatively rapid process (see Table 9), and results from precise synchronous interactions between the embryo and the uterus. The preimplantation stage is critical in this scheme, because injuries to the embryo at this time are likely to result either in death of the conceptus or in repair and recovery.

Based on morphological criteria, implantation can be divided into five phases: hatching, apposition, attachment/adhesion, invasion, and peri-implantation development; physiological correlates to these events ascribe these changes to interactions between progesterone and estrogen (48). Chemicals interfering with the timing of the entry of embryos into the uterus, the development of embryos, and the differentiation of the uterus will have a bearing on the occurrence or absence of implantation; a number have been described (49). From here on, the very early implanted embryo undergoes a complicated series of morphogenic events leading to an embryo with recognizable organ systems capable of insult by developmental toxins, the whole of which is outside the scope of this presentation. A very high rate of embryonic loss is a normal phenomenon in mammals, especially in the very early stages of pregnancy: Upon exposure to sperm, the probability of fertilization of a human ovum is estimated to be 84%, but by the time pregnancy is recognizable, one-half of all embryos have been lost (4). During the remainder of pregnancy, another 25% perish and are aborted, thus the entire process, from fertilization until birth, results in an estimated probability of a livebirth of only 31 out of 100.

## III. SOURCES OF REPRODUCTIVE HAZARDS

As alluded to earlier, there are a number of sources of environmental toxins that present a potential hazard to reproduction. Chief
among these are chemicals or groups of chemicals and/or physical
factors to which individuals are exposed in the workplace or in the
environment at large. There are also exposures to needed medica-
tions and usage of social chemicals and workplace situations in which
the specific hazards are yet to be even identified, yet alone proven.
Finally, there are accidental hazards in which chemical contaminants
through spills, leaks or other industrial accidents may provide significant exposures. We will consider these in turn.

### A. Environmental, Occupational Exposures

The largest source of reproductive hazards has been identified
through occupational or environmental exposures of specific chemicals,
chemical groups, or physical factors. Forty-six of these have been
characterized to date, of which 24 have been identified as affecting
only females (Table 3). Nine have been identified as affecting only
males, and 13 agents in this group affect both sexes and thus would
appear to constitute even greater hazard. These include cadmium,
carbon disulfide, chloroprene, estrogens, ethylene dibromide, gossypol, elevated temperature, lead, psychological stress, inorganic
mercury, toluene, vinyl chloride, and pesticides.

Additionally, a number of substances affect more than single endpoints in both sexes, and thus would also appear to constitute higher
priority factors for control. For example, carbon disulfide among
textile workers affects libido, induces sperm abnormalities, and causes
impotence in males, and produces menstrual irregularities, and results
in decreased fertility and increased spontaneous abortion in females.
Metals industries (lead and mercury) are other good workplace examples of sources of reproductive toxins affecting multiple endpoints.

The data generated thus far for agents in this group are admit-
tedly weak in a number of cases: chloroprene, DDT, dinitrodipropyl-
sulfanilamide, ethylene oxide, formaldehyde, methylparathion, non-
ionizing radiation, selenium, "stress," and styrene are examples
where evidence of reproductive toxicity is inadequate and additional
confirmatory data are needed.

Unfortunately, identification of a number of potent reproductive
toxins among agents in this group has evoked little change in industrial practice. In a few cases, there are restrictions on workers,
in the lead industry in Europe for instance. Some pesticides have
been banned from production and use, and extensive suits have been
litigated by affected DBCP workers, but precious little else has en-
sued either for protection of the worker or the individual exposed
through natural course in the environment.

Table 3  Environmental/Occupational Exposures:  Adverse Reproductive Outcomes

| Chemical/group | Occupation/situation | Effects on exposed | | Comments |
| --- | --- | --- | --- | --- |
| | | Males | Females | |
| Androgens | In manufacturing employees | | Altered menses (50) | |
| Anesthetics | Dental technicians, operating room personnel | | Increased spontaneous abortion (51,52), birth defects, decreased fertility, and low birth weight (53) | Some effects observed following *either* maternal or paternal exposure |
| Aniline | Occupational exposures | | Increased spontaneous abortion and infertility (cited, 21) | |
| Antimony | Occupational exposure to dust | | Spontaneous abortion, premature births, gynecological problems (54) | Evidence weak |
| Arsenic | Among women living close to or working in smelters emitting pollutants | | Increased spontaneous abortion (55), low birth weight (56) | |
| Benzene | With heavy occupational exposures | | Menstrual disorders (57), increased | Females more sensitive than males |

| Agent | Exposed population | Effects (male) | Effects (female) | Comments |
| --- | --- | --- | --- | --- |
| | | | spontaneous abortions, premature births (58) | Benzene exposures impossible to separate from petroleum and chlorinated hydrocarbon exposures |
| Boric acid | In manufacturing employees and high boron level in drinking water (Russia) | Reduced sexual function (59,60) | | |
| Butiphos | Agricultural workers occupationally (Russia) | | Aggravated parturition, stillbirths, birth defects (61) | |
| Cadmium | In manufacturing plant workers | Testicular damage (62) | Low birth weight (63) | Female effects refuted Food is also a major source of exposure |
| Caprolactam | Textile spinners | | Menstrual and childbearing disturbances (64) | |
| Carbaryl | Workers exposed during manufacture and application | Sperm abnormalities (65) | | |
| Carbon disulfide | Textile workers | Decreased libido, impotence, sperm abnormalities (66) | Menstrual irregularities (67), decreased fertility, and increased spontaneous abortion (68) | Female effects confirmed in other studies Declared reproductive hazard by NIOSH in 1985 |

Table 3 (continued)

| Chemical/group | Occupation/situation | Effects on exposed | | Comments |
| | | Males | Females | |
| --- | --- | --- | --- | --- |
| Carbon monoxide | Environmental exposure to gas | | Increased fetal death and neuropathy (cited, 69) | |
| Chlordecone (kepone) | Among manufacturing workers | Loss of libido (cited, 70), reduced sperm count and motility, abnormal sperm morphology (71), infertility (72) | | 76 Exposures in 1975; use banned in 1977 |
| Chloroprene | Factory workers and among wives of exposed *male* workers (Russia) | Sperm abnormalities (73) | Menstrual disorders (cited, 74), increased sterility and abortion (73) | Most claims anecdotal |
| Chromium | In manufacturing employees | | Menstrual disorders (75) | |
| DDT | Agricultural workers (Russia) | | Pregnancy complications (76), miscarriages, toxemia, and low birth weight (77) | Use halted in U.S. in 1972 |
| Dibromochloropropane (DBCP) | Agricultural workers and manufacturing employees | Testicular atrophy (78), infertility (79) | | Most potent testicular toxin yet found. |

310

| Agent | Population | Effect | Comments |
|---|---|---|---|
| Dimethylformamide | Environmental exposure | Increased abortion (81) | No recovery in severely affected cases<br>No adverse effects in families of exposed men (80)<br>Production partially banned in 1977 |
| Dinitro-dipropyl-sulfanilamide | Manufacturing plant spouses exposed | Miscarriage and birth defects (82) | Report unconfirmed |
| Estrogens | In manufacturing employees | Impotence (cited, 70), decreased libido, infertility (83)<br>Abnormal menses (83) | |
| Ethylene dibromide | Spouses of chemical manufacturing employees (females), manufacturing employees (males) | Decreased sperm counts (84)<br>Decreased fertility (85) | Study in females is inconclusive and requires confirmation<br>Currently under government study as testicular toxin |
| Ethylene oxide | Production plant workers | Increased gynecological disorders and abortions (86,87) | Data inadequate<br>A major industrial chemical |
| | Hospital workers | Increased spontaneous abortion (88) | |

**Table 3** (continued)

| Chemical/group | Occupation/situation | Effects on exposed | | Comments |
| | | Males | Females | |
|---|---|---|---|---|
| Formaldehyde | Occupational exposures | | Menstrual disorders, increased spontaneous abortion, increased infertility and low birth weight (89) | Limited study, inadequate for analysis Male study negative—further studies needed |
| Gasoline | Environmental, occupational contact | | Birth defects (90), altered menses, and impaired fertility (cited, 36) | |
| Gossypol | Exposure through cooking | Antispermatogenic effects (91) | Menstrual disturbances (cited, 21) | |
| High altitude | Environmental exposure | Decreased sperm, reduced motility, abnormal sperm (92) | | Data limited |
| High temperature | Occupational, environmental | Inhibition spermatogenesis, testicular pathology at 30–37°C (93) | Birth defects at >40°C (94) | |
| Insecticides (general) | Environmental exposures | | Fetal death and birth defects (95, 96) | |

| | | | | |
|---|---|---|---|---|
| Irradiation | Occupational exposure | Spermatogenesis alterations, reduced hormone levels (97) | | Testicular function altered at >15 rads |
| Lead | Pottery glazers Male workers in auto and storage battery plants | Sterility (98), abnormal sperm (99), hypogonadism (100) | Increased prematurity and spontaneous abortion, neurological defects in children (cited, 101), menstrual disorders (102) | Work restrictions on women in some countries |
| | Female refinery workers | | Increased abortion (103) | |
| Manganese | Mineworkers | Decreased libido (104), impotence (105) | | |
| Mercury (inorganic) | Industrial poisoning (male) Occupational exposures (female) | Reduced libido and potency, disturbed spermatogenesis (106) | Menstrual disturbances and increased spontaneous abortion (107, 108), abnormal ovarian function (109) | |
| Methyl parathion | Environmental exposure | | Fetal death and birth defects (110) | Assoication unconfirmed |
| Microwaves | Long-term occupational exposure | Decreased libido, sperm reduced motility, and abnormal sperm (111) | | Evidence in males incomplete, female studies indicated |
| Nonionizing radiation | Physiotherapists | | Perinatal death and birth defects (112) | Association weak |

**Table 3** (continued)

| Chemical/group | Occupation/situation | Effects on exposed | | Comments |
| | | Males | Females | |
| --- | --- | --- | --- | --- |
| Oral contraceptives | In formulating chemicals | | Altered menses (113) | |
| Pesticides (general) | In women producing organochlorine/phosphorus chemicals, environmental exposure in men spraying chemicals | Impotence (114) | Abnormal menses (115–118), ovarian malfunction (119), decreased fertility (120), gynecological disorders (121) | Adverse effects not confirmed in spouses of males (122) |
| Phthalate plasticizers | Among those manufacturing chemicals | | Abnormal menses and increased spontaneous abortion (123) | |
| Selenium | Laboratory workers | | Increased spontaneous abortion and birth defects (245) | Report unconfirmed |
| "Stress" | Environmental | Decreased sperm counts (cited, 4) | Anecdotal reports of amenorrhea | |

| | Source | | | Comments |
|---|---|---|---|---|
| Styrene | Plastics processing plant | | Menstrual disturbances (124,125) | |
| Tetraethyl lead | Exposure to fuel fumes | Reduced libido and potency with reduced semen volume, sperm count and motility, abnormal morphology (127,128) | | Human effects not corroborated (126) |
| Thallium | Poisoning | | Low birth weight (129) | |
| Toluene chemicals | Exposure in manufacturing industries, abuse | Sperm abnormalities (130) | Menstrual disorders (131), low birth weight (132), birth defects (133–135), spontaneous abortion (130) | Exposure to other solvents as well clouds effect of toluene |
| Vinyl chloride | Among manufacturing plant workers | Loss of libido and impotence (136) | Increased miscarriage, stillbirth (137,138), irregular menses (139) | Effects in females need validation |

## B. Occupational Exposure (Agent Unidentified)

There is a small group of occupations or industries that have been associated with adverse reproductive outcomes in females, but in which the specific agents inducing the effects have not been clearly identified. These have been tabulated in Table 4.

Little comment can be made of these sources of potential hazard except to indicate that in most cases the available data demonstrate these may represent likely sources of reproductive toxins. Additional epidemiological data are needed to isolate the agents responsible for this hazard.

## C. Drug Exposures

Another major source of reproductive hazards is therapeutic use of drugs. Table 5 is a list of 27 drugs or drug groups documented as having adverse reproductive effects in either males or females. The majority of adverse effects by drugs is on the male. By groups, the antihypertensives and antineoplastic agents are particularly effective gonadotoxins, but a number of other groups, including some CNS-acting agents (anticonvulsants, antidepressants, narcotics, phenothiazines), hormonal agents, and other drugs of varying therapeutic utility have effects as well.

Two drugs, DES and narcotics as a group, are potent reproductive toxins in both males and females. The former has marked antifertility activity, and is a recognized developmental toxin as well. The latter exert their toxicity via suppression of testosterone and luteinizing hormone.

## D. Social Uses/Abuses

Chemical exposures resulting from social habits constitute a significant source of hazard to reproductive health in the human (Table 6).

Alcohol use, in addition to being a major social problem in contemporary society, has significant implications on reproductive outcome. In men, its chronic use results in testicular toxicity, and in pregnant women, its use affects all systems of fetal development; it has been called in fact, the major teratogen of recent history (175).

Another major social habit, tobacco smoking, is also associated with adverse reproductive effects. It is the most important single preventable determinant of low birth weight and perinatal mortality in the United States (208).

Adverse reproductive effects have also been recorded in both sexes for "recreational drugs" and in females for excessive coffee (caffeine) consumption.

**Table 4**   Occupational Reproductive Hazards—Exposure Unidentified

| Occupation/ industry | Reproductive effects | Reference | Comments |
|---|---|---|---|
| Chemical | Increased spontaneous abortion | 140 | |
| | Abnormal menses | 141 | Chlorine responsible? |
| Electrical | Adverse reproductive effects | 142 | |
| Factory workers | Decreased viability and body weight at birth | 143 | |
| | Malformations | 144 | |
| Laboratory technicians | Increased spontaneous abortion | 145 | Effect not confirmed (246) |
| | Increased perinatal death rate | 146 | |
| | Malformations | 147–149 | Negative reports (146,150) |
| Leather-workers | Increased stillbirths and perinatal death | 413 | |
| Metals | Increased spontaneous abortion | 151 | |
| Plastics | Abnormal menses | 152–154 | |
| | Malformations | 155 | |
| | Increased spontaneous abortion | 140,156 | |
| Pulp and paper industry | Pregnancy complications | 157 | |
| Rubber | Altered menses | 158 | Hydrocarbons responsible? |
| Video display terminal operators | Abnormal pregnancy outcomes | 159 | Results not confirmed (160) Government studies underway |
| Wastewater treatment | Increased fetal loss | 161 | From *paternal* exposures |
| Workers, laborers (generalized) | Increased spontaneous abortion | 162 | |

Table 5  Drug Exposures:  Adverse Reproductive Outcomes

| Drug/group | Effects on | | Comments |
| --- | --- | --- | --- |
| | Males | Females | |
| Anticonvulsants | Diminished potency, decreased fertility, and abnormal sperm (163) | | |
| Antidepressants | Decreased libido, impotence (164) | | |
| Antihypertensives | Ejaculation disorders, impotence, sexual dysfunction, including depression of libido (cited, 165) | | Effects related to autonomic action |
| Antimalarials | Affect sperm motility (cited, 21) | | |
| Antineoplastic drugs | Azospermia, oligospermia, gonadal damage, infertility (cited, 165) | Ovarian failure (166) | Pubertal male gonads most sensitive Effects due to generalized toxicity |
| Butyrophenones | Abnormal sperm morphology (167) | | |
| Cimetidine | Reduced sperm counts (168), oligospermia (169), impotence (170) | | |

| Agent | | | |
|---|---|---|---|
| Clomiphene | Decreased sperm (171) | Increased multiple births (172) | |
| Colchicine | Azospermia (173) | | |
| Diamines | Azospermia, spermatid alterations in testis (174) | | |
| Diethylstilbestrol | Epididymal cysts, hypoplastic genitals and gonads, reduced semen volume, decreased sperm density and motility, infertility (cited, 175) | Vaginal abnormalities, uterine malignancy, irregular menses, reduced pregnancy rates, increased prematurity, perinatal mortality and fetal wastage (cited, 175) | |
| Disulfiram | Affected spermatogenesis and reduced potency (cited, 21) | | |
| 131I | Azospermia (176) | Fetal goiter (cited, 175) | |
| Methandrostenolene | Oligozoospermia (177) | | |
| Metronidazole | Decreased libido (cited, 165) | | |
| Narcotics | Reduced semen volume and libido, decreased sperm motility (178) | Disruption of menstrual cycle (179), increased neonatal morbidity (180), childhood neurobehavioral effects (181) | Marked depression of testosterone and LH |
| Niridazole | Oligozoospermia (182) | | |
| Nitrofurantoin | Affects spermatogenesis (183) | | |

**Table 5** (continued)

| Drug/group | Effects on | | |
| | Males | Females | Comments |
| --- | --- | --- | --- |
| Phenothiazine drugs | Decreased semen volume and sperm motility, oligospermia (184) | | |
| Propranolol | Impotence (185) | Reduced birth weights (186) | |
| Salicylates | Affect fertility (cited, 21) | Reduced birth weights and increased perinatal mortality (187) | |
| Spironolactone | Impotence (188), decreased libido, sperm density and motility (189) | Menstrual irregularities (414) | Affects androgen receptors in gonad |
| Sulfasalazine | Decreased sperm motility, oligospermia, abnormal sperm morphology (190–192) | | Effect reversible |
| Testosterone | Sterility (193) | | |
| Trimethoprim-sulfamethoxazole | Decreased sperm count, infertility (194) | | |
| Vaginal spermicides | | Reproductive loss (195) | Effect disputed (196) |
| Warfarin | | Abortion, stillbirths, IUGR and birth defects (cited, 175) | |

Table 6  Social Exposures: Adverse Reproductive Outcomes

| Chemical | Effects on exposed | | Comments |
|---|---|---|---|
| | Males | Females | |
| Alcohol | Testicular atrophy, azospermia, testicular pathology (197) | Low birth weight, retarded growth and mental development (198), decreased sexual responsiveness (cited, 21), birth defects: "FAS" (199), abortion (200) | A major teratogen and a direct testicular toxin |
| Caffeine (coffee) | | High rate reproductive loss (201), increased risk to low birth weight (17) | From *father's* exposure |
| "Recreational drugs" | Effects on libido, impotence, priapism, ejaculatory disturbances (202) | Low birthweight, short gestation, increased major malformations (marijuana) (415) | |
| Tobacco smoking | Abnormal sperm (203) | Increased spontaneous abortion (19), low birth weight (204), increased perinatal/neonatal mortality (205, 206), reduced fertility (207) | |

Table 7   Exposures Due to Accidental Contamination:   Reproductive Outcomes

| Location (date) | Chemical(s) identified | Source | Reproductive outcomes | Comments |
|---|---|---|---|---|
| Hiroshima/ Nagasaki (1945) | Atomic radiation | Wartime bombing | Birth defects (209) | |
| Minamata, Japan (1952) | Methylmercury salts | Entry into food chain | Death, birth defects (210) | Subsequently occurred in Sweden, Japan, U.S.S.R., U.S., Iraq Only putative chemical teratogen in human |
| Kyushon, Japan (1968) | PCBs | Entry into food chain | Menstrual dysfunction (211), low birth weight (212), "Cola" babies (213) | Poisoning termed "Yusho" Also in Taiwan in 1979 |
| Vietnam (1970– ) | 2,4,5-T/ Agent Orange (TCDD?) | Spraying/ contaminated drinking water | Abortion, stillbirths, birth defects (214–216) | Allegations refuted (217,218) |
| | | Direct contact | Birth defects from father's exposure (219) | Negative study published (221) |
| New Zealand, U.S., Gulf Islands (1972– ) | 2,4,5-T (TCDD?) | Spraying/ contaminated drinking water | Increased miscarriages and/or birth defects (222–227) | Negative studies on this issue have been published (228–234) |

| Location (year) | Chemical(s) | Source | Effects reported | Conclusion |
|---|---|---|---|---|
| Michigan (1974) | PBBs | Entry into food chain | Reproductive problems, birth defects (235) | Fetal mortality not affected (412) |
| Michigan (up to 1975) | TCDDs | Contact through manufacture | No adverse pregnancy outcomes from *father's* exposure (220) | |
| Seveso, Italy (1976) | TCDD | Plant explosion | Abortion (236), birth defects (237–239) | Effects not proven (240) |
| Love Canal, NY (1978) | Benzene Dichloroethylene Lindane Chloroform Toluene (of some 82 chemicals isolated) | Hazardous waste site | Increased miscarriages and birth defects (241) | Effects not corroborated (242) |
| Drake Waste Site, PA (1978) | Numerous chemicals | Hazardous wastes | No related birth defects could be ascertained (243) | |
| Three-Mile Island, PA (1979) | Radiation | Nuclear power plant accident | No increased spontaneous abortions (244) | |

## E. Accidental Contamination

There are a number of potential sources of reproductive hazards
due to strictly accidental exposure. These have been recorded for
wartime bombing, accidental contamination of food or water supplies,
or contact with the toxin through industrial or hazardous waste
(Table 7).

There are both well-documented and uncorroborated exposure
effects from agents in this list. Several of the agents are recognized developmental toxins in the human, including methyl mercury
and PCBs. Others, like 2,4,5-T and its incorporated contaminant
TCDD (dioxin) and PBBs have not been confirmed as reproductive
toxins, and their reported effects must be regarded as dubious.
Several other incidents, widely publicized in the press in recent
years, such as hazardous waste sites at Love Canal and situations
such as Times Beach, Three-Mile Island, and Bhopal also have not
been shown at present to have any detrimental effects on reproduction. Perhaps future research will prove differently.

## IV. LABORATORY METHODS AND ANIMAL MODELS
## FOR DETERMINING REPRODUCTIVE EFFECTS

## A. Male

The choice of a laboratory animal model to predict reproductive
hazards to the human male is conditioned in part by two factors,
the higher prevalence of infertility in humans than in laboratory
animals or in signal species, and the numbers of progressively motile
and morphologically normal sperm in human semen typically are inferior to values characteristic of males of other species (42). Human
testes may function at the threshold of pathology, and may be particularly sensitive to toxins compared with the testes of animals used
to study testicular function (33). Thus, it appears that men are
more vulnerable than animals to potential reproductive toxins and
raises the issue of whether animal models are really sensitive in detecting reproductive hazards in humans. Furthermore, the very
nature of the reproductive process in males (in contrast to females),
in which spermatogenesis is a continuous process and therefore usually fully restorative following chemical injury, necessitates an entirely different strategy in assessing reproductive parameters in the
laboratory.

Despite these factors, and as in other toxicity assessments, evaluation of potential reproductive toxins requires evaluation of one or
more laboratory species. Let it be stated at the onset that *no* animal
model has reproductive characteristics similar to those of humans,
but in general, rodents and rabbits offer several advantages in comparison to the dog and subhuman primate (33,42). Early age at

sexual maturity, short gestational and lactational periods, ease of handling, large litters, and cost are considerations in their favor (247). Of these species, the *rat* is probably preferable to the mouse or hamster for reasons of size, well-characterized reproductive processes, and widespread use in other toxicological studies. The major disadvantage of the rat in this context is that ejaculates cannot be collected, thus semen or spermatozoa cannot be evaluated by longitudinal protocol. The *rabbit* is an ideal second species because they are the smallest common species from which semen can be quantitatively and conveniently collected in longitudinal studies, and as in the rat, a wealth of background information exists for this species. Both species can be subjected to fertility testing, probably the most important criteria in selecting male laboratory models, although multigenerational use in the rabbit is not practical.

Among other laboratory species considered for use as models, the dog is suitable for semen collection, but impractical for use in fertility testing, and subhuman primates are sufficiently rare and too costly for routine use (42). Monkeys are also considered unsuitable for investigation of semen parameters (24). Other species recommended include the chicken (248) and hamster, tree shrew, guinea pig, and gerbil (249). Only the latter species of this group is considered acceptable by one investigator (249), but recent utility has not been explored.

Useful endpoints for studying reproduction in male animal models compared to those of the human are tabulated in Table 8. Methods for studying effects on reproduction include whole animal testing, routine methods of analyses of target organs (testes, semen), and other nonroutine and largely unvalidated methods, some of which may have potential for use in the future.

## 1. Whole Animal Model Testing

*Reproduction/Fertility Study.* The most commonly applied animal test for detecting effects on reproductive function is the reproduction or fertility (generation) study, usually carried out in the rodent.

The stereotypic design, promulgated in 1966 by the U.S. Food and Drug Administration (250), is used primarily for new drugs in this country, the United Kingdom (251), and Japan (252). The design is an elaboration of the older "2-litter" test originally intended for evaluating food additives and pesticides by the FDA. The multigeneration study evolved over the years, the current model being the one proposed in 1968 by Fitzhugh (253).

The basic test is typically termed a Segment I test or reproduction/fertility study. The test provides for treatment of the male (usually about 6 weeks of age) over the cycle of spermatogenesis prior to cohabitation with a female which has been treated over several estrous cycles prior to mating and usually through gestation and

**Table 8** Endpoints in Animal Models for Studying Male Reproductive Function[a]

| | Species | | | | | |
|---|---|---|---|---|---|---|
| | Mouse | Rat | Rabbit | Beagle dog | Rhesus monkey | Human |
| Age at sexual maturity (days) | 28–35 | 45–75 | 150–210 | 180–240 | 800 | 15.1 (yrs.) |
| Age at breeding (days) | 50 | 100 | 180 | 270–365 | 2190 | — |
| Cycle seminiferous epithelium (days) | 8.6 | 12.9 | 10.7 | 13.6 | 9.5 | 16.0 |
| Cycle spermatogenesis (days) | 35.0 | 51.6 | 48.0 | 54.4 | 70.0 | 64.0 |
| Testes weight (g) | 0.2 | 3.7 | 6.4 | 12.0 | 49 | 34 |
| Ejaculate volume (ml) | ? | ? | 1.0 | 0.8–3.1 | 1.1 | 3.4 |
| Sperm: | | | | | | |
| count ($10^6$/ml) | 1.1–2.0 | 50–60 | 50–250 | 60–600 | 100–600 | 80–110 |
| abnormal (%) | — | <3 | — | 10 | — | 12–27 |
| motile (%) | — | 32–50 | — | 80 | 58 | 58–65 |
| velocity (µm/sec) | — | 65–69 | — | — | — | 30–68 |
| Daily sperm production ($10^6$) | 5 | 86 | 160 | 300 | 1100 | 125 |
| Sperm reserves cauda ($10^6$) | 49 | 440 | 1600 | ? | 5700 | 420 |
| Sperm transit time through cauda (days) | 5.6 | 5.1 | 9.7 | ? | 5.6 | 3.7 |
| Breeding life (yrs) | 1–1.5 | 1 | 1–3 | 5–14 | 12–15 | 60 |

Compiled from numerous sources.

weaning (Fig. 4a). The British add behavioral and reproduction phases as well. In this manner, the effects of a test article over a broad spectrum of gonadal function, estrous cycles, mating behavior, conception, parturition, lactation, weaning, and growth and development of the resultant offspring can be assessed. Specifically, this is the sole test suggested by various regulatory agencies to determine *male* reproductive function. Alternatively, either males or females treated alone and bred to untreated mates in similar manner can be employed to isolate gender-specific effects. However, this is seldom necessary in actual practice.

A widely used variation of this test design and one used for potential food additives (254), pesticides (255), and regulated chemicals (256) in the United States is one that selects $F_1$ offspring at weaning to become parents of a second generation, with treatment continuing through the process, to weaning of $F_2$ offspring. This is the so-called 2-generation 1-litter study (Fig. 4b). A further variation, applied to Canadian pesticide registration (257) and stemming from the perception that the quality of litters varies between matings of the same parents, allows for two litters each ("a" and "b") being produced by $F_0$ and $F_1$ parents over two generations, the 2-generation 2-litter study. A third generation could be produced in a similar manner and a teratology phase added to the second or third generation if so desired (Fig. 4c). The primary objectives of multigeneration protocols are twofold: To detect injury to the developing gonads and to fertility from the progressive accumulation of body burdens, and to determine the potential adverse consequences of metabolic transformation (258). This type of study is the testing method of choice when there is need for an overall view of reproductive function that cannot be achieved by discrete, shorter tests. In terms of specific information obtained, the parental animals provide data on fertility and pregnancy. The first generation provides information on the uterine environment, lactation, and growth and maturation of offspring, and the second (and third) generation assess the effect of chemical accumulation and gene alteration (249). It should be noted that an Advisory Panel has questioned the value of multigeneration reproduction studies beyond the second filial generation (259). Reproduction/fertility tests carried out according to these different protocols vary in duration from about 3 to 13 months (Table 9).

While there is at present no strict uniformity in treatment duration among the various regulatory body guidelines under which these tests are regulated, there have been recent attempts at standardization. Fertility studies for drugs (250–252) require 60 days treatment for males and 2 weeks for females prior to mating. The FDA rules for additives (254) and European Organization (OECD) (260) share the recommendation that males be treated 10 weeks and females

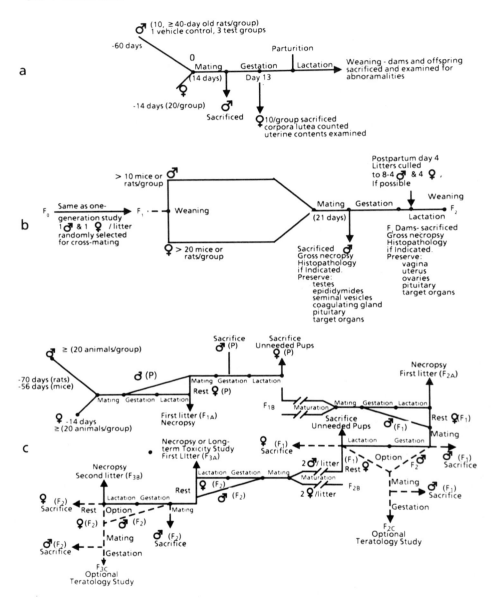

**Figure 4** Reproduction/fertility study schemes: (a) Segment I, (b) 2G 1-litter, (c) 3G 2-litter, with teratology phase (modified from Ref. 269).

**Table 9**   Characteristics of Reproduction/Fertility Studies

| Agency/year | Parental treatment (days premating) | | | Study duration (months) |
|---|---|---|---|---|
| | $F_0$ | $F_1$ | $F_2$ | |
| FDA (drugs) 1966 | 60 M, 14 F | | | 3.5 |
| OECD 1983 | 70 M, 14 F $----\blacktriangleright$ c. 91 | | | 4 or 10 |
| EPA FIFRA 1982 | 56 | 98 | | 10 |
| EPA TSCA 1985 | 70 | 77 | | 10 |
| FDA (additives) 1982 | 70 M, 14 F $\longrightarrow$ $------\blacktriangleright$ w/wo teratology | | | 11–12 or 20 |
| Japan MAFF 1985 | 56 $\longrightarrow$ | | | 8 |
| Canada (pesticides) 1981 | c.80 $\longrightarrow$ (2 litter) | | | 13 |
| United Kingdom 1974 | 60 M, 14 F $\longrightarrow$ | | | 7 |
| Japan (drugs) 1984 | 60 M, 14 F | | | 3.5 |

2 weeks, while Japanese MAFF (261) states 8 weeks treatment for both sexes. The recommendations by the EPA differ: Rules for pesticides state 8 and 14 weeks, respectively, for first- and second-generation animals (255), while TSCA rules indicate 10 and 11 weeks, respectively (256). Some consistency is in order.

Strictly speaking, since spermatogenesis requires over 4 cycles (about 52 days) of the seminiferous epithelium in the rat, a test to evaluate effects of an agent on spermatogenesis should extend over 6 cycles (77 days) for this species (33,42). The same concept for length of treatment applies to other species as well (i.e., rabbit, 65 days; dog, 82 days; rhesus monkey, 57 days). This interval is based on the time required to attain steady-state concentrations of the agent in the target organs, the concept that an agent acting on the germinal epithelium may require some time prior to degeneration of the affected cells, the fact that damage to the germinal epithelium is most evident by absence of more mature germ cells, and finally, by the knowledge that qualitative changes in germ cells may not be readily discernable until abnormal sperm pass into the cauda epididymis or ejaculated semen. For monitoring recovery, 12–18 complete cycles of the seminiferous epithelium are necessary (24,33).

Criticisms regarding all aspects of the currently utilized design for reproduction studies have been published (249,258,262-270,417). These center mainly on the limited group sizes, lack of testing $F_1$ progeny reproductive ability, excessively long premating periods, no provision for behavioral testing in protocols, undue complexity in study design, requirement of spermatogenesis testing of male animals, histopathology, and time and cost required for testing. Additional criticism of conventional fertility tests has also been made on the grounds that such tests are simply insensitive (42). In this context, it has been pointed out that since male rats produce and ejaculate 10 to 100 times more sperm than are necessary for normal fertility and litter size, the number of sperm available can be reduced by 90% before the decrease in ejaculate is sufficient to cause sterility. Thus, there may be difficulties in identifying reproductive toxicity even if they reduce sperm counts significantly. Also, the quality of measurements of conventional reproductive parameters from tests as currently performed are really not very good (268). In spite of these criticisms, generation reproduction studies of the types just described remain the primary method for reproductive toxicity testing. The methods of performing fertility and generational tests are crucial in obtaining the proper information for assessing reproductive hazards in the animal model, and the reader would do well to study closely the details in the publications cited above. Pitfalls and discussion pertinent to conducting fertility/reproduction studies is found in Section IV.B.1.

Parameters obtainable in males from reproduction/fertility studies include only endpoints relating to mating (e.g., libido and fertility). The ultimate index of male fertility is, of course, induction of successful pregnancy in the receptive female (24). Conventional indices are as follows:

$$\text{Copulatory index} = \frac{\text{no. males mating}}{\text{no. males paired}}$$

$$\text{Copulatory interval} = \text{Day (mean) animals paired until mating}$$

$$\text{Fertility index} = \frac{\text{no. males shown to be fertile}}{\text{no. males paired}}$$

$$\text{Conception rate} = \frac{\text{no. males shown to be fertile}}{\text{no. males mating}}$$

*Continuous Breeding.* In order to satisfy some criticisms of reproduction-type studies in cost-effective yet scientifically acceptable ways, another type of comprehensive reproductive toxicology protocol has been designed which tests both male and female reproductive function, with the mouse the animal model (271).

The design of the protocol maximizes the number of litters that can be measured by continuous breeding of paired mice over a 98-day period following a 7-day treatment period (Fig. 5). Through discarding the offspring as they are produced, several litters can result and at the end of 98 days, the last litter is followed through weaning. If effects are observed, crossover matings can be performed with control mice to assess sex-specific effects, and target organ toxicity can be determined through histopathology, if necessary. Should there be no effect, the weanlings can be treated, reared, and bred to test their reproductive capacity after prenatal, lactational, and developmental exposure.

Limited testing has shown the protocol to be predictive and sensitive in discriminating effects of several developmental toxicants (264, 272–274), but further validation is needed to determine if the pattern of reproductive toxicity of a number of different test chemicals can be shown. To data, some 40 chemicals from the glycol ether, polyglycol, phthalate ester, methylxanthine and other classes have been studied, but full results are not available at present (275). Of particular interest is the fact that the continuous breeding protocol has been accepted by U.S. agencies in lieu of the fertility or generational-type reproduction studies (276).

*Serial Mating.* Serial mating in rodents, such as used in so-called dominant lethal assay, is another type of test used, but it assesses male reproductive effects only.

The protocol for such tests consists of a short, 5–7 day treatment regimen at acute or subacute dosages to male mice or rats, followed by serial matings, usually to two untreated females each over short (usually 7 day) cohabitation periods over the total spermatogenesis cycle of 8–10 weeks. About two weeks after evidence of copulation, the females are sacrificed and evidence of dominant lethal mutations (decreased embryo viability) is assessed. The time that treatment affected viability indicates when the spermatogenesis process was interfered with. For example, decreased viability of implant sites in the first week of treatment in the mouse indicates an effect on epididymal sperm, whereas in the sixth week or earlier would point to effects on spermatogonia; intermediate intervals would affect spermatids and spermatocytes (277). It appears that few, if any, compounds tested exert their effect in one week only (278). Treatment-related decreases in sperm-positive matings might indicate effects on libido or semen quality. Thus, the serial mating protocol has proven to be a valuable tool in assessing the effects of chemicals on male reproductive function. Among the alternatives that can be used to serial mating as described above is to continue the treatment exposure over all stages of spermatogenesis and then conduct a single-mating trial. This procedure was successfully used to test one potential developmental toxicant, dimethyl methyl phosphonate in rats (cited, 264).

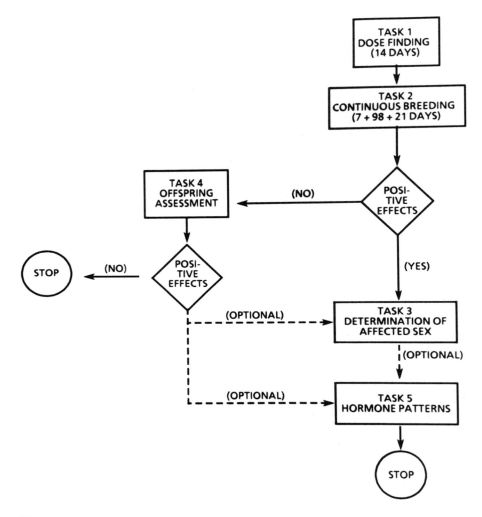

**Figure 5**   Continuous breeding scheme (from Ref. 264).

A number of criticisms of serial mating procedures, such as the propensity of the assay for showing preimplantation loss which is *not* correlated with dead implants, aberrancies in statistical analysis, dose-response problems, and the inordinate time to conduct the test have resulted in modifications leading to adoption of better protocols (279).

*Limited/Competitive Fertilization.* To compensate for the insensitivity of conventional reproduction/fertility tests due to excessive sperm production in rodents, several other approaches have been suggested.

The first is the use of artificial insemination, allowing introduction of a controlled and limited number of sperm into the reproductive tract of the female (42). In this way, insemination with only a number of sperm that is marginally adequate for normal fertility, a functional alteration in the number of sperm brought about by an agent could be detectable by a decrease in fertility.

Another approach that has been used is one termed "competitive fertilization." In this technique, sperm from a control and a treated male are placed in direct competition by simultaneously inseminating equal numbers of sperm from the two males into a single female (280). The parentage can be determined by any of several phenotypic marker systems. Such a technique was successfully employed to detect toxic levels of caffeine in semen in avian species (248).

*Copulatory Behavior.* One of the most logical endpoints for reproductive assessment is whether the animals are mating. In the most commonly used species, the rodent, mating is traditionally confirmed by inspection of the females for the presence of a vaginal or copulatory plug, or smearing of vaginal contents for the presence of sperm. Coitus usually occurs at night, thus examination is done the following morning. Presence of a vaginal plug is more predictive of pregnancy outcome than is presence of sperm in the vagina (281). In male rodents, multiple intromissions are the rule: Four or more penile intromissions are necessary to achieve successful pregnancy (282).

It is very important to correlate copulation with the actual results at termination of pregnancy of the female in order to detect sterile matings. This obviously is different from the situation where males do not mate, indicating potential behavioral and/or neuromuscular effects.

A simple method of assessing libido and fertility in the male was first detailed many years ago (253). A male is cohabitated with a female for two estrous cycles; if no copulation occurs, it is replaced by another male. The number of copulations divided by the number of pregnancies provides a mating index.

As part of the development of other models that could provide information on the overall function of the male reproductive system,

another simple scheme for assessing copulatory behavior in rodents
has been devised (283). In this model, male and female rats are
placed together at 100 days of age (maximum sperm production in the
male) and mating behavior observed following exposure to the chemical under test. Either subacute (5 days) or subchronic exposures
(70–80 days) are used. The mount latency (interval between introduction of male to female and the first mount), the number of mounts,
the number of intromissions, and ejaculation latency (interval between
first mount and ejaculation) are scored. The animals are then sacrificed and additional reproductive assays conducted if desired. Although not validated at present, this model has detected two chemicals that alter copulatory behavior, trichloroethylene and carbon
disulfide (283). Similar methods are underway in other laboratories
to assess adverse effects on the nervous system through disturbances
of behavior, libido, erection, and ejaculation in rats (284).

### 2. Target Organ Analysis

*Semen Assessment.* Semen analysis is considered to be very
useful in studies on the possible effects of drugs, chemicals and environmental hazards on testicular and epididymal function and on
male fertility (285). In fact, the single most sensitive and important
parameter for human fertility is the total number of motile sperm in
an ejaculate (33). Three lines of indirect evidence suggest that
monitoring sperm can indicate reproductive impairment (8): Male
exposures affect fetal loss independently of female factors; there is
a general association between fertility and sperm counts, proportion
of abnormally shaped sperm and proportion of motile sperm; sperm
quality is a sensitive indicator of testicular function, and impaired
quality is correlated with increased incidence of spontaneous abortion.
Sperm has additional advantages of being readily obtainable, is subject to objective evaluation, is regarded as a sensitive indicator of
recent exposures, is free from consideration of female factors, and
requires modest sample size to demonstrate presence or absence of
hazard (8).

Semen is a composite solution formed by the testes and accessory
male reproductive organs whose function is to provide a nutritive
medium of proper osmolality and volume for conveying sperm to the
endocervical mucus. Semen is assessed according to three main
parameters: sperm concentration or density (counts), motility, and
morphology. Semen characteristics (volume, color, consistency, pH)
themselves are of little value in assessing reproductive detriment.

Paradoxically, infertile human males tend to have increased semen
volume (286), while postcoital studies suggest that greatly decreased
semen values in men may result in poor penetration of cervical mucus
by the sperm (287). Much of the data related to semen analysis in
laboratory animals has come from the work of Amann and his associates,

and the reader desiring more detailed information is referred to those and other publications (2,42,288-292).

*Sperm Counts.* Measurements of sperm numbers are the most feasible component of semen evaluation (293). It is possible that reproductive toxicants can affect daily sperm production, thus this endpoint may be an important one in reproductive toxicology. However, only an accurate determination of the total number of sperm in an ejaculate can provide this information, and this is not feasible in many laboratory species (33,42). Nonetheless, sperm production can be assessed indirectly in any one of several ways.

Semen for quantitation in laboratory animals is typically taken from the cauda epididymides following sacrifice of the animal and counts of spermatozoa are performed in a hemacytometer. For larger laboratory animals like rabbits, and in humans, sperm counts may be made directly from ejaculates. In animal studies, a uniform interval of 1 or 2 days, or less ideally 3 or 4 days between semen collection is essential, and the series of ejaculates should extend over 20 days if semen is not collected continuously throughout the experiment (42, 288,289). The methods for counting sperm are simple and well established, and techniques exist for accurate quantitation. Background data on sperm production is provided for the common laboratory species in Table 8.

A low sperm count is in itself not a reason for infertility (285). In fact, sperm concentration is considered the least informative of all semen tests (292). Dysfunctional sperm, rather than a deficient number of sperm, is the probable cause of reduced fertility (294). Although 10 to 40 million spermatozoa/ml semen has been a dividing line between infertile and fertile (292), the only valid data concerning sperm count and its relationship to fertility has been the observation that men with sperm counts less than 20 million/ml were encountered more frequently in an infertile group than in a fertile group in an older, classic study (295). In reality, more than 80% of apparently infertile men have sperm counts which meet or exceed the normal standards (293). In fact, pregnancies have been achieved by men who had sperm counts below 2 million/ml upon semen analysis (296). A similar situation exists in animals. For instance, in one experiment in rats, the only disturbance of reproduction following an 80% reduction of morphologically normal, motile sperm by chemical administration was a small reduction in the number of implants per pregnant female (297).

The use of sperm counts for reproductive risk assessment is confounded by several other factors as well: Normal day-to-day variations in sperm count and the fact that sperm counts may reflect relatively late signs of testicular toxicity (293). Further, while there are a number of chemicals that can induce severe damage to spermatogenesis, much less is known about agents with weak or moderate inhibitory effects on spermatogenesis or sperm maturation.

*Sperm Motility.* Motility of spermatozoa is a functional parameter, because successful fertilization depends on the sperm being actively motile (47). It has been said that fertility potential is related to the total number of motile sperm (298); motility has been found to be a sensitive indicator of male fertility (295). Essentially, two aspects of motility can be distinguished: percent progressive motile sperm and velocity of sperm.

Percent progressive motile sperm can be quantitated from the same diluted semen sample collected from the cauda epididymides of the animal following sacrifice as was the sperm count, or ejaculated samples can be used. Though visual estimation of sperm motility is not ideal, it can be very useful provided the estimations are made in a careful manner, especially controlling for time and temperature after collection and dilution to allow proper visualization (42,289,299). Acceptable techniques and discrete criteria for categorizing motility have been published (289,300,301). While no rigid standardization exists for motility, it is felt by many investigators that semen should be considered abnormal if fewer than 60% of spermatozoa show progressive motion in specimens examined within three hours of collection (286).

Scientifically, rapidly declining motility seems compatible with fertility, while a low motility soon after ejaculation can be regarded a sign of decreased fertility, at least in the human (285). In rats, the presence of a high percentage of immotile sperm is clear evidence for abnormal testicular or epididymal function (42). A number of chemical agents are known to inhibit motility, enhance it, or immobilize sperm altogether (47).

The other motility factor important in assessment is velocity, or the swimming speed of sperm. According to one investigator, the velocity of spermatozoa may be the most important factor in predicting fertility in men (302). Freshly ejaculated sperm from fertile subjects in one study averaged 75 $\mu$m/second, but in men with impaired fertility, a high proportion of the sperm moved <40 $\mu$m/second (303). Spermatozoal velocity is assessed visually or by a number of techniques including photomicrography and turbidimetric methods. How sperm velocity is applicable in animal models is unclear at present.

*Sperm Morphology.* The morphological characteristics of sperm have long been regarded a parameter closely related to fertility as a measure of testicular toxicity. However, it remains difficult to define specific criteria for the shape and percentage of "normal" sperm necessary to establish fertility (4). Sperm morphology is regarded as the most stable and predictive semen parameter of fertility potential in animals (304). The mouse sperm morphology test has, in fact, been the predominant test conducted on sperm used as an indicator of germ cell mutation and it has been used in testing over 150 chemicals in the mouse (305–307). The test is based on the premise that an agent that induces abnormal forms of sperm is one that clearly interferes with the normal differentiation of germ cells, and about 27% of chemicals tested have had this propensity (307). Its full utility in assessing reproductive toxins is unconfirmed however, as is its applicability in other species (283); the test is feasible in rats, however (308).

There is no commonly accepted method of morphological assessment. One way of course, is to examine cells microscopically in a diluted sample of semen from that already procured from the cauda epididymides and that from which sperm counts and motility have been evaluated as described above. Sperm from ejaculates can also be utilized. Properly prepared stained smears should be used, and evaluation based on an appropriate classification scheme. Several techniques have been published (305,306,309,310).

Both head and tail of spermatozoa should be evaluated. Changes in sperm head shape have been associated with effects on fertility in humans and animals (42,311). In rats, the presence of sperm containing a proximal cytoplasmic droplet is clear evidence of abnormal testicular or epididymal function (42). In humans, excessive numbers of sperm with coiled tails have been correlated with infertility (285).

*Testicular Morphology*. Morphology of the testes can be evaluated subjectively or quantitatively; the latter being more sensitive (42). An understanding of spermatogenesis is essential for evaluation of testicular histology and function; the process has been described in detail (312).

Examination of suitably fixed testes can establish whether all cellular associations and types of germ cells are present in the tubules; however, subtle changes in spermatogenesis are not detectable. The various cell types which can be identified by relatively simple histological examination of the seminiferous tubules of the testis include spermatogonia, primary and secondary spermatocytes, spermatids, and spermatozoa. It is imperative that testes be properly prepared for these evaluations: Helly's, Bouin's, Zenker's, and formalin in descending order, have been established by one major laboratory as fixatives of preference for morphological studies with tissue embedding in methacrylate preferred (264).

For quantitative evaluations, different types of germ cells can be counted (e.g., leptotene spermatocytes, Sertoli cells). Counting spermatid nuclei in testicular homogenates is probably the most sensitive and simple approach for detecting degeneration or death of primary spermatocytes or spermatids according to one investigator (42). Enumeration of germ cells per Sertoli cell or per tubule cross section was the most sensitive measure of testicular response in a recent study in the rabbit with the testicular toxin, dibromochloropropane (416). Quantitation can also be applied by scoring tubule cross sections with respect to mature spermatid luminal alignment and evidence of active spermatogenesis. Significant deviations in these values between control and treated male rats would be clear evidence of treatment affect. It is also important to identify which cells are the first to be visibly affected by treatment with the compound under study. Appreciation of biological variability and spontaneous pathology of aging of the testis has been stressed in toxicity testing in the various species (24).

*Sex Organ Weights.* This parameter is useful because testicular size largely determines daily sperm production (288), and because testicular degeneration induced by toxins will result in reduction in testis size (42). However, it is not as sensitive as other tests for detecting testicular damage. For instance, a 50-60% weight reduction of the testes is correlative to an atrophic gland that has lost all or most of its germ cells (264).

One testis freed of the epididymis and spermatic cord of each male on test should be weighed as an indication of testicular toxicity (42). Since testes weight and body weight in adult males are independent variables, absolute testis weights are the appropriate parameter for assessment.

Weighing the distal half of the epididymis may also be an informative measurement (42). The weight of accessory male sex glands is an objective indicator of whether or not the androgen status of the animal has been significantly compromised (264); it is thought to be a crude bioassay of testosterone production by the testes and normalcy of the number of available steroid receptors (42).

A product of the sex organs, the postmating seminal plug, may be weighed, its size serving as a marker of hormone status since it is a product of androgen-dependent glands (283), but the method appears to have little practical significance.

*Endocrine Function.* Historically, the male endocrine system has been an infrequent target of reproductive toxicants. In some cases however, routine endocrine analyses may be desired. In fact, it is clearly established in all mammalian species investigated that an endocrine defect in the brain, pituitary or testis may inhibit spermatogenesis and normal sexual behavior (33).

Luteinizing hormone (LH) controls testosterone secretion by the testes which in turn, is responsible for the maintenance of accessory glands and spermatogenesis. Prolactin synergizes with LH in the regulation of testosterone synthesis, secretion, and inhibition (24). Follicle-stimulating hormone (FSH) on the other hand, controls Sertoli cell function and spermatogenesis, testosterone playing a pivotal role in the latter process. Thus, one infamous reproductive toxicant, dibromochloropropane (DBCP), through destruction of germ cells, induced a measurable increase in FSH without any concurrent changes in either testosterone or LH (313). In contrast, an experimental drug, PMHI, caused severe testicular weight depression and affected Sertoli cells without altering hormone levels (314).

Direct toxic effects on the testes can lead to abnormally high levels of gonadotropins because of the feedback relationship existing between the pituitary gland and the gonads (293). In such cases, radioimmunoassays for gonadotropins may provide useful information. However, laboratory assays of circulating hormones are likely to provide only late signs of reproductive effect.

### 3. Others

A number of qualitative and quantitative reproductive toxicity tests have been described (33). The following represent some of the assays currently being explored or already in limited use.

*Sperm Penetration Tests.* Since cervical mucus is a well-defined fluid accessible for laboratory study and sperm travel to the site of fertilization, passing first through it, important functions of the sperm cell can be assessed by examination of sperm interaction with the cervical mucus (315). Thus, sperm penetration of cervical mucus is one type of examination which may be useful in reproductive toxicology. The ability of sperm to penetrate cervical mucus has been correlated with fertility in humans (316). Several different in vitro methods are available to assess the ability of sperm cells to enter into the mucus and to characterize and/or quantify their swimming behavior (317,318).

Another sperm penetration test that may be useful utilizes hamster ova. Hamster ova treated enzymatically to digest the zona pellucida membrane can be fertilized by sperm from other species, including the human (319). Thus, the percentage of capacitated sperm observed to penetrate the zona pellucida-freed hamster egg and fuse can be determined. Clinically, there are a number of reports associating male fertility and the success of sperm fusion (320,321), but the test at present remains controversial, based largely on the fact that sperm unable to fuse hamster ova may not represent infertile sperm (293,294). This subject has been reviewed in detail recently (322).

*Double Y Bodies.* This test is based on staining of fluorescent spots in sperm by a quinacrine dye (323). The spots are thought to be Y chromosomes, thus sperm containing two Y bodies are thought to represent abnormal sperm due to meiotic nondisjunction (324). Unlike other tests on males discussed thus far, the double Y-body test has no direct counterpart in common laboratory species; it appears to be of unique applicability to humans and certain other primates (299).

*Acrosomal Proteolytic Activity.* Proteolytic activity in the sperm acrosome is essential for penetrating the zona pellucida of the ovum. Therefore, loss of this activity may reflect decreased fertility. A method has been developed to demonstrate proteolytic activity in sperm acrosomes based on staining of sperm suspensions with toluidine blue (325). The method has been used by one group of investigators in mice to successfully identify two reproductive toxicants, cyclophosphamide and mitomycin C (326). Further application of the method is in order.

*Semen Chemistry.* A number of tests have been used in the past in humans to evaluate different chemical entities in semen which may be markers of infertility. These include tests for seminal fructose (327), zinc (328), polyamines (329), fumarase (330), cyclic nucleotides (331), various cations (332), and adenine triphosphate (ATP) (333). Only ATP content of semen has been shown to be correlated with sperm count, motility and the ability of sperm to penetrate zona-free hamster ova (322). Application of these and other chemical analyses to animals warrants attention.

*Pubertal Development.* A testing protocol has been developed recently to screen chemicals for reproductive effects in male hamsters in order to identify potential reproductive toxicants for more thorough testing (418). A series of pubertal alterations are measured following chemical administration including preputial separation, flank gland development, sexual behavior, development of gonads, sperm motility, caudal sperm reserves, and pituitary hormone levels. The reproductive toxicant methoxychlor induced a number of changes in pubertal development, and indicates the screen may have future utility.

## B. Female

In contrast to the male, animal model selection and study design for assessing reproductive hazards in the female require a somewhat different strategy, due primarily to the fact that in the female, a *finite* number of germ cells (oocytes) is formed during the fetal period. Additional germ cells cannot be produced, thus chemical injury may be irreversible. Another important factor in these considerations is the cyclicity of reproductive functions which characterize the female (i.e., estrus or menses at fixed intervals), which have no true counterpart in the male. One additional factor influencing choice of animal models for determining reproductive effects in females is that laboratory animals, with the exception of primates, are polytocous. Thus, even more importantly than in males, no animal model has reproductive characteristics similar to those of human females.

Nonetheless, current viewpoints favor the use of one or more laboratory animal species to assess potential reproductive hazards to the female of different chemical agents. The choice of species rests largely on the negative aspects of most all species, leaving the *rat* and *rabbit*, as in male studies, as first and second species preferential in the study of effects on female reproductive processes.

Fertility testing can be carried out, timed ovulation is possible, and evaluation of oocytes, embryos, uterine morphology, hormone receptors, and longitudinal hormonal analyses can be conducted in both species (42). These species have the further advantage of having the potential of producing multiple numbers of large litters (6-8 in the rat, 7-11 in the rabbit) during their reproductive lives. Of several other species, the long anestrus, the inability to predict the onset of proestrus or to induce estrus or ovulation, together with the impossibility of conducting fertility testing in the bitch, severely limit the use of the dog (42). Inbred mice may represent the most sensitive species for oocyte and follicle toxicity assay (33). And while subhuman primates offer several advantages related primarily to having menstrual cycles and bearing single young, widespread use in reproductive toxicology is unlikely for a variety of reasons. The guinea pig is more satisfactory than other species for assessing the effects of toxicants on gonadotropic function or luteinization (33). Pigs and cows are desirable large species for steroidgenesis toxicity assays (33).

Useful endpoints for studying reproduction in female animal models compared to those of the human are tabulated in Table 10. Methods and techniques for assessing reproductive effects in female animal models include fertility-type studies (whole animal testing), a number of target organ (ovary) analyses, and nonroutine methods perhaps having potential utility in the future.

### 1. Whole Animal Model Testing

*Reproduction/Fertility Study.* As in assessing male reproductive function, the standard reproduction/fertility study in rodents remains the most sensitive indicator of chemical effects on reproduction in use at present as it relates to the female gender.

Reproduction/fertility studies in females provide a wide range of parameters which may reflect reproductive effects. One of these is evaluation of the estrous cycle. This is typically done prior to administration of a test chemical, prior to mating concurrent with chemical administration, and/or following chemical treatment during mating. One of the ways to assess estrus is to simply score the cycle in relation to normal duration of the stages, for example, in the rat, a diestrus greater than three consecutive days or shorter than two consecutive days, or proestrus, estrus or metestrus longer than 1 day. In this manner, adverse effects on normal reproductive cycling can be discerned. It is important to stress that changes observed with treatment are in fact different than they were in the untreated period, since there is some variation in cycle periodicity from animal to animal.

As already indicated, females in reproduction/fertility studies are usually administered the test chemical for periods ranging from

Table 10  Endpoints in Animal Models for Studying Female Reproductive Function[a]

| | | | Specie | | | |
|---|---|---|---|---|---|---|
| | Mouse | Rat | Rabbit | Beagle dog | Rhesus monkey | Human |
| Age at sexual maturity (days) | 28 | 46–53 | 120–240 | 270–425 | 1,642 | 15.2 (yrs) |
| Age at breeding (days) | 35–60 | 100 | 150–180 | 270–365 | 1,825 | — |
| Duration estrous/menstrual cycle (days) | 4–5 | 5 | N/A | 120–240 | 28 | 28 |
| Duration estrus (hr) | 10 | 13–15 | continuous | 168–216 | N/A | N/A |
| Conventional fertility rates (%) | c.90 | c.90 | >80 | — | — | 85 |
| Duration gestation (days) | 19 | 21 | 31 | 63 | 165 | 260 |

|  | | | | | | |
|---|---|---|---|---|---|---|
| Ovulation (hr from estrus onset) | 2–3 | 8–12.5 | 10–12[b] | 24–72 | 264–336[c] | 336[c] |
| Number oocytes ovulated | 10–12 | 12–14 | 8–10 | 6–12 | 1 | 1 |
| Fertilization (hr after ovulation) | 5 | 4 | immed. | c.48 | <48 | <36 |
| Implantation (days after coitus) | 4–5 | 5–6 | 7–8 | 18 | 9–11[d] | 7[d] |
| Litter size | 8–11 | 10–12 | 7–9 | 4–8 | 1 | 1 |
| Breeding life (yrs) | <1 (6–10 litters) | 1 | 1–3 | 5–10 | 10–15 | 30 |

[a]Compiled from numerous sources.
[b]After coitus.
[c]Of menstrual cycle.
[d]After ovulation.

two weeks to 14 weeks prior to mating (minimum 3 estrous cycles).
The females are paired with males in 1:1 preferably, or 2:1 ratios,
usually to treated animals, over 2- or 3-week mating intervals.  Appropriate subtests may also be performed to establish cause of sex-
induced infertility or offspring mortality due to maternal toxicity.
Several useful endpoints can be determined from these pairings to
include affects on libido and ability to copulate.  These are:

$$\text{Copulatory index (sometimes termed "mating index")} = \frac{\text{no. females mating}}{\text{no. females paired}}$$

$$\text{Mating index} = \frac{\text{no. females mating}}{\text{no. estrous cycles}}$$

The copulatory interval or precoital time (days animals paired
before mating) is also of interest here, but refers more to the male
than to the female.  At termination of gestation, the dams are either
sacrificed and the offspring taken by Cesarean section, or more
commonly, are allowed to deliver.  At this time, pregnancy status is
determined by any of several endpoints:

$$\text{Fertility index} = \frac{\text{no. pregnant}}{\text{no. females paired}}$$

$$\text{Pregnancy index ("fecundity index" = conception rate)} = \frac{\text{no. pregnant}}{\text{no. females mating}}$$

$$\text{Gestation index} = \frac{\text{no. live litters born}}{\text{no. pregnant}}$$

$$\text{Parturition index} = \frac{\text{no. deliveries}}{\text{no. females mated}}$$

Careful observations are made of delivery, since protracted or
difficult labor (dystocia) may be chemically induced.  An endpoint
of significance at this point in the reproductive process is concerned with viability of offspring at birth, assessed in the following
manner:

$$\text{Gestation survival index ("live birth index")} = \frac{\text{no. live pups at birth}}{\text{no. pups born}}$$

Another parameter evaluated at this time is data reflective of
litter size (live + dead term fetuses), since reductions may reflect
adverse chemical effects on early embryonic or fetal viability.

Growth and survival of the pups during lactation are then evaluated and are important on two counts. This is because reduced growth as measured by body weights and pup viability, quantitated by survival indices (see below), may be due to chemical toxicity. In the first instance, the dams, through inherent toxicity and/or behavioral alteration, or both, may affect nursing and/or care of their litters; as one might expect, maternal neglect can have profound effects on neonates. If there is chemical toxicity to the pups directly through in utero and/or nursing chemical exposure, failure to thrive and death may also ensue. Pups are usually culled to 8 or 10 per litter on day 4 (or 5) of lactation in order to minimize intra-litter competition during nursing. Traditional survival indices are as follows:

$$\text{Reproduction index} = \frac{\text{pups surviving 4 days}}{\text{no. pregnant animals}}$$

$$\frac{\text{4- (or 5-)day survival index}}{\text{("viability index")}} = \frac{\text{pups surviving 4 days}}{\text{live pups at birth}}$$

$$\text{7-day survival index} = \frac{\text{pups surviving 7 days}}{\text{live pups at 4 days}}$$

$$\text{14-day survival index} = \frac{\text{pups surviving 14 days}}{\text{live pups at 7 days}}$$

$$\text{21-day survival index} = \frac{\text{pups surviving 21 days}}{\text{live pups at 14 days}}$$

$$\text{Lactation index} = \frac{\text{pups surviving 21 days (weaned)}}{\text{pups retained day 4 (or 5)}}$$

There are a number of important considerations to be taken into account in order to avoid pitfalls in conducting reproduction/fertility studies, whether they be done to assess reproductive effects in males or females.

For the prototype fertility study of the Food and Drug Administration (250), separate protocols exist for treatment of males and females. In the author's opinion this is unwarranted as a general rule, and combined treatment of both sexes in a single study is appropriate. Actually, from practical experience, the necessity for conducting them separately would occur in less than 1% of cases according to one experienced investigator (266). Gender-specific effects can be determined in a combined study by adding additional groups of each sex to high dose and control groups and mated to each other as has been suggested by others (421), or simply repeating the study using treated animals of both sexes mated to untreated spouses in the rare case where such effects are suspected or realized.

Virtually all regulatory guidelines recommend a minimum of 20 animals per group for parental and litter observations. For all practical purposes, this requires placing 24, 26, or preferably 30 animals per group on study to ensure adequate numbers for evaluation. Otherwise, toxic, seasonal, or other factors may result in too few litters for adequate analysis. The advantages of group sizes even larger than 30 each in detecting reproductive effects have been described (268).

Another almost universal requirement of the various protocols is the criteria for dose selection. The highest dose should elicit toxicity of undefined quantity, but no mortality. Seldom are doses in reproduction studies the same as those for determining developmental toxicity; the higher doses used in the latter are deliberately set to induce maternal toxicity. At the lower levels the recommendation is minimal toxicity (again of undefined severity or nature) at the mid dose level, while the low dose should be a "no observable effect level" (NOEL). This ideal set of dosage criteria is difficult to achieve as a general condition.

The age at which the females are mated is a critical factor: they should be approximately 9-10 weeks of age at first mating (266); guidelines and regulations specify ages ranging from immediately after weaning to 9 weeks. Toxicants, particularly those that possess steroidal activity, will diminish the success of pregnancy and number of offspring of older but not those of younger females; thus while testing at earlier ages is more economical, it might yield false-negative results (33). Further, declining fertility as a normal phenomenon of advancing age can occur within the range of ages specified by some protocols for matings intended to produce litters from which a further generation will be derived, pointing further to the critical nature of this factor (249,422). Presently, treatment regimens range from 8 to 14 weeks, thus duration impacts directly on breeding age. It should be recognized too, that body weight is a more critical factor than age in the determination of reproductive capacity in rodents (266). The wide variability experienced in fertility rates among control animals is in itself a real concern in studies of this type (268).

At least one reproduction/fertility protocol, that of the United Kingdom (251), specifies that postnatal evaluation be conducted on $F_1$ issue. This protocol states that "late effects of the drug on the progeny in terms of auditory, visual and behavioral function should be assessed." What specific evaluation this statement is meant to convey is not known, but the reproductive toxicologist would be wise to include assessments concerned with postnatal maturation (e.g., eye opening, pinna detachment), reflexes (e.g., negative geotaxis,

Preyer's reflex), and learning (e.g., maze, shuttle box) from representatives of both sexes from each litter in order to provide sufficient data to satisfy these regulations.

The disposition of offspring as described in the various protocols is variable. Certainly the 13-day midterm embryo examination as defined in the FDA Fertility and General Reproductive Performance Study (250) can, in my judgment, be better replaced with sacrifice one day prior to term, primarily because direct and indirect fetal effects can be discriminated, and intrauterine growth can be more fully assessed. Detailed examination of offspring for malformations from reproduction studies as suggested in U.K (251) and Japanese guidelines (252) would appear to be a meaningless exercise since treatment is chronic in both designs and ends prior to organogenesis in the latter as well. Neither regimen could be expected to elicit teratogenicity under any but the most unusual circumstances.

Requirements for reproductive phases of the offspring also vary widely: Most protocols recommend production of one litter per generation, but the practice in Canada with pesticides (257) and the trend in the United States with additives (254) toward evaluation of *two* litters per generation is, in my opinion unfounded; the evidence provided to date (423) to indicate that sufficient information is gained from the second litter in such studies is less than convincing. In fact, it is my experience and that of others (266) that first matings are as successful as second matings in most litter parameters, and analysis of 20 multiple generation studies reported in the literature indicated that even *one generation* was sufficient for evaluation of reproductive effects (265).

Notwithstanding the large number of perhaps less significant variations (e.g., mating schemes, culling practices) in protocol design among the various international protocols, undoubtedly the most important consideration is the apparent lack of universal acceptability from country to country and agency to agency at the present time. Do sufficient scientific reasons exist to disallow in any country a fertility study in which adequate numbers of 1:1 mated rats are term sacrificed for fetal morphological examination, suitable numbers allowed to deliver and wean for postnatal testing and selection for producing a second generation, the treatment period encompassing all reproductive events? Global study designs typified by this oversimplified example would go a long way in standardizing testing requirements to the benefit of all, and without sacrificing scientific principles.

As pointed out by others (266), the chief concern with reproduction studies is with the interpretation of differences around the limits of normal variation, not with clear-cut dose-related toxicity; the validity of such studies can be seriously compromised by the coincidental or treatment-related death or infertility of an occasional male or more often, less than absolute mating performance and pregnancy rate. So it is that protocol design in these types of studies assumes great importance, and the inexperienced investigator would do well to take great care in planning reproduction studies for specific objectives.

*Reproductive Capacity.* The total reproductive efficiency assessment is very suitable for determining reproductive toxicity in rodents. It is particularly powerful for identification of chronic, low dose exposures. The test is based on the irreplaceable nature of oocytes; thus, animals are intentionally depleted of the ovarian complement of oocytes through repetitive matings. Single treated females are paired with single fertile males and as litters are born, the young are removed and the females bred repeatedly. The cumulative number of live young per dam over an extended period of time (usually 35 weeks) is a measure of reproductive capacity. Failed fertilization, preimplantation loss and dominant lethality are some of the reproductive parameters that can be assessed in this test. It has been used successfully to determine the reproductive capacity of mice following gestational exposure to a well-known reproductive toxicant, DES (334).

*Reproductive Behavior.* Sexual behavior is another important observation to make in the female. These are mainly indicators of hypothalamic function or dysfunction (33). In the mammalian female, a recurring estrous cycle ("heat") induced by gonadal hormones produces the two measurable behaviors proceptivity and receptivity (258). Proceptivity is a display of a variety of patterns including darting, hopping and ear vibration, obviously representing solicitation of the male. Receptivity then follows, with the female assuming the lordosis posture for mounting by the male. Methods for assessing sexual behavior and quantifying it have appeared (335–338). Since mating occurs in the dark hours in rodents, this assessment is inconvenient, if not difficult.

A notable example of alteration of female receptivity has been provided in a study reported in rats, in which females rejected males and practiced pseudocopulation with each other following treatment with a potentially new CNS drug (339).

## 2. Target Organ Analysis

Endpoints for quantitation of reproductive injury in the female take advantage of the fact that normal fertility is the result of the integration of normally differentiated, developed and maintained central nervous system, ovarian, and reproductive tract functioning (258). The endpoints specifically would include sexual differentiation and maturity, estrual cyclicity and stability, oocyte quantitation, corpora lutea function, follicle atresia, and reproductive senescence. Several other endpoints which might be included here, such as reproductive capacity and reproductive behavior are included more appropriately in Section IV.B.1.

*Sexual Differentiation and Maturity.* There are several ways to assess the level of sexual differentiation and maturation as might be influenced by reproductive toxicants. These assessments are particularly useful for toxicants having hormonal activity (33,258). The first externally visible affect with the reproductive hormones is androgenization of the vulva; with such masculinization, the anogenital distance is increased. This effect was reported in female pups of rats injected with androgens during gestation (340). A similar effect is the uterotrophic response, assessed either by alterations in uterine weight or in histology of the uterus following treatment. Still another method is through assay of estrogen receptor binding in target tissues. Another method with utility in assessing sexual development and maturity is examination of the female offspring to determine the time of appearance of the vaginal opening (after postnatal day 7 in the rat). Reproductive toxicants, especially those with hormonal activity, can advance or delay this process.

A testing protocol has been developed recently to screen chemicals for reproductive effects in female hamsters in order to identify potential reproductive toxicants requiring further testing (418). A number of pubertal alterations are measured following chemical administration including age at first behavioral estrus, estrus cyclicity, fertility, litter size, viability, and the number of implant sites. Methoxychlor induced a number of alterations, and the screen may be suitable for screening of other potential toxicants.

*Estrous Alterations.* Initiation of regular estrous cycles at the time of sexual maturity occurs shortly after vaginal opening and is dependent on hormone coordination that is reflected in mating behavior. Although the human does not have an estrous cycle, alterations found in a model species estrous cycle may signal possibly important though subtle changes in the menstrual cycle as well. Several characteristics can be evaluated, including simple cyclicity, senescence, and postpartum stability. It is important to remember that proper lighting is critical to estrous cycling in rodents (420).

The estrous cycle in the rat consists of a proestrus stage (12 hours), estrus or "heat" (12 hours), metestrus (21 hours), and diestrus (57 hours), the different stages characterized microscopically by vaginal cellular contents over a 4-5 day interval. The endpoint in mature animals is the cyclic appearance of leucocytes and non-cornified squamous cells in the vagina during the last two stages. Alterations in either the timeliness of the stages of estrous, or inability to cycle altogether is indicative of a disruption of a sensitive pituitary-ovarian balance, thus may reflect reproductive toxicity. Successful pregnancies in the presence of such changes however, may indicate minor, reversible or insignificant alterations. In this regard it has been shown that the copulatory response in the rat represents a better index of heat than does vaginal cornification, the marker for estrus (341).

Reproductive senescence may be determined in a similar manner by examining vaginal smears prior to and subsequent to resting intervals of 2–3 months duration. The lack of estrous cycling (anestrous) is indicative of senescence and may have possible relevance for humans. The method has been shown to be more predictive for chronic anovulation than is gonadotrophin assay (342).

A "stress test" of sorts has been devised to determine any cause for reduction in reproductive potential, predicated on the observation that within 8 to 10 hours after delivery in the rodent, the first postpartum estrus occurs in the majority of dams (258). On this basis, the test is conducted during four consecutive cycles by mating the postpartum females beginning 8 hours after delivery; the number of vaginal plugs and the number and weight of the offspring determined, with cumulative reproductive performances compared to controls.

*Quantitation of Oogenesis and Ovulation.* There are several quantitative measures that may demonstrate reproductive toxicity in the female animal. While the only direct method of assessing ovulation in laboratory animals depends on collecting free oocytes, there are several indirect methods that may be used to quantitate these processes based on morphological features of the ovary and reproductive outcome (343).

The first of these is determination of the number of oocytes in the ovary through histologic examination; the number observed represents a direct measure of oocyte toxicity. Determination of the precise developmental stage of oogenesis or folliculogenesis is indicative of when exposure to a reproductive toxicant occurred.

Another of these methods is serial counting of oocytes and/or ovarian follicles for detecting and measuring follicle atresia or destruction. Alteration of counts, especially those indicating accelerated loss of either oocytes or follicles might be reflective of reproductive toxicity. Another method of assessing follicular function is the simple but very subjective evaluation of secondary sex characteristics at the time of sexual maturation. Several other ways of assessing folliculogenesis have been described, but are indirect, and not feasible in many laboratories.

### 3. Others

A number of qualitative and quantitative reproductive toxicity tests have been described in addition to the ones just outlined (33) and some may hold promise for the future.

## V. USE AND PREDICTABILITY OF ANIMAL MODELS IN IDENTIFYING REPRODUCTIVE HAZARDS

The main source of relevant information relating to reproductive hazards in the human comes largely from animal studies. It is therefore pertinent to determine whether animal models have predictive value in identifying potential reproductive hazards. Several sources have inferred from review of comparative data that the predictive value of animal models in determination of potential reproductive chemical hazards is high in both males and females (344,345). To be sure, humans are certainly not less sensitive than animals with respect to reproductive effects, thus it appears reasonable to assume that where animal data do exist showing reproductive effects, it is also reasonable to conclude that there may be reproductive effects in humans as well. Let us see what the actual data show (Table 11).

Of the approximately 75–80 individual agents or groups of agents thus far identified as potential reproductive hazards in the human (Tables 3,5–7), 40 or about half have also demonstrated concordant reproductive effects in laboratory animal models. Thus, as a generality, identifiable reproductive hazards in humans at present have also been associated with reproductive effects in animals only about half of the time. Of these, effects in males were mimicked in 74% and effects in females were observed in 81%. Moreover, many other agents have been identified as inducing adverse reproductive effects in animals, but have not yet been confirmed as hazards in human reproduction. As far as the ability to successfully predict whether a given agent will be a reproductive hazard in humans because it produces reproductive effects in animals, it appears that this propensity is not very great.

Some reproductive effects, such as menstrual/estrous cycles and fertility appear to show good correlation in animals and humans because such effects are modulated much the same in the various species. Others, like specific effects on pregnancy, appear not to correlate closely, presumably because of basic biochemical and physiologic differences among species (e.g., pituitary and ovarian function is essential in rodent but not in human). Because of these differences, complete understanding of both site and mechanism of action of reproductive toxins will be necessary to extrapolate from experimental animal studies to evaluation of human risk (39).

## VI. SAFETY EVALUATION AND RISK MANAGEMENT

As the preceding discussion has demonstrated, there are thousands of potential reproductive hazards to which we are exposed. The 80

Table 11  Predictability of Animal Models in Identifying Reproductive Hazards

| Chemical/group | Effects in | | | | Comments |
| | Males | | Females | | |
| | Human[a] | Animal | Human[a] | Animal | |
|---|---|---|---|---|---|
| Alcohol | + | Reproductive dysfunction in rats (346) | + | "FAS" in mouse, dog, rat, and sheep (cited, 175) | Putative human teratogen |
| Antimony | o | | + | Abortion in rabbits (347) | |
| Antineoplastic drugs | + | Infertility in rats (348) | + | o | Putative human teratogens |
| Arsenic | o | | + | Fetal body weight reduced in mouse (349) and rat (350) with salts | |
| Benzene | o | | + | Estrous cycle changes in rats (351) | |
| Boric acid | + | Testicular atrophy in rats (352) and dogs (353) | o | | |
| Cadmium | + | Testicular damage and reduced fertility in mice, rats, | + | Reduced fetal body weight in rats (354) | |

| Agent | | | | | | |
|---|---|---|---|---|---|---|
| | | hamsters, rabbits, guinea pigs, dogs, and squirrel (cited, 345) | | | | |
| Carbon disulfide | + | Male sterility (355) and decreased sperm counts in rats (356) | + | | o | |
| Carbon monoxide | o | | + | Reduced fetal survival in mouse, rat, rabbit, sheep, and pig (cited, 345) | | |
| Chlordecone | + | Testicular atrophy in rat (357) and rabbit (358) | o | | o | Female effects reported in animals: persistent estrus and anovulation in rat (359) and mouse (360) |
| Chloroprene | + | Testicular degeneration in rat and cat (361) | | Reproductive effects in rats and mice (362) | | |
| Cimetidine | + | Antiandrogenic effects in rat (363). | o | | | |
| Clomiphene | + | Testicular lesions in rats (364) | + | | | |
| DDT | o | | + | Increased embryonic death and reduced fetal body weight in | | |

**Table 11** (continued)

| Chemical/group | Effects in | | | |
| --- | --- | --- | --- | --- |
| | Males | | Females | |
| | Human[a] | Animal | Human[a] | Animal | Comments |
| Diamines | + | Decreased fertility and sperm abnormalities in mouse, rat, dog, and monkey (366) | ○ | rabbit (365), anovulation and persistent estrus in rat (396) | |
| Dibromochloropropane | + | Testicular atrophy and infertility in rat, rabbit, and guinea pig (367,368) | ○ | | Animals less sensitive than humans |
| Diethylstilbestrol | + | Gonadal lesions in mice (369), rats (370), and primates (371) | + | Gonadal lesions in mice (372), rats (370), ferrets (373), hamsters (374), and primates (375) | |
| Ethylene dibromide | + | Suppression of reproduction in rats (376) | + | ○ | |

| Agent | | | | |
|---|---|---|---|---|
| Gossypol | + | Antifertility effects in rats, hamsters, and rabbits (377), mice (378), and monkeys (379) | + | o |
| High temperature | + | Testis lesions, lowered testosterone levels and abnormal sperm in rats (cited, 304) | + | Malformations readily induced in many species |
| Insecticides (general) | o | o | + | Developmental toxicity induced in multiple species by many (175) |
| $131_I$ | + | o | + | Fetal goiter in mice, rabbits, and guinea pigs (cited, 175) |
| Irradiation | + | Spermatogenesis alterations in mouse (380) | o | |
| Lead | + | Sperm abnormalities and infertility in rat and mouse (cited, 381) | + | o |
| Manganese | + | Testicular damage and infertility in mouse (382), rat (383), and rabbit (384) | o | |

Table 11   (continued)

| Chemical/group | Effects in | | | |
| --- | --- | --- | --- | --- |
| | Males | | Females | |
| | Human[a] | Animal | Human[a] | Animal | Comments |
| Mercury (inorganic) | + | Reduced fertility in mice (385) | + | Estrous effects in mouse (386), rat (387), and hamster (388) | |
| Methyl mercury | ○ | | + | Developmental toxicity in variety of species (cited, 175) | |
| Methyl parathion | ○ | | + | Increased fetal mortality in rat (389) | |
| Narcotics | + | ○ | + | Increased neonatal mortality in rat (390), disrupted estrus in rat (391) | |
| Nitrofurantoin | + | Reversible arrest of spermatogenesis in rats (392) | ○ | | |
| PCBs | ○ | | + | Prolonged estrus in mouse (393), primate (394), and rat (395) | |

356

| | | | |
|---|---|---|---|
| Phthalate plasticizers | o | + | Increased fetal mortality in rodents (123) |
| Salicylates | + | o | Reproductive effects produced in multiple species by many (175) |
| Spironolactone | + | + | Affects fertility in mice and rats (419) |
| Styrene | o | + | Estrous cycle effects in rats (397) |
| Thallium | o | + | Reduced fetal body weight in rat (398) |
| Tobacco smoking | + | + | Reduced fetal body weight in rat (399) and rabbit (400) |
| Toluene chemicals | + | + | Reduced fetal body weight in mouse and rat (401) |
| Vinyl chloride | + | + | Increased embryonic lethality in mouse and rat (402) |
| Warfarin | o | + | Abortion, fetal death in rabbits (403), mice (404), and rats (405) — Putative human teratogen |

[a]See Tables 3, 5, 6, and 7 for details.
o, no effect; +, effect.

or so chemicals that have been identified as possible toxicants constitute risks from occupational, therapeutic, or other exposure patterns. It would appear that altered reproductive function is definitely a major health endpoint of substantial proportions.

As pointed out by Schull (6), within the broad context of the workplace and environment, every individual is involved, but some by virtue of their occupations will have even greater risks; thus it is the working males and females of reproductive age in this group that are of special concern. A subset of these persons, whose risks may differ substantially, are *pregnant* women. They warrant special consideration for at least two reasons: Their physiology is altered as a consequence of pregnancy, and this factor may affect their own risks; and their exposure is inextricably confounded with that of the fetuses they carry. Moreover, they constitute a "visible susceptible" group, whereas most other high-risk groups are less readily identifiable.

As might be expected, reproductive hazards constitute multiple risk factors (406), primarily because of differing pregnancy outcomes, but for other reasons as well, including confounding factors leading to problems with data interpretation, synergistic effects, documentation of human exposures, and adequate sample sizes, among others.

A number of factors must be identified if assessment of risk to reproduction is to be made more precise (6). First, there is a need to understand more fully the relationships between the measurable endpoints and reproductive outcomes. As has already been discussed, sperm production in animal models must be reduced to critical levels before reproductive effects can even be ascertained, while in the human, we are not certain what levels of sperm density are associated with impaired fertility. We need to define more precisely just what endpoints are of greatest predictability in reproduction for both animals and humans.

Since observations on humans are limited and experimental results in animals will be the basis of human risk assessment, the choice of animal surrogates is critical. As we have already pointed out, while the rat and rabbit appear to be the most suitable models at present, they clearly are less desirable than some others with respect to certain endpoints, and additional species and other possible endpoints must be investigated. Very few comparisons of methods for assessing reproductive effects from the same chemical in the same animal species have been made. One recent study conducted on the testicular toxin dibromochloropropane (DBCP) in the rabbit demonstrated the most sensitive indicators of effect to be sperm morphology and elevation of FSH in contrast to sperm motility, ejaculate volume, sperm concentration, fertility rate, libido, and LH and testosterone levels (424). Similar studies on a variety of real and potential reproductive toxicants are in order to define appropriate methods for assessing reproductive hazards. Reproduction in its broadest sense is a very sensitive tool in toxicity testing (407), but methods are not sensitive enough and as we have shown, animal models have identified reproductive hazards only about half the time. Hardly convincing evidence for their use as models!

The current Segment I type fertility-reproduction and the multi-generation protocol for certain chemicals are likely for several reasons to remain the standard in vivo testing procedures to assess the potential of chemicals to disrupt reproduction. But the continuous breeding protocol now being subjected to validation procedures may prove to be a valuable tool in this regard as well. A testing strategy based on the biological activity of the compound under study would be meaningful (24): Toxicokinetics should be part of reproductive assessments (344), and characterization of the relationship between dose level and response in animals is crucial to this assessment (425). Ultimately, risk-benefit analysis relies heavily on judgement based on an understanding of both the relevance and limitations of experimental data obtained from animals. At present, extrapolation from no-effect levels in animals to presumably safe levels of human exposure should incorporate a safety margin sufficiently wide to take account of possible species differences in susceptability. The present 10- to 100-fold NOEL doses should be sufficient in this regard for all but the most unique and ubiquitous hazards.

Also, information routinely collected on potential reproductive hazards must be better utilized to make more valid predictions. Proper evaluation of existing information is critically important in this regard. For instance, it has been said that the infertility due to DBCP exposure at one manufacturing plant could have been identified within 4 years just from monitoring the numbers of births to their spouses, instead of the 20-year period that passed following notice by the workers (408). As already pointed out, reproduction data on individual toxicants and epidemiologic information on workers exposed to a chemical in production, let alone adverse reaction reports, are available only for a small number of chemicals. In fact, a large study conducted in 1981 of reproductive hazards could only identify two agents—smoking and alcohol, as having substantial effects in the general population and only two—anesthetic gases and lead, as risk factors to workers exposed in the workplace; data on others were considered fragmentary and incomplete (344).

Part of the formidable task of identifying reproductive hazards could be expedited if the mechanism of a chemical agent's action could be inferred from knowledge of its structure and physicochemical properties. Studies on these aspects need to be greatly expanded. Even in those instances where exposure to known reproductive toxins is believed to have occurred, it is not yet possible to assess the effects of low levels of exposure. Since in many instances it may be economically impracticable to remove completely a particular hazard, permissable levels of exposure will presumably have to be set for a number of toxicants, much as they have already been set for exposure to radiation, for instance.

Lastly, we must utilize more fully the information now available to minimize untoward occurrences in the workplace. Of the three major informational sources: alert observations by clinicians, systematic toxicological testing in nonhuman systems, and epidemiological studies and surveillance among humans, the observational report has been the most productive to date (409,410). Probably the best example is the effort by workers in a DBCP manufacturing plant to gain an explanation for their infertility.

One of the main problems in estimating risk from potential reproductive toxins is the number of chemicals, knowledge of exposure, numbers of potential victims of exposure, benefits and economics are radically different between drug and industrial chemical testing, and affect both the philosophy of testing and the acceptable risk.

## ACKNOWLEDGMENT

The author is grateful to Ms. Kathy Cox for aiding in the preparation of this manuscript.

## REFERENCES

1. Chamberlain, G. (ed.). (1984). *Pregnant Women at Work*, London, Macmillan.
2. Alexander, N. J. (1982). Male evaluation and semen analysis. *Clin. Obstet. Gynecol.* 25:463.
3. Steinberger, E. (1981). Current status of studies concerned with evaluation of toxic effects of chemicals on the testes. *Environ. Health Perspect.* 38:29.
4. *Reproductive Health Hazards in the Workplace.* (1985). Washington, D.C., OTA.
5. Lee, I. P. and Dixon, R. L. (1978). Factors influencing reproduction and genetic toxic effects on male gonads. *Environ. Health Perspect.* 24:117.
6. Schull, W. J. (1984). Reproductive problems: fertility, teratogenesis and mutagenesis. *Arch. Environ. Health* 39:207.
7. Chez, R. A., Haire, D., Quilligan, E. J., and Wingate, M. B. (1976). High risk pregnancies: obstetrical and perinatal factors. In *Prevention of Embryonic, Fetal, and Perinatal Disease.* Edited by R. L. Brent and M. I. Harris. DHEW Publ. No. (NIH) 76-853, pp. 67-95.

8. Rosenberg, M. J. (1984). Practical aspects of reproductive surveillance. In *Reproduction: The New Frontier in Occupational and Environmental Health Research*. Edited by J. E. Lockey, G. K. Lemasters, and W. R. Keye. New York, A. R. Liss, pp. 147–156.

9. Boue, J., Boue, A., and Lazar, P. (1975). Retrospective and prospective epidemiological studies of 1500 karyotyped spontaneous human abortions. *Teratology 12*:11.

10. Shepard, T. H. and Fantel, A. G. (1979). Embryonic and early fetal loss. *Clin. Perinatol. 6*:219.

11. Slater, B. C. S. (1965). The investigation of drug embryopathies in man. In *Embryopathic Activity of Drugs*. Edited by J. M. Robson, F. M. Sullivan, and R. L. Smith. Boston, Little, Brown & Co., pp. 241–260.

12. Hook, E. B. (1981). Human teratogenic and mutagenic markers in monitoring about point sources of pollution. *Environ. Res. 25*:178.

13. Sholtz, R., Goldstein, H., and Wallace, H. M. (1976). Incidence and impact of fetal and perinatal disease. In *Prevention of Embryonic, Fetal and Perinatal Disease*. Edited by R. L. Brent and M. I. Harris. DHEW Publ. No. (NIH) 76-853, pp. 1–18.

14. Byrne, J., Warburton, D., Kline, J., Blanc, W., and Stein, Z. (1985). Morphology of early fetal deaths and their chromosomal characteristics. *Teratology 32*:297.

15. Mattison, D. R. (1981). Effects of biologically foreign compounds on reproduction. In *Drugs During Pregnancy*. *Clinical Perspectives*. Philadelphia, George F. Stickley Co., pp. 101–125.

16. Stellman, J. M. (1979). The effects of toxic agents on reproduction. *Occup. Health Saf. 48*:36.

17. Hogue, C. J. (1981). Coffee in pregnancy. *Lancet 1*:554.

18. Coulam, C. B. (1982). The diagnosis and management of infertility. In *Gynecology and Obstetrics*. Edited by J. J. Sciarra. New York, Harper & Row, pp. 1–18.

19. Kline, J., Stein, Z. A., Susser, M., and Warburton, D. (1977). Smoking: A risk factor for spontaneous abortion. *N. Engl. J. Med. 297*:793.

20. Sever, L. E. and Hessol, N. A. (1984). Overall design considerations in male and female occupational reproductive studies. In *Reproduction: The New Frontier in Occupational and Environmental Health Research*. Edited by J. E. Lockey, G. K. Lemasters, and W. R. Keye. New York, A. R. Liss, pp. 15–47.

21. Schrag, S. D. and Dixon, R. L. (1985). Reproductive effects of chemical agents. In *Reproductive Toxicology*. Edited by R. L. Dixon. New York, Raven Press, pp. 301–319.

22. Phillips, J. C., Foster, P. M. D., and Gangolli, S. D. (1985). Chemically-induced injury to the male reproductive tract. In *Endocrine Toxicology*. Edited by J. A. Thomas, K. S. Korach, and J. A. McLachlan. New York, Raven Press, pp. 117–134.

23. Neumann, F. (1984). Effects of drugs and chemicals on spermatogenesis. *Arch. Toxicol.* 7(Suppl.):109.

24. Heywood, R. and James, R. W. (1985). Current laboratory approaches for assessing male reproductive toxicity: testicular toxicity in laboratory animals. In *Reproductive Toxicology*. Edited by R. L. Dixon. New York, Raven Press, pp. 147–160.

25. Dixon, R. L. (1984). Assessment of chemicals affecting the male reproductive system. *Arch. Toxicol.* 7(Suppl.):118.

26. Dixon, R. L. and Hall, J. L. (1982). Reproductive toxicology. In *Principles and Methods of Toxicology*. Edited by A. W. Hayes. New York, Raven Press, pp. 107–140.

27. Mattison, D. R. (1983). The mechanisms of action of reproductive toxins. *Am. J. Indust. Med.* 4:65.

28. Bergin, E. J. and Grandon, R. E. (1984). *How to Survive in Your Toxic Environment, The American Survival Guide*. New York, Avon.

29. Zenick, H. (1984). Mechanisms of environmental agents by class associated with adverse reproductive outcomes. In *Reproduction: The New Frontier in Occupational and Environmental Health Research*. Edited by J. E. Lockey, G. K. Lemasters, and W. R. Keye. New York, A. R. Liss, pp. 335–361.

30. Wyrobek, A. J., Watchmaker, C., and Gordon, L. (1984). An evaluation of sperm tests as indicators of germ-cell damage in men exposed to chemical or physical agents. In *Reproduction: The New Frontier in Occupational and Environmental Health Research*. Edited by J. E. Lockey, G. K. Lemasters, and W. R. Keye. New York, A. R. Liss, pp. 385–405.

31. Bernstein, M. E. (1984). Agents affecting the male reproductive system: effects of structure on activity. *Drug Metab. Rev.* 15:941.

32. Thomas, J. A. (1981). Reproductive hazards and environmental chemicals: a review. *Toxic Subst. J.* 2:318.

33. Anon. (1982). *Assessment of Risks to Human Reproduction and to Development of the Human Conceptus from Exposure to Environmental Substances*. Proc. U.S. EPA Conferences, Atlanta, 1980 and St. Louis, 1980 (EPA-600/9-82-001), NTIS.

34. Chapman, R. M. (1983). Gonadal injury resulting from chemotherapy. *Am. J. Ind. Med.* 4:149.

35. Mattison, D. R. and Thorgeirsson, S. S. (1978). Smoking and industrial pollution, and their effects on menopause and ovarian cancer. *Lancet* 1:187.

36. Mattison, D. R. (1985). Clinical manifestations of ovarian toxicity. In *Reproductive Toxicology*. Edited by R. L. Dixon. New York, Raven Press, pp. 109–130.

37. Mattison, D. R. (1981). Drugs, xenobiotics and the adolescent: implications for reproduction. In *Drug Metabolism in the Immature Human*. Edited by L. F. Soyka and G. P. Redmond. New York, Raven Press, pp. 129–143.

38. Hemminki, K., Axelson, O., Niemi, M-L., and Ahlborg, G. (1983). Assessment of methods and results of reproductive occupational epidemiology: spontaneous abortions and malformations in the offspring of working women. *Am. J. Ind. Med.* 4:293.

39. Mattison, D. R., Nightingale, M. S., and Shiromizu, K. (1983). Effects of toxic substances on female reproduction. *Environ. Health Perspect.* 48:43.

40. Steinberger, E. and Lloyd, J. A. (1985). Chemicals affecting the development of reproductive capacity. In *Reproductive Toxicology*. Edited by R. L. Dixon. New York, Raven Press, pp. 1–20.

41. Langman, J. (1981). *Medical Embryology*, 4th Ed. Baltimore, Williams & Wilkins.

42. Amann, R. P. (1982). Use of animal models for detecting specific alterations in reproduction. *Fund. Appl. Toxicol.* 2:13.

43. Desjardins, C. (1985). Morphological, physiological, and biochemical aspects of male reproduction. In *Reproductive Toxicology*. Edited by R. L. Dixon. New York, Raven Press, pp. 131–146.

44. Erickson, B. H. (1985). Effects of ionizing radiation on mammalian spermatogenesis: a model for chemical effects. In *Reproductive Toxicology*. Edited by R. L. Dixon. New York, Raven Press, pp. 35–46.

45. Keye, W. R. (1984). An overview of female reproduction: sexual differentiation, puberty, menstrual function, fertilization. In *Reproduction: The New Frontier in Occupational and Environmental Health Research*. Edited by J. E. Lockey, G. K. Lemasters, and W. R. Keye. New York, A. R. Liss, pp. 189–200.

46. Longo, F. J. (1985). Biological processes of fertilization. In *Reproductive Toxicology*. Edited by R. L. Dixon. New York, Raven Press, pp. 173–190.

47. Gwatkin, R. B. L. (1985). Effects of chemicals on fertilization. In *Reproductive Toxicology*. Edited by R. L. Dixon. New York, Raven Press, pp. 209–218.

48. Sherman, M. I. and Wudl, L. W. (1976). The implanting mouse blastocyst. In *The Cell Surface in Animal Embryogenesis and Development*. Edited by G. Poste and G. L. Nicolson. Amsterdam, Elsevier/North Holland, pp. 81–125.

49. Wu, J. T. (1985). Chemicals affecting implantation. In *Reproductive Toxicology*. Edited by R. L. Dixon. New York, Raven Press, pp. 239–249.

50. Agaponova, E. D., Markov, V. A., Shashkina, L. F., Tsarichenko, G. V., and Lyubchenko, P. N. (1973). Effects of

androgens on the bodies of women engaged in industrial work. *Gig. Truda. Prof. Zabol. 17*:24.

51. Askrog, V. F. and Harvold, B. (1970). Teratogenic effect of inhalation anaesthetics. *Nord. Med. 83*:498.

52. Nixon, G. S., Heisby, C. A., Gordon, H., Hytten, F. E., and Renson, C. E. (1979). Pregnancy outcome in female dentists. *Br. Dent. J. 146*:39.

53. Anon. (1974). Occupational disease among operating room personnel: A national study. Report of an ad hoc committee on the effect of trace anesthetics on the health of operating room personnel. American Society of Anesthesiologists. *Anesthesiology 41*:321.

54. Belyayeva, A. P. (1967). The effect of antimony on reproductive function. *Gig. Truda. Prof. Zabol. 11*:32.

55. Nordstrom, S., Beckman, L., and Nordenson, I. (1978). Occupational and environmental risks in and around a smelter in northern Sweden. III. Frequencies of spontaneous abortion. *Hereditas 88*:51.

56. Nordstrom, S., Beckman, L., and Nordenson, I. (1978). Occupational and environmental risks in and around a smelter in northern Sweden. I. Variations in birth weight. *Hereditas 88*:43.

57. Mikhailova, L. M., Kobyets, G. P., Lyubomudrov, V. E., and Braga, G. F. (1971). The influence of occupational factors on diseases of the female reproductive organs. *Pediatr. Akush. Ginekol. 33*:56.

58. Mukhametova, I. M. and Vozovaya, M. A. (1972). Reproductive power and the incidence of gynecological affections in female workers exposed to the combined effect of benzine and chlorinated hydrocarbons. *Gig. Truda. Prof. Zabol. 16*:6.

59. Tarasenko, N. Y., Kasparov, A. A., and Strongina, O. M. (1972). The effect of boric acid on the generative function in males. *Gig. Truda. Prof. Zabol. 16*:13.

60. Krasovskii, G. N., Varshavskaya, S. P., and Borisov, A. I. (1976). Toxic and gonadotropic effects of cadmium and boron relative to standards for these substances in drinking water. *Environ. Health Perspect. 13*:69.

61. Kasymova, R. A. (1976). Experimental and clinical data on the embryotoxic effect of butiphos. *Probl. Gig. Organ. Zdravookhr. Uzb. 5*:101.

62. Smith, J. P., Smith, J. C., and McCall, A. J. (1960). Chronic poisoning from cadmium fume. *J. Pathol. Bact. 80*:287.

63. Tsvetkova, R. P. (1970). Influence of cadmium compounds on the generative function. *Gig. Truda. Prof. Zabol. 14*:31.

64. Martynova, A. P., Lotis, V. M., Khadzieva, E. D., and Gaidova, E. S. (1972). Occupational hygiene of women engaged

in the production of capron (6-handecanone) fiber. *Gig. Truda. Prof. Zabol. 16*:9.

65. Wyrobek, A. J., Watchmaker, G., Gordon, L., Wong, K., Moore, D., and Whorton, D. (1981). Sperm shape abnormalities in carbaryl-exposed employees. *Environ. Health Perspect. 40*:255.

66. Lancranjan, I. (1972). Alterations of spermatic liquid in patients chemically poisoned by carbon disulphide. *Medna Lav. 63*:29.

67. Wiley, F. H., Hueper, W. C., and Von Oettingen, W. F. (1936). On toxic effects of low concentrations of carbon disulfide. *J. Ind. Hyg. Toxicol. 18*:733.

68. Ehrhardt, W. (1967). Experience with the employment of women exposed to carbon disulphide. In *International Symposium on Toxicology of Carbon Disulphide*. Amsterdam, Excerpta Medica, p. 240.

69. Longo, L. D. (1970). Carbon monoxide in the pregnant mother and fetus and its exchange across the placenta. *Ann. N.Y. Acad. Sci. 174*:313.

70. Sullivan, F. M. and Barlow, S. M. (1979). Congenital malformations and other reproductive hazards from environmental chemicals. *Proc. R. Soc. Lond. 205*:91.

71. Cohn, W. J., Boylan, J. J., Blanke, R. B., Fariss, M. W., Howell, J. R., and Guzelian, P. S. (1978). Treatment of chlordecone (Kepone) toxicity with cholestyramine (Results of a controlled clinical trial). *N. Engl. J. Med. 298*:243.

72. Cannon, S. B., Veazey, J. M., Jackson, R. S., Burse, V. W., Hayes, C., Straub, W. E., Landrigan, P. J., and Liddle, J. A. (1978). Epidemic Kepone poisoning in chemical workers. *Am. J. Epidemiol. 107*:529.

73. Sanotskii, I. V. (1976). Aspects of the toxicology of chloroprene: immediate and longterm effects. *Environ. Health Perspect. 17*:85.

74. U.S. Department of Health, Education and Welfare. (1977). Criteria document for a recommended standard: occupational exposure to chloroprene. DHEW (NIOSH) Publication No. 77-210.

75. Makarov, Y. V. and Shmitova, L. A. (1974). Occupational conditions and gynecological illnesses in workers engaged in the production of chromium compounds. In *Gigiena Truda Sostoyanie Spetsificheskikh Funkts. Rabot. Neftekhim. Khim. Prom-sti.* Edited by R. A. Malysheva. Sverdlovsk, USSR, Sverdl Nauchno-Issled Inst. Okhr Materum Mladenchestva Minzdrava, pp. 180–186.

76. Kagan, Yu.S., Fudel-Ossipova, S. I., Khaikina, B. J., Kuzminskaya, U. A., and Kouton, S. D. (1969). On the problem of the harmful effect of DDT and its mechanism of action. *Residue Rev. 27*:43.

77. Nikitina, Y. I. (1974). Course of labor and puerperium in the vineyard workers and milkmaids in Crimea. *Gig. Truda. Prof. Zabol. 18*:17.
78. Biava, C. G., Smuckler, E. A., and Whorton, D. (1978). The testicular morphology of individuals exposed to dibromochloropropane. *Exp. Mol. Pathol. 29*:448.
79. Whorton, D., Krauss, M. M., Marshal, S., and Milby, T. H. (1977). Infertility in male pesticide workers. *Lancet 1*:1259.
80. Goldsmith, J. R., Patasknic, G., and Israeli, R. (1984). Reproductive outcomes in families of DBCP-exposed men. *Arch. Environ. Health 39*:85.
81. Schottek, W. (1972). Chemicals (Dimethylformamide) having embryotoxic activity. In *Vop. Gig. Normirovaniya Izuch. Otdalennykh Posledstivil Vozdeistviya Prom. Veshchestv.* pp. 119–123.
82. Dickson, D. (1979). Herbicide claimed responsible for birth defects. *Nature 282*:220.
83. Harrington, J. M., Rivera, R. O., and Lowry, L. K. (1978). Occupational exposure to synthetic estrogens—the need to establish safety standards. *Am. Ind. Hyg. Assoc. J. 39*:139.
84. Mattison, D. R. (1985). Personal communication.
85. Wong, O., Utidjian, H. M. D., and Karten, V. S. (1979). Retrospective evaluation of reproductive performance of workers exposed to ethylene dibromide. *J. Occupat. Med. 21*:98.
86. Yakubova, Z. N., Shamova, N. A., Miftakhova, F. A., and Shilova, L. F. (1976). Gynecological disorders in workers engaged in ethylene oxide production. *Kazanskii Meditsinskii Zhurnal 57*:558.
87. Spasovski, M., Khristeva, V., Pervov, K., Kirkov, V., Dryanovska, T., Panova, Z., Bobev, G., Gincheva, D., and Ivanova, S. (1980). Healthstate of the workers in the production of ethylene and ethylene oxide. *Khig. Zdrav. 23*:41.
88. Hemminki, K., Mutanen, P., Saloniemi, I., Niemi, M-L., and Vainio, H. (1982). Spontaneous abortions in hospital staff engaged in sterilising instruments with chemical agents. *Br. Med. J. 285*:1461.
89. Shumilina, A. V. (1975). Menstrual and child-bearing functions of female workers occupationally exposed to the effects of formaldehyde. *Gig. Truda. Prof. Zabol. 12*:18.
90. Hunter, A. G. W., Thompson, D., and Evans, J. A. (1979). Is there a fetal gasoline syndrome? *Teratology 20*:75.
91. National Coordinating Group on Male Antifertility Agents. (1978). Gossypol, a New Antifertility Agent for Males. *Chinese Med. J. 4*:417.
92. Donayre, J., Guerra-Garcia, R., Moncloa, F., and Sobervilla, L. A. (1968). Endocrine studies at high altitude. IV. Changes in the semen of men. *J. Reprod. Fertil. 16*:55.

93. Hueper, W. C. (1942). Testes and occupation. *Urol. Cutaneous Rev. 46*:140.

94. Smith, D. W., Clarren, J. K., and Harvey, M. A. (1978). Hyperthermia as a possible teratogenic agent. *J. Pediatr. 92*:878.

95. Nora, J. J., Nora, A. H., Sommerville, R. J., Hill, R. M., and McNamara, D. G. (1967). Maternal exposure to potential teratogens. *JAMA 202*:1065.

96. Hall, J. G., Pallister, P. D., Clarren, S. K., Beckwith, J. B., Wiglesworth, F. W., Fraser, F. C., Cho, S., Benke, P. J., and Reed, S. D. (1980). Congenital hypothalamic hamartoblastoma, hypopituitarism, imperforate anus, and postaxial polydactyly—a new syndrome? Part I. Clinical, causal and pathogenetic considerations. *Am. J. Med. Genet. 7*:47.

97. Popescu, H. I., Klepsch, L., and Lancranjan, I. (1975). Elimination of pituitary gonadotropic hormones in men with protracted irradiation during occupational exposure. *Health Phys. 29*:385.

98. Hamilton, A. and Hardy, H. L. (1974). *Industrial Toxicology*, 3rd revised ed. New York, Publishing Science.

99. Lancranjan, I., Popescu, H. I., Gavanescu, O., Klepsch, I., and Serbanescu, M. (1975). Reproductive ability of workmen occupationally exposed to lead. *Arch. Environ. Health 30*:396.

100. Braunstein, G. P., Dahlgren, J., and Loriaux, D. L. (1978). Hypogonadism in chronically lead-poisoned men. *Infertility 1*:33.

101. Rom, W. N. (1976). Effects of lead on the female and reproduction: a review. *Mt. Sinai J. Med. NY 43*:542.

102. Panova, Z. (1973). Cytomorphological characteristics of menstrual cycles in women in occupational contact with inorganic lead. *Khig. Zdrav. 16*:549.

103. Nogaki, K. (1957). On action of lead on body of lead refinery workers: particularly conception, pregnancy and parturition in case of females and on vitality of their newborn. *Igaku Kenkyu 27*:1314.

104. Schuler, P., Oyanguren, H., Maturana, V., Valenzuela, A., Cruz, E., Plaza, V., Schmidt, E., and Haddad, R. (1957). Manganese poisoning, environmental and medical study at a Chilean mine. *Industr. Med. Surg. 26*:167.

105. Mena, I., Marin, O., Fuenzalida, S., Cotzias, G. C. (1967). Chronic manganese poisoning. Clinical picture and manganese turnover. *Neurology 17*:128.

106. McFarland, R. B. and Reigel, H. (1978). Chronic mercury poisoning from a single brief exposure. *J. Occupat. Med. 20*:532.

107. Marinova, G., Cakarova, O., and Kaneva, Y. (1973). A study on the reproductive function in women working with mercury. *Probl. Akush. Ginekol. 1*:75.

108. Goncharuk, G. A. (1977). Problems relating to occupational hygiene of women in production of mercury. *Gig. Truda. Prof. Zabol. 21*:17.

109. Panova, Z. and Dimitrov, G. (1974). Ovarian function in women occupationally exposed to metallic mercury. *Akush. Ginekol. 13*:29.

110. Ogi, D. and Hamada, A. (1965). Case reports on fetal deaths and malformations of extremities probably related to insecticide poisoning. *J. Jpn. Obstet. Gynecol. Soc. 17*:569.

111. Lancranjan, I., Marcanescu, M., Rafaila, E., Klepsch, I., and Popescu, H. I. (1975). Gonadic function in workmen with long-term exposure to microwaves. *Health Phys. 29*:381.

112. Kallen, B., Malmquist, G., and Moritz, U. (1982). Delivery outcome among physiotherapists in Sweden: is non-ionizing radiation a fetal hazard? *Arch. Environ. Health 37*:81.

113. DeMorales, A. V., Rivera, R. O., Harrington, J. M., and Stein, G. F. (1978). The occupational hazards of formulating oral contraceptives: A survey of plant employees. *Arch. Environ. Health 33*:12.

114. Espir, M. L. E., Hall, J. W., Shirreffs, J. G., and Stevens, D. L. (1970). Impotence in farm workers using toxic chemicals. *Br. Med. J. 1*:423.

115. Veis, V. P. (1970). Some data on the status of the sexual sphere in women who have been in contact with organochlorine compounds. *Pediatr. Akush. Ginekol. 32*:48.

116. Marinova, G., Osmankova, D., Deremendzhieva, L., Khadzhikolev, I., Chakurova, O., and Kaneva, Y. (1973). Professional injuries: pesticides and their effects on the reproductive functions of women working with pesticides. *Akush. Ginekol. 12*:138.

117. Nakazawa, T. (1974). Chronic organophosphorous intoxication in women. *J. Jpn. Assoc. Rural Med. 22*:756.

118. Makletsova, N. Y. (1979). Characteristics of the course of pregnancy, childbirth, and the period after birth in female workers in contact with the pesticide zineb. *Pediatr. Akush. Ginekol. 41*:45.

119. Blekherman, N. A. and Ilyina, V. I. (1973). Changes of ovary function in women in contact with organochlorine compounds. *Pediatriya 52*:57.

120. Ilyina, V. I. (1977). Status of the specific gynecological function of women exposed to polychloropinene in the fields. *Pediatr. Akush. Ginekol. 39*:40.

121. Makletsova, N. Yu. and Lanovoi, I. D. (1981). Status of gynecological morbidity of women with occupational contact with the pesticide zineb. *Pediatr. Akush. Ginekol. 43*:60.

122. Roan, C. C., Matanoski, G. E., Mcilnay, C. Q., Olds, K. L., Pylant, F., Trout, J. R., and Wheeler, P. (1984). Spontaneous abortions, stillbirths, and birth defects in families of agricultural pilots. *Arch. Environ. Health* 39:56.

123. Aldyreva, M. V., Klimona, T. S., Izyumova, A. S., and Timofievskaya, L. A. (1975). The influence of phthalate plasticisers on the generative function. *Gig. Truda. Prof. Zabol.* 19:25.

124. Pokrovskii, V. A. (1967). Peculiarities of the effect produced by some organic poisons on the female organism. *Gig. Truda. Prof. Zabol.* 11:17.

125. Zlobina, N. S., Izyumova, A. S., and Ragule, N. Y. (1975). The effect of low styrene concentrations on the specific functions of the female organism. *Gig. Truda. Prof. Zabol.* 19:21.

126. Harkonen, H. and Holmberg, P. C. (1982). Obstetric histories of women occupationally exposed to styrene. *Scand. J. Work Environ. Health* 8:74.

127. Vurdelja, N., Farago, F., Nikolic, V., and Vuckovic, S. (1967). Clinical experience with intoxications of fuel containing lead-tetraethyl. *Folia Facultatis Medicae, Universitas Comenianae* 5:133.

128. Neshkov, N. C. (1971). The influence of chronic intoxication of ethylated benzene on the spermatogenesis and sexual function of man. *Gig. Truda. Prof. Zabol.* 15:45.

129. Stevens, W. J. and Barbier, F. (1976). Thalliumintoxicatie Gedurende de Zwangerschap. *Acta Clinica Belgica* 31:188.

130. Hamill, P. V. V., Steinberger, E., Levine, R. J., Rodriguez-Rigau, L. J., Lemeshow, S., and Avrunin, J. S. (1982). The epidemiologic assessment of male reproductive hazard from occupational exposure to TDA and DNT. *J. Occup. Med.* 24:985.

131. Syrovadko, O. N., Skornin, V. F., Pronkova, E. N., Sorkina, N. S., Isyumova, A. S., Gribova, I. A., and Popova, A. F. (1973). Effect of working conditions on the health status and some specific functions of women handling white spirit. *Gig. Truda. Prof. Zabol.* 17:5.

132. Syrovadko, O. N. (1977). Working conditions and health status of women handling organosilicon varnishes containing toluene. *Gig. Truda. Prof. Zabol.* 21:15.

133. Euler, H. H. (1967). Animal experimental studies of an industrial noxa. *Arch. Gynakol.* 204:258.

134. Toutant, C. and Lippmann, S. (1979). Fetal solvents syndrome. *Lancet* 1:1356.

135. Hersh, J. H., Podruch, J. H., Rogers, G., and Weisskopf, B. (1985). Toluene embryopathy. *J. Pediatr.* 106:922.

136. Walker, A. E. (1975). A preliminary report of a vascular abnormality occurring in men engaged in the manufacture of vinyl chloride. *Br. J. Dermatol.* 93:22.

137. Infante, P. F. (1976). Oncogenic and mutagenic risks in communities with polyvinyl chloride production facilities. *Ann. N. Y. Acad. Sci.* 271:49.

138. Infante, P. F., McMichael, A. J., Wagoner, J. K., Waxweiler, R. J., and Falk, H. (1976). Genetic risks of vinyl chloride. *Lancet* 1:734.

139. Matysyak, V. G. and Yaroslavskii, V. K. (1973). Specific female organism functions in women engaged in polymer production. *Gig. Truda. Prof. Zabol.* 17:105.

140. Hemminki, K., Fransula, E., and Vainio, H. (1980). Spontaneous abortions among female chemical workers in Finland. *Int. Arch. Occup. Environ. Health* 45:123.

141. Alekperov, I. I., Sultanova, A. N., Palii, E. T., Elisuiskaya, R. V., and Lobodina, V. V. (1969). The course of pregnancy, birth and the postpartum period in women working in the chemical industry: A clinical-experimental study. *Gig. Truda. Prof. Zabol.* 13:52.

142. Nordstrom, S., Birke, E., and Gustavsson, L. (1983). Reproductive hazards among workers at high voltage substations. *Bioelectromagnetics* 4:91.

143. Czernielewska, I., Chrominska, H., and Bankowiak, D. (1976). The effect of working conditions of pregnant women on the development of fetus and the fates of newborn. *Zdrow. Publiczne* 87:174.

144. Hemminki, K., Mutanen, P., Luoma, K., and Saloniemi, I. (1980). Congenital malformations by the parental occupation in Finland. *Int. Arch. Occup. Environ. Health* 46:93.

145. Strandberg, M., Sandback, K., Axelson, O., and Sundell, L. (1978). Spontaneous abortions among women in hospital laboratory. *Lancet* 1:384.

146. Hansson, E., Jansa, S., Wande, H., Kallen, B., and Ostlund, E. (1980). Pregnancy outcome for women working in laboratories in some of the pharmaceutical industries in Sweden. *Scand. J. Work Environ. Health* 6:131.

147. Yager, J. W. (1973). Congenital malformations and environmental influence: the occupational environment of laboratory workers. *J. Occup. Med.* 15:724.

148. Ericson, A., Kallen, B., Meirik, O., and Westerholm, P. (1982). Gastrointestinal atresia and maternal occupation during pregnancy. *J. Occup. Med.* 24:515.

149. Meirik, O., Kallen, B., Gauffin, U., and Ericson, A. (1979). Major malformations in infants born of women who worked in laboratories while pregnant. *Lancet* 2:91.

150. Olsen, J. (1983). Risk of exposure to teratogens amongst laboratory staff and painters. *Dan. Med. Bull. 30*:24.

151. Hemminki, K., Niemi, M-L., Koskinen, K., and Vainio, H. (1980). Spontaneous abortions among women employed in the metal industry in Finland. *Int. Arch. Occup. Environ. Health 47*:53.

152. Loshenfeld, R. A. and Ivakina, N. P. (1973). Nature of the menstrual cycle in workers engaged in the production of polymers. *Sb. Nauch. Tr. Rostov. Gos. Med. Inst. 62*:149.

153. Panova, Z., Stamova, N., and Gincheva, N. (1977). Menstrual, generative function, and gynecological morbidity in women working in the production of polyamide fibers. *Khig. Zdrav. 20*:523.

154. Chobot, A. M. (1979). Menstrual function in workers of the polyacrylonitrile fiber industry. *Zdrav. Belor. 2*:24.

155. Holmberg, P. C. (1977). Central nervous defects in two children of mothers exposed to chemicals in the reinforced plastics industry. Chance or a causal relation? *Scand. J. Work Environ. Health 3*:212.

156. Hemminki, K., Lindbohm, M-L., Hemminki, T., and Vainio, H. (1984). In Reproductive hazards and plastic industry. *Industrial Hazards of Plastics and Synthetic Elastomers.* New York, A. R. Liss, pp. 79—87.

157. Blomqvist, U., Ericson, A., Kallen, B., and Westerholm, P. (1981). Delivery outcome for women working in the pulp and paper industry. *Scand. J. Work Environ. Health 7*:114.

158. Beskrovnaya, N. I., Khrustaleva, G. F., Zhigulina, G. A., and Davydkina, T. I. (1979). Gynecological illness in rubber industry workers. *Gig. Truda. Prof. Zabol. 23*:36.

159. Anon. (1982). NIOSH to probe births to VDT users: Panel recommends 5-hour VDT-day. *Guild Reporter 49*:20.

160. Kurppa, K., Holmberg, P. C., Rantala, K., and Nurminen, T. (1984). Birth defects and video display terminals. *Lancet 2*:1339.

161. Morgan, R., Kheifets, L., Obrinsky, D. L., Whorton, M. D., and Foliart, D. E. (1984). Fetal loss and work in a waste water treatment plant. *Am. J. Publ. Health 74*:499.

162. Hemminki, K., Saloniemi, I., Luoma, K., Salonen, T., Partanen, T., Vainio, H., and Hemminki, E. (1980). Transplacental carcinogens and mutagens: childhood cancer, malformations and abortions as risk indicators. *J. Toxicol. Environ. Health 6*:1115.

163. Christiansen, P., Dergaard, J., and Lund, M. (1975). Potency, fertility and sexual hormones in young male epileptics. *Ugeskr. Laeger 137*:2402.

164. Simpson, G. M., Blain, J. H., Iqbal, J., and Iqbal, F. (1966).
     A preliminary study of trimipramine in chronic schizophrenia.
     *Curr. Therap. Res.* 8:225.
165. Smith, C. G. (1982). Drug effects on male sexual function.
     *Clin. Obstet. Gynecol.* 25:525.
166. Koyama, H., Wada, J., Nishizawa, Y., Iwanaga, T., Aoki, T.,
     Terasawa, T., Kosaki, G., Yamamoto, T., and Wasa, A. (1977).
     Cyclophosphamide-induced ovarian failure and its therapeutic
     significance in patients with breast cancer. *Cancer* 39:1403.
167. Simpson, G. M., Blair, J. H., and Cranswick, E. H. (1964).
     Cutaneous effects of a new butyrophenone drug. *Clin.
     Pharmacol. Therap.* 5:310.
168. Van Thiel, D. H., Gavaler, B. S., Smith, W. I., and Paul, G.
     (1979). Hypothalamic-pituitary-gonadal dysfunction in men
     using cimetidine. *N. Engl. J. Med.* 300:1012.
169. Babb, R. R. (1980). Cimetidine. Clinical uses and possible
     side effects. *Postgrad. Med.* 68:87.
170. Wolf, M. M. (1979). Impotence on cimetidine treatment.
     *N. Engl. J. Med.* 300:94.
171. Heller, C. G., Rowle, M. J., and Heller, G. V. (1969). Clo-
     miphene citrate: a correlation of its effect on sperm concentra-
     tion and morphology, total gonadotropins, ICSH, estrogen and
     testosterone excretion, and testicular cytology in normal men.
     *J. Clin. Endocrinol. Metab.* 29:638.
172. Asch, R. H. and Greenblatt, R. B. (1976). Update on the
     safety and efficacy of clomiphene citrate as a therapeutic
     agent. *J. Reprod. Med.* 17:175.
173. Merlin, H. E. (1972). Azoospermia caused by colchicine—a
     case report. *Fertil. Steril.* 23:180.
174. Heller, C. G., Flageolle, B. Y., and Matson, L. J. (1973).
     Histopathology of the human testes as affected by bis(dichloro-
     acetyl)diamines. *Exp. Mol. Pathol.* 2(Suppl.):107.
175. Schardein, J. L. (1985). *Chemically Induced Birth Defects.*
     New York, Marcel Dekker.
176. Handelsman, D. J., Conway, A. J., Donnelly, P. E., and
     Turtle, J. R. (1980). Azoospermia after iodine-131 treatment
     for thyroid carcinoma. *Br. Med. J.* 281:1527.
177. Holma, P. (1977). Effects of an anabolic steroid (metandienone)
     on spermatogenesis. *Contraception* 15:151.
178. Cicero, T. J., Bell, R. D., Wiest, W. G., Allison, J. H.,
     Polakoski, K., and Robins, E. (1975). Function of the male
     sex organs in heroin and methadone users. *N. Engl. J. Med.*
     292:882.
179. Wikler, A. (1971). Drug dependence. In *Clinical Neurology.*
     Edited by A. Baker. New York, Harper & Row, Vol. 2, pp. 1–42.
180. Pierson, P. S., Howard, P., and Kleber, H. D. (1972).
     Sudden deaths in infants born to methadone-maintained addicts.
     *JAMA* 220:1733.

181. Rosen, T. S. and Johnson, H. I. (1982). Children of metha-
     done-maintained mothers: follow-up to 18 months of age.
     *J. Pediatr. 101*:192.
182. El-Beheiry, A., Kamel, M., and Gad, A. (1982). Niridazole
     and fertility in bilharizial men. *Arch. Androl. 8*:297.
183. Nelson, W. O. and Bunge, R. G. (1965). The effect of thera-
     peutic dosages of nitrofurantoin (Furadantoin) upon spermato-
     genesis in man. *J. Urol. 77*:275.
184. Shader, R. I. and DiMascio, A. (1968). Endocrine effects of
     psychotropic drugs: VI. Male sexual function. *Conn. Med.
     32*:847.
185. Miller, R. A. (1976). Propranolol and impotence. *Ann.
     Intern. Med. 85*:682.
186. Pruyn, S. C., Phelan, J. P., and Buchanan, G. C. (1979).
     Long-term propranalol therapy in pregnancy: maternal and
     fetal outcome. *Am. J. Obstet. Gynecol. 135*:485.
187. Turner, G. and Collins, E. (1975). Fetal effects of regular
     salicylate ingestion in pregnancy. *Lancet 2*:338.
188. Greenblatt, D. J. and Koch-Weser, J. (1973). Gynecomastia
     and impotence: complications of spironolactone therapy.
     *JAMA 223*:82.
189. Caminos-Torres, R., Ma, L., and Snyder, P. J. (1977).
     Gynecomastia and semen abnormalities induced by spironolactone
     in normal men. *J. Clin. Endocrinol. Metab. 45*:255.
190. Toth, A. (1979). Reversible toxic effect of salicylazosulfa-
     pyridine on semen quality. *Fertil. Steril. 31*:538.
191. Levi, A. J., Fisher, A. M., Hughes, L., and Hendry, W. F.
     (1979). Male infertility due to sulphasalazine. *Lancet 2*:276.
192. Traub, A. I., Thompson, W., and Carville, J. (1979). Male
     infertility due to salphasalazine. *Lancet 2*:639.
193. Steinberger, E. and Smith, K. D. (1977). Effect of chronic
     administration of testosterone enanthate on sperm production
     and plasma testosterone, follicle-stimulating hormone, and
     luteinizing hormone levels: a preliminary evaluation of a pos-
     sible male contraceptive. *Fertil. Steril. 28*:1320.
194. Murdia, A., Mathur, V., Kothari, L. K., and Singh, K. P.
     (1978). Sulphatrimethoprim combinations and male fertility.
     *Lancet 2*:375.
195. Jick, H., Shiota, K., Shepard, T. H., Hunter, J. R.,
     Stergachis, A., Madsen, S., and Porter, J. B. (1982).
     Vaginal spermicides and miscarriage seen primarily in the
     emergency room. *Teratog. Carcinog. Mutag. 2*:205.
196. Huggins, G., Vessey, M., Flavel, R., Yeates, D., and
     McPherson, K. (1982). Vaginal spermicides and outcome of
     pregnancy: findings in a large cohort study. *Contraception
     25*:219.

197. Turner, T. B., Mezey, F., and Kimball, A. W. (1977).
Measurement of alcohol-related effects in man: chronic effects
in relation to levels of alcohol consumption. *Johns Hopkins
Med. J. 141*:235.

198. Ulleland, C. N. (1972). The offspring of alcoholic mothers.
*Ann. N. Y. Acad. Sci. 197*:167.

199. Jones, K. L. and Smith, D. W. (1973). Recognition of the
fetal alcohol syndrome in early infancy. *Lancet 2*:999.

200. Kline, J., Shrout, P., Stein, Z., Susser, M., and Warburton, D. (1980). Drinking during pregnancy and spontaneous
abortion. *Lancet 2*:176.

201. Weathersbee, P. S., Olsen, L. K., and Lodge, J. R. (1977).
Caffeine and pregnancy: a retrospective study. *Postgrad.
Med. 62*:64.

202. Fabro, S. (1985). Drugs and male sexual function. *Reprod.
Toxicol. 4*:1.

203. Viczian, M. (1969). Ergebrisse von Spermauntersuchungen bei
Zigarettenrauchern. *Z. Haut. Geschlechtskr. 44*:183.

204. Meredith, H. V. (1975). Relation between tobacco smoking of
pregnant women and body size of their progeny: a compilation
and synthesis of published studies. *Hum. Biol. 47*:451.

205. Greenwood, S. G. (1979). Warning: cigarette smoking is
dangerous to reproductive health. *Fam. Plan. Perspect. 11*:
168.

206. Landesman-Dwyer, S. and Emanuel, I. (1979). Smoking during
pregnancy. *Teratology 19*:119.

207. Baird, D. D. and Wilcox, A. J. (1985). Cigarette smoking
associated with delayed conception. *JAMA 253*:2979.

208. Longo, L. D. (1982). Some health consequences of maternal
smoking: issues without answers. *Birth Defects 18*:13.

209. Plummer, G. (1952). Anomalies occurring in children exposed
in utero to the atomic bomb in Hiroshima. *Pediatrics 10*:687.

210. Kitamura, S., Hirano, Y., Noguchi, Y., Kojima, T., Kakita, T.,
and Kuwaki, H. (1959). The epidemiological survey on Minamata
disease (No. 2). *J. Kumamoto Med. Soc. 33*(Suppl. 3):569.

211. Wasserman, M., Wasserman, D., Cucos, S., and Miller, H. J.
(1979). World PCBs map: storage and effects in man and his
biologic environment in the 1970s. *Ann. N. Y. Acad. Sci.
320*:69.

212. Kuratsune, M., Yoshimura, T., Matsuyaka, J., and Yama-
guchi, A. (1972). Epidemiologic study on Yusho, a poisoning
caused by ingestion of rice-oil contaminated with commercial
brand of polychlorinated biphenyls. *Environ. Health Perspect.
1*:119.

213. Rogan, W. J. (1982). PCB's and cola-colored babies: Japan
1968, and Taiwan, 1979. *Teratology 26*:259.

214. Galston, A. W. (1970). Herbicides, no margin of safety. *Science 167*:237.

215. Funazaki, Z. (1971). Herbicides and deformities in Vietnam. *Jpn. J. Publ. Health Nurse 27*:54.

216. Laporte, J. R. (1977). Effects of dioxin exposure. *Lancet 1*:1049.

217. Cutting, R. T., Phuoc, T. H., Ballo, J. M., Benenson, M. W., and Evans, C. H. (1970). Congenital Malformation, Hydatiform Moles, and Stillbirths in the Republic of Vietnam 1960-1969. Washington, D.C., GPO.

218. Stevens, K. M. (1981). Agent Orange toxicity: a quantitative perspective. *Human Toxicol 1*:31.

219. Norman, C. (1983). Vietnam's herbicide legacy. *Science 219*:1196.

220. Townsend, J. C., Bodner, K. M., VanPeenen, P. F. D., Olson, R. D., and Cook, R. R. (1982). Survey of reproductive events of wives of employees exposed to chlorinated dioxins. *Am. J. Epidemiol. 115*:695.

221. Donovan, J. W., MacLennan, R., and Adena, M. (1984). Vietnam service and the risk of congenital anomalies. A case-control study. *Med. J. Austral. 140*:394.

222. Tung, T. T., Anh, T. K., Tuyen, B. Q., Tra, D. X., and Hugen, N. X. (1971). Clinical effects of massive and continuous utilization of defoliants on civilians. *Vietnamese Stud. 29*:53.

223. Sare, W. M. and Forbes, P. L. (1972). Possible dysmorphogenic effects of an agricultural chemical: 2,4,5-T. *NZ Med. J. 75*:37.

224. Lowry, R. B. and Allen, A. B. (1977). Herbicides and spina bifida. *Can. Med. Assoc. J. 117*:580.

225. EPA, Epidemiology Studies Division, U.S. EPA. (1979). Six years spontaneous abortion rates in Oregon areas in relation to forest 2,4,5-T spray practices.

226. Anon. (1979). EPA halts most use of herbicide 2,4,5-T. *Science 203*:1090.

227. Regenstein, L. (1982). *America the Poisoned.* Washington, D.C., Acropolis Books.

228. Nelson, C. J., Holson, J. F., Green, H. G., and Gaylor, D. W. (1979). Retrospective study of the relationship between agricultural use of 2,4,5-T and cleft palate occurrences in Arkansas. *Teratology 19*:377.

229. O'Neill, L. (1979). A letter from Alsea. *EPA J. 5*:4.

230. Field, B. and Kerr, C. (1979). Herbicide use and incidence of neural-tube defects. *Lancet 1*:1341.

231. Brogan, W. F., Brogan, C. E., and Dadd, J. T. (1980). Herbicides and cleft lip and palate. *Lancet 2*:597.

232. Thomas, H. F. (1980). 2,4,5-T use and congenital malformation rates in Hungary. *Lancet 2*:214.

233. Smith, A. H., Matheson, D. P., Fisher, D. O., and Chapman, C. J. (1981). Preliminary report of reproductive outcomes among pesticide applicators using 2,4,5-T. *NZ Med. J. 93*:177.

234. Hanify, J. A., Metcalf, P., Nobbs, C. L., and Worsley, K. J. (1981). Aerial spraying of 2,4,5-T and human birth malformations: An epidemiological investigation. *Science 212*:349.

235. Chen, E. (1979). *PBB: An American Tragedy*. Englewood Cliffs, NJ, Prentice-Hall.

236. Remotti, G., De Vibianco, V., and Candiani, G. B. (1981). The morphology of early trophoblast after dioxin poisoning in the Seveso area, Italy. *Placenta 2*:53.

237. Reggiani, G. (1978). Medical problems raised by the TCDD contamination in Seveso, Italy. *Arch. Toxicol. 40*:161.

238. Commoner, B. (1977). Seveso: the tragedy lingers on. *Clin. Toxicol. 11*:479.

239. Hay, A. (1977). Dioxin damage. *Nature 266*:7.

240. Abate, L., Basso, P., Belloni, A., Bisanti, L., Borgna, C., and others. (1982). Mortality and birth defects from 1976 to 1979 in the population living in the TCDD polluted area of Seveso. In *Chlorinated Dioxins and Related Compounds: Impact on the Environment*. Edited by O. Hutzinger, R. W. Frei, E. Merian, and F. Pocchiari. Oxford, Pergamon Press, pp. 571–587.

241. Tarlton, F. and Cassidy, J. J., (Eds.). (1981). *Love Canal: A Special Report to the Governor and Legislature*. N.Y. State Dept. of Health.

242. Vianna, N. J. (1980). Adverse pregnancy outcomes—potential endpoints of human toxicity in the Love Canal. Preliminary results. In *Human Embryonic and Fetal Death*. Edited by I. H. Porter and E. B. Hook. New York, Academic Press, pp. 165–168.

243. Budnick, L. D., Sokal, D. C., Falk, H., Logue, J. N., and Fox, J. M. (1984). Cancer and birth defects near the Drake Superfund Site, Pennsylvania. *Arch. Environ. Health 39*:409.

244. Johnson, C. (1984). Spontaneous abortions following Three-Mile Island accident. *Am. J. Publ. Health 74*:520.

245. Robertson, D. S. F. (1970). Selenium—a possible teratogen? *Lancet 1*:518.

246. Heidam, L. Z. (1984). Spontaneous abortions among laboratory workers, a follow-up study. *J. Epidemiol. Comm. Health 38*:36.

247. Dixon, R. L. (1985). Regulatory aspects of reproductive toxicity. In *Reproductive Toxicology*. Edited by R. L. Dixon. New York, Raven Press, pp. 321–328.

248. Hagen, D. R. and Dziuk, P. J. (1981). Detection of the effects of ingested caffeine on fertility of cocks by homospermic and heterospermic insemination. *J. Reprod. Fertil.* 63:11.

249. Collins, T. F. X. (1978). Multigeneration studies of reproduction. In *Handbook of Teratology*, Vol. 4. Edited by J. G. Wilson and F. C. Fraser. New York, Plenum Press, pp. 191–214.

250. Goldenthal, E. I. (1966). Guidelines for Reproduction Studies for Safety Evaluation of Drugs for Human Use, Drug Review Branch, Division of Toxicological Evaluation, Bureau of Science, FDA.

251. Committee of Safety of Medicines (1979). Notes for Guidance on Reproduction Studies (of Applicants for Product Licenses and Clinical Trial Certificates), Medicines Act 1968, Revised 1974 and subsequently (MAL 2). Department of Health and Social Security.

252. Guidelines of Toxicity Studies (1984). Notification No. 118 of the Pharmaceutical Affairs Bureau, Ministry of Health and Welfare. Yakugyo Jiho Co., Ltd., Tokyo, Japan.

253. Fitzhugh, O. G. (1968). Reproduction tests. In *Modern Trends in Toxicology*. Edited by E. Boyland and R. Goulding. New York, Appleton-Century-Crofts, pp. 75–85.

254. FDA (1982). Toxicological Principles for the Safety Assessment of Direct Food Additives and Color Additives Used in Food, Bureau of Foods.

255. EPA (1982). Pesticide Assessment Guidelines (FIFRA), Subdivision F, Hazard Evaluation: Human and Domestic Animals, Office of Pesticide Programs, EPA 540/9-82-025.

256. Health Effects Testing Guidelines (TSCA). (1985). *Fed. Reg.* 50:39397.

257. Guidelines for Pesticide Toxicology Data Requirements (1981). Health Protection Branch, Health and Welfare, Canada.

258. Heinrichs, W. L. (1985). Current laboratory approaches for assessing female reproductive toxicity. In *Reproductive Toxicology*. Edited by R. L. Dixon. New York, Raven Press, pp. 95–108.

259. Food and Drug Administration (1970). Advisory Committee on protocols for safety evaluations: Panel on reproduction, Report on reproduction studies in the safety evaluation of food additives and pesticide residues. *Toxicol. Appl. Pharmacol.* 16:264.

260. OECD Guidelines for Testing of Chemicals (1981). Director of Information, OECD, Paris, France.

261. Director General, Agricultural Production Bureau, Ministry of Agriculture, Forestry and Fisheries. (1985). Guidance on Toxicology Study Data for Application of Agricultural Chemical Registration, 59 NohSan No. 4200.

262. Christian, M. S. and Voytek, P. E. (1983). In vivo reproductive and mutagenicity tests. In *A Guide to General Toxicology*. Edited by F. Homburger, J. A. Hayes, and E. W. Pelikan. Basel, S. Karger, pp. 294–325.

263. Christian, M. S. and Hoberman, A. M. (1985). Current in vivo reproductive toxicity and teratology methods. In *Safety Evaluation and Regulation of Chemicals*. Basel, Karger, pp. 78–88.

264. Lamb, J. C. and Chapin, R. E. (1985). Experimental models of male reproductive toxicology. In *Endocrine Toxicology*. Edited by J. A. Thomas, K. S. Korach, and J. A. McLachlan. New York, Raven Press, pp. 85–116.

265. Christian, M. S. (1986). A critical review of multigeneration studies. *J. Am. Coll. Toxicol.* 5:161.

266. Palmer, A. K. (1981). Regulatory requirements for reproductive toxicology: theory and practice. In *Developmental Toxicology*. Edited by C. A. Kimmel and J. Buelke-Sam. New York, Raven Press, pp. 259–287.

267. Wright, P. L. (1978). Test procedures to evaluate effects of chemical exposure on fertility and reproduction. *Environ. Health Perspect.* 24:39.

268. Schwetz, B. A., Rao, K. S., and Park, C. N. (1980). Insensitivity of tests for reproductive problems. *J. Environ. Pathol. Toxicol.* 3:81.

269. Marks, T. A. (1985). Animal tests employed to assess the effects of drugs and chemicals on reproduction. In *Male Fertility and Its Regulation*. Edited by T. J. Lobl and E. S. E. Hafez. Boston, MTP Press, Ltd., pp. 245–267.

270. Christian, M. S. (1983). Reproduction and teratology studies: unique requirements for generation, interpretation, and reporting. *Drug Inform. J.* 17:163.

271. Lamb, J. C., Gulati, D. K., Russell, V. S., Hommel, L., and Sabharwal, P. S. (1984). Reproductive toxicity of ethylene glycol (EG) studied by a new continuous breeding protocol. *Toxicologist* 4:136.

272. Reel, J. R., Lawton, A. D., Wolkowski-Tyl, R., Davis, G. W., and Lamb, J. C. (1985). Evaluation of a new reproductive toxicology protocol using diethylstilbestrol (DES) as a positive control compound. *J. Am. Coll. Toxicol.* 4:147.

273. Lamb, J. C. (1985). Reproductive toxicity testing: evaluation and developing new test systems. *J. Am. Coll. Toxicol.* 4:163.

274. Lamb, J. C., Maronpot, R. R., Gulati, D. K., Russell, V. S., Hommel-Barnes, L., and Sabharwal, P. S. (1985). Reproductive

and developmental toxicity of ethylene glycol in the mouse. *Toxicol. Appl. Pharmacol. 81*:100.

275. NTP. (1986). Fiscal Year 1985, Annual Plan, Dept. of Health and Human Services and U. S. Public Health Service.

276. Lamb, J. C. (1985). Personal communication.

277. Bateman, A. J. (1973). The dominant lethal assay in the mouse. *Agents Actions 3*:73.

278. Green, S. and Springer, J. A. (1973). The dominant lethal test: Potential limitations and statistical considerations for safety evaluation. *Environ. Health Perspect. 6*:37.

279. Green, S., Auletta, A., Fabricant, J., Kapp, R., Manand-har, M., Sheu, C., Springer, J., and Whitefield, B. (1985). Current status of bioassays in genetic toxicology—the dominant lethal assay. *Mutat. Res. 150*:49.

280. Saacke, R. G., Vinson, W. E., O'Connor, M. L., Chandler, J. E., Mullins, J., Amann, R. P., Marshall, C. E., Wallace, R. A., Vincell, W. N., and Kellgren, H. C. (1980). The relationship of semen quality and fertility: a heterospermic study. *Proc. 8th Tech. Conf. Artif. Insem. Reprod.* Columbia, MO, Natl. Assn. Anim. Breeders, pp. 71–78.

281. Szabo, K. T., Free, S. M., Birkhead, H. A., and Gay, P. E. (1969). Predictability of pregnancy from various signs of mating in mice and rats. *Lab. Anim. Care 19*:822.

282. Wilson, J. R., Adler, N., and LeBoeuf, B. (1965). The effects of intromission frequency on successful pregnancy in the female rat. *Proc. Nat. Acad. Sci. 53*:1392.

283. Zenick, H., Blackburn, K., Hope, E., Oudiz, D., and Goeden, H. (1984). Evaluating male reproductive toxicity in rodents: a new animal model. *Teratog. Carcinog. Mutag. 4*:109.

284. Mercier, O., Perraud, J., Stadler, J., and Kessedjian, M. J. (1985). A standardized method to test the copulatory behavior of male rats: a basis of evaluation of drug effect. *Teratology 32*:28A.

285. Eliasson, R. (1978). Semen analysis. *Environ. Health Perspect. 24*:81.

286. Cannon, D. C. (1974). Examination of seminal fluid. In *Clinical Diagnosis*, 15th ed. Edited by I. Davidson and J. B. Henry. Philadelphia, W. B. Saunders, pp. 1300–1306.

287. MacLeod, J. (1965). The semen examination. *Clin. Obstet. Gynecol. 8*:115.

288. Amann, R. P. (1970). Sperm production rates. In *The Testis*, Vol. 1. Edited by A. D. Johnson, W. R. Gomes, and N. L. VanDermark. New York, Academic Press, pp. 433–482.

289. Amann, R. P. (1981). A critical review of methods for evaluation of spermatogenesis from seminal characteristics. *J. Androl. 2*:37.

290. Carson, W. S. and Amann, R. P. (1972). The male rabbit, VI. Effects of ejaculation and season on testicular size and function. *J. Anim. Sci.* 34:302.

291. Amann, R. P., Kavanaugh, J. F., Griel, L. C., and Voglmayr, J. K. (1974). Sperm production of Holstein bulls determined from testicular spermatid reserves, after cannulation of rete testis or vas deferens, and by daily ejaculation. *J. Dairy Sci.* 57:93.

292. Eliasson, R. (1985). Clinical effects of chemicals on male reproduction. In *Reproductive Toxicology*. Edited by R. L. Dixon. New York, Raven Press, pp. 161–172.

293. Overstreet, J. W. (1984). Assessment of disorders of spermatogenesis. In *Reproduction: The New Frontier in Occupational and Environmental Health Research*. Edited by J. E. Lockey, G. K. Lemasters, and W. R. Keye. New York, A. R. Liss, Inc., pp. 275–292.

294. Overstreet, J. W. (1983). Evaluation and control of the fertilizing power of sperm. In *The Sperm Cell*. Edited by J. Andre. Boston, Martinus Nijhoff Publ., p. 1.

295. MacLeod, J. and Gold, R. Z. (1951). The male factor in fertility and infertility. II. Spermatozoan counts in 1000 men of known fertility and in 1000 cases of infertile marriage. *J. Urol.* 66:436.

296. Barfield, A., Melo, J., Coutinho, E., Alvaez Sanchez, F., Faundes, A., Brache, V., Leon, P., Frick, J., Bartsch, G., Weisks, W. H., Brenner, P., Mishell, D., Bernstein, G., and Oritz, A. (1979). Pregnancies associated with sperm concentrations below 10 million/ml in clinical studies of a potential male contraceptive method, monthly depot medroxyprogesterone acetate and testosterone esters. *Contraception* 20:121.

297. Blazak, W. F., Rushbrook, C. J., Ernst, T. L., Stewart, B. E., Spak, D., DiBiasio-Erwin, D., and Black, V. (1985). Relationship between breeding performance and testicular/epididymal functioning in male Sprague-Dawley rats exposed to nitrobenzene (NB). *Toxicologist* 5:121.

298. Farris, E. J. (1949). The number of motile spermatozoa as an index of fertility in man: a study of 406 semen specimens. *J. Urol.* 61:1099.

299. Wyrobek, A. J. (1983). Methods for evaluating the effects of environmental chemicals on human sperm production. *Environ. Health Perspect.* 48:53.

300. Eliasson, R. (1975). Analysis of semen. In *Progress in Infertility*. Edited by S. J. Behrman and R. W. Kistner. Boston, Little Brown and Co., p. 691.

301. Mitchell, J. A., Nelson, L., and Hafez, E. S. E. (1976). Motility of spermatozoa. In *Human Semen and Fertility*

*regulation in Men.* Edited by E. S. E. Hafex. St. Louis, C. V. Mosby, pp. 89–99.

302. Blasco, L. (1984). Clinical tests of sperm fertilizing ability. *Fertil. Steril.* 41:177.

303. Harvey, C. (1960). The speed of human spermatozoa and the effect on it of various dilutants with some preliminary observations on clinical material. *J. Reprod. Fertil.* 1:84.

304. Manson, J. M. and Simons, R. (1979). Influence of environmental agents on male reproductive failure. In *Work and the Health of Women.* Edited by V. R. Hunt. Cleveland, CRC Press, pp. 155–179.

305. Wyrobek, A. J. and Bruce, W. R. (1975). Chemical induction of sperm abnormalities in mice. *Proc. Nat. Acad. Sci. (USA)* 72:4425.

306. Wyrobek, A. J. and Bruce, W. R. (1978). The induction of sperm-shape abnormalities in mice and humans. In *Chemical Mutagens. Principles and Methods for Their Detection,* Vol. 5. Edited by A. Hollaender and F. J. deSerres. New York, Plenum Press, pp. 257–281.

307. Wyrobek, J., Gordon, L. A., Burkhart, J. G., Francis, M. W., Kapp, R. W., Letz, G., Malling, H. V., Topham, J. C., and Whorton, M. D. (1983). An evaluation of mouse sperm morphology test and other sperm tests in nonhuman mammals. *Mutat. Res.* 115:1.

308. Lock, L. F. and Soares, E. R. (1980). Increases in morphologically abnormal sperm in rats exposed to $Co^{60}$ irradiation. *Environ. Mutag.* 2:125.

309. Byran, J. H. D. (1970). An eosin-fast green-naphthol yellow mixture for differential staining of cytologic components in mammalian spermatozoa. *Stain Tech.* 45:231.

310. Cassidy, S. L. (1981). Rodent testicular sperm head count— a useful method of detecting cytotoxic agents in reproductive toxicology. *Teratology* 24:35.

311. MacLeod, J. (1971). Human male infertility. *Obstet. Gynecol. Surv.* 26:335.

312. Setchell, B. P. (1978). *The Mammalian Testis.* Ithaca, Cornell University Press.

313. Potashnik, G., Yanai-Inbar, I., Sacks, M. I., and Israeli, R. (1979). Effect of dibromochloropropane on human testicular function. *Isr. J. Med. Sci.* 15:438.

314. Lobl, T. J., Bardin, C. W., and Chang, C. C. (1980). Pharmacological agents producing infertility by direct action on the male reproductive tract. In *Research Frontiers in Fertility Regulation.* Edited by G. I. Zatuchni. Hagerstown, MD, Harper and Row.

315. Moghissi, K. S. (1976). Postcoital test: physiologic basis, technique and interpretation. *Fertil. Steril.* 27:117.

316. Ulstein, M. and Fjallbrant, B. (1976). In vitro tests of sperm penetration in cervical mucus. In *Human Semen and Fertility Regulation in Men.* Edited by E. S. E. Hafez. St. Louis, C. V. Mosby, p. 383.

317. Kremer, J. (1965). A simple sperm penetration test. *Int. J. Fertil. 10:*209.

318. Katz, D. F., Overstreet, J. W., and Hanson, F. W. (1980). A new quantitative test for sperm penetration into cervical mucus. *Fertil. Steril. 33:*179.

319. Yanagimachi, R., Yanagimachi, H., and Rogers, B. J. (1976). The use of zona-free animal ova as a test-system for the assessment of the fertilizing capacity of human spermatozoa. *Biol. Reprod. 15:*471.

320. Rogers, B. J., VanCampen, H., Ueno, M., Lambert, H., Bronson, R., and Hale, R. (1979). Analysis of human spermatozoal fertilizing ability using zona-free ova. *Fertil. Steril. 32:*664.

321. Karp, L. E., Williamson, R. A., Moore, D. E., Sky, K. K., Plymate, S. R., and Smith, W. D. (1981). Sperm penetration assay: useful test in evaluation of male fertility. *Obstet. Gynecol. 57:*620.

322. Prasad, M. R. N. (1984). The in vitro sperm penetration test: a review. *Int. J. Androl. 7:*5.

323. Pearson, P. L., Bobrow, M., and Vosa, C. G. (1970). Technique for identifying Y chromosomes in human interphase nucleus. *Nature 226:*78.

324. Kapp, R. W. (1979). Detection of aneuploidy in human sperm. *Environ. Health Perspect. 31:*27.

325. Propping, D., Tauber, P. F., and Zaneveld, L. J. D. (1978). An improved assay technique for the proteolytic activity of individual human spermatozoa. *Int. J. Fertil. 23:*24.

326. Ginsberg, L. C., Johnson, S. C., Salama, N., and Ficsor, G. (1981). Acrosomal proteolytic assay for detection of mutagens in mammals. *Mutat. Res. 91:*415.

327. Phadke, A. M., Samant, N. R., and Deval, S. D. (1973). Significance of seminal fructose studies in male infertility. *Fertil. Steril. 24:*894.

328. Marmar, J. L., Katz, S., Praiss, D. E., and De Benedictis, T. J. (1975). Semen zinc levels in infertile and post-vasectomy patients and patient with prostatitis. *Fertil. Steril. 29:*539.

329. Fair, W. R., Clark, R. B., and Wehner, N. (1972). A correlation of seminal polyamine levels and semen analysis in the human. *Fertil. Steril. 23:*38.

330. Crabbe, M. J. C. (1977). The development of a qualitative assay for male fertility from a study of enzymes in human semen. *J. Reprod. Fertil. 51:*73.

331. Beck, K. J., Schonhofer, P. S., Rodermund, O. E., Dinnendahl, V., and Peters, H. D. (1976). Lack of relationship between cyclic nucleotide levels and spermatozoal function in human sperm. *Fertil. Steril.* 27:403.

332. Homonnai, Z. T., Matzkin, H., Fairman, N., Paz, G., and Kracier, P. F. (1978). The cation composition of human seminal plasma and prostatic fluid and its correlation to semen quality. *Fertil. Steril.* 29:539.

333. Comhaire, F., Vermuelen, L., Ghedira, K., Mas, G., and Irvine, S. (1983). Adenosine triphosphate (ATP) in human semen: a marker of its potential fertilizing capacity. *Am. Soc. Androl.* (Abstr.).

334. McLachlan, J. A., Newbold, R. R., Shah, H. C., Hogan, M., and Dixon, R. L. (1981). Reduced fertility in female mice exposed transplacentally to diethylstilbestrol. *Fertil. Steril.* 38:364.

335. McLachlan, J. A. and Dixon, R. L. (1976). Transplacental toxicity of diethylstilbestrol: A special problem in safety evaluation. In *Advances in Modern Toxicology: New Concepts in Safety Evaluation.* Edited by M. A. Mehlman, R. E. Shapiro, and H. Blumenthal, Washington, D.C., Hemisphere Publ. Co., Vol. I, Part I, pp. 423–448.

336. Gerall, A. A. and McCrady, R. E. (1970). Receptivity scores of female rats stimulated either manually or by males. *J. Endocrinol.* 46:55.

337. McClintock, M. K. and Adler, N. T. (1978). The role of the female during copulation in the wild and domestic Norway rat. *Behavior* 67:67.

338. Christian, M. S., Galbraith, W. M., Voytek, P., and Mehlman, M. A. (1983). Advances in modern environmental toxicology. In *Assessment of Reproductive and Teratogenic Hazards.* Princeton, NJ, Princeton Sci. Publ., Vol. III, p. 160.

339. Tuchmann-Duplessis, H. and Mercier-Parot, L. (1961). Diminution de la fertilite du rat soumis a un traitement chronique de niamide. *C. R. Acad. Sci. [D] (Paris)* 253:712.

340. Greene, R. R., Burrill, M. W., and Ivy, A. C. (1939). Experimental intersexuality: the effect of antenatal androgens on sexual development of female rats. *Am. J. Anat.* 65:415.

341. Rasmussen, E. W. and Kaada, B. R. (1965). Variation in length of heat periods in albino rats according to age. *J. Reprod. Fertil.* 10:9.

342. Gellert, R. J., Heinrichs, W. L., and Swerdloff, R. (1974). Effects of neonatally administered DDT homologs on reproductive function in male and female rats. *Neuroendocrinology* 16:84.

343. Faddy, M. J., Jones, E. C., and Edwards, R. G. (1976). An analytical model for follicular dynamics. *J. Exper. Zool.* 197:173.

344. Nisbet, I. C. T. and Karch, N. J. (1983). *Chemical Hazards to Human Reproduction.* Park Ridge, NJ, Noyes Data Corp.

345. Barlow, S. M. and Sullivan, F. M. (1982). *Reproductive Hazards of Industrial Chemicals, An Evaluation of Animal and Human Data.* London, Academic Press.

346. Klassen, R. W. and Persaud, T. V. N. (1978). Influence of alcohol on the reproductive system of the male rat. *Int. J. Fertil.* 23:176.

347. Bradley, W. R. and Frederick, W. G. (1941). The toxicity of antimony in animal studies. *Indust. Med. 10. Indust. Hyg. Sec.* 2:15.

348. Jackson, H., Fox, B. W., and Craig, A. W. (1959). The effect of alkylating agents on male rat fertility. *Br. J. Pharmacol.* 14:149.

349. Hood, R. D. and Bishop, S. L. (1972). Teratogenic effects of sodium arsenate in mice. *Arch. Environ. Health* 24:62.

350. Beaudoin, A. R. (1974). Teratogenicity of sodium arsenate in rats. *Teratology* 10:153.

351. Avilova, G. G. and Ulanova, I. P. (1975). Comparative characteristics of the effect of benzene on the reproductive function of adult and young animals. *Gig. Truda. Prof. Zabol.* 19:55.

352. Bouissou, H. and Castagnol, R. (1965). Action of boric acid on the testicle of the rat. *Arch. Mal. Profess. Med. Travail Secur. Soc.* 26:293.

353. Weir, R. J. and Fisher, R. S. (1972). Toxicologic studies on borax and boric acid. *Toxicol. Appl. Pharmacol.* 23:351.

354. Barr, M. (1973). The teratogenicity of cadmium chloride in two stocks of Wistar rats. *Teratology* 7:237.

355. Agranovskaya, B. A. (1973). Effect of prophylactic trace element-vitamin feedings on the generative function of white rats exposed to carbon disulfide. *Tr. Leningr. Sanit.-gig. Med. Inst.* 103:118.

356. Tepe, S. J. and Zenick, H. (1982). Assessment of male reproductive toxicity due to carbon disulfide: use of a new technique. *Toxicologist* 2:77.

357. Larson, P. S., Egle, J. L., Hennigar, G. R., Lane, R. W., and Borzelleca, J. F. (1979). Acute, subchronic, and chronic toxicity of chlordecone. *Toxicol. Appl. Pharmacol.* 48:29.

358. Epstein, S. S. (1978). Kepone-hazard evaluation. *Sci. Tot. Environ.* 9:1.

359. Hammond, B., Bahr, J., Dial, O., McConnel, J., and Metcalf, R. (1978). Reproductive toxicology of Mirex and Kepone. *Fed. Proc.* 37:501.

360. Huber, J. J. (1965). Some physiological effects of the insecticide Kepone in the laboratory mouse. *Toxicol. Appl. Pharmacol.* 7:516.

361. vonOettingen, W. F., Hueper, W. C., Deichmann-Gruebler, W., and Wiley, F. H. (1936). 2-Chloro-butadiene (chloroprene): its toxicity and pathology and the mechanism of its action. *J. Indust. Hyg. Toxicol. 18*:240.

362. Salnikova, L. S. and Fomenko, V. N. (1973). Experimental investigation of the influence produced by chloroprene on the embryogenesis. *Gig. Truda. Prof. Zabol. 17*:23.

363. Winters, S. J., Banks, J. L., and Loriaux, D. L. (1979). Cimetidine is an antiandrogen in the rat. *Gastroenterology 76*:504.

364. Kabra, S. P. and Prasad, M. R. (1967). Effect of clomiphene on fertility in male rats. *J. Reprod. Fertil. 14*:39.

365. Hart, M. M., Adamson, R. H., and Fabro, S. (1971). Prematurity and intrauterine growth retardation induced by DDT in the rabbit. *Arch. Int. Pharmacodyn. Ther. 192*:286.

366. Coulston, F., Beyler, A., and Drobeck, H. (1960). The biologic actions of a new series of bis(dichloroacetyl)-diamines. *Toxicol. Appl. Pharmacol. 2*:715.

367. Torkelson, T. R., Sadek, S. E., Rowe, V. K., Kodama, J. K., Anderson, H. H., Loquvam, G. S., and Hine, C. H. (1961). Toxicologic investigation of 1,2-dibromo-3-chloropropane. *Toxicol. Appl Pharmacol. 3*:545.

368. Rao, K. S., Murray, F. J., Crawford, A. A., John, J. A., Potts, W. J., Schwetz, B. A., Burek, J. D., and Parker, C. M. (1979). Effects of inhaled 1,2-dibromo-3-chloropropane (DBCP) on the semen of rabbits and the fertility of male and female rats. *Toxicol. Appl. Pharmacol. 48*:A137.

369. McLachlan, J. A., Newbold, R. R., and Bullock, B. (1975). Reproductive trace lesions in male mice exposed prenatally to diethylstilbestrol. *Science 190*:991.

370. Vorherr, H., Messer, R. H., Vorherr, U. F., Jordan, S. W., and Kornfeld, M. (1979). Teratogenesis and carcinogenesis in rat offspring after transplacental and transmammary exposure to diethylstilbestrol. *Biochem. Pharmacol. 28*:1865.

371. Wadsworth, P. F. and Heywood, R. (1978). The effect of prenatal exposure of Rhesus monkeys (Macaca mulatta) to diethylstilboestrol. *Toxicol. Lett. 2*:115.

372. Walker, B. E. (1980). Reproductive tract anomalies in mice after prenatal exposure to DES. *Teratology 21*:313.

373. Baggs, R. B. and Miller, R. K. (1983). Induction of urogenital malformation by diethylstilbestrol in the ferret. *Teratology 27*:28A.

374. Gilloteaux, J. P., Steggles, R. J., and Alan, W. (1982). Upper genital tract abnormalities in the Syrian hamster as a result of in utero exposure to diethylstilbestrol. *Virchows Arch. A: Pathol. Anat. Histopathol. 2*:163.

375. Hendrickx, A. G., Benirschke, K., Thompson, R. S., Ahern, J. K., Lucas, W. E., and Oi, R. H. (1979). The effects of prenatal diethylstilbestrol (DES) exposure on the genitalia of pubertal Macaca mulatta. I. Female offspring. *J. Reprod. Med. 22*:233.

376. Short, R. D., Minor, J. L., Winston, J. M., Seifter, J., and Lee, C. C. (1978). Inhalation of ethylene dibromide during gestation by rats and mice. *Toxicol. Appl. Pharmacol. 46*:173.

377. Chang, M. C., Gu, Z., and Saksena, S. K. (1980). Effect of gossypol on the fertility of male rats, hamsters and rabbits. *Contraception 21*:461.

378. Hahn, D. W., Rusticus, C., Probst, A., Homm, R., and Johnson, A. N. (1981). Antifertility and endocrine activities of gossypol in rodents. *Contraception 24*:97.

379. Shandilya, L., Clarkson, T. B., Adams, M. R., and Lewis, J. C. (1982). Effects of gossypol on reproductive and endocrine functions of male cynomolgus monkeys (Macaca fascicularis). *Biol. Reprod. 27*:241.

380. Ehling, U. H. (1971). Comparison of radiation- and chemically-induced dominant lethal mutations in male mice. *Mutat. Res. 11*:35.

381. Singhal, R. L. and Thomas, J. A. (Eds.). (1980). *Lead Toxicity*. Baltimore, Urban and Schwazenberg.

382. Gray, L. E. and Laskey, J. W. (1980). Multivariate analysis of the effects of manganese on the reproductive physiology and behaviour of the male house mouse. *J. Toxicol. Environ. Health 6*:861.

383. Chandra, S. V. (1971). Cellular changes induced by manganese in the rat testis-preliminary results. *Acta Pharmacologica et Toxicologica 29*:75.

384. Chandra, S. V., Ara, R., Nagar, N., and Seth, P. K. (1973). Sterility in experimental manganese toxicity. *Acta Biol. Med. Germanica 30*:857.

385. Lee, I. P. and Dixon, R. L. (1975). Effects of mercury on spermatogenesis studied by velocity sedimentation cell separation and serial mating. *J. Pharmacol. Exp. Therap. 194*:171.

386. Lach, H. and Srebro, Z. (1972). The oestrous cycle of mice during lead and mercury poisoning. *Acta Biologica Cracoviensia. Series Zoologia 15*:121.

387. Baranski, B. and Szymczyk, I. (1973). Effects of mercury vapours upon reproductive function on white female rats. *Medcyna Pracy 24*:249.

388. Lamperti, A. A. and Printz, R. H. (1973). Effects of mercuric chloride on the reproductive cycle of the female hamster. *Biol. Reprod. 8*:378.

389. Fish, S. A. (1966). Organophosphorus cholinesterase inhibitors and fetal development. *Am. J. Obstet. Gynecol.* *96*:1148.

390. Smith, D. J. and Joffe, J. M. (1975). Increased neonatal mortality in offspring of male rats treated with methadone or morphine before mating. *Nature* (London) *253*:202.

391. George, R. (1971). Hypothalamus: Anterior pituitary gland. In *Narcotic Drugs: Biochemical Pharmacology*. Edited by D. Clouet. New York, Plenum, pp. 283–296.

392. Davies, A. G. (1980). *Effects of Hormones, Drugs and Chemicals on Testicular Function*, Vol. 1. St. Albans, VT, Eden Press.

393. Orberg, J., Johansson, N., Kihlstrom, J. E., and Lundberg, C. (1972). Administration of DDT and PCB. *Ambio* *1*:148.

394. Barsotti, D. A., Marlar, R. J., and Allen, J. R. (1976). Reproductive dysfunction in rhesus monkeys exposed to low levels of polychlorinated biphenyls (Aroclor 1248). *Food Cosmet. Toxicol.* *14*:99.

395. Gellert, R. J. (1978). Uterotrophic activity of polychlorinated biphenyls (PCB) and induction of precocious reproductive aging in neonatally treated female rats. *Environ. Res.* *16*:123.

396. Heinrichs, W. L., Gellert, R. J., Bakke, J. L., and Lawrence, N. L. (1971). DDT administered to neonatal rats induces persistent estrus syndrome. *Science* *173*:642.

397. Izyumova, A. S. (1972). The action of small concentrations of styrol on the sexual function of albino rats. *Gig. Sanit.* *37*:29.

398. Gibson, J. E. and Becker, B. A. (1970). Placental transfer, embryotoxicity and teratogenicity of thallium sulphate in normal and potassium-deficient rats. *Toxicol. Appl. Pharmacol.* *16*: 120.

399. Younoszai, M. K., Peloso, J., and Haworth, J. C. (1969). Fetal growth retardation in rats exposed to cigarette smoke during pregnancy. *Am. J. Obstet. Gynecol.* *104*:1207.

400. Schoeneck, F. J. (1941). Cigarette smoking in pregnancy. *N.Y. State J. Med.* *41*:1945.

401. Hudak, A., Rodics, K., Stuber, I., and Ungvary, G. (1977). Effects of toluene inhalation on pregnant CFY rats and their offspring. *Munkavedelem 23*:(1–3 Suppl.) 25.

402. John, J. A., Smith, F. A., Leong, B. K. J., and Schwetz, B. A. (1977). The effects of maternally inhaled vinyl chloride on embryonal and fetal development in mice, rats and rabbits. *Toxicol. Appl. Pharmacol.* *39*:497.

403. Hirsh, J., Cade, J. F., and Gallus, A. S. (1970). Fetal effects of coumadin administered during pregnancy. *Blood* *36*:623.

404. McCallion, D., Phelps, N. E., Hirsh, J., and Cade, J. F. (1971). Effects of coumadin administered during pregnancy to rabbits and mice. *Teratology* 4:235.

405. Mirkova, B., Antov, G., Vasileva, L., Christeva, V., and Benchev, I. (1979). Study on the teratogenic effect of warfarin in rats. *Eur. Soc. Toxicol. Congr.* 21:115.

406. Hogue, C. J. R. (1984). The effect of common exposures on reproductive outcomes. *Teratol. Carcinog. Mutag.* 4:45.

407. Koeter, H. B. W. M. (1983). Relevance of parameters related to fertility and reproduction in toxicity testing. In *Reproductive Toxicity*. Edited by D. R. Mattison. New York, Alan R. Liss, pp. 81–86.

408. Levine, R. J., Blunden, P. B., DalCorso, R. D., Starr, T. B., and Ross, C. E. (1983). Superiority of reproductive histories to sperm counts in detecting infertility at a dibromochloropropane manufacturing plant. *J. Occup. Med.* 25:591.

409. Omenn, G. S. (1983). Environmental risk assessment: Relation to mutagenesis, teratogenesis, and reproductive effects. *J. Am. Coll. Toxicol.* 2:113.

410. Omenn, G. S. (1984). A framework for reproductive risk assessment and surveillance. *Teratog. Carcinog. Mutag.* 4:1.

411. Tuchmann-Duplessis, H., David, G., and Haegel, P. (Eds.) (1972). *Illustrated Human Embryology. Embryogenesis,* Vol. 1. New York, Springer-Verlag.

412. Humble, C. G. and Speizer, F. E. (1984). Polybrominated biphenyls and fetal mortality in Michigan. *Am. J. Public Health* 74:1130.

413. Clarke, M. and Mason, E. S. (1985). Leatherwork: a possible hazard to reproduction. *Br. Med. J.* 290:1235.

414. Levitt, J. I. (1970). Spironolactone therapy and amenorrhea. *JAMA* 211:2014.

415. Linn, S., Schoenbaum, S. C., Monson, R. R., Rosner, R., Stubblefield, P. C., and Ryan, K. J. (1983). The association of marijuana use with outcome of pregnancy. *Am. J. Publ. Health* 73:1161.

416. Foote, R. H., Berndtson, W. E., and Rounsaville, T. R. (1986). Use of quantitative testicular histology to assess the effect of dibromochloropropane (DBCP) on reproduction in rabbits. *Fund. Appl. Pharmacol.* 6:638.

417. Baeder, C., Wickramaratne, G. A. S., Hummler, H., Merkle, J., Schon, H., and Tuchmann-Duplessis, H. (1985). Identification and assessment of the effects of chemicals on reproduction and development (reproductive toxicology). *Food Chem. Toxicol.* 23:377.

418. Gray, L. E., Ferrell, J., Gray, K., and Ostby, J. (1986). Alterations in reproductive development in hamsters induced by methoxychlor (M). *Toxicologist* 6:294.

419. Nagi, S. and Virgo, B. B. (1982). The effects of spirono-lactone on reproductive functions in female rats and mice. *Toxicol. Appl. Pharmacol. 66*:221.

420. Tutak, L. S. and Arthur, A. T. (1986). Disruption of the reproductive process in female rats resulting from constant exposure to light. *Toxicologist 6*:99.

421. Christian, M. S., Diener, R. M., Hoar, R. L., and Staples, R. E. (1980). Reproduction, teratology and pediatrics. *PMA Guidelines*.

422. Bottomley, A. M. and Leeming, N. M. (1981). Effect of maternal bodyweight and age on outcome of mating. *Teratology 24*:35A.

423. Clegg, D. J. (1979). Animal reproduction and carcinogenicity studies in relation to human safety evaluation. *Dev. Toxicol. Environ. Sci. 4*:45.

424. Foote, R. H., Schermerhorn, E. C., and Simkin, M. E. (1986). Measurement of semen quality, fertility, and reproductive hormones to assess dibromochloropropane (DBCP) effects in live rabbits. *Fund. Appl. Toxicol. 6*:628.

425. Clegg, E. D. and Zenick, H. (1986). Issues in male repro-ductive risk assessment. *Toxicologist 6*:31.

# 11

# Developmental Toxicology

BETSY D. CARLTON* / *Battelle Columbus Division, Columbus, Ohio*

## I. INTRODUCTION

Although a true developmental approach to toxicology would include the periods from conception through senescence, thereby overlapping with the areas of mutagenesis, reproduction, teratology, geriatrics, and behavior, in this chapter the definition of developmental toxicology will be restricted to the study of physical effects of chemical exposure during the periods from conception through birth, to sexual maturity. Within this category of developmental toxicology, the relative strengths and weaknesses of protocols used to assess teratogenicity caused by exposure of the pregnant animal will be discussed. (Mutagenic effects acting via the sperm as would be detected using a dominant lethal assay in rodents have been discussed elsewhere in this volume.) Also included in this chapter will be a discussion of postnatal evaluations, including endpoints of pup viability and growth, and sexual maturation.

## II. TERATOLOGY

### A. Nature of the Problem

Teratology is the study of birth defects. Terata (birth defects) may result from genetic or chromosomal defects, the exposure of the pregnant individual to exogenous substances (xenobiotics), or the interaction of genetics and the environment. These xenobiotics may be physical agents such as ionizing radiation, drugs, chemicals,

---

*Current affiliation*: National Sanitation Foundation, Ann Arbor, Michigan.

environmental contaminants, over- or underexposure to essential
vitamins or trace elements, or infectious agents such as viruses,
bacteria, or protozoa. Approximately 7% of the children born in the
United States each year have identifiable birth defects (1), 65% of
which are of unknown etiology. Birth defects may be morphological,
biochemical, or behavioral. For the purpose of this chapter, only
morphological defects will be considered. In order to produce a
morphologic change in the conceptus, the exposure must occur during the period of organogenesis (exceptions being restriction malformations caused by physically restrictive conditions in the uterus
during development). In humans, this "critical period" essentially
covers the first trimester of pregnancy, a time period when many
women are unaware that they are pregnant. In rodents such as
rats and mice, the critical period extends approximately from day
6 through day 15 of gestation. This is not to be interpreted, however, as suggesting that birth defects cannot result from exposure
before or after this "window" in development. Ultimately, the sensitivity of each conceptus to teratogen exposure results from the interaction of the genetic character of both the mother and the offspring
with the teratogen. Teratology, as a practical science, seeks to
identify those chemicals or agents that might be teratogenic in humans
or animal species of interest. For both ethical and practical reasons,
rodents and other laboratory animals are used to estimate the teratogenic potential of xenobiotics. In general, when teratology data
are required in two species, a rodent (usually rat) and a nonrodent
species are chosen, theoretically to provide species with differing
sensitivities and different potential target organs. Realistically, however, this decision is based in tradition, probably resulting from laboratory evaluations of thalidomide, and might be disputed scientifically.

## B. Species

There are four species commonly used for teratology studies which
are accepted by governmental regulatory agencies: rats, mice, rabbits, and hamsters. While the largest historic data bases exist for
rats and rabbits, each of the four species has advantages and disadvantages. Each of the species exhibit differential sensitivities to
chemical insult; indeed, different strains within a species frequently
demonstrate a wide range of sensitivities. Rats are relatively inexpensive; are easy to handle, breed, and dose; have large litters
(8-13 fetuses per litter, the average litter size being dependent
upon the rat strain); and are the most commonly used species, although their placentation changes from a yolksac to a chorioallantoic
placenta at midgestation and differs from the type of placentation
found in humans. In addition, rats typically are the species of
choice for postnatal development and reproductive toxicology studies

and therefore should be used if additional reproductive data are to be collected so as to provide a more complete data set. Sprague-Dawley rats are one of the most frequently used strains for teratology studies.

Rabbits are more expensive and more difficult to handle than rats, and their litters may be somewhat more difficult to evaluate, but they have similarly large litters. Rabbits became the species of choice when it was shown that they were responsive to the terato-genic effects of the drug thalidomide in a manner similar to that shown by humans, whereas the rat strains used did not indicate the teratogenic risk posed by the drug. Upon further study it became apparent that certain strains of rabbits and rats were thalido-mide sensitive, while other strains of rats and rabbits were not. Tradition dies hard, however, and a sufficiently large database now exists for rabbits that they are second only to rats as the species of choice for teratology studies for regulatory submission. Rabbits should not be used for the teratologic evaluation of such substances as antibiotics, since normal gastrointestinal flora may be destroyed, leading to spurious maternal toxicity. New Zealand White rabbits are the most commonly used rabbit strain, but Dutch Belted rabbits are used frequently because they are smaller and easier to handle.

Syrian golden hamsters are the most common hamster strain used for teratology studies. They average 10–12 fetuses per litter, and the fetuses are only slightly smaller than those of rats (and are larger than mouse fetuses). Hamsters have several distinct ad-vantages: their 4-day estrous cycle is remarkably stable and can be determined prior to initiation of breeding by visually observing the quality of the discharge that can be expressed easily from the vagina; hamsters will breed 1–2 hours after lights-out for a period of approximately two hours, reducing gestation-age variability; and their gestation period is slightly less than 16 days. Conception rates are approximately 95%. Hamsters have not been routinely used for teratology studies conducted for regulatory agency submission, but have a moderate database, primarily from academic research laboratories.

While mice also demonstrate an ease of handling, are relatively inexpensive to purchase and house, have short gestation periods (18–21 days) and large litters (8–12 fetuses/litter), and an extensive database exists for numerous mouse strains, mice are not routinely used in teratology studies for regulatory submission. The primary reason for their infrequent use is the small size of the fetuses rela-tive to those of rats. Rats are therefore easier to study when only one rodent species is needed. Wide ranges of fertility, fecundity, and teratogen sensitivity can be observed when different mouse strains are compared. Mice are most frequently used when a par-ticular sensitivity is required. For instance, the A/J mouse strain

is most useful in the study of cleft palate because of the high spontaneous occurrence rate of the malformation in this strain, and C57Bl/6
are of greater utility in studying the effects of some trace element
deficiencies or supplementations than are random-bred CD-1 mice. In
general, random-bred animal strains are of greater utility in teratology
studies, mimicking the genetic diversity of the human population.
Comparisons of teratogenic outcome following chemical exposure in
several strains of inbred mice can, however, provide information on
the potential range of response to the test agent. When a random-bred
mouse strain is desired, CD-1 mice are routinely used.

Alternative animal species have been proposed, particularly as
nonrodent alternatives to the rabbit. The most commonly suggested
nonrodent species is the ferret. Ferrets are seasonal breeders and
therefore must be brought into a stage of sexual receptivity by manip-
ulating the light cycle. Like cats, ferrets are induced ovulators, and
can be bred once they are brought into season. Ferrets have large
litters (6–10 fetuses/litter), and a 41–44 day gestation period. The
use of ferrets has not yet gained widespread acceptance, as much because they must "compete" with an already well-accepted species with
a large database (rabbits) as because of the relative inconvenience of
using seasonal breeders.

Ideally, nonhuman primates would be the experimental animal of
choice for extrapolation of teratology data to humans. They are generally the most similar to humans in placentation, metabolic potential, and
development, but they are not identical to humans and will necessarily
differ in some responses. There are several disadvantages to the use
of nonhuman primates, however, which limit their utility. Nonhuman
primates such as cynomolgus or rhesus monkeys are both expensive to
purchase and house and have limited availability, are comparatively
difficult to breed and handle, have long menstrual cycles and gestation
periods, and, like humans, usually have only one offspring per
pregnancy.

## C. Exposure Regimen

A sufficient number of animals should be used to allow reasonable possibility of the statistical significance of any adverse findings to be
determined. Some practical considerations come into play at this point,
however. The most commonly accepted minimum numbers of animals
per dose group are 20 *pregnant* rodents or 12 *pregnant* rabbits per
dose group, although the use of 20 pregnant rabbits is encouraged.
A sufficient number of animals must be bred in excess of those required to obtain the desired number of dams per dose group. Both
the species and strain of test animal must be taken into consideration
when determining the number of breeding pairs necessary; breeding
efficiency differs significantly between species and strains.

A range-finding test should be conducted in pregnant animals to determine any differences in response to the test article between pregnant and nonpregnant animals, and also to determine the dose range which will provide both a no-effect level and a fetotoxic or maternally toxic dose for the teratology study. Usually 5 pregnant animals in each of 5 or 6 dose levels are treated using the dosing regimen that will be used for the teratology study. Litters are taken by hysterotomy and are weighed and examined for external malformations. Fetuses usually are preserved (for possible examination at a later time, if necessary), but are not evaluated for visceral or skeletal malformations prior to initiation of the teratology study.

To be able to adequately interpret the results of a teratology study in animals, a minimum of three dose levels and a concurrent control group should be used. If the test substance must be dissolved or suspended in a vehicle substance, the vehicle should be administered to the control group at a rate comparable to the test groups. If the vehicle volume varies with the test article dose level, controls should receive the greatest volume of vehicle used. A concurrent untreated control group can also be incorporated into the study design if an unusual vehicle substance is being used or if there is any indication that the vehicle itself might be teratogenic.

Exposure routes should most closely approximate the route of human exposure. Where human exposure is likely to occur via any of several routes, many factors should be considered when choosing the most appropriate exposure route for animal studies: (1) by which route will the greatest human exposure occur (considering frequency, duration, and dose)? (2) is the toxic potential of the test article greater when administered via one route when compared to another route? (3) which exposure route is both appropriate and practically and economically feasible? The test article can be administered by injection (intravenous, intramuscular, subcutaneous, intraperitoneal), by gavage, in the feed or water, or by inhalation. When the inhalation route is chosen, care must be taken that the test article aerosol or particle aerodynamic size distribution is in the respirable range.

As previously stated, the "critical period" for administration of the xenobiotic is during the period of organogenesis, when the developing organ systems are most sensitive. In rodents, this is generally interpreted as days 6–15; in rabbits, days 6–18; days 6–14 in hamsters; and the first trimester, particularly weeks 3–8, in humans. If information is to be gathered regarding the sensitivity of a particular organ system, the period of exposure may be restricted to a few days or be as limited as a particular postconceptional hour. Alternatively, if one is uncertain as to any particular target organ and prefers to maximize the possibility of observing teratogenic effects, then the time of dose administration can be increased to encompass both the embryonic and fetal periods (i.e., days 6–21 in rats).

## D. Endpoints

In any teratology study, fetuses are taken by ceasarean section shortly before the time of anticipated parturition, to preclude such confounding factors as cannibalism of any malformed offspring by the dam. The incidences of external, visceral, and skeletal anomalies and variations as well as the number and percent of live, dead, or resorbed fetuses are determined. The number of corpora lutea observable on each ovary are counted and compared to the number of implantation sites as an indicator of preimplantation loss. Live fetuses should be weighed, sexed if possible, and examined for grossly observable external malformations, including the presence of cleft palate. If sex is not determined at the time of necropsy, it should be determined when the fetuses are processed for visceral and skeletal evaluations. For rodent species, one-third to one-half of the fetuses should be examined for internal soft-tissue (visceral) anomalies. At the present time, two methods are routinely used: immediate visceral evaluation using the in situ dissection technique proposed by Staples (2), or the fetuses can be preserved in Bouin's solution and evaluated by Wilson's free-hand razor blade sectioning technique (3).

Each of the two techniques has its advantages and disadvantages. The Staples technique is best done using approximately 6–8 people at the time of necropsy to set up an "assembly line" to process the dams and fetuses in a timely manner. The most difficult part of the visceral dissection technique is cutting the fetal heart appropriately so that all cardiac chambers, valves, and septa can be visualized. The person performing this function must be well trained so that they can recognize any cardiac defects present, and can consistently assure that the cuts made in the heart are not only appropriately placed, but also at the correct angle and depth. One advantage of the Staples dissection technique is that fetal tissues are observed fresh, rather than being preserved, thereby allowing observation of tissue color as well as morphology and placement. An additional advantage is that anomalies of the major blood vessels are more easily visualized since they can be visualized intact. Using the Wilson technique, they must be traced through several sections, requiring the ability to visualize in three dimensions. All fetuses can be processed for skeletal evaluations as well as visceral, although most studies using the Staples technique include Wilson sectioning of half of the fetal heads. In contrast to the Wilson technique, at the completion of visceral evaluations using the Staples technique, the fetal remains are not suitable for preservation and future reference. If the fetuses are to be examined for visceral abnormalities using the Wilson technique, they are placed in Bouin's solution for at least 72 hours prior to evaluation. Serial sections of the head and trunk are made using free-hand cuts with a razor blade. All major organ systems are examined. An advantage of the Wilson technique is that fewer people are required at necropsy and one person can evaluate the fetuses at any time, accommodating the laboratory's work schedule. Fetuses processed for visceral examinations by the Wilson technique cannot be examined for skeletal anomalies. Sterz and Lehmann (4) reported that, in a comparison of the Wilson and in situ sectioning techniques, particular cardiac abnormalities such as missing ductus arteriosus and ventricular septal defects inferior to the aortic valves, were detected only by the in situ sectioning method and not by the Wilson technique. Rather than indicating a deficiency in the technique, however, this particular study indicates the absolute importance of having well-trained staff who cannot only recognize abnormalities when they occur, but also use the technique appropriately (these anomalies would have been detected in a correctly sectioned fetus).

Skeletal anomalies are determined in rodent fetuses that have been preserved in 70% ethanol, eviscerated, digested with potassium hydroxide (KOH), stained with alizarin red S, using the method of Dawson (5) or modifications thereof, and cleared in increasing concentrations of glycerin. Anomalies are usually classified as either variations or abnormalities as an indicator of the severity of the malformation and the historic frequency of occurrence in controls. Abnormalities in cartilage development can be examined by double staining the fetuses for skeletal examinations with both alizarin red S and alcian blue (6).

Rabbit fetuses and fetuses from other larger species are examined for gross external malformations and then are evaluated using in situ dissection techniques because the large fetal size precludes ease of serial section. Rabbit fetuses must be skinned prior to processing for skeletal evaluation, since the skin is not easily digested by KOH.

The uteri of apparently nonpregnant animals should be carefully examined for evidence of implantation sites. Mid- or late-gestation resorptions are usually easily visualized as yellow nodules found along the mesometrial margins of the uterine horns. Very early resorption sites may not be as easily visualized unless the uterine horns are carefully placed between two clear plexiglass plates and gentle pressure applied. An alternative method of visualization is to stain the uterus by immersion in an ammonium sulfide solution for 10 minutes, which clearly stains the early resorption sites dark blue-black (7).

Correlation of the number of implantation sites (live, dead, and resorbed fetuses) with the number of corpora lutea will provide an indication of preimplantation loss. The number of corpora lutea cannot be determined for preimplantation loss calculations if no implantation sites are evident or if all fetuses were resorbed early in gestation because the female would have resumed her natural estrous cycle, with new corpora lutea for each cycle.

## E. Male-Mediated Developmental Toxicology

Male-mediated developmental toxicology and dominant lethal effects
are two distinct entities. The latter refers to an effect of a xenobiotic on the genetic material in the sperm resulting in the in utero
death of the fetus, a subject discussed in the chapter on mutagenesis.
The former refers to perinatal toxicity or teratogenic outcome resulting from exposure of the male to a xenobiotic prior to mating. While
no single cause can be determined, the teratogenic agent may be
acting through damage to the sperm, the presence of the chemical
or metabolite in the semen, or alterations in the semen. Few male-
mediated developmental toxins have been documented. While concern
over the reproductive performance of men exposed to hazardous chemicals dates back to the 1800s, contemporary examination of male-
mediated teratology primarily dates to the 1970s when epidemiologic
reports indicated that wives of surgeons, operating room personnel,
and dentists using anesthetic gases such as halothane had a higher
incidence of miscarriages, stillbirths, and infants with birth defects
(8,9). Additionally, Yerushalmy's early epidemiologic studies (10)
of male cigarette smokers pointed to increased incidences of low birth
weight babies, neonatal mortality, and congenital anomalies. Smith
and Joffe (11) serendipitously discovered that morphine administered
to male rats lead to high neonatal mortality. Since then, these results have been confirmed, and other chemicals such as methadone,
thalidomide, lead, and caffeine have also been shown to adversely
affect the offspring (12–15). Male-mediated developmental toxicology
studies are conducted in a manner similar to standard teratology and
developmental toxicology studies, except that the test chemical is
administered to the male for 2–10 weeks prior to breeding, rather
than to the dam.

## F. In Vitro Teratology

### 1. General

Increased international consciousness of the need to conserve
resources, time, money, and animals has lead to significant explora-
tion of alternative in vitro test systems in toxicology research (16–18).
Several in vitro systems are currently proposed and are being tested
as screening methods for the examination of the teratogenic potential
of xenobiotics. These methods can be divided into mammalian cell
cultures, organ cultures, and whole embryo cultures, and submammalian test systems including *Xenopus*, *Hydra*, *Dugesia* (flatworms),
insects, sea urchins, and fish embryos. All of these alternative
models appear to share many of the same benefits and shortcomings.
All are short-term assays (usually 96 hours or less) and represent
a considerable monetary savings and a reduction in the number of

animals needed to test the toxicity or teratogenicity of a compound. In vitro alternatives, because they represent simplified systems relative to intact organisms, or because they are phylogenetically removed from humans, rarely can be used to identify or predict specific toxicities or target organs. They are best used as screening systems rather than as definitive tests for teratogenicity.

Mammalian development is based on a series of cytodifferentiative and morphologic events. Many of the in vitro tests proposed are based on mechanistic correlates of development, including interference with elaboration of developmental stage-specific enzymes or proteins. Cell morphogenesis is known to be dependent upon cell surface functions and properties. Disruption of cell adhesion properties by teratogens is the basis of the in vitro model described by Braun et al. (20,21).

All of the alternative models which will be described are maintained in aqueous media, thereby making the evaluation of water-insoluble test substances more difficult. Carrier vehicles may be employed, but may be toxic or teratogenic themselves if used in excessive concentrations, or for test substances such as heavy metals, may be inadequate. Most of the models possess nonexistent or immature metabolic systems, although hepatocytes or microsomal S-9 fractions can be added to ameliorate this problem. None of the in vitro systems currently under consideration provide any indication of increases or decreases in test compound-induced embryotoxicities brought about via maternal-fetal-placental interactions.

In general, teratogenic hazard can best be expressed as a relative teratogenic index (RTI), the relative merits of which were discussed by Fabro et al. (19). The RTI is calculated from the ratio of the lethal dose to the lowest dose resulting in observable terata (LD01/td05). In in vivo studies, this ratio would be calculated from the ratio of the maternally toxic dose to the teratogenic dose. The RTI allows a relative ranking of teratogenic potency and provides a mechanism for comparison of the various in vitro systems with each other and with in vivo data.

The literature on in vitro test systems is quite extensive and is growing daily. No attempt will be made in this chapter to discuss all available systems, to discuss any of the models in depth, or to provide an extensive bibliography, because this research area will have undergone significant changes before this text is in press and will continue to change at an increasing rate in the foreseeable future. A brief description of some of the more commonly used models is presented below.

### 2. Mammalian Systems

*Whole Embryo.* Rat whole embryo culture, a technique developed by New (22), is being used increasingly both as a screening system for the study of teratogenic potential, but also as a means to explore teratogenic mechanisms. As an in vitro alternative, rat whole embryo culture is one of the more labor-intensive systems being used. Whole rat embryos are dissected from the uterus with their extraembryonic membranes intact on gestation day 9.5, and cultured on serum containing the test article for approximately 48 hours. Embryos are scored for viability, size, spinal flexure, and the presence or absence of malformations of many of the major organ systems. Protein content of the embryos is also determined. While whole rat embryo cultures are observed too early in gestation to detect malformations in some organ systems such as the reproductive tract, it has a distinct advantage over the other in vitro systems in that it may suggest potential target organs in a mammalian system or mimic teratogenic sequelae observed in humans (23). Additionally, these embryos can be grown on serum from rodents, cows, monkeys, or humans, allowing the examination of the teratogenic potential of the parent compound and/or metabolites as they are present in the organism of interest (i.e., humans). Overviews of this experimental model have been written by Fantel, Sadler, and Klein (24–26) and their colleagues.

*Organ Culture.* The mammalian organ culture most commonly studied for teratology is the limb bud culture as described by Barrach and Neubert, and Kochhar (27–29). This method utilizes limb buds taken from mouse embryos of known gestational ages (usually 12.5 days), and cultured for 6 days. The limbs are scored both qualitatively for the presence or absence of malformations and quantitatively for the amount of cartilage present. A variety of endpoints can be examined, including cell proliferation or death, differential growth, size and shape of limb parts, chondrogenesis, and various biochemical parameters. The limb bud assay is relatively labor intensive and is not as rapid as some of the other alternatives currently proposed. Like the whole embryo culture, limb buds are cultured on serum, and therefore have the potential for use in examining the effects of serum taken from individuals exposed to the test article.

*Cell Culture.* Several cell culture systems are currently undergoing validation experiments. Two systems being tested are the human embryonic palate mesenchyme (HEPM) system proposed by Pratt et al. (30,31) and the mouse ovarian tumor cell attachment assay (MOT) developed by Braun et al. (20,21). The research by Pratt et al. indicated that HEPM cells, although they are a commercially available cell line (American Type Culture, Rockville, MD), are still representative of in vivo palatal mesenchyme cells in their growth profiles in response to epidermal growth factor (EGF) and ornithine decarboxylase activity. HEPM cells are used because they are representative of the in vivo cell response, because they are derived from a human embryo (thereby theoretically presenting an image of human cell response), and because cleft palate is one of the more commonly observed human teratogenic responses. Endpoints for this assay are cell death and cell growth expressed as percent of control.

As previously mentioned in Section II.F.1, the rationale behind the MOT assay system as discussed by Braun et al. (20) is based on teratogen-induced interference with cell attachment during development. In this assay system, mouse ovarian tumor cells are plated with lectin-coated disks in the presence or absence of various concentrations of the test article. The primary endpoints examined are inhibition of cell attachment and cell death.

Individually, these two models have fairly high false positive and false negative rates (i.e., 21% of the tested agents incorrectly classified in the MOT assay) (21). The HEPM and MOT assays have been proposed as complementary systems, each appropriately detecting the false positives and false negatives of the other model. According to Pratt et al. (31), the combined assay systems are reliable (90%), with low false negative rate (1 of 102) compounds examined. Both model systems have easily defined endpoints and are rapid and inexpensive. The MOT system, in particular, however, is not easily established by a new laboratory, and appears to require considerable "tinkering" before it provides consistent results within a laboratory. These two systems are currently undergoing validation under contract from a government agency.

### 3. Submammalian Systems

*Hydra*. This in vitro test, developed by Johnson et al. (32,33), is one of the few systems developed specifically to estimate teratogenic hazard. An artificial "embryo" is created by dissociating the cells of the adult hydra and pelleting the cells by gentle centrifugation. The dissociated, pelleted cells will then reaggregate and undergo all of the normal developmental processes characteristic of a hydra embryo, achieving whole body regeneration and tentacle formation. The ratio of adult and embryonic toxicities is determined by calculating the minimal toxic dose in adult hydra and minimal developmentally toxic dose level required to elicit toxicity in the "embryo." This assay system is inexpensive, and the data are easy to interpret. Although the assay is not very complex, it is relatively difficult to establish. The hydra is phylogenetically distant from mammals, however, and should therefore be used as a first screen, rather than as a definitive indicator of teratogenicity in mammalian systems.

*FETAX*. One of the more promising of the submammalian assays is the FETAX (Frog Embryo Teratogenesis Assay: *Xenopus*) proposed by Greenhouse, and Dumont and co-workers (34,35). Blastula-stage embryos are used for this assay. The embryos are maintained in the presence of the test substance for 96 hours. Embryos are examined at 24, 48, and 72 hours and evaluated at 96 hours and scored for viability, size, pigmentation, morphologic abnormalities, motility, and stage of development. Since many of the stages of amphibian development are similar to mammalian development, and the FETAX system utilizes whole amphibian embryos, the "developmental relevance" of FETAX is higher (36) than many of the other teratogenesis assays. The results appear to correlate well with mammalian teratogenicity data reported in the literature (37,38).

*Drosophila.* This method entails treating *Drosophila melanogaster* larvae, incorporating the test article into the medium over the entire metamorphosis period, from the egg through three instar stages to pupa formation. Adult flies are then examined under 25× magnification for external morphological anomalies. The *Drosophila* system has been evaluated by a government agency and others for applicability as a first-pass screening system for chemical teratogenic potential (39,40).

## III. POSTNATAL DEVELOPMENT

Study design for the examination of developmental toxicology can take many approaches. Dose exposure may be initiated prior to mating of the parental animals, and usually continues throughout breeding, gestation, and lactation. Postnatal evaluations such as would be conducted using a Segment III protocol for submission to the FDA generally examine chemical effects during the last half of gestation and throughout lactation. Postnatal measures include pup weight and viability, sex ratio within and between litters in a dose group, physical maturation as determined from key developmental landmarks such as eye opening, incisor eruption, or ear pinna detachment, behavioral developmental progression, and sexual development.

## A. General Development

In rodents, eye opening is one of the more commonly observed indicators of general development. Eye opening, defined as that lactational day when all pups in a litter are observed to have both eyes open (there is frequently a one-day delay between the time when a pup's first eye opens and the second eye opens and a delay of several days between the first and last pup in a litter), usually occurs between days 14 and 16 (begin examinations at day 10). Ear pinna detachment and incisor eruption routinely are observed in rodents at approximately days 2-4 and 9-12 (begin examinations at days 1 and 8), respectively. These general developmental indices are most frequently influenced by changes in pup body weight, but may be accelerated or delayed as a result of chemical exposure in the absence of chemically induced body weight changes.

## B. Sexual Development

The indicators of sexual maturity frequently examined in rodents are the observation of testicular descent or preputial separation in males, and the observation of vaginal patency, the first estrous vaginal smear, and the onset of regular estrous cycles in females. In hamsters, the development of the testosterone-dependent flank gland can also be determined. Chemical exposure may result in either a delay in, or acceleration of, these developmental landmarks.

In rats, the age of vaginal opening is approximately 31–34 days (begin examinations at day 25); the age at first estrus is 32–35 days, and the age at the first regular 4 or 5 day cycle is approximately 34–38 days (begin examination at the time of vaginal patency). The age of preputial separation in rats is approximately 40–44 days (begin examination at day 35). Full male sexual maturity (at which time breeding can be initiated for reproduction or developmental studies) will not be reached until approximately 10 weeks of age. In hamsters, sexual maturity in the female is similar to that found in the rat. Hamsters have an astoundingly regular 4-day estrous cycle. Male hamsters achieve preputial separation at an earlier age than rats, however, at days 34–38.

## IV. CAVEATS

While any of the in vivo or in vitro teratology assays discussed can be conducted by a competent technician under the supervision of a teratologist, it must be emphasized that appropriate training is of utmost importance. As was discussed in Section II.D, important malformations can be overlooked if the evaluations are conducted by personnel who are not well versed in the technique. Many studies must be repeated due to inadequate examination of the fetuses or poor interpretation and presentation of the results. A sufficiently large number of litters should be examined to allow statistical evaluation of the data. To reduce the effect of intralitter variability in teratogenic response and increase the validity of the data interpretation, the litter and not the individual fetus should be used as the unit of comparison for statistical purposes, although the total number and percent of dead or malformed fetuses may be taken into account in the final interpretation of study results.

While the in vitro techniques are comparatively easy to perform and endpoints are standardized, many of the techniques (cell, organ, and mammalian embryo assays, in particular) require practice and validation in the conducting laboratory to learn the "black magic" components, those small variations in technique that allow successful conduct of the assay but which are rarely published or even acknowledged.

Teratogenicity and embryo/fetotoxicity should be considered in light of any existing signs of maternal toxicity. Karnofsky argued that any substance has teratogenic potential if given at the appropriate dose level in an appropriate species. Substances that are teratogenic at doses close to the maternally toxic dose are usually considered to have a good margin of safety. Teratogenic or embryo/fetotoxic outcome seen only at maternally toxic doses may indicate that the test substance is not teratogenic or toxic to the conceptus directly, but may be acting indirectly only. In general, if a test article is teratogenic only at maternally toxic doses, it is not considered a true teratogen in that experimental system.

Decreased fetal weight or low birth weight should not be ignored or downplayed, but should be considered a significant toxicologic finding, particularly in the absence of overt maternal toxicity. In humans, low birth weight (small-for-date babies) is associated with increased perinatal morbidity and mortality. Increased frequency and severity of illness in the first year of life have been reported among low birth weight infants.

Although few, if any, compounds have been found teratogenic in humans and not in experimental animals, it should be noted that animal models in teratology evaluations should be used as indicators of the teratogenic potential of a test article in humans, and not as absolute predictors. It should be recognized that while the existence of teratogenic outcome indicates that the particular test article is a teratogen in that experimental system, the extrapolation of results between species or between strains is not clearcut. Differences in target organs and in sensitivity may be observed. While positive teratogenic outcome is indicative of teratogenicity, a lack of terata does not rule out that the xenobiotic may be teratogenic in other test systems or in humans.

## REFERENCES

1. Anonymous. (1975). *National Foundation/March of Dimes: Facts*, National Foundation, New York.
2. Stapels, R. E. (1974). Detection of visceral alterations in mammalian fetuses. *Teratology* 9:A37
3. Wilson, J. G. (1965). Methods for administering agents and detecting malformations in experimental animals. In *Teratology: Principles and Techniques*. Edited by J. G. Wilson and J. Warkany. Chicago, Univeristy of Chicago Press, p. 262.
4. Sterz, H. and Lehmann, H. (1985). A critical comparison of the freehand razor-blade dissection method according to Wilson with an in situ sectioning method for rat fetuses. *Teratogen. Carcinogen. Mutagen.* 5:347.

5. Dawson, A. B. (1926). Note on the staining of the skeleton of cleared specimens with alizarin red S. *Stain Technol.* 1:123.
6. Inouye, M. (1976). Differential staining of cartilage and bone in fetal mouse by alcian blue and alizarin red S. *Cong. Anom.* 16:171.
7. Salewski, V. E. (1964). Farbemethode zum makroskopischen nachweis von implantationsstellen am uterus der ratte. *Archiv. Path. Exp. Pharmacol.* 247:367.
8. Ad Hoc Committee on the effects of trace anesthetics on the health of operating room personnel. (1974). *Anesthesiology* 41: 321.
9. Cohen, E. N., Brown, Jr., B. W., Bruce, D. L., Cascorbi, H. F., Corbett, T. H., Jones, T. W., and Whitcher, C. E. (1975). A survey of anesthetic health hazards among dentists. *J. Am. Dent. Assoc.* 90:1291.
10. Yerushalmy, J. (1971). The relationship of parents' cigarette smoking to outcome of pregnancy—implications as to the problem of inferring causation from observed associations. *Am. J. Epidemiol.* 93:443.
11. Smith, D. J. and Joffe, J. M. (1975). Increased neonatal mortality in offspring of male rats treated with methadone or morphine before mating. *Nature* 253:202.
12. Soyka, L. F. and Joffe, J. M. (1980). Male mediated drug effects on offspring. In *Drug and Chemical Risks to the Fetus and Newborn.* Edited by R. H. Schwarz and S. J. Yaffe. New York, Alan R. Liss, p. 49.
13. Lutwak-Mann, C. (1984). Observations on progeny of thalido-mide-treated male rabbits. *Br. Med. J.* 1:1090.
14. Joffe, J. M. (1979). Influence of drug exposure of the father on perinatal outcome. *Clin. Perinatol.* 6:21.
15. Weathersbee, P. S., Olsen, L. K., and Lodge, J. R. (1977). Caffeine and pregnancy. A retrospective survey. *Postgrad. Med.* 62:64.
16. Kimmel, G. L., Smith, M. K., Kochhar, D. M., and Pratt, R. M. (1982). Proceedings of the consensus workshop on in vitro teratogenesis testing. *Teratogen. Carcinogen. Mutagen.* 2:i.
17. Balls, M., Riddell, R. J., and Worden, A. N. (Eds.). (1983). *Animals and Alternatives in Toxicity Testing.* New York, Academic Press, p. 197.
18. Homburger, F. and Marquis, J. (1985). Third international conference on safety evaluation and regulation and joint American-Swiss seminar on alternative embryotoxicity and teratogenicity tests. *J. Am. Coll. Toxicol.* 4:185.
19. Fabro, S., Shull, G., and Brown, N. A. (1982). The relative teratogenic index and teratogenic potency: proposed components of developmental toxicity risk assessment. *Teratogen. Carcinogen. Mutagen.* 2:61.

20. Braun, A. G., Emerson, D. J., and Nichison, B. B. (1979).
    Teratogenic drugs inhibit tumour cell attachment to lectin-coated
    surfaces. *Nature* 282:507.
21. Braun, A. G., Nichinson, B. B., and Horowicz, P. B. (1982).
    Inhibition of tumor cell attachment to Concanavalin A-coated
    surfaces as an assay for teratogenic agents: Approaches to
    validation. *Teratogen. Carcinogen. Mutagen.* 2:343.
22. New, D. A. T. (1978). Whole embryo culture and the study of
    mammalian embryos during organogenesis. *Biol. Rev.* 53:81.
23. Clapper, M. L., Clark, M. E., Klein, N. W., Kurtz, P. J.,
    Carlton, B. D., and Chhabra, R. S. (1986). Cardiovascular
    defects in rat embryos cultured on serum from rats chronically
    exposed to phenytoin. *Teratogen. Carcinogen. Mutagen.* 6:151.
24. Fantel, A. G. (1982). Culture of whole rodent embryos in
    teratogen screening. *Teratogen. Carcinogen. Mutagen.* 2:231.
25. Sadler, T. W., Horton, W. E., and Warner, C. W. (1982).
    Whole embryo culture: A screening technique for teratogens?
    *Teratogen. Carcinogen. Mutagen.* 2:243.
26. Klein, N. W., Chatot, C. L., Plenefisch, J. D., and Carey,
    S. W. (1983). Human serum teratogenicity studies using in vitro
    cultures of rat embryos. In *Short-Term Bioassays in the
    Analysis of Complex Environmental Mixtures III.* Edited by
    M. D. Waters, S. S. Sandhu, J. Lewtas, L. Claxton, N. Cher-
    noff, and S. Nesnow. New York, Plenum Press, p. 393.
27. Barrach, H.-J. and Neubert, D. (1980). Significance of organ
    culture techniques for evaluation of perinatal toxicity. *Arch.
    Toxicol.* 45:161.
28. Kochhar, D. M. (1975). The use of in vitro procedures in
    teratology. *Teratology* 11:273.
29. Kochhar, D. M. (1982). Embryonic limb bud organ culture in
    assessment of teratogenicity of environmental agents. *Teratogen.
    Carcinogen. Mutagen.* 2:303.
30. Wilk, A. L., Greenberg, J. H., Horigan, E. A., Pratt, R. M.,
    and Martin, G. R. (1980). Detection of teratogenic compounds
    using differentiating embryonic cells in culture. *In Vitro* 16:
    269.
31. Pratt, R. M., Grove, R. I., and Willis, W. D. (1982). Pre-
    screening for environmental teratogens using cultured mesen-
    chymal cells from the human embryonic palate. *Teratogen.
    Carcinogen. Mutagen.* 2:313.
32. Johnson, E. M. (1980). A subvertebrate system for rapid
    determination of potential teratogenic hazards. *J. Environ.
    Pathol. Toxicol.* 2:153.
33. Johnson, E. M., Gorman, R. M., Gabel, B. E. G., and
    George, M. E. (1982). The *Hydra attenuata* System for detec-
    tion of teratogenic hazards. *Teratogen. Carcinogen. Mutagen.*
    2:263.

34. Greenhouse, G. (1975). Effects of pollutants in embryos and larvae of frogs: a system for evaluating teratogenic effects of compounds in freshwater environments. *Proceedings of the Sixth Annual Conference of Environmental Toxicology*, National Technical Information Service, p. 493.

35. Dumont, J. N., Shultz, T. W., Buchanan, M., and Kao, G. (1983). Frog embryo teratogenesis assay: Xenopus (FETAX)— a short-term assay applicable to complex environmental mixtures. In *Short-Term Bioassays in the Analysis of Complex Environmental Mixtures III*. Edited by M. D. Waters, S. S. Sandhu, J. Lewtas, L. Claxton, N. Chernoff, and S. Nesnow. New York, Plenum Press, p. 393.

36. Smith, M. K., Kimmel, G. L., Kochhar, D. M., Shepard, T. H., Spielberg, S. P., and Wilson, J. G. (1983). A selection of candidate compounds for in vitro teratogenesis test validation. *Teratogen. Carcinogen. Mutagen.* 3:461.

37. Courchesne, C. L. and Bantle, J. A. (1985). Analysis of the activity of DNA, RNA, and protein synthesis inhibitors on *Xenopus* embryo development. *Teratogen. Carcinogen. Mutagen.* 5:177.

38. Sabourin, T. D., Faulk, R. T., and Goss, L. B. (1985). *Xenopus* embryos as teratogen screens: assays with NTP repository chemicals. *Soc. Environ. Toxicol. Chem.* Annual Meeting (Abstr.).

39. Hardin, B. D., Bond, G. P., Sikov, M. R., Andrew, F. D., Beliles, R. P., and Niemeier, R. W. (1981). Testing of selected workplace chemicals for teratogenic potential. *Scand. J. Environ. Health* 7:66.

40. Bournias-Vardiabasis, N. and Teplitz, R. L. (1982). Use of *Drosophila* embryo cell cultures as an in vitro teratogen assay. *Teratogen. Carcinogen. Mutagen.* 2:333.

# 12

# Evaluating the Biological Hazards of Combustion Products

HAROLD L. KAPLAN / Southwest Research Institute, San Antonio, Texas

## I. INTRODUCTION

The United States has the worst fire-fatality record of the industrial nations, with approximately 6000 deaths per year due to fire (1,2). Smoke inhalation is the primary cause of these deaths, accounting for about 80% of the victims (2). Carbon monoxide is the most prevalent toxic component of smoke and is responsible for the majority of deaths attributed to the inhalation of smoke or to asphyxia. Other highly toxic gases also may be produced, depending on the chemical composition of the material, as well as on the combustion conditions. The smoke generated by combustion of synthetic polymers, which contain elements not present in natural materials, may differ considerably from that evolved from commonly used natural products such as cotton and wood. It has been claimed that, in general, the smoke from decomposing synthetic polymers is faster acting and more toxic than smoke from wood (1). There is adequate experimental evidence from animal studies with a number of synthetics to support this claim (1,3).

Ideally, the most effective approach to reduce fatalities from smoke inhalation is to reduce the incidence of fires by means of fire detection and suppression systems. The use of these systems has become more widespread and, in some cases, mandatory, which has probably contributed to the continuing decline of fire-related deaths during the past five years. Other reasons suggested for this decline are mandatory ignition standards promulgated by the federal government and the State of California and the use of more ignition-resistant

materials in the construction of modern upholstered furniture (4).
Despite these improvements in fire safety, fire fatalities continue to
mount, with most due to the inhalation of toxic smoke. Three recent
examples of fires in which smoke toxicity was the primary cause of
multiple deaths are the fires in the MGM Grand Hotel in Las Vegas,
the Biloxi, Mississippi jail, and the Westchase Hilton Hotel in Houston,
Texas. Although the matter is controversial, there are claims that
highly toxic gases released from synthetic polymers were responsible
for many of the deaths in these fires.

An additional suggestion for reducing fire fatalities is material
selection, that is, using materials which generate the least toxic
combustion products, when a choice of materials is available. For
this approach to be effective, other fire safety properties of a
material, such as ignitability, flame spread rate, rate of heat release,
and smoke generation rate, also must be considered in the selection
process. Standardized test methods and criteria for compliance with
codes and regulations have been established for flammability properties, which are easily measured. In contrast, standardized test
methods do not exist for evaluating the toxicity of the combustion
atmospheres produced by materials. In fact, there is considerable
disagreement in the fire safety community as to how the toxicity of
combustion products of materials should be evaluated. A major reason
for this disagreement is the potential economic impact on manufacturers of certain synthetic polymers if criteria for rejection of materials
on the basis of smoke toxicity are adopted by regulatory agencies.
Nevertheless, the adoption of a meaningful test method and appropriate criteria can enable the selection of materials with the least potentially adverse fire safety properties and the identification of those
materials which are most hazardous in a fire environment. In addition, regulatory actions requiring toxicity testing would provide an
impetus to the manufacturers of synthetic materials to produce materials with improved toxicity as well as flammability characteristics.

It is the objective of this chapter to present an approach and
methodology which can provide a meaningful evaluation of the toxicity of the thermal decomposition products of materials. To accomplish this objective, it is necessary to review the state of the art
of combustion toxicology. This review will provide the toxicologist
outside of this discipline with an understanding of the problems
unique to combustion toxicology, the methods available for testing
materials, the capabilities and limitations of these methods and deficiencies in our knowledge. Although the focus of this chapter will
be on the evaluation of the toxic hazards of combustion products,
the reader should be fully aware that the toxicity of combustion
products represents only one element in the total potential hazard
of a material in a fire.

## II. HISTORICAL REVIEW

The beginning of combustion toxicology has been ascribed to Zapp (5), who, in 1951, reported in "The Toxicology of Fire" that fire fatalities were often caused by smoke inhalation and thermal damage to the respiratory tract (6). Although other scientists became interested in the toxicity of smoke during the next twenty years, it was during the mid-1970s that research in the area of smoke toxicity rapidly expanded. The impetus for the intensified interest in, and concern for, the toxicity of smoke was the finding in 1974 of a neurotoxic organophosphate ester in the smoke produced by combustion of a noncommercial polyurethane foam (7). As a consequence of this finding, the Products Research Committee was formed in 1974, with substantial resources provided by industry for support of research in the behavior of cellular plastics in fire. With funding by this committee as well as by government agencies, numerous laboratories became involved in various areas of fire research.

One of the unfortunate consequences of the sudden availability of research funds was the evolution of a plethora of laboratory test methods for assessing the toxicity of smoke produced by the combustion of materials. Some of these methods were developed by scientists with expertise relevant to combustion methodology but who had no or little training in toxicology. The various methods that evolved during this period utilized different combustion devices and conditions, different animal exposure chambers and, in some cases, different indices of toxicity and different species of test animals. Because of these marked differences, data obtained with one laboratory test method generally had little relevance to data obtained with a different method. In addition, some investigators, unfamiliar with fundamental toxicology principles, merely compiled and published table after table of meaningless data. A few investigators who appreciated the complexity of smoke atmospheres developed test methods to enable a comprehensive evaluation of the toxicity of combustion products and to understand the mechanisms of their toxicity.

During the 1980s, the emphasis in combustion toxicology shifted from the development of test methodologies to the promulgation of a standardized toxicity test method. In 1980, the Center for Fire Research of the National Bureau of Standards (NBS) published the NBS test method (8). The method was developed by the NBS, with assistance by an ad hoc working group composed of members from academia, industry, and government, for the purpose of establishing a standardized procedure for evaluating the toxicity of combustion products. Investigators began to use this method to compare and rank materials according to the toxicity of their combustion products, a use that is vehemently opposed by the plastics industry. In 1982, the NBS published a modification of the method, with a revised statement of its purpose that "this test method is primarily intended for research and preliminary screening purposes" (9). At the present time, this method and three other methods are being considered by American Society of Testing Materials (ASTM) task groups for recommendation as a standard ASTM test method. Other significant advances in combustion toxicology during this period include the use of primates in studies of the physiological and behavioral effects of fire gases and combustion atmospheres, the development of mathematical models for predicting the toxic effects of major combustion gases in rodents and the development of computer models for hazard analysis/risk assessment of materials in fires.

During the past two years, a number of state legislatures have considered the adoption of toxicity tests for building materials and furnishings in an effort to reduce fire fatalities due to smoke inhalation. At the present time, only New York State has initiated any action requiring testing. In May of 1984, the Secretary of State for New York made the recommendation that toxicity data on smoke produced by polymeric materials, as determined by the Uniform Fire Prevention and Building Code Council, be filed at the Department of State (10). Under proposed Article 15 of New York's Uniform Fire Prevention and Building Code (11), manufacturers of regulated products are required to submit combustion toxicity data, in addition to data on ignitability, flame spread, and other properties of materials, to the Secretary of State for filing in a publicly accessible data bank. This requirement has met with strong opposition by the plastics industry and may be challenged in the courts or even by federal governmental agencies sympathetic to this industry. In the event combustion toxicity testing is not mandated, it is doubtful that any significant effort to evaluate and improve the combustion toxicity of materials will be forthcoming. But even worse would be the adoption of a so-called "toxicity screening test," based solely on the lethality of rodents, which would not adequately evaluate the toxicity of combustion products. Such a test would result only in additional cost to the consumer without any reduction in the incidence of smoke inhalation deaths.

## III. THE TOXICITY OF SMOKE

### A. The Nature of Smoke and Its Toxic Effects

In combustion toxicology, smoke is commonly defined as a complex mixture of the airborne solid and liquid particulates and gases evolved when a material undergoes thermal decomposition (12). Thermal decomposition of a material may occur as a result of anaerobic pyrolysis, oxidative pyrolysis (commonly referred to as "smoldering"), and/or flaming combustion. Although all of these processes may

**Table 1**    Volatile Combustion Products of Polyvinyl Chloride

| Combustion product | Quantity (mg/g) | Combustion product | Quantity (mg/g) |
|---|---|---|---|
| Hydrogen chloride | 583.0 | Butane | 0.28 |
| Acetic acid | — | Isopentene | 0.02 |
| Carbon dioxide | 729.0 | 1-Pentene | 0.06 |
| Carbon monoxide | 442.0 | Pentane | 0.16 |
| Methane | 4.6 | Cyclopentene | 0.05 |
| Ethylene | 0.58 | Cyclopentane | 0.05 |
| Ethane | 2.2 | 1-Hexene | 0.05 |
| Propylene | 0.47 | Hexane | 0.12 |
| Propane | 0.84 | Methylcyclopentane | 0.04 |
| Vinyl chloride | 0.60 | Benzene | 36.0 |
| 1-Butene | 0.18 | Toluene | 1.3 |

*Source*:   From Ref. 13.

occur at some point in a real fire, few fires start or progress anaerobically (6). Consequently, almost all laboratory test methods have been designed to decompose materials under oxidative pyrolysis and/or flaming combustion conditions.

When a material is thermally decomposed, a wide variety of chemical species are produced. For example, 50 chemical compounds were detected in the volatile combustion products of a commercial sample of polyvinyl chloride (13); those which were identified and quantitated are listed in Table 1. Mitera and Michal (14) identified 55 compounds in the combustion products of polyethylene, 56 in the combustion products of polypropylene and more than 30 in those of both polystyrene and polyamide. Even with a natural material such as Douglas fir, more than 75 different chemicals have been identified in the smoke produced by the combustion of this wood (15). The specific thermal decomposition products of any material, as well as the quantities and rates of evolution of these products, are highly dependent on the conditions under which the material is decomposed. These conditions include temperature, rate of heating, combustion mode (nonflaming or flaming), and oxygen availability (4,12,16).

Almost all natural and synthetic polymers contain carbon and, when combusted, generate carbon monoxide (CO) and/or carbon dioxide

($CO_2$). The ratio of the quantities of the two gases evolved depends on the amount of oxygen present at the site of combustion. In addition to these two prevalent toxicants, various polymer decomposition products are evolved as simple saturated and unsaturated hydrocarbons (e.g., methane, ethane, ethylene), partially oxidized species (e.g., acetaldehyde, acrolein) and more complex aromatics (e.g., benzene, toluene). Many materials contain nitrogen, sulfur, and halogens in addition to carbon and hydrogen. When these materials are thermally decomposed, hydrogen cyanide (HCN), nitrogen oxides ($NO_x$), sulfur dioxide ($SO_2$), ammonia ($NH_3$), and halogen acids (HCl, HBr, and HF) may be evolved. Also, other decomposition products, including isocyanates and nitriles may be formed. The common gases (other than CO and $CO_2$) produced by thermal decomposition of materials and the toxicological effects of these gases are summarized in Table 2 (17).

The large number of diverse chemical species present in smoke must affect many organ systems of the body and cause myriad physiological alterations. Many of these alterations are masked by the effects of the major toxicants (CO, HCN, and irritant gases) which are the most prevalent components of smoke and generally are present in the highest concentrations. Consequently, it has become common practice in combustion toxicology to categorize the major fire effluents into two classes, the hypoxia-producing gases or asphyxiants and the irritants. A third catchall class has been designated for those chemicals with "other and unusual specific toxicities" (18). Many components of smoke may fit into this category, but these compounds generally are present in low concentrations and are not analyzed for. With few exceptions, the effects of these chemicals have not been evident in postmortem examinations of fire victims or in experimental studies with animals. Nevertheless, it is possible that some of these compounds contribute to the incapacitating and lethal effects of smoke inhalation, even though the effects of the hypoxia-producing toxicants and the irritants predominate.

## B. Causes of Death In Smoke Inhalation Victims

### 1. Postmortem Studies of Fire Victims

The search for specific toxicants responsible for smoke inhalation fatalities has consisted of two principal approaches. In the first approach, data have been obtained from postmortem examinations of fire victims in an attempt to identify the causes of death. Some studies have analyzed data accumulated from many fires whereas others have investigated the fatalities in specific fires. Results of these studies have established that carbon monoxide is the primary cause of death of most fire victims, and that other factors, including cardiovascular disease, alcohol, HCN, HCl, and particulates, have been or may have been involved in some deaths.

Table 2  Toxicological Effects of Fire Gases

| Toxicant | Sources | Toxicological effects | Estimate of short-term (10-min) lethal concentration (ppm) |
|---|---|---|---|
| Hydrogen cyanide (HCN) | From combustion of wool, silk, polyacrylonitrile, nylon, polyurethane, and paper. | A rapidly fatal asphyxiant poison. | 350 |
| Nitrogen dioxide ($NO_2$) and other oxides of nitrogen | Produced in small quantities from fabrics and in larger quantities from cellulose nitrate and celluloid. | Strong pulmonary irritant capable of causing immediate death as well as delayed injury. | >200 |
| Ammonia ($NH_3$) | Produced in combustion of wool, silk, nylon, and melamine, concentrations generally low in ordinary building fires. | Pungent, unbearable odor; irritant to eyes and nose. | >1000 |
| Hydrogen chloride (HCl) | From combustion of polyvinyl chloride (PVC), and some fire-retardant-treated materials. | Respiratory irritant; potential toxicity of HCl coated on particulate may be greater than that for an equivalent amount of gaseous HCl. | >500, if particulate is absent |
| Other halogen acid gases (HF and HBr) | From combustion of fluorinated resins or films and some fire-retardant materials containing bromine. | Respiratory irritants. | HF ~ 400 HBR > 500 |

**Table 2** (continued)

| Toxicant | Sources | Toxicological effects | Estimate of short-term (10-min) lethal concentration (ppm) |
|---|---|---|---|
| Sulfur dioxide (SO$_2$) | From materials containing sulfur. | A strong irritant, intolerable well below lethal concentrations. | >500 |
| Isocyanates | From urethane polymers; pyrolysis products, such as toluene −2, 4-diisocyanate (TDI), have been reported in small-scale laboratory studies; their significance in actual fires is undefined. | Potent respiratory irritants; believed the major irritants in smoke of isocyanate-based urethanes. | ∼100 (TDI) |
| Acrolein | From pyrolysis of polyolefins and cellulosics at lower temperatures (∼400°C). | Potent respiratory irritant. | 30 to 100 |

*Source:* From Ref. 17.

One of the major studies of postmortem data was a 6-year study by the Johns Hopkins University of 530 fire fatalities from 398 primarily residential fires in Maryland (19). The postmortem examinations consisted of (1) analyses of carboxyhemoglobin, cyanide, and alcohol in the blood and other tissues, (2) heavy metal analyses of trachea and bronchi, and (3) pathological examinations of victims' hearts. Results of analyses for blood COHb (Table 3) showed that approximately 60% of the victims had blood COHb levels equal to or greater than 50%, which is generally considered evidence of CO-induced death (20). In 40% of the victims in which COHb levels were below 50%, the investigators attributed death to CO plus cardiovascular disease in 20%, to burns in 11%, and to "unexplained" causes (possibly other toxicants) in 9% of the victims. In a similar 3-year study of 182 fire fatalities in Glasgow, Scotland, lethal blood levels of COHb were measured in most of the victims and heart disease was prevalent in victims in which COHb levels were below 50% (4). In both the Maryland and Glasgow studies, intoxicating levels of alcohol were present in a large percentage of the victims.

Hydrogen cyanide has been implicated as a possible cause of smoke-inhalation fatalities by a number of studies which have shown cyanide in the blood of victims at levels considered toxic or even

**Table 3**   Distribution of Fire Victims
According to Blood CO Saturation Levels

| COHb (%) | Number of victims | Percent |
|---|---|---|
| 0-9 | 48 | 9 |
| 10-19 | 42 | 8 |
| 20-29 | 37 | 7 |
| 30-39 | 38 | 7 |
| 40-49 | 43 | 8 |
| 50-59 | 58 | 11 |
| 60-69 | 79 | 15 |
| 70-79 | 111 | 21 |
| ≥80 | 74 | 14 |
| Total | 530 | 100 |

*Source*: From Ref. 19.

lethal. In the 272 Maryland fire fatalities in which blood cyanide concentrations were measured, almost 70% had levels above "normal" (0-0.25 µg/ml) and 10% had levels considered "probably toxic" (>2.00 µg/ml) by the investigators (19). In another study, in which the blood of 10 of 42 victims of the Tennessee jail fire was analyzed for COHb and cyanide, all of the victims except one had elevated cyanide levels (21). However, elevated blood cyanide levels in victims of this and other fires were almost always accompanied by lethal levels of COHb. One exception was the Houston Westchase Hilton fire in which blood cyanide levels were elevated in 9 of 10 victims, but COHb levels of 50% or greater were present in only two victims (22). The cause of death of two victims in which 8.0 and 10.0 µg/ml of cyanide were measured was attributed by the medical examiner to "asphyxia due to soot, carbon monoxide and cyanide inhalation." Because high COHb levels almost always accompany elevated cyanide levels, it has not been possible to determine the role of HCN in causing fatalities attributed to smoke inhalation. In addition, blood cyanide data appear to be less definitive than COHb levels because of analytical difficulties with cyanide, possible blood storage effects on cyanide concentrations, and incomplete understanding of the pharmacokinetics of HCN (19,23). It is the opinion of some investigators that elevated cyanide and lethal COHb levels in the blood of fire victims indicate that HCN caused early incapacitation of the victims, resulting in continued inhalation of CO and subsequent death (22,24).

Irritant gases are prevalent in combustion atmospheres and are capable of producing severe effects on the eyes and respiratory tract. However, the contribution of these gases to fire fatalities that have been attributed to smoke inhalation is not well understood. Evidence that these gases may play a significant role in some deaths has been based primarily on findings of respiratory tract damage in some victims, because it is rarely possible to detect irritant gases in postmortem analyses of blood and other tissues. In the Westchase Hilton Hotel fire, hydrogen chloride was considered to have had a contributory role in some of the fire fatalities (22). The basis for this conclusion was the detection of chloride in soot samples from the room of origin and pathological findings of respiratory tract damage and pulmonary edema in two fatalities and of corneal burns in one survivor of the fire. In an earlier report, Dyer and Esch found extensive pulmonary hemorrhaging and edema in a fireman who died 24 hours after being present in a fire involving "amounts of PVC and Teflon" (25).

## 2. Analytical Studies of Fire Atmospheres

The second approach to identify toxicants responsible for fire fatalities has consisted of analytical studies of smoke from real fires.

Table 4 Analyses of Atmospheres in San Antonio and Boston Building Fires

| | TLV-STEL[a] (15 min) | STLC[b] (10 min) | San Antonio study | | | Boston study | | |
|---|---|---|---|---|---|---|---|---|
| | | | % Samples | Median | Maximum | % Samples | Median | Maximum |
| Carbon monoxide | 400 | 5000 | 90 | 50 | 7450 | >90 | 23 | 4800 |
| Acrolein | 0.3 | 30–100 | 6 | ND | 4 | >50 | 0.4 | 98 |
| Acetaldehyde | 150 | – | 19 | ND | 7 | NA | NA | NA |
| Benzene | 25 | 20,000 | 100 | 2 | 17 | 92 | 0.7 | 180 |
| Hydrogen chloride | 5[c] | >500 | 53 | 4 | 232 | 36 | <1 | 280 |
| Hydrogen cyanide | 10[c] | 350 | 89 | 0.2 | 9 | 11 | <0.2 | 4 |
| Nitrogen dioxide | 5 | >200 | NA | NA | NA | – | <0.2 | 8 |
| Carbon dioxide (%) | 1.5 | 10 | 93 | 0.07 | 1.6 | 100 | 0.2 | 7.5 |
| Oxygen depletion (%) | 5 | 10 | 100 | <1 | 1.3 | NA | NA | NA |
| Particulate (g/m$^3$) | – | – | 69 | 0.04 | 0.9 | – | 0.03 | 18 |

[a]Threshold limit value-short-term exposure limit (TLV-STEL): The maximal concentration to which workers can be exposed for up to 15 minutes continuously without irritation, tissue damage, or narcosis.
[b]Short-term lethal concentration (STLC): The concentration at which lethality may be anticipated after a 10-min exposure.
[c]Threshold limit value ceiling (TLV-C): The concentration that should not be exceeded even instantaneously.
ND: Not detected.
NA: Not analyzed.
Source: From Ref. 12.

In these studies, which have been limited in number, samples of
fire atmospheres were obtained by firefighters equipped with portable
collection devices and were subsequently analyzed in the laboratory.
The most recent and extensive studies were conducted by the Harvard
School of Public Health in 1979 (26), the Southwest Research Institute
(SwRI) in 1981 (27), and the Southwestern Institute of Forensic
Sciences in 1985 (28). In the Harvard study, firefighters from the
Boston Fire Department collected 275 smoke samples from nearly 200
fires in multistory dwellings. The samples were analyzed for CO,
$CO_2$, HCl, HCN, $NO_2$, acrolein, benzene, and total particulate. In
the SwRI study, firefighters from the San Antonio Fire Department
collected 38 samples of smoke from fires involving single-story,
single-family frame dwellings. These samples were analyzed for
particulates and for the same gases as in the Harvard study, except
that $NO_2$ was not analyzed and acetaldehyde and oxygen were analyzed in the SwRI study. In the study by the Southwestern Institute of Forensic Sciences, samples obtained by firefighters of the
Dallas Fire Department were analyzed for CO, HCl, HCN, aldehydes
(formaldehyde and acetaldehyde), total hydrocarbons and various
organic compounds.

Little definitive information as to which toxicants in smoke are
responsible for fire fatalities has been obtained from these analytical
studies fo fire atmospheres. The results (Tables 4 and 5) have been
consistent in demonstrating that CO is the most prevalent toxic combustion product in smoke. Although the concentrations of this gas
in many of the samples were low, some samples did contain hazardous
concentrations. Hydrogen cyanide, HCl, acrolein, acetaldehyde,
and $NO_2$ also were detected in many samples in at least one of the
studies, but mostly at low concentrations. In the Southwestern

Table 5    Analyses of Atmospheres in Dallas Fires

| Gas | Maximum (ppm) | Range (ppm) | Average (ppm) |
|---|---|---|---|
| Carbon monoxide (CO) | 15,000 | 0–15,000 | 1450 |
| Hydrochloric acid (HCl) | 40 | 0–40 | 1.1 |
| Hydrocyanic acid | 40 | 0–40 | 3.7 |
| Aldehydes (formaldehyde and acetaldehyde) | 15 | 1–15 | 5 |
| Total hydrocarbons | 1200 | 500–1200 | 800 |

*Source*: Adapted from Ref. 28.

Institute of Forensic Sciences study, CO was measured at concentrations that exceeded the IDLH and STLC levels in only 10.5% of the fires. The investigators concluded that none of the gases analyzed could be responsible for smoke inhalation fatalities and suggested a possible role of free radical species. However, the results of all of these analytical studies must be interpreted with caution. Inasmuch as a sample collected by a firefighter is representative of the fire atmosphere at only one small point or interval of time, it is possible that any of the gases measured was present at considerably higher or lower concentrations prior to the collection of the sample. The presence of low concentrations of these gases, or even their absence, in isolated samples taken by firefighters after a fire has developed should not be considered evidence that some unknown toxicants are responsible for fire fatalities. In combustion toxicity tests, it is often possible to account for observed toxic effects in animals with analytical data for the major toxicants, but these data must be obtained continuously or at least frequently during combustion of the test material.

## IV. REVIEW OF COMBUSTION TEST METHODS

### A. Laboratory Bioassay Methods

Laboratory test methods for evaluating the acute toxicity of combustion atmospheres generated by materials have been reviewed by Birky (29), the National Academy of Sciences (6), Kaplan et al. (12), and most recently by Alarie (1). In the comprehensive review by Kaplan and co-workers (12), the apparatus and methodology of each of six principal test methods were described in detail, data obtained with each method were presented and the advantages and limitations of each method were discussed. These methods are (1) the DIN method; (2) the Federal Aviation Administration (FAA) method; (3) the National Bureau of Standards (NBS) method; (4) the Radiant Heat Test method; (5) the University of Pittsburgh (PITT) method; and (6) the University of San Francisco (USF) method. In addition to these, several minor methods which have been used in the combustion toxicity testing of materials were reviewed. The reader is referred to this publication for specific details of test methods.

All laboratory test methods which utilize animals for evaluating the toxicity of combustion atmospheres have four primary elements. These are: (1) a device for combustion of the material; (2) a chamber for exposure of test animals; (3) toxicological measurements of animal responses; and (4) chemical analyses of the chamber atmosphere for selected gases and of the blood of test animals for COHb. It is obvious from Table 6, in which the major features of the principal test methods are summarized, that there are marked differences

**Table 6** Summary of Principal Laboratory Test Methods

| Method | Combustion device | Furnace temperature | Air Flow | Quantity of material |
|---|---|---|---|---|
| DIN | Movable annular tube furnace | Fixed, 200–600°C | Dynamic | Fixed, same volume or weight |
| FAA | Tube furnace | Fixed, 625°C[a] | Static, recirculating | Fixed, 0.75 g[a] |
| NBS | Crucible furnace | Fixed, 25°C below and above auto ignition temperature | Static | Varied, 8 g maximum |
| Radiant heat | Radiant heat furnace | Fixed, heat fluxes up to 5 W/cm$^2$ | Static | Surface area varied |
| PITT | Tube furnace | Ramped to 600°C above 0.2% weight loss temperature | Dynamic | Varied |
| USF | Tube furnace | Fixed or ramped, 200–800°C | Static or dynamic | Normally fixed, 1.0 g; varied to obtain LC$_{50}$ |

[a]FAA method modified for fixed or ramped heating, flaming or nonflaming combustion and determination of LC$_{50}$.
[b]Optional 10-minute exposure to 30 mg/L if LC$_{50} \geq 2$ mg/L to determine if material rapidly produces toxic products.
[c]Except for determination of sensory irritation.
[d]Modified to vary quantity of material and measure LC$_{50}$ and LT$_{50}$.
*Source*: From Ref. 12.

| Animals/ no. per test | Exposure mode | Exposure duration | Toxicity measurements | Chemical analyses |
|---|---|---|---|---|
| Rats, at least 5, usually 20 | Head-only or whole body | 30 min | $LC_{50}$ (30 min + 14 day) | $CO$, $CO_2$, $O_2$, selected gases, COHb |
| Rats, 3; at least 3 tests | Whole body | 30 min | $t_i$ and $t_d$[a] | $CO$, $CO_2$, $O_2$, HCN, selected gases |
| Rats, 6 | Head-only | 30 min[b] | $LC_{50}$ (30 min + 14 day) | $CO$, $CO_2$, $O_2$, COHb |
| Rats, 6 | Head-only | 30 min | $LA_{50}$, $t_i$, and gross respiratory tract pathology | $CO$, $CO_2$, $O_2$ |
| Mice, 4 | Head-only | 30 min, from 0.2% weight loss[c] | $RD_{50}$, $LC_{50}$ (30 min + 10 min), SI, asphyxiation range, histopathology, $LT_{50}$ | $CO$, $CO_2$, $O_2$, HCN, selected gases |
| Mice, 4; at least 2 tests | Whole body | 30 min | $t_i$ and $t_d$[d] | $CO$, $O_2$, $CO_2$, selected gases |

among test methods in the combustion device, and conditions, the mode of exposure of test animals and the measurements used for assessment of toxicity.

### 1. Combustion Devices

The most commonly used methods for thermally decomposing materials in laboratory toxicity studies utilize the tube furnace, the crucible ("cup") furnace or the radiant heat device.

*The Tube Furnace.* In methods which utilize the tube furnace, the sample of material in a glass tube or other container is thermally decomposed in a furnace equipped with a temperature controller and the products of combustion are carried to an animal exposure chamber by means of a stream of air passing through the tube. The combustion atmosphere may be cooled and diluted by mixing with an additional air stream prior to entry into the exposure system. The exposure chamber, in conjunction with the tube furnace, may be operated in either the static mode (FAA method), the dynamic mode (DIN, University of Pittsburgh methods), or both modes (USF). Variations of this basic scheme also have been used in combustion toxicity studies. For example, in the DIN 53 436 method, a movable annular electric oven tightly encloses a section of a quartz combustion tube and moves along the tube and test material at a fixed rate, thermally decomposing a constant quantity of the material per unit time (30). Cited as advantages of the tube furnace system by researchers are accurate temperature control, capability for monitoring weight loss, versatility in thermally decomposing materials at a fixed temperature or by ramping the temperature at a fixed rate (4,12). Disadvantages of the tube furnace are the limitation of the system to relatively small samples and the potential loss of smoke components on the walls of the combustion tube.

*The Crucible (Cup) Furnace.* The crucible furnace, also referred to as the cup furnace, basically consists of a quartz beaker, crucible, or other container mounted in a furnace equipped with a temperature controller. In the NBS test method, the cup furnace is interfaced with the bottom of the exposure chamber, which allows the smoke to be transported into the chamber by convection (9). Advantages of the cup furnace are that larger sample sizes can be thermally decomposed in the cup than in the tube furnace, there is less opportunity for loss of smoke components than with the tube furnace and the cup furnace provides close control of decomposition temperature (4,12). Disadvantages are that air flow into the cup appears to be limited, heat transfer to low density samples is inefficient and there is no provision for continuous monitoring of weight loss of the sample.

*Radiant Heat Devices.* Radiant heat devices have been of several different designs, but all of these devices thermally decompose materials by radiating infrared energy to the test materials. In one proposed test method, a radiant heat device is interfaced to the bottom of the NBS chamber in place of the cup furnace (12). Although this method has been used to evaluate the toxicity of combustion products of materials, the test results have not been published in the literature. Cited as advantages of radiant heat devices are that they provide more realistic combustion of composite or multilayer materials than other devices and that they allow materials to be tested in their end-use configuration and the weight loss of materials to be continuously monitored (4,12). Disadvantages of radiant heat devices are that the same heat flux may produce different surface temperatures with different materials because of variations in color and surface temperature, smoke may interfere with transfer of radiant heat energy and there may be a severe shortage of oxygen during combustion.

There has been considerable controversy over which is the most appropriate combustion device for use in evaluating the toxicity of the thermal decompsoition products of materials. Investigators have often suggested that the relevance of the combustion conditions to real fires is the most appropriate criterion for selection of the combustion device (12). Others are of the opinion that the utility of the combustion method depends largely on what the test method is intended to accomplish (4). Although none of the combustion devices can simulate all stages of a real fire or all fire scenarios, proponents of each type can identify similarities of the method to some phases of a fire or to certain fire scenarios. Those advocating use of radiant heat devices point out that the primary mode of heat transfer in a real fire is radiation of infrared energy. There is some recent experimental evidence that the cup furnace and the tube furnace can yield combustion atmospheres similar to those present in certain stages of full-scale laboratory fires. In these experiments, the investigators reported that the relative concentrations of selected smoke components produced by the tube furnace were comparable to those in the later, well-developed stages of the full-scale fire (31). The chemical profile generated by the cup furnace compared well with that in earlier stages. These experiments were limited to the combustion of wood, polypropylene, and polymethylmethacrylate.

In test methods that use the tube furnace for combustion, the furnace can be operated at one or more fixed temperatures or can be ramped through a range of temperatures at a fixed rate. In contrast, the cup furnace is operated only at fixed temperatures. Investigators who advocate ramping of temperature to decompose materials emphasize that this mode of heating simulates the development of many real fires. Decomposition of materials at one or more fixed temperatures, in the opinion of others, allows the evaluation of materials under "worst case" combustion conditions or at selected stages of a real fire. In the opinion of Alarie (1), the fixed temperature and ramped temperature systems of combustion are equally valid for evaluating the potential toxicity of materials.

### 2. Exposure Chambers

The parameters of the exposure chambers used in the various test methods are determined by the mode of exposure (dynamic versus static) (whole body versus head only), the rodent species, the type and location of the combustion device, and the toxicity measurements. There is considerable variation in the size, configuration and construction materials of these chambers. For example, the exposure chamber of the University of Pittsburgh test method is a 2.3 liter glass cylinder, whereas the NBS method uses a 200 liter polymethylmethacrylate (or polycarbonate) rectangular chamber. With most methods, test animals are exposed in the head-only mode to reduce heat stress of the animals and to prevent ingestion of combustion products deposited on the fur of the animals. Additional advantages of this mode are that it facilitates blood sampling of animals and respiratory monitoring during the exposure.

The principal difference in the design and operation of the various chambers is determined by whether the test animals are exposed under static or dynamic conditions. In the static mode of exposure, the combustion products enter the chamber and remain until the exposure is terminated. In the dynamic mode, there is a continuous flow of combustion products from the furnace into and through the chamber. Proponents of each mode can identify similarities of the mode to certain real fire scenarios or to some stages of a real fire. It has been suggested that the static exposure (NBS, USF methods) simulates fire conditions in which there is limited flow-through ventilation so that combustion products accumulate in or near the room of origin (4). In contrast, the dynamic exposure system (DIN, University of Pittsburgh method) simulates fire environments in which victims are exposed to a continuous flow of combustion products. In the DIN fixed-temperature method, the composition of the atmosphere remains constant, whereas, under the ramped heating condition of the University of Pittsburgh method, the composition of smoke to which the animals are exposed changes during the exposure.

### 3. Toxicity Measurements

The toxicity measurements of the various test methods are almost as diverse as the combustion devices and the exposure chambers. These measurements have been made by techniques that range from simple observations of test animals to monitoring of complex physiological and behavioral responses. With most test methods, incapacitation and lethality of either mice or rats have been the most commonly used indices of toxicity. The University of Pittsburgh test method also provides for the evaluation of sensory irritation by measuring the respiratory rate depression of mice (32). In addition, the electrocardiogram of the rat has been monitored during exposure to pure fire gases and smoke, but this physiological measurement has been used to a very limited extent (33).

*Lethality and LC50 Values.* The primary index of toxicity used by almost all combustion toxicity test methods has been lethality. Whereas lethality is recognized by toxicologists as a customary starting point in toxicity evaluations of chemicals, unfortunately, many combustion toxicologists consider the $LC_{50}$ value synonymous with toxicity. With some test methods, lethality has been reported as the ratio of the number of dead animals to the number of exposed animals, but generally a concentration–response curve and an $LC_{50}$ value have been obtained. The $LC_{50}$, in classical inhalation toxicology, is defined as the concentration of gas or vapor that results in death of 50% of the test animals. Because smoke consists of a mixture of particulates and gases, the percentage of animals responding should be related to the concentration of the smoke mixture rather than to the concentration of any single gas in deriving the $LC_{50}$ value. This concentration can be calculated by relating the weight loss of the material to the volume of the exposure chamber in a static system or to the total airflow through a dynamic system. In practice, however, investigators using the cup furnace in the NBS method (static mode), generally report the $LC_{50}$ value as the ratio of the quantity of material that kills 50% of the animals (the sample charge) to the chamber volume. With the tube furnace used in the dynamic mode, the University of Pittsburgh method reports the $LC_{50}$ value as the quantity of material that kills 50% of the animals whereas, in the DIN method, the weight loss of the material and air dilutions are used in deriving an $LC_{50}$ value. Because of these differences among test methods, it is not often possible to compare $LC_{50}$ values obtained with different methods unless the reported data are expressed on a common basis.

Time to lethality also is considered an important toxicity index of combustion atmospheres because survival and escape from a fire environment are critically dependent on the rapidity of the lethal effects of the fire environment (4). A number of investigators have conducted combustion toxicity studies in which animals were exposed to combustion atmospheres until lethality (or some other effect) occurred in all animals. The average times to lethality caused by smoke generated by different materials have been used to compare and rank materials (34,35). This approach has been criticized by Alarie (1) who considers the use of the average time to death of all exposed animals invalid as a measure of toxicity. However, Alarie and his co-workers (3) have used time to death in conjunction with $LC_{50}$ values to compare the toxicity of combustion atmospheres generated by different materials. The investigators proposed a system for classifying the toxicity of materials (when combusted) in comparison to Douglas fir on the basis of their $LC_{50}$ and $LT_{50}$ values. The $LT_{50}$

value is defined as the time at which 50% of the animals die at the LC50 sample weight, or the weight nearest above it. The LC50 and LT50 values of a variety of materials are listed in Table 7 and the classification of most of these materials in comparison to Douglas fir is shown in Figure 1.

Incapacitation. The key to survival in a fire is rapid escape from the fire environment. Delay or prevention of escape leads to further inhalation of toxic smoke and continued exposure to other hazards, and possible subsequent injury or even death. The potential impairment by smoke of mental and motor functions that are necessary for escape was recognized by the National Academy of Sciences in its recommendation that combustion toxicity test methods should include measurements of the loss of capacity to escape and of other behavioral effects (6). A variety of behavioral and physiological methods were developed and/or applied to combustion toxicity tests during the 1970s in order to obtain a measure of the potential of smoke generated by a material to incapacitate an animal. These methods have been reviewed in detail by Kaplan and Hartzell (36) and by Clarke et al. (4).

Behavioral methods that have been used to measure the incapacitating effects of gases and/or smoke include leg flexion shock avoidance response (37), the motor-driven activity wheel (34), the pole-climb conditioned avoidance/escape response (38), the rotarod (39), and the shuttlebox (40,41). In addition, incapacitation of animals has been evaluated by physiological and observational techniques. Of the behavioral methods, the leg flexion shock avoidance response has been used most widely and has the largest data base. It is the only method that allows measurement of incapacitation in animals exposed in the head-only mode and location of the behavioral apparatus outside of the exposure chamber. For this method, the rat is positioned in a tubular restrainer such that an electric shock (approximately 4.5 ma) is delivered to one hind leg upon contact with a metal platform suspended below the leg. Approximately 10–15 minutes of training are required for the rat to learn to avoid the shock by raising its leg above the metal platform. When the animal is unable to avoid the shock during an exposure, incapacitation is deemed to have occurred. As many as 6 rats have been instrumented to measure incapacitation in smoke toxicity tests.

The second most widely used method is the motor-driven exercise wheel (tumble cage). Although the size and configuration of the equipment vary, the apparatus basically consists of a wire-mesh cage in the form of a wheel which is rotated at a slow constant speed by an electric motor. The animal instinctively moves in a direction counter to that of wheel rotation in an attempt to remain upright in the cage. When the animal is no longer capable of maintaining its movement and begins to slide or tumble as the cage is rotated, incapacitation is considered to have occurred.

Table 7   LC$_{50}$ and LT$_{50}$ Values and Classification of Materials

| Abbreviation | Sample name—description | LC$_{50}$ (g) | LT$_{50}$ (min) | LCt$_{50}$ (g min) | Class[a] |
|---|---|---|---|---|---|
| PRC materials[b] | | | | | |
| GM 21 | Flexible polyurethane foam | 12.9 | 13 | 168 | B |
| GM 23 | Same as GM 21, with fire retardant | 10.4 | 18 | 187 | B |
| GM 25 | High resilience, flexible polyurethane foam | 8.3 | 19 | 158 | B |
| GM 27 | Same as GM 25, with fire retardant | 14.4 | 15 | 216 | B |
| GM 29 | Rigid polyurethane foam | 10.4 | 28 | 291 | B |
| GM 31 | Same as GM 29, with fire retardant | 8.2 | 23 | 189 | B |
| GM 35 | Rigid polyurethane foam, fluorocarbon blown | 7.5 | 17 | 128 | B |
| GM 37 | Same ad GM 35, CO$_2$ blown | 8.0 | 15 | 120 | B |
| GM 41 | Rigid isocyanurate foam | 6.4 | 18 | 115 | B |
| GM 43 | Same as GM 41, contains some polyurethane | 6.1 | 16 | 98 | B |
| GM 47 | Polystyrene expanded | 5.8 | 11 | 64 | B |
| GM 49 | Same as GM 47, with fire retardant | 10.0 | 9 | 90 | B |
| GM 57 | Phenol formaldehyde—phenol resin, expanded with blowing agent | 6.3 | 20 | 126 | B |
| Non-PRC materials | | | | | |
| PTFE | Polytetrafluoroethylene resin | 0.64 | 8 | 5 | C |
| PVC | Polyvinylchloride (92% homopolymer) | 7.0 | 10 | 70 | B |

**Table 7** (continued)

| Abbreviation | Sample name—description | LC50 (g) | LT50 (min) | LCt50 (g min) | Class[a] |
|---|---|---|---|---|---|
| PVC-CN | Polyvinylchloride (92% homopolymer + 5% zinc ferrocyanide) | 2.3 | 7 | 16 | C |
| PCP-CN | Polychloroprene (92% homopolymer + 5% zinc ferrocyanide) | 2.5 | 6 | 15 | C |
| ABS-3 | Standard acrylonitrile/butadiene/styrene | 6.3 | 9 | 57 | B |
| Mod. | Modacrylic | 4.9 | 18 | 88 | B |
| Wool | Wool fibers—undyed | 3.0 | 27 | 81 | B |
| UF | Urea formaldehyde foam | 2.5 | 22 | 55 | B |
| Cellulose | Blowing type cellulose fiber insulation | 11.9 | 21 | 250 | B |
| D. Fir | Douglas fir | 63.8 | 22 | 1404 | A |
| Fiberglas | Fiberglas building insulation, 3.5 in. thick with paper and vapor barrier | 35.7 | 25 | 893 | A |
| P.E.I | Polyester resin—commercial acrylic modified unsaturated | 34.8 | 14 | 487 | B |
| P.E.II | Polyester resin—experimental acrylic modified unsaturated | 57.4 | 18 | 1033 | A |
| H.P.E. | Polyester resin—styrenated halogen modified | 14.4 | 16 | 230 | B |
| SPF wood | Compressed spruce, pine, fir slab | 48.7 | 19 | 925 | A |

[a]From Figure 1.
[b]Obtained from the Product Research Committee (PRC) sample bank at the National Bureal of Standards.
*Source:* From Ref. 3.

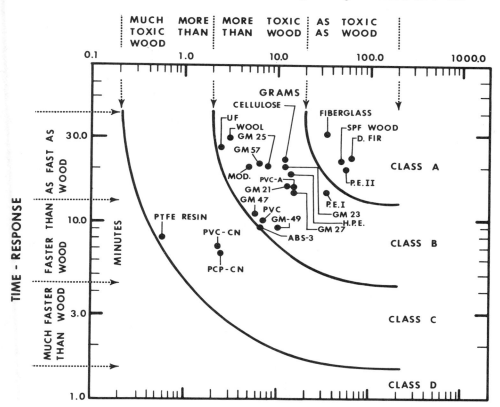

**Figure 1**   Classification of materials by LC₅₀ and LT₅₀ values. Each point represents the amount of material (gram on the X axis) which produced sufficient smoke to kill 50% of the animals (LC₅₀) and the time (minutes on the Y axis) required to kill 50% of the animals (LT₅₀) using that amount of material. Reading the graph vertically each material is classified in terms of potency while each material is classified in terms of onset of action by reading horizontally. To combine both, parallel quadrants separate class A, B, C, and D. (See Table 7 for identification of material abbreviations.) (From Ref. 3.)

Behavioral methods have been used to study the incapacitating effects of pure gases, including CO, HCN, HCl, and acrolein, as well as the effects of combustion atmospheres produced by materials. With a few of these methods, concentration–response curves, $IC_{50}$ values (the concentration that incapacitates 50% of the exposed animals), and concentration–time curves have been derived for incapacitation by some of the major toxicants. These data are useful in establishing whether a particular toxicant in a combustion atmosphere is responsible for the incapacitating effects of the atmosphere. In many studies, however, behavioral methods have been used to obtain time-to-incapacitation data for the smoke generated by a fixed quantity of a material and to compare and rank materials by incapacitation times. It is doubtful whether these data, without additional toxicity information, serve any meaningful purpose.

In order to evaluate the sensitivities of the various behavioral methods for measuring the incapacitating effects of CO and HCN, Kaplan and Hartzell (36) utilized data from available literature studies of incapacitation by these gases in rodents and nonhuman primates. Because of the variability in the form of reported data, concentration-time (Ct) products were calculated from reported concentrations and exposure times necessary for incapacitation in order to establish a common basis for comparison. The data (Table 8) indicate that the sensitivites of most of the methods used to assess incapacitation of rats by CO are comparable and that incapacitation generally occurs after an exposure intensity or magnitude of approximately 30,000 to 40,000 ppm-minutes. This exposure intensity for incapacitation is approximately one-third of the CO Ct product necessary to produce lethality in rats (36). These investigators also reported some Ct products associated with incapacitation by HCN but the data were too limited and variable to compare the sensitivities of the behavioral methods.

Although behavioral methods are sensitive to the incapacitating effects of hypoxia-producing agents, this methodology appears to have limited utility in evaluating the incapacitating effects of irritant gases. Data obtained from experiments in which rats were exposed to either pure HCl or acrolein show that rats are extremely tolerant to irritant gases. When concentrations of these gases are sufficiently high to incapacitate animals, the animals die within a short time afterward (41,42). Even those concentrations which are not high enough to incapacitate rats may cause a high incidence of mortalities during the usual 14-day postexposure period. This tolerance of rodents to irritant gases may be a serious limitation to the use of this animal model in combustion toxicity tests.

Physiological indices that have been used to assess the incapacitating effects of gases and/or combustion atmospheres include the depression of respiratory rate and the onset of cardiac arrhythmias.

Table 8    Exposure Intensity (Ct Product) of CO
Associated with Incapacitation

| Subject/method | CO Ct[a]<br>ppm-min |
|---|---|
| Baboons (SwRI) | 35,000 (active) |
| Monkeys (Huntingdon) | 25,000 (active)<br>50,000 (restrained) |
| Rats[b] | |
|   Leg flexion (Utah) | 30,000–40,000 |
|   (SwRI) | 30,000–40,000 |
| Activity wheel (FAA) | 37,000 |
|   (Michigan) | 30,750 |
|   (McDonnell Douglas) | 22,000–36,000 |
| Pole-climb avoidance (SRI) | 48,000 |
| Rotarod (Michigan) | 31,500 |
|   (SwRI) | 36,000–44,000 |
| Shuttlebox (Michigan) | 41,000–53,000 |
|   (SwRI) | 33,900 |

[a]Ct products are presented as single values, rather
than ranges, when data for only one concentration
or time were available or an EC50 was reported.
[b]Animals are active in all methods except leg
flexion which requires animals to be restrained.
*Source:*  Adapted from Ref. 36.

Most of the studies of the effects of gases and smoke on the inhibition of respiration have been conducted at the University of
Pittsburgh and are reviewed in the next section on sensory irritation.  In the only study of the utility of cardiac arrhythmias to
assess incapacitation, Gaume and others (43) reported that arrhythmias occurred slightly prior to incapacitation of rats by CO in an
activity wheel.  In the University of San Francisco test method,
incapacitation has been assessed by observation of the loss of equilibrium (staggering), prostration, convulsions, or collapse (44).
However, observational techniques are highly subjective and, in
general, are less desirable than other methods.

    *Sensory Irritation.*  Sensory irritants are prevalent in combustion
atmospheres and may play a significant role in fire fatalities attributed

to smoke inhalation. These chemicals irritate the eyes, causing pain, blinking, and lachrimation, which may interfere with vision. They also affect the upper respiratory tract, causing a reflex inhibition of respiratory rate and a burning sensation in the nose, mouth, and throat. Severe irritation may result in inflammation, swelling of the larynx and trachea, laryngeal spasms, and bronchoconstriction (45). It is quite possible that the effects of sensory irritants delay the escape of individuals from the fire environment and even incapacitate them. Continued inhalation of CO would result in high blood COHb levels so that death would be attributed by postmortem examination to CO.

The only test method that provides a direct measurement of sensory irritation of combustion atmospheres is the University of Pittsburgh method (46). The measurement is based on the reflex inhibition of respiratory rate caused by stimulation of trigeminal nerve endings in the nasal mucosa. Respiratory rate is monitored in four mice in body plethysmographs during exposure and a concentration-response relationship for respiratory depression and an $RD_{50}$ value are determined by varying the quantity of material decomposed in successive experiments. The $RD_{50}$ is defined as the quantity of material that produces a 50% decrease in respiratory rate. It has been claimed that the $RD_{50}$ concentration in mice is equivalent to an intolerable level of sensory irritation for humans and will incapacitate a human within 3-5 minutes (32,47,48). Although data obtained in human volunteers exposed to the smoke from Red Oak are not consistent with this claim (49), it is possible that some factor of the $RD_{50}$ value may be useful in predicting the incapacitating concentration of gases and smoke in humans. For example, Alarie (50) correlated $RD_{50}$ values with ACGIH TLV-TWA values for 25 chemicals and proposed that the 0.03 $RD_{50}$ value may be useful in establishing TLV-TWA values for airborne chemicals.

*Other Toxicity Indices.* In later studies by Alarie and his co-workers (3,32,51), the University of Pittsburgh test method was modified and expanded to provide a more comprehensive evaluation of the toxicity of combustion atmospheres. In addition to sensory irritation, measurements of stress, lethality, asphyxiation, and histo-pathological changes were included in the test protocol. According to Alarie and his co-workers (3,32), sensory irritation evokes a series of physiological adjustments, including changes in heart rate, blood pressure, and blood vessel size, to compensate for the reduced breathing rate and apneic periods. Therefore, a stress index (SI), calculated from the rate of onset and recovery of the respiratory effect and the degree of respiratory depression, was used as an index of the stress of a combustion atmosphere. A concentration-response relationship was established for physiological stress and a SI 100 value (the sample size associated with a stress value of 100) was derived. The SI 100, RD$_{50}$, and LC$_{50}$ values of combustion atmospheres produced by various materials (Table 9) were used to classify materials in comparison to Douglas fir (3). Asphyxiant effects were evaluated from the characteristic alterations of the respiratory pattern of the animal as well as by the absence of body movements. An asphyxiant range (i.e., the sample weight range in which asphyxiation was observed) was reported as an index of toxicity. Finally, histopathological examinations were made of the major organs of exposed animals sacrificed at 24 hours following exposure. Numerical ratings were used to indicate the severity of damage to the upper respiratory tract and, in other organs, the absence or presence of lesions was noted.

## B. Analytical Methods

Although biological approaches have been predominant, a few investigators have proposed chemical or analytical approaches to evaluate the toxicity of combustion atmospheres. Sumi and Tsuchiya (52), for example, defined a "toxicity" factor, $t = C/C_f$, for each gaseous component of smoke, where C is the concentration of the gas in smoke and $C_f$ is the concentration that is fatal to humans within 30 minutes. The total toxicity of a combustion atmosphere is obtained by summation of the t factors for the gases in the atmosphere. Tsuchiya (53) subsequently expanded on this concept in developing a "dynamic toxicity factor," TD, which takes into account the rate of production of toxic gases per unit surface area of the material as well as the toxicities of the gases. An analytical approach also was developed by Spurgeon (54) who correlated the times to incapacitation of rats with chemical analyses of the combustion atmospheres of 75 aircraft interior materials. A mathematical expression was developed for calcualtion of incapacitation time based on the yield of nine combustion gases, CO, HCN, H$_2$S, NO$_2$, SO$_2$, HCl, CH$_2$O, HB$_r$, and HF.

All methods based solely on chemical analyses have the same major deficiency, which is that the prediction of potential toxicity from chemical analyses for common toxicants is not always reliable. Two examples of materials which produce combustion atmospheres whose toxic effects are not predictable from analyses of the atmospheres are Teflon 100 (fluorinated ethylene/fluorinated propylene) and Tefzel 200 (ethylene-tetrafluoroethylene). In a study of the combustion toxicity of halogenated polymers, Kaplan and others (55) reported that insufficient quantities of CO, HF, and COF$_2$ were produced by these two materials to account for the observed toxicity. Even when the major toxicants in a combustion atmosphere can be identified, the prediction of toxicity from these analyses may be speculative because of possible biological interactions between these

Table 9  Classification of Thermal Decomposition Products from Tested Materials[a] in Comparison to Wood[b]

| Toxicity indices measured as | Classification | | | |
|---|---|---|---|---|
| | Much more toxic than wood | More toxic than wood | Similar to wood | Less toxic than wood |
| Acute mortality (LC50)[c] | LC50 = 0.2–2 g PTFE | LC50 = 2–20 g All materials except PTFE and wood | LC50 = 20–200 g Fiberglass | LC50 > 200 g None found |
| Physiological stress (SI100) | SI100 = 0.012–0.12 g None found | SI100 = 0.12–1.2 g GM 29, GM 31, GM 35, GM 37, GM 41, GM 43, GM 57, UF, PVC-A | SI100 = 1.2–12 g GM 21, GM 23, GM 25, GM 27, GM 47, wood | SI100 12 g GM 49 |
| Sensory irritation (RD50) | RD50 = 0.1–1 mg None found | RD50 = 1–10 mg GM 21, GM 23, GM 25, GM 27 | RD50 = 10–100 mg GM 31, GM 35, GM 39, UF, PTFE, PVC-A | RD50 > 100 mg GM 29, GM 41 |

[a]Materials are identified in Table 7.
[b]Wood taken as Douglas fir.
[c]Calculated on the basis of deaths recorded during the 30-minute exposure and 10 minutes of recovery.
Source: Adapted from Ref. 3.

chemicals. Therefore, the use of animals is necessary in combustion toxicity tests of materials to detect the presence not only of unusual or uncommon toxicants but also of biological interactions between common gases.

## V. METHODS FOR EVALUATING THE BIOLOGICAL HAZARDS OF COMBUSTION PRODUCTS

### A. Objective and Requirements of Evaluation Methods

The primary objective of any method for evaluating the biological or toxicological hazards of exposure to a chemical is the determination of the chemical's potential to cause adverse effects in humans. In the case of chemicals present in the industrial and occupational environments, data from epidemiological studies and industrial and occupational human exposures often are sufficient for this assessment. When such data are not available, toxicological studies in which animals are exposed to the chemical of concern must be conducted. These studies must identify the nature of the toxic effects, the target organs affected and the mechanism of action of the chemical to enable a valid extrapolation to humans. This same requirement is applicable to methods for evaluating the biological hazards of combustion atmospheres produced by thermal decomposition of materials.

### B. Screening Versus Evaluating

In recent years, there has been considerable controversy among the fire science community over the need for a standardized "toxicity screening test." In addition, proponents of a screening test have different views regarding what the test should accomplish. Some are of the opinion that the purpose of the test should be to identify those materials that generate "highly" or "unusually" toxic combustion atmospheres. Although the criterion for unusual toxicity is not clearly defined, there is universal agreement that smoke produced by polytetrafluoroethylene (PTFE) is representative of that category since $LC_{50}$ values for all other materials tested to date are at least an order of magnitude greater than that of PTFE smoke. Proponents of the "unusually toxic" screening test generally claim that these other materials should "pass" the test because none of their $LC_{50}$ values differ by more than a factor of 10. In view of the fact that a single experiment with any of the available test methods is capable of differentiating between the toxic potency of PTFE smoke and that of other materials, the adoption of this type of toxicity screening test would have minimum economic impact on manufacturers and consumers. The test, however, would not reduce the incidence of fire fatalities or serve any other useful purpose.

Other advocates of a screening test insist that a screening test
must yield numbers that can be assigned to materials on the basis
of the "toxicity" of their combustion atmospheres. These individuals argue that, because numbers are used to rate certain flammability
properties of materials, a comparable numbering system can be established for the toxicity of combustion products for use by code
officials and regulatory agencies. The $LC_{50}$ values required under
proposed Article 15 of New York State's Uniform Fire Prevention and
Building Code (11) is an example of a numbering system, although
the purpose is to make the data available to the public rather than
for regulatory action. The assignment of numbers to materials is
strongly opposed by plastics manufacturers, who contend, and right-
fully so, that numbers imply differences in toxicity even though
these differences often are not of any significance. In addition,
these numbers may be misinterpreted by individuals. To avoid this
possible misinterpretation, some advocates of a screening test propose
that materials be separated into classes or categories on the basis
of the $LC_{50}$ values of their combustion atmospheres. With this system, minor differences in $LC_{50}$ values would not be apparent.

Regardless of whether $LC_{50}$ values or classes of toxic potency
are used, any "toxicity screening test" based solely on the lethality
of rodents has limited relevance and utility. This type of test only
provides a measure of the toxic potency of the combustion atmosphere of a material in rodents. It does not necessarily provide a
measure of the toxic potency to humans nor does it evaluate the potential of the atmosphere to cause adverse effects in humans. One
of the major deficiencies of a screening test based on lethality is its
failure to take into account the nature and rapidity of the toxic
effects of a combustion atmosphere and the mechanism of action of
the toxicants. For example, it is evident that the toxicity and potential hazard of the combustion atmospheres of the five materials
shown in Table 10 differ considerably although their $LC_{50}$ values are
very similar. The toxic hazard of a combustion atmosphere containing HCN and CO is certainly not the same as one containing primarily
CO even though the two atmospheres have comparable $LC_{50}$ values.
Similarly, the toxicity and hazard to humans of an atmosphere that is
highly irritating and causes postexposure deaths in rodents are not the
same as one in which CO is the major toxicant, despite similar lethal
potencies in rodents. Another major deficiency in the use of a screening test based on toxic potency is that the lethality of rodents does not
appear to be a suitable toxicity index for evaluating the effects of irritant gases in humans. Recent studies of the effects of HCl in primates
have shown that the respiratory response of rodents to sensory irritants is markedly different than that of primates and could lead to an
inaccurate evaluation of the potential of these gases to, particularly
when hypoxia-producing gases also are present, cause injury and
death in humans (57).

Table 10  LC$_{50}$ Values, Toxic Effects, and Primary Toxicants of Combustion Atmospheres Generated by Materials[a]

| Material | Combustion mode | LC$_{50}$ (mg/L) | Toxic effects | Analytical data | Primary toxicants |
|---|---|---|---|---|---|
| Douglas fir | Flaming | 37.6 | Lethalities during exposure | High concentrations of CO, high COHb levels at death | CO |
| Douglas fir | Nonflaming | 32.8 | Most lethalities post-exposure, some during exposure | High concentrations of CO, high COHb levels in exposure lethalities | CO, irritants |
| Kynar | Flaming | 27.3 | All postexposure lethalities | High concentrations HF, low concentrations of HCl, CO, COF$_2$ | HF |
| Tefzel 200 | Flaming | 30.2 | Most lethalities during exposure, some postexposure | Low concentrations of HF, HCl, CO, COF$_2$ | Unknown |
| Acrylic product | Nonflaming | 36.8 | Lethalities during exposure | High concentrations of HCN, medium concentrations of CO | HCN, CO |

[a]NBS test method used for all materials.
*Source:* From Refs. 55 and 56.

## C. Approach For Evaluating the Toxicity of Combustion Atmospheres

The recommended approach for evaluating the potential of combustion atmospheres to cause adverse effects in humans consists of two separate phases. In the first phase, the toxicity of an atmosphere is characterized by animal experimentation and correlated with analytical data in an attempt to identify the major toxicants. When the identities of the major toxicants are established, available human data for these gases can be utilized in the second phase to evaluate the toxicological hazard of the combustion atmosphere. Considerable experience has shown that, in the case of many combustion atmospheres, the integration of toxicological and analytical data can establish the identity of the causative species, particularly when CO and/or HCN are the major toxicants. In addition, sufficient animal data have been obtained in studies with HCl and HF to establish whether these gases were responsible for or contributed to the observed toxicity. In the event the toxic effects of a combustion atmosphere are not consistent with the analytical findings, further analytical work will be required to identify the causative species.

The major limitation to this two-phased approach is that considerable analytical effort may be required to establish the identity of the major toxicants of some combustion atmospheres. In most cases, these toxicants will be irritant gases, perhaps various aldehydes, organic acids, $NO_2$, nitriles, or isocyanates, which cause irritation of the eyes and respiratory tract and postexposure deaths in rodents. If the identity of these gases can be established, available human data often are sufficient to enable an assessment of the hazards of the combustion atmosphere to humans. In the event major toxicants are not identified, the results of animal experimentation should be used with caution in evaluating the toxic hazard of these atmospheres to humans. Another limitation to this or any approach is our limited knowledge of the combined effects of hypoxia-producing gases, such as CO and HCN, or of irritant and hypoxia-producing gases in humans. Although biological interaction of some combustion gases have been investigated in rodents, results of recent studies with nonhuman primates indicate that investigation of the combined effects of combustion gases in primate species is warranted.

## D. Applicable Concepts

### 1. Concentration-Time Product

In a classical inhalation toxicity study of a gas or vapor, animals generally are exposed to a constant concentration of the chemical for a specified period of time. The exposure is described in terms of the concentration and the time of exposure. In contrast, in combustion toxicity experiments, animals are exposed to a mixture of gases, the concentrations of which are not constant during the usual 30-minute exposure period because these gases are evolved at different rates. It is possible to describe the intensity or magnitude of exposure to the major components of the smoke in terms of a concentration-time product (Ct), provided that these gases are continuously monitored or that frequent samples are taken and analyzed. The concentration-time product of a gas is equal to the integrated area under the concentration-time curve and may be expressed in units of ppm-minutes, mg/L·min, or $mg/m^3$·min. A concentration-time curve for CO and for HF obtained during a nonflaming combustion toxicity test of Kynar is shown in Figure 2. It also is possible to describe the intensity of exposure to the total combustion atmosphere, rather than to individual gases, in terms of a Ct product calculated from the weight loss of the material with time (2).

As pointed out by MacFarland (58), the Ct product cannot be the dose of the toxicant because the dose is an amount or quantity of material. However, it is a measure of the magnitude or intensity of the exposure conditions and does bear some proportionality to the dose. As either the concentration of the gas or the time of exposure increases, the quantity of material that enters the respiratory tract increases (assuming ventilation does not decrease) and, therefore, the dose increases.

### 2. Haber's Rule

Haber's rule states that the Ct product necessary to elicit a fixed response is constant, in other words, Ct = k (58). Thus, according to the rule, if $C_1t_1$ causes 50% mortality, $C_2t_2$ will also result in death of half of the exposed animals, provided $C_2t_2 = C_1t_1$. When tested experimentally, the rule has been found to hold reasonably well for a limited range over which C or t is varied. The range over which the Ct product is constant occurs in the curved portion of the hyperbolic concentration-time curve for a response (Fig. 3). Deviations from the rule occur with both high and low concentrations of a gas (and short and long exposure times) so that the ends of the hyperbola become asymptotic. Despite these deviations, Ct products have utility in evaluating whether major toxicants, such as CO, HCN, and HCl, are responsible for certain observed effects (incapacitation and lethality) of combustion atmospheres. For these evaluations, the Ct products necessary to produce these effects must be determined in pure gas experiments.

### E. Methodology

#### 1. Recommended Test Method

All of the combustion toxicity test methods have advantages and limitations, which have been reviewed in detail by Kaplan, et al. (12)

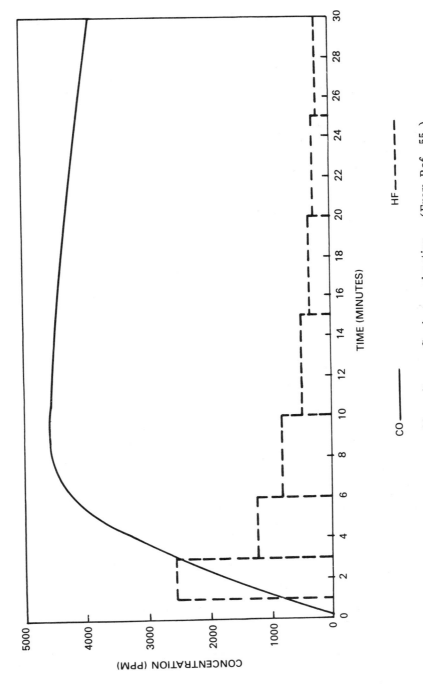

**Figure 2** Gas evolution from Kynar, 23 mg/L, nonflaming combustion. (From Ref. 55.)

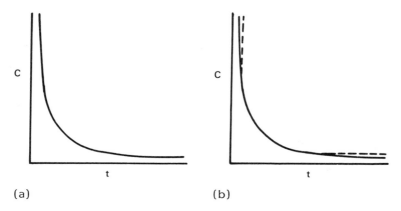

(a)                              (b)

Figure 3   Haber's rule: (a) theoretical, (b) showing the deviations usually encountered. (From Ref. 58.)

and by Clarke and others (4). The University of Pittsburgh and NBS test methods have considerable data bases and, in the opinion of the author, are the methods of choice for evaluating the toxicological hazards of combustion atmospheres. Because considerably more pure gas data and analytical results have been reported with the NBS method, this method, with modifications, is recommended as the test method for the approach designated in this chapter. The NBS test method is described in detail in NBSIR 82-2532, "Further Development of a Test Method for the Assessment of the Acute Inhalation Toxicity of Combustion Products" (9). Recommended modifications to the method include measurements of incapacitation and of sensory irritation, histopathological examination of animals, and additional chemical analyses.

*Combustion.* The conductive type furnace (Fig. 4) described by Potts and Lederer is utilized as the combustion device. Nonflaming combustion experiments are conducted at 25°C below the predetermined autoignition temperature; flaming combustion experiments are conducted at 25°C above this temperature, except when higher temperatures may be necessary to maintain flaming combustion. The autoignition temperature of a test material is established in a series of experimental trials without animals, by decreasing or increasing the furnace temperature from an initial estimated starting temperature, with an upper limit of 800°C.

*Exposure Chamber.* Test animals are exposed to combustion atmospheres in a nominal 200-L exposure chamber (Fig. 5) with interior dimensions of 122 × 36 × 46 cm and constructed of clear polymethylmethacrylate or polycarbonate. Animal ports constructed

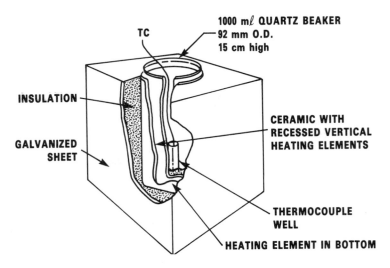

**Figure 4** Cutaway drawing of the pyrolysis/combustion furnace. (From Ref. 9.)

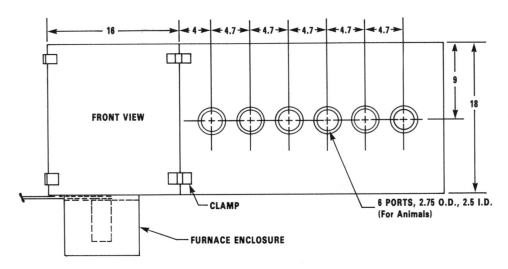

**Figure 5** Animal exposure chamber in NBS test method. (From Ref. 9.)

of polymethylmethacrylate tubing permit exposure of 6 rats in the head-only mode to the smoke generated within the chamber.

*Animal Exposures.* Adult male Sprague-Dawley rats, weighing 250–350 g, are used to characterize the toxicity of the combustion atmospheres generated by a material. Prior to the start of each experiment, 6 animals are weighed and placed in tubular aluminum restrainers which are inserted into the chamber. The experiment is initiated with the addition of a weighed sample of the test material into the tared quartz beaker after equilibration of the selected furnace temperature. In each experiment, 6 animals are exposed to the combustion atmosphere for a total of 30 minutes. At least five experiments are conducted with varying quantities of the material in both the flaming and nonflaming combustion modes in order to derive concentration-response curves and LC$_{50}$ values. The sample weight used in an experiment is related to the chamber volume and expressed as the sample "charge" or sample concentration in mg/liter units.

*Toxicity Measurements. Incapacitation.* Five of the six animals are used for measurement of incapacitation by the leg flexion shock avoidance response. Each animal's responses and time of responses are recorded on a strip chart.

*Lethality.* The five test animals in which incapacitation is measured are observed for lethality during exposure and for 14 days postexposure. Animals that expire during exposure or the first hour postexposure are considered exposure lethalities; those that expire after the first postexposure hour are considered postexposure lethalities. The concentration-response relationship and slope are established for lethality and an LC$_{50}$ value with confidence limits (30-min exposure and 14-days postexposure) are derived by the probit method of Finney (60) or by another appropriate statistical method.

*Blood COHb Analyses.* The sixth animal is used to obtain a measure of the percent COHb saturation at the median time of incapacitation. Immediately after incapacitation of the third of the five test animals, the sixth animal is removed and a blood sample is obtained by intraorbital venous puncture. In the event none of the animals are incapacitated, a blood sample is obtained from the sixth animal at the end of the exposure. Blood samples also are obtained by cardiac puncture from all animals that expire during exposure.

*Toxic Signs and Pathology.* Animals that survive the exposure are observed for toxic signs such as respiratory abnormalities, ataxia, and loss of righting reflex during the first hour postexposure and periodically for 14 days. Animal body weights are recorded preexposure and on days 1, 7, and 14 postexposure for comparison with body weight growth patterns of control animals. Animals that die during exposure or postexposure are necropsied and major organs (respiratory tract, heart, kidneys, liver, and spleen) are examined grossly and by light microscopy.

*Combustion Atmosphere Analyses.* Analyses of the combustion atmosphere during exposure are made continuously for $O_2$, $CO_2$, and CO, and either continuously or at frequent intervals for other major toxicants to enable calculation of Ct products for these toxicants. Analyses are performed for HCN, HCl, and HF as warranted by the chemical structure of the material. Analyses for additional compounds, including aldehydes, nitriles and isocyanates, may be required to establish the identity of major toxicants in the combustion atmospheres generated by some materials.

*Sensory Irritation.* Although the measurement of sensory irritation is not specified in the NBS test protocol, sensory irritation is, in the opinion of the author, an important toxicity parameter of combustion atmospheres. Relatively simple modifications to the NBS exposure chamber to allow the monitoring of respiratory response of rats to gases and combustion atmospheres have been described by Hartzell and others (61). By conducting a series of experiments with different quantities of a material, a concentration-response relationship for respiratory depression and an $RD_{50}$ value may be derived. These experiments generally require smaller quantities of materials than for incapacitation and lethality of animals and cannot be conducted in conjunction with the experiments in which incapacitation and lethality are measured.

### 2. Toxic Effects of Major Combustion Gases in Rodents

An essential element in evaluating the toxicological hazards of combustion atmospheres is the determination of the major toxicants responsible for the observed toxic effects. Analytical data alone often are insufficient for this determination because gases which are not routinely analyzed for may be the major toxicants. In addition, chemical analyses cannot detect toxic effects that may occur as a result of biological interactions between toxicants. Consequently, analytical data must be correlated with toxicological results to determine whether the common toxicants are the causative species or whether additional analyses for uncommon chemicals are warranted. The determination of whether common toxicants are responsible for the observed toxic effects is based on toxicity data obtained in studies with the pure gases.

*Carbon Monoxide.* There is an extensive data base on the incapacitating and lethal effects of CO in rats for determining whether the observed toxicity of a combustion atmosphere is due solely to CO intoxication (18,36). In a study of CO by Hartzell and others (18), concentration-time curves for incapacitation using leg-flexion shock avoidance (Fig. 6) and for lethality (Fig. 7) were linearized by

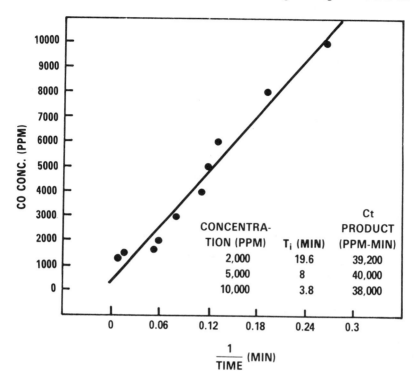

**Figure 6** Concentration-time curve for incapacitation (leg flexion shock avoidance) by CO and Ct products associated with incapacitation. (Adapted from Ref. 18.)

plotting the concentration of CO against the reciprocal of the time to incapacitation or to death. At CO concentrations of 2000 to 10,000 ppm, the Ct products which incapacitate the rat range from approximately 38,000 to 40,000 ppm-minutes. The Ct products necessary to cause lethality in the rat range from 125,000 to 147,000 ppm-minutes at concentrations of 5000–10,000 ppm and are approximately three times greater than those necessary to incapacitate the rat. As a guide, a Ct product of approximately 35,000 ppm-min or greater may be considered evidence that CO was responsible for incapacitation of the rat by a combustion atmosphere and a Ct product of approximately 100,000 ppm-min is evidence of CO-induced lethality. The blood COHb saturation levels in rats incapacitated by CO generally are 65% or greater and the levels in animals that die from exposure to CO generally exceed 75% (56).

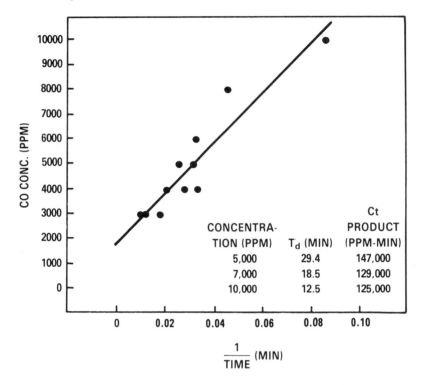

The table within the figure:

| CONCENTRATION (PPM) | $T_d$ (MIN) | Ct PRODUCT (PPM-MIN) |
|---|---|---|
| 5,000 | 29.4 | 147,000 |
| 7,000 | 18.5 | 129,000 |
| 10,000 | 12.5 | 125,000 |

Figure 7   Concentration-time curve for lethality of rats by CO and Ct products associated with lethality. (Adapted from Ref. 18.)

*Carbon Monoxide and Sensory Irritants.* Data from combustion toxicity tests of certain materials have shown that incapacitation and, possibly lethality, of rats have occurred later than expected from the concentration-time curves for CO. Although incapacitation or death appeared to have been delayed, blood COHb saturation levels were consistent with a CO-induced effect, that is, >65% COHb at incapacitation and >75% COHb at death. In such tests, there generally is clinical evidence of the presence of sensory irritants, including severe irritation of the eyes, respiratory abnormalities, severe weight loss, and postexposure lethalities. Because sensory irritants cause a reflex inhibition of respiratory rate in rodents, these delayed effects of CO could be due to a decreased rate of loading of CO. This "protective" inhibition of respiration by irritants in rats is not observed in nonhuman primates which respond to high concentrations of irritant gases with a brief and transient holding of the breath followed by an increase in respiratory rate (57).

The effect of HCl and CO intoxication of rats has been investigated in a recent study by Hartzell and others (61). These investigators reported that HCl caused decreases in respiratory rate, ranging from a 35% decrease at 200 ppm to a 67% decrease at 1500 ppm. In experiments in which rats were exposed to 1000 ppm of HCl in combination with various concentrations of CO, CO (3000–5000 ppm) Ct products were approximately 65,000 ppm-minutes for incapacitation or almost 75% greater than the Ct product necessary for incapacitation by CO alone. Thus, times to incapacitation from exposure to 3000–5000 ppm of CO were almost doubled in the presence of 1000 ppm of HCl. Although the data were somewhat erratic, 2500 ppm HCl did not cause a greater increase in time to incapacitation than 1000 ppm of HCl. Times to lethality caused by CO also appeared to be increased somewhat by the presence of 1000 ppm or 2500 ppm of HCl, but not as much as times to incapacitation. These data indicate that, in combustion toxicity tests of materials, the presence of irritants may "protect" rodents from the incapacitating or lethal effects of CO during the 30-min exposure and lead to an artificial increase in the $IC_{50}$ or $LC_{50}$ value of the material. This is another reason why screening tests based on toxic potency of combustion atmospheres in rodents may yield invalid information for evaluating toxic hazard in humans.

*Hydrogen Cyanide.* Although the incapacitating and lethal effects of HCN have not been studied as much as those of CO, there is an adequate data base to evaluate whether HCN is a major toxicant of a combustion atmosphere. It is evident from the linearized concentration-time curve for incapacitation (Fig. 8) that even low concentrations of HCN are rapidly incapacitating and that Haber's rule is valid for a much narrower range of concentrations of HCN than of CO. Even so, at HCN concentrations of approximately 150–500 ppm, a Ct product of approximately 800 ppm-minutes or greater may be considered evidence that HCN was responsible for the incapacitation of test animals. Thus, on the basis of Ct values, the intensity of exposure required to incapacitate rats with HCN is approximately 1/40 of the intensity required with CO, except perhaps at the extremities of the time–concentration curves where large deviations from Haber's rule occur. The concentration-time relationship for lethality (Fig. 9) also shows greater deviation from Haber's rule with HCN than with CO. These data, as well as data from studies by Levin et al. (62) and Higgins and others (63), indicate that a Ct product of approximately 2500 ppm-minutes or greater may be used as a guide to evaluate whether HCN was responsible for the deaths of animals in combustion toxicity tests. This product is approximately 1/40 the Ct product necessary for CO to cause lethality.

*Hydrogen Cyanide and Carbon Monoxide.* Because CO interferes with the transport of oxygen by the blood and HCN interferes with the utilization of oxygen by cells, one might expect that exposure to the two gases simultaneously would result in additive effects.

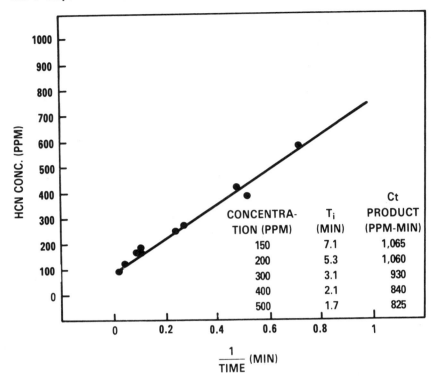

Figure 8   Concentration-time curve for incapacitation (leg flexion shock avoidance) of rats by HCN and Ct products associated with incapacitation.   (Adapted from Ref. 18.)

Experimental studies of the combined effects of HCN and CO, however, have yielded conflicting results.  In a study by Higgins and others (63), $LC_{50}$ values of a 5-min exposure to HCN in rats (503 ppm) and in mice (323 ppm) were not statistically different from those of a mixture of HCN and CO at a concentration that produced a 25% blood COHb level.  Even when animals were exposed to HCN after an exposure to CO that produced blood COHb levels of 25 or 50%, additive effects of the two gases were not evident.  In contrast, Smith (64) and Lynch (65) have reported that, based on times to incapacitation/death and $L(Ct)_{50}$ values, respectively, simultaneous exposure to HCN and CO results in additive effects.  The results of incomplete experiments at Southwest Research Institute (56) also suggest that the two gases are additive when time to incapacitation or death is measured, but low or high concentrations of either gas may

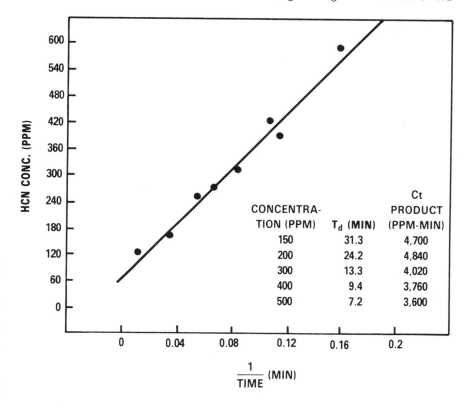

**Figure 9** Concentration-time curve for lethality of rats by HCN and Ct products associated with lethality. (Adapted from Ref. 18.)

yield inconsistent and considerably variable results. In view of the inconsistent results obtained by different investigators, a comprehensive study of the combined effects of CO and HCN in both rodents and nonhuman primates is warranted. Until more definitive data are available, it should be assumed that additive effects do occur and a combined Ct product should be calculated for the two gases to evaluate whether HCN and CO were responsible for incapacitation or death of animals. A combined Ct product for CO equivalents may be calculated as the product of the exposure time and the sum of the CO concentration and 40 times (the equivalent potency factor) the HCN concentration. Accordingly, a mixture of 200 ppm of HCN and 4000 ppm CO would have a combined equivalent concentration of 12,000 ppm of CO and would be expected to incapacitate rats in approximately 3 min (36,000 ppm-min CO equivalents) and cause death in approximately 8 min (96,000 ppm-min CO equivalents).

*Irritant Gases*. In combustion toxicity tests of materials, the toxic effects of irritant gases generally consist of irritation and lacrimation of the eyes, even corneal opacities, respiratory abnormalities, body weight loss, and postexposure lethalities. The severity of these effects varies with the specific irritants present in the smoke and their concentrations. Gross pathological and histopathological abnormalities may be evident in the eyes and respiratory tract of animals exposed to irritant gases. Although the NBS test method protocol provides for the observation of clinical signs and the pathological examination of animals, most combustion toxicity tests have neglected the toxic effects of irritant gases, except for the measurement of postexposure lethality. The notable exception is one of the University of Pittsburgh test protocols which evaluates sensory irritation by measurement of respiratory rate depression in mice and provides for determination of $RD_{50}$ values of gases and combustion atmospheres. It is apparent from the $RD_{50}$ values reported by Barrow and others (32) in Table 11 that gases as well as combustion atmospheres produced by materials may differ considerably in the severity of their irritating effects and, consequently, in their potential hazard to humans in a fire environment.

The identification of irritant gases as major toxicants in combustion atmospheres is much more difficult than that of either CO or HCN for several reasons. First is that, except for respiratory rate depression, the only effect of irritants that is measured in combustion toxicity tests and can be correlated with analytical data, is postexposure lethality. This is a delayed effect, however, to which other toxicants and factors, including animal health status and environmental conditions, may contribute. Consequently, there may be considerable variability in the occurrence of postexposure lethality in animals exposed to an irritant gas or a combustion atmosphere. A second reason is that, because studies of relatively few pure irritant gases have been conducted, there is a limited data base for identifying an irritant gas as a major toxicant. Finally, with few exceptions, automated instrumentation for analyses of irritant gases is not available, and the analyses of these gases generally are more complex and time-consuming than those of CO and HCN.

Hydrogen chloride has received the most attention in studies of the irritant gases. Most of the experimental work with HCl has been conducted with rodents, although a few studies with nonhuman primates have been reported. The rat can tolerate high concentrations of this gas without incapacitation or lethality occurring during exposure. Sufficiently high concentrations (greater than approximately 80,000 ppm) have been reported to incapacitate the rat in the motor-driven exercise wheel and shuttlebox within a few minutes,

**Table 11** RD50 Concentrations for the Thermal Decomposition Products of Various Polymers and Several Single Airborne Chemical Irritants

| Thermal decomposition products for various polymers | $RD_{50}$ (mg/L) | 95% Confidence limits |
|---|---|---|
| Flexible polyurethane foam | 0.06 | 0.04–0.09 |
| Fiberglass-reinforced polyester | 0.14 | 0.12–0.17 |
| Polystyrene (oxidative pyrolysis) | 0.18 | 0.08–0.42 |
| Douglas fir | 0.24 | 0.15–0.35 |
| Polytetrafluoroethylene | 0.25 | 0.18–0.35 |
| Polyvinyl chloride (no plasticizer or fire retardant) | 0.50 | 0.32–0.78 |
| Polyvinyl chloride (plasticized) | 0.19 | 0.17–0.22 |
| Polystyrene (flaming combustion) | 6.0 | 4.4–8.4 |

| Single chemicals | $RD_{50}$ (ppm) | 95% Confidence limits | $RD_{50}$ (mg/L) |
|---|---|---|---|
| Toluene diisocyanate | 0.39 | 0.31–0.49 | 0.0028 |
| Chlorine | 9.3 | 5.2–16.9 | 0.027 |
| Sulfur dioxide | 117 | 67–204 | 0.31 |
| Ammonia | 303 | 188–490 | 0.21 |
| Hydrogen chloride | 309 | 219–435 | 0.45 |

*Source*: From Ref. 32.

with death occurring shortly thereafter (41,42). A number of investigators have reported $LC_{50}$ values in rats exposed to HCl for
different time periods. There are discrepancies between these
values, which may be due to differences in the postexposure periods
of observation as well as to difficulties in analyzing HCl. For example, Darmer and others (66) reported $LC_{50}$ values of 40,989 ppm
(34,803–48,272) for a 5-min exposure and of 4701 ppm (4129–5352)
for a 30-min exposure, with 7-day postexposure observation periods.
Hartzell and others (67) reported an $LC_{50}$ value of 15,900 ppm
(11,540–21,890) for a 5-min exposure of rats and an $LC_{50}$ value of
3715 ppm (2,540–5,435) for a 30-min exposure, but lethalities during the 14-day postexposure period were included in these values.
These investigators also determined $LC_{50}$ values for other exposure
times. From the linearized plot of the $LC_{50}$ value as a function of
the reciprocal of exposure time (Fig. 10), it is evident that the
range of $LC_{50}t$ products is wide, varying from 80,000 ppm-min at
a concentration of 16,000 ppm to 132,000 ppm-min at 4000 ppm of
HCl. The data reported in this study indicate that a Ct product of
approximately 60,000 ppm-min may be used as a guide to evaluate
whether HCl in a combustion atmosphere may have been responsible
for postexposure deaths.

Limited data are available for assessing whether other irritants
are major toxicants in the combustion atmospheres of materials. In
an unpublished study of acrolein by Crane (68), rats were incapacitated in the motor-driven exercise wheel after a 5-min exposure of
5000–10,000 ppm of acrolein, with death occurring shortly thereafter.
Higgins and others (63) investigated the toxicity of 5-min exposures
of mice and rats to HF and $NO_2$, with and without CO. The $LC_{50}$
values (7-day postexposure observations) in rats of 18,200 ppm
(15,965–20,748) for HF and 831 ppm (566–1240) for $NO_2$ were not
significantly different than those obtained in rats exposed to each
gas with CO sufficient to produce a 25% COHb level.

*Carbon Dioxide.* Carbon dioxide stimulates the respiratory center
and is capable of causing a marked increase in the respiratory minute
volume of animals. Ventilation in humans is increased by 50% by a
concentration of 18,000 ppm of $CO_2$ in air and by 100% by a concentration of 25,000 ppm (30). This increased ventilatory effect of $CO_2$
would be expected to increase the uptake of CO and other gases
and possibly cause an increase in their toxicity. Studies of the
combined effects of CO and $CO_2$ have yielded conflicting results.
Levin (69) found that 2500 ppm of CO is twice as toxic in the
presence of 5% $CO_2$, with lethality as the index of toxicity. In a
study by Rodkey and Collison (70), the presence of 4.5% $CO_2$ was
found to decrease the time of death of rats exposed to 6000 ppm of
CO from 22.4 ± 0.8 min to 16.8 ± 0.6 min. In contrast to these
results, Crane (71) did not find a significant change in the time to

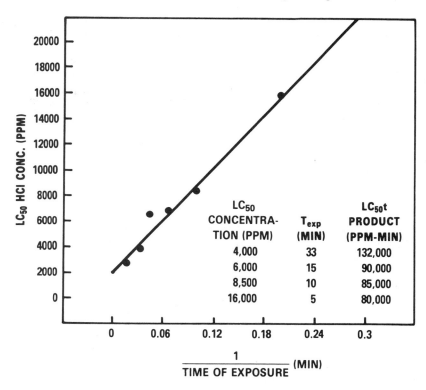

| LC$_{50}$ CONCENTRA-TION (PPM) | T$_{exp}$ (MIN) | LC$_{50}$t PRODUCT (PPM-MIN) |
|---|---|---|
| 4,000 | 33 | 132,000 |
| 6,000 | 15 | 90,000 |
| 8,500 | 10 | 85,000 |
| 16,000 | 5 | 80,000 |

Figure 10   LC$_{50}$ values of HCl in rats (14-day postexposure observation) as a function of exposure time and Ct products for the LC$_{50}$ values.  (Adapted from Ref. 68.)

incapacitation or death of rats exposed to 5000 ppm of CO when concentrations of 4 to 13% of CO$_2$ were added to the CO.   Similarly, Hartzell and Switzer (72) reported that 5% CO$_2$ did not significantly change the time to incapacitation of rats exposed to 3500 ppm of CO.

### 3.  *Identification of Major Toxicants by Correlation of Toxicity and Analytical Data*

Combustion toxicity studies of a wide variety of both natural and synthetic materials have been reported in the literature.   In most of these studies, however, analyses of combustion gases have been very limited in scope.   The data obtained in very few of these studies allow the correlation of toxicological and analytical results in order to establish the identity of the major toxicants of the combustion atmospheres. Detailed analytical data have been obtained in other combustion toxicity studies of materials, but the results are proprietary in nature and have not been published in the literature. Consequently, limited examples of combustion toxicity studies are available to demonstrate the correlation of toxicity and analytical data.

One comprehensive study in which chemical analyses were used to establish the identity of major toxicants was reported by Kaplan and others (55). The pertinent data from this study of five halogenated polymers used as electrical wire coatings are summarized in Table 12. In the case of three of the materials, Halar 500, Halar 555, and Kynar, the investigators were able to identify the primary toxicants in both the flaming and nonflaming combustion atmospheres.

Table 12   Summary of Toxicity and Analytical Data in Combustion Tests of Five Halogenated Polymers

| Material | Combustion mode | $LC_{50}$ (mg/L) | Predominant toxic effects[a] |
|---|---|---|---|
| Halar 500 (Ethylene-chlorotri-fluoroethylene) | Flaming | 15.1 | Postexposure lethality |
| | Nonflaming | 20.1 | Incapacitation, lethality during exposure, some lethality postexposure |
| Halar 555 (Blown ethylene-chlorotrifluoro-ethylene) | Flaming | 20 | Postexposure lethality |
| | Nonflaming | 28.9 | Incapacitation, some lethality during exposure, some lethality postexposure |
| Kynar (Polyvinylidene) | Flaming | 27.3 | Postexposure lethality |
| | Nonflaming | 24.3 | Incapacitation, lethality during exposure |

In the nonflaming mode, incapacitation and lethalities of rats during the exposures correlated well with blood COHb levels and the Ct products for CO during the 30-min exposures. Sufficient quantities of HF and/or HCl also were present to account for the postexposure lethalities that were observed in the experiments. Under flaming combustion conditions, postexposure lethality was the predominent toxic effect and was consistent with the analytical data for HCl and/or HF. The absence of incapacitation and lethality during exposure was consistent with the low quantities of CO measured in the combustion atmospheres and low blood COHb levels in animals. In the case of the other two materials, Teflon 100 and Tefzel 200, the quantities of CO, HCl, HF, and $COF_2$ that were evolved were insufficient to account for the observed toxic effects and the primary toxicants in their combustion atmospheres were not identified.

| Percent COHb[b] | Ct product (approx. ppm-min)[c] | | | $COF_2$[d] (Max. ppm) | Major toxicants |
|---|---|---|---|---|---|
| | CO | HF | HCl | | |
| 29% - End of test | 24,000– 29,000 | 12,000– 17,000 | 37,000– 47,000 | NA | HF, HCl |
| 67% - Incapacitation 79% - Lethality | 101,000– 133,000 | 8,000– 12,000 | 39,000– 54,000 | ND | CO, HF, HCl |
| 27% - End of test | 20,000– 23,000 | 8,000– 12,000 | 33,000– 42,000 | ND | HF, HCl |
| 75% - Incapacitation 80% - Lethality | 98,000– 117,000 | 8,900– 15,000 | 41,000– 47,000 | 40 | CO, HF, HCl |
| 38% - End of test | 30,000– 46,000 | 13,000– 37,000 | 500– 1,600 | 860 | HF |
| 68% - Incapacitation 81% - Lethality | 120,000– 132,000 | 19,000– 29,000 | 700– 1,200 | 200 | CO, HF |

Table 12    (continued)

| Material | Combustion mode | LC50 (mg/L) | Predominant toxic effects[a] |
|----------|-----------------|-------------|------------------------------|
| Teflon 100 (Fluorinated ethylene/fluorinated propylene) | Flaming | 0.075 | Postexposure lethality at low concentrations Incapacitation, lethality during exposure at high concentrations |
| | Nonflaming | 0.05 | Postexposure lethality |
| Tefzel 200 (Ethylene-tetra-fluoroethylene) | Flaming | 30.2 | Lethality during exposure, some postexposure lethality |
| | Nonflaming | 3.3 | Incapacitation, lethality during exposure, some postexposure lethality |

[a]Toxic effects represent the predominant effects observed during the series of experiments.
[b]Percent COHb are average values of relevant experiments.
[c]Range of Ct products in experiments in which sample charge is near LC50 value.
[d]COF2 was measured in only one experiment and not necessarily at the LC50 sample charge.
*Source*:  From Ref. 55.

Douglas fir, which has often been used as a reference standard for comparing the combustion toxicity of materials, is another example of a material whose primary combustion toxicants have been investigated by correlating toxicity and analytical data.  Data from a study of Douglas fir by Kaplan and others (73) who used a modified NBS test method are summarized in Table 13.  The predominant toxic effects of the nonflaming combustion atmospheres were incapacitation and a low incidence of lethality during exposure, with a high incidence of postexposure lethality.  Although blood COHb levels were typical for CO-induced incapacitation and lethality, times to

| Percent COHb[b] | Ct product (approx. ppm-min)[c] | | | COF$_2$[d] (Max. ppm) | toxicants |
|---|---|---|---|---|---|
| | CO | HF | HCl | | |
| 1.5% - End of test | ND | 200– 1,700 | 60– 100 | NA | Unknown |
| 3.5% - Incapacitation 3.5% - Lethality | 1,300– 13,000 | 4,000– 16,000 | 3,000 | 70 | Unknown |
| 1.5% - End of test | ND | 70–200 | ND | 150 | Unknown |
| 20% - End of test 30% - Lethality | 11,000– 29,000 | 6,800– 9,600 | 300– 600 | 60 | Unknown |
| 5% - End of test 7% - Lethality | 2,800– 5,400 | 3,000– 5,200 | 120 | 650 | Unknown |

incapacitation and the low incidence of exposure lethality were not consistent with the analytical data for CO. The CO Ct products at incapacitation (61,000–71,000 ppm-minutes) are almost twice as large as those necessary for a CO-induced effect and should have resulted in a more rapid incapacitation of animals. Also, the CO Ct products at 30 minutes (102,000–128,000 ppm-min) would be expected to produce a higher incidence of exposure lethality than was observed. These inconsistencies and the high incidence of postexposure lethality indicate that irritant(s) were present in the combustion atmospheres, which delayed the loading of CO and its toxic effects. The investigators

Table 13 Summary of Animal Exposure and Analytical Data
Douglas Fir (DF) Autoignition Temperature 425–460°C

| Test ref. no. | Sample conc. (mg/L) | Percent weight loss | Incapacitation | | % Lethality | |
|---|---|---|---|---|---|---|
| | | | No. of animals | Mean time | Exposure | Total |
| Nonflaming, $LC_{50}$ = 32.8 mg/L (28.9 – 37.3) | | | | | | |
| NF-8 | 32.5 | 98 | 4 | – | 0 | 0 |
| NF-6 | 30 | 88 | 5 | 27:29 | 0 | 20 |
| NF-11 | 32.5 | 97 | 5 | 24:22 | 20 | 40 |
| NF-9 | 35 | 96 | 5 | 23:50 | 20 | 100 |
| NF-7 | 40 | 98 | 5 | 22:28 | 20 | 80 |
| Flaming, $LC_{50}$ = 37.6 mg/L (34.3 – 41.2) | | | | | | |
| F-7 | 30 | 100 | 5 | 17:11 | 0 | 0 |
| F-6 | 35 | 100 | 5 | 16:03 | 40 | 40 |
| F-5 | 40 | 99 | 5 | 13:31 | 60 | 60 |
| F-4 | 50 | 100 | 5 | 11:40 | 100 | 100 |

Source: From Ref. 73.

also reported that toxic signs and body weight growth patterns in exposed animals were typical of those caused by irritant gases. Acrolein, which is generated in substantial quantities by nonflaming combustion of wood, was probably one of the primary irritants, although this gas was not analyzed in the study.

Under flaming combustion, the predominant toxic effects were incapacitation and lethality during exposure. Carbon monoxide was evolved in large quantities and the analytical data for CO (large Ct products) were consistent with the incidence of exposure lethality. Blood COHb levels at incapacitation and death were consistent with levels associated with these effects when caused by exposure to pure CO. Thus, in contrast to the nonflaming combustion mode, the data indicated that CO alone was the primary toxicant in flaming combustion atmospheres and that irritant gases were not present in sufficient concentrations to contribute to the toxicity of these atmospheres.

| Incapaci-tation | Percent COHb End of test | Mean expo. deaths | Carbon monoxide Max. (ppm) | Incap. Ct (ppm-min) | 30-min Ct (ppm-min) |
|---|---|---|---|---|---|
| Nonflaming, $LC_{50}$ = 32.8 mg/L (28.9 − 37.3) | | | | | |
| 70.0 | — | — | 5,300 | — | 73,050 |
| 78.1 | — | — | 6,000 | 65,070 | 79,380 |
| 74.0 | — | 85.7 | 7,150 | 71,500 | 111,090 |
| — | — | 82.7 | 7,225 | 61,330 | 101,910 |
| 81.5 | — | 87.4 | 8,230 | 69,530 | 127,860 |
| Flaming, $LC_{50}$ = 37.6 mg/L (34.3 − 41.2) | | | | | |
| 78.9 | — | — | 4,175 | 45,190 | 93,990 |
| 80.5 | — | 83.6 | 5,200 | 38,940 | 109,290 |
| 76.0 | — | 86.8 | 5,770 | 37,140 | 129,630 |
| 68.9 | — | 88.9 | 7,575 | 38,880 | 172,740 |

Analytical data also have been obtained in combustion toxicity studies of other materials, particularly nitrogen-containing materials. The results of many of these studies were reviewed by Kimmerle (30), who concluded that CO and/or HCN were the primary toxicants of atmospheres generated by some of these materials under certain combustion conditions. The analytical data, however, were very limited in scope and, in the opinion of this author, did not support any definite conclusions.

### 4. Extrapolation of Laboratory Toxicity Test Results in Assessing Toxicological Hazard to Humans

In order to assess the toxic hazards of combustion atmospheres to humans in a fire environment, the identities and the concentrations of the major toxicants in these atmospheres must be known.

Table 14  Hazardous Concentrations of Major Toxicants Generated by Thermal Decomposition of Materials

| Toxicant | ACGIH TLV-C[a] (ppm) | ACGIH TLV-STEL[b] (ppm) | IDLH[c] (ppm) | STLC[d] (ppm) | Hazardous/ lethal within a few min[e] (ppm or %) |
|---|---|---|---|---|---|
| Carbon monoxide | — | 400 | 1500 | 5000 | 8000 |
| Hydrogen cyanide | 10 | — | 50 | 350 | 280 |
| Carbon dioxide | — | 30,000[f] | 50,000 | — | 12% |
| Oxygen depletion | — | — | — | — | <12% |
| Hydrogen chloride | 5 | — | 100 | >500 | 1000–2000 |
| Hydrogen bromide | 3[f] | — | 50 | >500 | — |
| Hydrogen fluoride | 3[f] | — | 20 | ~400 | 50–100 |
| Ammonia | — | 35 | 500 | >1000 | 2000 |
| Acrolein | — | 0.3 | 5 | 30–100 | >10 |
| Formaldehyde | — | 2[f] | 100 | — | >50 |

| | | | | | |
|---|---|---|---|---|---|
| Sulfur dioxide | — | —[g] | 100 | >500 | 600–800 |
| Nitrogen dioxide | — | 5 | 50 | >200 | 250 |
| Styrene | — | 100 | 5000 | — | — |
| Toluene-2,4-diisocyanate | — | 0.02 | 10 | ~100 | — |

[a] American Conference of Governmental Industrial Hygienists (1984–85) threshold limit value-ceiling: The concentration that should not be exceeded even instnatly in the work environment.

[b] ACGIH threshold limit value-short-term exposure limit: The concentration to which workers can be exposed continuously for a short period of time (15 min) without suffering from (1) irritation, (2) chronic or irreversible tissue damage, or (3) narcosis of sufficient degree to increase the likelihood of accidental injury, impair self-resuce, or materially reduce work efficiency.

[c] Immediately dangerous to life or health: The maximum concentration from which one could escape within 30 minutes without any escape-impairing symptoms or any irreversible health effects. These IDLH levels were established in the NIOSH/OSHA Standards Completion Program.

[d] Short-term (10 min) lethal concentrations from Terrill and others (Ref. 17).

[e] From Kimmerle (Ref. 30) except for hydrogen chloride values from Haggard, H. W. and Y. Henderson, *Noxious Gases*, 2nd Edition, NY, Reinhold, pp. 126–127 (1943).

[f] Proposed change value.

[g] Proposed deletion of STEL value.

At the present time, a number of investigators are developing mathematical models to provide this information. These computer models will predict the concentration of smoke and concentrations of toxicants in a particular location in a building by integrating a variety of data, including the quantities and types of materials involved in the fire, the major toxicants generated by these materials, the rates of evolution of these toxicants, the effects of various factors on their rates of evolution, and the rate of transport or movement of smoke through buildings.

Once the concentration of smoke and the concentrations of the major toxicants in a room or other location have been established, it should be possible to predict the toxicological hazard to humans exposed to that smoke for various periods of time. The approach that is currently being developed by the National Bureau of Standards Center for Fire Research to make this prediction is based on the determination of $LC_{50}$ values in rats for major toxicants and for various exposure durations. These $LC_{50}$ values will then be used, with a safety factor, to predict how long occupants in a particular room or in a particular location in a fire environment may be exposed to smoke before death occurs. A major deficiency of this approach is that it is based on the very simplistic assumption that $LC_{50}$ values of combustion gases in rats are a valid measure of the lethal potency of these gases in humans. The approach does not take into account differences between rodents and humans in their responses to the various toxicants. Such differences do exist and may be significant, as evidenced by the marked difference in response of rodents and nonhuman primates to HCl and probably to other sensory irritants. In rats, HCl causes a decreased respiratory minute volume, thereby slowing the rate of uptake of CO (and possibly of other gases) so that incapacitation and death from exposure to CO are delayed and may not occur during the exposure period (61). This protective effect of sensory irritants in rodents probably does not occur in humans, based on studies by Kaplan and others (57) which have shown that baboons increase their respiratory minute volume in response to concentrations of HCl as low as 500 ppm. In fact, in baboons, high concentrations of HCl, and probably other sensory irritants, cause a severe hypoxemia which may enhance the effects of hypoxia-producing gases such as CO and HCN. Thus, whereas sensory irritants result in a protective effect in rodents, these gases may result in enhanced toxic effects of chemical asphyxiants in humans.

It is inconceivable that investigators would use $LC_{50}$ values in rats for predicting lethal hazard to humans when hazardous levels for humans have been established for many of the major toxicants in smoke. These hazardous levels are shown in Table 14 and should be used to predict the toxic hazard to humans when the identities and concentrations of these gases in a combustion atmosphere have been established.  However, even when it is possible to identify all of the major toxicants in a combustion atmosphere, the possibility of biological interactions between toxicants must be considered in evaluating the total toxicological hazard of the atmosphere.  For example, although additive effects between CO and HCN have been demonstrated only in rodents, it should be assumed that these gases, as well as oxygen depletion, also will interact in an additive manner in humans.  Also, until more definitive information becomes available, the assumption probably should be made that high concentrations of irritant gases including $NH_3$, HCl, HF, acrolein, and formaldehyde will enhance the toxicity of hypoxia-producing gases or conditions.

Some materials generate uncommon major toxicants which cannot be identified in combustion toxicity tests without a major analytical effort.  In these cases, rodent data must be used to predict the contribution of these toxicants to the potential toxic hazard of the combustion atmosphere to humans.  These data must not be restricted to $LC_{50}$ values.  Other information also must be evaluated, including the observations of clinical signs (particularly the severity of irritant effects), the rapidity of incapacitation and lethality, the target organs affected, and the nature and severity of pathological changes in these organs.  Utilization of all of these toxicological data will enable a more meaningful prediction of toxicological hazard to humans than the use of only $LC_{50}$ values in rodents.  However, even when the prediction is based on a comprehensive toxicity assessment in rodents, the deficiencies inherent in any direct extrapolation of rodent data to humans should be recognized.

## REFERENCES

1.  Alarie, Y. (1985).  The toxicity of smoke from polymeric materials during thermal decomposition. *Ann. Rev. Pharmacol. Toxicol.* 25:35.
2.  Alexeeff, G. and Packham, S. C. (1984).  Evaluation of smoke toxicity using concentration-time products. *J. Fire Sci.* 2:362.
3.  Alarie, Y. and Anderson, R. C. (1981).  Toxicologic classification of thermal decomposition products of synthetic and natural polymers. *Toxicol. Appl. Pharmacol.* 57:181.
4.  Clarke, III, F. B., Benjamin, I. A., and Clayton, J. W. (1982).  An analysis of current knowledge in toxicity of the products of combustion.  In *Report to committee on the toxicity of the products of combustion of the National Fire Protection Association.*  Morgan Technical Library, Batterymarch Park, Quincy, MA.
5.  Zapp, J. A. (1951).  The toxicology of fire. *Medical Division Special Report No. 4.*  U.S. Army Chemical Center, Maryland, p. 92.

6. National Materials Advisory Board. (1978). *Smoke and Toxicity (Combustion Toxicology of Polymers)*, Vol. 3. Publication No. NMAB 318-3, Washington, DC, National Academy of Sciences, pp. 1-55.

7. Petajan, J. H., Voorhees, K. J., Packham, S. C., Baldwin, R. C., Einhorn, I. N., Grunnet, M. L., Dinger, B. G., and Birky, M. M. (1975). Extreme toxicity from combustion products of a fire-retarded polyurethane foam. *Science 187*:742.

8. Birky, M. M., Paabo, M., Levin, B. C., Womble, S. E., and Malek, D. (1980). Development of recommended test method for toxicological assessment of inhaled combustion products. NBSIR 80-2077. Washington, DC, National Bureau of Standards.

9. Levin, B. C., Fowell, A. J., Birky, M. M., Paabo, M., Stolte, A., and Malelz, D. (1982). Further development of a test method for the assessment of the acute inhalation toxicity of combustion products. NBSIR 82-2532, Washington, DC, National Bureau of Standards.

10. Shaffer, G. S. (1984) Fire gas toxicity. Recommendations of the Secretary of State to the Uniform Fire Prevention and Building Code Council. Albany, NY: State of New York, Department of State, 12231.

11. Proposed Article 15, Part 1120 Combustion Toxicity Testing. (1985). Uniform Fire Prevention and Building Code Council, Albany, New York: State of New York, Department of State, 12231.

12. Kaplan, H. L., Grand, A. F., and Hartzell, G. E. (1983). *Combustion Toxicology: Principles and Test Methods*. Lancaster, PA, Technomic Publishing Company, Inc., pp. 1-174.

13. Autian, J. (1970). Toxicologic aspects of flammability and combustion of polymeric materials. *J. Fire Flamm. 1*:239.

14. Mitera, J. and Michal, J. (1985). The combustion products of polymeric materials, II GC-MS analysis of the combustion products of polyethylene, polypropylene, polystyrene and polyamide. *Fire Materials 9*:111.

15. Packham, S. C. and Hartzell, G. E. (1981). Fundamentals of combustion toxicology in fire hazard assessment. *J. Test. Eval. 9*:341.

16. Gad, S. C. and Smith, A. C. (1983). Influence of heating rates on the toxicity of evolved combustion products: results and a system for research. *J. Fire Sci. 1*:465.

17. Terrill, J. B., Montgomery, R. R., and Reinhardt, C. F. (1978). Toxic gases from fires. *Science 200*:1343.

18. Hartzell, G. E., Priest, D. N., and Switzer, W. G. (1985). Modeling of toxicological effects of fire gases: II. Mathematical modeling of intoxication of rats by carbon monoxide and hydrogen cyanide. *J. Fire Sci. 3*:115.

19. Birky, M. M., Halpin, B. M., Caplan, Y. H., Fisher, R. S., McAllister, J. M., and Dixon, A. M. (1979). Fire fatality study. *Fire Materials 3*:211.
20. Halpin, B. M. and Berl, W. G. (1979). Human fatalities from unwanted fires. *Fire J. 73*:105.
21. Birky, M. M., Paabo, M., and Brown, J. E. (1979). Correlation of autopsy data and materials involved in the Tennessee jail fire. *Fire Safety J. 2*:17.
22. Birky, M. M. (1982). "Westchase Hilton fire report, Part II," The Foundation for Fire Safety News, Rosslyn, Virginia, pp. 1–17.
23. Ballantyne, B. (1976). Changes in blood cyanide as a function of storage time and temperature. *J. Forensic Sci. Soc. 10*:305.
24. Purser, D. A. and Woolley, W. D. (1983). Biological studies of combustion atmospheres. *J. Fire Sci. 1*:118.
25. Dyer, R. F. and Esch, V. H. (1976). Polyvinyl chloride toxicity in fires, hydrogen chloride toxicity in fire fighters. *JAMA 235*:393.
26. Burgess, W. A., Treitman, R. D., and Gold, A. (1979). Air Contaminants in Structural Firefighting. Final Report to the National Fire Prevention and Control Administration and the Society of the Plastics Industry, Inc., Harvard School of Public Health, Cambridge, MA.
27. Grand, A. F., Kaplan, H. L., and Lee, G. H. (1981). Investigation of Combustion Atmospheres in Real Building Fires. Southwest Research Institute, Project Report No. 01-6067, San Antonio, Texas.
28. Lowry, W. T., Juarez, J., Petty, C. S., and Roberts, B. (1985). Studies of toxic gas production during actual structural fires in the Dallas area. *J. Forensic Sci. 30*:59.
29. Birky, M. M. (1977). Hazard characteristics of combustion products in fires: the state-of-the-art review, NBSIR 77-1234, Washington, DC, National Bureau of Standards.
30. Kimmerle, G. (1974). Aspects and methodology for the evaluation of toxicological parameters during fire exposure. *J. Fire Flamm./Comb. Tox. 1*:4.
31. Edgerly, P., Rogowski, Z., and Wooley, W. (1982). A Study of the Combustion Processes of the Pott's Pott Method and DIN Method Using Wood, Polypropylene and Polymethylmethacrylate. Proceedings of Interflam Conference 1982, London, England.
32. Barrow, C. S., Alarie, Y., and Stock, M. F. (1978). Sensory irritation and incapacitation evoked by thermal decomposition products of polymers and comparisons with known sensory irritants. *Arch. Environ. Health 33*:79.
33. Gaume, J. G. (1980). Instrumental animal systems for toxic assessment of materials. *J. Comb. Tox. 7*:124.

34. Crane, C. R., Sanders, D. C., Endecott, B. R., Abbott, J. K., and Smith, P. W. (1977). Inhalation Toxicology: I. Design of a Small-Animal Test System. II. Determination of the Relative Toxic Hazards of 75 Aircraft Cabin Materials. Report No. FAA-AM-77-9, Department of Transportation, Federal Aviation Administration. Washington, DC, Office of Aviation Medicine.

35. Hilado, C. J., Slattengren, C. L., and Furst, A. (1976). Relative toxicity of pyrolysis products of some synthetic polymers. *J. Comb. Tox.* 3:270.

36. Kaplan, H. L. and Hartzell, G. E. (1984). Modeling of toxicological effects of fire gases: I. Incapacitating effects of narcotic fire gases. *J. Fire Sci.* 2:286.

37. Packham, S. C., Jeppsen, R. B., McCandless, J. B., Blank, T. L., and Petajan, J. H. (1978). The toxicologic contribution of carbon monoxide as a component of wood smoke. *J. Comb. Tox.* 5:11.

38. Dilley, J. V., Martin, S. B., McKee, R., and Pryor, G. T. (1979). A smoke toxicity methodology. *J. Comb. Tox.* 6:20.

39. Hartung, R., Ball, G. L., Boettner, E. A., Rosenbaum, R., and Hollingsworth, Z. R. (1977). The performance of rats on a rotorod during exposure to combustion products of rigid polyurethane foams and wood. *J. Comb. Tox.* 4:506.

40. Boettner, E. A. and Hartung, R. (1978). The Analysis and Toxicity of the Combustion Products o/ Natural and Synthetic Materials. Final Report to the Society of the Plastics Industry, Inc. and the Manufacturing Chemists Association.

41. Kaplan, H. L., Grand, A. F., Switzer, W. G., Mitchell, D. S., Rogers, W. R., and Hartzell, G. E. (1985). Effects of combustion gases on escape performance of the baboon and the rat. *J. Fire Sci.* 3:228.

42. Crane, C. R., Sanders, D. C., Endecott, B. R., and Abbott, J. K. (1985). Inhalation Toxicology IV. Times to Incapacitation and Death for Rats Exposed Continuously to Atmospheric Hydrogen Chloride Gas. FAA-AM-85-4, Civil Aeromedical Institute, Oklahoma City, OK, Federal Aviation Administration.

43. Gaume, J. G., Reibold, R. C., and Spieth, H. H. (1981). Initial tests of the combined ECG/T$_i$ animal systems using carbon monoxide exposure. *J. Comb. Tox.* 8:125.

44. Hilado, C. J., Saxton, G. L., Kourtides, D. A., Parker, J. A., and Gilwee, W. J. (1976). Relative toxicity of pyrolysis products of some cellular polymers. *J. Comb. Tox.* 3:259.

45. Alarie, Y. (1966). Irritating properties of airborne materials to the upper respiratory tract. *Arch. Environ. Health* 13:433.

46. Barrow, C. S., Alarie, Y., and Stock, M. F. (1976). Sensory irritation evoked by the thermal decomposition products of plasticized polyvinyl chloride. *Fire Materials* 1:147.

47. Alarie, Y. (1973). Sensory irritation by airborne chemicals. *CRC Crit. Rev. Toxicol.* 2:299.
48. Kane, L. E., Barrow, C. S., and Alarie, Y. (1979). A short-term test to predict acceptable levels of exposure to airborne sensory irritants. *Am. Ind. Hyg. Assoc. J.* 40:207.
49. Potts, W. J. and Lederer, T. S. (1978). Some limitations in the use of sensory irritation method as an end-point in measurement of smoke toxicity. *J. Comb. Tox.* 5:182.
50. Alarie, Y. (1981). Dose-response analysis in animal studies: Prediction of human responses. *Environ. Health Perspect.* 42:9.
51. Barrow, C. S., Lucia, H., Stock, M. F., and Alarie, Y. (1979). Development of methodologies to assess the relative hazards from thermal decomposition products of polymeric materials. *Am. Ind. Hyg. Assoc. J.* 40:408.
52. Sumi, K. and Tsuchiya, Y. (1975). Toxicity of decomposition products. *JFF/Comb. Tox.* 2:213.
53. Tsuchiya, Y. (1981). Dynamic toxicity factor—evaluating fire gas toxicity. *J. Comb. Tox.* 8:187.
54. Spurgeon, J. (1978). The Correlation of Animal Response Data with the Yields of Selected Thermal Decomposition Products for Typical Aircraft Interior Materials. FAA-NA-78-45, Civil Aeromedical Institute. Oklahoma City, OK, Federal Aviation Administration.
55. Kaplan, H. L., Grand, A. F., Switzer, W. G., and Gad, S. C. (1984). Acute inhalation toxicity of the smoke produced by five halogenated polymers. *J. Fire Sci.* 2:154.
56. Kaplan, H. L. (1985). Unpublished toxicity test results.
57. Kaplan, H. L., Anzueto, A., Switzer, W. G., and Hinderer, R. K. (1986). Respiratory effects of hydrogen chloride in the baboon. *The Toxicologist* 6:52.
58. MacFarland, H. N. (1977). Respiratory toxicology. In *Essays in Toxicology, Vol. 7.* Edited by W. Hayes, Jr. New York, Academic Press, p. 141.
59. Potts, W. J. and Lederer, T. S. (1977). A method for comparative testing of smoke toxicity. *J. Comb. Tox.* 4:114.
60. Finney, D. J. (1971). *Probit Analysis*, 3rd edition. Cambridge, The University Press.
61. Hartzell, G. E., Stacy, H. W., Switzer, W. G., Priest, D. N., and Packham, S. C. (1985). Modeling of toxicological effects of fire gases: IV. Intoxication of rats by carbon monoxide in the presence of an irritant. *J. Fire Sci.* 3:263.
62. Levin, B. C., Gurman, J. L., Paabo, M., Baier, L., Procell, L., and Newball, H. H. (1986). Acute inhalation toxicity of hydrogen cyanide. *The Toxicologist* 6:59.
63. Higgins, E. A., Fiorca, V., Thomas, A. A., and Davis, H. V. (1972). Acute toxicity of brief exposures to HF, HCl, $NO_2$ and HCN with and without CO. *Fire Technol.* 8:120.

64. Smith, P. W. (1976). FAA Studies of the Toxicity of Products of Combustion. Proceedings of the First Conference and Workshop on Fire Casualties, Publication APL/JHU FPP 1376-1. Baltimore, Maryland, Johns Hopkins University, pp. 173–184.

65. Lynch, R. D. (1975). On the nonexistence of synergism between inhaled hydrogen cyanide and carbon monoxide. Fire Research Note No. 1035, Fire Research Station, Borehamwood, England.

66. Darmer, Jr., K. I., Kinkead, E. R., and DiPasquale, L. C. (1974). Acute toxicity in rats and mice exposed to hydrogen chloride gas and aerosols. J. Am. Ind. Hyg. Assoc. 35:623.

67. Hartzell, G. E., Packham, S. C., Grand, A. F., and Switzer, W. G. (1985). Modeling of toxicological effects of fire gases: III. Quantification of postexposure lethality of rats from exposure to HCl atmospheres. J. Fire Sci. 3:195.

68. Crane, C. R. (1983). Personal communication of unpublished experimental results with acrolein.

69. Chemical and Engineering News, American Chemical Society, pp. 35–38, (May 20, 1985).

70. Rodkey, F. L. and Collison, H. A. (1979). Effects of oxygen and carbon dioxide on carbon monoxide toxicity. J. Comb. Tox. 6:208.

71. Crane, C. R. (1985). Are the combined toxicities of CO and $CO_2$ synergistic. J. Fire Sci. 3:143.

72. Hartzell, G. E. and Switzer, W. G. (1985). On the toxicities of atmospheres containing both CO and $CO_2$. J. Fire Sci. 3:307.

73. Kaplan, H. L., Switzer, W. G., and Gad, S. C. (1984). Comparative inhalation toxicity of the combustion products of two nylons and Douglas fir. The Toxicologist 4:70.

# 13

# Practical Statistical Analysis

SHAYNE COX GAD / *G. D. Searle and Company, Skokie, Illinois*

## I. INTRODUCTION

This chapter is for both the practicing toxicologist and product safety individual as a practical guide to the common statistical problem encountered in toxicology and the methodologies that are available to solve them. It has been enriched by the inclusion of discussions of why a particular procedure or interpretation is suggested, and of examples of problems and pitfalls encountered in the day-to-day conduct and interpretation of studies. This chapter focuses on approaches, decisions, and issues, as opposed to techniques. Readers are directed to *Statistics and Experimental Design for Toxicologists* (1) if they wish to pursue details of actual statistical techniques.

Because of societal and regulatory requirements, studies are being designed and executed to generate increased amounts of data which are then utilized to address various areas of concern. As the resulting problems of data analysis have become more complex due to the nature of the field, toxicology and safety evaluation have come to draw more deeply from the well of available statistical techniques. In fact, however, the field of statistics has also been very active and growing during the last 25 years—to some extent, at least, because of the very growth of toxicology. These simultaneous changes have led to an increasing complexity of data and, unfortunately, to the introduction of numerous confounding factors which severely limit the utility of the resulting data in all too many cases.

One (and perhaps the major) difficulty is that there is a very real necessity of having an understanding of the biological realities and implications of a problem, and of knowing the peculiarities of toxicological data before procedures are selected and employed for analysis. Some of these characteristics include the following.

1. The need to work with a relatively small sample set of data collected from the members of a population (laboratory animals, cultured cells, and bacterial cultures) which is not actually our population of interest (that is, people or a wildlife population).

2. Dealing frequently with data resulting from a sample which was censored on a basis other than investigator design. By censoring, of course, we mean that not all data points were collected as might be desired. This censoring could be the result of either a biological factor (the test animal being dead or too debilitated to manipulate) or a logistic factor (equipment being inoperative or a tissue being missed in necropsy).

3. The conditions for which our experiments are supposed to predict outcome are very open-ended. In pharmacology (the closest cousin to at least classical toxicology), the possible conditions of interaction of a chemical or physical agent with a person are limited to a small range of doses via a single route over a short course of treatment to a defined patient population. In toxicology however, all these things (a dose, route, time span, and subject population) are virtually wide open.

4. The time frames available to solve our problems are limited by practical and economic factors. This frequently means that there is not time to repeat a critical study if the first attempt fails. So a true iterative approach is not possible.

Unfortunately, there are very few toxicologists or product safety professionals who are also statisticians, or vice versa. In fact, the training of most toxicologists in statistics has been limited to a single introductory course which concentrates on some theoretical basics. As a result, the armimentarium of statistical techniques of most toxicologists are limited and the tools that are usually present (t-tests, chi-square, analysis of variance, and linear regression) are neither fully developed nor well understood. It is hoped that this chapter will help in changing this situation.

As a point of departure toward this objective, it is essential that any data and analysis be interpreted by a professional who firmly understands three concepts; the difference between biological significance and statistical significance, the nature and value of different types of data, and causality.

For the first concept, we should consider the four possible combinations of these two different types of significance, for which we find the relationship shown below

|  |  | Statistical significance | |
|  |  | No | Yes |
| Biological | No | Case I | Case II |
| Significance | Yes | Case III | Case IV |

Cases I and IV give us no problems, for the answers are the same statistically and biologically. But cases II and III present problems. In Case II (the "false positive"), we have a circumstance where there is a statistical significance in the measured difference between treated and control groups, but there is no true biological significance to the finding. This is not an uncommon happening, for example, in the case of clinical chemistry parameters. This is called type I error by statisticians, and the probability of this happening is called $\alpha$ (alpha) level. In case III (the "false negative"), we have no statistical significance, but the differences between groups are biologically/toxicologically significant. This is called type II error by statisticians, and the probability of such an error happening by random chance is called the $\beta$ (beta) level. An example of this second situation is when we see a few of a very rare tumor type in treated animals. In both of these latter cases, numerical analysis, no matter how well done, is no substitute for professional judgment. Along with this, however, must come a feeling for the different types of data and for the value of each.

We will explore more fully the types of data (the second major concept) and their value (and the implications of value of data to such things as animal usage) in the next section.

The reasons that biological and statistical significance are not identical are multiple, but a central one is certainly causality. Through our consideration of statistics, we should keep in mind that just because a treatment and a change in an observed organism are seemingly or actually associated with each other does not "prove" that the former caused the latter. Though this fact is now widely appreciated for correlation (for example, the fact that the number of storks' nests found each year in England is correlated with the number of human births that year does not mean that storks bring babies), it is just as true in the general case for significance. Timely establishment and proof that treatment causes an effect requires an understanding of the underlying mechanism and proof of its validity. At the same time, it is important that we realize that not finding a good correlation or suitable significance associated with a treatment and an effect likewise does not prove that the two are not associated— that a treatment does not cause an effect. At best, it gives us a certain level of confidence that under the conditions of the current test, these items are not associated.

## II. BASIC PRINCIPLES

Let us first introduce (or review) a few simple terms and concepts which are fundamental to an understanding of statistics.

Each measurement we make, that is, each individual piece of experimental information we gather, is called a datum. It is extremely unusual, however, to either obtain or attempt to analyze a datum.

Rather, we gather and analyze multiple pieces at one time, the resulting collection being called data.

Data are collected on the basis of their association with a treatment (intended or otherwise) as an effect (a property) that is measured in the experimental subjects of a study, such as body weights. These identifiers (that is, treatment and effect) are termed variables. Our treatment variables (those that the researcher or nature control, and which can be directly controlled) are termed independent, while our effect variables (such as weight, life span, and number of neoplasms) are termed dependent variables because their outcome is believed to depend on the "treatment" bein0 studied.

All the possible measures of a given set of variables in all the possible subjects that exist is termed the population for those variables. Such a population of variables cannot be truly measured, for example, one would have to obtain, treat, and measure the weights of all the Fischer-344 rats that were, are, or ever will be. Instead, we settle for dealing with a representative group or sample. If our sample of data is appropriately collected and of sufficient size, it serves to provide good estimates of the characteristics of the parent population from which it was drawn.

Two terms refer to the quality and reproducibility of our measurements of variables. The first, accuracy, is an expression of the closeness of a measured or computed value to its actual or "true" value in nature. The second, precision, reflects the closeness or reproducibility of a series of repeated measurements of the same quantity.

If we arrange all of our measurements of a particular variable in order as a point on an axis marked as to the values of that variable, and if our sample were large enough, the pattern of distribution of the data in the sample would begin to become apparent. This pattern is a representation of the frequency distribution of a given population of data, that is, of the incidence of different measurements, their central tendency, and dispersion.

The most common frequency distribution and one we will talk about throughout this chapter, is the normal (or Gaussian) distribution. This distribution is so common in nature that two-thirds of all values are within one standard deviation (defined below) of the mean (or average value for the entire population) and 95% are within 1.96 standard deviations of the mean. There are other frequency distributions such as the binomial, Poisson, and chi square, which are encountered from time to time, but none of these are as pervasive as the normal distribution.

In all areas of biological research, optimal design and appropriate interpretation of experiments require that the researcher understand both the biological and technological underpinnings of the system being studied and of the data being generated. From the point of view of the statistician, it is vitally important that the experimenter

Table 1    Types of Variables (Data) and Examples of Each Type

| Classified by | Type | Example[a] |
|---|---|---|
| Scale | | |
| Continuous | Scalar | Body weight |
| | Ranked | Severity of a lesion |
| Discontinuous | Scalar | Weeks until the first observation of a tumor in a carcinogenicity study |
| | Ranked | Clinical observations in animals |
| | Attribute | Eye colors in fruit flies |
| | Quantal | Dead/alive or present/absent |
| Frequency distribution | Normal | Body weights |
| | Bimodal | Some clinical chemistry parameters |
| | Others | Measures of time-to-incapacitation |

[a]It should be kept in mind that though these examples are most commonly of the data types assigned above, it is not always the case.

both know and be able to communicate the nature of the data, and understand its limitations.  One classification of data types is presented in Table 1.

The nature of the data collected is determined by three considerations.  These are the biological source of the data (the system being studied), the instrumentation and techniques being used to make measurements, and the design of the experiment.  The researcher has some degree of control over each of these:  the least over the biological system (he/she normally has a choice of one of several models to study) and the most over the design of the experiment or study.  Such choices, in fact, dictate the type of data generated by a study.

Statistical methods are each based on specific assumptions. Parametric statistics, those that are most familiar to the majority of scientists, have more stringent sets of underlying assumptions than do nonparametric statistics. Among these underlying assumptions (for many parametric statistical methods, such as analysis of variance) is that the data are continuous. The nature of the data associated with a variable (as described above) imparts a "value" to that data, the value being the power of the statistical tests which can be employed.

Continuous variables are those which can at least theoretically assume any of an infinite number of values between any two fixed points (such as measurements of body weight between 2.0 and 3.0 kg). Discontinuous variables, meanwhile, are those which can have only certain fixed values, with no possible intermediate values (such as counts of 5 or 6 dead animals, respectively).

Limitations on our ability to measure constrain the extent to which the real-world situation approaches the theoretical here, but many of the variables studied in toxicology are in fact continuous. Examples of these are lengths, weights, concentrations, temperatures, periods of time, and percentages. For these continuous variables, we may describe the character of a sample with measures of central tendency and dispersion that we are most familiar with: the mean, denoted by the symbol $\bar{X}$ and also called the arithmetic average, and the standard deviation (SD, which is denoted by the symbol $\sigma$) and is calculated as being equal to

$$\sqrt{\frac{\Sigma X^2 - \frac{(\Sigma X)^2}{N}}{N - 1}}$$

where X is the individual datum and N is the total number of data in the group.

Contrasted with these continuous data, however, we have discontinuous (or discrete) data, which can only assume certain fixed numerical values. In these cases our selection of types of statistical tools or tests is more limited. A lot of data in toxicology fits into this category.

## A. Probability

Probability is simply the likelihood that in a sufficiently large sample a particular event would occur or a particular value be found. Hypothesis testing, for example, is generally structured so that the likelihood of a treatment group being the same as a control group (the so called "null hypothesis") can be assessed as being less than a selected low level (very frequently 5%, which implies that we are 95% (that is, $1.0 - 0.05$ or 95% sure that the groups are *not* equivalent).

## B. Functions of Statistics

Statistical methods may serve to do any combination of three possible tasks. The one we are most familiar with is hypothesis testing, that is, determining if two (or more) groups of data differ from each other at a predetermined level of confidence. A second function is the construction and use of models which may be used to predict future outcomes of chemical–biological interactions. This is most commonly seen as linear regression or as the derivation of some form of correlation coefficient. Model fitting allows us to relate one variable (typically a treatment or "independent" variables) to another. The third function, reduction of dimensionality, continues to be less commonly utilized than the first two. In this final category are the methods for reducing the number of variables in a system while only minimally reducing the amount of information, therefore making a problem easier to visualize and to understand. Examples of such techniques are factor analysis and cluster analysis. A subset of this last function, discussed later under descriptive statistics, is the reduction of raw data to single expressions of central tendency and variability (such as the mean and standard deviation).

There is also a special subset which is part of both the second and third functions of statistics. This is data transformation, which includes such things as the conversion of numbers to log or probit values.

## C. Descriptive Statistics

Descriptive statistics are used to convey, in a summarized manner, the general nature of the data. As such, the parameters describing any single group of data have two components. One of these describes the location of the data, while the other gives a measure of the dispersion of the data in and about this location. Often overlooked is that the choice of what parameters are used to give these pieces of information implies a particular nature of distribution for the data.

Most commonly, location is described by giving the (arithmetic) mean and the dispersion by giving the standard deviation (SD) or the standard error of the mean (SEM). The calculation of the first two of these has already been described. If we again denote the total number of data in a group as N, then the SEM would be calculated as

$$SEM = \frac{SD}{\sqrt{N}}$$

### 1. Comparison of SD and SEM

The standard deviation and the standard error of the mean are related to each other but yet are quite different. To compare these two, let us first demonstrate their calculation from the same set of 15 observations.

Sum ($\Sigma$)

Date Points ($X_i$):  1, 2, 3, 4, 4, 5, 5, 5, 6, 6, 6, 7, 7, 8, 9

78

Squares ($X_i^2$):  1, 4, 9, 16, 16, 25, 25, 25, 36, 36, 36, 49, 49, 64, 81

472

The standard deviation can then be calculated as:

$$SD = \sqrt{\frac{472 - \frac{(78)^2}{15}}{15 - 1}} = \sqrt{\frac{472 - \frac{(6084)}{15}}{14}}$$

$$= \frac{472 - 405.6}{14} = 4.742851 = 2.1778$$

with a mean ($\overline{X}$) of 78/15 = 5.2 for the data group. The SEM for the same set of data, however, is

$$SEM = \frac{2.1778}{\sqrt{15}} = \frac{2.1778}{3.8730} = 0.562301$$

The SEM is quite a bit smaller than the SD, making it very attractive to use in reporting data. This relative size is due to the SEM actually being an estimate of the error (or variability) involved in measuring the data from which means are calculated. This is implied by the central limit theorem, which has three main points associated with it.

The distribution of sample means will be approximately normal regardless of the distribution of values in the original population from which the samples were drawn.

The mean value of the collection of all possible sample means will equal the mean of the original population.

The standard deviation of the collection of all possible means of samples of a given size, called the standard error of the mean, depends on both the standard deviation of the original population and the size of the sample.

The SEM should be used only when the uncertainty of the estimate of the mean is of concern, which is almost never the case
in toxicology. Rather, we are concerned with an estimate of the
variability of the population, for which the standard deviation is
appropriate.

The use of the mean with either the SD or SEM implies, however,
that we have reason to believe that the data being summarized are
from a population which is at least approximately normally distributed.
If this is not the case, then we should rather use a set of terms
which do not have such a rigid underpinning. These are the median,
for location, and the semiquartile distance, for a measure of dispersion. These somewhat less commonly familiar parameters are characterized as follows.

## 2. Median

When all the numbers in a group are arranged in a ranked order
(that is, from smallest to largest), the median is the middle value.
If there is an odd number of values in a group then the middle value
is obvious (in the case of 13 values, for example, the seventh largest
is the median). When the number of values in the sample is even,
the median is calculated as the midpoint between the $[N/2]$th and the
$([N/2] + 1)$th number. For example, in the series of numbers 7,
12, 13, 19, the median value would be the midpoint between 12 and
13, which is 12.5.

## 3. Semiquartile Distance

When all the data in a group are ranked, a quartile of the data
contains one ordered quarter of the values. Typically, we are most
interested in the borders of the middle two quartiles. $Q_1$ and $Q_2$,
which together represent the semiquartile distance and which contain
the median as their center. Given that there are N values in an
ordered group of data, the upper limit of the jth quartile ($Q_j$) may
be computed as being equal to the $[j(N + 1)/4$th$]$ value. Once we
have used this formula to calculate the upper limits of $Q_1$ and $Q_3$,
we can then compute the semiquartile distance (which is also called
the quartile deviation, and as such is abbreviated as the QD) with
the formula $QD = (Q_3 - Q_1)/2$.

For example, for the 15 value data set 1, 2, 3, 4, 4, 5, 5, 5,
6, 6, 6, 7, 7, 8, 9, we can calcualte the upper limits of $Q_1$ and $Q_3$ as

$$Q_1 = \frac{1(15 + 1)}{4} = \frac{16}{4} = 4$$

$$Q_3 = \frac{3(15 + 1)}{4} = \frac{48}{4} = 12$$

The 4th and 12th values in this data set are 4 and 7, respectively. The semiquartile distance can then be calculated as

$$QD = \frac{12 - 4}{2} = 4$$

There are times when it is desired to describe the relative variability of one or more sets of data. The most common way of doing this is to compute the coefficient of variation (CV), which is calculated simply as the ratio of the standard deviation to the mean, or

$$CV = \frac{SD}{\bar{X}}$$

A CV of 0.2 or 20% thus means that the standard deviation is 20% of the mean. In toxicology, the CV is frequently between 20 and 50% and may at times exceed 100%.

## D. Outliers

Outliers are extreme (high or low) values which are widely divergent from the main body of a group of data and from what is our common experience. They may arise from an instrument (such as a balance) being faulty, the seeming natural urge of some animals to frustrate research, or they may be indicative of a "real" value. Outlying values can be detected by visual inspection of the data, use of a scattergram (as will be discussed later), or (if the data set is small enough, which is usually the case in toxicology) by a large increase in the parameter estimating the dispersion of data, such as the standard deviation.

When we can solidly tie one of the above error-producing processes (such as a balance being faulty) to an outlier, we can safely delete it from consideration. But if we cannot solidly tie such a cause to an outlier (even if we have strong suspicions), we have a much more complicated problem, for then such a value may be one of several other things. It could be a result of a particular cause that is the grounds for the entire study: that is, the very "effect" that we are looking for, or it could be because of the collection of legitimate effects which constitute sample error. As will be discussed later under exploratory data analysis, and as is now becoming more widely appreciated, in animal studies outliers can be an indication of a biologically significant effect which is not yet statistically significant. Variance inflation can be the result of such outliers, and can be used to detect them. Outliers, in fact, by increasing the variability within a sample, decrease the sensitivity of our statistical tests and actually preclude our having a statistically significant result (Beckman and Cook).

Alternatively, the outlier may be the result of an unobserved technician error, for example, and may be such as to change the decisions that would result from a set of data.

In this last case we want to reject the data point, to exclude it from consideration with the rest of the data. But how can one identify these legitimate statistical rejection cases?

There are a wide variety of techniques for data rejection. Their proper use depends on one's understanding of the nature of the distribution of the data. For normally distributed data with a single extreme value, a simple method such as Chauvenet's criterion (2) may legitimately be employed. This states that if the probability of a value deviating /rom the mean is greater than $1/2N$, one should consider that there are adequate grounds for its rejection.

A second relatively straightforward approach, for when the data are normally distributed but contain several extreme values, is to "winsorize" the data. Though there are a number of variations on this approach, the simplest (called the G-1 method) calls for replacing the highest and lowest values in a set of data. In a group of data consisting of the values 54, 22, 18, 15, 14, 13, 11, and 4, we would replace 54 with a second 22 and 4 with a replicate 11. This would give us a group consisting of 22, 22, 18, 15, 14, 14, 13, 11, and 11, which we would then treat as our original data. Winsorizing should not be performed, however, if the extreme values constitute more than a small minority of the entire data set.

Yet another approach is to use Dixon's test (3) to determine if extreme values should be rejected. In Dixon's test, the set of observations is first ordered according to magnitude (as we did earlier for the data set used to demonstrate quartile deviations, though there this step was simply to make the case clearer). The ratio of the difference of an extreme value from one of its nearest neighbor values to the range of values in the sample is then calculated, using a formula which varies with sample size. This ratio is then compared to a table value, and if found to be equal or greater, is considered to be an outlier at the $p \leqslant 0.05$ level. The formula for the ratio varies with sample size and according to whether it is the smallest or largest value that is suspect. If we have more information as to the nature of the data or the type of analysis to be performed, there are yet better ways to handle outliers.

## E. Sampling

Sampling or the selection of which individual data points will be collected, whether in the form of selecting certain animals to collect blood from or removing a portion of a diet mix to analyze, is an essential step upon which all other efforts toward a good experiment or study are based.

There are three assumptions about sampling which are common to most of the statistical analysis techniques that are used in toxicology: that sample is collected without bias, that each member of a sample is collected independently of the others, and that members of a sample are collected with replacements. Precluding bias, both intentional and unintentional, means that at the time of selection of a sample to measure, each portion of the population from which that selection is to be made has an equal chance of being selected. Ways of precluding bias are discussed in detail in the section on experimental design.

Independence means that the selection of any portion of the sample is not affected by and does not affect the selection or measurement of any other portion.

Finally, the assumption of sampling with replacement means that in theory, after each portion is selected and measured, it is returned to the total sample pool and thus has the opportunity to be selected again. This is a corollary of the assumption of independence. Violation of this assumption (which is almost always the case in toxicology and all the life sciences) does not have serious consequences as long as the total pool from which samples are being drawn is large enough (say 20 or greater) that the chance of reselecting that portion is small anyway.

There are four major types of sampling methods: random, stratified, systematic, and cluster. Random is by far the most commonly employed method in toxicology. It stresses the fulfillment of the assumption of avoiding bias. When the entire pool of possibilities is mixed or randomized (procedures for randomization are presented in a later section), then the preselected members of the pool are selected as they appear.

Stratified sampling is performed by first dividing the entire pool into subsets or strata, then doing randomized sampling from each strata. This method is employed when the total pool contains subsets which are distinctly different but in which each subset contains similar members. An example is a large batch of a powdered pesticide in which it is desired to determine the nature of the particle size distribution. Larger pieces or particles are on the top, while progressively smaller particles have settled lower in the container and at the very bottom, the material has been packed and compressed into aggregates. To determine a timely representative answer, proportionately sized subsets from each layer or strata should be selected, mixed, and randomly sampled. This method is used most commonly in diet studies.

In systematic sampling, a sample is taken at set intervals (such as every fifth container of reagent or taking a sample of water from a fixed sample point in a flowing stream every hour). This is most commonly employed in quality assurance or (in the clinical chemistry lab) in quality control.

To perform cluster sampling, the pool is already divided into numerous separate groups (such as bottles of tablets), and we select small sets of groups (such as several bottles of tablets), then select a few members from each small set. What one gets then is a cluster of measures. Again, this is a method most commonly used in quality control or in environmental studies when the effort and expense of physically collecting a small group of units is significant.

In classical toxicology studies, sampling arises in a practical sense in a limited number of situations. The most common of these are:

1.  Selecting a subset of animals or test systems from a study to make some measurement (which is either destructive or stressing of the measured system or is expensive) at an interval during a study. This may include doing interim necropsies in a chronic study or collecting and analyzing blood samples from some animals during a subchronic study.

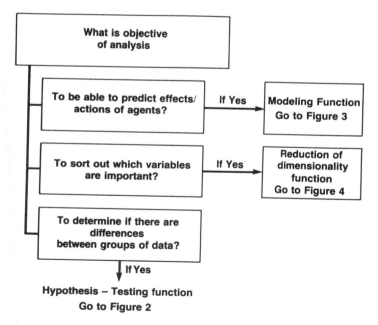

Figure 1   Overall decision tree for selecting hypothesis testing procedures.

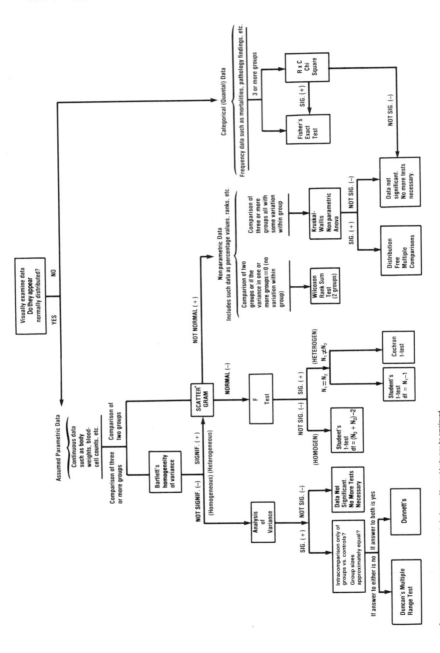

*If plot does not clearly demonstrate lack of normality exact tests may be employed.
–If continuous data, Kolmogorov Smirnov test.
–If discontinuous data, Chi-Square Goodness-of-Fit test may be used.

Figure 2   Decision tree for selecting hypothesis-testing procedures.

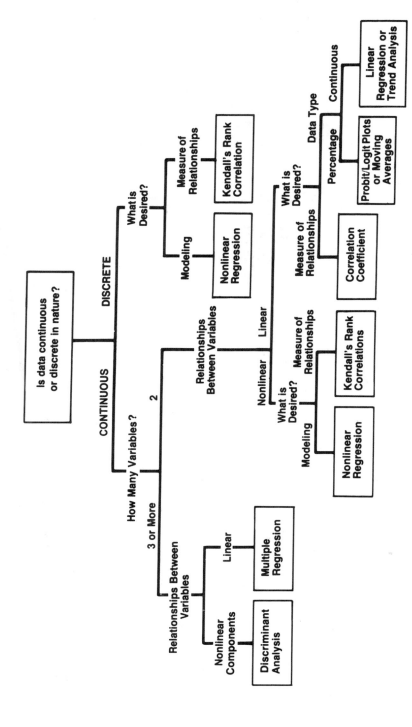

Figure 3    Decision tree for selecting modeling procedures.

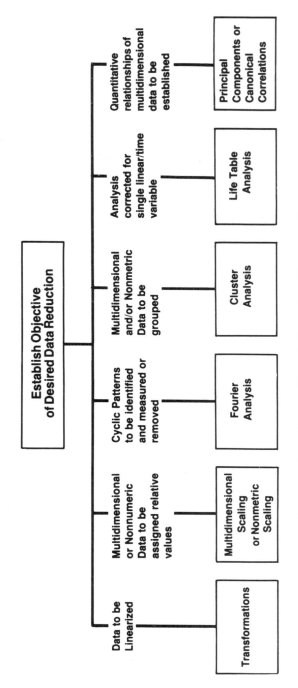

Figure 4   Decision tree for selection of reduction of dimensionality procedures.

2. Analyzing inhalation chamber atmospheres to characterize aerosol distributions with a new generation system.
3. Analyzing diet in which test material has been incorporated.
4. Performing quality control on an analytical chemistry operation by having duplicate analyses performed on some materials.
5. Selecting data to audit for quality assurance purposes.

## F. Generalized Methodology Selection

One approach for the selection of appropriate techniques to employ in a particular situation is to use a decision-tree method. Figure 1 is a decision tree that leads to the choice of one of three other trees to assist in technique selection, with each of the subsequent trees addressing one of the three functions of statistics that was defined earlier in this chapter. Figure 2 is for the selection of hypothesis-testing procedures, Figure 3 for modeling procedures, and Figure 4 for reduction of dimensionality procedures. For the vast majority of situations, these trees will guide the user into the choice of the proper technique. The specifics of the tests in these trees are beyond the scope of this chapter and should be pursued elsewhere (1).

## III. EXPERIMENTAL DESIGN

In toxicology, we generally carry out experiments for a twofold purpose. The first question we ask is whether or not an agent results in an effect on a biological system. Our second question, which is never far behind, is how much of an effect is present. Both the cost to perform research to answer such questions and the value that society places upon the results of such efforts have continued to increase rapidly. Additionally, it has become increasingly desirable that the results of studies aimed at assessing the effects of environmental agents allow as straightforward conclusions as possible. As these trends seem to have little likelihood of changing in the foreseeable future, it is essential that every experiment and study yield as much information as possible, and that (more specifically) the results of each study provide possible answers to the questions it was conducted to address. The statistical aspects of such efforts, as they are aimed at structuring experiments in design to maximize the possibilities of success, are called experimental design.

We have now become accustomed to developing exhaustively detailed protocols for an experiment or study prior to its conduct. But, typically, such protocols do not include or reflect a detailed plan for the statistical analysis of the data generated by the study and certainly even less frequently, reflect such considerations in their design. A priori selection of statistical methodology (as

opposed to the post hoc approach) is as significant a portion of the
process of protocol development and experimental design as any other
and can measurably enhance the value of the experiment or study.
Such prior selection of statistical methodologies is essential for effective detailing of such other portions of a protocol as the number
of animals per group and the sampling intervals for body weight.
Implied in such a selection is that the toxicologist has both an indepth knowledge of the area of investigation and an understanding
of the general principles of experimental design, for the analysis of
any set of data is dictated to a large extent by the manner in which
the data are obtained.

The four basic statistical principles of experimental design are
replication, randomization, concurrent ("local") control, and balance.
In abbreviated form, these may be summarized as follows.

## A. Replication

Any treatment must be applied to more than one experimental unit
(animal, plate of cells, litter of offspring, etc.). This provides
more accuracy in the measurement of a response than can be obtained
from a single observation, since underlying experimental errors tend
to cancel each other out. It also supplies an estimate of the experimental error derived from the variability among each of the measurements taken (or "replicates"). In practice, this means that an
experiment should have enough experimental units in each treatment
group (that is, a large enough "N") so that reasonably sensitive
statistical analysis of data can be performed. The estimation of what
is a large enough sample size is addressed in detail later in this
chapter.

## B. Randomization

This practice ensures that every treatment shall have its fair share
of extreme high and extreme low values or of hyper- and hyporespond-
ing individuals. It also serves to allow the toxicologist to proceed as
if the assumption of "independence" is valid. That is, there is no
avoidable (known) systematic bias in how one obtains data.

## C. Concurrent Control

Comparisons between treatments should be made to the maximum extent possible between experimental units from the same closely defined
population. Therefore, animals used as a "control" group should
come from the same source, lot, age, etc. as test group animals.
Except for the treatment being evaluated, test and control animals
should be maintained and handled in exactly the same manner.

## D. Balance

If the effect of several different factors is being evaluated simultaneously, the experiment should be laid out in such a way that the contributions of the different factors can be separately distinguished and estimated. There are several ways of accomplishing this end by using one of several different forms of design, as will be discussed below.

There are four basic types of experimental designs which are utilized in toxicology. These are the randomized block, latin square, factorial design, and nested design. Other designs that are used are really combinations of these basic designs, and furthermore are very rarely employed in toxicology. Before examining these four basic types, however, we must first examine the basic concept of blocking.

Blocking is, simply put, the arrangement or sorting of the members of a population (such as all of an available group of test animals) into groups based on certain characteristics which may (but are not sure to) alter an experimental outcome. Such factors which may cause a treatment to give a differential effect are genetic background, age, sex, overall activity levels, and so on. The process of blocking then acts (or attempts to act), so that each experimental group (or block) is assigned its fair share of the members of each of these subgroups.

We should now recall that randomization is aimed at spreading out the effects of undetectable or unsuspected characteristics in a population of animals or some portion of this population. The merging of the two concepts of randomization and blocking leads to the most basic experimental design, the randomized block. This type of design requires that each treatment group have at least one member of each recognized characteristic group (such as age), the exact members of each block being assigned in an unbiased (or random) fashion.

A second concept and its understanding are essential to the design of experiments in toxicology, that of censoring. Censoring is the exclusion of measurements of certain experimental units, or indeed of the experimental units themselves, from consideration in data analysis or inclusion in the experiment at all, respectively. Censoring may occur either prior to initiation of an experiment (where, in modern toxicology, this is almost always a planned procedure), during the course of an experiment (when they are almost universally unplanned, resulting from, for example, the death of animals on test), or after the conclusion of an experiment (when, usually, data are excluded because of being identifird as some form of outlier).

In practice, a priori censoring in toxicology studies occurs in the assignment of experimental units to test groups. The most familiar example is in the common practice of assignment of test animals to acute, subacute, subchronic, and chronic studies, where the results of otherwise random assignments are evaluated for body weights of the assigned members. If the mean weights are found not to be comparable by some pre-established criterion (such as a 90% probability of difference by analysis of variance) then members are reassigned (censored) to achieve comparability in terms of starting body weights. Such a procedure of animal assignment to groups is a censored randomization.

The first precise or calculable aspect of experimental design to be considered is determining what are sufficient test and control group sizes to allow one to have an adequate level of confidence in the results of a study. This number (N) can be calculated by using the formula

$$N = \frac{(t_1 + t_2)^2 \, s^2}{d^2}$$

where $t_1$ is the one-tailed t value with N-1 degrees of freedom corresponding to the desired level of confidence, and $t_2$ is the one-tailed t value with N-1 degrees of freedom corresponding to the probability that the sample size will be adequate to achieve the desired precision, and S is the sample standard deviation, derived typically from historical data and calculated as (with V being the variable of interest)

$$S = \sqrt{\frac{1}{N-1} \Sigma (V_1 - V_2)^2}$$

and d is the acceptable range of variation in the variable of interest.

A good approximation can be generated by substituting the t values (from a table of t values) for an infinite number of degrees of freedom. This entire process is demonstrated in the following example.

*Example*

In a subchronic dermal study in rabbits, the principal point of concern is the extent to which the compound causes oxidative damage to the erythrocytes. To quantitate this, the laboraotry will be measuring the numbers of reticulocytes in the blood. What then would be an adequate sample size to allow the question at hand to be addressed with reasonable certitude of an answer?

To do this, we use the one-tailed t value for an infinite number of degrees of freedom at 95% confidence level (that is, $p \leq 0.05$).

Going to a set of t tables, we find this number to be 1.645. From prior experience, we know that the usual values for reticulocytes in rabbit blood are from 0.5 to 1.9. The acceptable range of variation, 0, is therefore equal to the span of this range, or 1.4. Likewise, examining the control data from previous rabbit studies, we find our sample standard deviation to be 0.825. When we insert all of these numbers into the equation (presented above) for sample size, we can calculate the required sample size (N) to be

$$= \frac{(1.645 + 1.645)^2}{(1.4)^2} \, 0.825$$

$$= \frac{10.824}{1.96} \, (0.825)$$

$$= 4.556$$

In other words, in this case where there is little natural variability, measuring the reticulocyte counts of groups of only five animals each should be sufficient to answer the question.

There are a number of aspects of experimental design which are specific to the actual practice to toxicology. Before we look at a suggestion for step-by-step development of experimental designs, these aspects should first be considered as follows.

1. Frequently, the data gathered from specific measurements of animal characteristics are such that there is wide variability in the data. Often, such wide variability is not present in a control or low dose group, but in an intermediate dosage group variance inflation may occur. That is, there may be a large standard deviation associated with the measurements from this intermediate group. In the face of such a data set, the conclusion that there is no biological effect based on a finding of no statistically significant effect might well be erroneous.

2. In designing experiments, a toxicologist should keep in mind the potential effect of involuntary censoring on sample size. In other words, though the study described in the example might start with five dogs per group, this provides no margin should any die before the study is ended and blood samples are collected and analyzed. Just enough experimental units per group frequently leaves too few at the end to allow meaningful statistical analysis, and allowances should be made accordingly in establishing group sizes.

3. It is certainly possible to pool the data from several identical toxicological studies. For example, after first having performed an acute inhalation study where only three treatment group animals survived to the point at which a critical measure (such as analysis

of blood samples) was performed, we would not have enough data to perform a meaningful statistical analysis. We could then repeat the protocol with new control and treatment group animals from the same source. At the end, after assuring ourselves that the two sets of data are comparable, we could combine (or pool) the data from survivors of the second study with those from the first. The costs of this approach, however, would then be both a greater degree of effort expended (than if we had performed a single study with larger groups) and increased variability in the pooled samples (decreasing the power of our statistics).

4. Another frequently overlooked design option in toxicology is the use of an unbalanced design, that is, of different group sizes for different levels of treatment.

There is no requirement that each group in a study (control, low dose, intermediate dose, and high dose) have an equal number of experimental units assigned to it. Indeed, there are frequently good reasons in toxicology to assign more experimental units to one group than to the others, and, as we shall see later, all the major statistical methodologies have provisions to adjust for such inequalities, within certain limits. The two most common uses of the unbalanced design have larger groups assigned to either the highest dose to compensate for losses due to possible deaths during the study or to the lowest dose to give more sensitivity in detecting effects at levels close to a threshold of effect, or more confidence that there is not an effect.

5. Frequently, we are confronted in toxicology with the situation that an undesired variable is influencing our experimental results in a nonrandom fashion. Such a variable is called a confounding variable and its presence, as discussed earlier, makes clear attribution and analysis of effects at best difficult, and at worst impossible. Sometimes such confounding variables are the result of conscious design or management decisions, such as the use of different instruments, personnel, facilities, or procedures for different test groups within the same study. Occassionally, however, such confounding variables are the result of unintentional factors or actions, in which case it is called a lurking variable. Examples of such variables are almost always the result of standard operating procedures being violated: water not being connected to a rack of animals over a weekend, a set of racks not being cleaned as frequently as others, or a contaminated batch of feed or vehicle being used.

6. Finally, some thought must be given to the clear definition of what is meant by experimental unit and concurrent control.

The experimental unit in toxicology encompasses a wide variety of possibilities. It may be cells, plates of microorganisms, individual animals, litters of animals, and so forth. The importance of clearly defining the experimental unit is that the number of such units per group is the "N" which is used in statistical calculations or analysis resulting from studies, and there, critically affects the power of such calculations.

The experimental unit is the unit which receives treatments and yields a response which is measured and becomes a datum. What this means in practice is that, for example, in reproduction or teratology studies where we treat the parental-generation females and then determine results by counting or evaluating offspring, the experimental unit is still the parent. Therefore, the number of litters, not the number of offspring, is the N (4).

A true concurrent control is one that is identical in every manner with the treatment groups except for the treatment being evaluated. This means that all manipulations, including gavaging with equivalent volumes of vehicle or exposing to equivalent rates of air exchanges in an inhalation chamber, should be duplicated in the control groups just as they occur in the treatment.

The goal of the four principles of experimental design is good statistical efficiency and economy of resources. An alternative way of looking at this in a step-wise logical manner is to do a logic flow analysis of the problem. Such an undertaking is conducted in three steps, and should be performed every time any major study or project is initiated or indeed, at regular periods during the course of conduct of a series of "standard" smaller studies. These steps are detailed below.

1.  Define the objective of the study: get a clear statement of what questions are being asked.
    A.  Can the question, in fact, be broken down into a set of subquestions?
    B.  Are we asking one or more of these questions repeatedly? For example, does "X" develop at 30, 60, 90+ days and/or does it progress/regress or recover?
    C.  What is our model to be in answering this/these questions? Is it appropriate and acceptably sensitive?
2.  For each subquestion (i.e., separate major variable to be studied):
    A.  How is the variable of interest to be measured?
    B.  What is the nature of the data generated by the measure? Are we getting an efficient set of data? Or are we buying too little information, and would another technique improve the quality of the information generated to the point that it becomes a higher "class" of data? Or too much information (i.e., does some underlying aspect of of the measure limit the class of data obtainable within the bounds of feasibility of effort)?
    C.  Are there possible interactions between measurements? Can they be separated/identified?

D. Is our N (sample size) both sufficient and efficient?

E. What is the control (formal or informal)? Is it appropriate?

F. Are we needlessly adding confounding variables (asking inadvertent or unwanted questions)?

G. Are there "lurking variables" present? These are undesired and not readily recognized differences which can affect results, such as different technicians observing different groups of animals?

H. How large an effect will be considered biologically significant? This is a question which can only be resolved by reference to experience or historical control data.

3. What are the possible outcomes of the study, that is, what answers are possible to both our subquestions and to our major question?

A. How do we use these answers?

B. Do the possible answers offer a reasonable expectation of achieving the objectives that caused us to initiate the study?

C. What new questions may these answers cause us to ask? Can the study be redesigned, before it is actually started, so that these "revealed" questions may be answered in the original study?

A practical example of the application of this approach can be demonstrated in the process of designing a chronic inhalation study. Although in such a situation the primary question being asked is usually "does the chemical result in cancer by this route?", even at the beginning there are a number of other questions that it is expected that the study will answer. Two of these questions are (1) if cancer is caused, what is the relative risk associated with it and (2) are there other expressions of toxicity associated with chronic exposure? Several, if not all, of the above questions are actually to be asked repeatedly during the course of the study. Before the study starts, a plan and arrangements must be formed and criteria established against which to measure the answers to these questions.

The last phase of our logic analysis must start by considering each of the things which may go wrong during the study. These include the occurrence of an infectious disease (Do we continue or stop exposures? How will we now separate what portions of observed effects are due to the chemical under study and what is due to the disease process?), finding that extreme nasal and respiratory irritation was occurring in test animals, or revealing the existence of some hidden variable. Can we preclude (or minimize) the possibility of a disease outbreak by doing a more extensive health surveillance and quarantine on our test animals prior to the start of the study?

Could we select a better test model, that is, one that is not as sensitive to upper respiratory or nasal irritation?

If the reader has a greater degree of interest in experimental design, there are many tests available that provide detailed guidance on the statistical aspects of experimental design. Among those that are recommended are Cochran and Cox (99); Diamond (100); Federer (101); Hicks (102); and Myers (2).

## IV. DATA ANALYSIS APPLICATIONS IN TOXICOLOGY

Having reviewed the necessary basic principles and provided a set of methods for statistical handling of data, the remainder of this book will address the practical aspects and difficulties encountered in day-to-day toxicology.

As a starting point, we present an overview of data types actually encountered in toxicology (Table 2) classified by type (as presented at the beginning of this book). It should be stressed, however, that this classification is of the most frequent nature of each sort of observation (such as body weight) and will not be universally true.

There are now common practices in the analysis of toxicology data, though they are not necessarily the best. These are discussed in the remainder of this chapter, which seeks to review statistical methods on a use-by-use basis and to provide a foundation for selection of alternatives in specific situations.

### A. Median Lethal and Effective Doses

For many years, the starting point for evaluating the toxicity of an agent was to determine its $LD_{50}$ or $LC_{50}$, which are the dose or concentration of a material at which half of a specified dosed or exposed population of animals would be expected to die. These figures are analogous to the $ED_{50}$ (effective dose for half a population) used in pharmacologic activities, and are derived by the same means.

To calculate either of these figures the data we have before us are, at each of several dosage (or exposure) levels, the number of animals dosed and the number that died. If we are seeking only to establish the median effective dose in a range-finding test, then 4 or 5 animals per dose level, using the Thompson and Weil (5) method of moving averages is the most efficient and will give a sufficiently accurate solution. With two dose levels, if the ratio between the high and low dose is two or less, even total or no mortality at these two dose levels will yield an acceptably accurate median lethal dose, although a partial mortality is desirable. If, however, we wish to estimate a number of toxicity levels ($LD_{10}$, $LD_{90}$) and are interested

**Table 2**  Classification of Data Commonly Encountered in Toxicology by Type

| | |
|---|---|
| Continuous normal: | Body weights |
| | Food consumption |
| | Organ weights: absolute and relative |
| | Mouse ear swelling test (MEST) measurements |
| | Pregnancy rates |
| | Survival rates |
| | Crown-rump lengths |
| | Hematology (some) |
| | Clinical chemistry (some) |
| Continuous but not normal: | Hematology (some-WBC) |
| | Clinical chemistry (some) |
| | Urinalysis |
| Scalar data: | Neurobehavioral signs (some) |
| | PDI scores |
| | Histopathology (some) |
| Count data: | Resorption sites |
| | Implantation sites |
| | Stillborns |
| | Hematology (some-reticulocyte counts/Howel-Jolly/WBC differentials) |
| Categorical data: | Clinical signs |
| | Neurobehavioral signs (some) |
| | Ocular scores |
| | GP sensitization scores |
| | Mouse ear swelling tests (MEST) sensitization counts |
| | Fetal abnormalities |
| | Dose/mortality data |
| | Sex ratios |
| | Histopathology data (most) |

in more precisely establishing the slope of the dose/lethality curve, the use of at least 10 animals per dosage level with the log/probit regression technique is most commonly used.

Note that in the equation $Y_i = a + bx_i$, b is the slope of the regression line, and that our method already allows us to calculate 95% confidence intervals about any point on this line. Note that the confidence interval at any one point will be different from the interval at other points, and must be calculated separately. Additionally, the nature of the probit transform is such that toward the extremes ($LD_{10}$ and $LD_{90}$) the confidence intervals will "balloon." That is, they become very wide. Since the slope of the fitted line in these assays has a very large uncertainty, in relation to the uncertainty of the $LD_{50}$ itself (the midpoint of the distribution), caution must be used with calculated $LD_x$s other than $LD_{50}$s. The imprecision of the $LD_{35}$, a value close to the $LD_{50}$, is discussed by Weil (6), as is that of the slope of the log dose-probit line (7). Debanne and Haller recently reviewed the statistical aspects of different methodologies for estimating a median effective dose.

There have been questions for years as to the value of $LD_{50}$ and the efficiency of the current study design (which uses large numbers of animals) for determining it. As long ago as 1953, Weil et al. (8) presented forceful arguments that an estimate having only minimally reduced precision could be made using significantly fewer animals. More recently, the last few years have brought forth an increased level of concern over the numbers and manners of use of animals in research and testing, and have produced additional strong arguments against the existing methodologies for determining the $LD_{50}$, or even the need to produce this estimate of lethality at all (9). In response, a number of suggestions for alternative methodologies have been advanced (10-12).

These methods center around one of two techniques. The first of these (as Gad et al. (11) propose) use an approach with probes and a staggered dosing procedure. Prior to the start of an acute study comprising sufficient numbers of animals to permit conclusions to be drawn, single animals are treated on successive days at a series of dose levels. The first level probed is one which is either the maximum level required to be tested (based on regulatory criteria, e.g., 2 g/kg in a dermal study) or at a lower level if a material is judged to have a greater potential for lethality. One or two days later, based on the observed results in the single probe animal, an additional animal is dosed. If death or severe signs of toxicity occur in the initial animal, the second animal is given a lower dose, for example, at one-third or one-tenth of the initial dose level depending on the speed of observed response. If no severe signs of toxicity are observed, the probe dose is the maximum required to be tested, the initial dose is followed for a week postdosing. If it survives, the main study is initiated with the high dose group receiving the same dose level as the probe. If no severe toxicity is observed and the level tested was one based on judgment (i.e., not the maximum required), an additional animal is dosed at a level two to three times the initial test level. This process, a variation on the up-and-down methodology, commonly results in allowing us to state that "the $LD_{50}$ is greater than" the highest test level we actually evaluate in the main study.

Where the lethality results are of concern for regulatory purposes (such as finding that an oral probe animal dies at 50 mg/kg, raising the possibility that the material needs to be labelled as a poison), a full group of animals is dosed at the decision-point level. Otherwise, the highest dose level tested is just below what is expected to be a 100% lethal level, as testing a full group at a higher level would only serve to confirm lethality at that level while precluding the investigation of mechanisms or other expressions of toxicity.

The actual study is performed in a staggered start-up manner. That is, the high dose and vehicle control groups are dosed on onr day. After two days of measurements and observations, one or two additional groups are dosed at levels based on the observed results from the high dose group. If the response in the high dose group has been minimal or unremarkable, only one additional group is dosed, at a lower level such as one-half to one-third of the high dose level. If signs of toxicity were more marked, two groups are dosed at levels ranging from one-third to one-tenth of the high dose. The nature of effects observed for is modified in response to the results seen in the high dose. If the second set of groups shows signs of toxicity within two days, an additional group of animals is dosed at a yet lower level. Those animals brought in for a study but not utilized because additional dose levels are not needed provide probe animals for subsequent studies.

The second approach, the up-and-down methods, were proposed by Bruce (12). This is an adaptive procedure for conducting dose-response experiments having a yes-no endpoint. Using this strategy for acute toxicity testing, animals are dosed one at a time, starting the first animal at the toxicologist's best estimate of the $LD_{50}$. If this animal survives, then the next animal receives a higher dose, while if the first animal dies, the next animal receives a lower dose. Doses are usually adjusted by a constant multiplicative factor, such as 1.3 or 2. The dose for each successive animal is adjusted up or down depending upon the outcome for the previous animal. It can be seen that this method of experimentation causes the doses to be rapidly adjusted toward the $LD_{50}$ and then to be maintained in the region of the $LD_{50}$. The procedure concentrates experimental effort in the region of the interest and, as a result, uses animals in a very efficient manner.

## B. Body and Organ Weights

Among the sets of data commonly collected in studies where animals are dosed with (or exposed to) a chemical are body weight and the weights of selected organs. In fact, gain in body weight (also called "growth") is frequently the most sensitive parameter to indicate an adverse effect. How to best analyze this and in what form to analyze the organ weight data (as absolute weights, weight changes, or percentages of body weight) have been the subject of a number of articles in the past (4, 13-15).

Both absolute body weights and rates of body weight change (calculated as changes from a baseline measurement value which is traditionally the animal's weight immediately prior to the first dosing with or exposure to test material) are almost universally best analyzed by analysis of variance (ANOVA) followed, if called for, by a post hoc test. Even if the groups were randomized properly at the beginning of a study (no group being significantly different in mean body weight from any other group, and all animals in all groups within two standard deviations of the overall mean body weight), there is an advantage to performing the computationally slightly more cumbersome (compared to absolute body weights) changes in body weight analysis.

This advantage is an increase in sensitivity due to the adjustment of starting points (the setting of initial weights as a "zero" value) acting to reduce the amount of initial variability. In this case, Bartlett's test is first performed in ensure homogeneity of variance and the appropriate sequence of analysis is followed.

With smaller sample sizes, the normality of the data becomes increasingly uncertain and nonparametric methods such as Kruskal-Wallis may be more appropriate (16).

Analysis of relative (to body weight) organ weights is a valuable tool for identifying possible target organs (11). How to perform this analysis is still a matter of some disagreement, however.

Weil (14) presented evidence that organ weight data expressed as percentages of body weight should be analyzed separately for each sex. Furthermore, as the conclusions from organ weight data of the males differed so often from those of females, data from animals of each sex should be used in this measurement. Also, Weil (4, 17), Boyd (18), and Boyd and Knight (19), have discussed in detail other factors which influence organ weights and must be taken into account.

The two competing approaches to analyzing relative organ weights call for either: (1) calculating organ weights as percentages of total body weights (at the time of necropsy) and analyzing the results by analysis of variance (ANOVA), or (2) analyzing results by analysis of covariance (ANCOVA) with body weights as the covariates as previously discussed by the author (15).

A number of considerations should be kept in mind when these questions are addressed. First, one must keep a firm grasp on the concept of biological significance as opposed to statistical significance. In the case of these particular considerations, we are particularly concerned with examining organ weights when an organ weight changes out of proportion to changes in whole body weight. Second, we are now being required to detect smaller and smaller changes while still retaining a similar sensitivity (i.e., the $p < 0.05$ level).

There are several devices to attain the desired increase in power. Onr is to use larger and larger sample sizes (number of animals) and the other is to utilize the most powerful test we can. The use of even currently employed numbers of animals is being vigorously questioned. The power of statistical tests must, therefore, now assume increased importance in our considerations.

The biological rationale behind analyzing both absolute body weight and the organ weight to body weight ratio (this latter as opposed to a covariance analysis of organ weights) is that in the majority of cases, except for the brain, the organs of interest in the body change weight (except in extreme cases of obesity or starvation) in a parallel manner with the body overall. And it is the cases where this is not so that we are particularly interested in detecting. Analysis of actual data from several hundred studies (unpublished data) has shown no significant difference in rates of weight change of target organs (other than the brain) compared to those of the body itself for healthy animals in those species commonly used for repeated dose studies (rats, mice, rabbits, and dogs). Furthermore, it should be noted that analysis of covariance is of questionable validity in analyzing body weights and related organ weight changes, as it has as a primary assumption the fact that it is independent of treatment, that is, that the relationship of the two variables is the same for all treatments (20). Pointedly, in toxicology this is not true.

In cases where the differences between the error mean squares are much greater, the ratio of F ratios will diverge in precision from the result of the efficiency of covariance adjustment. These cases occur either when sample sizes are much larger or where the differences between means themselves are much larger. This latter case is one which does not occur in the designs under discussion in any manner that would leave analysis of covariance as a valid approach, because group means start out being very similar and cannot diverge markedly unless there is a treatment effect. As we have discussed earlier, a treatment effect invalidates a prime underpinning assumption of analysis of covariance (ANCOVA).

Finally, in cases where ANCOVA does reveal a difference between groups, one is somewhat hampered in determining where the difference lies if the adjustment was critical to the sensitivity of the analysis.

## C. Clinical Chemistry

A number of clinical chemistry parameters are commonly determined on the blood and urine collected from the animals in chronic and subchronic (and occasionally acute) toxicity studies. In the past (and still, in some places), the accepted practice has been to evaluate these data using univariate parametric methods (primarily t tests and/or ANOVA). However, this can be shown to be not the best approach on a number of grounds.

First, such biochemical parameters are rarely independent of each other. Neither is our interest often focused on just one of the parameters. Rather, there are batteries of parameters associated with toxic actions at particular target organs. For example, increases in creatinine phosphokinase (CPK), hydroxybutyrate dehydrogenase (HBDH), and lactate dehydrogenase (LDH) occurring together are strongly indicative of myocardial damage. In such cases, we are not just interested in a significant increase in one of these, but in all three. Table 3 gives a brief overview of the association of various parameters with actions at particular target organs. More detailed coverage of the interpretation of such clinical laboratory tests can be found in Wallach (21).

Similarly, changes in serum electrolytes (sodium, potassium, and calcium) interact with each other; a decrease in one is frequently tied to an increase in one of the others. Furthermore, the nature of the data (in the case of some parameters), because of either the biological background of the parameter or the way in which it is measured, frequently is either not normally distributed (particularly because of being markedly sdewed) or not continuous in nature. This can be seen in some of the reference data for experimental animals in Mitruka and Rawnsley (23) or Weil (24) in, for example, the cases of creatinine, sodium, potassium, chloride, calcium, and blood urea nitrogen. It should be remembered that both normal distribution and continuous data are underlying assumptions in the parametric statistical techniques described in this chapter. Such data has also been as termed being from "contaminated" normal distributions.

## D. Hematology

Much of what we said about clinical chemistry parameters is also true for the hematologic measurements made in toxicology studies. The pragmatic approach of evaluating which test to perform by use of a decision tree should be taken until one becomes confident as to which are the most appropriate methods. Keeping in mind that both sets of values and (in some cases) population distribution vary not only between species, but also between the commonly used strains

Table 3  Association of Changes in Biochemical Parameters with Actions at Particular Target Organs

| Parameter | Organ System | | | | | | | | Notes |
|---|---|---|---|---|---|---|---|---|---|
| | Blood | Heart | Lung | Kidney | Liver | Bone | Intestine | Pancreas | |
| Albumin | — | — | — | ↓ | ↓ | — | — | — | Produced by liver—very significant reductions require (or indicate) extensive liver damage. |
| ALP (alkaline phosphatase) | — | — | — | — | ↑ | ↑ | ↑ | — | Elevations usually associated with cholestasis. Bone alkaline phosphatase tends to be higher in young animals. |
| Bilirubin (total) | ↑ | — | — | — | ↑ | — | — | — | Usually elevated due to cholestasis, due either to obstruction or hepatopathy. |
| BUN (blood urea nitrogen) | — | — | — | ↑ | ↓ | — | — | — | Estimates blood filtering capacity of the kidneys. Doesn't become significantly elevated until kidney function is reduced 60–75%. |
| Calcium | — | — | — | ↑ | — | — | — | — | Can be life threatening and result in acute death. |

| Test | | | | | | | | | Comments |
|---|---|---|---|---|---|---|---|---|---|
| Cholinesterase | — | — | — | ↑ | — | — | — | ↓ | Found in plasma, brain and RBC. |
| CPK (creatinine phosphokinase) | — | ↑ | — | — | — | — | — | — | Most often elevated due to skeletal muscle damage but can also be produced by cardiac muscle damage. Can be more sensitive than histopathology. |
| Creatinine | — | — | — | ↑ | — | — | — | — | Also estimates blood filtering capacity of kidney as BUN does. More specific than BUN. |
| Glucose | — | — | — | — | — | ↑ | — | — | Alterations other than those associated with stress are uncommon and reflect an effect on the pancreatic islets or anorexia. |
| GGT (gamma glutamyl transferase) | — | — | — | — | — | ↑ | — | — | Elevated in cholestasis. This is a microsomal enzyme and levels often increase in response to microsomal enzyme induction. |
| HBDH (hydroxybutyric dehydrogenase) | — | ↑ | — | — | — | ↑ | — | — | |

Table 3 (continued)

| Parameter | Organ System | | | | | | | | Notes |
|---|---|---|---|---|---|---|---|---|---|
| | Blood | Heart | Lung | Kidney | Liver | Bone | Intestine | Pancreas | |
| LDH (lactic dehydrogenase) | — | ↑ | ↑ | ↑ | ↑ | — | — | — | Increase usually due to skeletal muscle, cardiac muscle and liver damage. Not very specific. |
| Protein (total) | — | — | — | ↓ | ↓ | — | — | — | Absolute alterations are usually associated with decreased production (liver) or increased loss (kidney). |
| SGOT (serum glutamicoxaloacetic transaminase) (also called AST) | — | ↑ | — | ↑ | ↑ | — | — | ↑ | Present in skeletal muscle and heart and most commonly associated with damage to these. |
| SGPT (serum glutamicpyruvic transaminase) (also called ALT) | — | — | — | — | ↑ | — | — | — | Elevations usually associated with hepatic damage or disease. |
| SDH (sorbitol dehydrogenase) | — | — | — | — | ↑ or ↓ | — | — | — | Liver enzyme which can be quite sensitive but is fairly unstable. Samples should be processed as soon as possible. |

Arrow indicates increase (↑) or decrease (↓) of chemistry values from control values/ranges.

of species (and that the "control" or "standard" values will "drift"
over the course of only a few years), familiarity should not be taken
for granted.

The majority of these parameters are, again, interrelated and
highly dependent on the method used to determine them. Red blood
cell count (RBC), platelet counts, and mean corpuscular volume
(MCV) may be determined by a device such as a Coulter counter
taking direct measurements, and the resulting data are usually suitable for parametric methods. The hematocrit, however, may actually
be a value calculated from the RBC and MCV values and, if so, is
dependent on them. If the hematocrit is measured directly, instead
of being calculated from the RBC and MCV, it may be compared by
parametric methods.

Hemoglobin is directly measured and is an independent and continuous variable. However, probably because at any one time a number of forms and conformations (oxyhemoglobin, deoxyhemoglobin,
methemoglobin, etc.) of hemoglobin are actually present, the distribution seen is not typically a normal one, but rather may be a multi-
modal one. Here a nonparametric technique such as the Wilcoxon or
multiple rank-sum test is called for.

Consideration of the white blood cell (WBC) and differential
counts leads to another problem. The total WBC is, typically, a
normal population amenable to parametric analysis, but differential
counts are normally determined by counting, manually, one or more
sets of 100 cells each. The resulting relative percentages of neutro-
phils are then reported as either percentages or are multiplied by
the total WBC count with the resulting "count" being reported as
the "absolute" differential WBC. Such data, particularly in the case
of eosinophils (where the distribution do not approach normality and
should usually be analyzed by nonparametric methods. It is widely
believed that "relative" (%) differential data should not be reported
because they are likely to be misleading.

Lastly, it should always be kept in mind that it is rare for a
change in any single hematologic parameter to be meaningful. Rather,
because these parameters are so interrelated, patterns of changes
in parameters should be expected if a real effect is present, and
analysis and interpretation of results should focus on such patterns
of changes. Classification analysis techniques often provide the
basis for a useful approach to such problems.

## E.  Histopathologic Lesion Incidence

In the last 20 years, there has been an increasing emphasis on
histopathological examination of many tissues collected from animals
in subchronic and chronic toxicity studies. While it is not true that
only those lesions which occur at a statistically significantly increased
rate in treated/exposed animals are of concern (for there are the

cases where a lesion may be of such a rare type that the occurrence of only one or a few such in treated animals "raises a flag"), it is true that, in most cases, a statistical evaluation is the only way to determine if what we are seeing in treated animals is significantly worse than what has been seen in control animals. And although cancer is not our only concern, it is the category of lesions that is of the greatest interest.

Typically, comparison of incidences of any one type of lesion between controls and treated animals are made using multiple 2 × 2 chi square or Fisher's exact test with a modification of the numbers as the denominators. Too often, experimenters exclude from consideration all those animals (in both groups) which died prior to the first animals being found with a lesion at that site. The special case of carcinogenicity bioassays will be discussed in detail in a later section and the last chapter.

An option which should be kept in mind is that frequently a pathologist can and will not just identify a lesion as present, but also grade those that are present as to severity. This represents a significant increase in the information content of the data which should not be given up by performing an analysis based only on the perceived quantal nature (present/absent) of the data. Quantal data, analyzed by chi-square or Fisher's exact tests, are a subset (the 2 × 2 case) of categorical or contingency table data. On the case under discussion it also becomes ranked (or "ordinal") data, in other words, the categories are naturally ordered (for example, no effect > mild lesion > moderate lesion > severe lesion). This gives a 2 × R table if only one treatment and one control group are involved, or an N × R ("multiway") table if there are three or more groups of animals.

The traditional method of analyzing multiple cross-classified data has been to collapse the N × R contingency table over all but two of the variables, and to follow this with the computation of some measure of association between these variables. For an N-dimensional table this results in $N(N - 1)/2$ separate analyses. The result is very crude, "giving away" information and even (by inappropriately pooling data) yielding a faulty understanding of the meaning of data. Though computationally more laborious, a multiway (N × R table) analysis should be utilized.

## F. Reproduction

Reproductive implications of the toxic effects of chemicals are becoming increasingly important. Because of this, reproduction studies, along with other closely related types of studies (such as teratogenesis, dominant lethal, and mutagenesis studies, which are discussed later in this chapter), are now common companions to chronic toxicity studies.

One point that must be kept in mind with all the reproduction-related studies is the nature of the appropriate sampling unit. Put another way: What is the appropriate N in such a study—the number of individual pups or the number of litters (or pregnant females)? Fortunately, it is now fairly well accepted that the first case (using the number of offspring as the N) is inappropriate (4). The real effects in such studies are actually occurring in the female that receives the dosage or exposure to the chemical, or that is mated to a male which received a dosage or exposure. What happens to her, and to the development of the litter she is carrying, is biologically independent of what happens to every other female/litter in the study. This cannot be said for each offspring in each litter; the death of, or other change in, one member of a litter can and will be related to what happens to every other member in numerous ways. Or the effect on all of the offspring might be similar for all of those from one female and different or lacking in another.

As defined by Oser and Oser (22), there are four primary variables of interest in a reproduction study. First, there is the fertility index (FI) which may be defined as the percentage of attempted matings (i.e., each female housed with a male) which resulted in pregnancy, with pregnancy being determined by a method such as the presence of implantation sites in the female. Second, there is the gestation index (GI) which is defined as the percentage of mated females, as evidenced by a vaginal plug being dropped or a positive vaginal smear, which deliver viable litters (i.e., litters with at least on live pup). Two related variables which may also be studied are the mean number of pups born per litter and the percentage of total pups per litter that are stillborn. Third, there is the viability index (VI), which is defined as the percentage of offspring born that survive at least 4 days after birth. Finally (in this four-variable system) there is the lactation index (LI), which is the percentage of those animals per litter alive at 4 days which survive to weaning. In rats and mice, this is classically taken to be until 21 days after birth. An additional variable which may reasonably be included in such a study is the mean weight gain per pup per litter.

Given that our N is at least 10 (we will further explore proper sample size under the topic of teratology), we may test each of these variables for significance using a method such as the Wilcoxon-Mann-Whitney U test, or the Kruskal-Wallis nonparametric ANOVA. If N is less than 10, then we cannot expect the central limit theorem to be operative and should use the Wilcoxon sum of ranks (for two groups) or the Kruskal-Wallis nonparametric ANOVA (for three or more groups) to compare groups.

## G. Teratology

When the primary concern of a reproductive/developmental study is the occurrence of birth defects or deformations (terata, either structural or functional) in the offspring of exposed animals, the study is one of teratology. In the analysis of the data from such a study, we must consider several points.

First is sample size. Earlier in this book we reviewed the general concerns with this topic, and presented a method to estimate what a sufficient sample size would be. The difficulties with applying these methods here revolve around two points: (1) selecting a sufficient level of sensitivity for detecting an effect and (2) factoring in how many animals will be removed from study (without contributing a datum) by either not becoming pregnant or not surviving to a sufficiently late stage of pregnancy. Experience generally dictates that one should attempt to have 20 pregnant animals per study group if a pilot study has provided some confidence that the pregnant test animals will survive the dose levels selected. Again, it is essential to recognize that the litter, not the fetus, is the basic independent unit for each variable.

A more fundamental consideration, as we alluded to in the section on reproduction, is that as we use more animals, the mean of means (each variable will be such in a mathematical sense) will approach normality in its distribution. This is one of the implications of the central limit theorem; even when the individual data are not normally distributed, their means will approach normality in their distribution. At a sample size of ten or greater, the approximation of normality is such that we may use a parametric test (such as a t test or ANOVA) to evaluate results. At sample sizes less than ten, a nonparametric test (Wilcoxon rank-sum or Kruskal-Wallis nonparametric ANOVA) is more appropriate. Other methodologies have been suggested (25,26) but do not offer any widespread acceptance of usage. One nonparametric method that is widely used in the Mann-Whitney U test, which was described earlier. Williams and Buschbom (27) further discuss some of the available statistical options and their consequences, and Rai and Van Ryzin (28) have recommended a dose-responsive model.

## H. Dominant Lethal Assay

The dominant lethal study is essentially a reproduction study which seeks to study the end point of lethality to the fetuses after implantation and before delivery. The proper identification of the sampling unit (the pregnant female) and the design of an experiment so that a sufficiently large sample is available for analysis are the prime statistical considerations of concern. The question of sampling unit has been adequately addressed in earlier sections. Sample size is of concern here because the hypothesis-testing techniques which are appropriate with small samples are of relatively low power, as the variability about the mean in such cases is relatively large. With sufficient sample size [e.g., from 30 to 50 pregnant females per dose level per week (29)], variability about the mean and the nature of the distribution allow sensitive statistical techniques to be employed.

The variables of concern that are typically recorded and included in analysis are (for each level/week): (a) the number of pregnant females, (b) live fetuses/pregnancy, (c) total implants/pregnancy, (d) early fetal deaths (early resorptions)/pregnancy, and (e) late fetal deaths/pregnancy.

A wide variety of techniques for analysis of these data have been (and are) used. Most common is the use of ANOVA after the data have been transformed by the arc sine transform (30).

Beta binomial (31,32) and Poisson distributions (33) have also been attributed to these data, and transforms and appropriate tests have been proposed for use in each of these cases (in each case with the note that the transforms serve to "stabilize the variance" of the data). With sufficient sample size, as defined earlier in this section, the Mann-Whitney U test is to be recommended for use here. Smaller sample sizes should necessitate the use of the Wilcoxon rank-sum test.

## I. Diet and Chamber Analysis

Earlier we presented the basic principles and methods for sampling. Sampling is important for many aspects of toxicology, and here we address its application in diet preparation and the analysis of atmospheres from inhalation chambers.

In feeding studies, we seek to deliver desired doses of a material to animals by mixing the material with their diet. Similarly, in an inhalation study we mix a material with the air the test animals breathe.

In both cases, we must then sample the medium (food or atmosphere) and analyze these samples to determine what levels or concentrations of material were actually present and to assure ourselves that the test material is homogeneously distributed. Having an accurate picture of these delivered concentrations, and how they varied over the course of time, is essential on a number of grounds:

1. The regulatory agencies and sound scientific practice require that analyzed diet and mean daily inhalation atmosphere levels be ±10% of the target level.
2. Marked peak concentrations, because of the overloading of metabolic and repair systems, could result in extreme acute effects that would lead to apparent results in a chronic

study which are not truly indicative of the chronic low level effects of the compound, but rather of periods of metabolic and physiologic overload. Such results could be misinterpreted if the true exposure or diet levels were not maintained at a relatively constant level.

Sampling strategies are not just a matter of numbers (for the statistical aspects), but of geometry, so that the contents of a container or the entire atmosphere in a chamber is truly sampled; and of time, in accordance with the stability of the test compound. The samples must be both randomly collected and "representative" of the entire mass of what one is trying to characterize. In the special case of sampling and characterizing the physical properties of aerosols in an inhalation study, some special considerations and terminology apply. Because of the physiologic characteristics of the respiration of humans and of test animals, our concern is very largely limited to those particles or droplets which are of respirable size. Unfortunately, "respirable size" is a somewhat complexly defined characteristic based on aerodynamic diameter, density, and physiological characteristics. A second misfortune is that while those particles with an aerodynamic diameter of less than 10 μm are generally agreed to be respirable in humans (that is, they can be drawn down to the deep portions of the lungs), in the rat this characteristic is more realistically limited to those particles below 3 μm in aerodynamic diameter. The one favorable factor is that there are now available a selection of instruments which accurately (and relatively easily) collect and measure aerodynamically sized particles or droplets. These measurements result in concentrations in a defined volume of gas, and can be expressed as either a number concentration or a mass concentration (the latter being more common). Such measurements generate categorical data or concentrations measured in each of a series of aerodynamic size groups (such as > 100 μm, 100–25 μm, 25–10 μm, 10–3 μm, etc.). The appropriate descriptive statistics for this class of data are the geometric mean and its standard deviation. These aspects and the statistical interpretation of the data that are finally collected should be considered after sufficient interaction with the appropriate professionals. Typically, it then becomes a matter of the calculation of measures of central tendency and dispersion statistics, with the identification of those values which are beyond acceptable limits (34).

## J. Mutagenesis

In the last 15 years a wide variety of tests (see Kilbey et al., Ref. 35 for an overview of available tests) for mutagenicity have been developed and brought into use. These tests give us a quicker and cheaper (though not as conclusive) way of predicting whether a material of interest is a mutagen, and possibly a carcinogen, than do longer term whole-animal studies.

How to analyze the results of this multitude of tests (Ames, DNA repair, micronucleus, host-mediated, cell transformation, sister chromatid exchange, and *Drosophila* SLRL, just to name a few) is a new and extremely important question. Some workers in the field hold that it is not possible (or necessary) to perform statistical analysis, that the tests can simply be judged to be positive or not positive on the basis of whather or not they achieve a particular degree of increase in the incidence of mutations in the test organism. This is plainly not an acceptable response, when societal needs are not limited to yes/no answers but rather include at least relative quantitation of potencies (particularly in mutagenesis, where we have come to recognize the existence of a nonzero background level of activity from naturally occurring factors and agents). Such quantitations of potency are complicated by the fact that we are dealing with a nonlinear phenomenon. For though low doses of most mutagens produce a linear response curve, with increasing doses, the curve will flatten out (and even turn into a declining curve) as higher doses take the target systems into levels of acute toxicity to the test system.

Several concepts, different from those we have discussed previously need to be examined, for our concern has now shifted from how a multicellular organism acts in response to one of a number of complex actions to how a mutational event is expressed, most frequently by a single cell. Given that we can handle much larger numbers of experimental units in these systems that use smaller test organisms, we can seek to detect both weak and strong mutagens.

Conducting the appropriate statistical analysis, and utilizing the results of such an analysis properly, must start with understanding the biological system involved and, from this understanding developing the correct model and hypothesis. We start such a process by considering each of five interacting factors (36,37)

1. $\alpha$, which is the probability of our committing a type I error (saying an agent is mutagenic when it is not, equivalent to our p in such earlier considered designs as the Fisher's exact test); false positive;

2. $\beta$, which is the probability of our committing a type II error (saying an agent is not mutagenic when it is); false negative;

3. $\Delta$, our desired sensitivity in an assay system (such as being ablr to detect an increase of 10% in mutations in a population);

4. $\sigma$, the variability of the biological system and the effects of chance errors; and

5. n, the necessary sample size to achieve each of these (we can only, by our actions, change this one portion of the equation) as n is proportional to:

$$\frac{\sigma}{\alpha, \ \beta, \ \text{and} \ \Delta}$$

The implications of this are, therefore, that (a) the greater $\sigma$ is, the larger n must be to achieve the desired levels of $\alpha$, $\beta$, and $\Delta$, (b) the smaller the desired levels of $\alpha$, $\beta$, and/or $\Delta$, if n is constant, the larger our $\sigma$ is.

What is the background mutation level and the variability in our technique? As any good genetic or general toxicologist will acknowledge, matched concurrent control groups are essential. Fortunately, with these test systems large n's are readily attainable, though there are other complications to this problem, which we shall consider later. An example of the confusion that would otherwise result in illustrated in the intralaboratory comparisons of some of these methods done to date, such as that reviewed by Weil (40).

New statistical tests based on these assumptions and upon the underlying population distributions have been proposed, along with the necessary computational background to allow one to alter one of the input variables ($\alpha$, $\beta$, or $\Delta$). A set that shows particular promise is that proposed by Katz (38,39) in his two articles. He described two separate test statistics: $\phi$ for when we can accurately estimate the number of individuals in both the experimental and control groups, and $\theta$, for when we do not actually estimate the number of surviving individuals in each group, and we can assume that the test material is only mildly toxic in terms of killing the test organisms. Each of these two test statistics is also formulated on the basis of only a single exposure of the organisms to the test chemicals. Given this, then we may compute

$$\phi = \frac{\alpha(M_E - 0.5) - Kb(M_C + 0.5)}{\sqrt{Kab(M_E + M_C)}}$$

where a and b are the number of groups of control (c) and experimental (e) organisms, respectively.

$N_C$ and $N_E$ are the numbers of surviving microorganisms.

$$[K = N_E/N_C]$$

$M_E$ and $M_C$ are the numbers of mutations in experimental and control groups.

$\mu_e$ and $\mu_c$ are the true (but unknown) mutation rates (as $\mu_c$ gets smaller, N's must increase).

We may compute the second case as

$$\theta = \frac{\sigma(M_e - 0.5) + (M_c + 0.5)}{ab(M_e + M_c)}$$

with the same constituents.

In both cases, at a confidence level for $\alpha$ of 0.05, we accept that $\mu_c = \mu_e$ if the test statistic (either $\phi$ or $\theta$) is less than 1.64. If it is equal to or greater than 1.64, we may conclude that we have a mutagenic effect (at $\alpha = 0.05$).

In the second case ($\theta$, where we do not have separate estimates of population sizes for the control and experimental groups) if K deviates widely from 1.0 (if the material is markedly toxic), we should use more containers of control organisms [tables for the proportions of each to use given different survival frequencies may be found in Katz (39)]. If different levels are desired, tables for $\theta$ and $\phi$ may be found in Kastenbaum and Bowman (41).

An outgrowth of this is that the mutation rate per surviving cells ($\mu_c$ and $\mu_e$) can be determined. It must be remembered that if the control mutation rate is high enough that a reduction in mutation rates can be achieved by the test compound, these test statistics must be adjusted to allow for a two-sided hypothesis (42). The levels may likewise be adjusted in each case, or tested for, if what we want to do is assure ourselves that we do have a mutagenic effect at a certain level of confidence (note that this is different from disproving the null hypothesis).

It should be noted that there are numerous specific recommendations for statistical methods designed for individual mutagenicity techniques, such as that of Bernstein et al. (43) for the Ames test. Exploring each of them is beyond the scope of this chapter, however.

## K. Behavioral Toxicology

A brief review of the types of studies/experiments conducted in the area of behavioral toxicology, and a classification of these into groups is in order. Although there are a small number of studies which do not fit into the following classification, the great majority may be fitted into one of the following four groups. Many of these points were first covered by one of the authors in an earlier article (44).

Observational score-type studies are based on observing and grading the response of an animal to its normal environment or to a stimulus which is imprecisely controlled. This type of result is generated by one of two major sorts of studies. Open-field studies involve placing an animal in the center of a flat, open area and counting each occurrence of several types of activities (e.g., grooming, moving outside a designated central area, rearing) or timing until the first occurrence of each type of activity. The data generated are scalar of either a continuous or discontinuous nature, but frequently are not of a normal distribution. Tilson et al. (45) have presented some examples of this. Observational screen studies involve a combination of observing behavior or evoking a response to a simple stimulus, the resulting observation being graded as normal or as deviating from normal on a graded scale. Most of the data so generated are of a rank nature, with some portions being quantal or interval in nature. Irwin (46) and Gad (47) have presented schemes for the conduct of such studies.

The second type of study is one which generates rates of response as data. The studies are based on the number of responses to a discrete controlled stimulus or are free of direct connection to a stimulus. The three most frequently measured parameters are licking of a liquid (milk, sugar water, ethanol, or a psychoactive agent in water), gross locomotor activity (measured by a photocell or electromagnetic device), or lever pulling. Work presenting examples of such studies has been published by Annau (48) and Norton (49). The data generated are most often of a discontinuous or continuous scalar nature, and are often complicated by underlying patterns of biological rhythm (to be discussed more fully later).

The third type of study generates a variety of data which is classified as error rates. These are studies based on animals learning a response to a stimulus or memorizing a simple task (such as running a maze or a Skinner box-type shock avoidance system). These tests or trials are structured so that animals can pass or fail on each of a number of successive trials. The resulting data are quantal, though frequently expressed as a percentage.

The final major type of study is that which results in data which are measures of the time to an endpoint. They are based on animals being exposed to or dosed with a toxicant; then the time until an effect is observed is measured. Usually the endpoint is failure to continue to be able to perform a task. The endpoints can, therefore, be death, incapacitation, or the learning of a response to a discrete stimulus. Burt (50) and Johnson et al. (51) present data of this form. The data are always o/ a censored nature, that is, the period of observation is always artificially limited on one end, such as in measuring time to incapacitation in combustion toxicology data, where animals are exposed to the thermal decomposition gases of test materials for a period of 30 minutes. If incapacitation is not observed during these 30 minutes, it is judged not to occur. The data generated by these studies are continuous, discontinuous, or rank in nature. They are discontinuous because the researcher may check, or may be restricted to checking for the occurrence of the endpoint only at certain discrete points in time. On the other hand, they are rank if the periods to check for occurrence of the endpoint are far enough apart, in which case one may actually only know that the endpoint occurred during a broad period of time, but not where in that period.

There is a special class of test which should also be considered at this point: the behavioral teratology or reproduction study. These studies are based on dosing or exposing either parental animals during selected periods in the mating and gestation process or pregnant females at selected periods during gestation. The resulting offspring are then tested for developmental defects of a neurological and behavioral nature. Analysis is complicated by a number of facts: (1) the parental animals are the actual targets for toxic effects, but observations are made on offspring; (2) the toxic effects in the parental generation may alter the performance of the mother in rearing its offspring, which in turn can lead to confusion of behaviors develop at different times (which will be discussed further below).

A researcher can, by varying the selection of the animal model (species, strain, sex), modify the nature of the data generated and the degree of dispersion of these data. Particularly in behavioral studies, limiting the within-group variability of data is a significant problem and generally should be a highly desirable goal.

Most, if not all, behavioral toxicology studies depend on at least some instrumentation. Very frequently overlooked here (and, indeed, in most research) is that instrumentation, by its operating characteristics and limitations, goes a long way toward determining the nature of the data generated by it. An activity monitor measures motor activity in discrete segments. If it is a "jiggle cage" type monitor these segments are restricted so that only a distinctly limited number of counts can be achieved in a given period of time and then only if they are of the appropriate magnitude. Likewise, technique can also readily determine the nature of data. In measuring response to pain, for example, one could record it as a quantal measure (present or absent), a rank score (on a scale of 1–5 for from decreased to increased responsiveness, with 3 being "normal"), or as scalar data (by using an analgesia meter which determines either how much pressure or heat is required to evoke a response).

Study design factors are probably the most widely recognized of the factors which influence the type of data resulting from a study. Number of animals used, frequency of measures, and length of period of observation are three obvious design factors which are readily under the control of the researcher and which directly help to determine the nature of the data.

Table 4   Overview of Statistical Testing for Behavioral Toxicology: Tests Commonly Used[a] as Opposed to Those Most Frequently Appropriate

| Type of observation | Most commonly used procedures[a] | Suggested procedures |
|---|---|---|
| Observational scores | Either Student's t-test or one-way ANOVA | Kruskal-Wallis nonparametric ANOVA or Wilcoxon Rank sum |
| Response rates | Either Student's t-test or one-way | Kruskal-Wallis ANOVA or one-way ANOVA |
| Error rates | ANOVA followed by a posthoc test | Fisher's exact, or RXC Chi square, or Mann-Whitney U-test |
| Times to | Either Student's t-test or one-way ANOVA | ANOVA then a posthoc test or Kruskal-Wallis ANOVA |
| Teratology and | ANOVA followed by a posthoc test | Fisher's exact test, Kruskal-Wallis ANOVA, or Mann-Whitney U-test |

[a]That these are the most commonly used procedures was established by an extensive literature review which is beyond the scope of this book.  The reader need only, however, look at the example articles cited in the text of Gad and Weil (1) to verify this fact.

Finally it is appropriate to review each of the types of studies presently seen in behavioral toxicology, according to the classification presented at the beginning of this section, in terms of which statistical methods are used now and what procedures should be recommended for use.  The recommendations, of course, should be viewed critically.  They are intended with current experimental design and technique in mind and can only claim to be the best when one is limited to addressing the most common problems from a "library" of readily and commonly available and understood tests.

Table 4 summarizes this review and recommendation process in a straightforward form.

## V. CARCINOGENESIS AND RISK ASSESSMENT

Both carcinogenesis and the broader realm of risk assessment (as it applies to toxicology) have in common that, based on experimental results in a nonhuman species at some relatively high dose or exposure level, an attempt is made to predict a result of extreme impact in humans at much lower levels. In this section we will examine the assumptions involved in these undertakings, review the aspects of design and interpretation of animal carcinogenicity studies, and present the framework on which risk assessment is based.

The reader should first understand that, contrary to popular belief, risk assessment in toxicology is not limited to carcinogenesis. Rather, it may be applied to all the possible deferred toxicologic consequences of exposure to chemicals or agents which are of a truly severe nature. That is, those things (such as carcinogenesis, teratogenesis, or reproductive impairment) that threaten life (either existing or prospective) at a time distant to the actual exposure to the chemical or agent. Because the consequences of these toxic events are so extreme yet are detached from the actual cause by time (unlike when a person dies from overexposure to an acutely lethal agent, such as carbon monoxide), society is willing to accept only a low level of risk while maintaining the benefits of use of the agent. Though the most familiar (and, to date, best developed) case is that of carcinogenesis, much of what is presented for risk assessment may also be applied to the other endpoints of concern.

### A. Carcinogenicity Bioassays

At least in a general way, we now understand what appear to be most of the mechanisms underlying chemical- and radiation-induced carcinogenesis. A review of these mechanisms is not germane to this chapter [readers wishing a good short review are advised to read Miller and Miller (52)], but it is now clear that cancer as seen in humans is the result of a multifocal set of causes. The single most important statistical consideration in the design of bioassays in the past was based on the point of view that what was being observed and evaluated was a simple quantal response (cancer occurred or it did not), and that a sufficient number of animals needed to be used to have reasonable expectations of detecting such an effect. Though the single fact of whether or not the simple incidence of neoplastic tumors is increased due to an agent of concern is of interest, a much more complex model must now be considered. The time-to-tumor, patterns of tumor incidence, effects on survival rate, and age at first tumor all must now be included in a model.

### 1. Bioassay Design

As presented earlier in the section on experimental design, the first step which must be taken is to clearly state the objective of the study to be undertaken. Carcinogenicity bioassays have two possible objectives, though (as we shall see) the second is now more important and (as our understanding of carcinogenesis has grown) is increasingly crowding out the first.

The first objective is to detect possible carcinogens. Compounds are evaluated to determine if they can or cannot induce a statistically detectable increase of tumor rates over background levels, and only by happenstance is information generated which is useful in risk assssessment. Most older studies have such detection as their objective. Current thought is that at least two species must be used for detection to be adequately sensitive.

The second objective for a bioassay is to provide a range of dose response information (with tumor incidence being the response) so that a risk assessment may be performed. Unlike detection, which requires only one treatment group with adequate survival times (to allow expression of the endpoint of interest as tumors), dose response requires at least three treatment groups with adequate survival. We will shortly look at the selection of dose levels for this case. However, given that the species is known to be responsive, only one species of animal need be used for this objective.

To address either or both of these objectives, three major types of study designs have evolved. First is the classical skin painting study, usually performed in mice. A single easily detected endpoint (the formation of skin tumors) is evaluated during the course of the study. Though dose response can be evaluated in such a study (dose usually being varied by using different concentrations of test material in volatile solvent), most often detection is the objective of such a study. Though others have used different frequencies of application of test material to vary dose, there are data to suggest that this only serves to introduce an additional variable (53). Traditionally, both test and control groups in such a study consist of 50 or 100 mice of one sex (males being preferred because of their very low spontaneous tumor rate). This design is also used in tumor initiation/promotion studies.

The second common type of design is the original National Cancer Institute (NCI) bioassay. The announced objective of these studies was detection of moderate to strong carcinogens, though the results have also been used in attempts at risk assessment. Both mice and rats were used in parallel studies. Each study used 50 males and 50 females at each of two dose levels (high and low) plus an equal sized control group. The National Toxicology Program (NTP) has recently moved away from this design because of a recognition of its inherent limitations.

Finally, there is the standard industrial toxicology design, which uses at least two species (usually rats and mice) in groups of no fewer than 100 males and females each. Each study has three dose groups and at least one control. Frequently additional numbers

of animals are included to allow for interim terminations and histopathological evaluations. In both this and the NCI design, a long
list of organs and tissues are collected, processed, and examined
microscopically. This design seeks to address both the detection
and dose-response objectives with a moderate degree of success.

Selecting the number of animals to use for dose groups in a
study requires consideration of both biological (expected survival
rates, background tumor rates, etc.) and statistical factors. The
prime statistical consideration is reflected in Table 5, where it can
be seen that if, for example, we were studying a compound which
caused liver tumors, and were using mice (with a background or
control incidence of 30%), we would have to use 389 animals per sex
per group to be able to demonstrate that an incidence rate of 40%
in treatment animals was significant compared to the controls at the
p ≤ 0.05 level.

Perhaps the most difficult aspect of designing a good carcinogenicity study is the selection of the dose levels to be used. At
the start, it is necessary to consider the first underlying assumption
in the design and use of animal cancer bioassays, the need to test
at the highest possible dose for the longest practical period.

The rationale behind this assumption is that although humans may
be exposed at very low levels, statistically detecting the resulting
small increase (over background) in incidence of tumors would require the use of an impractically large number of test animals per
group. This point is illustrated by Table 6 where while only 46
animals (per group) are needed to show a 10% increase over a zero
background (that is, a rarely occurring tumor type), 770,000 animals
(per group) would be needed to detect a tenth of a percent increase
above a 5% background. As we increase dose, however, the incidence
of tumors (the response) will also increase until it reaches the point
where a modest increase (say 10%) over a reasonably small background level (say 1%) could be detected using an acceptably small
sized group of test animals (in Table 5 we see that 51 animals would
be needed for this example case). There are, however, at least two
real limitations on how high the highest dose may be. First is that
the test rodent population must have a sufficient survival rate after
receiving a lifetime (or two years) of regular doses to allow for
meaningful statistical analysis. The second is that we really want
the metabolism and mechanism of action of the chemical at the highest level tested to be the same as those at the low levels where
human exposure would occur. Unfortunately, we usually must select
the high dose level based only on the information provided by a
subchronic or range-finding study. Selection of too low a dose will
make the study invalid for detection of carcinogenicity, and may
seriously impair the use of the results for risk assessment.

There are several approaches to this problem. One has been
the rather simplistic approach of the NTP Bioassay Program, which

Table 5  Sample Size Required to Obtain a Specified Sensitivity at $p < 0.05$

| Background tumor incidence | $p^a$ | Treatment Group Incidence | | | | | | | | | |
|---|---|---|---|---|---|---|---|---|---|---|---|
| | | 0.95 | 0.90 | 0.80 | 0.70 | 0.60 | 0.50 | 0.40 | 0.30 | 0.20 | 0.10 |
| 0.30 | 0.90 | 10 | 12 | 18 | 31 | 46 | 102 | 389 | | | |
|      | 0.50 | 6  | 6  | 9  | 12 | 22 | 32  | 123 | | | |
| 0.20 | 0.90 | 8  | 10 | 12 | 18 | 30 | 42  | 88  | 320 | | |
|      | 0.50 | 5  | 5  | 6  | 9  | 12 | 19  | 28  | 101 | | |
| 0.10 | 0.90 | 6  | 8  | 10 | 12 | 17 | 25  | 33  | 65  | 214 | |
|      | 0.50 | 3  | 3  | 5  | 6  | 9  | 11  | 17  | 31  | 68  | |
| 0.05 | 0.90 | 5  | 6  | 8  | 10 | 13 | 18  | 25  | 35  | 76  | 464 |
|      | 0.50 | 3  | 3  | 5  | 6  | 7  | 9   | 12  | 19  | 24  | 147 |
| 0.01 | 0.90 | 5  | 5  | 7  | 8  | 10 | 13  | 19  | 27  | 46  | 114 |
|      | 0.50 | 3  | 3  | 5  | 5  | 6  | 8   | 10  | 13  | 25  | 56  |

[a] p = Power for each comparison of treatment group with background tumor incidence.

Table 6  Average Number of Animals Needed to Detect a Significant Increase in the Incidence of an Event (Tumors, Anomalies, etc.) Over the Background Incidence (Control) at Several Expected Incidence Levels Using the Fisher Exact Probability Test ($p \leq 0.05$)

| Background incidence (%) | Expected increase in incidence (%) | | | | | |
|---|---|---|---|---|---|---|
| | 0.01 | 0.1 | 1 | 3 | 5 | 10 |
| 0 | 46,000,000[a] | 460,000 | 4,600 | 511 | 164 | 46 |
| 0.01 | 46,000,000 | 460,000 | 4,600 | 511 | 164 | 46 |
| 0.1 | 47,000,000 | 470,000 | 4,700 | 520 | 168 | 47 |
| 1 | 51,000,000 | 510,000 | 5,100 | 570 | 204 | 51 |
| 5 | 77,000,000 | 770,000 | 7,700 | 856 | 304 | 77 |
| 10 | 100,000,000 | 1,000,000 | 10,000 | 1,100 | 400 | 100 |
| 20 | 148,000,000 | 1,480,000 | 14,800 | 1,644 | 592 | 148 |
| 25 | 160,000,000 | 1,600,000 | 16,000 | 1,840 | 664 | 166 |

[a]Number of animals needed in each group, controls as well as treated.

is to conduct a 3-month range-finding study with sufficient dose levels to establish a level which significantly (10%) decreases the rate of body weight gain. This dose is defined as the maximum tolerated dose (MTD) and is selected as the highest dose. Two other levels, generally one half MTD and one quarter MTD, are selected for testing as the intermediate and low dose levels. In many earlier NCI studies, only one other level was used.

The dose range-finding study is a must in most cases, but the suppression of body weight gain is a scientifically questionable bench mark when dealing with establishment of safety factors. Physiologic, pharmacologic, or metabolic markers generally serve as better indicators of the systemic response than body weight. A series of well-defined acute and subchronic studies designed to determine the "chronicity factor" and to study onset of pathology can be more predictive for dose setting than body weight suppression.

Also, the NTP's MTD may well be at a level that the metabolic mechanisms for handling a compound at real-life exposure levels have been saturated or overwhelmed, bringing into play entirely artifactual metabolic and physiologic mechanisms (54). The regulatory response to the questioning of the appropriateness of the MTD as a high dose level [exemplified by Haseman (55)] has been to acknowledge that occasionally an excessively high dose is selected, but to counter that using lower doses would seriously decrease the sensitivity of the detection function.

Selection of levels for the intermediate and lower doses for a study is easy only in comparison to the selection of the high dose. If an objective of the study is to generate dose-response data, then the optimal placement of the doses below the high is such that they cover as much of the range of a response curve as possible and yet still have the lowest dose at a high enough level that one can detect and quantify a response. If the objective is detection, then having too great a distance between the highest and next highest dose creates a risk to the validity of the study. If survival in the high dose is too low, yet the next highest dose does not show non-neoplastic results (that is, cause other than neoplastic adverse biological effects) so as to support it being a high enough dose to have detected a strong or moderate carcinogen, the entire study may have to be rejected as inadequate to address its objective. Portier and Hoel (56) have proposed statistical guidelines (for setting dose levels below the high) based on response surfaces. In so doing they suggest that the lowest dose be no less than 10% of the highest.

While it is universally agreed that the appropriate animal model for testing a chemical for carcinogenicity would be one whose metabolism, pharmacokinetics, and biological responses were most similar to humans, economic considerations have largely constrained the actual choices to rats and mice. The use of both sexes of both species is preferred on the grounds that it provides for (in the face of a lack of understanding of which species would actually be most like humans for a particular agent) a greater likelihood of utilizing the more sensitive species. Use of the mouse is both advocated and defended on these grounds and because of the economic advantages and the species' historical utilization (57). There are those who believe that the use of the mouse is redundant and represents a diversion of resources while yielding little additional information (58) citing a "unique contribution" for mouse data in 273 bioassays of only 13.6% of the cases (that is, 37 cases). Others question the use of the mouse based on the belief that it gives artifactual liver carcinogenesis results. One suggestion for the interpretation of mouse bioassays is, that in those cases where there is only an increase in liver tumors in mice (or lung tumors in strain A mice) and no supporting mutagenicity findings (a situation characteristic of some classes of chemicals), the test compound should not be considered an overt carcinogen (59). This last question, however, is even more strongly focused on the strain of mouse that is used than on the use of the species itself.

The NCI/NTP (National Toxicology Program) currently recommends an F1 hybrid cross between two inbred strains, the C57B1/6 female and the C3H male, the results being commonly designated as the B6C3F1. This mouse was found to be very successful in a large-scale pesticide testing program in the mid-1960s. It is a hardy animal with good survival, easy to breed, disease resistant, and was reported to have a relatively low spontaneous tumor incidence. Usually, up to 24 months termination, at least 80% of the control mice are still alive.

The problem is that, contrary to what was originally believed (60), the spontaneous liver tumor incidence in male B6C3F1 mice is not 15.7%, but more like 32.1% (61). The issue of spontaneous tumor rates and their impact on the design and interpretation of studies will be discussed more fully later. Thus, use of a cross of two inbred mouse strains is also a point of controversy. Haseman and Hoel (52) have presented data to support the idea that inbred strains have lower degrees of variability of biological functions and tumor rates, making them more sensitive detectors and quantitators. These authors also suggest that the use of a cross from two such inbred strains allows one to more readily detect tumor incidence increases. On the other hand, it is argued that such genetically homogeneous strains do not properly reflect the diversity of metabolic functions (particularly ones which would serve to detoxify or act as defense mechanisms) which are present in the human population.

Study length and frequency of treatment are design aspects which must also be considered. These are aspects where the objectives of detection and dose-response definition conflict.

For the greatest confidence in a "negative" detection result, an agent should be administered continuously for the majority of an animal's lifespan. The NTP considers that 2 years is a practical treatment period in rats and mice, although the animals currently used in such studies may survive an additional 6–12 months. Study lengths of 15–18 months are considered adequate for shorter-lived species such as hamsters. An acceptable exposure/observation period for dogs is considered to be 7–10 years, an age equivalent to about 45–60 years in humans. For dietary treatments, continuous exposure is considered desirable and practical. With other routes, practical considerations may dictate interrupted treatments. For example, inhalation treatment for 6–8 hr/day on a 5 day/week schedule is the usual practice. Regimens requiring special handling of animals, such as parenteral injections, are usually on a 5 day/week basis. With some compounds intermittent exposures may be required because of toxicity. Various types of recovery can occur during exposure-free periods, which may either enhance or decrease chances of carcinogenicity. In view of the objective of assessing the carcinogenicity as the initial step, intermittent exposures on a 3–5 day/week basis is considered both practical and desirable for most compounds.

Following cessation of dosing or exposure, continued observation during a nontreatment period may be required before termination of the experiment. Such a period is considered desirable because (1) induced lesions may progress to more readily observable lesions, and (2) morphologically similar but noncarcinogenic proliferative lesions that are stress related may regress. Neoplastic or "neoplastic-like" lesions that persist long after removal of the stimulus are considered of serious consequence, from the hazard viewpoint. Many expert anatomical pathologists, however, feel able to diagnose and determine the biological nature of tumorous lesions existing at the time of treatment without the added benefit of a treatment-free period.

In determining the length of an observation period, several factors must be considered: period of exposure, survival pattern of both treated and control animals, nature of lesions found in animals that have already died, tissue storage and retention of the chemical, and results of other studies that would suggest induction of late-occurring tumors. The usual length of a treatment-free observation period is 3 months in mice and hamsters and 6 months in rats. An alternative would be to terminate the experiment or an individual treatment group on the basis of survival (say at the point at which 50% of the group with the lowest survival has died).

The arguments against such prolonged treatment and maintenance on study revolve around the relationship between age and tumor incidence. As test animals (or humans) become older, the background ("naturally occurring") incidence of turmors increases (63) and it becomes increasingly more difficult to identify a treatment effect apart from the background effect. Salsburg (64) has published an analysis of patterns of senile lesions in mice and rats, citing what he calls the principle of biological confounding. "If a particular lesion (e.g., pituitary tumor) is part of a larger syndrome induced by the treatment, it is impossible to determine whether the treatment has 'caused' that lesion."

This could lead to a situation where any real carcinogen would be nonidentifiable. If the usual pattern of old-age lesions for a given species or strain of animals includes tumors, then almost every biologically active treatment can be expected to influence the incidence of tumors in some cluster of lesions at a sufficiently high dose.

Reconsidering our basic principles of experimental design, it is clear that we should try to design bioassays so that any carcinogenesis is a clear-cut single event, unconfounded by the occurrence of significant numbers of lesions due to other causes (such as age). One answer to this problem is the use of interim termination groups. When an evaluation of tumor incidences in an interim sacrifice (sample) of animals indicates that background incidences are becoming a source of confounding data, termination plans for the study can be altered to minimize the loss of power. Several authors (65) have presented such adaptive sacrifice plans.

A number of other possible confounding factors can enter into a bioassay unless design precludes them. These include (a) cage and litter effects (which can be avoided by proper prestudy randomization of animals and rotation of cage locations), (b) vehicle (corn oil, for example, has been found to be a promoter for liver carcinogens), and (c) the use of the potential hazard route for humans, for example, dietary inclusion instead of gastric intubation. Other general aspects of the design of carcinogenicity bioassay may be found in Robens et al. (66).

### 2. Bioassay Interpretation

The interpretation of the results of even the best designed carcinogenesis bioassay is a complex statistical and biological problem. In addressing the statistical aspects, we shall have to overview some biological points (which have statistical implications) along the way.

First, all such bioassays are evaluated by comparison of the observed results in treatment groups with those in one or more control groups. These control groups always include at least one group that is concurrent, but because of concern about the variability in background tumor rates, a historical control group is also considered in at least some manner.

The underlying problem in the use of concurrent controls alone is the belief that the selected populations of animals are subject both to an inordinate degree of variability in their spontaneous tumor incidence rates and that the strains maintained at separate breeding facilities are each subject to a slow but significant degree of genetic drift. The first case raises concern that, by chance, the animals selected to be controls for any particular study will be either "too high" or "too low" in their tumor incidences, leading to either a false positive or false negative statistical test result when test animals are compared to these controls. The second problem leads to the concern that over the years, different laboratories will be using different standards (control groups) against which to compare the outcome of their tests, making any kind of relative comparison between either compounds or laboratories impossible.

The last 10 years have seen at least 8 separate publications reporting on 5 sets of background tumor incidences in test animals. These 8 publications are summarized and compared in Tables 7 and 8 for B6C3F1 mice and Fischer 344 rats, respectively.

It should be kept in mind in considering these separate columns of numbers that there are some overlaps in the populations being reported. For example, it is almost certain that some NCI/NTP study control groups were incorporated in several separate publications. At the same time, the related survival and growth data on control animals (broken out by type of treatment and vehicle) has also been published (67), allowing for some assessment of comparability of control animal populations based on grounds other than just tumor incidences. It is interesting that in these NCI/NTP bioassay program control populations, mean survival of B6C3F1 mice was greater than that of F344 rats.

Generally, historical control group data are used primarily as a check to ensure that the statistical evaluations used in comparing treatment groups to concurrent controls have a sound starting point (68).

Dempster et al. (69) have, however, proposed a method for incorporating historical control data in the actual process of statistical analysis. A variable degree of pooling (combining) of historical with concurrent controls is performed based on the extent to which the historical data fit an assumed normal logistic (log transform) model.

Age (either animals or humans) is clearly related to both "background" cancer incidence and chemically induced carcinogenesis. Indeed, one view of chemically induced carcinogenesis is that it serves in many, if not all, cases to accelerate the rate at which developing deficiencies in the body's defense system allow cancers to be expressed. As either a carcinogen becomes more potent or a larger dose is used, neoplasms successfully overcome or evade defense mechanisms and are expressed as tumors. In some cases, clearly the effect of a test chemical has been to result in the earlier

Table 7  Reported Background Tumor Incidences in B6C3F1 Mice

| Organ/tissue | Chu (68) | | Fears et al. (70,71), page (60), Gart et al. (72) | | Chu et al. (68) | | Tarone et al. (73) (Ranges) | |
|---|---|---|---|---|---|---|---|---|
| | M | F | M | F | M | F | M | F |
| Brain | .9 | .1 | <1.0 | 0 | <.1 | .1 | — | — |
| Skin/subcutaneous | 1.9 | 1.6 | 1 | <1.0 | 3.1 | 1.7 | — | — |
| Mammary gland | — | .8 | — | <1.0 | — | 1.3 | — | — |
| Circulatory system | 2.4 | 1.7 | <1.0 | <1.0 | 2.9 | 2.4 | — | — |
| Lung/trachea | 11.7 | 4.4 | 9.2 | 3.5 | 13.7 | 5.2 | 10.6-21.9 | 3.6-7.1 |
| Heart | .1 | .1 | <1.0 | 0 | — | — | — | — |
| Liver | 21.9 | 4.0 | 15.6 | 2.5 | 24.6 | 4.7 | 25.0-40.1 | 4.6-9.7 |
| Pancreas | .1 | .1 | <1.0 | <1.0 | 2.1 | < .1 | — | — |
| Stomach | .3 | .3 | 1.1 | <1.0 | .4 | .4 | — | — |
| Intestines | .4 | .4 | <1.0 | <1.0 | .5 | .2 | — | — |
| Kidney | .2 | .1 | <1.0 | <1.0 | .3 | < .1 | — | — |
| Urinary/bladder | .1 | .1 | 0 | <1.0 | <.1 | < .1 | — | — |
| Preputial gland | — | — | — | — | — | — | — | — |
| Testis | .5 | NA | <1.0 | NA | .4 | NA | — | — |
| Ovary | NA | .7 | NA | <1.0 | NA | .9 | — | — |

Table 7  (continued)

| Organ/tissue | Chu (68) M | Chu (68) F | Fears et al. (70, 71), page (60), Gart et al. (72) M | Fears et al. (70, 71), page (60), Gart et al. (72) F | Chu et al. (73) M | Chu et al. (73) F | Tarone et al. (73) M (Ranges) | Tarone et al. (73) F (Ranges) |
|---|---|---|---|---|---|---|---|---|
| Uterus | NA | 1.2 | NA | 1.9 | NA | 1.6 | — | — |
| Pituitary | .2 | 3.2 | <1.0 | 3.5 | .3 | 3.6 | — | — |
| Adrenal | .9 | .7 | <1.0 | <1.0 | 1.4 | .6 | — | — |
| Thyroid | 1.0 | 1.3 | 1.1 | <1.0 | 1.0 | 1.7 | — | — |
| Pancreatic islets | .3 | .1 | <1.0 | <1.0 | .4 | .2 | — | — |
| Body cavities | .1 | .3 | <1.0 | <1.0 | .4 | .3 | — | — |
| Leukemia/lymphoma | 5.6 | 12.7 | 1.6 | 6.8 | 10.3 | 20.6 | 7.2-12.2 | 1.7-30.4 |
| N | 2355 | 2365 | 1132 | 1176 | 3543 | 3617 | ? | ? |

Table 8   Reported Background Tumor Incidences in Fischer 344 Rats

| Organ/tissue | Chu (68) M | Chu (68) F | Fears et al. (70), page (60) Gart et al. (72) M | Fears et al. (70), page (60) Gart et al. (72) F | Goodman et al. (74)[a] M | Goodman et al. (74)[a] F | Chu et al. (68) M | Chu et al. (68) F | Tarone et al. (73) M | Tarone et al. (73) F |
|---|---|---|---|---|---|---|---|---|---|---|
| Brain | .9 | .6 | 1.3 | <1.0 | .81 | .55 | .8 | .6 | — | — |
| Skin/subcutaneous | 6.6 | 3.2 | 5.7 | 2.5 | 6.4 | 3.0 | 7.8 | 3.2 | — | — |
| Mammary gland | 1.4 | 17.9 | 0 | 18.8 | 1.54 | 8.5 | 1.5 | 20.9 | — | — |
| Circulatory system | .4 | .5 | <1.0 | <1.0 | .38 | .27 | .7 | .4 | — | — |
| Lung/trachea | 3.1 | 1.8 | 2.4 | <1.0 | 2.9 | 2.0 | 3.0 | 1.9 | — | — |
| Heart | .3 | .1 | <1.0 | <1.0 | .2 | .05 | — | — | — | — |
| Liver | 1.8 | 3.1 | 1.2 | 1.3 | 1.74 | 3.9 | 2.2 | 1.9 | 0.7-3.4 | 0.5-2.9 |
| Pancreas | .2 | — | <1.0 | 0 | .16 | 0 | .2 | — | — | — |
| Stomach | .3 | .2 | <1.0 | <1.0 | .32 | .2 | .3 | — | — | — |
| Intestines | .3 | .5 | <1.0 | <1.0 | .31 | .36 | .6 | .2 | — | — |
| Kidney | .4 | .2 | <1.0 | <1.0 | .38 | .16 | .5 | .3 | — | — |
| Urinary/bladder | .1 | .2 | <1.0 | <1.0 | .1 | .22 | .1 | .2 | — | — |
| Preputial gland | 1.4 | 1.2 | — | — | 1.4 | 1.2 | 2.4 | 1.8 | — | — |
| Testis | 80.6 | NA | 76.2 | NA | 80.1 | NA | 2.3 | NA | — | — |

Table 8 (continued)

| Organ/tissue | Chu (68) | | Fears et al. (70), page (60) Gart et al. (72) | | Goodman et al. (74)[a] | | Chu et al. (73) | | Tarone et al. (73) | |
|---|---|---|---|---|---|---|---|---|---|---|
| | M | F | M | F | M | F | M | F | M | F |
| Ovary | NA | .3 | NA | <1.0 | NA | .33 | NA | .4 | — | — |
| Uterus | NA | 15.6 | NA | 16.8 | NA | 5.55 | NA | 17 | — | — |
| Pituitary | 11.5 | 30.5 | 10.2 | 29.5 | 11.4 | 0.3 | 4.7 | 34.9 | 7.5-31.2 | 31.0-58.6 |
| Adrenal | 10.0 | 4.6 | 8.7 | 4.0 | 9.95 | 4.58 | 2.4 | 5.2 | — | — |
| Thyroid | 7.1 | 6.5 | 5.1 | 5.6 | 7.16 | 6.65 | 8.2 | 6.8 | 3.6-9.0 | 4.7-7.0 |
| Pancreatic islets | .8 | 1.0 | 3.2 | 1.3 | 3.89 | 1.05 | 3.9 | .8 | — | — |
| Body cavities | 1.1 | .3 | <1.0 | <1.0 | 2.51 | .38 | 2.6 | .4 | 2.8-9.0 | 1.0-1.9 |
| Leukemia/lymphoma | 11.7 | 9.1 | 6.5 | 5.5 | 12.3 | 9.9 | 9.9 | 13.4 | 9.1-23.6 | 7.5-15.4 |
| N | 1806 | 1765 | 846 | 840 | 1794 | 1754 | 2960 | 2924 | b | b |

[a]Gives detailed breakdown of neoplastic and nonneoplastic lesions in aged animals.
[b]Range of averages, 6 different laboratories.

appearance of tumors in a test animal population than in nontreated members of the same population. Unelss a study is designed and conducted so that a reasonably accurate measurement of time-to-tumor can be made, one is left with only the incidence of tumors found at the end of the study and the variable incidence in animals that die on study, and cannot rule out that though the terminal incidences were comparable, the test chemical resulted in an earlier development or expression of these same tumors. This is one of the strengths of the traditional skin painting studies, which allow easy detection of skin tumors as soon as they appear and tracking of their progress.

If the target organ is not the skin, the only reasonably sensitive manner of evaluating time-to-tumor (unless the tumors are rapidly life threatening and there is an accordingly high early mortality rate leading to necropsy of spontaneous deaths in test animals) is to periodically, during the study, terminate, necropsy, and histopatho-logically evaluate random samples of test and control animals. The traditional NCI bioasay had no such interim or serial sacrifices (73) and therefore could not address such issues.

Such serial sacrifices are usually conducted on at least 20 animals per sex per group starting at one year into the study. Several statistical methods other than life table procedures are available for analysis of such data (75,76).

A related issue is the age at which to terminate the animals. We have already presented the point that as a study progresses, the rise in the background level of tumors makes it more and more dif-ficult to clearly partition out treatment-effect tumors from age-effect tumors. Swenberg (77) and Solleveld et al. (78) have made the point that the incidence of many tumor types has increased from 100 to 500% when control rat results from two-year studies (rats 100–116 weeks of age) were comapred to those from life-span studies (140–146 weeks of age). If such an increase in age (25%) can result in such extreme increases in spontaneous tumors, what is the effect on interpretation of incidence rates seen in concurrent treatment groups? This is especially the case if, as Salsburg (64) has suggested, any biologically active treatment will result in a shift in the patterns of neoplastic lesions occurring in aging animals. The current practice is to interpret tumor incidence on an independent site-by-site basis (on the assumption that what happens at each tissue site is inde-pendent of what happens elsewhere), and no allowance or factoring is made for the fact that what may be occurring in animals over a life span (as expressed by tumor incidence levels at an advanced age) is merely a shifting of patterns from one tumor site to another. In other words, commonly the "significantly" increased incidence of liver tumors is focused on, while the just as statistically significant decrease in kidney tumors compared to controls is ignored. Clearly, we should not be trying to analyze tumor data from animals that are advancing into senescence in the same manner that we do the data from those which lack these confounding factors. Where should a cut-off point be? This is a problem requiring some work, but clearly the data of Cameron et al. (67) suggest that the growth curves of 9,385 B6C3F1 mice and 10,023 F344 rats from control groups in NCI/NTP studies show consistent patterns of decline in body weights from these animals starting at the following ages (in weeks).

|                | Males | Females |
|----------------|-------|---------|
| B6C3F1 mice    | 96    | 101     |
| Fisher 344 rats | 91   | 106     |

A consideration of similar data on tumor incidences (unfortunately not available from NCI/NTP studies) would certainly improve confidence in selecting cutoff points for age, but the above ages merit consideration as termination points.

Having reviewed the preceding biological factors, we may now begin to directly address the statistical interpretation of carcinogenesis bioassays. Such interpretation, once believed to be a simple problem of calculating the statistical significance of increases of tumor incidences in treatment groups at each of a number of tissue sites, is now clearly of itself a more complex task. Assuming dose level and route were appropriate, at least four separate questions must still be addressed in such an interpretation of incidence.

1. Are the data resulting from the bioassay sufficient to warrant analysis and interpretation? Factors which may invalidate a bioassay include inadequate survival in test or control groups, extreme (high or low) control group tumor incidence levels, excessive loss of tissues from autolysis, infection during the study, and the use of contaminated diet or water.

2. Are there increases in tumor incidences in test groups compared to those in control groups? If so, then we must proceed to do an incidence comparison on some form of contingency table arrangement of the data. Such comparisons are traditionally performed using a series of Fisher's exact tests.

3. If there is a significant increase in tumor incidence, is there a trend (dose response) in the data for these sites which concurs with what we know about biological responses to toxicants? That is, as dose increases, response should increase. A significant increase occurring only in a low

dose group (with the incidence levels in the higher dose groups being comparable to controls), would be of very questionable biological significance.

4. If significant incidence and trend are present, is there supporting evidence of the material being a carcinogen? An example of this was cited earlier in the case of mouse liver tumors where the presence of positive mutagenicity findings would support a belief of biological significance and concern about real-life exposure of humans.

Two major controversial questions are involved in such comparisons: (a) Should they be based on one-tailed or two-tailed distribution, and (b) what are the effects and implications of multiple comparisons? The one-or-two-tailed controversy revolves around the question of which hypothesis we are properly testing in a study such as a chronic carcinogenicity study. Is the tumor incidence different between the control and treated groups? In such cases, it is a bidirectional hypothesis and, therefore, a two-tailed distribution we are testing against. Or are we asking is the tumor incidence greater in the treated group than in the control group? In the latter case, it is a unidirectional hypothesis and we are contemplating only the right-hand tail of the distribution. The implications of the answer to this question are more than theoretical; significance is much greater (exactly double, in fact, for Fisher's exact test) in the one-tailed case than in the two-tailed. For example, a set of data analyzed by Fisher's exact test which would have a two-tailed p level of 0.098 and one-tailed level of 0.049 would be flagged, therefore, as significantly different if the one-tailed test were employed. Feinstein (79) provides excellent discussion of the background in a nonmathematical way. Determination of the correct approach must rest on a clear definition by the researcher, beforehand, of the objective of his study and of the possible outcomes (if a bidirectional outcome is possible, are we justified in using a one-tailed test statistic?).

The multiple comparisons problem is a much more lively one. In chronic studies, we test lesion/tumor incidence on each of a number of tissues, for each sex and species, with each result being flagged if it exceeds the fiducial limit of $p \leq 0.05$.

The point we must ponder here is the meaning "$p \leq 0.05$." This is the level of the probability of our making a type I error (incorrectly concluding we have an effect when, in fact, we do not). So we have accepted the fact that there is a 5% chance of our producing a false positive from this study. Our trade-off is a much lower chance (typically 1%) of a type II error, that is, of our passing as safe a compound which is not safe. These two error levels are connected; to achieve a lower type II level inflates our type I level. The problem in this case is that when we make a large number of such comparisons, we are repeatedly taking the chance that we will "find" a false positive result. The set of lesions and/or tumor comparisons described above may number more than 70 tests for significance in a single study, which will result in a large inflation of our false positive level. The extent of this inflated false positive rate (and how to reduce its effects) has been discussed and estimated with a great degree of variability. Salsburg (80) has estimated that the typical original National Cancer Institute (NCI) type cancer bioassay has a probability of type I error ranging between 20 and 50%. Fears and colleagues (70,71), however, have estimated it as being between 6 and 24%. Haseman and Hoel (55) have also reviewed some of Salsburg's calculations and stated that correcting for multiple counting of individual animals and adjusting for survival differences markedly reduced the false positive rate. Without some form of correction factor, the "false positive" rate of a series of multiple tests can be calculated as being equal to $1-0.05^N$ where N is the number of tests and the selected alpha level is 0.05. Salsburg (80) expressed the concern that such an exaggerated false positive result may cause a good compound to be banned. Though Haseman (81) challenged this on the point that a much more mature decision process than this is used by the regulatory agencies, Salsburg has pointed out at least two cases, however, where the decision to ban was based purely on such a single statistical significance. What, then, is a proper use of such results? Or, conversely, how can we control for such an inflated error rate?

There are statistical methods available for dealing with this multiple comparisons problem. One such is the use of Bonferroni inequalities to correct for successive multiple comparisons (82). This method has the drawback that there is some accompanying loss of power expressed as an inability to identify true positives properly. A method proposed by McKnight and Crowley (83), if information from frequent interim terminations is present, provides a reasonably sensitive yet unbiased means of evaluating such data. Similarly, Meng and Dempster (84) have proposed a Bayesian approach to such analysis to solve the multiple comparisons problem. In this, a logistically distributed (or log-transformed) model which accommodates the incidences of all tumor types or sites observed in the current experiment simultaneously as well as their historical control incidences, is developed. Exchangeable normal expected values are assumed for certain linear terms in the model. Posterior means, standard deviatione, and Bayesian p values are computed for an overall treatment effect as well as for the effects on individual tumor types or tissue sites. Model assumptions are then evaluated using probability plots and the sensitivity of the parameter estimates to alternative expected values is analyzed.

The third and fourth questions presented earlier are parts of what is evolving as a second set of approaches to the interpretation of bioassay results.

These new second approaches use the information in a more mature decision making process. First, the historical control incidence rates such as are given for the B6C3F1 mouse and the Fischer-344 rats in Tables 7 and 8 should be considered; as we have seen, some background incidences are so high that these tissues are "null and void" for making decisions. Second, we should look not just for a single significant incidence in a tissue, but rather for a trend. For example, we might have the following percentages o, a liver tumor incidence in the female rats of a study: (a) control = 3%, (b) 10 mg/kg = 6%, (c) 50 mg/kg = 17%, and (d) 250 mg/kg = 54%. In this study only the incidence at the 250 mg/kg level might be statistically significant. However, the trend through each of the levels is suggestive of a dose-response. Looking for such a trend is an essential step in a scientific assessment of the results, and one of the available trend analysis techniques, such as presented in Gad and Weil (1), should be utilized. Another method for determining whether statistically significant incidences are merely random occurrences is to compare the results of the quantitative variables to two or more concurrently run control groups. Often the mean of one variable will differ from only one of these controls and be numerically within the range of this same variable of the two control means. If so, the statistical significance compared to the one control must be seriously questioned as to its being associated with a biological significance. Three different such stepwise interpretative procedures are common. These are the NCI method, the weight-of-evidence method, and the Peto method. The NCI approach is somewhat complex, involving each of the four steps outlined earlier in a process overviewed by Tarone et al. (73). The statistical aspects of this are outlined below.

## B. NCI Bioassay Method

1. Survival Analysis. By sex, species, and organ, exclude all animals dying prior to first incidence of tumor at that site. Do a life-table analysis for survival at the same time.
2. Use Fisher exact test to obtain one-tailed p at each site using the survival adjusted ratwos obtained in 1 above.
3. Utilize the Bonferroni correction using r (where r = the number of dose levels; not k = the number of total comparisons); multiply the computed p by r to maintain overall error rate. Significance is claimed only if p is less than $\alpha/r$.
4. Perform tests for linear trend using Cochran-Armitage test (dose response curve must be significantly different from zero, and positive).

*Notes*: In 100 animal bioassays, you need 5 or more animals to have tumors achieve a one-tailed $p \geqslant 0.05$. With Bonferroni correction, 7 or more are needed.
NCI believes and practices the rare tumor incidence flag mechanism. (See Refs. 96-98.)

The 9 possible interpretations of an analysis of tumor incidence and survival analysis are smmmarized in Table 9.

The weight of evidence approach consists primarily of the four steps of interpretation presented earlier, with emphasis on the last step (integration of related and supporting information into the evaluation process) as opposed to the NCI approach (which places emphasis on the two "statistical" steps). The weight of evidence approach poses difficulty in the regulatory and legal fields because it requires judgment and is not overtly quantitative. However, it does represent a scientifically valid approach for distinguishing important differences in the potential of chemicals to induce cancer. The greatest weight of evidence should be given to chemicals that induce dose-related increases in malignant tumors at multiple sites, in both sexes and in multiple species using appropriate routes of administration. At the other end of the spectrum, much less weight should be given to chemicals that induce only an increased incidence of a benign neoplasm, whose incidence is normally quite variable, and is found only in the high dose group of one sex of a single species. One must also integrate a significant amount of additional information.

For example, the shape and extent of the dose-response curve should be known in relation to factors such as the chemical's pharmacokinetics, its overwhelming of host defenses, or saturation of metabolic systems. Is the chemical genotoxic? How do the site and dose response for toxicity compare with those for carcinogenicity? This knowledge is highly relevant when attempting to understand the mechanismr involved in carcinogenesis for each specific chemical, and can and should be incorporated into both hazard identification and risk assessment to improve their accuracy. It is widely believed to be appropriate to test a chemical at the MTD in order to gain assurance that it has been adequately tested. However, if a chemical is not genotoxic, but induces frank cytotoxicity in the liver only at doses at which it also induces liver tumors, it should be considered differently than a chemical that is genotoxic and induces liver tumors over a large dose range including noncytotoxic doses.

The Peto procedure (85) is actually a collection of approaches arising from the central belief that it is possible to generate an additional vital set of data from a well run bioassay, and that we should utilize these same pieces of data in interpreting results.

The data in question constitute an evaluation of the likelihood that each individual tumor would (or would not) be life threatening.

Table 9  Interpretation of the Analysis of Tumor Incidence and Survival Analysis (Life Table)

| Outcome type | Tumor association with treatment[a] | Mortality association with treatment | Interpretation[b] |
|---|---|---|---|
| A | + | + | Unadjusted test may underestimate tumorigenicity of treatment. |
| B | + | + | Unadjusted test gives valid picture of tumorigenicity of treatment. |
| C | + | – | Tumors found in treated groups may reflect longer survival of treated groups. Time adjusted analysis is indicated. |
| D | – | + | Apparent negative findings in tumors may be due to the shorter survival in treated groups. Time-adjusted analysis and/or a retest at lower doses is indicated. |
| E | – | 0 | Unadjusted test gives a valid picture of the possible tumor-preventive capacity of the treatment. |
| F | – | – | Unadjusted test may underestimate the possible tumor-preventive capacity of the treatment. |
| G | 0 | + | High mortality in treated groups may lead to un-adjusted test missing a possible tumorigen. Adjusted analysis and/or retest at lower doses is indicated. |
| H | 0 | 0 | Unadjusted test gives valid picture of lack of association with treatment. |

Table 9 (continued)

| Outcome type | Tumor association with treatment[a] | Mortality association with treatment | Interpretation[b] |
|---|---|---|---|
| I | 0 | - | Longer survival in treated groups may mask tumor-preventive capacity of treatment. |

[a] + = Yes, - = No and 0 = No bearing on discussion.
[b] The unadjusted test referred to here is a contingency table type analysis of incidence, such as a Fisher's exact test.

The approach calls for the pathologist on a study to not only identify a mass or tumor as neoplastic or not, but also to categorize each neoplasm in one of several possible classes as to the risk it presents to the survival of the host organism. Such classification is generally in one of at least five different categories:

1. Tumor did or would definitely cause death of animal.
2. Tumor probably did or could cause death of animal.
3. Cannot be determined.
4. Tumor probably didn't or wouldn't cause death of animal.
5. Tumor didn't or wouldn't cause death of animal.

Such data can then be employed in a more precise interpretation of the meaning of the bioassay. An entire separate, sensitive set of significance tests based on such data have been proposed by Peto et al. (85).

The last point to be addressed under the topic of carcinogenicity bioassay is the use of the resulting data for the conduct of carcinogenic potency comparisons. Such a potency comparison would both be valuable in a scientific sense and provide a basis for prioritization of regulatory actions.

Potency and dose response of carcinogens for any single species of animals may be expressed in one of two manners, either as the incidence rate of tumors at the end of a set period of time or as the time lag from treatment to a specified incidence rate of tumors. This second way has also been extended to determining time to death as a result of tumors produced by a carcinogen (86).

Squire (87) has proposed a ranking system for animal carcinogens based on data from NTP bioassays (that is, in the absence of time-to-tumor information). The major considerations are:

1. Number of species affected.
2. Number of different types of neoplasms induced in one or more species.
3. A negative correction for the spontaneous incidence in control groups of induced neoplasms.
4. Cumulative dose or exposure per kilogram body weight in affected groups.
5. The proportion of induced neoplasms which were malignant.
6. The degree of supporting genotoxicity (mutagenicity) data.

Of course, our real interest in the potency of carcinogens is in humans, which means an interspecies comparison. Crouch and Wilson (1979), using the results of some 70 NCI/NTP bioassays where carcinogenicity was established in both rats and mice, reported that a comparison demonstrated empirically that good correlations exist

between these two species for suitably defined carcinogenic potencies
for various chemicals. Such a correlation would allow sufficient accuracy in extrapolating from animal data to human risk to support a
logical scheme for the evaluation of such risks. More recently,
however, Bernstein et al. (88) examined a larger NCI/NTP Bioassay
Program data base. They observed that there is a very high correlation of the maximum doses tested (max-d) for rats and mice on
a milligram per kilogram body weight per day basis. Calculating the
carcinogenic potency (b-defined in their paper), they found it to
be restricted to an approximately 30-fold range surrounding $\log(2)/$
max-d, which has a biological as well as a statistical basis. Since
the max-d's for the set of NCI/NTP test chemicals varied over many
orders of magnitude, it necessarily follows statistically that the carcinogenic potencies will be highly correlated. This "artifact" of
potency estimation does not imply that there is no basis for extrapolating animal results to humans. They concluded that "it does suggest, however, that the interpretation of correlation studies of carcinogenic potency needs much further thought."

On an intermediate level, others have suggested a class of Bayesian statistical methods for the interspecies extrapolation of potency
functions that allows for the combining of data from different substances and species of animals, using the results as one constructs
the model to estimate interexperimental error between the different
sources of data being combined.

## C. Areas of Controversy in Statistics As Used for Toxicology

It should now be clear to the reader that the use of statistics in
toxicology is not a cut and dried matter. There are a number of
areas which are (and have been) the subject of honest controversy,
and it should be expected that others will arise as the two fields
advance.

There remain three areas to be addressed which are somewhat
peculiar to toxicology. These are the effects of censoring on data,
the direction of hypothesis testing, and the use of unbalanced
designs.

### 1. Censoring

Censoring is practiced when not all the possible data arising from
an experiment are available for or used in analysis. Though some
would make the distinction that censored data are different from
missing data in that the values for the former can be accurately
estimated and those for missing data cannot, here the term is used
to mea all data not included in analysis for whatever reasons. There
are four major reasons for data being censored in toxicology studies,

and the degree of accuracy for which the value of such censored values can be estimated varies, depending on the reason for censoring.

1. The most common reason for censoring in toxicology is because of death; not all the animals which start a study end it. In these cases we have no basis to accurately estimate the observations that would have been made had the animal (or animals) lived. Censoring by death is an example of "left censoring;" unplanned without recourse and generally during a period when the information lost would be of interest. Right censoring, on the other hand, generally is planned, there is recourse to get the information if needed and the information potentially lost is of minimal if any interest.

2. Data may be censored by having samples lost to measurement at intermittent periods. Such losses are the result of occurrences such as clotting of blood samples prior to analysis, loss of tissues during necropsy, and breakdown of instruments at critical times. Usually the values of the last observations can be estimated with some accuracy. And most such cases can be remedied by resampling (collecting more blood, for example).

3. When we judge an extreme value to be an outlier and reject it, we are censoring it. If the value is cleanly discarded, we are de facto saying we cannot accurately estimate its value. If, however, we use a procedure such as winsorizing and replace it with a less extreme value, we are in fact estimating the most probable true value of the observations.

4. Finally, some observations may be censored because their values are beyond the range at which the instruments we use can accurately measure. An example is in measuring rabbit methemoglobin with an instrument designed for humans. Extreme low values are not accurately measured, and are reported as negative percentage values. In this case, we can accurately estimate a censored value as being "less than" or "greater than" a known value.

What are the consequences of censoring? The answer depends on the nature and extent of the censoring process. If only a few of a large number of values are lost and the pattern of loss is randomly distributed among all groups on study, little if any harm is done. If the extent of data loss is too severe, for example, because the majority of the animals in a group die, the entire experiment may have to be discarded. An intermediate case is when the extent of censoring is low but the censoring is not random. This is not uncommon in toxicology, where censoring because of death tends to be concentrated in the high dose groups. In these cases, the experiment is not lost but rather truncated, that is, some effects cannot be addressed with reference to the treatment used in highly censored groups. And, as we will discuss a little later, it may imbalance a design.

An additional common effect of censoring that should be kept in mind is on the normality of the sample. If all values above a certain level (say of serum electrolytes) are censored because animals having such values die before the measurements are made, we are left with a truncated normal distribution. A special case of this was discussed by Gad and Smith (89) in that the time-to-incapacitation values in combustion toxicology are censored because they are only measured to 30 minutes, and not beyond. Such truncated populations cannot be treated as normal for purposes of statistical analysis.

An entire family of methods have been developed to address censored data sets. Bishop et al. (90) present an excellent overview of some of these.

## 2. Direction of Hypothesis Testing

Which direction (or directions) we are testing a hypothesis in can be restated as asking whether we are to use a one-tailed or a two-tailed test. This is of consequence because one-tailed tests are always more sensitive (more likely to find an effect) than are two-tailed tests.

Generally, such a selection must be made prior to the start of an experiment, based on a clear statement of the question being asked (that is, the objective of the study). If we are asking if a chemical increases the incidence of cancer, then our question is one-tailed—we are not interested in the detection of any significant decrease in the incidence of cancer. Most toxicology studies, however, are of a "shot gun" nature. They are designed to detect and identify any and all effects. This is a two-tailed question: can a chemical either increase or decrease the incidence of cancer?

Feinstein (79) provides a clear discussion of questions of direction of effect as they relate to biostatistics.

## 3. Unbalanced Designs

One of the principles of experimental design presented earlier was that of balance. This held that group sizes should be at least approximately equal. As we have reviewed the different methods presented in this book, we have noted that a number of them have impaired performance if the sizes of the groups are not equivalent.

Yet, it is not uncommon to lose data because of censoring in toxicology studies, and if such censoring is related to a compound or treatment effect, it is very likely that the most affected groups will not be equivalent in size to our control group at the end of an experiment.

At the same time, it should be clear that it is easier to statistically detect large effects than small effects. In the vast majority of cases, larger effects occur in high dose groups (not infrequently to the extent that no statistical analysis is necessary), while it is in the lower dose groups that the guidance provided by statistical analysis is most needed.

These reasons argue for the use of unbalanced designs in toxicology. In other words, those treatments where it is expected that more statistical power will be needed or which are expected to suffer from an increased level of censoring due to death (where death itself is not the variable of interest) should be administered to larger test groups. Farmer et al. (91) have reviewed a number of options for deciding on the degree of imbalance with which to start a study.

### 4. Use of Computerized Statistical Packages

Finally, we must recognize that for many toxicology laboratories, the approach to statistical analysis of data is to use one of the mainframe packages which automatically selects and utilizes statistical tests. It is critically important in these cases to understand the limitations and proper uses of statistical tests that are automatically employed.

### 5. Screens

One major set of activities in toxicology (and also in pharmacology, for that matter) is screening for the presence or absence of an effect. Such screens are almost always focused on detecting a single endpoint of effect (such as mutagenicity, lethality, neuro or developmental toxicity, etc.) and have a particular set of operating characteristics in common.

1. A large number of compounds are to be evaluated, so that ease of performance (which can also be considered efficiency) is a major desirable characteristic.
2. The screen must be very sensitive in its detection of potential effective agents. An absolute minimum of effictive agents should escape detection, that is, there should be very few false negatives (in other words, the type II error rate or $\beta$ should be low).
3. It is desirable that the number of false positives be small (that is, that there be a low type I error rate or $\alpha$ level).
4. Items 1–3 are all to some degree contradictory, requiring the involved researchers to agree on a set of compromises. These typically start with acceptance of a relatively high $\alpha$ level (0.10 or more).

5.  In an effort to better serve item 1, such screens are fre-
    quently performed in batteries so that multiple endpoints
    are measured in the same mode. Additionally, smch measure-
    ments may be repeated over a period of time in each model.

In an early screen, a relatively large number of compounds will
be tested. It is unlikely that one will stand out so much as to be
statistically significantly more important than all the other compounds.
A more or less continuous range of activities will be found. Compounds showing the highest activity will proceed to the next assay
in the series, and may be used as lead compounds in a new cycle of
testing and evaluation.

Each assay can have an associated activity criterion. If the result for a particular test compound meets this criterion, the compound
may pass to the next stage. This criterion could be based on statistical significance (i.e., all compounds with observed activities
significantly greater than the control at the 5% level could be tagged).
However, for early screens such a criterion may be too strict and
few compounds may go through to further testing.

A useful indicator of the efficiency of an assay series is the
frequency of discovery of truly active compounds. This is related
to the probability of discovery and to the degree of risk associated
with a compound. These two factors in turn depend on the distribution of activities in the test series and the changes at each stage of
rejecting and accepting compounds with given activities.

Statistical modelling of the assay system may lead to the improvement of the design of the system to reduce the interval between dis-
civeries. Preliminary results suggest that in the early screens it
may be beneficial to increase the number of compounds tested, decrease the numbers of animals per group, and increase the range
and number of doses. The result will be less information on more
structures, but an overall increase in the frequency of discovery
(assuming that truly active compounds are entering the system at a
steady rate).

The design of each assay and the choice of the activity criterion
should therefore be adjusted bearing in mind the relative costs of
retaining false positives and rejecting false negatives. Decreasing
the group sizes in the early assays reduces the chance of obtaining
significance at any particular level (such as 5%) so that the activity
criterion must be relaxed, in a statistical sense, to allow more compounds through. At some stage, however, it becomes too expensive
to continue screening many false positives and the criteria must be
tightened up accordingly.

An excellent introduction to this subject is Redman's (92) interesting approach which identifies four characteristics of an assay.
It is assumed that a compound is either active or inactive, and that

the proportion of actives can be estimated from past experience.
After testing, a compound will be classified as positive or negative.
It is then possible to design the assay to optimize the following
characteristics:

a. Sensitivity. The ratio of true positives to total actives;
b. Specificity. The ratio of true negatives to total inactives;
c. Positive accuracy. The ratio of true to observed positives;
d. Negative accuracy. The ratio of true to observed negatiges.

An advantage of testing more compounds is that it gives the opportunity to average activity evidence over structural classes, or study
quantitative structure-activity relationships (QSARs). QSARs can
be used to predict the activity of new compounds and thus reduce
the chance of in vivo testing on negative compounds. It can increase
the proportion of truly active compounds passing through the system.

In conclusion, it may be said that maximization of the performance
of a series of screening assays requires close collaboration between
the biologist, chemist, and statistician. It should be noted, however, that screening forms only part of a much larger research and
development context.

Screens may thus truly be considered the biological equivalent
of exploratory data analysis (EDA). EDA methods, in fact, provide
a number of useful possibilities for less rigid and yet quite utilitarian
approaches to the statistical analysis of the data from screens. A
brief presentation of such methods comprises the final section of
this chapter.

As an example of such an approach, a set of devices called
quality control charts may be advantageously constructed and used
during assay development and in routine screening procedures.
During the development of assay methodology, for example, by keeping records of assay results, an initial estimate of the assay standard
deviation is available when full-scale use starts. The initial estimate
can then be revised as more data is generated.

The following example shows the usefulness of control charts for
control measurements in a screening procedure. Our example test
for screening potential immune suppressive agents measures reduction
of edema (mouse ear volume) by test compounds compared to a control treatment. A control chart was established to monitor the performance of the control agent (a) to establish the mean and variability of the control, and (b) to ensure that the results of the control for a given experiment are within reasonable limits (a validation
of the assay procedure). The average ear volume difference (ear
volume before treatment − ear volume after treatment) and the average range for a series of experiments are shown in Table 10.

As in quality control charts, the mean and average range of the
assay were determined from previous experiments. In this example,

**Table 10** Average Paw Volume Difference and Range for Screening Procedure (Four Guinea Pigs per Test Group)

| Test number | Mean | Range | Test number | Mean | Range |
|---|---|---|---|---|---|
| 1 | 38 | 4 | 11 | 28 | 12 |
| 2 | 43 | 3 | 12 | 41 | 10 |
| 3 | 34 | 3 | 13 | 40 | 22 |
| 4 | 48 | 6 | 14 | 34 | 5 |
| 5 | 38 | 24 | 15 | 37 | 4 |
| 6 | 45 | 4 | 16 | 43 | 14 |
| 7 | 49 | 5 | 17 | 37 | 6 |
| 8 | 32 | 9 | 18 | 45 | 8 |
| 9 | 48 | 5 | 19 | 32 | 7 |
| 10 | 34 | 8 | 20 | 42 | 13 |

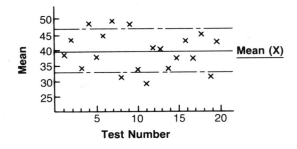

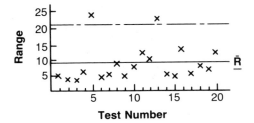

**Figure 5** Quality control chart for means and range for control group in screening procedure for mouse ear swelling agents.

**Table 11**  Values for Determining Upper and Lower Limits for Mean ($\bar{X}$) and Range Charts

| Sample size of subgroup (N) | A: Factor for $\bar{X}$ chart | Range chart factors | |
|---|---|---|---|
| | | Lower limit ($D_L$) | Upper limit ($D_u$) |
| 2 | 1.88 | 0 | 3.27 |
| 3 | 1.02 | 0 | 2.57 |
| 4 | 0.73 | 0 | 2.28 |
| 5 | 0.58 | 0 | 2.11 |
| 6 | 0.48 | 0 | 2.00 |
| 7 | 0.42 | 0.08 | 1.92 |
| 8 | 0.37 | 0.14 | 1.86 |
| 9 | 0.34 | 0.18 | 1.82 |
| 10 | 0.31 | 0.22 | 1.78 |
| 20 | 0.18 | 0.41 | 1.59 |

the screen had been run 20 times previous to the data of Table 10. These initial data showed a mean ear volume difference of 40 and a mean range ($\bar{R}$) of 9. These values were used for the control charts shown in Figure 5. The subgroups are of size 4. Using the values provided in Table 11, the action limits for the $\bar{X}$ and range charts were calculated as follows:

$$\bar{X} \pm 0.73\bar{R} = 40 \pm 0.73(9) = 33.4 \text{ to } 46.6 \ (\bar{X} \text{ chart})$$

$$\bar{R}(2.28) = 9(2.28) = 20.5 \text{ the upper limit for the range.}$$

Note that the lower limit for the range of subgroups consisting of four units is zero. Six of the 20 means are out of limits. Efforts to find a cause for the large intertest variation failed. The procedures were standardized and followed carefully, and the animals appeared to be homogeneous. Because different shipments of animals were needed to proceed with these tests over time, the investigators felt that there was no way to reduce the variability of the procedure. Therefore, a new control chart was prepared based on the variability between test means. A moving average was recommended using five successive averages.

Based on historical data, $\bar{X}$ was calculated as 39.7 with an average moving range of 12.5. The limits for the moving average graph are

$$39.7 \pm 0.73(12.5) - 30.6 \text{ to } 48.8$$

The factor 0.73 is obtained from Table 11 for subgroup samples of size 4.

Such charts may also be constructed and used for proportion or count type data. By constructing such charts for the range of control data, we may then use them as a rapid and efficient tool for detecting effects in groups being assessed for that same screen endpoint.

### 6. Exploratory Data Analysis

Over the past 10 years, an entirely new approach has been developed to get the most information out of the increasingly larger and more complex data sets facing scientific researchers. This approach involves the use of a very diverse set of fairly simple techniques which comprise exploratory data analysis (EDA). As expounded by Tukey (93), there are four major ingredients to EDA:

Displays: These visually reveal the behavior of the data and suggest a framework for analysis. The scatterplot (presented earlier) is an example of this approach.

Residuals: These are what remain of a set of data after a fitted model (such as linear regression) or some similar level of analysis has been subtracted out.

Re-expressions: These involve the questions of what scale would serve to best simplify and improve the analysis of the data. Simple transformations, such as presented earlier in this chapter, are used to simplify data behavior (such as linearizing or normalizing it) and clarify analysis.

Resistance: This is a matter of decreasing the sensitivity of analysis and summary of data to misbehavior. This means that the occurrence of a few outliers will nto invalidate or make too difficult the methods used to analyze the data. For example, in summarizing the location of a set of data, the median (but not the arithmetic mean) is highly resistant.

These four ingredients are utilized in a process falling into two broad phases: an exploratory phase and a confirmatory phase. The exploratory phase isolates patterns and features of the data and reveals them, allowing for inspection of the data before there is any firm choice of actual hypothesis testing or modeling methods.

Confirmatory analysis allows evaluation of the reproducibility of the observed patterns or effects. Its role is close to that of classical hypothesis testing, but also often includes steps such as (a) incorporating information from an analysis of another, closely related set of data and (b) validating a result by assembling and analyzing additional data (Fig. 6 shows an example of this approach).

These techniques are in general beyond the scope of this text. Velleman and Hoaglin (94) and Hoaglin et al. (95) present a clear overview of the more important methods, along with the codes for their performance on the microcomputer (they have also now been incorporated into Minitab). A short examination of a single case of the use of these methods, however, is in order.

Toxicology has long recognized that no population, animal or human, is completely uniform in its response to any particular toxicant. Rather, a population is composed of a (presumably normal) distribution of individuals; some resistant to intoxication (hyporesponders), the bulk that respond close to a central value (such as an LD50), and some that are very sensitive to intoxication (hyperresponders). This distribution of population can, in fact, result in additional statistical techniques. The sensitivity of techniques such as ANOVA is reduced markedly by the occurrence of outliers (extreme high or low values including hyper- and hyporesponders) which, in fact, serve to markedly inflate the variance (standard deviation) associated with a sample. Such a variance inflation effect

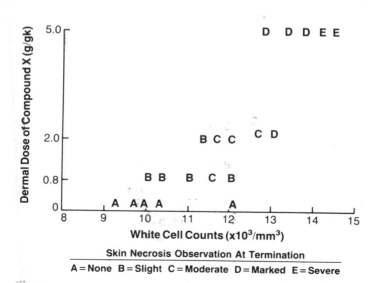

Figure 6   Exploratory data analysis:  correlative plots.

is particularly common in small groups that are exposed or dosed at just over or under a threshold level, causing a small number of individuals in the sample (who are more sensitive than the other members) to respond markedly. Such a situation is displayed in Figure 7 which plots the mean and standard deviations of methemoglobin levels in a series of groups of animals exposed to successively higher levels of a hemolytic agent.

Though the mean level of methemoglobin in group C is more than double that of control group A, no hypothesis test will show this difference to be significant because of the large standard deviation associated with it. Yet this "inflated" variance exists because a single individual has such a marked response. Such inflation certainly indicates that the data need to be examined closely. Indeed, all tabular data in toxicology should be visually inspected for both trend and variance inflation.

A concept related (but not identical) to resistance and exploratory data analysis is that of robustness. Robustness generally implies insensitivity to departures from assumptions surrounding an underlying model such as normality.

In summarizing the location of data the median, though highly resistant, is not extremely robust. But the mean is both badly nonresistant and badly nonrobust.

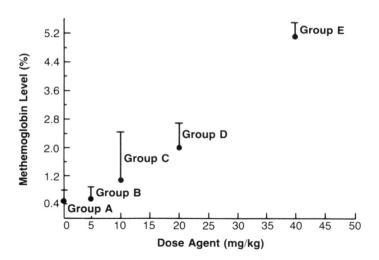

Figure 7    Variance inflation.    Points are means; error bars are +1 S.D.

REFERENCES

1. Gad, S. C. and Weil, C. S. (1986). *Statistical and Experimental Design for Toxicologists.* Caldwell, NJ, Telford Press.
2. Myers, J. L.(1972). *Fundamentals of Experimental Design.* Boston, Allyn and Bacon.
3. Dixon, W. J. and Massey, F. J., Jr. (1969). *Introduction to Statistical Analysis,* 3rd ed. New York, McGraw-Hill.
4. Weil, C. S. (1970). Selection of the valid number of sampling units and a consideration of their combination in toxicological studies involving reproduction, teratogenesis or carcinogenesis. *Food Cosmet. Toxicol. 8:*177–182.
5. Thompson, W. R. and Weil, C. S. (1952). On the construction of tables for moving average interpolation. *Biometrics 8:*51–54.
6. Weil, C. S. (1972). Statistics vs. safety factors and scientific judgement in the evaluation of safety for man. *Toxicol. Appl. Pharmacol. 21:*459.
7. Weil, C. S. (1975). Toxicology experimental design and conduct as measured by interlaboratory collaboration studies. *J. Assoc. Off. Anal. Chem. 58:*687–688.
8. Weil, C. S., Carpenter, C. P., and Smith, H. I. (1953). Specifications for calculating the median effective dose. *Am. Indust. Hyg. Assoc. Quart. 14:*200–206.
9. Zbiden, G. and Flury-Roversi, M. (1981). Significant of the LD$_{50}$ test for the toxicological evaluation of chemical substances. *Arch. Toxicol. 47:*77–99.
10. DePass, L. R., Myers, R. C., Weaver, E. V., and Weil, C. S. (1984). An assessment of the importance of number of dosage levels, number of animals per dosage level, sex and method of LD$_{50}$ and slope calculations in acute toxicity studies. In *Alternate Methods in Toxicology, Vol. 2: Acute Toxicity Testing: Alternate Approaches.* Edited by A. M. Goldberg. New York, Mary Ann Liebert, Inc.
11. Gad, S. C., Smith, A. C., Cramp, A. L., Gavigan, F. A., and Derelanko, M. J. (1984). Innovative designs and practices for acute systemic toxicity studies. *Drug Chem. Toxicol. 7:*423–434.
12. Bruce, R. D. (1985). An up-and-down procedure for acute toxicity testing. *Fund. App. Toxicol. 5:*151–157.
13. Jackson, B. (1962). Statistical analysis of body weight data. *Toxicol. Appl. Pharmacol. 4:*432–443.
14. Weil, C. S. (1962). Applications of methods of statistical analysis to efficient repeated-dose toxicological tests. I. General considerations and problems involved. Sex differences in rat liver and kidney weights. *Toxicol. Appl. Pharmacol. 4:*561–571.
15. Weil, C. S. and Gad, S. C. (1980). Applications of methods of statistical analysis to efficient repeated-dose toxicologic tests. 2.

Methods for analysis of body, liver and kidney weight data. *Toxicol. Appl. Pharmacol.* 52:214–226.

16. Zar, J. H. (1974). *Biostatistical Analysis.* Englewood Cliffs, NJ, Prentice-Hall, p. 50.

17. Weil, C. S. (1973). Experimental design and interpretation of data from prolonged toxicity studies. In *Proc. 5th Int. Congr. Pharmacol.* San Francisco, Vol. 2, pp. 4–12.

18. Boyd, E. M. (1972). *Predictive Toxicometrics.* Baltimore, Williams & Wilkins.

19. Boyd, E. M. and Knight, L. M. (1963). Postmortem shifts in the weight and water levels of body organs. *Tox. Appl. Pharm.* 5:119–128.

20. Ridgemen, W. J. (1975). *Experimentation in Biology.* New York, pp. 214–215.

21. Wallach, J. (1978). *Interpretation of Diagnostic Tests.* Boston, Little, Brown and Company.

22. Oser, B. L. and Oser, M. (1956). Nutritional studies in rats on diets containing high levels of partial ester emulsifiers. II. Reproduction and loctation. *J. Nutr.* 60:429.

23. Mitruka, B. M. an0 Rawnsley, H. M. (1977). *Clinical Biochemical and Hematological Reference Values in Normal Experimental Animals.* New York, Masson.

24. Weil, C. S. (1982). Statistical analysis and normality of selected hematologic and clinical chemistry measurements used in toxicologic studies. *Arch. Toxicol. (Suppl.)* 5:237–253.

25. Kupper, L. L. and Haseman, J. K. (1978). The use of a correlated binomial model for the analysis of certain toxicological experiments. *Biometrics* 34:69–76.

26. Nelson, C. J. and Holson, J. F. (1978). Statistical analysis of teratologic data: Problems and advancements. *J. Environ. Pathol. Toxicol.* 2:187–199.

27. Williams, R. and Buschbom, R. L. (1982). Statistical analysis of litter experiments in teratology. *Battelle PNL-4425.* 15 pp.

28. Rai, K. and Van Ryzin, J. (1985). A dose-response model for teratological experiments involving quantal responses. *Biometrics* 41:1–9.

29. Bateman, A. T. (1977). The dominant lethal assay in the male mouse. In *Handbook of Mutagenicity Test Procedures.* Edited by B. J. Kilbey, M. Legator, W. Nichols, and C. Ramel. New York, Elsevier, pp. 325–334.

30. Mosteller, F. and Youtz, C. (1961). Tables of the Freeman-Tukey transformations for the binomial and Poisson distributions. *Biometrika* 48:433–440.

31. Aeschbacher, H. U., Vautaz, L., Sotek, J., and Stalder, R. (1977). Use of the beta binomial distribution in dominant-lethal testing for "weak mutagenic acitivity," Part 1. *Mutat. Res.* 44:369–390.

32. Vuataz, L. and Sotek, J. (1978). Use of the beta-binomial distribution in dominant-lethal testing for "weak mutagenic activity," Part 2. *Mutat. Res. 52*:211–230.
33. Dean, B. J. and Johnston, A. (1977). Dominant lethal assays in the male mice: evaluation of experimental design, statistical methods and the sensitivity of Charles River (CD1) mice. *Mutat. Res. 42*:269–278.
34. Bliss, C. I. (1965). Statistical relations in fertilizer inspection. Connecticut Agricultural Experiment Station, New Haven, CT. *Bulletin* p. 674.
35. Kilbey, B. J., Legator, M., Nicholas, W., and Ramel, C. (1977). *Handbook of Mutagenicity Test Procedures*. New York, Elsevier, pp. 425–433.
36. Grafe, A. and Vollmar, J. (1977). Small numbers in mutagenicity tests. *Arch. Toxicol. 38*:27–34.
37. Vollmar, J. (1977). Statistical problems in mutagenicity tests. *Arch. Toxicol. 38*:13–25.
38. Katz, A. J. (1978). Design and analysis of experiments on mutagenicity. I. Minimal sample sizes. *Mutat. Res. 50*:301–307.
39. Katz, A. J. (1979). Design and analysis of experiments on mutagenicity. II. Assays involving micro-organisms. *Mutat. Res. 64*:61–77.
40. Weil, C. S. (1978). A critique of the collaborative cytogenetics study to measure and minimize interlaboratory variation. *Mutat. Res. 50*:285–291.
41. Kastenbaum, M. A. and Bowman, K. O. (1970). Tables for determining the statistical significance of mutation frequencies. *Mutat. Res. 5*:61–77.
42. Ehrenberg, L. (1977). Aspects of statistical inference in testing genetic toxicity. In *Handbook of Mutagenicity Test Procedures*. Edited by B. J. Kilbey, M. Legator, W. Nichols, and C. Ramel. New York, Elsevier, pp. 419–459.
43. Bernstein, L., Kaldor, J., McCann, J., and Pike, M. C. (1982). An empirical approach to the statistical analysis of mutagenesis data from the *Salmonella* test. *Mutat. Res. 97*:267–281.
44. Gad, S. C. (1982). Statistical analysis of behavioral toxicology data and studies. *Arch. Toxicol. (Suppl.) 5*:256–266.
45. Tilson, H. A., Cabe, P. A., and Burne, T. A. (1980). Behavioral procedures for the assessment of neurotoxicity. In *Experimental and Clinical Neurotoxicology*. Edited by P. S. Spencer and N. H. Schaumburg. Baltimore, Williams & Wilkins, pp. 758–766.
46. Irwin, S. (1968). Comprehensive observational assessment. In Systematic, quantitative procedure for assessing the behavioral and physiologic state of the mouse. *Psychopharmacologia 13*: 222–257.

47. Gad, S. C. (1982). A neuromuscular screen for use in industrial toxicology. *J. Toxicol. Env. Health* 9:691–704.
48. Annua, Z. (1972). The comparative effects of hypoxia and carbon monoxide hypoxia on behavior. In *Behavioral Toxicology*. Edited by B. Weiss and V. G. Laties. New York, Plenum Press, pp. 105–127.
49. Norton, S. (1973). Amphetamine as a model for hyperactivity in the rat. *Physiol. Behav.* 11:181–186.
50. Burt, G. S. (1972). Use of behavioral techniques in the assessment of environmental contaminants. In *Behavioral Toxicology*. Edited by B. Weiss and V. G. Laties. New York, Plenum Press, pp. 241–263.
51. Johnson, B. L., Anger, W. K., Setzer, J. V., and Xinytaras, C. (1972). The application of a computer controlled time discrimination performance to problems. In *Behavioral Toxicology*. Edited by B. Weiss and V. G. Laties. New York, Plenum Press, pp. 129–153.
52. Miller, E. C. and Miller J. A. (1981). Mechanisms of chemical carcinogenesis. *Cancer* 47:1055–1064.
53. Wilson, J. S. and Holland, L. M. (1982). The effect of application frequency on epidermal carcinogenesis assays. *Toxicology* 24:45–53.
54. Gehring, P. J. and Blau, G. E. (1977). Mechanisms of carcinogenicity: Dose response. *J. Environ. Pathol. Toxicol.* 1:163–179.
55. Haseman, J. K. and Hoel, D. G. (1979). Statistical design of toxicity assays: Role of genetic structure of test animal population. *J. Toxicol. Environ. Health* 5:89–101.
56. Portier, C. J. and Hoel, D. H. (1984). Design of animal carcinogenicity studies for goodness-of-fit of multistage models. *Fund. Appl. Toxicol.* 4:949–959.
57. Grasso, P. and Crampton, R. F. (1972). The value of the mouse in carcinogenicity testing. *Fund. Cosmet. Toxicol.* 10:418–426.
58. Wittenau, M. S. and Estes/ P. (1983). The redundancy of mouse carcinogenicity bioassays. *Fund. Appl. Toxicol.* 3:631–639.
59. Ward, J. M., Griesemer, R. A., and Weisburger, E. K. (1979). The mouse liver tumor as an endpoint in carcinogenesis tests. *Toxicol. Appl. Pharmacol.* 51:389–397.
60. Page, N. P. (1977). Concepts of a bioassay program in environmental carcinogenesis. In *Environmental Cancer*. Edited by H. F. Kraybill and M. A. Mehlman. New York, Hemisphere Publishing, pp. 87–171.
61. Nutrition Foundation. (1983). *The Relevance of Mouse Liver Heptoma To Human Carcinogenic Risk*. Washington, DC, Nutrition Foundation.

62. Haseman, J. K. (1985). Issues in carcinogenicity testing: Dose selection. *Fund. Appl. Toxicol.* 5:66-78.

63. Dix, D. and Cohen, P. (1980). On the role of aging in cancer incidence. *J. Theor. Biol.* 83:163-173.

64. Salsburg, D. (1980). The effects of lifetime feeding studies on patterns of senile lesions in mice and rats. *Drug Chem. Tox.* 3:1-33.

65. Ciminera, J. L. (1985). Some issues in the design, evaluation and interpretation of tumorigenicity studies in animals. Presented at the Symposium on Long-term Animal Carcinogenicity Studies: A Statistical Perspective, March 4-6, 1985, Bethesda, MD.

66. Robens, J. F., Joiner, J. J., and Schueler, R. L. (1982). Methods in testing for carcinogenesis. In *Principles and Methods of Toxicology*. Edited by A. W. Hayes. New York, Raven Press, pp. 79-105.

67. Cameron, T. P., Hickman, R. L., Korneich, M. R., and Tarone, R. E. (1985). History, survival and growth patterns of B6C3F1 mice and F344 rats in the National Cancer Institute carcinogenesis testing program. *Fund. Appl. Toxicol.* 5: 526-538.

68. Chu, K. (1977). *Percent Spontaneous Primary Tumors in Untreated Species Used at NCI for Carcinogen Bioassays*. NCI Clearing House.

69. Dempster, A. P., Selwyn, M. R., and Weeks, B. J. (1983). Combining historical and randomized controls for assessing trends in proportions. *J. Am. Stat. Assoc.* 78:221-227.

70. Fears, T. R., Tarone, R. E., and Chu, K. C. (1977). False-positive and false-negative rates for carcinogenicity screens. *Cancer Res.* 27:1941-1945.

71. Fears, T. R. and Tarone, R. E. (1977). Response to "Use of Statistics When Examining Life Time Studies in Rodents to Detect Carcinogenicity." *J. Tox. Environ. Health* 3:629-632.

72. Gart, J. J., Chu, K. C., and Tarone, R. E. (1979). Statistical issues in interpretation of chronic bioassay tests for carcinogenicity. *J. Natl. Cancer Inst.* 62:957-974.

73. Tarone, R. E., Chu, K. C., and Ward, J. M. (1981). Variability in the rates of some common naturally occurring tumors in Fischer 344 rats and (C57BL/6NXC3H/HEN)F[1] (B6C3F1) mice. *J. Natl. Cancer Inst* 66:1175-1181.

74. Goodman, D. G., Ward, J. M., Squire, R. A., Chu, K. C., and Linhart, M. S. (1979). Neoplastic and nonneoplastic lesions in aging F344 rats. *Toxicol. Appl. Pharmacol.* 48:237-248.

75. Bratcher, T. L. (1977). Bayesian analysis of a dose-response experiment with serial sacrifices. *J. Environ. Pathol. Toxicol.* 1:287-292.

76. Dinse, G. E. (1985). Estimating tumor prevalence, lethality, and mortality. Presented at the Symposium on Long-term Animal Carcinogenicity Studies: A Statistical Perspective, March 4-6, 1985. Bethesda, MD.

77. Swenberg, J. A. (1985). The interpretation and use of data from long-term carcinogenesis studies in animals. *CIIT Activities* 5(6):1-6.

78. Solleveld, H. A., Hasemen, J. K., and McConnel, E. E. (1984). Natural history of body weight gain, survival, and neoplasia in the F344 rat. *J. Natl. Cancer Inst.* 72:929-940.

79. Feinstein, A. R. (1975). Clinical biostatistics XXII: Biologic dependency, hypothesis testing, unilateral probabilities, and other issues in scientific direction vs. statistical duplexity. *Clin. Pharmacol. Ther.* 17:499-513.

80. Salsburg, D. S. (1977). Use of statistics when examining life time studies in rodents to detect carcinogenicity. *J. Toxicol. Environ. Health* 3:611-628.

81. Haseman, J. K. (1977). Response to use of statistics when examining life time studies in rodents to detect carcinogenicity. *J. Toxicol. Environ. Health* 3:633-636.

82. Wilks, S. S. (1962). *Mathematical Statistics.* New York, John Wiley, pp. 290-291.

83. McKnight, B. and Crowley, J. (1984). Tests for differences in tumor incidence based on animal carcinogenesis experiments. *J. Am. Stat. Assoc.* 79:639-648.

84. Meng, C. and Dempster, A. P. (1985). A Bayesian approach to the multiplicity problem for significance testing with binomial data. Presented at the Symposium on Long-term Animal Carcinogenicity Studies: A Statistical Perspective, March 4-6, 1985, Bethesda, MD.

85. Peto, R., Pike, M., Day, N., Gray, R., Lee, P., Parish, S., Peto, J., Richards, S., and Wahrendorf, J. (1980). Guidelines for Simple, Sensitive Significance Tests for Carcinogenic Effects in Long-Term Animal Experiments. In *IARC Monographs on the Evaluation of the Carcinogenic Risk of Chemicals to Humans, Supplement 2, Long-Term and Short-Term Screening Assays for Carcinogens: A Critical Appraisal.* Lyon, International Agency for Research in Cancer, pp. 311-346.

86. Lijinsky, W., Reuber, M. D., and Riggs, C. W. (1981). Dose response studies of carcinogenesis in rats by nitrosodiethylamine. *Cancer Res.* 41:4997-5003.

87. Squire, R. A. (1981). Ranking animal carcinogens: A proposed regulatory approach. *Science* 214:877-880.

88. Bernstein, L., Gold, L. S., Ames, B. N., Pike, M. C., and Hoel, D. G. (1985). Some tautologous aspects of the comparison

of carcinogenic potency in rats and mice. *Fund. Appl. Toxicol.* 5:79–86.

89. Gad, S. C. and Smith, A. C. (1984). Influence of heating rates on the toxicity of evolved combustion products: Results and a System for Research. *J. Fire Sci. 1*(6):465–479.

90. Bishop, Y., Fujii, K., Arnold, E., and Epstein, S. S. (1971). Censored distribution techniques in analysis of toxicological data. *Experientia 27*:1056–1059.

91. Farmer, J. H., Uhler, R. J., and Haley, T. J. (1977). An unbalanced experimental design for dose response studies. *J. Environ. Pathol. Toxicol. 1*:293–299.

92. Redman, C. E. (1981). Screening compounds for clinically active drugs. In *Statistics in the Pharmaceutical Industry.* Edited by C. R. Buncher and J. Tsay. New York, Marcel Dekker, pp. 19–42.

93. Tukey, J. W. (1977). *Exploratory Data Analysis.* Reading, MA, Addison-Wesley Publishing Co.

94. Velleman, P. F. and Hoaglin, D. C. (1981). *Applications, Basics and Computing of Exploratory Data Analysis.* Boston, MA, Duxbury Press.

95. Hoaglin, D. C., Mosteller, F., and Tukey, J. W. (1983). *Understanding Robust and Explanatory Data Analysis.* New York, John Wiley.

96. Miller, R. G. (1966). *Simultaneous Statistical Inference.* New York, McGraw-Hill, pp. 6–10.

97. Tarone, R. E. (1975). Tests for trend in life tables analysis. *Biometrika 62*:679–682.

98. Armitage, P. (1955). Tests for linear trends in proportions and frequencies. *Biomet. II*:375–386.

99. Cochran, W. G. and Cox, G. M. (1975). *Experimental Designs.* New York, John Wiley.

100. Diamond, W. J. (1981). *Practical Experimental Designs.* Belmont, CA, Lifetime Learning Publications.

101. Federer, W. T. (1955). *Experimental Design.* New York, Macmillan.

102. Hicks, C. R. (1982). *Fundamental Concepts in the Design of Experiments.* New York, Holt, Rinehart and Winston.

# 14

# Placing and Monitoring Testing at External Facilities

ANN C. SMITH / *Allied-Signal Inc., Morristown, New Jersey*

## I. INTRODUCTION

Companies needing to evaluate the toxicity of their materials (products, raw materials, intermediates, etc.) may not have the capability to perform the required testing. Alternatively, although the capability may exist, the company's laboratory schedule may not be able to accommodate a rush study. At some time, for various reasons, industry will need to contract studies to external facilities, whether they are commercial contract laboratories, university laboratories, or even a member company's laboratory as in the case of a consortium study. As with all contractual arrangements, thorough preparation is required in order to obtain the desired product or service, to avoid confusion and misunderstanding, and to produce a timely result. This chapter is a practical guide for sponsors who need to place their studies at external laboratories. The information provided is drawn from a number of readily available sources as well as from the author's experience gained from visiting numerous laboratories in this country and abroad.

## II. DEFINING THE STUDY

### A. Preliminary Study Plan

The first step in placing a study externally is to define the study. A detailed study protocol will be part of the contract, and will be negotiated during the agreement phase. However, in the early stages of finding a laboratory, a preliminary study design is needed

before screening prospective laboratories. Some laboratories will not
be able to do certain specialty studies, such as teratology or phytotoxicity evaluations. Others may be able to do the basic work, but
not subsequent aspects (pathology, electron microscopy, statistical
evaluation) which are essential. So the first step is to define clearly
the study to be performed.

A large part of this definition may simply be an iteration of
regulatory requirements. Consideration of specifically required data
sets should certainly be made before seeking an outside laboratory.
For more complex studies which lie outside regulatory guidance, a
list of the specific objectives of the study and definition of the
methodology to approach their resolution will serve as a general
study guide. See Chapter 1 for further guidance on defining study
objectives.

### B. Distinguishing Essential from Negotiable Study Elements

An important step is to determine which parts of the study must be
included. It is desirable to maximize the amount of information to be
obtained, while also considering time, number of animals, and use of
other resources. It may not be realistic to try to accomplish all the
objectives which can be stated during the early stages of study design. This distinction of essential and negotiable study elements is
a critical step which will enable the study sponsor to select a suitable laboratory as well as to negotiate the specific components of the
study.

### C. Designating the Study Monitor

Another early aspect to consider in external placement concerns
personnel, specifically, the study's director. It is not uncommon
that the employee who functions as a study monitor on behalf of
the sponsor is called the "study director." This is a difficult concept to grasp, since the responsibilities of the study director imply
being intimately involved with and overseeing the day-to-day activities
of the study and can therefore be discharged only by an employee
of the laboratory contracted to perform the study. Regardless of
what the on-site study director is called, the sponsor needs to provide sufficient authority to allow important decisions to be made
without prolonged discussions on the telephone, or worse yet, emergency site visits by the sponsor.

For complex or long-term studies, the laboratory should provide
an alternate study director to ensure both continuing internal oversight as well as a contact for the sponsor if the primary study
director is unavailable.

Having defined the work to be done, ranked the elements of the study as essential or negotiable, and selected a study monitor from within the sponsor's organization, a laboratory must be found which can do the necessary work.

## III. IDENTIFYING COMPETENT LABORATORIES

The first step is to obtain a list of laboratories engaged in contract toxicological testing. Although other opportunities exist, for example, university laboratories, laboratories of a consortium member's company, and, in some cases, government laboratories, the vast majority of externally placed studies involve the contracting party (the "sponsor") placing a study in a "contract laboratory." Therefore, this situation will be used as the model for the rest of this chapter.

### A. Published Lists

Several lists of contract laboratories exist (1,2). These lists are updated from time to time, since the contract laboratory industry is dynamic and the capabilities of an individual laboratory change over time.

These compendia serve as basic information for finding laboratories capable of performing a specific study. More detailed information can be obtained by writing to the individual laboratories.

### B. Information Available at Meetings

A great deal of information about contract laboratories can be obtained at professional and trade meetings. Brochures which explain the types of study the laboratory is capable of conducting, and descriptions of facilities, staff, and price ranges for standard studies are displayed at such meetings by many contract laboratories. Laboratory sales representatives attend these meetings frequently to discuss specific study needs with prospective sponsors.

A second source of information available at meetings is the experience of professional colleagues, who may be able to provide advice on where to have certain kinds of studies conducted, having had similar work done previously. Of particular importance is information about where their work was done, its perceived quality, and how to avoid mistakes or misunderstandings in dealing with a particular contract laboratory.

This latter source of information needs to be taken with the proverbial "grain of salt." Almost anyone who has contracted studies has had some problems; those who have contracted many studies have had at least one study with a major problem; and probably every good contract laboratory has been inappropriately criticized for poor work at least once. A distorted evaluation is altogether possible if, for example, uncontrollable events (power shutdowns, shipping strikes, etc.) might have affected study results and the sponsor's overall impression of the laboratory.

For highly specialized studies, choices in laboratories may be very limited. Phytotoxicity testing, for example, is still a relative rarity. Teratological evaluations, although offered by many laboratories, are tricky, demanding and performed well by only a few. Genetic toxicity testing is in similar circumstances. An even more complex situation involves tests requiring several kinds of relatively unusual expertise or equipment. A teratology study which requires inhalation exposure, for example, may limit laboratory selection to only a few facilities. Contract laboratories will usually provide information on the availability of services in specialized areas, if they are unable to provide such testing themselves.

## C. "Freedom of Information" Requests

Copies of reports of laboratory inspections conducted by federal agencies are available under the Freedom of Information (FOI) Act. These reports generally follow the format of the laboratory inspection guidance given to Food and Drug Administration (FDA) or Environmental Protection Agency (EPA) investigators, and provide a great deal of information of varying utility. Since they are purged of references to proprietary activities, trademarks, specific sponsorship of studies, and much other information, it is sometimes difficult to understand the intent of the report. In addition, they present the opinions of individual investigators concerning isolated activities and events and therefore may not be truly representative of a laboratory's usual practices.

On the other hand, since the laboratory inspection procedures used by a particular agency are consistent, the FOI reports permit some comparison among laboratories. This information, coupled with other inputs, is therefore valuable and should not be ignored.

FOI requests should be made to the specific agency which conducted the inspection. Since FDA's inspection program has been in existence for some time, they are the logical first agency to call in seeking inspection reports on particular laboratories (3).

Having developed a list of laboratories able to do the study in question, the most critical part of getting a good job done is in selecting *the* laboratory at which to place the study. The rest of this chapter will be spent reviewing selection criteria in detail.

## IV. LABORATORY SELECTION CRITERIA

A number of criteria serve as guides in selecting a laboratory. Particular studies might require additional selection criteria. What

follows is a minimal list of aspects of the laboratory which will have
to be evaluated. Presumably there exists in the sponsor's company
a standard against which all individual laboratories will be evaluated.
Certain aspects may be more important than others, but all laboratories will have to meet this minimum standard.

## A. Physical Resources

An essential element in producing a good product is the availability
of sufficient physical resources at a contract laboratory to ensure
the uninterrupted progress of the study from beginning to end.
The complex array of personnel, materials, and financial resources
for successful progression of the study begins with consideration
of the physical resources of the laboratory. Elements to consider
include: space, fuel and water supply, power (with back up),
heating, ventilation and air conditioning, equipment needed to run
the study, etc. Financial resources should be sufficient to run the
study from the creation of the draft protocol to the production of the
final report and beyond, if revisions are needed. Laboratory failures do occur so the prudent study sponsor must select carefully.
One of the aims is to obtain a stable laboratory which will remain in
business beyond study termination.

Laboratory animal care facilities may be accredited by the American Association for Accreditation of Laboratory Animal Care (AAALAC).
This is a voluntary body which accredits laboratories based on its
own standards as supplemented and reinforced by those of other
organizations. Accreditation is based on elements of several major
activities, programs or capabilities of the individual laboratory, such
as veterinary resources, physical resources, administrative matters
and the presence and activity of an animal care and use (animal
welfare) committee. AAALAC accreditation is frequently the only
objective symbol of the general compliance of the laboratory with
standards of good practice in animal use and care, veterinary,
physical plant, and administrative areas. Although no guarantee
that the laboratory does good testing, AAALAC accreditation represents a worthwhile first step toward excellence.

## B. Personnel and Technical Expertise

Does the laboratory employ personnel trained in the needed specialty?
What about ancillary expertise (pathology, statistics)? If not directly employed by the laboratory, are trained specialists available
on a consulting basis? For example, if the major emphasis of a
study is the determination of the inhalation toxicity of a test agent,
but a minor component concerns teratogenic effects, the selected
laboratory will require skilled, experienced inhalation toxicologists
on staff. The laboratory does not necessarily have to employ its

own teratologists, however, since coverage of these evaluations may reasonably be effected by consultants in this specialty.

A skilled, competent staff will be necessary to the conduct of the work. Prospective laboratories' personnel environments should be scrutinized for signs of frequent or rapid staff turnover, difficulties in recruiting and retaining new staff and lack of career pathways for staff currently employed.

Many laboratories rely on independent organization certification to demonstrate a standard of achievement and competence on the part of their technical and scientific staff. For example, both the American Board of Toxicology and the American College of Toxicology have certification programs for toxicologists. Likewise, the American Association of Laboratory Animal Sciences (AALAS) has three stages for certification of laboratory animal technical staff. Other specialties have similar certification programs based on some combination of experience and achievement demonstrated by written and practical testing.

Hand in hand with personnel availability is the selection criterion of technical expertise. Many different specialties are brought to bear on a particular study. The more complex the study, the greater the difficulty in finding a contract laboratory with all the necessary expertise.

In attempting to evaluate the qualifications of contract laboratory staff, organizational charts and curricula vitae should be obtained. These documents are standard tools which are used by contract laboratories as marketing aids. Both FDA's and EPA's Good Laboratory Practice (GLP) regulations (4–7) require laboratories to maintain documentation of the training, experience and job descriptions of personnel. This is usually done by means of compilations of curricula vitae.

Another important point in evaluating staff capabilities is the number of people employed by the laboratory. The proposed study staff should be sufficient to perform all the work required. Attention should be directed to the laboratory's overall workload relative to available staff.

## C. Standard Operating Procedures

A large portion of the initial visit to prospective contract laboratories can usefully be spent in reviewing standard operating procedures (SOPs). These should be written for all routinely performed activities.

GLPs require that SOPs be established in the following general areas: animal room preparation, animal care, test and control substance management, test system (animal) observations, laboratory tests, management of on-study dead or moribund animals, necropsy, specimen collection and identification, histopathology, data management, equipment maintenance and calibration, identification of animals, and quality assurance. Although not specifically required by GLP regulations, the laboratory should also have SOPs for archiving activities. In each of these areas, numerous individual SOPs should be in place. For example, in the area of histopathology, SOPs should be available to describe tissue selection, preparation, processing, staining, and coverslipping; slide labeling and packaging; and storage and retention of wet tissues, blocks, and slides. Similarly, SOPs should be available for maintenance and calibration of all equipment and instrumentation which requires these activities.

The laboratory's SOPs should be clear, understandable, and sufficiently detailed to permit a technically experienced person to perform them. They should be up to date, and the method for keeping them current should be described. They should have the sanction of facility management, usually provided by signature of the person responsible for the pertinent laboratory activity.

To be effective, SOPs should be available to those who need them. For example, animal care SOPs should be available to vivarium workers, as analytical and clinical chemistry SOPs should be available in these laboratories. Compendia of SOPs which sit pristinely on shelves in offices may not reflect what is actually occurring in the laboratories and animal quarters. Likewise, SOPs which have not been reviewed or revised in several years should be viewed with suspicion. Improvements in actual methods occur frequently, and should be reflected in the written procedures.

If the laboratory has contracts with other laboratories, SOPs should be available for the secondary laboratories as well. Both the SOPs and these contracts should be reviewed in the same way.

## D. Cost

A key factor in laboratory selection for most sponsors is the cost of the study. This single element can largely affect the quality of a study. "Caveat emptor" applies equally to the toxicologist as to the home consumer. Many of the negotiable elements of a carefully defined study will not be performed in a similarly titled study at a different laboratory for a lower cost. Conversely, some of the extras offered for a higher priced study should not be included for extra cost if they are neither necessary nor desirable. The objective in considering the cost of a study is to select the laboratory which offers all the essential study elements at the lowest cost consistent with good quality. Good quality in turn relies on the other criteria previously discussed. When a laboratory is found which can perform all desired elements of the study, does high quality work, and offers a lower price for the study than its competitors, this is probably the laboratory to choose to perform the study.

In discussing costs, the sponsor should attempt to determine whether the laboratory will be able to add elements to the study if this appears desirable as the study progresses. The laboratory should have the capability to expand the original study design. Sponsor and laboratory should attempt to foresee how the cost of such additions would be determined.

## E. Ease of Monitoring

A consideration in selection of contract laboratories is the sponsor's ease of monitoring the study, which is largely a function of distance between the sponsor and the laboratory. In some studies, this may be a major consideration; in others, not worthy of mention. If the study is complex and requires frequent oversight, a trade-off may need to be made between the best laboratory relative to the previously mentioned selection criteria and monitoring ease.

On the other hand, sponsors do not plan complex studies unless they anticipate substantial product safety evaluation concerns, and therefore, considerable potential profit. If this is the case, the relatively small additional sum spent in the increased cost of frequent or distant monitoring may be minuscule in the eyes of those selecting the laboratory.

## F. Reputation

The reputation held by particular contract laboratories is clearly a guide in laboratory selection. Although not an absolutely reliable indicator of the worth of a contract laboratory's efforts, by and large laboratories earn their reputations over time. Beware of laboratories which submit low bids for studies and either cut corners to stay within their quoted cost or include add-ons, at the sponsor's expense, through the course of the study. Study additions can significantly increase the actual cost if the contract requires the sponsor to pay for them.

Other laboratories try to foresee likely additional aspects of the study, which may increase the quoted cost but yield a much better product. Producing the study at the price quoted is only one part of a contract laboratory's reputation. Quality, professional qualifications of staff, activity in scientific professional societies, accreditation, regulatory interface, and many other issues are important as well.

## G. Protection of Client Confidentiality

Most contract laboratories expend considerable effort in trying to maintain confidentiality on behalf of their clients. In walking through a laboratory, clients should not be able to see proprietary labels on test material containers, or cage labels which state company names. A contract laboratory concerned about client confidentiality will be careful not to allow visible evidence to be seen by other potential clients. Confidentiality is usually of significant concern and should be discussed with laboratory management. The laboratory's master schedule should maintain client confidentiality as well.

## H. Prior Experience

Prior experience with specific contract laboratories simplifies the task of selecting a laboratory. Establishing a continuing relationship with one or several laboratories in the case of routine testing provides an opportunity to fine-tune study protocols. This will be discussed in greater detail in Section X below.

## I. Scheduling

Undoubtedly, starting the study as soon as possible is important. The ability of the laboratory to begin the study soon may well determine where the study is performed. Most of the larger contract houses can start all but very large studies within 4–6 weeks. Some studies may be able to be initiated on even shorter notice. Certainly for shorter studies, less complicated protocols are needed and generally less lead time is required to begin the study. The converse is equally true, so if the study is large, long-term, or complicated, a fairly long time before study initiation will be needed to get the details of the study worked out with the laboratory. As a result, a laboratory which is willing to start a lengthy or complex study before the details have been settled should generally be avoided.

## V. SITE VISITS OF PROSPECTIVE CONTRACT LABORATORIES

In scheduling site visits with contract laboratories, the objectives should be clearly defined. Meeting those people who will be directing and contributing importantly to the study provides an opportunity to evaluate their understanding of the nature of the questions or problems which may arise. Ancillary contributors (pathologists, statisticians) should be interviewed carefully as well, since their contributions can be of fundamental significance to the quality and outcome of the study.

The facilities should be toured, looking for appropriate size, construction, spacing and design. GLP regulations as promulgated under the Food, Drug and Cosmetic Act, the Toxic Substances Control Act, or the Federal Insecticide, Fungicide and Rodenticide Act provide guidance as to the general facility, equipment and operational requirements of laboratories.

Storage areas for extra racks and cages, feed and bedding, and so forth are frequently inadequate in laboratories, and these facilities should be inspected and evaluated.

Both EPA and FDA provide their field investigators who conduct laboratory inspections for compliance with GLPs with "Compliance Guidance Manuals" (8,9). These are comprehensive documents which use a checklist approach to inspecting a laboratory for adherence to all the elements of GLP regulations. They can be obtained from the agencies, and can be used as guidance for study sponsors in evaluating prospective laboratories. An advantage of using this approach is that the sponsor will not omit an important element in inspecting a prospective laboratory. However, the sponsor should not get so bogged down in reviewing checklist items that actual observation of the laboratory is abbreviated.

## VI. THE CONTRACT

A sound contract is an important element in placing a study at an external laboratory. If negotiated carefully, it will pay off in improved communication at all stages of the study and should reduce the possibility of misunderstanding.

### A. General Terms

General terms of the contract should address such aspects as timeliness, proprietary rights, confidentiality, adherence to regulatory requirements (in the research effort and in the laboratory's practices in waste disposal, workers' protection, and safety, etc.), type and frequency of reports, communications between parties, conditions under which the study may be aborted and restarted, timing and method of payment, and the like. Such a contract ", . . . should be negotiated by a team of lawyers and scientists who have a thorough understanding of the problems to be investigated, including both the scientific issues and the potential business implications. . . . Armed with this . . . understanding, the lawyers can then proceed to develop a contract that is appropriate to the situation. . . . Much of the language will be routine or 'boiler plate,' the type commonly found in agreements of various kinds" (10).

The contract should specify who does what in the furtherance of the study. For example, if analysis is necessary, the sponsor may wish to retain the responsibility to analyze the test material as a means of keeping its identity confidential. The derivative concern about documentation of the analysis is presumably also retained by the sponsor, but the contract should be clear on the responsibilities of both parties.

When discussing study personnel, various degrees of authority are vested in contract laboratory study staff by the sponsor. The study contract should define as clearly as possible the degree of authority vested in the contract laboratory staff and at what point the sponsor would be consulted for a decision when unforeseen situations arise. In general terms, then, the contract should define the rights and responsibilities of both parties.

The contract should also address financial matters, such as the cost of the study and the method and timing of payment. Certain unanticipated activities not directly related to the study may increase the cost to the laboratory; the contract should attempt to anticipate these events and establish reasonable incremental costs to the sponsor to deal with them. For example, study-specific inspections by agencies authorized to review a study (FDA or EPA) may add to the cost to the laboratory for additional staff time to accompany inspectors, copy documents, and otherwise field the inspections. If the sponsor wishes to be present at such inspections, additional direct costs will be incurred. Although many readers would view this simply as part of the laboratory's cost of doing business, the contract should anticipate how each party is expected to respond financially if the inspection becomes very time-consuming or onerous.

Likewise, poststudy activities and responsibilities should be defined in the contract. Who will archive tissue and other samples and specimens? For how long? If statistical analysis is to be performed, of what does it consist? Who decides? If further analysis appears desirable after evaluation of the data, will the sponsor incur extra costs?

## B. The Study Protocol

The most important part of site visits to laboratories will be the discussion of the study and establishment of the protocol. Extensive prior experience of the sponsor in conducting the contemplated study is helpful although many elements may still have to be negotiated. If the sponsor has limited experience, the importance of the protocol increases, since it contains the specific language of the contract between sponsor and laboratory which governs the conduct of the study.

To write a protocol with little flexibility may preclude the study director's judgment and may actually compromise the quality of the study. Each party must feel comfortable that the study protocol provides sufficient detail to specify what is to be done, when, and under what conditions. However, the protocol must not be so rigid that the study director is hampered in responding to changing conditions and events as they occur. Since unanticipated events almost always occur, the objective is to provide a protocol which permits the study to be conducted as closely as possible to the original study plan and to answer all the important study questions.

## C. Other Terms

### 1. Authorship

The question of authorship of publications resulting from the proposed study should be covered in the contract. Not all work is worthy of publication nor do contract laboratory staff often get an opportunity to author papers. But if the laboratory has contributed significantly to the work, and a publication is contemplated, help in writing portions of the manuscript should be solicited from members of the study staff, for which coauthorship is a deserved reward.

### 2. Reports

The contract should specify the nature and frequency of reports which the laboratory will make to the sponsor. For example, a short-term study (two weeks or less) may require only telephone confirmation of study start, status of the animals at the halfway point, confirmation of termination, and the usual draft and final report (see Sect. VIII below).

For a longer study, the sponsor may request written status reports at regular intervals. In the case of chronic studies the sponsor may wish to have formal interim reports prepared by the laboratory. The contract should clearly specify the expectations of both parties concerning reports.

### 3. Inspections by the Sponsor

Most contract laboratories do not like the thought of unscheduled site visits by study sponsors, for understandable reasons. Under ordinary circumstances, a large amount of staff time is spent escorting visitors through the laboratory. Unscheduled visitors therefore place an additional burden on already stretched resources.

Nevertheless, the right to monitor study progress at any reasonable time should be explicitly affirmed in the contract. This right, although perhaps never exercised by the sponsor, should not be relinquished. As a practical matter, unscheduled monitoring visits almost never occur, since the sponsor must recognize that the study staff may be unavailable at the time of the visit, making the trip a wasted one.

Likewise, the contract should explicitly grant the sponsor access to the laboratory's quality assurance (QA) inspection reports of the study. These reports are ordinarily *not* available to government investigators, and some contract laboratories prefer not to share them. However, a sponsor should ensure that the contract grants access to the QA reports.

## VII. IN-PROGRESS MONITORING

As mentioned before, "Compliance Inspection Manuals" which are used by inspectors in their agency laboratory inspection programs are available from EPA and FDA. The manuals offer a systematic and thorough means of reviewing elements of GLP compliance and can serve as guides regarding standardized aspects of laboratories and studies.

Having carefully evaluated the laboratory before contracting the study, the focus of in-progress monitoring changes from general to specific. Whereas initially the animal feed room was inspected for cleanliness, good housekeeping and a rodent-free environment, now the feed should be inspected to see if it is segregated and logged out at suitable times and in amounts proportional to specific study needs.

Likewise, much of the other in-progress monitoring will focus on data which have already been gathered. In performing this review, notes should be made and a list of items prepared for discussion with facility and study management at an exit conference. In-progress monitoring should also include review of vivarium conditions (temperature, humidity) and animal husbandry records. Although not the most fascinating data to review, the conditions under which the animals are housed can seriously influence the study's outcome, both from a biological point of view as well as relative to the study's acceptability by regulatory agencies.

All data pertaining to clinical observations, blood and clinical chemistry analyses, weights, and feed consumption statistics should be reviewed. Not all of these may apply and some studies will have more complex in-life observations than described here.

The laboratory's QA inspection reports should be reviewed at this time. These reports should demonstrate that QA inspections are being carried out according to QA SOPs. The content of the reports should be reviewed as a means of ensuring adherence to the study protocol and the laboratory's standard operating procedures.

The purpose of an in-progress monitoring visit is to review all the data collected since the last visit in order to ascertain that the study is progressing smoothly and without major problems. The data reviewed should be generally consistent with the sponsor's understanding of study progress derived from previous inspections or reports from the laboratory. If the study appears to be changing in unsuspected ways, the sponsor and the study director should discuss the possibility of alteration of the study design: adding more or different observations, adjusting doses or dosing schedules, inserting an unplanned interim sacrifice. The study protocol is designed to accommodate all reasonably foreseeable events in the study. However, some events may occur which were unexpected, particularly in a complex study. The monitoring visit allows the opportunity for the sponsor and study director to adapt the study design, if necessary.

If the study design has been changed since the sponsor's last visit, protocol amendments which clearly state the change, its scope, and the reason for the change should be found in the study documentation. If the amendment was authorized by the sponsor during a previous communication, this should be referred to.

The facility's SOPs should again be checked to ensure that relevant procedures are being followed (from cage washing to histological preparation). Most procedures generate some kind of documentation which should be reviewed.

When all available documentation has been reviewed, the sponsor will have a list of items for discussion with study management. Sponsor and study director, together with other pertinent laboratory staff (pathologist, animal care supervisor, quality assurance staff) should meet to resolve these issues.

Generally, the questions can be resolved fairly easily. Sometimes things go wrong which are beyond the control of facility management, such as temperature or humidity excursions in the animal room. If not numerous, extreme, or cyclical, such excursions are probably of little importance. However, if patterns of consistent difficulties are detected, facility management should be required to improve its control over environmental conditions. This may involve moving the study to a different room for completion or providing the facility maintenance staff with additional instruction and training. Whatever the cause, the desired effect is correction of excessive environmental variation.

Since the laboratory was selected on the basis of a thorough preplacement evaluation, now is the time to ask laboratory management to bring its expertise to bear on whatever problems have arisen in the study.

What if major problems arise which warrant aborting the study and restarting it? A frank discussion with study management (and your own management!) should be the starting point. If the sponsor's judgment to abort comes as the result of in-progress monitoring without any previous idea that such serious deficiencies existed, the sponsor's and the study director's views are apparently far apart. If, on the other hand, the sponsor's inspection is the result of the laboratory's report of problems, then the decision to restart the study may be easily and jointly reached.

The contract confers rights and responsibilities on both parties, and should therefore be consulted if study abortion and restart is contemplated. If the contract clearly permits the sponsor to judge at what point a major problem or a series of minor problems constitutes grounds for aborting the study, the decision to do so should be made expeditiously. Having learned from the experience, sponsor and study director should proceed to restart the study with as little delay as possible.

## VIII. THE STUDY REPORT

Most sponsors will want interim reports for major long-term studies. Since the interim reports will form the basis for the final report, they should be read carefully and critically. If misinformation, confidential business information, or poor interpretations of data are presented in the interim reports, they should be corrected at once. Interim reports may also be sought by regulators, so they should be held to the same exacting standards of thoroughness and accuracy as the final report.

The final report should be presented to the sponsor in draft form. Several years ago, this was a contested notion, with many contract laboratories objecting to draft reports. However, the current practice is for contract laboratories to submit drafts for review by sponsors.

The study report should contain all essential elements, generally those covered in GLP regulations. Additional data may be included, for example, information about the test material, interpretative statements by sponsor scientists, references to other studies of the test material, or a host of other information. The sponsor should make such inclusions after receipt of the final report from the testing laboratory. For example, if previous study data are relevant, they might usefully be included in a discussion section.

Much report information required by GLPs deals with methodological details which should have been carefully described in the protocol. Appending the protocol to the study report can serve to fulfill these requirements. This saves time and retains the study plan as a historical document. If the protocol was not strictly followed or if it required extensive alterations, a new description of methodology may be preferable.

The final study report should contain the signatures of all required parties: study director, QA inspector, pathologist, statistician, clinical chemist, and any other scientists who contributed significantly to the work. It is also a good idea to list the study personnel. Such personnel can change frequently, and personnel lists may not be available if there is a need to identify study staff at some time in the future.

The study report should take no more than two drafts in order for sponsor and contract laboratory to agree on a final version. If the sponsor feels that additional drafts are needed, this should be resolved quickly with the contract laboratory. Frequently there is a reluctance to rewrite reports many times, and the zeal with which the perfect report is pursued will diminish with time. A qualified scientist is entitled to disagree with conclusions reached by another in an addendum to the report, although agreeing on the conclusions drawn from the study at the outset is a less awkward means of presenting conclusions in the report. Nevertheless it is not uncommon for a sponsor's final report to include statements of opinion differing from those offered by the contract laboratory.

## IX. ANCILLARY SERVICES

The contract laboratory may not have available all the services needed to complete the study. For example, some laboratories use contract pathology services. Archiving of raw data, specimens, samples, and interim and final reports may be done at a commercial archiving operation rather than at the laboratory. Prior to contracting, decisions need to be made concerning services which the laboratory itself will not provide. In the case where pathology is subcontracted, the sponsor should be able to specify a pathology laboratory other than the one the contract laboratory usually uses. Likewise, if the contractor does not have its own archive space, the samples could be retained by the sponsor, rather than having them sent to a commercial archivist or warehouse. These issues should be anticipated and addressed in the contract. If circumstances require a change in the planned provider of these services, sponsor and contract laboratory should keep each other informed.

## X. ONGOING CONTRACTS

Having successfully completed a contracted study, if the sponsor anticipates a continuing need, developing an ongoing contract with this laboratory for future work should be considered. Establishing a continuing relationship with one or several laboratories enables the sponsor to familiarize the laboratory thoroughly with the sponsor's study methods as well as with any idiosyncrasies of reporting or data gathering. In addition, economies can usually be effected on the basis of volume and/or regular scheduling. Also, establishing an ongoing relationship with a contract laboratory may improve the turnaround time of "rush" studies, since the laboratory might be able to accommodate such a request more easily for an established than for a onetime customer.

Many sponsors have found it useful to establish such ongoing testing contracts with several laboratories simultaneously. Some advantages of this approach are: expanding the possibilities of squeezing in a "rush" study, extending the standardization of test methodology from the sponsor's perspective, and increasing the objectivity of the overall testing program by bringing several observation and judgment capabilities to bear on similar methods and data sets.

A fourth advantage is that failures of individual contract laboratories will not leave a sponsor's testing program grounded so that the process of finding a suitable laboratory must be begun again.

Some specialties are well practiced in only a handful of laboratories. In these cases the objective must be to get a good study done each time. More and closer overseeing may be required in such cases than if several laboratories are adept and ready to do the required testing.

## REFERENCES

There is a relative paucity of literature in the general area covered in this chapter. Several specific references have been cited, and these are listed below. However, certain other articles and books may be of value to the reader; these are offered as suggestions for further reading.

### Cited References

1. Jackson, F. M. (1985). *International Directory of Contract Laboratories*. New York, Marcel Dekker, Inc.
2. Texas Research Institute. (1986). *Directory of Toxicology Testing Institutions*. Houston, Texas Research Institute.
3. To obtain inspection reports from FDA, call their FOI office at (301) 443-6310. For EPA reports, the telephone number of their FOI office is (202) 382-4048. The respective addresses are: Department of Health and Human Services, 200 Independence Ave., SW, Washington, DC 20201; FOI Office (A-101), USEPA, 401 M Street, NW, Washington, DC 20460.
4. Code of Federal Regulations, Title 21, Part 58 (Food, Drug and Cosmetic Act).
5. Code of Federal Regulations, Title 40, Part 792 (Toxic Substances Control Act).
6. Code of Federal Regulations, Title 40, Part 160 (Federal Insecticide, Fungicide and Rodenticide Act).
7. Principles of Good Laboratory Practice have been enumerated by the Organization for Economic Cooperation and Development. Other countries (Japan, United Kingdom, The Netherlands) and the European Economic Community have also proposed or finalized GLP guidelines and requirements.
8. Good Laboratory Practice Compliance Inspections of Laboratories Conducting Health Effects Studies, Inspectors' Manual. (1985). Washington, DC, USEPA, Office of Pesticides and Toxic Substances, Office of Compliance Monitoring.
9. *Compliance Program Guidance Manual*, Chapter 48, Human drugs and biologics: Bio research monitoring. (1984). Washington, DC, Food and Drug Administration.

10. Macdougall, I. C. (1981). Some contractual and legal aspects of toxicological research. In *Scientific Considerations in Monitoring and Evaluating Toxicological Research*. Edited by E. J. Gralla. Washington, DC, Hemisphere Publishing Corporation, p. 193.

## Additional Reading

Food and Drug Administration's Good Laboratory Practice Regulations original proposal, *Fed. Reg. 41*:51206–51230 (1976). This details the reasons for the proposed GLPs and includes a catalog of deficiencies found in laboratories which performed studies in support of FDA regulated products.

Guide for the Care and Use of Laboratory Animals, DHEW Publ. No. (NIH) 78-23, revised 1985.

Gralla, E. J. (Ed.). (1981). *Scientific Considerations in Monitoring and Evaluating Toxicological Research*. Washington, DC, Hemisphere Publishing Corporation.

Jackson, E. M. (1984). How to choose a contract laboratory: Utilizing a laboratory clearance procedure. *J. Toxicol. Cut. Ocular Toxicol. 3*:83–92.

James, J. W. (1982). Good Laboratory Practice, ChemTech, 162–165, March 1982.

Hoover, B. K., Baldwin, J. K., Uelner, A. F., Whitmire, C. E., Davies, C. L., and Bristol, D. W. (Eds.). (1986). *Managing Conduct and Data Quality of Toxicology Studies*. Princeton, Princeton Scientific Publishing Co., Inc.

Paget, G. E. (1977). *Quality Control in Toxicology*. Baltimore, MD, University Park Press.

Paget, G. E. (1979). *Good Laboratory Practice*. Baltimore, MD, University Park Press.

Paget, G. E. and Thompson, R. (Eds.). (1979). *Standard Operating Procedures in Toxicology*. Baltimore, MD, University Park Press.

Paget, G. E. and Thompson, R. (Eds.). (1979). *Standard Operating Procedures in Pathology*. Baltimore, MD, University Park Press.

# 15

# Hazard and Risk Assessment

MICHAEL A. JAYJOCK / Rohm and Haas Company, Philadelphia, Pennsylvania

SHAYNE COX GAD / G. D. Searle and Company, Skokie, Illinois

## I. INTRODUCTION

The problem of understanding the hazards and risks associated with unintentional or coincidental exposures to chemicals is a complex one which has multiple uncertainties built into it. All too many members of our society either fail or refuse to understand this fundamental fact. Worse, all too many, including scientists, do not understand that toxicity (the potential of a chemical to cause health effects under a laboratory situation) and hazard (the practical consideration of whether such an adverse health effect could occur in real life) though related, are neither the same or directly correlated.

It must also be understood that contrary to popular belief, risk assessment in toxicology is not limited to carcinogenesis. Rather, it may be applied to any of the possible deferred catastrophic toxicological consequences of exposure to chemicals or agents where the effect is separated in time from the putative cause, and where the effect (say a birth defect) is also something that occurs at some low baseline incidence level in the human population. That is, those things (such as carcinogenesis, teratogenesis, or reproductive impairment) that threaten life (either existing or prospective) at a time distant to the actual exposure to the chemical or agent. Because the consequences of these toxic events are extreme, yet are distanced from the actual cause by time (unlike overexposure to an acutely lethal agent, such as carbon monoxide), society is willing to accept only some low level of risk while maintaining the benefits of use of the agent. Though the most familiar (and, to date, best developed) case is that of carcinogenesis, much of what is presented here for risk assessment may also be applied to the other endpoints of concern.

Finally it is necessary to understand that risk assessment is a multistep process, and each step in the process is subject to varying degrees of uncertainty and calls for sound scientific judgement. There are at least five major steps in the process. These steps and the uncertainties and judgements associated with them are:

1. *Physical, Chemical, and Manufacturing/Use Characteristics.* The starting point for understanding the exposure and subsequent risk associated with a chemical entity and its use is to understand both the innate characteristics of the entity (physical state, vapor pressure, boiling point, flash point, etc.) and its life cycle (how it is made, transported, used, and disposed of). These are crucial points to truly characterize and understand a material—the toxicity and hazard cannot be separated from these factors (particularly how it is used). These factors are also the easiest to characterize with minimal uncertainty.

2. *Data Qualification.* Evaluating available pertinent data sets (such as human epidemiology studies and animal bioassays) for adequacy and suitability, and then selecting which will be used to build a risk assessment model is the initial first step. Data sets of adequate (but not first rate) quality can be used later to "check" the model for accuracy.

3. *Low Dose Extrapolation.* Using the selected mathematical model, the dose-response information from one or more animal studies is extrapolated from the levels at which we have dose-response data to the dose/exposure region of concern (that is, where there is likely human exposure, generally four or more orders of magnitude distant from our actual data).

4. *Cross Species Extrapolation* (also called scaling). Now, having a dose-response model for what happens to an animal species at a low dose level, we must relate what happens in the species used in bioassays (usually mice and rats) to human. Methods for doing this will be reviewed toward the end of this chapter. Though they generally have much better biological basis than the low-dose extrapolation methods (which really have no biological basis), the uncertainty associated with them is still generally a couple of orders of magnitude.

5. *Real Life Exposure Estimation.* The last step in the process is estimating human exposure: how many people (and who)

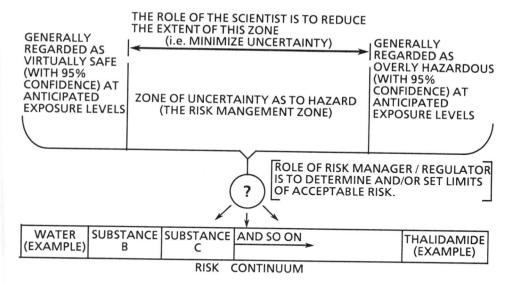

Figure 1    Risk assessment uncertainty and risk management.

are exposed to how much?  As we shall see, this final step
again has significant uncertainty associated with it.

So we have multiple steps, each with a level of uncertainty
attached to it.  The objective of the entire process (given the uncertainties involved) is to identify a level of exposure associated
with an unacceptable degree of concern as to human health effects.
One can then compare this region of exposure which represents unacceptable risk with that which contains human exposure to determine
if risk is acceptable.

There are two major approaches to dealing with this uncertainty.

*Most Conservative*

Based on worst case answer to any element of uncertainty,
including

    most sensitive species

    most sensitive strain

    most sensitive sex

    assumption of no threshold

    use of upper confidence limits of VSD (virtually safe dose)

*Most Appropriate*
  Based on judgement, including
    most appropriate route
    best data (i.e., with least uncertainty)
    no *prima facie* acceptance or rejection of a threshold or
      of linearity (or lack of it) in the dose response at
      regions beyond our data

Just as it is inappropriate to substitute the term "safe" for "virtually safe" or "having acceptable risk" when describing very low-level exposures to the classes of toxic agents we are speaking of, it is also not correct or acceptable to equate "most conservative" with "best science." The best science approach is that which minimizes the uncertainty associated with each of these steps to the extent possible. In the face of continuing uncertainty, the most conservative approach *within the bounds of the data* is appropriate and should be selected.

Our challenge then, is to select and utilize those methods which minimize the uncertainty in the entire risk assessment process. This process is presented diagramatically in Figure 1.


## II.  PHYSICAL, CHEMICAL, AND MANUFACTURING/USE CHARACTERISTICS

For a chemical entity to cause any of the adverse health effects that are of concern in this chapter, it is first necessary that the material gain entry into the body. Such entry is determined by two sets of requirements: first, exposure must occur. The determinants of such exposure will be looked at in more detail under exposure assessment (Sect. III). The second, however, is whether such materials will be absorbed. And the major determinants of absorption (and, indeed, of generation of the potential for exposure to a chemical) are its innate chemical and physical characteristics.

There is a long list of chemical and physical factors which may potentially influence exposure and absorption of chemicals. We will only briefly look at four of these here: physical state, vapor pressure, boiling point, and chemical stability.

Physical state (whether a material is a gas, liquid, or solid at room temperature, and if a solid whether it is a powder or gum, for example) is important in that it determines both in what ways a material can be handled and transported and if there is a potential for inhalation exposure. Gases, liquids which can be aerosolized, or solids which are low-density fine powders all can find their way into the atmosphere of the work place, and from there be absorbed.

Likewise, vapor pressures of liquids determine how much of the material will be in the gas phase at room temperatures. In addition, gases possess the greatest potential to be inhaled.

Boiling point is closely related to vapor pressure, and is of interest for similar reasons. The actual temperatures and atmospheric pressures at which a material is handled will determine how much material is vaporized; for vapor pressures are traditionally characterized for "standard" conditions. But not all work places meet such conditions. Some factories may be located in areas where ambient temperatures are higher (the South) or where atmospheric pressure is lower (such as in Denver); both of these conditions would increase the real potential of a nominal liquid to convert to the gas phase.

Chemical stability in industry is of concern for a host of reasons. But one reason which may be overlooked is that working with a chemical of low stability may lead to exposure of a worker to a compound other than the one being manufactured.

Directly interfacing with chemical and physical characteristics are the details of the substance life cycle. This cycle includes the manufacturing process, any formulation that may occur, transportation, use, and finally, the disposal of a material. Chemical and physical properties influence each of these steps, and the details of each step (in conjunction with these same physical and chemical characteristics) determine how much and what kind of worker and population exposure will occur.

## III. EXPOSURE IDENTIFICATION AND ASSESSMENT

Determining the significance of any exposure is impossible without consideration of the inherent hazard or toxicity of the material. Similarly, the practical consequences of a material's intrinsic hazard is meaningless without evaluation of the exposure or dose that is delivered to the site of action. The following algorithm illustrates this simple but profound relationship between exposure and hazard in the estimation of risk:

Risk = f (exposure)(hazard)

Risk is directly proportional to the level of exposure and hazard and both must be present for there to be any consequence. These two entities of exposure and hazard are inextricably connected in the risk-assessment process. In practice, the risk assessor usually runs an iterative process weighing his or her knowledge of the one versus the other to help focus attention and actions to arrive at a reasoned conclusion. For example, a situation with a very low exposure potential can tolerate considerable inherent hazard (i.e., toxicity) without resulting in a conclusion of unreasonable risk.

The level of scientific uncertainty with either the nature or the objective level of exposure or hazard colors our actions or conclusions in the overall risk assessment. The interfacing of the uncertainties around hazard and exposure has consequences with regard to how far one needs to go in the analysis. Take an example of a low exposure application with a material of unknown but potentially high hazard. If we had a high confidence in the low exposure potential of the use scenarios of this material we could tolerate a high degree of uncertainty in our knowledge of the hazard of the material even though it has an ascribed hazard level that is relatively high. In this case, reasonable and easily defensible worst-case assumptions of hazard render a conclusion of acceptable risk when viewed in the context of the total assessment. This approach precludes the necessity for expending precious resources on sharpening our understanding of the compound's hazard. It's not difficult for the reader to imagine situations where the opposite is true, that is, when one has a high degree of confidence in the material's inherent hazard as being low but much less certainty about its exposure patterns. The challenge comes in the typically intermediate situation where "gray" levels of exposure and hazard exist. Here the assessor needs to decide where the resources should be best spent to render the required decisions.

Since risk assessment is dependent on both exposure and hazard the exposure-assessment process properly involves close iterative interaction with that of the hazard evaluation. In this scheme uncertainty is addressed by using the upper bounds of exposure and hazard from the objective evidence at hand. Each examination of hazard or exposure then drives the other until enough resources are committed to the evaluation and the assessor finds him or herself with a reasonable determination of acceptable or unacceptable risk based on the accumulated data.

With this inseparable interactive relationship of exposure and hazard firmly in mind, we can seek to characterize the elements of each separately.

## A. Preliminary Exposure Assessment

### 1. Chemical and Physical Properties

Characterization of critical chemical and physical properties for compounds with potential adverse health impact establishes a basis for subsequent exposure analysis. An insoluble solid without fines will have virtually no inhalation exposure potential, while a volatile liquid in an open vessel can offer significant inhalation potential. Since it helps to focus attention and activity, property characterization should be the first task for the investigator. Some critical properties related to exposure potential are listed below:

*Vapor Pressure-Boiling Point.* Assuming a constant area of air-liquid interface, the vapor pressure of the liquid is a direct measure of its exposure potential. Indeed, knowing the vapor pressure allows one to calculate the worse case of vapor exposure:

Saturation Concentration (ppm v/v) = (VP/760)(1,000,000)

where VP is the vapor pressure in torr or mmHg.

A scheme for the reasonable estimation of vapor pressure at various temperatures when the compound's structure and boiling point (at normal or reduced pressure) or its vapor pressure at a prescribed temperature are known is presented in Ref. 1.

*Particle Size Distribution of Bulk Powders.* Particles greater than 100 μm in diameter settle rapidly and thus offer little inhalation potential in most instances. Similarly, particles larger than about 10 μm tend to be removed in the upper respiratory tract and rarely make it to deep lung tissue of humans. Thus, knowledge of the particle size distribution of granular material offers important information relative to its inhalation potential.

*Solubility and Octanol/Water Coefficient.* The solubility of a substance in water (or lipids) can in large measure determine the fate of the material in the environment or in the body. For instance, a material with a high octanol/water coefficient will tend to partition and be found in the organic-rich sediment of a lake or stream rather than in the water column. In another instance, insoluble particulates that reach the deep lung because of small particle size tend to remain in the alveolar region and will not be distributed throughout the systemic circulation.

## 2. Site-Specific Characteristics

Airborne exposure potential to vapors from liquids is directly related to the ambient use temperature and the surface area of exposed liquid. With all other conditions held steady, the exposure potential of any application will also be proportional to the quantity of material transferred per unit time.

## 3. Absorbed Versus Available Dose

The most meaningful description of exposure is a quantification of the amount of toxicant per unit time that reaches the site of toxic action in the physiology of the species involved. This is rarely achieved and assessors usually settle for less direct measures of exposure; namely, the dose that is available for absorption by the organism. Thus, human inhalation exposure is gauged by measuring the concentration of the toxicant in the air that might be breathed by an individual. This concentration is multiplied by the individuals' residence time in and their inhalation rate of this air to arrive at an estimate of exposure.

### 4. Dose

Absorption of the dose is more often not addressed or it is implicitly assumed to be 100% of the available dose. The situation with dermal exposure is even less precise. The simplest schemes estimate the amount of material applied or remaining on the skin and then assume a certain percentage (5–100%) of percutaneous absorption into the systemic circulation (2). More sophisticated approaches attempt to estimate the kinetic transfer rate of toxicant through the skin multiplied by the affected surface area of skin to give a systemically absorbed dose (3–5).

### 5. Monitoring Versus Modelling

Estimation of available dose from inhalation of air contaminant can be accomplished by analytical sampling of the ambient air. The details of what constitutes statistically valid and reliable sampling are presented elsewhere (6,7). Protocols for the sampling of dermal dosing are also available (8–10). These direct sampling techniques require the development and validation of analytical protocols that are specific to the compound(s) of concern. Assuming proper validation and sampling strategies are employed, these data represent the best (i.e., the most precise and accurate) measure of the exposure potential based on available dose.

A more general approach involves exposure estimation based on physicochemical principles or an empirically derived data base or a combination of these two techniques.

The decision whether to monitor or model an exposure is dependent primarily on the precision needs of the analysis and the availability of validated monitoring and modeling tools. If anticipated exposures are close to ascribed exposure limits, then monitoring methods and sampling strategies that render a high level of statistical evaluative power may be necessary. Conversely, in scenarios where exposure potential is low, modeling using conservative (i.e., overestimating) assumptions may show a lack of significant exposure potential vis-a-vis exposure limits and thus allow a conclusion of relative safety without the need for or the expense of direct measurements. Thus, the first step in any exposure assessment should be the use of conservative models of exposure potential in a preliminary screening. Monitoring or model refinement remain as possible next

steps in the process if the worst-case model does not allow a conclusion of relative safety.

The state of development for exposure models for the estimation
of inhalation or percutaneous exposure of occupationally exposed
workers is relatively crude. Their current value lies in the above
mentioned preliminary screening. Assessors who want or need to
refine their estimates of exposure beyond this stage can choose
either to refine the model or do monitoring. Historically they have
almost invariably chosen the latter because it gives a direct answer
and in the short run is certainly less expensive. Refined and validated models remain a highly viable but essentially untapped resource
for cost-effective exposure assessment. Specific discussion of the
research needs in this area are presented later.

Exposure models in the areas of outdoor ambient air and surface
and ground water are more highly developed than models developed
for occupational exposure indoors. Part of the reason for this is
the above mentioned tendency of industrial hygienists to directly
monitor exposures. This luxury is often unavailable to the assessor
trying the gauge ambient exposure levels in the environment. Direct
measurement may be impossible or highly impractical because of the
large areas involved or the generally lower (often analytically undetectable concentrations) of toxicants found in the multiple and
interacting compartments of the general environment.

## B. Distribution of Xenobiotics

The highest concentrations of xenobiotic agents available to affect
human health are usually found in the workplace. Conditions that
enhance the exposure potential are large quantities of chemical toxicants existent in occupational settings as raw materials, intermediates, or products which may be handled in operations which are
somewhat "open." Relatively high exposures are also possible in
living quarters from direct product use (e.g., pesticides) or in-
cidental contaminants (e.g., formaldehyde from building materials).
Recent studies (11) have shown significant levels of indoor air contamination and subsequent health risk in some homes from naturally
occurring radon gas seeping into the structures from the ground.

Any contaminant entering the general air volume in the indoor
environment will have a comparatively long residence time in that
volume because indoor ventilation rates are, for the most part, much
lower than those outdoors. This assumes that the incoming ventilatory air is essentially free of the contaminant and thus dilutes and
purges it. Overall ventilation rates in private residences are typically
much lower than those found in industrial rooms (12).

If the source of the xenobiotic contaminant is not in or directly
proximate to the indoor industrial or residential environment then it

must travel through time and space to be available for human exposure. Ambient air contamination can come from specific industrial
point sources or general and highly disperse "line" or "area" sources
such as motor vehicles on a highway or in a congested city. The
scale of these contaminant concentrations are measured in fractions
of miles to hundreds or even thousands of miles while the scale of
indoor exposure fields from proximate sources is measured in feet.

General contamination of the soil or surface water and ground
water can allow toxicants to travel to human targets either directly
or through possible accumulation or concentration in food. The
physical scale of these contaminant soil and surface water fields are
also quite large compared to specific local indoor environments and
the time scale of these events is usually much longer than those for
air contamination. It takes considerably longer to contaminate (or
clean up) an aquafer or a lake than it does to foul (or clear) the air.

## C. Air Concentration Modeling

Modeling of air concentrations of toxicants like many other exposure
models is typically based on the conservation of mass. Contaminant
mass is generated, injected into the air, and then accounted for as
it disperses, deposits, or transforms with time. The elements can
be divided into three areas of characterization:

Source. The strength (mass/time) and location of contaminant
release.
Dispersion. A quantitative description of contaminant transport
in the air.
Depuration. The time-dependent loss of contaminant form an
air volume of interest. Mechanisms of loss include ventilatory
dilution and purging from a specified volume of air, deposition losses onto environmental surfaces, and chemical
transformation.

The level to which we can identify and quantify each of the
above is the extent that our models will be true simulations of
reality.

### 1. Workplace

The following equation describes the conservation of mass in the
workroom air:

$$VdC = Gdt - QCdt - KCdt \tag{1}$$

V = room volume
C = contaminant concentration (weight/volume)

G = contaminant input rate (weight/time)
Q = ventilation rate (volume/time)
K = nonventilatory depuration coefficient (dimensionless)

This equation simply states that in any "snapshot" of time (dt), the amount of toxicant in the workroom air (VdC) will be equal to the amount that went in (Gdt) minus the amount that comes out by ventilation-purging (QCdt) and other clearing mechanisms (KCdt).

This model assumes complete if not perfectly efficient mixing of air and contaminant. As such it predicts there will be a uniform concentration within the volume of the room with no concentration gradient. This assumption has been tested and validated in relatively small industrial rooms (13). However, its ability to predict the maximum exposure potential in larger rooms is questionable.

Recent studies have shown that in some industrial ventilation fields, point sources in large rooms result in essentially spherical or hemispheric diffusion patterns from the source with diatomically decreasing concentration from the source to distal points in the room (14–16). Thus, the maximum concentration and exposure potential in many industrial ventilation fields appear to be concentrated within a relatively short distance from the source.

Adequate treatment of ventilatory purging in the real world requires one to account for the incomplete mixing of the incoming clean air with contaminated air. This is typically expressed as an effective ventilation rate (Q') which is the nominal ventilation rate (Q) lowered by a mixing factor (m) between 0 (poor) and 1.0 (perfect mixing).

$$Q' = (Q)(m) \tag{2}$$

Thus, Q' replaces Q in Eq. (1).

Input into the system (Gdt) is estimated by determining how much contaminant is injected into the room volume (V) per unit time. Injection can occur from such operations as spraying, drumming with subsequent displacement of vapors into the workroom air, fugitive emissions from pressure vessels, and simple evaporation. Models for the estimation of input (G) from these types of sources are presented elsewhere (17–20). These source term models use measured or estimated physicochemical properties of the contaminant as a neat material or in solution.

Very little work has been done to measure the effect of non-ventilatory depuration (KCdt). Work reported on $SO_2$, $NO_2$, and $O_3$ indicate that these mechanisms could be as effective as typical ventilation rates in lowering contaminant levels (21–23); however, very little work has been done on other gases and vapors and without quantification with objective data, K is usually ignored and the term is dropped. As such, models without nonventilatory depuration could seriously overestimate concentration and exposure.

Ignoring K and assuming a constant source and ventilation rate yields a simple solution to the above equation at steady-state equilibrium viz:

$$Ceq = G/(m)(Q) \tag{3}$$

Thus, inhalation exposure potential estimated by this model is directly proportional to the rate of source generation and inversely proportional to nominal ventilation rate and mixing efficiency.

A simple approach to the problem of modeling maximum exposure potential in a large industrial room is to use the above conservation of mass model but restrict the volume to that in the immediate vicinity of the source (24). The modeler then predicts equilibrium concentration in this "affected volume" around the source by calculating the source strength (G) using one of the above methods, applying a mixing factor between 0.2 and 1, and estimating the general ventilation that is actually entering or leaving this "affected volume." An affected volume of 8000 ft$^3$ (20 foot cube) around the source has been suggested from theoretical considerations (24). Given a nominal ventilation rate of 3 air changes/hour yields a ventilation rate in this affected volume around the source of 400 cfm. Using a conservatively low mixing factor of 0.3 gives the following simple model for equilibrium concentration estimation:

$$Ceq = G/(3.4) \tag{4}$$

where Ceq is estimated workroom air concentration of contaminant in milligrams per cubic meter (mg/m$^3$) and G is the amount of contaminant entering the affected volume per unit time in milligrams per minute.

The above treatment is valid for systems in which the rate of contaminant generation is relatively constant and essentially continuous. The estimation of concentration averages for short-term activities (i.e., those of a few hours duration or less) requires a more general and computationally complicated solution to the above conservation of mass equation. Integrating Eq. (1) to solve for average concentration C over time (t − t$_0$) with the assumption of constant contaminant release starting at t = 0 yields:

$$C_{avg} = G/(Qm + K) - [GV/(t(Qm + K)^2)](1 - e^{(-t(Qm + K)/V)}) \tag{5}$$

$C_{avg}$ = average concentration.

    t = elapsed time.

    e = natural log base number (2.7182 . . .)

If one assumes K = 0, average concentrations calculated for "long" time intervals (i.e., large values of the quantity (tQm/V) approach the equilibrium concentration presented in Eqs. (3) or (4). However, low ventilation rates, large volumes, and poor mixing will dramatically decrease the actual integrated dose for any person exposed during a batch operation. For example, consider a batch job lasting one hour in a room with poor mixing (m = 0.1) and 14,160 1pm (500 cfm) general ventilation in a 6.1 m (20 ft) cube. The one-hour time-weighed exposure or dose is less than 20% of that calculated by using Ceq.

It should be noted that the above model inputs are suggested for use in large industrial rooms with ventilation rates of 1–5 air changes per hour and low levels of air turbulence. Rooms with significantly higher levels of air turnover or turbulence (e.g., mixing fans) will not have a strong exposure gradient around sources and a larger "affected volume" with generally higher mixing factors and ventilation rates will render better predictions of exposure.

### 2. Community

Models used for the estimation of outdoor concentrations and subsequent exposure to toxicant sources also address the basic issues of source strength, dispersion, and extinction; however, instead of conserving mass in a defined "box" of air the approach has been to provide a stochastic description of the dispersion of a plume of contaminant as it diffuses downwind. These models divide the diffusion into vertical and horizontal directions; it assumes the diffusion in each direction will conform to a normal or distribution around the centerline (see Fig. 2). Downwind concentrations are predicted from the following basic relationship:

$Cc = G/((\sigma y)(\sigma z)(u)(\pi))$
$Cc$ = centerline concentration (with ground level release)
 $G$ = contaminant source rate (weight/time)
$\sigma y$ = horizontal dispersion coefficient (length)
$\sigma z$ = vertical dispersion coefficient (length)
 $u$ = wind speed (length/time)

The dispersion coefficients are empirically derived and dependent on conditions of atmospheric stability and terrain. Details on this modeling technique are available elsewhere (25). Suffice it to say that these models have been claimed to be accurate to within a factor of 2 or 3 (26).

## D. Dermal Exposure Modeling

Biological monitoring for the contaminant or its metabolite(s) can offer a direct indication of the level of percutaneous absorption through

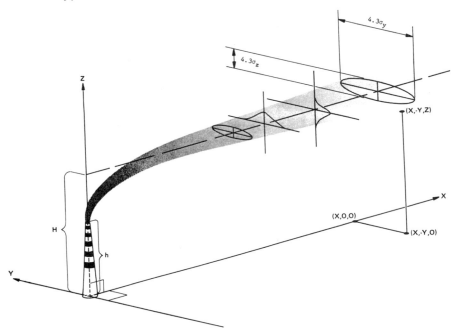

**Figure 2** Coordinate system showing Gaussian distribution in the horizontal and vertical. (Courtesy R. H. Schultz, Trinity Consultants.)

dermal exposure. Assuming the opportunities for ingestion and inhalation are relatively low, the monitoring data can reveal the level of toxicant that is most likely entering the body via dermal absorption. A published assessment of wood preservative workers' exposure to pentachlorophenol (27) used this technique to estimate that 93% of the workers' total exposure was from "non-respiratory routes."

It is important to note that any estimation of worker dosage to a toxicant requires a consideration of the fact that the actual dose is a combination of the equally important factors of toxicant concentration, time of exposure, and fraction of the applied dose that is absorbed. Monitoring the biological levels or effect gives one an integrated endpoint of these factors. Biological monitoring data can be particularly enlightening with regard to percutaneous exposure which is more difficult to model than inhalation.

In most cases, the exposure limits for inhalation of contaminants are set based on some physical response to an airborne concentration multiplied by a safety factor. Thus the risk-assessment process simply monitors or estimates the level of airborne contamination and

compares it with the established exposure limit. The simplicity of
this system is not available to the exposure-risk assessor of cutaneous exposure. The relationship between applied dermal exposure and
subsequent systemic dose is more uncertain and is more tentative,
especially when comparing or attempting to predict the response of
different species. Thus, if actual direct and quantitative evidence
of human percutaneous absorption is available, it is of the utmost
value to the risk-assessment process, particularly if it can be related to at least qualitative levels of dermal exposure.

### 1. Absolute Worst Case: Instantaneous Systemic Absorption

This modeling scenario assumes that liquid splashed or flowed
over the skin will remain on the skin as a thin film and then all or
a percentage of the toxic compound will be rapidly and completely
absorbed into the systemic circulation. Experimental work (28)
indicates that the worst case of completely immersing and withdraw-
ing a hand from liquid will result in approximately 3 mg/cm$^2$ retention
of water and 14 mg/cm$^2$ retention of mineral oil. Using these data,
the above assumptions, an estimate of affected surface area(s), and
the number of exposures per day will allow one to directly calculate
a worst-case dose. This approach can be grossly conservative
(depending on the percentage ascribed to the absorbed dose) but
usable as a "first-tier" assessment for compounds with low orders
of toxic hazard or exposure.

### 2. Realistic Worst Case: Diffusional Absorption

In addition to having the potential for being too conservative,
the total absorption assessment method outlined above is essentially
unusable in any exposure scenario in which part or the whole body
is totally immersed for extended periods of time. Attempting to use
the total absorption technique in these settings will result in the
assumption that all or a percentage of the available toxicant in solution is immediately available for absorption. The calculated dose
from dissolved compounds in a swimming pool or lake would be massive indeed! Other than being very conservative, this instantaneous absorption model has a critical flaw. In treating dermal exposure
as a process independent of time, it is incapable of estimating continuous dermal exposure. As mentioned above, its value lies as a
screening tool in those applications where its assumptions and con-
servativeness are acceptable.

A kinetic approach seeks to determine transport rate of toxicant
through the skin in order to estimate the level of systemic absorption per unit of skin area and time of cutaneous exposure [i.e.,
weight of toxicant absorbed/(skin area)(time of exposure)]. A

straight-forward model aimed at this determination (3) assumes the uppermost layer of skin, the *stratum corneum* (SC) is the rate-limiting skin barrier and purely Fickian or passive diffusion in the dominant transport mechanism. These assumptions render a very simple relationship for dermal absorption:

$$J = (Kp)(Cv)$$

J = the absorption rate per unit area and time ($mg/cm^2$ hr)
Kp = the permeability constant (cm/hr)
Cv = concentration of toxicant ($mg/cm^3$)

An expanded version is also presented (3):

$$J = \frac{(Km)(Cv)(Dm)}{(Z)}$$

Km = the SC:vehicle partition coefficient
DM = the diffusion constant of the toxicant in the SC layer
Z = the thickness of the SC layer

Measured permeability constants for human skin range (3) from approximately $10^{-6}$ to $10^{-2}$ cm/hr. Where necessary, in vitro testing techniques offer expeditious, germane, and relatively inexpensive means of determining these critical permeability constants. It is important to note that a lag time to steady state exists during the transport of the toxicant across the epidermis and this time is often quite long. The lag time represents an important piece of the potential exposure assessment and should be carefully characterized.

A rational approach for the modeling of discreet instances of dermal dosing is contained in a recently proposed biophysically based kinetic model of chemical absorption via human skin (4). This model also assumes passive diffusion of compounds and includes first-order rate expressions for transport first across the SC, then further across viable epidermal tissue to the blood, and finally to the urine. Reverse diffusion from the viable epidermis to the SC, reflecting the compound's relative affinity for the SC over viable tissue is also considered. This non-steady-state model allows one to calculate the percent of the applied compound appearing in the urine as a function of time. The most intriguing aspect of this model is that all but one of the first-order rate constants are calculated from physical properties. Only the rate constant for elimination from blood to urine requires experimental determination.

These kinetic models are still in the developmental stage; however, they exemplify the innovative approaches to dermal exposure modeling that are currently and will continue to be needed to realistically assess risk.

*Example*: Consider a person sampling a hypothetical amine in a propylene glycol solution (100 mg amine/g of glycol solution) once per hour. We will assume he/she is quite sloppy and covers both hands with the material for the 5 minutes it takes to sample the material. Given 8 exposures/day, 1300 cm$^2$ of exposed skin, 5% absorption and 3 mg/cm$^2$ retained solution per exposure results in a calculated dose of:

$$(8/\text{day})(1300 \text{ cm}^2)(3 \text{ mg/cm}^2)(0.05)(0.1) = 156 \text{ mg/(person)(day)}$$

Estimating the percutaneous dose by diffusion transport modeling requires the determination of the kinetic rate coefficient (Kp) discussed above. Literature values for this coefficient typically range from $10^{-6}$ to $10^{-2}$ cm/hr. Assume we tested our solution and the steady-state kinetic transport rate for the amine in propylene glycol is in the middle of this range at $10^{-4}$ cm/hr. Given unit density for the liquid mixture, the rate of transfer of the amine at steady state is:

$$J = (\text{Kp})(\text{Cv}) = (10^{-4} \text{ cm/hr})(100 \text{ mg/cm}^3)$$
$$= 0.01 \text{ mg/((cm}^2)(\text{hr}))$$

Assuming 40 minutes of total exposure daily to 1300 cm$^2$ of skin:

$$(1300 \text{ cm}^2)(40/60 \text{ hr})(0.01 \text{ mg/((cm}^2)(\text{hr})) = 9 \text{ mg/((person)(day))}$$

Equilibrium or steady-state percutaneous absorption is somewhat analogous to the equilibrium airborne concentration of contaminant (Ceq) in the general ventilation model. Both require a finite period of time to achieve this equilibrium and the time-integrated dose for many batch exposure scenarios will be substantially lower than that calculated assuming steady-state conditions. As such, the above represents a conservative estimate of the percutaneous dose.

## E. Demographics and Exposure Profile

As mentioned above, actual human exposure or delivered dose results from the time-weighted integration of contaminant concentration and uptake rate. Obviously, concentration modeling alone will not suffice to completely answer questions of how much toxicant was delivered. Ultimately the models or combination of monitoring/modeling must render an acceptable estimation of dose and be validated against measured data of human exposure in various settings.

Job exposure profiling is a process that seeks to characterize a specific job or worker's exposure. Different approaches are used, one being to use historical personal monitoring data (or observations in the case of dermal exposure) to characterize the exposure for a particular job. Another measures or estimates spatial and temporal contaminant and worker position patterns in an area, which in turn allows estimation of job exposures within this work space. Regardless of the method, job exposure profiling represents a vital piece of the occupational exposure–risk-assessment process. Air concentration measurements and models mean little if the amount of well characterized air inhaled during a work day is unknown. The job-exposure profile is critical because it places and times the worker in the workroom environment and allows a more reasonable estimation of available dose and hopefully a data base for model verification.

A similar concept is available for assessing exposure and subsequent risk to the general population. Combining demographic data with estimated environmental concentrations will allow for an integrated estimation of total risk associated with any release. Recent government publications offer a wealth of specific information for exposure profiling in the general population (29).

## F. Future Research

Experimental work designed to refine and validate ventilation and dermal exposure models remains the single most important element in the future success of the exposure assessment process. As mentioned above, the magnitude and form of the extinction factor (K) in the ventilation model will only be available experimentally using a range of representative materials. Similarly, the choice of predictive scheme(s) for the estimation of evaporative generation rates (G) will only be adequately decided with real data.

Before laboratory simulation can properly validate any indoor exposure model, however, a statistical description of ventilation fields or resultant isopleth concentrations typically present in industrial rooms needs to be available in much more detail than is currently available. The indoor ventilation model presented in this chapter assumes random omnidirectional air movement. This assumption needs to be tested by characterizing ventilation field data in a number of representative indoor settings. Once this critical information is in hand, experimental model validation can proceed.

## IV. HAZARD IDENTIFICATION

The initial process of identifying which compounds have the potential to be hazardous is, indeed, the process of toxicology testing. Such testing and its proper conduct are the subject of many of the preceding chapters. This testing serves to generate the initial biological information—hopefully, the only biological system data that will be available for most chemicals.

## V. DATA QUALIFICATION

Are the studies from which the toxicology data are generated adequate? Some are totally sound, most are somewhat flawed but the data still are usable, and some are such that no data from them may be used in the risk-assessment process. I will not attempt to address evaluation of all the types of studies associated with risk assessment, but rather as an example point out common flaws in animal carcinogenicity studies. These flaws arise from the wrong answers to the following questions.

Is test animal survival sufficient?

Were there enough animals in groups to start with?

Are there both statistical and biological trends associated with the observed evidence of carcinogenesis? Statistical trend is demonstrated by the presence of a dose-responsive increase in tumor incidence. Biological trend is demonstrated by evidence of preneoplastic tissue alterations in animals which do not have frank tumors.

Is the target tissue a "null" one? That is, one such that due to high control group incidences of the same tumor a judgement as to either statistical or biological significance cannot be made.

Was the tissue sampling (for histopathology) adequate (both sufficient in number and unbiased)?

Is the target organ a problem tissue? That is, is it one such that the occurrence of a tumor at that site in the test animal is of unclear significance to humans. Examples are mouse liver and rat forestomach tumors. In such cases, the existence of supporting (or negative) mutagenicity data can help to clarify the issue.

Animal carcinogenicity bioassays are of two types in terms of their objectives: detection screens and dose-response quantifiers. Traditional NCI bioassays and current NTP bioassays were intended as screens; they have high sensitivity, limited discrimination, and do not serve well in estimating risk, but they do very well in serving their objective, which is to detect potentially carcinogenic "bad actors" in an efficient and economical manner. Dose-response quantifiers generally start at a lower high dose (than the MTD), cover a broader range of doses, and use more animals (particularly in the lower dose groups, employing an "unbalanced" design).

Properly designed, they should also have at least three dose groups in the response range.

The interpretation of the results of even the best designed carcinogenesis bioassay is a complex statistical and biological problem. In addressing the statistical aspects, we shall have to review some biological points which have statistical implications as we proceed.

First, all such bioassays are evaluated by comparison of the observed results in treatment groups with those in one or more control groups. These control groups always include at least one group that is concurrent, but because of concern about variability in background tumor rates, a historical control "group" is also considered in at least some manner.

The underlying problem in the use of concurrent controls alone is the belief that the selected populations of animals are subject both to an inordinate degree of variability in their spontaneous tumor incidence rates and that the strains maintained at separate breeding facilities are each subject to a slow but significant degree of genetic drift. The first problem raises concern that, by chance, the animals selected to be controls for any particular study will be either "too high" or "too low" in their tumor incidences, leading to either a false positive or false negative statistical test result when test animals are compared to these controls. The second problem leads to concern that, over the years, different laboratories will be using different standards (control groups) against which to compare the outcome of their tests, making any kind of relative comparison between compounds or laboratories impossible.

The last decade has seen at least eight separate publications reporting 5 sets of background tumor incidences in test animals (30). These publications are summarized and compared for B6C3F1 mice and Fischer 344 rats in Gad and Weil (31). The related survival and growth data on control animals (broken out by type of treatment and vehicle) has also been published (32).

Historical control incidences should not be used to generate an "exclusion zone" associated with its range. Such data should be evaluated as to where the mean historical incidence of tumors at a site are and what the density function is and if this historical data represents the same population; animals in the same laboratory during recent history. But extreme outlier values in a range (either high or low) are not appropriately used to sort out and discard data. The local (concurrent) control group data is generally much more important in any evaluation, and historical control group data (as a general rule) are used primarily as a check to ensure that the statistical evaluations used in comparing treatment groups to concurrent controls have a sound starting point.

Dempster et al. (33) have, however, proposed a method for incorporating historical control data in the actual process of statistical analysis. A variable degree of pooling (combining) of historical with concurrent controls is performed based on the extent to which the historical data fit an assumed normal logistic (log transformed) model.

Having selected which studies to use to develop a model on, that is, those of the highest quality which have the least uncertainty associated with them, risks should then be calculated on the basis of highest tumor incidence rates at any single organ site, and not on combined total incidences of tumors in control animals at only those sites where test animals have higher incidences than control animals.

The decision on which tumor count to use (highest single site or total animals with tumors at those sites showing significant increases in controls) makes minimal difference in some cases, as there are few animals with tumors at other than one site. This, of course, excludes mammary and forestomach tumors as "null" tissues in rats for predicting human effects. More importantly, I believe that competing risks makes the combining of *selected* tumor sites inappropriate. If we look at more than one site, should we not look at the total incidence of animals with any malignant tumor in each group as a comparator, and then adjust the increased risk (if any) of being in a test group downward for the baseline level of incidence seen in controls? In other words, if we look at total tumor incidences, we must address the question: are we only shifting age-related patterns of tumor incidence, as some investigators (Salsburg (34) for example] have suggested.

## VI. STATISTICAL MODELS FOR LOW-DOSE EXTRAPOLATION

Given knowledge of what happens at relatively high doses by one or more routes in one or more animal species, one must next predict what would happen in the same species at much lower dose levels. These doses may be separated by as much as seven orders of magnitude. It should be remembered at this point that risk assessment is not limited to carcinogenesis, but rather is generally applicable to any catastrophic irreversible effect where real human exposures are at much lower levels than those of animals and where the cause (exposure to a chemical) is separated significantly in time from the effect (such as cancer) which also occurs at some background level in the normal course of human events. None of the mathematical models we use has a sound biological basis (in fact, most have no biological basis). They can give vastly different (by five or more orders of magnitude) answers, and have very wide regions of uncertainty (called 95% confidence intervals, which may range from two to as high as five orders of magnitude) associated with them.

Which model to choose should depend on the data and how well it fits the model in the small region (usually only across a range of two orders of magnitude at most) where we actually have data. Pharmacokinetic data may tell us if we are dealing with a linear or nonlinear (either "hockey stick" or curvilinear) dose-response surface. Choice of a model may also, as we will see, depend on whether or not it is accepted (or denied) on faith that there is a threshold for the effect of interest (most often, carcinogenesis). The question of threshold is beyond the scope of this chapter and the reader is referred to Gad and Weil (31) for a thorough discussion, or to Epstein (35), Claus et al. (36), Albert et al. (37), Mantel and Schneiderman (38), Guess and Hoel (39), Klaassen and Doull (40), Dinman (41), Kraybill (42), Miller (43), and Stokinger (44) for presentations of individual points of view.

Those characteristics of the toxicologic response which are both known and agreed on, however, certainly should be accommodated in any risk-assessment model. In the case of carcinogenesis, for example, the interrelationships of the variables dose, time-to-tumor (or latency), and probability of response (that is, incidence levels of tumors) must be accommodated. As the dose of a carcinogen is increased over a suitable range, two things happen: the incidence (proportion) of tumors in the exposed population increases, and the time between exposure and the appearance of tumors in the population (the latency period) decreases. The reverse of these two relationships is also true. In the case of time, there are cases (at least in animals) where it is clear that the carcinogen is merely speeding up a natural process by decreasing the latency period. But the reverse relationship, it should be noted, is the basis for one argument for threshold. As Jones and Grendon (45) put it, "low dosage exposure at some levels is virtually without risks because the expected lifetime of those exposed is exceeded by the time necessary for low concentrations of altered cells to develop into cancer."

There are at least eight different models for extrapolating a line or curve from a high-dose region to a low-dose region. In this section we will examine each of these models, and compare them in terms of characteristics and outcome. Not discussed here (but rather at the end of this chapter) is the safety factor approach. Some of these models are such that they handle only quantal (also called dichotomous) data, while others will also accommodate time-to-tumor information. All have quantal-type data as their starting point, however.

In the models below, certain standard symbols are used. Most of these models express the probability of a response P, as a function, f, of dosage, D, so that $P = f(D)$ and the models differ only with respect to choice of function, f. The nonthreshold models assume that if proportion p of control animals respond to a dose that $f(D) = p$ only for D equal to zero, and that for any nonzero D, f(D) → p (that is, there is a response). Threshold models assume the existence of a $D_0$ such that for all $D < D_0$, f(D) = p (that is, that there is some dose below which there is no response). If safety is defined as zero increase over control response, then a nonthreshold model would require that any nonzero dosage be associated with some finite risk.

## A. One-Hit Model

This most basic model is based on the assumption that cancer initiates from a single cell as a result of a random occurrence or "hit" that causes an irreversible alteration in the DNA of a susceptible cell type. It is also assumed that the likelihood of this hit is directly proportional to the level of carcinogen exposure. This suggests a direct linear dose response such that if one is to diminish the risk from $10^{-2}$ to $10^{-8}$, then the dose should be divided by $10^6$.

Accordingly, the one-hit model is also called the linear model, though a number of the other models also behave in a linear manner at lower doses. Based on the concept that a single receptor molecule of some form responds after an animal has been exposed to some single unit of an agent, the probability of tumor induction by exposure to the agent is then

$$P(D) = 1 - \exp(-\lambda D)$$

where

$$D \geqslant 0, \ 0 \leqslant P(D) \leqslant 1,$$

$\lambda$ is an unknown rate constant (or slope) and D is the expected number of hits at a given dose level. The term "dose" is used in a broad sense, and may mean the total, accumulated dose or the dosage rate in terms of body weight, surface area approximations, or concentration in the diet. The model makes no allowance for the pattern of exposure, but rather implies that it is the total "dose" (no matter how recieved) which determines risk. There are ample data in the literature [such as that on chromates(46)] which are contrary to this assumption. Computing the estimated incidence of effect from the one-hit model in terms of the exponential series produces

$$P(D) = \frac{\lambda D}{1} \frac{(\lambda D)^2}{1 \cdot 2} + \frac{(\lambda D)^3}{1 \cdot 2 \cdot 3} \ \cdots$$

which, for small values of P(D), is well approximated by

$$P(D) = \lambda D$$

Though Hoel et al. (47) have argued that this model is consistent with a reasonable set of biological assumptions, there is now almost universal agreement that the model is excessively conservative. The concept of a hit is a model for a variety of possible elementary biochemical events and the equation must be considered descriptive rather than mechanistic (that is, it attempts to describe what is seen rather than what may actually occur). This model is essentially equivalent to assuming that the dose-response curve is linear in the low-dose region. Thus, the slope of the one-hit curve at dose D is $[1 - P(D)]$, and at dose levels for which $P(D) < .05$, it varies by less than 5%, in other words, it is essentially constant and equal to $\lambda$. The linear model is one of two models, the other being the probit model, originally specified by the Environmental Protection Agency (1976) in its interim guidelines for assessment of the health risk of suspected carcinogens. Recently the EPA (48) has published guidelines which call for the use of the restricted multistage model (also called the linearized multistage model) which in fact behaves exactly like the one-hit model with most available data sets. The assumption of low-dose linearity will generally lead to a very low, virtually safe dose (VSD), so low as to lead the Food and Drug Administration Advisory Committee to remark that assuming linearity ". . . would lead to few conflicts with the results of applying the Delaney clause." The one-hit model, having only one disposable parameter, $\lambda$, will often fail to provide a satisfactory fit to dose-response data in the observable range. Other models described below, by introducing additional parameters, often lead to reasonable fits in the observable range.

An additional level of conservatism is provided by extrapolating from the upper confidence limit (UCL) for the excess tumor rate (highest incidence in a treatment group minus the control incidence) down to a zero dose level. The linear model assumes that the tumor rate is proportional to dose, or that $P(D) = \lambda D$. The upper confidence limit for the slope ($\lambda$) is then the UCL divided by the experimental dosage. Thus an estimate of an upper limit for the incidence of tumor-bearing animals, $P_u$, for a given dose D is

$$P_u = \frac{UCL(D)}{D_e}$$

where $D_e$ is the experimental dosage. Conversely, the dose D for a given $P_u$ can be calculated as

$$D = \frac{P_u D_e}{UCL}$$

The linear model can also serve as a conservative upper boundary for probit dose-response curves. This upper boundary on the proportion of tumor-bearing animals may not, however, be as conservative as one might imagine, depending on the shape of the actual incidence curve. Crump et al. (49), Peto (50), and Guess et al. (100) have shown that the curvilinear dose-response curve resulting from the multistage model is well approximated by the linear model at low dose levels. Gross et al. (51) discussed the statistical aspects of a linear model for extrapolation.

The example below illustrates this linear extrapolation model in practice.

A compound is administered as 5% (50,000 ppm) in diet for 2 years to a group of 100 animals. At the end of the study, 22 of these test animals and 6 of 100 control animals are found to have developed liver tumors.

Thus, upper confidence limit on the excess tumor rate is approximately equal to

$$(p_t - p_c) + z \sqrt{\frac{p_t(1 - p_t)}{n_t} + \frac{p_c(1 - p_c)}{n_c}}$$

where $p_t$ is the proportion of animals with tumors in $n_t$ treated animals, $p_c$ is the proportion of animals with tumors in $n_c$ control animals, and z is the normal deviate corresponding to the level of confidence desired.

The upper 99% confidence level for this example is thus

$$(0.22 - 0.06) + 2.33 \sqrt{\frac{0.22 \times 0.78}{100} + \frac{0.06 \times 0.94}{100}}$$

$$= (0.16) + 2.33 \sqrt{.001716 + .000564}$$

$$= 0.16 + 2.33 (0.0477493)$$

$$= 0.271256$$

If it is then desired to estimate an upper limit of risk associated with exposure to 10 ppm of the material in the diet this would be

$$= \frac{0.271256}{50,000} \times 10 = 5.43 \times 10^{-5}$$

## B.  The Probit Model

This model assumes that the log tolerances have a normal distribution with mean $\mu$ and standard deviation $\sigma$. The proportion of individuals responding to dose D, say P(D), is then simply

$$P(D) = \phi[(\log D - \mu)/\sigma] = \phi(\alpha + \beta \log D),$$

where $\phi(x)$ is the standard normal integral from $-\alpha$ to X, $\alpha = -\mu/\sigma$, and $\beta = 1/\sigma$. This dose-response curve has $P(D)$ near zero if D is near zero and $P(D)$ increasing to unity as the dose increases. A plot of a typical probit dose-response is given by an S-shaped (sigmoid) curve. The quantity above is referred to as the slope of the probit line, where

$$Y = \phi^{-1}[P(D)] = \alpha + \beta \log D$$

and $Y + 5$ is the probit of P.

This is the same model presented earlier in this volume for linearizing a special case of quantal response, the data for $LD_{50}$'s. Despite its nonthreshold assumption, it is a characteristic of the probit curve that as dose decreases, zero response is approached very rapidly, more rapidly than any power of dose. Other curves to be considered later approach zero response more slowly than the probit.

An alternative derivation of the probit model which relates it to time-to-response has been given by Chand and Hoel (52) using the Druckrey observation that median time to tumor, T, is related to dose, D, by the equation $DT^n = C$, where n and C are constants unrelated to D (53). Combining this relation with an assumed log normal distribution of response time then gives the $P(D)$ as probability of response to any given time, $T_0$, where $\alpha$ and $\beta$ are simple functions of n, C, $T_0$ and the standard deviation is of the distribution of response times.

The actual method which has the probit model as its basis is the Mantel-Bryan procedure (54). In its initial form, this procedure used the probit model but with a preassigned slope of unity when the dose was expressed as a logarithm. The rationale for this slope was that as all observed probit-transformed carcinogen slopes at the time of the proposal exceeded that value, the procedure could therefore be considered conservative. An additional conservative feature involves use of the upper 99% confidence limit of the proportion responding at a dose level, rather than the observed proportion. The procedure then extrapolates downward to a response level of $10^{-8}$, using each separate dose level in the experiment, or combinations, taking as the virtually safe dose (VSD) the lowest of the values obtained. A conservative method of taking account of the response of the control group was also given. An improved version of the procedure, which included several sets of independent data and better methods of handling background response rates and responses at multiple doses has since been published (98).

A dosage $D_0$ is said to be virtually safe if $f(D_0) \geqslant p + (1 - p)P_0$, where $P_0$ is some near-zero lifetime risk, such as $10^{-8}$ or $10^{-6}$ (the value adopted by the FDA). The virtually safe dose (VSD) may then be calculated as $f^{-1}[p + (1 - p)P_0]$. The calculation thus requires choosing a model ($f$), determining the value of its contained variables from observations in the known range, and then extrapolating down to the unknown response region, $P_0$, to determine the VSD. This method is illustrated in the example below.

From the data in the example for the one-hit model we have already calculated an upper 99% confidence interval of 0.271, corresponding to a normal deviate of −0.61. If it is desired to determine the level corresponding to a tumor probability of less than one in a million (which has a normal deviate of −4.753), the extrapolation proceeds along the probit-log dosage line with a slope of 1 from the normal deviate of the upper 99% confidence limit on the observed result to the normal deviate for the selected probability or −0.61 − (−4.753) = 4.143 standard deviations.

The dose level corresponding to this risk is then

$$\frac{50,000 \text{ ppm}}{10^{4.143}}$$

$$= \frac{5 \times 10^4}{1.39 \times 10^4}$$

$$= 3.597 \text{ ppm}$$

One of the advantages of the Mantel-Bryan procedure is that it rewards a larger experiment by reducing the upper confidence limit, which results in a larger dose for a selected proportion of tumor-bearing animals. Table 1 shows some dosages for a series of sample sizes; all yield observed tumor rates of 4%, with no tumors in the controls for predicted tumor probability of less than one in a million.

Some situations, such as cigarette smoking in humans and diethylstilbestrol in mice, have indicated slopes on the order of 1. Thus one must be careful to establish that the slope of the dose-response is sufficiently large before applying the Mantel-Bryan procedure, reinforcing the desorability of multiple-dose experiments.

According to Mantel and Schneiderman (38), the Mantel-Bryan methodology has several advantages:

1. It does not need an experimental estimate of the slope.
2. Statistical significance is not needed.
3. It takes into account a nonzero spontaneous background tumor incidence.

**Table 1** Mantel-Bryan Dosages for Various Sample Sizes with the Same Proportion of Experimental Animals with Tumors[a]

| Sample size | No. of animals with tumors | Upper 99% confidence limit | Dosage (fraction of experimental dosage) |
|---|---|---|---|
| 50 | 2 | 0.158 | 1/5630 |
| 100 | 4 | 0.112 | 1/3430 |
| 200 | 8 | 0.085 | 1/2400 |
| 400 | 16 | 0.069 | 1/1860 |

[a]Predicted tumor probability $<10^{-6}$.

4.  It considers multiple-dose studies.
5.  Any arbitrary acceptable risk can be calculated.
6.  It avoids categorizing a substance in absolute terms.
7.  It permits the investigator flexibility in study design.

Mantel and Bryan (54) provided an example of an actual study in which the carcinogen 3-methylcholanthrene was given to mice as a single injection, with 12 different dose levels used. Table 2 provides the methodology and findings of the Mantel-Bryan procedure resulting from that experiment.

Some criticisms of the Mantel-Bryan procedure are:

1.  The normal distribution may not offer as accurate a description in the tails of the distribution as it does in the central parts, especially if one proceeds out to $10^{-6}$ to $10^{-8}$ (this results from the behavior of the probit transform in the extremes of its range).
2.  The use of the arbitrarily low slope of unity for downward extrapolation has been criticized because of the lack of observational support.
3.  The procedure does not mechanistically incorporate any of the present understandings of the process of carcinogenesis.
4.  The model is insufficiently conservative, because the extrapolated probability approaches zero with decreasing dose more rapidly than any polynomial function of dose, and, in particular, more rapidly than a linear function of dose and hence may underestimate probability at low dose.
5.  The model is excessively conservative, because it does not postulate a threshold or accommodate time to tumor data.

Table 2  Illustration of Methodology for Determining the "Safe" Dose from Results at Several Dose Levels (54, 102)

| Dose per mouse (mg) | Log dose | Result | | Maximum p value 99% assurance | Corresponding normal deviate | Calculated "safe" (1/100 million) log dose (2)-(6)-5.612 |
| | | No. of tumors/ No. of mice | No. of tumors/ No. of mice | | | |
| (1) | (2) | (3) | (4) | (5) | (6) | (7) |
| 0.000244 | 6.388-10 | 0/79 | 0/158 | 0.0288 | -1.899 | 2.675-10 |
| 0.000975 | 6.990-10 | 0/41 | 0/79 | 0.0566 | -1.584 | 2.962-10 |
| 0.00195 | 7.291-10 | 0/19 | 0/38 | 0.1141 | -1.205 | 2.884-10 |
| 0.0039 | 7.592-10 | 0/19 | 0/19 | 0.2152 | -0.789 | 2.769-10 |
| 0.0078 | 7.893-10 | 3/17 | 3/17 | 0.480 | -0.050 | 2.331-10 |
| 0.0156 | 8.194-10 | 6/18 | 6/18 | 0.729 | +0.610 | 1.972-10 |
| 0.0312 | 8.495-10 | 13/20 | 13/20 | 0.871 | +1.131 | 1.752-10 |
| 0.0625 | 8.796-10 | 17/21 | 17/21 | 0.958 | +1.728 | 1.456-10 |
| 0.125 | 9.097-10 | 21/21 | — | — | — | — |
| 0.25 | 9.398-10 | 21/21 | — | — | — | — |
| 0.50 | 9.699-10 | 21/21 | — | — | — | — |
| 1.0 | 10.000-10 | 20/20 | — | — | — | — |

## C. Multistage

The multistage model (49,55) represents a generalization of the one-hit model and assumes that the carcinogenic process is composed of an unknown number of stages that are needed for cancer expression. Inherent in this model is the additional assumption that the effect of the carcinogenic agent in question is additive to a carcinogenic effect produced by external stimuli at the same stages. Such an assumption generally leads one to expect a linear dose-response curve at low exposure levels.

This assumes that carcinogenesis occurs in a single cell as a point of origin and, according to the multistage model, is the result of several stages which may include somatic mutation. The transitional events are individually assumed to depend linearly on dose rate. This then leads in general to a model in which the probability of tumor approximates a low-order polynomial in dose rate. In the low dose region, which would relate to environmental levels, one finds that the responses are well approximated by a linear function of dose rate. The characteristic in which the low dose probability is proportional to the kth power of dose, where k is the number of stages, was considered by Armitage and Doll (55) to be quite inconsistent with observation. They derived a multistage model, which by assuming that the effect of the agent at some stages was additive to an effect induced by external stimuli at those stages, led to a lower power than k for D. Crump et al. (49) discussed this model and, by assuming additivity at all stages, have obtained as an expression for the required probability

$$P(D) = 1 - \exp[- \sum_{i=0}^{K} (\alpha_i + \beta_i D)]$$

where $\alpha_i$ and $\beta_i$ are positive numbers. Hartley and Sielken (56) combined this model with time to response, obtaining a more general result. For $\alpha_i > 0$ these models also imply low dose linearity since

$$\lim P'(D) = \alpha_1 \exp(-\alpha_0)$$

as $D \to 0$.

Armitage and Doll cited data relating lung cancer mortality to previous smoking habits as indicating the presence of a linear dose-response curve, but errors in reporting the amount smoked would lead to such a curve even if the true curve were convex. This would then support the view that the apparent low-dose linearity in many epidemiologic studies is an artifact of errors in the reporting of dose. Crump et al. (49) stressed the crucial nature of the additivity assumption, pointing out that it can make orders of magnitude differences in the estimated risk associated with the low dose exposure.

Crump et al. (57) describes a procedure for low-dose extrapolation in the presence of background which, although based on the generalized model above, reduces (when upper confidence limits are used) to an extrapolation using low-dose linearity. This is because the use of upper confidence limits on $x_1$ on the model is equivalent to admitting the possibility of a positive value of $x_1$, which at low doses dominates the expression. Once upper confidence limits on the VSD or risk at a given dose are used, there may therefore be little practical difference, between use of the one-hit model and the generalization given by the Crump et al. equation above.

Hartley and Sielken (56) have developed a procedure based on maximum likelihood for the Armitage-Doll model. Their program is very general and allows for the inclusion of the effect of the time to a tumor.

In practice, these two approaches result in fitting a polynomial model to the dose response curve such that (where t is time):

$$\frac{p(D,t)}{1 - P(D,t)} = g(D)h(t)$$

where $P(D,t)$ is the probability of the observance of a tumor in an animal by time t at a dosage D,

$$p(D,t) = \frac{DP(D,t)}{Dt}$$

where $g(D)$ is a function of dose such that

$$g(\text{dose}) = (a_1 + b_1 \text{ dose})(a_2 + b_2 \text{ dose}) \ldots (a_n + b_n \text{ dose})$$
$$= c_0 + c_1 \text{ dose} + c_2 \text{ dose}^2 + \ldots + c_n \text{ dose},$$

where $a_i$, $b_i$, $c_i \geqslant 0$ are parameters that vary from chemical to chemical and $h(t)$ is a function of time. The probability of a tumor by time t and dosage D is then

$$P(D,t) = 1 - \exp\left[-g(D)H(t)\right]$$

where

$$H(t) = \int_0^t h(t) \, Dt$$

This function generally fits well in the range where we have experimental data but has limited applicability to the estimation of potential risk at low doses. The limitations arise, first, because the model cannot reflect changes in kinetics, metabolism, and mechanisms at low doses and, second, because low dose estimates are highly sensitive to a change of even a few observed tumors at the lowest experimental dose (which is the pivotal point for this model). A logical statistical approach to account for the random variation in tumor frequencies is to express the results in terms of best estimates and measures of uncertainty.

Important biological mechanisms of activation and detoxification are not usually specifically considered. However, a steady-state kinetic model that incorporates the process of deactivation as well as other pharmacokinetic considerations has been offered by Cornfield (58). He noted that whenever the detoxification response is irreversible, low exposure levels are predicted to be harmless. However, the presence of a reversible response suggests linearity at low-dose exposures. He additionally predicted that when multiple protective responses are sequentially operational, the dose-response relationship will look like a hockey stick "with the striking part flat or nearly flat and the handle rising steeply once the protective mechanisms are saturated." Despite its seemingly greater biological veracity, the Food Safety Council (59) challenged the multistage model general assumption of low-dose linearity on the basis of (1) the general absence of support for dosewise additivity seen in many studies in which additivity has been evaluated and (2) studies that showed the effects of one carcinogenic agent offset or prevented the carcinogenic effects of another.

Crump (60) has noted that biostatistical models such as the multistage model assume that the quantity of carcinogen finding its way to the critical sites is proportional to the total body exposure, which is clearly not the case across the entire dose range covered by the model.

Criticisms of these models can be summarized as below.

1. These models do not consider the variation in susceptibility of the members of the population when deriving their dose-response relationships.
2. Low-dose linearity is not consistently found in experimental systems.
3. Low-dose linearity is assumed to occur by a mechanism of additivity to background levels, however, there is a lack of data supporting the additivity hypothesis.
4. They do not sufficiently recognize pharmacokinetic considerations including rates of absorption, tissue distribution, detoxification processes, repair, and excretion. (This would apply to the Mantel-Bryan model as well.)

## D. Multihit

This model is also called the restricted multistage, the k-hit, or gamma multihit model, and is a generalization of the one-hit model.

If k or more hits of a "target" (gene, cell, or enzymatic receptor) are required to induce cancer, the probable incidence of tumors as a function of exposure to a dose (D) is given by

$$P(D) = 1 - \sum_{i=0}^{k-1} \frac{(\lambda D)^i e^{\lambda D}}{i!} \frac{(\lambda D)^k}{k!}$$

For low dose or small values of $\lambda$, the model may be approximated by

$$P(D) = \gamma D^k$$

or

$$\log P(D) = \log \gamma + k \log D$$

Thus k (the number of critical "hits") represents the slope of log P(D) versus log D. By the same reasoning, if at least k hits are required for a response, then

$$P(D) = P(X \geqslant k) = \frac{\int_0^{\lambda D} u^{k-\gamma} e^{-u} du}{(k-1)!}$$

Because this equation contains an additional parameter (k) to that in the linear model, it may ordinarily provide a better description of dose-response data than the one-parameter curve. This can be further generalized by allowing k to be any positive number (not limited to whole numbers, that is). In this case the above formula can be described as the dose-response curve which assumes a gamma distribution of tolerances with the shape parameter k. It should be noted that

$$\lim[P(D)/D^k] = \text{constant}$$

as

$$D \to 0$$

Thus, in the low-dose region, the equation is linear for k = 1, concave for k < 1 and convex for k > 1. At higher doses the gamma and the log normal distributions are difficult to distinguish. It is therefore suggested that the model provides a compromise mixture of the probit model at high dose levels and the logit model at low ones.

Procedures for estimating the parameters of the k-hit model by nonlinear maximum likelihood estimation have been developed by Rai and Van Ryzin (61). This method has the advantage of permitting the data to determine the number of hits needed to describe the results without introducing more than two parameters. When only one dose level gives responses greater than zero and less than 100%, unique values of the two parameters can no longer be estimated. The background effect in this model is taken care of using Abbott's correction, though the assumptions behind this use are open to question by some (62).

The multihit model is discussed in some detail in the Food Safety Council report (59). One derivation of this model follows from the assumption that k hits or molecular interactions are necessary to induce the formation of a tumor and the distribution of these molecular events over time follows a Poisson process. In practice, the model appears to fit some data sets reasonably well and to give low-dose predictions that are similar to the other models. There are cases, however, in which the predicted values are inconsistent with the predictions of other models by many orders of magnitude. For instance, the virtually safe dose as predicted by the multihit model appears to be too high for nitrilotriacetic acid and far too low for vinyl chlorides (59).

## E. Pharmacokinetic Models

In general, these are really an add-on or preliminary step to use of another model, as they represent an attempt to integrate an under-standing of compound specific metabolic and pharmacokinetic dif-ferences between dose levels and species. This would then act to decrease or eliminate some of the large variations between tumor incidences predicted by conservative models and what is actually seen in the real world. The aim is to convert the administered doses to blood levels or concentrations of reactive species at the receptor sites. Multiple examples exist of differences between the ratios of dose to concentration in different species. These ratios also vary with route, but oral and inhalation are generally more comparable across species than is dermal (63). Pharmacokinetic models have often been used to predict the concentration of the parent compound and metabolites in the blood and at reactive sites, if identifiable. Cornfield (58), Gehring and Blau (64), and Anderson et al. (65) have extended this concept to include rates for macromolecular events (e.g., DNA damage and repair and enzymatic protective factors) involved in the carcinogenic process. The addition of statistical distributions for the rate parameters and a stochastic component representing the probabilistic nature of molecular events and selection processes may represent a useful conceptual framework for describing the tumorigenic mechanism of many chemicals. Pharmacokinetic data are presently useful only in specific parts of the risk-assessment process, but this is somewhat a reflection of the limited availability of such data. A more complete understanding of the mechanism of chemically induced carcinogenesis would allow a more complete utilization of pharmacokinetic data. Pharmacokinetic comparisons between animals and humans are presently most useful for making species conversions and for understanding qualitative and quantitative species differences. The modeling of blood concentrations and metabolite concentrations identifies the existence of saturated pathways and adds to an understanding of the mechanism of toxicity in many cases.

Taking advantage of the similarity of the probit and some pharmacokinetic models in the 5% to 95% range, Cornfield (58) developed an approximate method of estimating its parameters, particularly the value of T, the saturation dose for protective and repair factors. Risks at dosages below T are crucially dependent on K*, the relative speed of the reverse, deactivation reaction. This cannot be well estimated from responses at dosages above T, so that low-dose assessment using this model are more dependent on further pharmacokinetic experimentation than on further statistical developments.

This model considers an agent subjected to simultaneous activation and deactivation reactions, both reversible, with the probability of a response being proportional (linearly related) to the amount of activated complex. Denoting total amount of substrate in the system by S and protective factors by T and the ratios of the rate constants governing the forward and reverse reactions by K for the activation step and K* for the deactivation step, the model is, for D > T

$$P(D) = \frac{D - S[P(D)] - y}{D - S[P(D)] - y + K}$$

where $y = K[P(D)] / \{K[P(D)] + K*[1 - P(D)]\}$ and for D < T

$$D < TP(D) \stackrel{\sim}{=} \frac{D}{S + K\left(1 + \dfrac{T}{K*}\right)}$$

These equations follow from standard steady state mass action equations. Thus, at low dose levels, D < T, the dose-response curve is nearly linear, but for deactivating reactions in which the rate of the reverse reaction is small compared to that of the forward reaction, K* will be quite small and the slope of the curve will be near zero. In fact, in the limiting case in which K* = 0 the dose-response curve has a threshold at $D = T$, but since the model is steady state and does not depend on the time course of the reaction, it cannot be considered to have established the existence of a threshold. For $K^* > 0$, the dose-response curve is shaped like a hockey stick with the striking part nearly flat and rising sharply once the administered dose exceeds the dose, $T$, which saturated the system. Because of the great sensitivity of the slope at low doses to the value of $K^*/K$, and insensitivity at high doses, responses at dose levels above $D = T$ probably cannot be used to predict those below $T$. This can be considered a limitation of the model, but it can equally well be considered a limitation of high dose experimentation in the absence of detailed pharmacokinetic knowledge of metabolic pathways. The model can be generalized to cover a chain of simultaneous activating and deactivating reactions intervening between the introduction of $D$ and the formation of activated complex, but this does not appear to change its qualitative characteristics. The kinetic constants, $S$, $T$, $K$, and $K^*$ are presumably subject to animal-to-animal variation. This variation is not formally incorporated in the model, so that the possibility of negative estimates of one or more of these constants cannot be excluded.

## F. Weibull Model

Another generalization of the one-hit model is the Weibull model:

$$P(D) = 1 - \exp - (\alpha + \beta D^m)$$

where $m$, $\alpha$, and $\beta$ are parameters. Since $\alpha$ is frequently very near zero, it may be dropped from the equation as the dose approaches zero. Note that

$$\lim [P(D)/D^m =] = \text{constant}$$

as the dose approaches zero. Thus, in the low-dose region, this last equation is linear for $m = 1$, concave for $m < 1$, and convex for $m > 1$. With a typical set of data, the Weibull model tends to give an estimated risk at a low dose which lies between the estimates for the gamma multihit and the Armitage-Doll models. The Weibull distribution for time-to-tumors has been suggested as fitting observed incidences of human cancers (66,67).

$$P = bD^m (t - w)^k$$

where $P$ is the incidence rate of tumors at time $t$, $b$ is a constant depending on experimental conditions, $D$ is dosage, $w$ the minimum time to the occurrence of an observable tumor, m and k are parameters to be estimated. Also, Day (68), Peto et al. (69), and Peto and Lee (70) have considered the Weibull distribution for time-to-tumor occurrence. Theoretical models of carcinogenesis also predict the Weibull distribution (71). Theoretical arguments and some experimental data suggest the Weibull distribution where tumor incidence is a polynomial in dose multiplied by a function of age. Hartley and Sielken (56) adopted the form

$$H(t) = \sum_{i=1} \xi_i t^i$$

where $\xi \geqslant 0$. They noted that this function can be regarded as a weighted average of Weibull hazard rates with positive weight coefficients, $\xi$. The conventional statistical procedure of weighted least-squares provides one method of fitting the Weibull model to a set of data. With a background response measured by the parameter p, the model, using Abbott's correction is:

$$P = p + (1 - p)(1 - \exp(-\beta D^m)) = 1 - \exp(-(\alpha + \beta D^m)),$$

where $\alpha = -\ln(1 - p)$. With the transformation $Y = -\ln(1 - P)$, the model becomes

$$Y = \alpha + \beta D^m$$

With a nonlinear weighted least-squares regression program, one can estimate the three parameters ($m$, $\alpha$, $\beta$) directly. With only a linear weighted least-squares regression program, one can use trial and error on m to find the values of the three parameters which produce a minimum error sum of squares. A program for one electronic calculator (the TI-59) which conveniently handles up to nine data points is available from the Food Safety Council.

A nonlinear maximum likelihood method to obtain estimates of the parameters in the Weibull model can also be used. The use of the Weibull distribution for time-to-tumor leads to an extreme value distribution relating tumor response to dosage (52). Hoel (71) gives techniques for cases in which adjustments must be made for competing causes of death.

## G. Logit Model

As with the probit model, this leads to a sigmoid dose-response curve, symmetric about the 50% response point. Its equation (74) is:

$$P(D) = 1/[(1 + \exp)\{-(\alpha + \beta \log D)\}]$$

It approaches zero response as D decreases more slowly than even the probit curve, since

$$\lim [P(D)/D] = K$$

as the dose (D) approaches zero and where K is a constant.

The practical implication of this feature is that the logit model yields a lower VSD than the probit model (1/25th as much in calculations reported by Cornfield et al. (73) even when both models are equally descriptive of the data collected in bioassays.

Albert and Altshuler (71) have developed a related model for predicting tumor incidence and life shortening based on the work of Blum (75) on skin tumor response and of Druckrey (53) for a variety of chemical carcinogens in rodents. They had investigated cancer in mice exposed to radium. The basic relationship used was $Dt^n = c$, where D is dosage, t is the median time to occurrence of tumors, n is a parameter greater than 1, and c is a constant depending on the given experimental conditions. It is of interest to determine the time it takes for a small proportion of the population to develop tumors. With this formulation, as the dosage is increased, the time to tumor occurrence is shortened. Albert and Altshuler (74) used the log normal distribution to represent time-to-tumor occurrence, assuming the standard deviation to be independent of dosage.

The log normal distribution of tumor times corresponds closely to the probit transformation as employed in the Mantel-Bryan procedure.

## H. Log-Probit

The log-probit model assumes that the individual tolerances follow a log normal distribution due to each animal having its own threshold dose. Specific steps in the complex chain of events that lead to carcinogenesis are likely to have log normal distributions. For example, it is reasonable to assume that the distribution of a population of kinetic rate constants for detoxification, metabolism, elimination, in addition to the distribution of immunosuppression surveillance capacity and DNA repair capacity, can be adequately approximated by normal or log normal distribution.

Tolerance distribution models have been found to adequately model many types of biological dose-response data, but it would be an overly simplistic expectation to represent the entire carcinogenic process by one tolerance distribution. A tolerance distribution model may give a good description of the observed data, but from a mechanistic point of view there is no reason to expect extrapolation to be valid. The probit model extrapolation has, however, fit well in some instances (76).

The log-probit model has been used extensively in the bioassay of dichotomous responses (77) such as lethality. A distinguishing feature of this model is that it assumes that each animal has its own distinct threshold dose below which no response occurs and above which a tumor is produced by exposure to a chemical. An animal population has a range of thresholds encompassing the individual thresholds. The log-probit model assumes that the distribution of these log dose thresholds is normal. This model is based on the belief that there are relatively few either extremely sensitive or extremely resistant animals in a population. Accordingly, the probability of a tumor being induced in a population by an exposure to a dose D of a chemical can be calculated as

$$P(D) = \phi(\alpha + \beta \log D)$$

where $\phi$ denotes the standard cumulative Gaussian (normal) distribution. In support of this, Chand and Hoel (52) have shown that this dose response is obtained when the time-to-tumor distribution is log normal under certain conditions.

## I. Miscellaneous Models

There are a large number of other proposed models for low-dose extrapolation, although these others have not gained any large following. Two examples are the extreme value and no-effect-level models.

Chand and Hoel (52) demonstrated that if the time-to-tumor distribution is a Weibull distribution, the dose-response model would become an extreme value model under certain conditions, such that

$$P(D) = 1 - \exp[-\exp(\alpha + \beta \log D)]$$

Park and Snee (78) made the observation that many biological responses vary linearly with the logarithm of dose, and that practical thresholds exist, and therefore the responses can be represented by the following model:

$$\text{Response} = B_1 \qquad \text{if dose} < D^*$$

$$\text{Response} = B_1 + B_2 \log (\text{dose}/D^*) \log \qquad \text{if dose} \geqslant D^*$$

This model incorporates a parameter $D^*$ that represents a threshold below which no dose-related response occurs. In this model, $B_1$ is the constant response level at doses less than D*, and $B_2$ is the slope of the log-dose response curve at doses $\geqslant$ D*. It has been empirically found that many quantitative toxicological endpoints can be adequately described by the no-effect-level model. This model may, therefore, be useful for establishing thresholds for endpoints related to the carcinogenic process in situations where information other than the simple presence or absence of a tumor is available. Both the model and predicted threshold are of value when carcinogenicity is a secondary event.

## J. Comparison of Models

None of the models presented here (or any other mathematical models for this same use) can be "proved" on the basis of biological arguments or available experimental data, but some are more attractive than others on these grounds in a case-by-case basis. The multistage model appears to be the most general model according to the values of the parameters, but frequently we lack many of these parameters. Unfortunately, most of these models fit experimental bioassay data equally well for the observable response rates at experimental dosage levels, but they give extremely different estimated responses when extrapolated to low dosage levels. There are now numerous sets of data which have been used to compare two or more of the models against each other, but these comparisons all too often are based on one or a few data sets which favor particular operating characteristics. Gad and Weil (31) present and review four such limited data set comparisons.

Table 3 attempts to summarize the major characteristics of the eight models presented here in terms of their operating characteristics. The performance of each model in any one particular case is dependent on the nature of the observed dose-response curve. All fit true linear data well, but respond differently to concave or convex response curves. The actual choice of model must depend on available information and on the professional judgment of the investigator. The author believes that to attempt to use any purely mathematical model is wrong—that an understanding of the pharmacokinetics and mechanisms of toxicity across the dose range is an essential initial step in the risk assessment of carcinogens. Any mathematical model must utilize such data, and as there is now significant evidence that many of these actual response curves are multiphasic (nonlinear), only models which can accommodate such nonlinear response surfaces have a chance of being useful in the broad general case.

## K. Cross-Species Extrapolation

This is also called species-to-species extrapolation or scaling. Our efforts and projections to this point are (generally) for the animal

Table 3   Characteristics and Requirements for Use of Major Low Dose Extrapolation Models

| | Low dose linearity | Extrapolates low dose levels | Estimates virtual safe dose | Mechanistic (M) or tolerance distribution (T) | Requires metabolic data | Accommodates threshold | Takes time-to-tumor into account | Estimate of potential risk of low doses[a] |
|---|---|---|---|---|---|---|---|---|
| One-hit (linear) | X | X | X | M | | | | Highest |
| Multistage (Armitage-Doll) | X | X | X | M | | | | High |
| Weibull (Chand and Hoel) | X | | X | T | | X | X | High |
| Multihit | X | X | X | M | | | | Medium |
| Logit (Albert and Altshuler) | X | | X | T | | X | X | Medium |
| Probit (Mantel-Bryan) | X | | X | T | | | | Medium |
| Log-probit (Gehring et al.) | | | X | M | X | X | X | Low |
| Pharmacokinetic (Cornfield) | | X | X | M | X | X | X | Lowest |

[a]If real curve is convex.

specie(s) that toxicology data is available in. Now it is necessary to predict what this means in humans. What conversion factor can we derive that allows us to equate "X" dose in rats to a dose in humans that would evoke the same result? The first option would again be some form of pharmacokinetic model, but such is usually not available. So we must use one of several mathematical methods (generally based on either portion of total dietary intake or body weight or body surface area). Though there is some biological basis for these conversions, it is not on a point for point basis and one to two orders of magnitude of uncertainty are generally involved. This extrapolation has both qualitative and quantitative aspects.

The qualitative aspects of species-to-species extrapolations are best addressed by a form of classification analysis tailored to the exact problem at hand. This approach identifies the physiological, metabolic, and other factors which may be involved in the risk-producing process in the model species (for example, the carcinogenesis process in test mice), establishes the similarities and differences between these factors and those in humans, and comes up with means to bridge the gaps between these two (or to identify the fact that there is no possible bridge).

Tomatis (79) had provided an excellent evaluation of the comparability of carcinogenicity findings between rodents and humans, in general finding the former to be good predictors of the endpoint in the latter. However, in his 1984 Stokinger lecture, Weil (80) pointed out that the model species should respond biologically to the material as similarly as possible to humans; that the routes of exposure (actual and possible) should be the same; and that there are known wide variations in response to carcinogens. Deichmann (81), for example, has reviewed studies demonstrating that 2-naphthylamine is a human and dog carcinogen, but not active in the mouse, rat, guinea pig, or rabbit.

Smith (82) discussed interspecies variations of response to carcinogens, including N-2-fluorenyl-acetamide, which is potent for the dog, rabbit, hamster, and rat (believed to be due to formation of an active metabolite by N-hydroxylation), but not in the guinea pig or steppe lemming, which do not form this metabolic derivative.

Table 4 presents an overview of the classes of factors which should be considered in the first step of a species extrapolation. Examples of such actual differences which can be classified as one of these factors are almost endless.

The absorption of compounds from the gastrointestinal tract and from the lungs is comparable among vertebrate and mammalian species. There are, however, differences between herbivorous animals and omnivorous animals due to differences in stomach structure. The problem of distribution within the body probably relates less to species than to size, and will be discussed later under scaling. Metabolism, xenobiotic metabolism of foreign compounds, metabolic

**Table 4** Classes of Factors to be Considered in Species-to-Species Extrapolations in Risk Assessment

---

I. Sensitivity of model animal (relative to humans)
   A. Pharmacologic
   B. Receptor
   C. Life span
   D. Size
   E. Metabolic function
   F. Physiological
   G. Anatomic
   H. Nutritional requirements
   I. Reproductive and developmental processes
   J. Diet
   K. Critical reflex and behavioral responses (as emetic reflex)
   L. Behavioral
   M. Rate of cell division
   N. Other defense mechanisms

II. Relative population differences
   A. Size
   B. Heterogeneity
   C. Selected "high class" nature of test population

III. Differences between test and real world environment
   A. Physical (temperature, humidity, etc.)
   B. Chemical
   C. Nutritional

---

activation, or toxification/detoxification mechanisms (by whatever name) is perhaps the critical factor, and this can differ widely from species to species. The increasing realization that the original compound administered is not necessarily the ultimate carcinogen makes the further study of these matabolic patterns critical.

In terms of excretory rates, the differences between the species are not very great: small animals tend to excrete compounds more rapidly than large ones in a rather systematic way. The various cellular and intercellular barriers seem to be surprisingly constant throughout the vertebrate phylum. In addition, it is beginning to be appreciated that the receptors, such as DNA, are comparable throughout the mammalian species.

There are life-span (or temporal) differences that have not been considered adequately, either now or in the past. It takes time to develop a tumor, and at least some of that time may be taken up by the actual cell division process. Cell division rates appear to be significantly higher in smaller animals. Mouse and rat cells turn over faster than human cells—perhaps at twice the rate. On the other hand, the latent period for development of tumors is much shorter in small animals than in large ones.

Another problem is that the life-span of humans is about 35 times that of the mouse or rat; thus there is a much longer time for a tumor to appear. These sorts of temporal considerations are of considerable importance.

Body size, irrespective of species, seems to be important in the rate of distribution of foreign compounds throughout the body. A simple example of this is that the cardiac output of the mouse is on the order of 1 ml/min, and the mouse has a blood volume of about 1 ml. The mouse is turning its blood volume over every minute. In humans, the cardiac output per minute is only 1/20 of its blood volume. So the mouse turns its blood over and distributes whatever is in the blood or collects excretory products over 20 times faster than humans.

Another aspect of the size difference which should be considered is that the large animal has a very much greater number of susceptible cells that may interact with potential carcinogenic agents, though there is also a proportionately increased number of "dummy" cells.

Rall (83,84), Oser (85), and Borzelleca (86) have published articles reviewing such factors and Calabrese (87) has published an excellent book on the subject.

Having delineated and quantified species differences (even if only having factored in comparative body weights and food consumption rates), we can now proceed to some form of quantitative extrapolation. This process as pointed out earlier, is called scaling.

There are currently three major approaches to scaling in use in risk assessment. These are by fraction of diet, by body weight, and by body surface area (87,88). These three are all single variable or two-dimensional models, and the latter two are one form or another of what are called allometric equations. Davidson et al. (89) have presented the generalized form of this equation as $Y = aW^n$ where W = body size, n is the slope of the derived line, and a is a scaling factor. Recently there have been proposals (90) that a multidimensional model would be more accurate, which in turn would be but more complex forms of the allometric equation.

The "fraction of diet" method is based on converting the results in the experimental animal model to man on a mg (of test substance)/kg (diet)/day basis. When the experimental model is the mouse, this leads to an extrapolation factor which is sixfold lower than on a body weight (mg/kg) basis (91). Fraction of diet factors are not considered accurate indices of actual dosages since the latter are influenced not only by voluntary food intake, as affected by palatability and caloric density of the diet and by single or multiple caging, but more particularly by the age of the animal. During the early stages of life, anatomic, physiologic, metabolic, and immunologic capabilities are not fully developed. Moreover, the potential for toxic effect in an animal is a function of the dose ingested, ultimately, of the number of active molecules reaching the target cell. Additionally, many agents of concern do not have ingestion as the major route of intake in humans. Both the Environmental Protection Agency (EPA) and the Consumer Product Safety Commission (CPSC) frequently employ a fraction of diet scaling factor.

Human diets are generally assumed to be 600–700 g/day, while that in mice is 4 g/day and in rats 25 g/day (the equivalent of 50 g/kg/day).

The second, or body weight approach, is the most common general approach to scaling in toxicology. There are several ways to perform a scaling operation on a body weight basis. The most common is to simply calculate a conversion factor (K) as

$$\frac{\text{Weight of human (70 kg)}}{\text{Weight of test animal (0.4 kg for rat)}} = K$$

More exotic methods for doing this, such as that based on a form of linear regression, are reviewed by Calabrese (87) who believes that the body wieght method is preferable.

A difficulty with this approach is that the body weights of both animals and humans change throughout life. An "ideal man" (70 kg for men and 50 kg for women) or "ideal rat" (for which there is no real consensus) weight is therefore utilized.

Finally, there are the body surface area methods, which attempt to factor in differences in metabolic rates based on the principle that these change in proportion with body surface area (since as the ratio of body surface area to body weight increases, the more energy is required to maintain constant body temperature). As long ago as 1938, Benedict (92) published a comparison of body weight versus basal metabolic rates for species from mice to elephants which showed a linear relationship between the two variables. There are several methods for doing this, each having a ratio of dose to the animal's body weight (in mg/kg) as a starting point, resulting in a conversion factor with $mg/m^2$ as the units.

The EPA version is generally calculated as:

$$(M_{human}/M_{animal})^{1/3} = \text{surface factor}$$

where M = mass in kilograms. Another form is calculated based on constants that have been developed for a multitude of species of animals by actual surface area measurements (93). The resulting formula for this is:

$$A = KW^{2/3}$$

where A = surface area in $cm^2$; K = constant, specific for each
species; and W = weight in grams.

A scaling factor is then simply calculated as a ratio of the surface area of man over that of the model species.

The "best" scaling factor is not generally agreed upon. Though
the majority opinion is that surface area is preferable where a metabolic activation or deactivation is known to be both critical to the
risk producing process and present in both the model species and
human, these assumptions may not always be valid. Table 5 presents a comparison of the weight and surface area extrapolation
methods for eight species.

Schneiderman et al. (94) and Dixon (95) have published comparisons of these methods, but Schmidt-Nielsen (88) should be considered the primary source on scaling in interspecies comparisons.

**Table 5** Extrapolation of a Dose of 100 mg/kg in the Mouse to
Other Species

|  |  |  | Extrapolated dose (mg) based on | | |
| Species | Weight (g) | Surface area[a] ($cm^2$) | Body weight (A) | Body surface area (B) | Ratio A/B |
|---|---|---|---|---|---|
| Mouse | 20 | 46.4 | 2 | 2 | 1.0 |
| Rat | 400 | 516.7 | 40 | 22.3 | 1.80 |
| Guinea pig | 400 | 564.5 | 40 | 24.3 | 1.65 |
| Rabbit | 1500 | 1272.0 | 150 | 54.8 | 2.74 |
| Dog | 12000 | 5766.0 | 1200 | 248.5 | 4.82 |
| Cat | 2000 | 1381.0 | 200 | 59.5 | 3.46 |
| Monkey | 4000 | 2975.0 | 400 | 128.2 | 3.12 |
| Human | 70000 | 18000.0 | 7000 | 775.8 | 9.8 |

[a]Surface area (except in case of human) calculated from formula:

$$\text{Surface area } (cm^2) = K(W^{2/3})$$

where K is a constant for each species and W is body weight (values
of K and surface area of human taken from Ref. 92).

On an intermediate level, DuMouchel and Harris (96) have suggested a class of Bayesian statistical methods for combining data from different substances and species of animals, using the results as one constructs each stage of the model to estimate interexperimental error between the different sources of data being combined. In the same paper they proposed a means of using such data to rank the relative potency of carcinogenic agents.

## L. Estimating Human Exposure

The most toxic material in existance would not have risk associated with it if there wasn't any exposure. Having now produced a model that will estimate risk to humans at any given dose (with a noticeable degree of uncertainty already in hand), measurements or estimates of human exposure (both incidence and extent) must be generated.

This remaining step in performing a risk assessment (quantitating the exposure of the human population, both in terms of how many people are exposed by what routes and to what quantities of an agent they are exposed) unfortunately, also has uncertainties associated with it.

With the exception of some key points, the process of identifying and quantitating exposure groups within the human population is beyond the scope of this text. Classification methods are again the key tool for identifying and properly delimiting human populations at risk. An investigator must first understand the process involved in making, shipping, using, and disposing of a material. EPA recently proposed guidelines for such identification and exposure quantitation (97). The exposure groups can be very large or relatively small subpopulations, each with a markedly different potential for exposure. For di-(2-ethyl-hexyl)phthalate (DEHP), for example, the following at-risk populations have been identified:

IV Route
    3,000,000 receiving blood transfusions (50 mg/year)
      50,000 dialysis patients (4500 mg/year)
      10,000 hemophiliacs (760 mg/year)
Oral Route
      10,800,000 children under 3 years of age (434 mg/year)
    220,000,000 adults (dietary contamination of 1.1 mg/year)

Not quantitated were possible inhalation and dermal exposures.

All such estimates of exposure in humans (and of the number of humans exposed), again, are subject to a large degree of uncertainty.

An alternative approach to achieving society's objective for the entire risk assessment procedure, namely protecting the human population from unacceptable levels of known risks, is the classical approach of using safety factors. In 1972, Weil (100) summarized this approach as "In summary, for the evaluation of safety for man, it is necessary to: (1) design and conduct appropriate toxicologic tests, (2) statistically compare the data from treated and control animals, (3) delineate the minimum effect and maximum no ill-effect levels (NIEL) for these animals, and (4) if the material is to be used, apply an appropriate safety factor, e.g., (a) 1/100 (NIEL) or 1/500 (NIEL) for some effects or (b) 1/500 (NIEL), if the effect was a significant increase in cancer in an appropriate test." This approach has served society reasonably well over the years, once the experimental work has identified the potential hazards and quantitated the observable dose-response relationships. The safety factor approach has not generally been accepted or seriously entertained by regulatory agencies, until such time as the most elegant risk assessment procedures can instill greater public confidence, the use of the safety factor approach should perhaps not be abandoned so readily for more "mathematically precise" methodologies.

As a final sanity check to this multistep process, the data points generated by other studies addressing the endpoint of interest should be evaluated to determine if they fall within the 95% confidence bounds of the projection. If we find that real data do not fit our extrapolation model at this point, then as scientists we have no choice but to reject such a model and start anew.

## VII. CONCLUSION

As scientists, we must clearly communicate the uncertainty associated with our extrapolations; to do otherwise is dishonest and only serves to abandon the job to others such as the news media. We must tell others not just what the results are, but also what they mean. Given our degree of uncertainty (with all our real data up in one small corner of the range), maybe we should evaluate and communicate the risks of chemical carcinogens in a rank order manner which would more clearly and honestly convey the quality of our "data" and understanding of its real life meanings.

Figure 1, presented at the beginning of this chapter, should serve to summarize our problem in completing this entire risk-assessment process. Our most vigorous efforts must be focused on those activities which best allow us to address these problems. Such activities should include designing better studies from the perspective of risk assessment (that is, covering a broader range of doses with an unbalanced design and selecting the doses for such studies on a knowledge of the underlying pharmacokinetics of the compound) and developing a better understanding of the underlying mechanisms on a molecular and cellular basis.

# REFERENCES

1. Hass, H. B. and Newton, R. F. (1978). Correction of boiling points to standard pressure. In *CRC Handbook of Chemistry and Physics, 59th Edition*. West Palm Beach, FL, CRC Press, p. D-228.
2. U.S. Environmental Protection Agency. Office of Toxic Substances. (1984). *A Manual for the Preparation of Engineering Assessments*. Unpublished draft, Chemical Engineering Branch, Economics and Technology Division, Washington, D.C., September 1, 1984.
3. Dugard, P. H. (1983). Skin permeability theory in relation to measurements of percutaneous absorption in toxicology. In *Dermatotoxicology*, 2nd ed. Edited by F. N. Marzulli and H. I. Maibach, New York, Hemisphere Publishing Corp., Chap. 3.
4. Guy, R. H., Hadgraft, J., and Maibach, H. J. (1985). Percutaneous absorption in man: A kinetic approach. *Toxicol. Appl. Pharmacol.*, 78:1213–1129.
5. Gale, R. M. and Shaw, J. E. (1983). *Percutaneous Absorption and Pharmacokinetics*. Pharmacokinetics and Topically Applied Cosmetics Symposium Proceedings CTFA Scientific Monograph Series No. 1. Washington, D.C., CTFA, pp. 11–28.
6. Hosey, A. D. (1973). General principles in evaluating the occupational environment. In *Industrial Environment—its Evaluation and Control*. USDHEW/NIOSH, Superintendent of Documents, Washington, D.C., U.S. Government Printing Office, Chap. 10.
7. Bar-Shalom, Y., Budenaers, D., Schainker, R., and Segall, A. (1975). *Handbook of Statistical Test for Evaluating Employee Exposure at Air Contaminants*. USDHEW/NIOSH, Contract No. HSM 99-73-78, Superintendent of Documents, Washington, D.C., U.S. Government Printing Office, April.
8. Davis, J. E. (1980). Minimizing occupational exposure to pesticides: Personal monitoring. *Residue Rev.* 75:33–50.
9. Durham, W. F. and Wolfe, H. R. (1962). Measurement of the exposure of workers to pesticides. *Bull. WHO* 26:75–91.
10. Wolfe, H. R. (1976). Field exposure to airborne pesticides. In *Air Pollution from Pesticides and Agricultural Processes*. Edited by R. E. Lee, Jr. Cleveland, OH, CRC Press, pp. 137–161.
11. Colle, R. and McNeil, Jr., P. E. (Eds.). (1980). *Radon in Buildings*. Proceedings of a Roundtable Discussion, NBS SP-581, Library of Congress Catalog Card Number: 80:600069, June.
12. Handley, T. H. and Barton, C. J. (1973). Home Ventilation Rates: A Literature Survey. Atomic Energy Commission Report ORNL-TM-4318.

13. Drivas, P. J., Simmonds, P. G., and Shair, F. H. (1972).
    Experimental characterization of venilation systems in buildings.
    *Environ. Sci. Technol. Curr. Res.* 6(7):609–614.
14. Jones, B. and Harris, R. L. (1983). Calculation of time-
    weighted average concentrations: A computer mapping applica-
    tion. *Am. Ind. Hyg. J.* 44:795–801.
15. Franke, J. R. and Wadden, R. A. (1985). Eddy diffusivities
    measured inside a light industrial building, Poster #107.
    American Industrial Hygiene Conference, Las Vegas, Nevada,
    May 23, 1985.
16. Cooper, D. W. and Horowitz, M. (1986). Exposures from
    indoor powder releases: Models and experiments. *Am. Ind.
    Hyg. J.* 47:214–218.
17. Berman, D. W. (1982). *Methods for Estimating Workplace
    Exposure to PMN Substances.* EPA Contract No. 68-01-6065
    (for the USEPA Economics and Technology Division). Arlington,
    VA, Clements Associates, Inc., October 5, 1982.
18. Kunkel, B. A. (1983). A comparison of evaporative source
    strength models for toxic chemical spills. *Air Force Surveys
    in Geophysics, No. 446.* Atmospheric Sciences Division Project
    6670, Hanscom AFB, MA, Air Force Geophysics Laboratory,
    November 16, 1983.
19. Astelford, W. J., Morrow, T. B., Magott, R. J., Prevost,
    R. J., Kaplan, H. L., Bass, R. L., and Buckingham, J. C.
    (1983). *Investigation of the Hazards Posed by Chemical Vapors
    Released in Marine Operations—Phase II.* DOT/U.S. Coast
    Guard, National Technical Information Service, Springfield,
    VA, January, 1983.
20. Wu, J. and Schroy, J. (1979). Emissions from spills. Paper
    presented at conference sponsored by Air Pollution Control
    Association, Gainesville, Florida, February, 1979.
21. Sutton, D. J., Nodolf, K. M., and Makino, K. K. (1976).
    Predicting ozone concentrations in residential structures.
    *ASHRAE J.* 21–26.
22. Wade, W. A., Cote, W. A., and Yocum, J. E. (1975). A
    study of indoor air pollution. *J. Air Pollut. Control Assoc.*
    25:933–939.
23. Walsh, M. A., Black, A., and Morgan, A. (1977). Sorption
    of SO2 by typical indoor surfaces including wool carpets, wall-
    paper, and paint. *Atmos. Environ. J.* 11:1107–1111.
24. Jayjock, M. A. (1986). Assessment of inhalation exposure and
    health risk from organic vapors. Paper presented at the
    American Industrial Hygiene Conference (AIHA), Dallas, Texas,
    May, 1986.
25. Schulze, R. H. (1977). *Notes on Dispersion Modeling.* Dallas,
    Trinity Consultants.

26. Turner, D. B. (1970). *Workshop of Atmospheric Dispersion Estimates*, U.S. EPA, 1970.
27. U.S. Department of Agriculture. (1980). *The Biological and Economic Assessment of Penachlorophenol—Inorganic Arsenicals—Creosote Volume 1: Wood Preservatives*. Technical Bulletin No. 1658-I, page 78, Washington, D.C., November 4, 1980.
28. Anonymous: Draft Report-Exposure Assessment for Retention of Chemical Liquids on Hands. Contract No. 68-01-6271, Task No. 56. Prepared for USEPA, Exposure Evaluation Division, by Vesar Inc., Springfield, Virginia, February 8, 1984.
29. USEPA (1985). *Methods for Assessing Expsoure to Chemical Substances*, Vols. 1–9. EPA 560/5-85-004, Washington, D.C., Office of Toxic Substances.
30. Chu, K. (1977). Percent Spontaneous Primary Tumors in Untreated Species Used at NCI for Carcinogen Bioassays. NCI Clearing House.
31. Gad, S. C. and Weil, C. S. (1986). *Statistics and Experimental Design for Toxicologists*. Caldwell, NJ, Telford Press, 380 pp.
32. Cameron, T. P., Hickman, R. L., Korneich, M. R., and Tarone, R. E. (1985). History survival and growth patterns of B6C3F1 mice and F344 rats in the National Cancer Institute Carcinogenesis Testing Program. *Gund. Appl. Toxicol. 5:* 526–538.
33. Dempster, A. P., Selwyn, M. R., and Weeks, B. J. (1983). Combining historical and randomized controls for assessing trends in proportions. *J. Am. Stat. Assoc. 78:*221–227.
34. Salsburg, D. (1980). The effects of lifetime feeding studies on patterns of senile lesions in mice and rats. *Drug Chem. Toxicol. 3:*1–33.
35. Epstein, S. S. (1973). The Delaney Amendment. *Ecologist 3:* 424–430.
36. Claus, G., Krisko, I., and Bolander, K. (1974). Chemical carcinogens in the environment and in the human diet: Can a threshold be established? *Food Cosmet. Toxicol., 12:*737-746.
37. Albert, R. E., Burns, F. J., and Altshuler, B. (1979). Reinterpretation of the linear non-threshold dose-response model in terms of the initiation—promotion mouse skin tumorgenesis. In *New Concepts in Safety Evaluation*. Edited by M. A. Mehlman, R. E. Shapiro, and H. Blumenthal. New York, Hemisphere Publishing, pp. 88–95.
38. Mantel, N. and Schneiderman, M. A. (1875). Estimating "safe" levels. A hazardous undertaking. *Cancer Res. 35:*1379–1386.
39. Guess, H. A. and Hoel, D. G. (1977). The effect of dose on cancer latency period. *J. Environ. Path. Toxicol. 1:*2179–2186.

40. Klaasen, C. D. and Doull, J. (1980). Evaluation of safety: Toxicology evaluation. In *Casarett and Doull's Toxicology*. Edited by J. Doull, C. D. Klaassen, and M. O. Amdur. New York, Macmillan Publishing Company, p. 26.

41. Dinman, B. D. (1972). "Non-concept" of "non-threshold" chemicals in the environment. *Science 175*:495–497.

42. Kraybill, H. F. (1977). Newer approaches in assessment of Environmental Carcinogenesis. In *Mycotoxins In Human and Animal Health*. Park Forest South, IL, Pathotox Publishers, pp. 675–686.

43. Miller, E. C. (1978). Some current perspectives on chemical carcinogens in humans and experimental animals: Presidential address. *Cancer Res. 38*:1471.

44. Stokinger, H. E. (1977). Toxicology and drinking water contaminants. *J. Am. Water Works Assoc.* July:399–402.

45. Jones, H. B. and Grendon, A. (1975). Environmental factors in the origin of cancer and estimation of the possible hazard to man. *Food Cosmet. Toxicol. 13*:251–268.

46. Steinhoff, D., Gad, S. C., Hatfield, G. K., and Mohr, U. (1986). Carcinogenicity study with sodium dichromate in rats. *Exp. Pathol. 30*:1219–1241.

47. Hoel, D. G., Gayle, D. W., Kirschstein, R. L. Saffiotti, V., and Schneiderman, M. A. (1975). Estimation of risks of irreversible delayed toxicity. *J. Toxicol. Environ. Health 1*:133.

48. EPA (1986). Guidelines for carcinogen risk assessment. *Fed. Reg. 51*(185) (September 24), 33992–34054.

49. Crump, K. S., Hoel, D. G., Langley, C. H. J., and Peto, R. (1976). Fundamental carcinogenic processes and their implications for low dose risk assessment. *Cancer Res. 36*:2973.

50. Peto, R. (1978). The carcinogenic effects of chronic exposure to very low levels o, toxic substances. *Environ. Health Perspectives 22*:155–159.

51. Gross, M. A., Fitzhugh, O. G., and Mantel, N. (1970). Evaluation of safety for food additives: An illustration involving the influence of methyl salicylate on rat reproduction. *Biometrics 26*:181–194.

52. Chand, N. and Hoel, D. G. (1974). A comparison of models for determining safe levels of environmental agents. In *Reliability and Biometry Statistical Analysis of Lifelength*. Edited by F. Proschan and R. J. Serfling. Philadelphia, SIAM.

53. Druckrey, H. (1967). Quantitative aspects in chemical carcinogenesis. In *Potential Carcinogenic Hazards from Drugs*, UICC Monograph Series, Vol. 7. Edited by R. Truhaut. Berlin, Springer-Verlag, p. 60.

54. Mantel, N. and Bryan, W. R. (1961). Safety testing of carcinogenic agents. *J. Natl. Canc. Inst. 27*:455–470.

55. Armitage, P. and Doll, R. (1961). Stochastic models for carcinogenesis from the Berkeley symposium on mathematical statistics and probability. Berkeley, University of California Press, pp. 19–38.

56. Hartley, H. O. and Sielken, R. L. (1977). Estimation of "safe doses" in carcinogenic experiments. *Biometrics 33*:1–30.

57. Crump, K. S., Guess, H. A., and Deal, K. L. (1977). Confidence intervals and est of hypotheses concerning dose response relations inferred from animal carcinogenicity data. *Biometrics 33*:437–451.

58. Cornfield, J. (1977). Carcinogenic risk assessment. *Science,* continuous carcinogenesis experiments. *Biometrics 29*:457–470.

59. Food Safety Council. (1980). Quantitative risk assessment. *Food Cosmet. Toxicol. 18*:711–734.

60. Crump, K. W. (1979). Dose response problems in carcinogenesis. *Biometrics 35*:157–167.

61. Rai, K. and Van Ryzin, J. (1979). Risk assessment of toxic environmental substances based on a generalized multihit model. In *Energy and Health*. Philadelphia, SIAM Press, pp. 99–177.

62. Haseman, J. K., Hoel, D. G., and Jennrich, R. J. (1981). Some practical problems arising from use of the gamma multihit model for risk estimation. *J. Toxicol. Environ. Health 8*: 379–386.

63. Garattini, S. (1985). Toxic effects of chemicals: Difficulties in extrapolating data from animals to man. *Crit. Rev. Toxicol. 16*:1–29.

64. Gehring, P. J. and Blau, G. E. (1977). Mechanisms of carcinogenicity: Dose response. *J. Env. Path. Toxicol. 1*:163–179.

65. Anderson, M. W., Hoel, D. G., and Kaplan, N. L. (1980). A general scheme for the incorporation of pharmacokinetics in low-dose risk estimation for chemical carcinogenesis: Example-vinyl chloride. *Toxicol. Appl. Pharmacol. 55*:154–161.

66. Cook, P. J., Doll, R., and Fellingham, S. A. (1969). A mathematical model for the age distribution of cancer in man. *Int. J. Cancer 4*:93–112.

67. Lee, P. N. and O'Neill, J. A. (1971). The effect of both time and dose applied on tumor incidence fate in benzopyrene skin painting experiments. *Br. J. Cancer 25*:759–770.

68. Day, T. D. (1967). Carcinogenic action of cigarette smoke condensate on mouse skin. *Br. J. Cancer 21*:56–81.

69. Peto, R., Lee, P. N., and Paige, W. S. (1972). Statistical analysis of the bioassay of continuous carcinogens. *Roy. J. Cancer 26*:258–261.

70. Pike, M. C. (1966). A method of analysis of a certain class of experiments in carcinogenesis. *Biometrics 22*:142–161.

71. Hoel, D. G. (1972). A representation of mortality data by competing risks. *Biometrics 28*:475–488.

72. Berkson, J. (1944). Application of the logistic function to bio-assay. *J. Am. Stat. Assoc. 39*:357-365.

73. Cornfield, J., Carlborg, P. W., and Van Ryzin, J. (1978). Setting tolerance on the basis of mathematical treatment of dose-response data extrapolated to low doses. *Proc. of the First Internat. Toxicol. Congress.* New York, Academic Press, pp. 143-164.

74. Albert, R. E. and Altshuler, B. (1973). Considerations relating to the formulation of limits for unavoidable population exposures to environmental carcinogens. In *Radionuclide Carcinogenesis.* Edited by J. E. Ballou et al. NTIS Springfield, AEC Symposium Series, CONF-72050, pp. 233-253.

75. Blum, H. F. (1959). *Carcinogenesis by Ultraviolet Light.* Princeton, Princeton University Press.

76. Gehring, P. G., Watanabe, P. G., and Park, C. N. (1979). Risk of angiosarcome in workers exposed to vinyl chloride as predicted from studies in rats. *Toxicol. Appl. Pharmacol. 49*: 15-21.

77. Finney, D. J. (1952). *Statistical Methods in Biological Assay.* New York, Hafner.

78. Park, C. N. and Snee, R. D. (1983). Quantitative risk assessment. State-of-the-art for carcinogenesis. *Am. Stat. 37*: 427-441.

79. Tomatis, L. (1979). The predictive value of rodent carcinogenicity tests in the evaluation of human risks. *Ann. Rev. Pharmacol. Toxicol. 19*:511-530.

80. Weil, C. S. (1984). Some questions and opinions: Issues in toxicology and risk assessment. *Am. Ind. Hyg. Assoc. J. 45*: 663-670.

81. Deichmann, W. B. (1975). Cummings Memorial Lecture-1975. The market basket: Food for thought. *Am. Ind. Hyg. Assoc. J. 36*:411.

82. Smith, R. L. (1974). The problem of species variations. *Ann. Nutr. Alim. 28*:335.

83. Rall, D. P. (1977). Species differences in carcinogenicity testing. In *Origins of Human Cancer.* Edited by H. H. Hiatt, J. D. Watson, and J. A. Winsten. Cold Spring Harbor, NY, Cold Spring Harbor Laboratories, pp. 1283-1290.

84. Rall, D. P. (1979). Relevance of animal experiments to humans. *Environ. Health Perspect. 32*:297-300.

85. Oser, B. L. (1981). The rat as a model for human toxicology evaluation. *J. Toxicol. Envir. Health 8*:521-542.

86. Borzelleca, J. F. (1984). Extrapolation of animal data to man. In *Concepts in Toxicology*, vol. I. Edited by A. S. Tegeris. New York, Karger, pp. 294-304.

87. Calabrese, E. J. (1983). *Principles of Animal Extrapolation.* New York, John Wiley.

88. Schmidt-Nielsen, F. (1984). *Scaling: Why Is Animal Size So Important?* New York, Cartridge University Press.
89. Davidson, I. W. F., Parker, J. C., and Beliles, P. R. (1986). Biological basis for extrapolation across mammalian species. *Reg. Tox. Pharmacol. 6:*211–237.
90. Yates, F. E. and Kugler, P. N. (1986). Similarity principles and intrinsic geometries: Contrasting approaches to inter-species sealing. *J. Pharm. Sci. 75:*1019–1027.
91. Association of Food and Drug Officials of the U.S. (1959). *Appraisal of the Safety of Chemicals in Foods, Drugs and Cosmetics.* Washington, D.C.
92. Benedict, F. C. (1938). Vita energeics: A study in comparative basal metabolism.
93. Spector, W. S. (1956). *Handbook of Biological Data.* Philadelphia, W. B. Saunders.
94. Schneiderman, M. A., Mantel, N., and Brown, C. C. (1975). *Ann. NY Acad. Sci. 246:*237–248.
95. Dixon, R. L. (1976). Problems in extrapolating toxicity data from laboratory animals to man. *Envir. Health Perspect. 13:* 43–50.
96. Dumouchel, W. H. and Harris, J. E. (1983). Bayes methods for combining the results of cancer studies in humans and other species. *J. Am. Stat. Assoc. 78:*293–315.
97. EPA (1984). Proposed Guidelines for Exposure Assessment. *Fed. Reg. 49(*227) (November 23):46304–46312.
98. Weil, C. S. (1972). Statistics vs. safety factors and scientific judgment in the evaluation of safety for man. *Toxicol. Appl. Pharmacol. 21:*454–463.
99. Mantel, N., Schidar, N. R., Brown, C. C., Ciminera, J. L., and Tukey, J. W. (1975). An improved Mantel-Bryan procedure for "safety" testing of carcinogens. *Cancer Res. 35:*865–872.
100. Guess, H. A., Crump, K. S., and Peto, R. (1977). Uncertainty estimates for low-dose-rate extrapolations of animal carcinogenicity data. *Cancer Res. 37:*3475–3483.

# Index

RA
1199
.P77
1988

RA
1199
.P77

1988

145.00